CHINESE ZODIAC
—SIGNS—

CHINESE ZODIAC
—SIGNS—

TREASURE PRESS

First published in Great Britain in 1982 by Arrow Books Limited as
twelve individual volumes: *Year of the Rat, Year of the Ox, Year
of the Tiger, Year of the Rabbit, Year of the Dragon, Year of the
Snake, Year of the Horse, Year of the Goat, Year of the Monkey,
Year of the Rooster, Year of the Dog and Year of the Pig*

© M.A. Editions 1982

This omnibus edition first published in
Great Britain in 1988 by
Treasure Press
Michelin House
81 Fulham Road
London SW3 6RB

Arrangement of this edition copyright © 1988
Octopus Publishing Group Ltd

Original text in French by Catherine Aubier
English edition arranged by Eugène Braun-Muuk
Translated by Eileen Finletter and Ian Murray
Designed by Julie Francis

ISBN 1 85051 331 7

Printed in Czechoslovakia

52 177

CONTENTS

General table of the years corresponding to the Chinese signs

THE RAT	THE OX	THE TIGER
31.1.1900/18.2.1901	19.2.1901/ 7.2.1902	8.2.1902/28.1.1903
18.2.1912/ 5.2.1913	6.2.1913/25.1.1914	26.1.1914/13.2.1915
5.2.1924/24.1.1925	25.1.1925/12.2.1926	13.2.1926/ 1.2.1927
24.1.1936/10.2.1937	11.2.1937/30.1.1938	31.1.1938/18.2.1939
10.2.1948/28.1.1949	29.1.1949/16.2.1950	17.2.1950/ 5.2.1951
28.1.1960/14.2.1961	15.2.1961/ 4.2.1962	5.2.1962/24.1.1963
15.2.1972/ 2.2.1973	3.2.1973/22.1.1974	23.1.1974/10.2.1975
2.2.1984/19.2.1985	20.2.1985/ 8.2.1986	9.2.1986/28.1.1987

THE RABBIT	THE DRAGON	THE SNAKE
29.1.1903/15.2.1904	16.2.1904/ 3.2.1905	4.2.1905/24.1.1906
14.2.1915/ 2.2.1916	3.2.1916/22.1.1917	23.1.1917/10.2.1918
2.2.1927/22.1.1928	23.1.1928/ 9.2.1929	10.2.1929/29.1.1930
19.2.1939/ 7.2.1940	8.2.1940/26.1.1941	27.1.1941/14.2.1942
6.2.1951/26.1.1952	27.1.1952/13.2.1953	14.2.1953/ 2.2.1954
25.1.1963/12.2.1964	13.2.1964/ 1.2.1965	2.2.1965/20.1.1966
11.2.1975/30.1.1976	31.1.1976/17.2.1977	18.2.1977/ 6.2.1978
29.1.1987/16.2.1988	17.2.1988/ 5.2.1989	6.2.1989/26.1.1990

THE HORSE	THE GOAT	THE MONKEY
25.1.1906/12.2.1907	13.2.1907/ 1.2.1908	2.2.1908/21.1.1909
11.2.1918/31.1.1919	1.2.1919/19.2.1920	20.2.1920/ 7.2.1921
30.1.1930/16.2.1931	17.2.1931/ 5.2.1932	6.2.1932/25.1.1933
15.2.1942/ 4.2.1943	5.2.1943/24.1.1944	25.1.1944/12.2.1945
3.2.1954/23.1.1955	24.1.1955/11.2.1956	12.2.1956/30.1.1957
21.1.1966/ 8.2.1967	9.2.1967/28.1.1968	29.1.1968/16.2.1969
7.2.1978/27.1.1979	28.1.1979/15.2.1980	16.2.1980/ 4.2.1981
27.1.1990/14.2.1991	15.2.1991/ 3.2.1992	4.2.1992/22.1.1993

THE ROOSTER	THE DOG	THE PIG
22.1.1909/ 9.2.1910	10.2.1910/29.1.1911	30.1.1911/17.2.1912
8.2.1921/27.1.1922	28.1.1922/15.2.1923	16.2.1923/ 4.2.1924
26.1.1933/13.2.1934	14.2.1934/ 3.2.1935	4.2.1935/23.1.1936
13.2.1945/ 1.2.1946	2.2.1946/21.1.1947	22.1.1947/ 9.2.1948
31.1.1957/15.2.1958	16.2.1958/ 7.2.1959	8.2.1959/27.1.1960
17.2.1969/ 5.2.1970	6.2.1970/26.1.1971	27.1.1971/14.2.1972
5.2.1981/24.1.1982	25.1.1982/12.2.1983	13.2.1983/ 1.2.1984
23.1.1993/ 9.2.1994	10.2.1994/30.1.1995	31.1.1995/18.2.1996

*The dates indicated specify the **first** and the **last** day of the year of the sign.*

HOW TO USE THIS BOOK

Each section of this book gives a detailed description of the character, personality and partnership possibilities of the twelve signs of the Chinese zodiac. The characteristics of the signs are described in conjunction with the respective important ascendant sign.

– There is also a synthesis of the Chinese zodiac and the more familiar Western zodiac. Together these give new meaning and depth to the description and prediction of an individual's personality, the main tendencies of his character, his behaviour and the broad outline of his destiny.

This book is divided into twelve sections, each one devoted to a different sign of the Chinese zodiac. The arrangement of each section is as follows:

A description of the characteristics of your specific Chinese sign, determined by the *year of your birth.*

The best (and worst) partners for that Sign, determined by *the hour of your birth.*

The combination and interaction of your sign with the Ascendant Element: Earth, Water, Fire, Wood, Metal.

The comparison and combination of the two zodiacs – Chinese and Western (for example, the Sagittarian Rat, the Virgo Rat) – highlight many subtleties which enable you to clarify your psychological portrait.

The astrological game of the I Ching, which adapts the ancient Taoist 'Book of Mutations' to each Chinese sign. This simple game offers the reader the opportunity to obtain wise and appropriate answers to abstract as well as everyday questions.

THE MYSTERIES OF CHINESE ASTROLOGY

中國星相
學之神秘

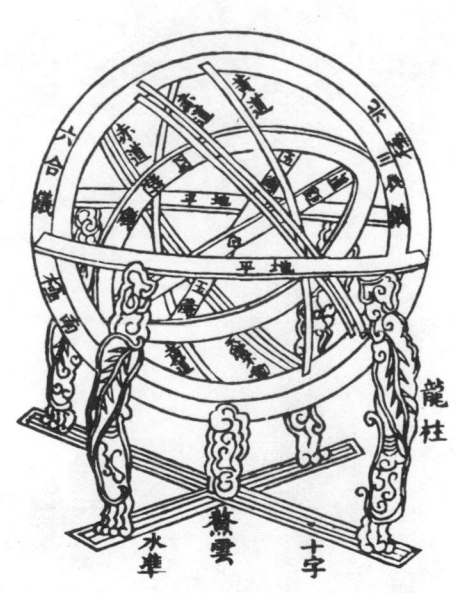

The legend of Buddha

One Chinese New Year more than five centuries before Christ, Buddha invited all the animals in creation to come to him, promising them recompense appropriate to his all-powerful and miraculous kindness and generosity. However, dimmed by their preoccupations of the moment (is it not said in the West that the characteristic of the animal is merely to eat, sleep, couple and fear?), almost all of them ignored the call of the Divine Sage. Yet twelve of the animals did go to him. They were, in order of their arrival, the Rat, Ox, Tiger, Rabbit, Dragon, Snake, Horse, Goat, Monkey, Rooster, Dog and Pig (other traditions replace the Rabbit with the Cat and the Pig with the Wild Boar).

To thank them Buddha offered each a year which would be dedicated to him alone through the ages. This year would carry the animal's name, and express his symbolic character and his specific psychological traits, marking the personality and behaviour of people born during that year.

Thus a cycle of twelve years was established, fitting exactly the sequence and rhythm of this improbable bestiary (one can imagine the dizzying amount of work which would have faced the astrologer if all of the animals had answered Buddha's invitation!).

Such is the legend.

The lunar cycle

Actually, Chinese astrology precedes the development of Far Eastern Buddhism, which began only in the 5th century of the Christian era, or about one thousand years after Buddha's appearance on earth. However, astrologers were already practising their art in China ten centuries before Christ; but the very origins of this astrology are as controversial as they are immemorial.

One point cannot be disputed: contrary to the West, which developed a solar astrology based on the apparent displacements of the daily star as its position in the Western zodiac changed from month to month, the Far East constructed a lunar astrology based on the annual cycle of lunar movements. This is why the Asian New Year – The Tet celebration among the Vietnamese – never falls exactly on the same date.

While the phases of the moon are equally important for a Western astrologer, their context is inscribed differently, with the result that their play of correspondence — and so their meanings and implications — are not comparable to those of Eastern astrology.

Without entering too deeply into scientific considerations which would lead us away from the purposes of this book, let us simply remind ourselves of the obvious and multiple influences of the moon, for example the movement of the tides, as well as more subtle levels, such as the female cycles and the obscure depths of the psyche. The term 'lunatic' has a precise and, indeed, clinical meaning. Recent statistical studies, for example, have made it possible to establish a strange and significant increase in acts of violence and criminality on nights when there is a full moon. Also, rigorous tests have established the direct impact of the moon on the chemical composition of certain bodies whose molecular structure can be modified depending on whether or not they have been exposed to lunar light.

Nuances of Chinese astrology

So, here we are with our twelve animals, the *Emblems* of Chinese astrology. Does this mean that all persons born in the same year as, say, the Rat or the Horse, will be subject to the same formulae of character and destiny? No more so than that those born under the sign of Aries or Libra are all confined to the same zodiacal script.

In Western astrology, the position of the planets, the calculation of the Ascendant and the Golden Mean of the Sky and its Mansions, allows the astrologer to refine and individualize a given theme considerably. In the same way, in Chinese astrology one obtains some surprisingly detailed and complex results. This is achieved by integrating with the intitial data factors such as the *Companion in Life* (determined by the hour of birth, but not to be confused with the Western Ascendant), and the predominant *Element*, which refers to the five Elements: Earth, Water, Fire, Wood and Metal.

This triple point of view — the *Emblematic Animal*, the *Companion in Life* and the *Element* — provide the reader with a greater diversity of references and a totality of perspectives both more rich and more precise than those found in Western astrology. To this we have added a detailed interpretation of the relationship between the Chinese and Western signs. The two astrologies are by nature distinct but never contradictory, and therefore complementary aspects and fusion can only result in a more profound understanding of the psychological types emanating from them. However, it is important to stress that although the concept of analogy holds an important place in Chinese astrology, it bears neither the same sense nor the same overall significance as in Western astrology.

Each Chinese sign is a universe in itself, a small cosmos

with its own laws and domains, completely independent of all other signs. Each of these living creatures is given specific powers and functions, becoming an emblematic animal endowed with a particular dimension peculiar unto itself. It creates its own jungle or cavern, and defines by its rhythm its own cadences and breathing. In this way it secretes its own chemistry — or, rather, its own alchemy. It is a supple, mobile, fluctuating image, governed by its own internal metamorphoses and contradictions.

Once we understand this, we will see that it is fatal to impose a fixed framework or clearly circumscribed area of mental categories and psychological equations in order to protect or reassure an anguished ego seeking a comforting or flattering projection of its own desires and fears.

Our alignment to a Chinese sign cannot be defined by exclusive formulae or linear classifications. The Chinese symbol unfolds slowly, a gift of the Gods, of Time and of Mystery; a delectable or poisoned gift which an Oriental person accepts with humility because he knows that its flavour may be born of the poison, as its poison may be born of the flavour.

Sometimes, in the course of a lifetime, it is circumstances more than a character trait which seem to determine and crystallize the principal tendencies of a sign. In such cases a thread of major or minor events will tend to form a symphonic background to the style of, say, a Dragon or a Rat.

To Have and To Be

Through the centuries Chinese astrology has permeated and inspired the mental attitudes and behaviour of hundreds of millions of people in the Far East, to an extent that is difficult for us to accept or even appreciate.

To understand better the spirit in which these people rely on the art of contemplation in handling the problems of daily life, a cardinal point must be emphasized — one which probably constituted the essential and fundamental difference between Eastern and Western civilizations, and poses a virtually impassable dividing line between them.

In our Western 'consumer society' — irrespective of the admiring or negative feelings we may associate with this expression — the fundamental question, from birth to death and at all levels of activity, is: 'What can I have?'. We are continuously asking what we might possess or enjoy; what material goods, fortune, luck, honours or power might be had; whether we will achieve success in love, prestige, a good job, family, health, home, friends or, on another level, culture and knowledge. It is always a question of, 'What can I obtain, preserve, enlarge?' which underlies the totality of our motivations.

Think of the *models* that are held up to us: the successful politicians, business tycoons, film and stage stars, celebrated artists or scientist, sports champions, heroes of crime novels or comic strips. Idols of all kinds incarnate the triumph and glory of 'to have'. All will say, 'I have the most power, the most money, the most diplomas and abilities', or even, 'Mine is the greatest love affair'. Or, why not 'Mine is the most terrible drama, the most frightful illness'? Esteem is won exclusively from what one *has*.

Still more obvious is advertising, which is omnipresent today, and proclaims that one must absolutely *have* such and such a product in order *to be:* dynamic, seductive, happy, at ease with oneself or wholly fulfilled.

For Orientals, the decisive question is not 'What can I have?' but 'Whom can I be?' The model aspired to is not the great leader, the hero or the champion, but the poor, naked Sage who has attained total freedom and perfect peace within himself. Princes and great businessmen bow low before him, for he is the image of the highest self-realization possible to man. In this perspective, the Sage renounces nothing; on the contrary, since he has attained the supreme reality, he is immeasurably richer than the most powerful ruler.

It is we who, due to our fragmented and illusory

attachments, our infantile whims and our incessant conflicts, continually forgo the most marvellous felicity of all — God.

'Who am I?' Whatever approaches and methods, schools, sects or forms of asceticism are followed, this question, in appearance so simple and banal, lies at the base of and is the key to all Oriental culture. Through it lies the way to true liberation, by way of those roads to genuine understanding and knowledge known as Yoga, Vedanta, Tantra, Tao and Zen — to cite only the best known.

All this may cause the Chinese approach to astrology to seem disconcerting to us. The Oriental does not think 'I have such and such predispositions, aptitudes or weaknesses inherent in my horoscope', but rather, 'How can I be a Rat (or a Goat or a Dog) in all the circumstances of my life?'

The Oriental's goal is not 'to have' in the same way in which we in the West say 'I possess such and such a quality or defect'. For him, it is instead a question of directions, implying a subtle and rhythmic progression; a sort of poetic dance of destiny, with each animal possessing its own steps and pirouettes — an entire choreography of its own.

These subtleties must be perceived clearly by those who wish to evolve without losing their way or turning round in circles in this immense domain of shimmering and shifting aspects of understanding.

The astrological I Ching

In this book, we present a game inspired by the oracles of the I Ching and adapted to each sign.

In his book *Zen Buddhism*, Alan Watts wrote: 'The I Ching is a work of divination containing oracles based on 64 abstract figures, each composed of six traits. These traits are of two sorts: divided or negative and undivided or positive. A modern psychologist would recognize an analogy with the Rorschach test, whose aim is to establish the mental portrait of an individual according to the spontaneous images suggested to him by an inkspot or an over-elaborate design. A subject whose images are inspired by the inkspot should be able to use his subsequent perceptions to deduce the necessary practical information to guide his future behaviour. Considered in this way, the divinatory art of the I Ching cannot be attacked as a vulgar superstition.'

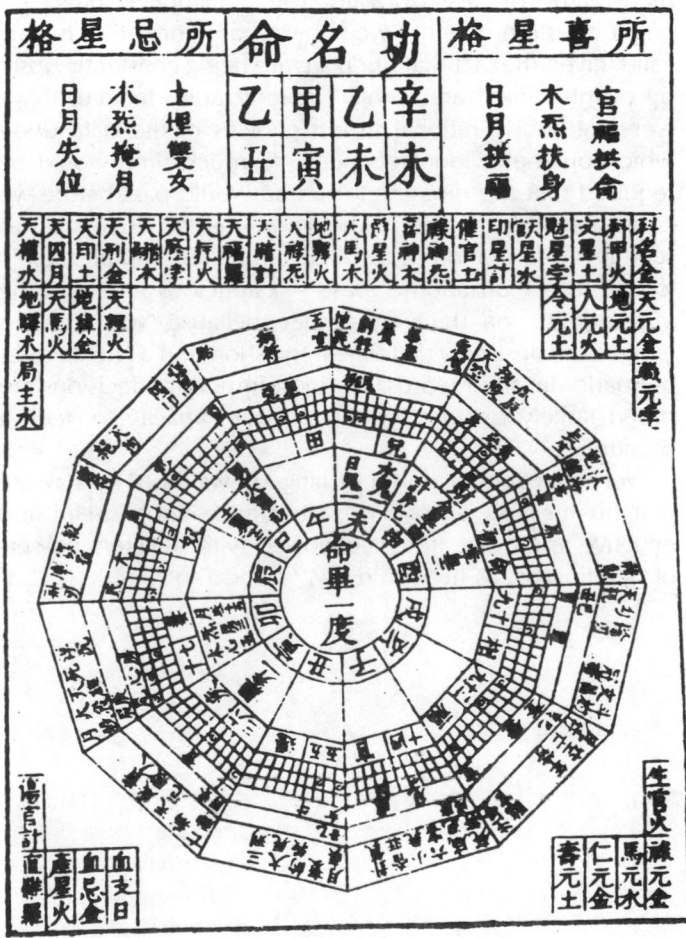

The relationship between the Signs and the Lunar Mansions

The practitioner of the I Ching commands an entire critical survey of the methods available when important decisions have to be made. We, on the other hand, are convinced that our decisions are rational because we depend upon a cluster of valid data affecting a problem; not for us to leave it to a mere game of heads or tails. The practitioner, however, might question whether we know what information is truly valid, given the fact that our plans are being constantly upset by events which are wholly unpredictable. Indeed, if we were rigorously rational in our choices of the data upon which our behaviour depended, so much time would be required that the moment for action would pass before we could assemble the data. Although we may set out initially to seek this information in a scientific manner, we are rapidly forced to act on another basis — capricious intuition, the impossibility of thinking further because we are too exhausted, or simply that time is too short and a choice must be made. In other words, our most important decisions are based largely on impressions, on our capacity to 'feel' a situation.

Every practitioner of the I Ching knows this. He is aware that his method is not an exact science but a useful and effective approach, if he is endowed with sufficient powers of intuition or, as he would say, 'in the Tao'.

THE YIN AND THE YANG

The *Yin* and the *Yang* are the symbols of two opposing and complementary principles whose indissoluble play and constant metamorphosis represent the roots, indeed the very tissues of the universe in action. They represent the eternal opposites — Positive-Negative, Yes-No, White-Black, Day-Night, Full-Empty, Active-Passive, Masculine-Feminine, and so on. Each contains within itself the germ of the other. That is why the man (Yang) bears within himself a feminine component (Yin), and the woman (Yin) a masculine one (Yang).

The Yin-Yang coupling is both indissoluble and changeable, each of the two terms being also its opposite and complementary term. This is expressed by the traditional figure:

At the moment when the Yang (white, active) is at its apogee — the bulging, enlarged part — the Yin (black, passive) imperceptibly takes its place — the tapering part — and vice verse.

The Yin and the Yang have no 'moral' character, neither is superior nor inferior to the other. Their antithesis is as necessary and as little in conflict as that of the left hand and the right hand striking together to applaud.

THE YIN AND THE YANG TYPES

The Rat, Ox, Rabbit, Monkey, Dog and Pig are **Yin**.
The Tiger, Horse, Dragon, Snake, Goat and Rooster are **Yang**.

The Yin man

Appearance: The Yin man is often corpulent, of medium height and muscularly well developed. He is physically resilient to a marked degree and his health is sound. He often has a round face and does not smile much.

Psychology: The Yin man is above all self-preoccupied and inclined to consider himself the centre of the universe. Though his behaviour appears calm, his moods are unstable and susceptible to his immediate environment. He has great confidence in himself, yet fears failure. Sociable, hospitable, he is optimistic vis-à-vis himself and others. His life is active; he is pragmatic and efficient.

The Yang man

Appearance: He is of average weight, often tall and slender, even willowy. His face is smiling and he prefers strong colours. Of delicate health, he should be advised to prevent rather than wait to cure illness.

Psychology: The Yang man is an individualist and attracted to introspective meditation. He is intelligent, independent and at times solitary. He prefers his own company and communing with nature to living with the crowd. Contrary to the Yin man, he seeks his equilibrium within himself instead of finding it amongst others.

YEAR OF THE RAT

 1900·1912·1924
1936·1948·1960
1972·1984·1996

THE DOMAINS OF THE RAT

十二生肖

DUHAMEL

THE RAT AND ITS SYMBOLISM

The Rat is an animal of the Yin tendency. He comes from the north and belongs to the winter solstice.

'The Rat is Yin because it is a creature which lives principally at night. Supposed to enjoy a life-span of three hundred years, the Rat turns white after its hundredth year. Extremely generous to those whom he likes, he is a symbol of wealth and prosperity. The Rat's home is well-furnished and elegant. He is, most usefully, endowed with the gift of second sight....'

In order to comprehend this quotation, we must delve into the very heart of Chinese mythology and folklore disclosed by the Chinese zodiac, the origin of which is very obscure. Only here can we learn about the origin and the choice of these twelve animals, all of them heroes of ancient legends.

There is no inauspicious animal, none is 'good' nor 'bad'. All participate in the same equilibrium, in one harmonious whole. So, let us break down our rational frontiers and set out on a search for our animal by way of the myths and legends, bordering the real and the imaginary.

The approaches are difficult for the Rat is master of the underground world, of those forces 'from below', which perhaps explains his gift for second sight. Brother of the serpent and the mole, he participates in that world of burrowing beings, curling under the earth, in the depths of caves or the warmth of replenished granaries.

'Creature of the entrails', hollowing out a deep tunnel, symbol of nocturnal and clandestine activities, he will at times experience both fear and cupidity, and also, misery; he then becomes an abominable tyrant.

'Extremely generous towards those whom he likes' . . . Those free from fear, who know how to recognize his quality, may benefit from his gift of second sight.

This brother of the serpent and the mole occupies a place of honour next to Daikoku, the Japanese god of wealth.

Even in Siberia the Rat is the emblem of prosperity. . .

. . . So, Rat venerated or Rat detested? We are free to choose, as with our destiny.

La Fontaine knew how to make us smile, how to touch our hearts with his joyous comrades at a feast interrupted by a feline race in 'The Town Rat and the Field-Mouse' In 'The Cat and the Old Rat' he concludes:

> *'He was experienced,*
> *And knew that lack of trust*
> *Is Mother of security.'*

Another Rat-Mouse, Disney's Mickey, prince of laughter and of the world of childhood, knew how to vanquish our fears, with laughter prevailing over the tragic. Let us not denigrate the world of the comic strip and recognize that it is a source of magic. It would seem that this is the best way to exorcize our inner demons — to dive deep into legend, searching our roots.

However, it is in India that the Rat — here a Rat-Mouse called Mushaka — is most fully revealed to us, being in character the most representative, the most whimsical, the most imaginative and the least predictable.

Imagine a tiny rat serving as a mount for a divinity named Ganesha. Ganesha represents the appeal to spiritual forces. He is the Guide, the Lord of Obstacles who both creates obstacles for the spiritual training of man and teaches him to surmount them by sublimating and conjuring with the apparently hostile forces rather than by destroying them. Half-man, half-elephant, he possesses a great trunk and strong defences. A mixture of the grotesque and the solemn, greedy and wily, he sits astride the Rat-Mouse Mushaka.

Together they live through all the possible adventures in our illogical world, a world made up of appearances and realities that are equally ephemeral. Here they are — partners, accomplices, sometimes denounced as thieves or hoaxers, appropriating material and spiritual riches and even going so far as to defraud holy men and gurus.

This Rat is a sort of Lucifer, a great Advocate who does not hesitate to misrepresent the truth and to falsify the evidence, but always, finally obliges the disciple to refine his feelings and pitilessly dispel any false pretences.

In short, one must trust appearances. Let us learn the Rat's language. This rodent has more than one trick up his sleeve; he is undeniably a magician!

A few notes on the Rat

Principal qualities: Charm, intelligence, imagination.

Principal defects: Aggressive and individualistic. Insists upon living only at his own rhythm.

In work: Clever and opportunistic. Not one for group work, unless·everyone depends on him.

Best role: Confidential agent.

Worst role: Administrative employee.

Money: Greedy and spendthrift.

Luck: To be born on a summer's night, for in winter the granaries are empty and he must work very hard to feed himself.

Cannot live without: Passion.

Adores: Everything off the beaten track, such as haunted castles, fried potatoes in Morocco, couscous in Sweden, frogs' legs in England, suet pudding and treacle in California.

Detests: Agendas, alarm clocks, family photograph albums.

Leisure activities: Any voyage at all, provided he thinks that he is the first to take it.

Favourite places: Grottoes, catacombs, caverns, underground passages, undiscovered caves.

Colours: Red and black.

Plants: Savory, wormwood.

Flowers: Orchid, tuberose and thistle.

Skills: Salesman, commercial traveller, legal or financial expert, broker, critic, writer, politician (of an extreme party, *never* the centre), speleologist, doctor, anaesthetist, anatomical pathologist, criminologist, detective and, of course, spy.

The four ages in the life of the Rat, according to Chinese tradition

The *infancy*, *childhood* and *youth* of the Rat will be without problems. He will live through them with insouciance, yet entranced by new discoveries. Adolescence may often cause problems, however, for this is an extremely sexual sign.

The Rat's *maturity* will be more difficult. Engaged by material struggles, he will be subject to financial ups and downs. An extremist on the sentimental level, the Rat will find it difficult to resist temptations and to avoid making brutal decisions.

In *old age* the Rat will be more peaceful. At this time he can master and even shed his aggressive instincts and greed, and finally accept the fact that he is a social animal belonging to a specific milieu within a certain historical and social context.

THE PSYCHOLOGY OF THE RAT

The Chinese zodiac embodies signs which, for the Western world, challenge and call for a rejection of our accepted 'way of life', our habit of a *priori* thinking and detached objective reflection. How should we view the Rat? The Rat, just like the Snake, has the unhappy knack of provoking romantic swoons or Homeric brawls. Why are people so susceptible, so easily provoked by him? Why are some people terrified by a rat rather than by a weasel, dog or chicken? Reflecting on it, one can be certain that this animal presents no real danger to man. Yet our history, our imaginative 'baggage', is filled with rats, from the rats off the ships that introduced the Plague to those that inhabit our barns. Harbingers of ruin as well as of opportunity, they haunt our unconscious and, in the stories we tell in the evening beside the fire, in old country houses replete with dreams and creaking floorboards, they are never far away.

Let us get rid of our preconceived ideas and render justice. As an animal, the Rat is considered to be the most 'intelligent' in our bestiary, along with the spider and the dolphin. In Chinese astrology he is the first of the Twelve to have answered the Buddha's call, which says a great deal for his opportunism. And have you ever heard of a rat discovered in any empty barn?

This animal, that so frightens us, holds a privileged place in Chinese astrology: he is number one. He is therefore solitary, individualistic and self-willed. He is constantly alert and watchful. It is extremely difficult, if not impossible, to influence him, much less dictate a course of conduct to him.

I have never encountered anyone born under the sign of the Rat who was not excessively jealous of his personal liberty and autonomy. I have also never met any stupid Rats, though they must surely exist.

At first glance, the Rat is likeable. He has a mysterious charm, a silky skin, an attractive face. He is astonishingly seductive. But is this totally natural? Not really, because the Rat is calculating rather than spontaneous; he aims to please. Usually incapable of making concessions, the Rat can make enormous efforts, if he wishes, to fascinate someone over whom he intends to establish an ascendancy. A taste for power? Indubitably. But still more important is his need to feel secure. The more you depend on the Rat, the more he has influence over you and the more he is reassured. At rest and confident again, he seems as charming as he first appeared to be. The more he gives the impression of being devoid of bad intentions, the more dangerous he becomes, if only because he has a natural power of auto-suggestion.

The Rat's aim, in fact, is to protect the deepest aspects of his personality, which combines profound disquiet with an aggressive reaction to all investigations. Master of the subterranean world, the Rat does not easily deliver his secrets; he guards them ferociously. Yet this does not make him happy. That would be too simple, and our Rat is not simple. He wants very much to be understood, but as soon as you try to step into his domain, to bring light to it, he reacts violently, becoming biting, critical, vindictive and spiteful. And he does this while hoping that you will not let yourself be intimidated by this 'honourable' fight of his and will continue to believe in him. Truly, the Rat wants to feel understood, while at the same time retaining a deep reserve and continuing to complain that he is misunderstood.

Since the Rat is essentially an introvert, although in appearance he can easily be mistaken for an extrovert, his aggressiveness frequently turns against him. From this there results a rather morbid capacity for guilt, a vicious circle of self-accusation and resentment due to thinking himself excluded, and a fear of impotence. He is incapable of embracing the middle way. Morally, he lives in a minefield, danger intoxicates him; but physically, he refrains from taking risks. The Rat likes to toy with his spiritual fate, to brush up against and even to exceed his limits and venture into forbidden territories. Otherwise, in accepting a mundane life, he would die of boredom.

The Rat is active and highly strung. Only hard mental effort with a concrete goal in view can assuage him. When he does nothing, he suffers from extreme anxiety, turns around in circles and becomes over-critical and odious. The stimulation of the struggle is vital for him. Anti-conformist in the extreme, he cannot endure daily life with its mundane obligations. In fact, he bristles at everything which might prevent him from behaving as he pleases — except when he is very much in love, but we will see about that later.

The Rat is often original at any price. The unforeseen and the baroque charm him. He is the kind who forgets birthdays and wedding anniversaries, but, with the delight of a child who has played a good trick, he will invent new festivities. He will leap for your throat if you ask him the time, because it will remind him of time passing, daily bread and other horrible details. To the Rat, life is not a dreary succession of days and nights, but a series of exceptional events and intense sensations.

The Rat respects the law only when it is his own, otherwise he likes to transgress the rules, overthrow taboos and defy the established order; his morality is personal.

THE RAT AS A CHILD

The child born under the sign of the Rat is easy to live with on one condition: that you create a setting that makes him feel secure, while leaving him free to his own experiences.

The very young Rat has an acute need of love — which will last all his life — and what really matters to him is the sincerity and quality of this love. He will be as happy in a hut as in a penthouse if his parents respond to his intellectual curiosity and cocoon him with tenderness. This affectionate climate, by disarming his aggressive instincts at an early age, will render the Rat less virulent in the future.

It is important to cultivate the child-Rat's gregariousness, rather than permit him to indulge his ingrained taste for secrecy. He will have no equal in leading his little friends into exciting explorations. When I was a small girl, I reverently followed a gang of boys whose leader, born under the sign of the Rat, organized Indian war games on a bit of waste land near the hotel where we were on holiday. What happened is what necessarily had to happen: our parents discovered that our playground was littered with mines from the bombardments of 1944. Informed of this, our leader-Rat laughingly declared: 'Of course I knew that, otherwise it wouldn't have been worth it.' While he was totally relaxed, our parents were in a state of confusion.

The child-Rat is adventurous and off-hand. He does well at school because everything interests him. He is alert, intelligent and curious. He seeks at an early age to distinguish between appearance and reality. He tends to be literary rather than mathematical, and is rarely a hard worker. He is also greedy, and at this age adores sweets.

Later, as he reaches the age of puberty and sexual awakening, the young Rat becomes acutely aware that his or her sex has been imposed upon him or her, and it is then that Rats acquire the habit of distinguishing themselves from others.

Parents should remember that young Rats are extremely modest, both physically and morally, and consider any pressure on their privacy akin to rape. So, be cautious and discreet!

LOVE LIFE

Anxious, tormented and often reacting aggressively, Rats never win the prize for being the easiest to get on with. They leave that to the Pig. On the other hand, they are never boring; and they are extremely romantic, indulging in passions as violent as those they wish to inspire.

The Rat's emotional life is never simple, for mad attractions, inflamed liaisons and excessive emotions are difficult to assimilate with work-a-day life and so frighten many people away. This is a point of view detested by our Rat, infatuated as he is with heightened sensations and bizarre situations. Often insisting that he is misunderstood, he is unable to confide in others. There is, as it were, a chasm between them and him which he cannot bring himself to bridge.

An egoist in his social life, when he is in love he is capable of unlimited generosity. He also has an unquestionable gift for getting himself into fearfully complicated situations, passing from the role of victim to that of aggressor without anyone being able to grasp exactly what has happened or why. The Rat is slightly sado-masochistic. 'I can support anything', he will say, 'but the absence of passion.'

A happy Rat, who feels properly understood, is bound to be faithful — deeply and passionately so — but the commitment is fragile: a failure in complicity, some disappointment or disagreement will ruin it all. He will then look elsewhere for love. If you reproach him, he will give you his point of view with touching sincerity. Inevitably, you will feel that he is speaking in bad faith and react against it. But the Rat is unbeatable at this game and conveys the sincerity of the great advocate.

Sexually, he is passionate (as always!), loves to vary his pleasures and does not lack imagination. A worthwhile partner.

FAMILY LIFE

The fireside, the soft and safe atmosphere of the average home in which, on Sundays, the men play cards while their wives discuss their difficulties with their children, their knitting or needlework always to hand — none of this holds any appeal for the Rat. It is not that he has anything against it, for he is no fool and appreciates its utility, especially within the context of the family. But the Rat hates to be involved in the problems of others; his own preoccupy him enough.

The true Rat needs to escape from time to time into his own domain, away from routes that have already been mapped out, and all the more so if he has been raised in a conventional milieu. Conventional terms, such as 'what will people think?', rile him to such an extent that he will appear to be transformed into a rabid revolutionary or snarling anarchist.

The Rat will be more at ease if he has children, but even with his own family his attitudes will be disconcerting. These little creatures will grow up in a strange atmosphere in which the oddest fantasies will intrude upon an otherwise rigorous regime. Visitors will receive an impression of total disorganization at first, but then will be astonished to discover that the Rat's children go to bed on time, the roast beef is properly cooked and that everyone is relaxed and the atmosphere agreeable.

The Rat makes an excellent parent because he exercises authority, even though he is hardly a conformist. He is alert with his children, encourages every little shoot of their young intelligence and imagination, and is adept at thinking up novel ways to learn, understand and experiment. He does everything possible to ensure that they have rich food — nutritionally as well as intellectually.

The Rat's children will feel protected and encouraged, especially if they have the good luck to be born in the year of the Ox, Rabbit, Pig or Goat. But Rat parents will have trouble with children born in the year of the Monkey, who will slip between their fingers; as well as those born in the year of the Snake, who will never obey, and the Tiger and the Horse who are too independent to tolerate the weight of parental authority. As for a Dragon child, this one will be able to do anything he pleases with Rat parents. The Rat parent will not have an easy time with a Dog child, because each will suffer from anxieties so acute that this will lead to mutual anguish.

PROFESSIONAL LIFE

Independent and active, the Rat dislikes administrative work, except when he has an imperative need for material security, which will have drawn him to inhabit some dusty offices. There, sheltered behind a mass of old filing cabinets, he will spend much of his time criticizing his superiors and speaking ill of his colleagues, whom he will consider no more than a large herd of cattle grown stupid by clocking in and out at milking time. The Rat who has failed is bitter and more aggressive than usual.

The majority of Rats manage to achieve something interesting in their lives, whether on a financial or creative level. In any case, a Rat is never banal. Having the blood of a fighter and a competitive spirit, a true Rat will institute a discreet campaign from the bottom of the ladder, silently undermining it during the hours of darkness in order, when daylight comes, to supplant those whom he considers to be less gifted than he is for undertaking the work in hand. He is capable, astute and, with good reason, relies on his native ability. He knows that when the chips are down he is more resourceful than others and will find a way while they dither.

However, beware: for the Rat, 'charity begins at home'. The Rat rarely believes in work for its own sake. Clever at getting others to work, especially manual work which he is disinclined to do, the Rat is fired by the profit motive.

The Rat's skills are generally more intellectual than manual. We meet many businessmen, but also many writers and artists, born under the sign of the Rat.

As to lady Rats, they are also excellent housekeepers.

MATERIAL LIFE

The Rat's behaviour vis-à-vis money is ambiguous. His great fear is to be in need, even to want for ready cash, and this compels him to be something of a hoarder. However, he uses his hoard not for himself alone and can be generous simultaneously to a small group of friends whose love he relies on and who therefore, in his eyes, both deserve and require his affection.

If the friends are not there, he will likely construct a Fort Knox with arms at the ready. But he will become bored, disarm the fort, take his money and gaily spend it. For the Rat is the sort of profiteer who likes to enjoy life and detests denying himself anything. Apparently rich one day, he will be penniless the next.

We must understand that the Rat is self-seeking. If he gives you a present, it is, of course, in order to give you pleasure. But you may be sure that he has already worked out what he can obtain in exchange, morally and materially; he has a great gift for barter.

Some words of advice: never ask a Rat to lend you money, unless you intend to pay him interest on it until the end of your days. Also, never ask him to buy something for you at the sales because he loves them and will buy absolutely anything under the pretext of 'saving money'.

ENVIRONMENT

The Rat perennially dreams of haunted castles, their draw-bridges and secret dungeons. Recounting these, teasing his guests, he will toss in a few skeletons in cupboards to complete the effect. Actually, the Rat is too meticulous to believe in all this, the dust of the past would make him sneeze. Plunged into the phantasmagoric atmosphere of his private dreams, he would not last a week before taking out the vacuum cleaner, setting up a list of household duties for the phantoms and polishing their chains. His dislike for receiving orders is accompanied curiously enough by an unbridled taste for order, which he creates and maintains. Mrs Rat is a remarkably fine housekeeper, and Mr Rat is constantly improving his home. In consequence, the Rat's home is comfortable and well organized, equipped with the most up-to-date household appliances, including a functional kitchen. Its interiors will be decorated with curious effigies — preferred enemies, sorcerers' cauldrons, African masks, and the like. There will also be an impressive library and a stereo on which he is as likely to play religious music as the tom-tom.

So that his happiness can be complete, the Rat must also have a cellar supplied with secret trap-doors; such means of escape are vital for him.

A guide to personal relations with a Rat
Methods of seduction:
He: Takes you to a romantic and mysterious spot one foggy night and asks you outright if you want to sleep with him.
She: Transforms herself into a strange, veiled mood which alternates between warm, whispered confidences and scratching you; an iron hand in a velvet glove.
If he loves you: He will say so and will give you the impression that nothing is too good for you. If you ask him for the moon, he is capable of getting it for you.
He expects of you: That you be madly in love with him.
To keep you: He or she offers you unforgettable and exhausting nights of love.

If he is unfaithful: It is by chance. Moreover, he instantly regrets it, feels guilty and finds excuses with unbelievable and touching bad faith.

If you are unfaithful: He will be unfaithful as well.

In the event of a breach between you: He will engineer it so that you make the decision so that he can reproach you later; or, if he wants to end things quickly, he will use any means to provoke an irreparable parting.

If you wish to give him a gift: Offer him a strange object that seems to have come from a far-away, exotic place. No need for it to be useful; bring it to him wrapped in newspaper and whisper that you stole it from a Hindu temple or an Egyptian tomb. Never admit that you found it at an Oriental exhibition at Harrods.

If you want to seduce him: Take him to your grandmother's abandoned house, make a bonfire of old letters and improvise a dinner by candlelight. The menu will be unimportant, but the wine must be excellent.

If you want to get rid of him: Take him home for lunch on a Sunday when an aunt and uncle from the country are there with their small children and holiday photographs are offered for inspection.

THE RAT
AND OTHER CHINESE SIGNS

Rat/Rat

It remains to be seen which of the two will be more complicated. To begin with, they will be amazed by their similarities, and, when observing each other, moved because for each of them it will be like looking in a mirror. Their passion will be all-embracing, irrational, exalted.

But such an impulsion is rarely enduring for two Rats together, unless they belong to opposing signs in the Western zodiac. Otherwise, they too easily drown in a sea of their resemblances.

It is the *lasting quality* that will be the weak point of this relationship. It is, though, good for the Rat to experience such a love affair; it will at least help him to understand why his love life is sometimes so difficult, provided that he learns to recognize his own tendencies in those of the other.

Friendship between two Rats is tricky, for though they are accomplices on many levels, there is a risk that they will compete with each other for control, since each wants his own way in most things.

Rat/Ox

The Rat and the Ox get along very well together. Both are individualists and therefore well placed to respect and admit the independence of the other. In this situation, the Rat needs to be taken seriously, and the Ox always takes everything very seriously! Also, little disposed to gossip, the Ox will respect his partner's secrets. Things will go less well when the Rat, for whom the charm of confidences is irresistible, especially when they are somewhat improper, reveals to his closest chums the more intimate appetites of the Ox. The latter will be enraged if this type of information leaks out.

The Rat's passionate nature may not always be entirely satisfied because the Ox does not think only 'of that'. Before going to bed, the Ox likes to do his accounts and check that the gas is turned off. But the Ox is faithful and reliable; both the male and the female take their responsibilities seriously. In fact, the Rat can count on him, while the Ox, in his everyday life, will enjoy and respond to the intelligence and the vivacity of his companion.

Rat/Tiger

The Rat is always fascinated by those signs who prove themselves to be capable of taking risks and this is one of the more effective ways to earn his admiration. In this respect, the Tiger holds all the aces.

The relationship between these two will not be peaceful, but certainly passionate! They will both find great satisfaction in each other. But the Tiger has the soul of a hunter and, from time to time, as a good feline must, he leaves his lair to search out available prey.

The apprehensive Rat wil have a hard time accepting that these conquests are only a game, a way for the Tiger to prove to himself that he is irresistible. But if he realizes that these conquests are rarely more than escapades, he and the Tiger can establish lasting ties.

One small snag: the Tiger is a realist but at the same time carefree. The Rat's greed, his fear of tomorrow, are completely foreign to him and he will not give a hoot about such things. Later, the Tiger may, of course, be pleased to find some meat in the freezer which otherwise he would have left to rot. Finally, though they may argue on this subject, they will prove to be complementary to each other.

Rat/Rabbit

Delighting in tranquillity and harmony, persons born during the year of the Rabbit hate extreme situations and are ill-equipped to deal with strain or stress.

The Rat, not realizing that his native disquiet creates a common ground with these graceful animals, will immediately label the Rabbit's prudence as pusillanimity. The latter will bristle at the Rat's tart criticism.

There is an undeniable, deep-rooted antipathy between the Rat and the Rabbit; if a Rat loves a Rabbit, he will not understand that the latter is at one and the same time adaptable, unstable and yet clings to security. And the Rat will have nothing to do with tranquillity and harmony; he prefers to live balanced on a tightrope, ever liable to have his fingers burnt. It is, of course, well known that the maxim 'once bitten, twice shy' applies to the Rabbit. Therefore, although the two have to make a strong effort to live together on an emotional level, as brother and sister or as friends, their differences can provide the opportunity for a profitable experience.

Rat/Dragon

This is an extremely positive alliance for the Rat; the Dragon's brilliance will compel his admiration, amaze and exhilarate him. The Rat will freely display an attachment both violent and irrational; he, so clever, so clear-headed, will embark without a qualm on the greatest of follies, simply to attract a blazing glance from this Prince of the Sky.

Yet here we may ask, does the Dragon really 'see' the Rat? Well, not always. From time to time he will be taken up with some new enthusiasm and forget him. But the Dragon so loves to be adored, adulated and admired, that the Rat's passion will act like a balm on his scales, as cool rain on his hot, dry breath.

Therefore, a lasting sentiment can unite them on the amorous, friendly or professional level. They can complete each other: the Dragon shines in peace, and so before each battle the attentive Rat will anticipate the obstacles in his path and, whispering into his ear, explain his adversary's weak points. The Rat will be very happy playing this occult role, which makes him feel indispensable. Then, blinded by his love, he will have no occasion to look for defects in the Dragon's armour. All will be 'for the best in the best of all possible worlds'.

Rat/Snake

This is a strange mixture. At first glance both are calm, clever and opportunistic, which makes for a positive common ground, above all in the field of business. The Rat is active, while the Snake prefers a minimum of effort. The one will shake up the other, who in turn will calm him. Both are possessive, and the Snake has a completely relative notion of fidelity. If he is unfaithful to his partner, he will only grudgingly accept that his partner is likely to do the same. The Rat will unsheath his claws; the Snake will try to smother him. Life will become increasingly complicated.

The Rat and the Snake, in fact, do not need each other, for they are capable, as the occasion requires, of using the same weapons with equal efficiency. But as comrades they respect each other. Sharing a taste for black comedy, they have fun together. If they establish an emotional tie, this will depend on a mutual tolerance — a quality not notable in either — however, that is the only way that they will be able to get along as a couple. Generally speaking, they understand each other and the Snake's quiet smile always calms the Rat's aggressiveness. But beware: this complicity is deep and secret; only they can sustain it.

Rat/Horse

The Rat and the Horse share a fault: both are egoists and capable of behaving very stupidly when carried away by passion. However, the Rat when passionate remains lucid, and even during his most excessive transports he remains capable of listening to the small voice of wisdom, of recognizing with a flash of lucidity the limits that would really be too dangerous to pass.

Not so the Horse! Acknowledging no limits, the great attraction to him is the love which drives him beyond the frontiers of the possible. He does not think things over; he plunges in like a bumblebee pollinating flowers.

Given their natures, the Rat will always be critical of the excesses and outbursts of the Horse; he will judge him to be superficial. The Horse, on the other hand, will think the Rat is spiteful and ill-natured. Neither of them will be completely wrong.

Understandably, Chinese astrological tradition advises these two signs to avoid an amorous liaison with each other. That is not difficult, for they are not much attracted to each other.

Rat/Goat

Here again is a relationship scarcely encouraged by tradition. It is accepted that the specific traits of these two signs are not in harmony: the Rat is too asiduous, too selfish, too critical and too lucid to tolerate for more than a very short time the casual unconcern and the fantasies of the Goat. And, although imaginative, the Rat is neither supple nor subtle enough, nor enough of an aesthete to follow the Goat in his quest for 'beauty at any price'.

The Goat will be disappointed in this relationship. He will feel misunderstood and will hate the Rat's criticisms. The Rat, irritated by what he feels to be an inconsistency in the Goat, will become even more biting. Since one belongs under the earth and the other lives in the clouds, it is, in any case, difficult for them to meet on any level.

A true Rat likes security, but he admires those who are capable of procuring it for themselves. This is not at all the Goat's 'forte'; he usually needs a patron. Unless the Western signs are especially encouraging, this relationship between such different personalities is hardly advisable.

Rat/Monkey

It is difficult in the case of a relationship between a Rat and a Monkey to advise them to avoid each other like the Plague. However, by doing so they will avoid many worries and complications. The trouble is that they both love complications. They therefore run the risk of experiencing a rather tortuous union.

Alike on many levels, the Rat and the Monkey can feel like accomplices and enjoy an amusing time together, but one will always try to get the better of the other, to dominate him in a rather underhand way. Each of them will say, 'I won that round, I really got him that time, didn't I?', and they will both be wrong.

If they are friends or colleagues, this alliance will be unstable but dynamic. In love, the hazards are greater, for the lucid Monkey cannot reciprocate the Rat's deep passions and give him all the attention and care that he pines for. In a pinch the Monkey can be charming and attentive, intoxicating his Rat with startling suggestions and compliments. But more often he will be cold, indifferent and thoughtless. This treatment can emasculate the Rat. He should take care: his equilibrium is endangered, because the Monkey will dominate him too much for his own good.

Rat/Rooster

One always fears that the Rat sees only the defects of the Rooster and becomes hypnotized by them. Then and there he will refuse to engage with this individual, so horribly sure of himself, and will pronouce him vain and superficial.

If the Rat takes the trouble to delve beneath appearances, he will discover qualities in the Rooster which please him. Once they get together, they will merrily criticize their circle of friends and acquaintances.

On the other hand, if they should turn their aggressions and their critical capacities against each other, a real boxing match will develop. Then, too, neither of them has any idea of economy. They would become broke and ruin each other in no time, at first with gifts and then with lawsuits.

A combination of a male Rat and female Rooster works better, because the female Rooster is level-headed and knows how to handle day-to-day life, even though it irritates her. If it is the Rat who is female, they will do well to open a shop for cut-rate goods, hire an amiable sales-girl and contrive not to eat up all their capital.

Rat/Dog

Why not? The Rat, who is always haunted by the vague thought of the morsels of grain which he will need when he is old, is well-placed to understand the deep anxieties of the Dog.

The Dog, who carefully protects his territorial limits, will not be offended by his companion's mania for secrecy. They will accept their differences without conflict and will delight in their resemblances. They will pursue their way, discreet accomplices, travelling only at night and never speaking to strangers.

This alliance will develop their reciprocal taste for mystery and, curiously enough, make them feel secure, for they give each other confidence: the Dog because he is faithful, which the Rat needs, and the Rat because he knows how to defend himself in case of difficulties.

In short, this is an advisable relationship, both in matters of the heart as well as in those of business.

Rat/Pig

The Rat and the Pig have in common the fact that they are unrepentant sensualists who like to profit from life, and sometimes go so far as to burn the candle at both ends. There is no doubt that they derive great pleasure from being together, goad each other on and will have fantastic experiences on all levels.

However, the Rat runs the risk of being irritated by the Pig's naiveté, especially if he is not in love or if the relationship is of the professional or family order.

But if passion is involved, our Rat, gratified by the kindness, the attentiveness and serenity of his partner, will never fail to take up his defence, encourage him and push him to be more dynamic. He will also teach him some profitable little tricks, such as how to avoid paying parking fines without getting caught. The Pig will be a bit shocked, but will then come round.

SOME RAT CELEBRITIES

Adenauer, Lucretia Borgia, Werner Von Braun, Charlotte Brontë, Luis Bunuel, Jimmy Carter, Pablo Casals, Charles I, Chateaubriand, Maurice Chevalier, Clausewitz, Disraeli, Manuel de Falla, Galileo, Haydn, Himmler, Ibsen, Ionesco, Lawrence of Arabia, Jack London, Mata-Hari, Monet, Mozart, Peter the Great, Rodin, Rossini, Shakespeare, Shelley, Johann Strauss, Tchaikovsky, Chiang Kai-shek, Leo Tolstoy, Torquemada, Toulouse-Lautrec, Washington, Emile Zola.

YOUR COMPANION IN LIFE

生命伴侣

After the Chinese sign of your year of birth, here is the sign of your hour of birth

What is a Companion in Life, as understood in Chinese astrology? It is a sort of 'ascendant' sign corresponding to your hour of birth This Companion is another animal belonging to the Chinese cycle of the twelve emblematic beasts, who falls into step with you and accompanies you, ever ready to help you brave the traps and ambushes along your route. A permanent and benevolent shadow, he can render the impossible possible.

He is your counterpart, but with his own character and tendencies and with a different psychology. Both guardian angel and devil's advocate, he will be a witness to your life and an actor in it.

Have you ever felt, deep inside yourself, the subtle presence of another 'myself' inhabiting you and with whom you live, at times in harmony, at others in conflict? Another self who sometimes criticizes you and at others encourages you? That is your Companion in Life.

There are times when he will appear to be an imposter or an intruder. Certainly, he often questions your habits and your moral or spiritual complacency. Accompanied by this companion, a shadow within, the route is less monotonous and the voyager multiplies his chances of arriving at his chosen destination. This, however, in itself matters little, for it is the journey and the manner in which it is conducted that are important. Indolence is the greatest danger: your Companion is capable of arousing you from a lassitude of spirit and, to that end, if necessary, robbing you of your certainties, trampling on your secret gardens and, finally, tearing away the great veil of illusion.

It sometimes happens that your Companion is of the same sign as your year of birth, a twin brother in a way — for example, a Rat/Rat. In this case, you must recognize that he will compel you to realize yourself fully and to live the double aspect — the Yin and the Yang — that your bear

50

within yourself. In any case, you also bear within yourself the twelve animals. So, set out on the long route, ready for the great adventure: the beautiful voyage during which you will encounter the harmoniously entangled, the solemn and the grotesque, the ephemeral reality, the dream and the imagined.

Table of hours corresponding to the twelve emblematic animals

If you were **born** between		your **companion** is	
11 pm and	1 am		Rat
1 am and	3 am		Ox
3 am and	5 am		Tiger
5 am and	7 am		Rabbit
7 am and	9 am		Dragon
9 am and	11 am		Snake
11 am and	1 pm		Horse
1 pm and	3 pm		Goat
3 pm and	5 pm		Monkey
5 pm and	7 pm		Rooster
7 pm and	9 pm		Dog
9 pm and	11 pm		Pig

These figures correspond to the *solar hour* of your birth. If necessary, you should check the summer times (Daylight Savings Time) and make the appropriate adjustment (sometimes two hours before or after statutory time).

THE RAT AND ITS COMPANION IN LIFE

 **Rat/Rat**

Make no mistake about it, this animal can only be master or slave. He can be master of the art of trickery and of prudence, instigator of plots, puller of strings behind the political scene or a great militarist and emperor of strategy. That is unless, from his earliest childhood, this Rat/Rat turns out to be a frentic individualist, rejecting dogmas and principles, constraints and proprieties, perpetually on the hunt for food and lodging with the aggressiveness to be expected of such a rodent.

In his other aspect, as a slave, he will be in a state of permanent conflict with himself, having chosen the servitude of the 'domestic rat', which, despite its apparent advantages, will always be at war with his instinctive need to be independent and self-supporting. As a slave, he has to renounce his desire to bewitch and fascinate others. This Rat/Rat will not frighten anyone but himself.

 **Rat/Ox**

Here the Companion is a striking example of a pseudo guardian angel. The aggressions of the Rat are tempered by the tranquil force of the Ox. The Rat explores in depth, the Ox on the surface. Both being creators, it is the Ox who sometimes, by butting with his horns, will force the Rat to leave his underground passages, jostling him from his fortifications. A lover of liberty, the Buffalo will rarely be sidetracked. If the Rat symbolizes perpetual movement, the other symbolizes slowness; and if Ox dreams of virgin territory, the Rat dreams of impenetrable universes. The Rat/Ox will be realistic, prudent and will know how to reinforce his success.

 **Rat/Tiger**

When a rodent is coupled with a carnivorous animal, the voyage will not be very peaceful; count on the Tiger, he will see to it that you do not fall asleep on your laurels! The hunt is his domain, the jungle his universe; the way will be strewn with traps and nothing will escape his vigilance. As a sentinel, he is unsurpassed. However, do not forget that the Tiger is a noble lord, who will expect to be first. In roaming various territories, he will appropriate them, and the individualistic Rat nature will respond with violent revolt, which may result in your being emotionally torn. Do not despair. The Tiger is also a symbol of moderation. He is an excellent guide, in every sense of the term, and the Rat, at times a usurper himself, will gain in tolerance and loyalty

 **Rat/Rabbit**

This is a curious mixture, to say the least. Are not these hereditary enemies 'condemned' to travel the same route? But do not be fooled, for this may be the best way to accomplish the voyage. An apprehensive Rat coupled with the eternally stalking Rabbit will not be easily deceived. Suspicious, both adaptable and aggressive, he will be ready to protect himself from predators and to go to any lengths to secure his comfort and vested interests. Also, the influence of the Rabbit will make the Rat less vulnerable to outbursts of passion. Calm and efficient, the Rat/Rabbit illustrates the aphorism 'Better to risk an intelligent friend than indulge a stupid one.'

Rat/Dragon

This is a lucky combination, for the Dragon is an excellent companion for the Rat. The voyage will be magical. In deepest harmony with himself, the Rat will leave his bottomless depths and will ride his scaled companion across the Milky Way, his muzzle in the stars. But be careful! If you allow yourself to be spellbound by the Dragon within you, you will pay dearly for it. You idolize him; he is fond of you. He reassures you; but in the end makes your decisions for you. The Dragon is prone to terrible rages; you will hide away. You must know how to make the most of your luck. Imagine it as a voyage in the watery depths and through the heavens, which also embraces the terrestrial world and its deeper recesses. Only do not forget that sometimes you must fight the Dragon in order to prevail, and that he is a ferocious sentinel.

Here is a Companion strong enough for the Rat, master of forces from below.

Rat/Snake

These two are brothers, but they fight each other mercilessly. Their territory is identical, but they have won it with bites and scratches, venom and trickery. The Rat and Snake are masters of the art of attack; moreover they are intuitive, professional spellbinders, who run the risk of putting each other to sleep by using mutual hypnosis. Alas, in this situation, the Rat cannot reverse roles.

The Snake will not lend himself to this little game. For the Rat the Snake Companion will always remain a mysterious reptile, coiled up under a stone, waiting to drag him at times into perilous labyrinths.

Rat/Horse

This coupling brings about an interchange between ardour and prudence. The Rat/Horse will go on often tumultuous voyages: What battles lie in wait! It will be difficult to temper the ardour of the Horse galloping under the blazing sun, while the anxious and prudent Rat will be busy securing his underground fortresses.

The ill-loved Rat must take dark and twisting paths to reach the light, while, for the Horse, it is intolerable to gallop in the shade. He needs the luminous Royal Way, and seeks the crowd and worldly success. The poor Rat must, however, straddle this charger and accept him as his guide. Lacking the power to bridle the magician, the Rat can always discover the joys of riding.

Rat/Goat

Here is an excellent Companion for the Rat, very different from him, whose nature is gay and free from care. An intuitive and subtle artist, the Goat will be prodigiously therapeutic for our ill-loved and anxious rodent. Moreover, the Goat responds to charm and appreciates sympathetic magic, and will not be bored by these qualities in the Rat.

Both will have a tendency to float about in a world of illusions, but, since they will get something worthwhile out of it, it is no matter if they seem blind and deaf; for these two it can be a useful technique.

 **Rat/Monkey**

Before leaving on a trip, these two should prepare a first aid kit; their journey is more likely to resemble a hazardous undertaking than an agreeable outing. These two companions believe in the principle of 'an eye for an eye, a tooth for a tooth', and repay each other accordingly. The Monkey will have but one idea: to devour the small rodent. The Rat will use all his tricks, including the most perverse, to make his companion fall into physical, moral and even spiritual traps. These two strange companions will have no tenderness for each other and will give each other no respite. Their journey will become an encounter staged in a prize-fighter's ring, where all blows are allowed and no rules are observed. May the more formidable win!

 **Rat/Rooster**

The Rooster, announcing the rising of the sun, and the Rat, busy with his nocturnal activities, are two companions who will hardly have time for sleep. For these two dissimilar characters, a true understanding may seem impossible, yet it is precisely in this that they may prove to be complementary to each other. The Rooster will perch; the Rat will burrow. Each has a lively nature. The one is a sun symbol, the other a symbol of night. They will mutually strengthen each other. Rat will offer his world of the underground on a gold platter to the Rooster at the very moment when the Rooster, ruffling his feathers, is rising on his spurs awaiting the moment of dawn's song. This is a daily offering on which the Rat would do well to meditate. For Master Rat, so often taking but rarely giving, this generous Rooster will be a source of strength, if he knows how to take what is offered.

Rat/Dog

He can be the ideal Companion for the Rat. The Dog is the guide for souls during their 'voyages' and is the guardian of the beyond. Like the rodent, he moves between subterranean and invisible worlds, He is, moreover, a faithful and mysterious Companion, slightly pessimistic for, symbolically, he is often associated with the idea of death. Since the Rat shares this association, the Dog's presence is not always welcome.

Perhaps one day the Rat will try to kill the Dog within him and, in battling against this guardian of the gates, he will break through his constraints. The Companion is sometimes a victim who must be sacrificed during the voyage.

Rat/Pig

On the one hand, the Pig is eager to cultivate the art of solitude'. He will avoid the main routes, preferring bushy paths with their odour of humus and a quiet night lying under the stars. On the other hand, a Rat/Pig is a complete materialist. Hoarder and profiteer, he will know how to capitalize not only on money, but on the fruits of his experiences.

The Rat/Pig will know only white or black; for him there are no shades of grey, no half-measures. His route will be scattered with obstructions which he will ruthlessly overcome. Do not count on him to have scruples; he will not know the meaning of the word.

Be careful! The Pig is credulous and this, added to the curiousity of the Rat, will spring a few traps. So, Rat/Pig, before you set forth, lay in your provisions of cheese and acorns.

THE RAT
AND THE FIVE
ELEMENTS

五行

YOUR ELEMENT

In Chinese astrology, each year is joined to an Element. There are five Elements: *Water, Fire, Wood, Metal, Earth.*

Each of the twelve emblematic animals is linked successively to each of the five Elements. For example, in the year 1900 the Rat was Metal, in 1912 he was Water, in 1924 he was Wood, in 1936, Fire and in 1948 he was Earth. Therefore, for the twelve years from 1900 he was linked to Metal, for the next twelve years to Water, and, for every succeeding period of twelve years, to each of the other Elements, in succession.

In order to determine the Element corresponding to the year of your birth, use the table below:

Years whose digits end in: 2 and 3 — Water
6 and 7 — Fire
4 and 5 — Wood
0 and 1 — Metal
8 and 9 — Earth

The same union of *Animal-Element* repeats every sixty years, for example, Rat-Metal appeared in 1720, 1780, 1840, 1900, 1960 and so on.

The five Elements are the primary forces affecting the universe. It is their particular association with each of the signs which provides the basis for every horoscope. Movement and fluctuation, Yin and Yang, these symbolic forces are in a perpetual state of action and interaction.

Wood gives birth to Fire, which gives birth to Earth, which gives birth to Metal, which gives birth to Water, which in turn gives birth to Wood.

RAT/WATER
(you were born in 1912 or 1972)

Water descends to earth from the cold of the northern sky. For the Chinese, Water is considered more a synonym for coldness and ice than as a source of heat and fertility.

Characteristics of the Rat/Water

Water of winter nights, rigour and severity; calm and deep water to be feared and respected; still water sheltering underwater demons asleep in its depths; fetid and muddy water of the marsh, a refuge of crawling creatures. All these the Rat/Water should beware of, for there he meets his season, his night, his coldness, his own components.

This element could become for the Rat a curb, indeed a swamp, in which his ideas and passions could be engulfed. In other words, Water can be a gilded trap for the Rat; he will be sheltered, but at the price of his liberty.

Health of the Rat/Water

The Water organ is the kidney. Its flavour is salted, causing tears if the Rat/Water swims too long between underground passages and ponds. Look out particularly for the usual kidney ailments; water must circulate freely, without restraint.

The Rat/Water and others

The Rat marked by Water knows how to listen. He is calm and placid; he might easily rule the masses, knowing how to contain his passions•and avoid unnecessary outpourings. He will live without fuss or trouble, and might also be a skilled craftsman, a prudent tradesman, a defender of peace, a convinced and determined humanist. Water soothes the aggressive impulses of the Rat, rendering him more humane and less anxious.

Some advice for a Rat/Water

Be less reserved; melt the ice which envelops and protects

you. Tear off your mask, let your inner demons come forth, for, if you are too passive, you will be encroached upon and sterility and slow death will follow.

The Rat/Water year

The culminating point in the Rat/Water year will be winter, a period of gestation. The Yin influence reinforces itself and the northern Rat will remain in the north, linked to his Water element.

The Water Rat in a Water year will have a tendency to splash and flounder in the mud. He should make use of this year to mature his ideas, time being on his side, but not to the extent that he should allow himself to be undermined by inertia.

The tendencies for such a year suggest that it can be excellent for women — for creative work, legal schemes and change — but there is a risk that plans entered into precipitously will be frustrated. Reflection will be more valuable than impulse.

Historical example of a Rat/Water year
1792

The French *emigres* from the new regime resorted to their kind in Europe. They also found a fellow-feeling in England. As J. H. Plumb writes: 'The more they indulged themselves the more separated they became from the hard purposeful world beneath them. The great Whig families . . . still had great empires to rule which gave them a natural position of authority in government. The political responsibility helped to keep the world of society on an even keel and saved it from the utter futility of its French counterpart which it ressembled more closely than most English historians have been willing to admit. There is the same grotesque extravagance, the same heightened class consciousness, the same feckless attitude to crises in politics or society . . . these were the years of England's ancien regime.'*

It is important to remember the extent of this fellow-feeling naturally conjured by the *emigres* from France. The first wave left after the storming of the Bastille; the second, and more influential, since they had sustained three years of revolution, occurred in 1792 and included Layafette. For them, the events of this year were decisive.

The conclusion of an Austro-Prussian protective alliance in February incited the French to a pre-emptive declaration of war against Austria in April. The intense feelings of the French were epitomized by Roger de Lisle's 'Marseillaise'. Their fervour was rewarded at the minor, but significant, battle of Valmy which caused the retreat of the Austrian forces within their territory and the more significant victory at Jamappes which enabled General Dumarrez to occupy Belgium. These were the lessons taught by a tigress at bay.

They were not ignored by the *emigres*, whose reaction was nevertheless misjudged. By their Declaration of Brunswick they called for the liberation of their King. The response in France was spontaneous and swift. The King and his family were promptly interned in 'The Temple' and the prisons 'cleared', a presage of the terror to come. The ultimate fate of the King was no longer in doubt. His arraignment and execution proceeded. A curtain had fallen on the days of the Enlightenment which the surviving monarchs were eager to raise. For this, however, they would have to look to England, the Paymaster of Europe.

RAT/WOOD
(you were born in 1924 or 1984)

To the East the wind blows, and from its warm caress of the earth Wood is born.

*England in the Eighteenth Century, Pelican, 1950.

Characteristics of the Rat/Wood

Wood is the coefficient fo equilibrium for the Rat. Wood is of the morning, springtime, a temperate nature, a lover of harmony, beauty and elegance. As an Element of the Rat, who originates from the north and belongs to the winter solstice, Wood brings the mildness that characterizes its season and also its creative force. It is in the spring that nature is reborn, after germinating beneath the earth, symbol of the rodent. Wood, which stretches its branches towards the sky, towards harmony, while plunging its tentacular roots into the belly of Mother Earth, is by its nature, a factor of equilibrium for the Rat. But Wood is also a passionate Element, with a distressing habit of self-destruction. It is at once susceptible and excessive, but without losing its dignity. It will even supply 'Wood' for our Rat's saw-mill! For the latter does not hold back from his aggressive impulses, his outbursts of anger, interminable sulks and dangerous passions.

Health of the Rat/Wood

The organ of Wood is the liver; its flavour is acid. The Rat, over-anxious and given to fretfulness, ought to keep a particularly close eye on his liver and refrain from drinking too much.

The Rat/Wood and others

He is inclined to be carefree, and it is best that he adopt a relaxed style in all his encounters. Faced with a conventional situation, he must improvize and allow his imagination and his inventive and creative mind free rein. The Rat/Wood could be a poet, a painter or even a farmer, thus uniting freedom and space, sky and earth and the wind, whose son he is.

Some advice for a Rat/Wood

You are handsome and passionate, ready at times to transform the social structure. An advocate of liberty, perhaps?

Politics, the stage, the arts await you. So leave your subterranean passages, leave your deep hole, and be carefree and relaxed.

The Rat/Wood year

The culminating point of a Rat/Wood year will be springtime, the period of growth and prosperity. Leaving winter behind him, the Rat will move away from his northern territory and travel east. His Yin aspect will tend towards the dynamism of the Yang. The Rat should profit from this season to brave new worlds and to create. Be supple in all senses of the term, know how to adapt yourself; this will be your winning card.

Tendency of the year: A year for diplomacy and suppleness, favourable for international relations; a year also for expanding agricultural activities and for an increase in the family. But an egotistical attitude will bring about disasters and a pervasive climate of anarchy.

Historical example of a Rat/Wood year
1804

England was again at war with France and Napoleon, proclaimed Emperor on 15 May, had already made his intentions clear. He was determined on invasion. For this purpose the Grand Army was mustered in the region of the Pas de Calais and every shipwright in Europe was recruited for the construction of the invasion fleet. A formidable armada was assembled.

England was without allies and short of troops at home. The government called for volunteers. The response was astonishing in a country which traditionally attracted only the 'scum of the earth' to its armed forces; but the island was called upon to defend itself, and defence was certainly needed against the conqueror of Italy and Egypt whose designs extended to California and Australia. Some half a million men joined the local volunteer organizations. The flood overwhelmed their administrative capacities and recruiting had to be stopped. The volunteers could scarcely be armed; in some districts, pikes were issued.

The situation remained intemperate and confused, for Napoleon himself never joined his army and, until the recall of Pitt to office, the orders from Whitehall gave little evidence of a plan for the national defence. In the country, fervour gave way to frustration.

Napoleon had his opportunities. He had the men and he probably had the ships; but he shrank from an act which might be as fatal as it could be decisive. With his army in being he would remain master of Europe: if committed across the Channel, he might lose it. Moreover the English fleets were at their old blockading stations and might fall upon his transports. Naval tactics imposed different considerations to those he could resolve by flair and instinct on land. Finally the element of surprise which he had nearly achieved in Egypt could never be repeated in the narrow waters of the English Channel, closely watched by English sloops.

There was possibly another element, too. Proclaimed Emperor of the French in May, Napoleon required the presence of the Pope at his coronation. In this, the Corsican meteor succumbed to the mystique of historical associations. On 2 December he crowned himself at Notre-Dame — but the Papal presence legitimized his dynasty. By then the season for invasion was past.

RAT/FIRE
(you were born in 1936)

Heat is born in the southern sky, descends to earth and fertilizes it. From their union Fire is born.

Characteristics of the Rat/Fire
The Fire element is of midday, of the south, of summer. Fire

is Yang, it is the element which heats, burns, transforms, confuses. For the Rat it can become internal Fire, a creative flame, a live and rapid force, but this can represent great danger, for it also devours, consumes and transmutes. Its great power can be destructive. Allied to the Rat it can bring death or light.

Health of the Rat/Fire

The organ of Fire is the heart; its flavour is bitter. The Rat/Fire should beware of the change in seasons. Moreover, the explosive and burning nature of this rodent should kindle his heart but not burn it out, for, like all of us, Rats have only one.

The Rat/Fire and others

Fire if often synonymous with war. It is lucid and clairvoyant, but also violent, irascible and impassioned. The Rat possesses within himself these same elements, and Fire will reinforce them. The Rat/Fire could become both an impassioned and a lucid man of action.

Fire inflames him, but it also brings him light and purifies him. It is this, which Earth does not nourish, Water does not slake and Metal does not harden, that might make of the Rat/Fire a warrior and a military leader. If he becomes an artist, he will reject the academic, conformist way of seeing and expressing.

Some advice for a Rat/Fire

You will be attracted to chimerical deities, but you are not made of 'Wood'; your inner Fire will not always be of the divine order. Beware of excesses.

The Rat/Fire year

The culminating point of the Rat/Fire will be summer, the period of creation, of material or spiritual advances, an active period but one which tends to become devouring. Leaving winter behind him, the Rat will move away from his northern territory and travel south, to warm himself under the summer sun. Abandoning his Yin aspect, he will stretch towards the hyperdynamic 'great Yang'.

Tendency of the year: This is a year favourable to cultural development, but there lurks a danger of over-reaction in all areas, often synonymous with a general sense of uneasiness, sometimes disguised by a destructive whirl of activity.

Historical example of a Rat/Fire year 1936

This was a year of grave domestic crisis in England which both threatened the institution of monarchy itself and tended to obscure, for the English, the significance of events in other parts of the world.

When the young Edward VIII succeeded to the English throne he was a popular figure who had shown a genuine if impotent concern for the plight of the unemployed, much to the displeasure of the Establishment. In contrast to his taciturn father he was bid fair to become the darling of the people. Then rumours of his attachment to Mrs Simpson began to spread. The truth soon emerged. He wished to marry a divorced American and to make her the Queen of England. The romantics took his side but the English people, innately conservative irrespective of their political allegiance, did not. They looked to the Monarchy for example, specifically for moral rectitude. The outcome was inevitable; Baldwin, then Prime Minister, and the formidable weight of the English Establishment had their way. In a moving speech to the nation, broadcast by the BBC, the young king announced his abdication. He was, he said, compelled to marry the woman he loved. A shy and unwilling Duke of York succeeded to the throne as George VI. He had the inestimable advantage of being married to the former Elizabeth Bowes Lyon of Glamis, in Scotland.

Before the German occupation of the Rhineland, the Italian invasion of Abyssinia and the outbreak of the Spanish civil war, the British government dithered, a policy later to be refined by the description 'appeasement'.

Almost unnoticed by the British public Mao Tse-tung completed his victorious long march in China and Stalin instituted his great purge in Russia. It was left to President Roosevelt of the United States to warn the world of the dangers facing it. Symbolically, the great American black athlete, Jesse Owens, triumphed at Hitler's Olympic Games.

RAT/EARTH
(you were born in 1948)

Earth was born from the slowly falling elements of the sky at its humid zenith.

Characteristics of the Rat/Earth
This is an afternoon earth; the humid and hot earth of summer. It is an undreamt of element for a Rat, this Earth, symbol of a soft, downy nest, of comfort and abundance; earth of slow transformatons and subterranean passages, muddled, spilling over until infiltration, inundation, decay and mouldiness sets in. The Rat/Earth will have a tendency to meditate, but such an effort at contemplation is unlikely to be auspicious for him. He needs action and the public life. Without these, master Rat will run the risk of asphyxiation from slowness and prudence.

Health of the Rat/Earth
The Earth's organ is the spleen, its flavour is sweet. The Rat/Earth will have a tendency to become fat and to be neurotic; he should engage in sports, and be careful about what he eats.

The Rat/Earth and others
The Rat/Earth is often a materialist, prudent to the point of egotism. Symbol of realism and of labourious productivity he is also crafty, a knowledgeable businessman or a subtle

financier. At home, he will be very much the family man and have a tendency to be despotic. Mrs Rat will be the archetype of the interfering mother.

Some advice for a Rat/Earth

Go out as much as possible, do not hide away in one of your many retreats, using meditation and contemplation as a pretext. You need activity, a touch of aggressiveness. In the matter of seduction, 'sages' rarely loose those passions of which you are so fond. Put some effort into it, show the sinews of war or of creativity, do not hesitate to adopt drastic measures, to carve your way, to get ahead. You must have faith in your good sense and cultivate your instincts. If you hide away cozily in the deepest heart of the warm earth, you risk being trapped — like a rat.

The Rat/Earth year

The culminating point — summer.
The Rat/Earth will be extremely well-provided for, indeed well-off. Summer being the period of abundance, he will not have to search for nourishment. Freed from material contingencies, he should give himself to others, not imprison himself in a comfort essentially gangrenous and self-destructive.

Tendency for the year: Creativity and productivity; knowing how to receive without forgetting to give!

Historical example of a Rat/Earth year
1648

This was the climactic year of the English civil war fought between the Cavaliers, supporters of Charles Stuart, King of England, and the Roundheads, led by Oliver Cromwell. In the style of the time it was a war ostensibly justified, promoted and stimulated by religious issues, but these had served to foment more material dissensions. Charles I believed in the high prerogative power of the Crown. Unlike his counterpart on the French throne he could not appeal to papal sanction to reinforce his claims. Genuinely a devout Christian, he was king of a Protestant country and supreme head of its Church. Unable to call upon the sanctions obtainable from the supreme Pontiff, his practical sanctions were reduced to the legalistic, a notoriously tricky field for any English monarch. Charles had run ignominiously aground upon the rocks of the English common law thrown up by Chief Justice Coke. Nor did his appeal to the Divine Right of Kings avail him, since his Puritan opponents claimed an equal acquaintance with the divinity.

Like many pious and devout men whose power has slipped, Charles I was devious, both in mind and in action. Promises rigorously enforced on his subjects by his Assize Courts could, by him, be broken, for the ends of God justified all means available to an annointed king. Breaking his word, Charles called on the Scots to invade England in his cause, a second and fatal incursion. They were routed by Cromwell at Preston. Arraigned with a great, if false, show of legality the King of England was accused of treason and beheaded the following January.

In the Paris parliament the young Louis XIV was abruptly addressed, but in terms that the English King would have welcomed: 'You are, Sire, our sovereign ruler. Your Majesty's power comes from above and owes only to its own conscience, after God, for its actions. . . '

RAT/METAL
(you were born in 1900 or 1960)

In the sky, coming from the West, drought will graze the skin of the earth and give birth to Metal. Winds come from the faraway steppes, seeking the vital sap.

Characteristics of the Rat/Metal
Metal is of the night, of autumn and of cold. It symbolizes clarity, purity and firmness. The Rat/Metal decides and cuts

through. His temperament is rigid and chaste, his remarks stinging. He oscillates between beauty and destruction. In other respects he is expert at putting plans into effect. At harvest time he is the blade that gleans. Alas, too much rigour engenders sadness and moroseness. In his perpetual search for nourishment, for equilibrium and for mystical summits, the Rat/Metal will often be tortured and will seek refuge in solitude, fleeing social gatherings which oppress him.

Health of the Rat/Metal

Metal's organ is the lung, its flavour is pungent. The Rat/Metal should seek fresh air and learn to control his breathing. It is by the free circulation of air in his lungs and in his body, rather similar to that of the Rat/Water, that the spiritual improvement he craves can be attained. He should avoid blockages of any kind and dryness of body and of heart.

The Rat/Metal and others

The Rat/Metal is an energetic, faithful man, true to his word. He may be the one who carries the lance in war or a man of law, a jurist or a lawyer, who sanctions, directs, forms judgements, decides. He has a sense of organization. A bit too stubborn, he has a tendency to lack subtlety and tact in some situations. He should be careful of being too cutting, for in this way he will risk the amputation of something inside him — his soul, perhaps. Since the Rat/Metal lacks suppleness and warmth, he should cultivate an easier manner, get outside himself sometimes, go out for a breath of fresh air — he needs it!

Some advice for a Rat/Metal

Relax, you are too stiff-necked. Discover fantasies and dreams. If you analyze too much, you will end by slipping into your own trap.

The Rat/Metal year

The culminating point will be autumn, when he must beware of self-destruction.

The winter Rat will leave the north for the west, his Yin tendency will be reinforced by the Yin of autumn, and this may be accompanied by a loss of speed, of energy and of dynamism. There is a danger of regression.

Tendency of the year: A period of dryness, of hardening; a period favourable for a dictatorial regime favouring a military state.

Historical example of a Rat/Metal year
1900

In England, as on the Continent, the twentieth century opened in an atmosphere of stability and continuing enterprise. Queen Victoria still reigned, but also as Empress of India. The Continental powers were at peace within themselves and with each other, despite the strains of great industrial change. France had settled for a parliamentary structure which encouraged a political debate commensurate with the effervescent artistic debates her genius released. In Germany, the centralized and essentially autocratic regime fostered by Bismark appeared well suited to the overt energies of its people. By 1900 the Emperor Franz Joseph had reigned for 52 years over a close and powerful union of two nations. In Russia, Tsar Nicholas II had won the support, if not the entire approbation of the second generation of peasant proprietors.

Yet this settled atmosphere was by no means somnolent. The imperialist ideal was at its zenith — the idea that the advanced culture owed a duty to the more backward one to impose on it the moral values and the merchandise of its superior civilization. In this context, the British received a sharp and brutal rebuff, meeting with a force of nationalism they had themselves fostered for a millennium. In China, a consortium of great powers mounted a punitive expedition as if against the Infidel and overtly in pursuit of trade. Neither contest proved satisfactory in the long run. The coveted trade with China quietly evaporated; the culture and obsessions of the Boers dominated South Africa.

By 1900 the opening up of the middle west and the industrial development in the United States had profoundly affected the economies of Europe and the very standards by which each of the Nation States measured its power. This involved an almost psychological change in political rhetoric. Thus, Germany sought expansion on account of its growing industrial capacities. The worth of work asserted a moral right to supremacy.

In France, the Capetian preoccupations prevailed beneath the charming gloss of *La Belle Epoque*. The humiliation of Sedan in 1870 could not be forgotten, nor the ceding of Alsace Lorraine.

Analogical Table
of the Different Elements

Elements	Wood	Fire	Earth	Metal	Water
Years ending in	4 and 5	6 and 7	8 and 9	0 and 1	2 and 3
Colours	Green	Red	Yellow	White	Blue
Seasons	Spring	Summer	End of summer	Autumn	Winter
Climates	Wind	Heat	Humid	Dry	Cold
Flavours	Acid	Bitter	Sweet	Pungent	Salty
Principal organ	Liver	Heart	Spleen	Lungs	Kidneys
Secondary organ	Gallbladder	Small intestine	Stomach	Large intestine	Bladder
Food	Wheat, poultry	Rice, lamb	Corn, beef	Oats, horse	Peas, pork

Table of Harmony
Between the Elements

		Wood Female	Fire Female	Earth Female	Metal Female	Water Female
○○○ Excellent prosperity	Male Wood	● ●	○	○ ○ ○	○	○ ○
○○ Good harmony, understanding	Male Fire	○	○	○ ○	●	● ●
○ Effort needed	Male Earth	● ●	○ ○	○ ○	○ ○ ○	●
● Rivalries and problems of reciprocal domination	Male Metal	○	● ●	●	● ●	○ ○ ○
● ● Misunderstanding and incomprehension	Male Water	○ ○	● ●	●	○ ○ ○	○

THE FOUR SEASONS OF THE RAT

四季

If you were born in spring
Rat/Aries

The alliance with Aries magnifies the aggressiveness of the Rat, while at the same time easing his inner anxiety. Instead of choosing his ground carefully, he charges indiscriminately from his underground exits. If he runs into obstacles, he stops, reflects, calculates his trajectory and starts out again. He is terribly efficient, and his motto could well be 'who wills the end desires the means'. Rather frank and direct for a Rat, very sociable, but not famous for his patience, he can be delightful to live with, on condition that you take care to keep up with him. He can be a marvellous lover, even though he may forget to telephone you for several weeks afterwards. That is normal, because he has no sense of time.

He must be left totally free. He is terribly independent and hates having anyone constantly underfoot or treading on his toes.

It is useles to go on about your childhood memories or to build castles in Spain; what interests him is the present. He needs to be busy, even continually overworked, otherwise he is likely to become unhappy and intolerable to others. What vitality!

Rat/Taurus

What charm! This Rat knows how to go about things and, from the nun to the whore — passing by Little Red Riding Hood and her grandmother — one cannot see who would be able to, or even wish to, resist this unholy mixture of fatal seduction and simple kindness. He knows very well what he wants, and he wants a lot, because he hungers for comfort, security — and love. Rather tranquil, he does become agitated when his plan of action is upset or his ambitions disturbed. Then he becomes frankly disagreeable.

Everything is to be gained by behaving gently with him, letting him exercize his authority, which is benevolent, by placing yourself under his protection — and staying there. For he hates to be dispossessed — that is the secret nightmare that haunts him. Taking all these conditions together, he is agreeable to live with, above all within the family circle. He will allow no one to lack for anything — himself least of all. But look out: never try to violate his privacy, to probe his secrets. One day you will discover them. It will be wonderful, extraordinary and brief. In fact, he only confides in someone when he wishes — and this only in a highly intimate atmosphere.

Rat/Gemini
Elusive Rat. Be careful: he is a virtuoso at this acrobatic game the end of which is to safeguard his independence and his autonomy. When he speaks of himself it is difficult to find one's bearings, and he cannot find his own either, for he becomes a veritable kaleidoscope.

His usual tactic is a zigzag flight, luring his enemy into the most unexpected traps. His favourite weapon is a smoke-screen; his oxygen, fog.

On the surface he is extremely sociable and remarkably at ease, quick to adapt to the thorniest of situations. This amuses him, but does not seriously involve him. Nothing can curb his capricious search, which amounts to an avid need for diverse experiences. He is capable of forgetting his mother and father when fascinated by a ticklish problem, an enigma or a mystery. Infinitely curious, endowed with a brilliant, perspicacious mind, he is one of those persons who does not know how to resist the challenge of whatever sphinx he runs across. You can consider yourself lucky if he does not mistake for a sphinx the first emaciated alley-cat that comes to prowl about the back streets of his insatiable and fruitful imagination.

If you were born in summer
Rat/Cancer
This is a soft, velvety Rat lying beside the hearth, which one wants very much to caress. He seems calm, tender, affectionate. Beware! Under a peaceful, transparent exterior, he

contribute to his interior equilibrium. He needs action and must spend physical and mental energy; he has a passion for living to the fullest. He is not a lukewarm Rat and his ambitions will never be banal. If his life should become mundane, it will be tragic. He will change into a caged Leo the Lion, bitter, aggressive and demanding.

Do not forget that the Rat is one of the most intelligent members of the animal kingdom, and was the first to answer the Buddha's call. Leo does not like to be second, either. In order to blossom and not to decay, the Rat/Leo will need the admiration and compliments of everyone, especially those close to him. Adulated, esteemed by his followers, he will be happy and generous.

Rat/Virgo

A quiet, unobtrusive Rat, he seems so organized, so careful to preserve each thing in its proper place, that he appears too good to be true. There are points in common between the Rat's greed a Virgo's need for security. The individual marked by this combination risks spending a good part of his life piling up an enormous amount of reserves; but these will never seem adequate. Touched by constant anxiety, he will always need to contemplate his subterranean hoard, replete with carefully catalogued victuals. And what of predatory beasts? To eliminate them, he sets traps. And friends who are hungry? He simply does not admit to them that he has reserves, though this, more often that not, makes him feel guilty. And what of those who find the way to his bunker? They had better not try to make away with even a slice of sausage; it might be one of those he has poisoned, fearing just such an eventuality.

Anxious, conservative, unbelievably nervous, in case of poverty the Rat/Virgo will be a godsend to his family; but he will be immediately transformed into a hissing serpent at the least attack coming from those outside.

Another important point in common between these two signs is their sexuality. Repressed but violent in Virgo, is secretive and complicated. He has no equal for fabricating a believable but fictitious personage, with the sole aim of hiding from a world he judges to be hostile to the detours of his dreamy, imaginative soul. In order to remain soft and velvety, he need an enormous amount of tenderness, loving care and security. At the same time he finds it difficult to tolerate well-intentioned, decent people who intervene when he is experiencing one of his cyclical crises of independence. He needs to get out on his own. This absolute freedom slightly frightens him, but he enjoys the shiver of anticipation.

Defensive rather than aggressive, he is unpredictable because one never knows exactly if one is addressing his fictitious personality or his real self. He always says that no one understands him, and he is often right. If he seems to be proud of his differences from others, do not believe in that too much: in truth it makes him unhappy, for he is hyper-sensitive, susceptible and deeply in need of appreciation.

Provided with remarkable creative powers, hating to be catalogued, he can succeed, but at his own rhythm, which at times is exceedingly slow and at others of surprising rapidity. Be on your guard against a sleeping Rat.

Rat/Leo

This is a Rat who roars. It is not advisable to bar his route. Active, crafty, enterprising, knowing how to be marvellously charming and authoritarian in turn, he likes to be taken seriously and does everything he can to achieve that end. If you are caught between his sharp claws, it is not certain that you will escape. He appears both invulnerable and danger-ous. At bottom, he is in conflict with himself and easily upset, for it is not easy to reconcile his tortuous Rat side with his superb Leo side.

He is capable of perpetrating both great gestures for self-seeking and even petty motives, and complicated and underhanded dealings with a noble end in view. This may make him unbeatable on any ground, but it does not intense in the Rat, this can lead to curious alternations of prudishness and dissipation.

If you were born in autumn
Rat/Libra
This is the gentlest, sweetest and least aggressive of Rats. Each time that his critical spirit whispers a virulent reply to him, he keeps quiet and says no more. A miracle! He forgets it and, in its place, says something vaguely banal but kind, as though trying to be pardoned for his wicked thoughts. It is really necessary to walk over the Rat/Libra's feet in hob-nailed boots to make him react, which he does in a pleasant voice, saying 'you know, dear friend, you are standing on my foot'.

The common point between these two signs is their emotional greed. It is intense in both cases. Libras are incapable of living alone. Rats are loving but demanding. If you are a poor orphan, an unhappy, lost soul who dreams of nice, warm soups, of quiet interiors and an embracing tenderness, look no further, you have found your ideal — on condition that you do not decide one day to go where the grass is greener. That could end in bloodshed! If your Rat is very Libran, he will be capable of throwing himself from the top of the highest building. If he is very Rat, he will take you with him — but *he* will have a parachute.

Rat/Scorpio
A Rat to hold with the tips of your fingers and not to come near without a good antidote for venom. He adores charming, fascinating, seducing and, on this level, he is incomparable. He will be a financier with financiers, an artist with artists, a beggar with beggars. Then, affirming his most visceral desire, which is to amaze and disconcert, he will transform himself, no sooner said than done, into a gentleman thief, a sorcerer or a millionaire with a Rolls-Royce. The Rat/Scorpio at bottom feels so different from others that he

often chooses to accentuate his differences and thus to give free rein to his aggressiveness.

Nothing escapes him: he is a walking radar, perfectly tuned and well-armed. It wouldn't take much for him to whistle like one of the robots in *Star Wars*. But he has a weak point: he is passionate, sensitive and a romantic, even if he doesn't want to admit it. When he finds someone strong enough to stand up to him, it is his nature to be faithful. He is also a remarkable critic, and would do better to make it his profession rather than use it against those close to him. He is the most lucid, the most secret, the most baffling of Rats. The richest also, perhaps — but one never sees any signs of it. His advice is always useful, indispensable, even when difficult to accept.

Rat/Sagittarius

This sociable and dynamic Rat is a born leader. He is gifted in debates; his talent for convincing is unparalled. Moreover, his ideas are generous, honest, practicable. He is a builder: his role will be to lay the first stone. Later on, he will be the one to intervene when there are labour problems. Then he will give the inaugural speech, and suddenly the Empire State Building, the Aswan Dam or the Great Wall of China will be unveiled. The Rat/Sagittarius prefers far-reaching enterprises. He is tireless and will prove to be indispensable and unbelievably useful — on condition, of course, that he is not saddled with the accounts. It is not that he would make off with the cash, but he would have a nervous breakdown. His job is to lead, to imagine, to invent, to carry out; not to follow or to count.

You can trust him not to leave empty-handed. But his earnings will have been honestly gained, along with other advantages, such as a house with swimming pool, stables, tennis courts, and a bevy of lovely hostesses. He will never lack for anything and will know how to get the best of everything. But his love life, often relegated to the background, will remain vaguely unfulfilled and melancholic.

If you were born in winter
Rat/Capricorn

A wise, thoughtful and efficacious Rat. His qualities of tenacity are allied to the perseverance of Capricorn, who canalizes his aggressiveness and directs it into paths where it will be most useful. His charm, though not obvious, is nonetheless considerable, for he appeals to those who seek security in a lasting passion.

The Rat/Capricorn appears to be serious and, no doubt, if he asks you to share his life, it means that he has thought a great deal about it and that he really wants you. But he is not very demonstrative. He almost always drags along behind him a vague, bitter love story which he has trouble overcoming. He is suspicious, secretive, and afraid of appearing ridiculous when he wishes to make a declaraton of love. You can be certain that he is faithful, trustworthy, discreetly affectionate; and also that he never repeats the same thing — 'I love you' included. You should appreciate that he is uneasy and much less cynical than he seems. Take the chance, if you can, to envelop him with tenderness, and do not take his rebuffs seriously. This Rat is beyond comparison at home, but he is an authoritarian. Warning: take him seriously.

Rat/Aquarius

This intelligent, inventive and idealistic Rat is not content with following beaten tracks. He lives on two levels. One is turned inward, highly self-protective, secretive — a forbidden planet. Though he may not seek to set traps around himself like the Rat/Virgo, he can send out a soporific ray or transform you into a toad. No, do not laugh, because this Rat is little sorcerer.

On the other level, the social, he is very different — enthusiastic, ready to fight for great causes, to battle for an ideal. The greater the difficulty, the more he will push ahead. A Don Quixote lies dormant within the Rat/Aquarius. But his need to seduce, to charm, to possess; the aggressiveness of certain of his reactions, will prevent some people from feeling sympathetic towards him. This matters little to him, however. He quickly tires of others when he does not attract their undivided attention. He leaves, looking for other pastures.

He is the vagabond of our double zodiac, of the mind as well as of the body. But he is unequalled at decoding a secret letter, communicating with extra-terrestrials, repairing a computer or inventing a time-machine. Ingenious, imaginative, full of both brilliant ideas and cock-and-bull ones, he is never boring — unless he has a wife who dotes on housekeeping, or she a husband who likes to cook. They will become too easily depressed in front of a burned meal. But they will be quickly consoled, for the Rat/Aquarius, though not noted for little attentions, is very understanding.

Rat/Pisces
A Rat with fins: his underground is aquatic and flows in all directions. Opportunist, generous, avid for affection — sometimes to the point of subordinating his life to a single love — wary of wasted effort, he only seeks adventure in trustworthy company and when confident of success. Capable of great generosity, of a devotion at times self-abnegating, he demands unconditionally to be taken seriously. If he is irritated, teased or made fun of, his aggressiveness comes to the fore, an aggressiveness which even in water remains rustproof.

The Rat/Pisces is gifted with remarkable receptivity and clairvoyance, which he can successfully cultivate. But he will often have a difficult time conciliating his desire to help others in a disinterested fashion with his profound greed. This can produce a large, smiling fish who attracts you with his melodious songs, then eats you up with great regret, for he would have loved to get to know you better. Could it be that the Sirens of Ulysses were Rats/Pisces?

THE
I CHING

易经

THE I CHING AND THE RAT

In the I Ching game, you ask a question and you obtain an answer. It is therefore a divining game. But the question you ask is posed through your Rat identity; the wheels, the complex mechanism of your mind and spirit, begin to turn. You ask a Rat question and the I Ching answers with a Rat 'solution', on which you then meditate as a Rat before arriving at a Rat conclusion.

The player is presented with a hexagram which contains the 'hypothesis-response' to his question, or, more exactly, a synthesis of forces affecting the concern or event inquired about.

For you, Master Rat, here are the sixty-four hexagrams of the I Ching and sixty-four hypotheses.

How to proceed
1. The question
Ask a question regarding any problem at all, past, present or future, personally concerning you. (If the question concerns a friend, consult the I Ching game in the book corresponding to his Chinese sign.)

2. Method of play
It must be done with concentration.

Take **three ordinary and similar coins** — for example, three 50p coins.

Heads will equal the number 3.

Tails will equal the number 2.

Throw the coins.

If the result is two coins showing Heads and one Tails, write 3+3+2. You thus obtain a total of 8 which you represent by a continuous line: ━━━

Draw the same continuous line if you have three coins showing Heads $(3+3+3=9)$.

If you throw two coins showing Tails and one Heads $(2+2+3=7)$, or all three showing Tails $(2+2+2=6)$, draw two separate lines: ▬ ▬

To sum up, 8 and 9 correspond to: ▬▬▬ (Yin)

6 and 7 correspond to: ▬ ▬ (Yang)

Repeat this operation *six times*, noting at the time of each throw the figure obtained on a piece of paper, proceeding from the first to the sixth figure, from bottom to top.

The final result, including a trigram from the bottom, or lower trigram (example: ▬▬), and a trigram of the top, or upper trigram (example: ▬▬), will be a hexagram of the I Ching. In our example this would look like:

Now merely look for the hexagram number in the table on page 88, and then consult the list of hexagrams with their descriptions to find the given answer. *In our example,* the hexagram obtained is number 63, entitled **After completion.**

Table of Hexagrams

Trigrams / Lower lines	Upper lines ☰	☷	☶
☰	1	11	34
☷	12	2	16
☶	25	24	51
☵	6	7	40
☴	33	15	62
☳	44	46	32
☲	13	36	55
☱	10	19	54

Use this table to find the number of your hexagrams. The meeting point between the lower and upper trigrams indicates the number of the hexagram that you are seeking.

5	26	9	14	43
8	23	20	35	45
3	27	42	21	17
29	4	59	64	47
39	52	53	56	31
48	18	57	50	28
63	22	37	30	49
60	41	61	38	58

THE HEXAGRAMS OF THE RAT

CH'IEN

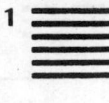

1 *The creative:* Energy, strength and will, creative spirit. Time will be your ally, but you chafe at restraint, nibble away at your reserves. You will have to learn to wait. Patience will prove more valuable than strength and will You must know how to leave at the right time.

K'UN

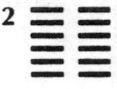

2 *The receptive:* Do not scorn those around you, the earth that bears you, the tools that serve you. It is with several grains of sand that one builds a castle. The grain sprouts by way of love.

CHUN

3 *The initial difficulty:* Unravel, seek the cause of the trouble, get rid of it. There are no bad reapings or sowings, only the bad farmer. Do not blame the earth and sky. The Rat should sometimes search within himself.

MÊNG

4 *Youthful folly:* 'It is not I who seeks the young fool, but the young fool who seeks me.' Do not set yourself up as a master: one transmits, one does not teach. There is some good in folly, but folly is not always good.

HSÜ

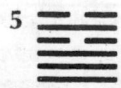

5 *Waiting:* Everything comes to he who has the patience to wait! The Rat should meditate at length. Prudence and reflection are not the enemies of instinct and action.

SUNG

6 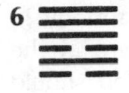 *Conflict:* Be conciliatory. Use craft and diplomacy, and so avoid law suits. Control your aggressiveness; sometimes you dig your own traps.

SHIH

7 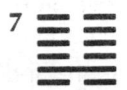 *The army:* Submission and discipline to achieve a collective aim. Do not shut yourself up in your ivory tower when the foundations are weakened. Strength comes through union. The world is not remade by sitting in one's room and calculating the dimensions of one's navel.

PI

8 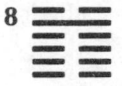 *Holding together (union):* When one likes to receive, one must also know how to give. Solitude is one of your eccentricities; do not transform it into a technique of 'anything goes'.

SHIAO CH'U

9  *The taming power of the small:* It is by improving small things and accomplishing them with love, without scorn or condescension that one builds great edifices. Do not put the cart before the horse.

LÜ

10  *Treading:* 'Tread on the tail of the Tiger, he does not bite Man.' Do not bristle, do not grind your teeth, extinguish the red gleam in your eyes, relax, breathe deeply, empty your mind. If you put away aggressiveness and fear, no animal, even the naturally ferocious, will refuse to allow himself to be tamed.

T'AI

11 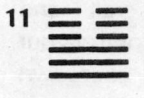 *Peace:* Or to know how to find harmony in contraries. There is not one truth, there are the truths which lead to 'the' truth. You should seek a dialogue. Stop sharpening your eye-teeth; they chew away at affinities and continue the confusion.

P'I

12 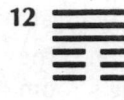 *Standstill:* You must know how to retire and wait. Inaction is a form of action. Nothing ripens in haste. The Rat must feel at ease in this situation and take advantage of it.

T'UNG JÊN

13 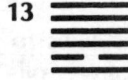 *Fellowship with men:* Daylight and sun, much love and faith are needed to build a cathedral. Success is achieved in union.

TA YU

14 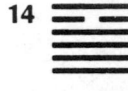 *Possession in great measure:* Whether materialist or spiritualist, the Rat who does not waste his energies will be able to manage well and be successful.

CH'IEN

15 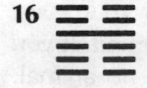 *Modesty:* Should not be transformed into false modesty. It is in the search for equality, in moderation, in controlling excess that you will find your equilibrium.

YÜ

16 *Enthusiasm:* Fair words are not enough. You must bring new ideas, excite the imagination, but do not forget that your partners expect something concrete; do not throw too much dust in their eyes.

SUI

17  *Following:* It is not enough to sow, you must know how to be patient in order to reap. It is the moment to use your powers of seduction, but you must be diplomatic. Understand that there are truths better left unsaid, even with charm.

KU

18  *Work on what has been spoiled:* Do not accuse your dog of having rabies simply because you wish to get rid of it. If your garden wall falls down, do not blame the mason, but rather your own negligence.

LIN

19 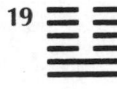 *Approach:* Beautiful summer days herald the autumn. Do not be content with the present; envisage the future. After the culminating point comes the beginning of decline.

KUAN

20 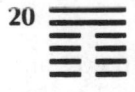 *Contemplation:* The Rat will be able to mount to the summit of a tower to contemplate the world. But he must not forget that he is exposing himself to the eyes of others. It is not by putting himself forward as a model that he will be able to have a true view of himself and of others.

SHIH HO

21  *Biting through (or clearly defined penalties):* One does not build a house on a marsh. A lie isolates and eats away at union. Be steady and know how to pledge your word. Cut down the weeds to let light enter the garden. The bite is sometimes an excellent legal penalty.

PI

22 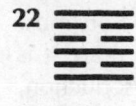 *Grace:* You are sensitive to appearances, touched by beauty. But grace is a state and not an end. Do not apply the formula 'what matters the bottle so long as one is drunk'.

PO

23 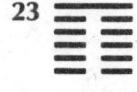 *Splitting apart:* Defer decisions. It is sometimes from within that destruction comes. Before climbing the tree, make sure that the branch is not rotten.

FU

24 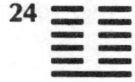 *Return — the turning point:* The wheel turns. After the dark, the light; after rain, the sun. Leave your burrows, the time is right for you.

WU WANG

25  *Innocence:* Give free rein to your intuition, on condition that it is in the service not of self-interest but of justice: although your instinct may guide you it should not, in addition, permit you to be the judge.

TA CH'U

26  *The taming of the great:* Symbol of power and of force. By selectivity and by renewal a plant grows. However, it is necessary to know how to 'take cuttings' in order to strengthen the stock. Assess your competence before taking on responsibility.

I

27  *The corners of the mouth:* Symbol of the nourishment of the body and of the spirit. 'Tell me what you read and I will tell you who you are.' Wholesome food is as salutary for the mind as spiritual nourishment is necessary for the harmony of the body.

TA KUO

28 *Preponderance of the great:* Do not take in hand what you are unable to sustain. Your vessel's equilibrium depends on its method of lading and its trim. One has to know how to adjust the strains.

K'AN

29 *The fathomless water:* Comes from above. Do not allow yourself to be overcome by panic; follow your subterranean nature. If you are sincere, you will have nothing to fear. The spring which gushes from the mountain runs and circulates; nothing can arrest its flow.

LI

30 *The clinging, fire:* Do not persist too much; do not burn up your energies uselessly. You must learn to be detached, to step back from a situation before you judge it. There are bonds one must know how to unloosen.

HSIEN

31 *Influence:* Favourable meetings, unions, associations. But you must leave your hole and forge ahead. Never sell the skin of a bear without first having killed it.

HÊNG

32 *Duration:* When the corn is ripe, it must be harvested. You must look into yourself anew and take stock. Inaction and complacency harden the arteries.

TUN

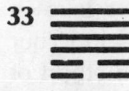 **33** *Retreat:* When the exits are blocked, it is best to retreat. Do not let this make you feel a failure and lead you to masochistic resignation, but rather make a wily and masterly move.

TA CHUANG

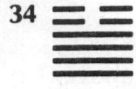 **34** *The power of the great:* Do not let yourself be carried away by the bustle of life as if it were a symbol of success and of obstacles overcome at full gallop. Too precipitous a charge will lead to a loss of control.

CHIN

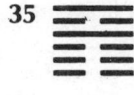 **35** *Progress:* You are blessed with attributes and talents more than sufficient for someone far better placed than you are. However, be content with your position as 'prince' without envying that of the 'sovereign'. Both have a role to play in striving for common objectives.

MING I

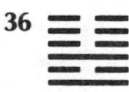 **36** *Darkening of the light:* As master of the underground and of darkness, you are well served! Sit out the crisis. Darkness reigns outside and in. Work on yourself; this is still the best remedy.

CHIA JÊN

 37 *The family:* An attachment must not become a prison, but one cannot live without some bond, some structure. Integration does not mean alienation.

K'UEI

 **38** *Opposition:* Respect the ideas of others if you wish them to respect your own. Harmony is born of diversity.

CHIEN

39  *Obstruction:* Obstinacy will get you nowhere. Look reality in the face, and do not refuse to take the hand held out to you.

HSIEH

40  *Deliverance:* After darkness, light. Do not be left with a sense of failure. One can only redeem bad work by accomplishing perfect work.

SUN

41  *Decrease:* Times are hard. Do not be taken in by what glitters. The flowers of the field can be as lovely as the rose, but you must know how to look at them.

I

42  *Increase:* Opportunity smiles at you. Do not put off until tomorrow what you can do today.

KUAI

43 *Breakthrough:* Truth sometimes springs from scandal.

KOU

44 *Coming to meet:* Sometimes one has to scratch beneath the veneer and not trust appearances. Do not accept compromises, otherwise your freedom will be forfeit and you will be led to disaster.

TS'UI

45 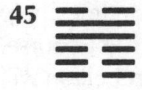 *Gathering together:* Know how to come close together, to gather in a group fired by the same ideal. Beware of any infiltration; it can only lead to ruin and slow destruction.

SHÊNG

46 *Pushing upwards:* Give proof of rectitude; be meticulous and do not neglect the finer details. Act methodically.

K'UN

47 *Oppression:* Take care, you are drying up. You lack energy and confidence in yourself. Overcome this; rely on yourself and do not wait to be attacked.

CHING

48 *The well:* You must not change the order of things. Evolution is movement; it does not mean destruction of the past.

KO

49 *Revolution:* Transformation is a vital need. 'One cannot make omelettes without breaking eggs.'

TING

50 *The cauldron:* Represents all five Elements. The cauldron sits upon the Earth, Wood kindles the Fire which heats it; its casing is Metal; within the Water boils. Nothing can be omitted from container to contained. Matter and spirit are ingredients both necessary and complementary.

CHÊN

51 *The arousing (shock, thunder):* There is electricity in the air, a swirling wind sweeps round your head. Ordeals can sometimes help you to see the light and find your right course. Know how to accept the situation; rebellion will get you nowhere.

KÊN

52  *Keeping still:* Try to empty your mind and spirit and perhaps momentarily the space about you. From this solitude calm is born. Silence after a storm is always a good thing.

CHIEN

53 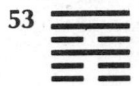 *Development (gradual progress):* Do not try to take short cuts. Do not skip the rungs of the ladder or you will fall.

KUEI MEI

54 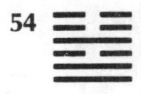 *The bride:* Do not confuse impulses with feelings. Before you commit yourself, be sure that your affection will be reciprocated and be steadfast in your choice.

FÊNG

55 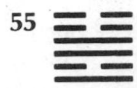 *Abundance:* A little prosperity and abundance harm nobody. Make use of this material and moral plenitude. But do not forget that after the good times come the lean.

LÜ

56 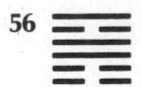 *The Wanderer:* It is sometimes necessary to put a distance between yourself and a problem in order to see things clearly. When the time comes to make a decision, secure your bases and forget revenge.

SUN

57  *The gentle:* Violence is not the best way to convince. It is by repetition that the perfection and purity of an act is attained. Make a continuous effort: it will achieve your purpose better than by violent attack.

TUI

58 *The serene, the joyous:* Persevere and communicate; be supple.

HUAN

59 *Dissolution:* You have a tendency to spread yourself too widely, a sign of confusion and egotism. Look for peace in retreat; participate in community work.

CHIEH

60 *Limitation:* You have not only rights but also duties. It is by assuming them that you become free. Also, if you pray, do not think that you are obliged to kneel on a bed of thorns.

CHUNG FU

61 *Inner truth:* Do not strike your neighbour on the head as you have been in the habit of doing. 'Actions speak louder than words', so try to do good deeds and not rely on fine words. Otherwise, you may discourage good will.

HSIAO KUO

62 *Preponderance of the small:* Sincere humility is its own reward. Do not scorn small things while dreaming of great ones. 'Do not trample on wild flowers while reciting poetry.'

CHI CHI

63 *After completion:* Always remember that a small cloud in a perfect blue sky can bring rain. Having reached the top of the mountain, you must provide for the descent.

WEI CHI

64 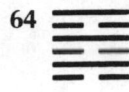 *Before completion:* As autumn gives way to winter, and spring announces summer, it is necessary to work towards a final outcome. Every end contains a new beginning, so plan without fear of the future.

YEAR OF THE OX

 1901·1913·1925
1937·1949·1961
1973·1985·1997

THE DOMAINS OF THE OX

十二生肖

THE OX AND ITS SYMBOLISM

The Ox is an animal of the Yin tendency; he comes from the North and belongs to the winter solstice.

'The Ox was born from the essence of a very old pine tree. It is Yin because it seems to rise from the moist soil of the grasslands ... A sign of longevity: Lao-Tse, the great Chinese philosopher, rode astride an Ox during his voyages to the mountains in search of immortality. The transcendent Ox can live for thousands of years.'

To understand this quotation, we must delve into the very heart of the Chinese mythology and folklore revealed by the Chinese zodiac, the origin of which is obscure. Only by doing this can we learn about the origins and the choices of these twelve animals, all of which are heroes of ancient legends.

There is no unlucky animal, none 'good' nor 'bad'. All participate in the same equilibrium, in one harmonious whole. So, let us break down our rational frontiers and set out on a search for our animal among these myths and legends, all of which border on the real and the imaginary.

The approaches to the Ox are difficult, for he is slow and secretive. It is he who loosens and ploughs the earth; but, unlike the Rat who burrows into the earth to hide away, the Ox works the earth to make it fertile. His is a slow, calm, obstinate and tenacious force. It seems as though nothing can stop him in his forward march. The Ox loves work to be well done. His power, combined with his contemplative spirit, makes him the perfect symbol of the Earth Element, a weighty, thick substance whose texture is composed of interlaced roots of humus and clay, of mud and rock. His habitat can be a rice field or a succulent prairie with grasses stretching for miles. The Ox treads on, tramples, ploughs; he could be an alchemist or a silent officiant of labour's rhythm.

In all civilizations the Ox is a precious auxiliary of man; gracefully and without apparent resistance he draws his plough, conquering the virgin earth; immutable and peaceful, he advances; emblem of Yin, mount of Lao-Tse, symbol of passive wisdom, impassive and invulnerable.

From one end of Asia to the other the Ox is an object of respect and veneration. It is easy to speak ironically of the sacred cows traditional to India that incarnate the most vibrant image of fertile motherhood, the source of nourishment and protection. Is it not the cow which yields milk and its products, the basis of all India's nourishment, and which is indispensable to the progress of India's agriculture?

Having sunk our feet in the imprints of his heavy hooves — in the solid, humid and heavy earth — in an attempt to understand this peaceful and contemplative beast we must choose other, more subterranean routes if we are to discover the Minotaur, guardian of Hell's circles in Dante's *Divine Comedy*; or seek for him under the bull's mask assumed by Jupiter when seducing and kidnapping Europa.

'He bellows', wrote Ovid in his *Metamorphoses*, 'and promenades his handsome shape over the tender grass: his colour is that of the snow on which no foot has yet placed its heavy imprint, and as yet unsoaked by the humid breath of the South Wind. His neck is swollen with muscles, his dewlaps fall to his shoulders. His horns are so small, one could believe that they were fashioned by a sculptor's hand, yet they also outshine a gem of pure water in their brilliance. His brow bodes nothing menacing, his eyes nothing dangerous. His face holds an expression of peace. The daughter of Agenor marvelled at the sight of so strong and handsome a beast whose aspect was so remote from the combative. However, despite such apparent gentleness, she at first feared to touch him. Then, approaching, she tendered to his mouth flowers of spotless purity. Her lover, overcome with joy and in expectation of the pleasure awaiting him, covered her hands with kisses. Now it was difficult for him, yes difficult, to leave the rest for later. At one moment he gambolled and bounded about the green grass; at another, he reclined his snow-white flank on the tawny sands. The princess, unaware that it was a god who carried her, even dared to sit on the bull's back. Further and further he went, carrying his quarry towards the open sea...'

One may wonder which of the two took the place of the other: was it Jupiter who disguised himself as a bull, or the bull as Jupiter? The Ox indulges in a game which consists of leading his partners astray in the heart of obscure labyrinths. Does not his need for solitude and his self-searching signify that the Ox is perpetually seeking his ultimate identity?

A few notes on the Ox

Principal qualities: A hard worker, well balanced, patient.
Principal defects: Stubborn, a bad loser. Has difficulty understanding those unlike himself. Not particularly lucid about what concerns him personally.
Work: Honest and persevering. A great sense of responsibility.
Best role: Moral arbiter.
Worst role: Salesman of tricks and jokes.
Money: Thrifty, somewhat stingy at times.
Luck: To be born in winter. In summer he has a huge amount of work to do in the grasslands. He cannot stop working.
Cannot live without: Contact with nature.
Adores: Taking care of his garden, breathing tranquilly, taking his time.
Detests: Being put in the wrong, feeling imprisoned or being lost in a crowd.
Leisure activities: Gardening, digging. If he has enough time to spare, conquering virgin land.
Favourite places: Freshly ploughed fields, quiet ponds. A spot unknown to others.
Colour: Green.
Plants: Thyme, ivy, sage.
Flowers: Peony, violet.
Professions: Statesman, man of action or of war, architect, archaeologist, managing director of a company, disting-

uished economist, farmer, gardener, leader of a religious sect (fanatic, naturally), dictator, policeman and, you can count on it, patron of the arts.

The four ages in the life of the Ox, according to Chinese tradition

The *childhood* and *youth* of the Ox are without problems; he will be too busy learning and working to get into mischief. His *maturity* will often be beset by emotional disappointments. Careless of the feelings of others, he has a sardonic attitude when revealing his more tender emotions. His *old age* will be calm and stable on the material level. He should put it to good use by taking an interest in others and learning to be indulgent.

THE PSYCHOLOGY OF THE OX

When the Buddha invited all of the animals in creation to come to him, the Ox was the second to arrive. He was preceded by the quick and opportunistic Rat, but was ahead of all the others. Yet the Ox is a slow, placid being who discounts gossip and does not make rash decisions. To get him to gallop one has to push him to the limit, to free his hooves from the soil in which he has been rooted for generations. And yet the Ox arrived in second place — for the simple reason that the Buddha had called him. Whereas the Tiger took time off for a bit of hunting, the Snake for a little nap and the Goat for a small dream, the Ox was not going to lose time en route. The others played around and the Ox beat them, just like the tortoise left the hare behind in the fable.

This little tale helps us to understand this second Chinese sign. The Ox is like a generator: while he ruminates, apparently indifferent to the world around him, he is in fact building up fantastic reserves of strength and power for the next battle. He saves his strength, prepares himself and takes a good look at himself. He waits for the moment to act and observes events through half-closed eyes, without participating. If he has not yet made up his mind, you can wave as many red capes as you like; he will not react.

On the other hand, if he is motivated (the Ox's motivations are simple: work, family and country), he shakes himself and gets under way. An Ox starting up is often impressive to watch, beginning with a spreading in breadth, especially if male, then continuing with an agitation of the skin surface and a rippling of the muscles. He then quickens his pace and, raising a cloud of dust, charges his objective and tosses his adversaries to the ground. It is extremely imprudent to provoke an Ox. If you really need to, send an experienced diplomat ahead of you, set down your arguments on paper and pack a suitcase. If, despite all these precautions, the Ox becomes angry before you have stated your case, take from your suitcase the machine gun you took the precaution to pack.

The Ox is of a choleric temperament. He is subject to enormous outbreaks of fury which are attributed to persons of calm behaviour who constantly discipline themselves. When the cork pops, it makes a very loud noise indeed!

Oxen always consider their rages justifiable; indeed, circumstances do usually justify them and they are, after all, extremely rare. But they leave an effect comparable to an earthquake.

For quite some time I worked with a female Ox, and I must admit that her efficiency was unequalled. She managed to run her house, care for a sick aunt and work nine hours a day (she was supposed to work for only eight hours, but an Ox never leaves unfinished work behind). She was charming and perfectly organized: an embodiment of good sense; loyal, devoted and obliging — to such a degree that everyone around her felt guilty.

But let a grain of sand slip into the well-oiled gears of her timetable; let an untimely demand upset her personal rhythm; in a word, let someone impose some other order than her own — and boom! Our nice Ox lady would explode like Vesuvius, heaping invective on all who had the lamentable idea of joining in the fray.

All Oxen are like this in differing degrees: they are the most honest, hardworking and efficient people on earth. In fact, they do everything so well that some opportunists willingly leave them all the burdens of responsibility. But Oxen will not complain, and, in fact, they like it. They are tough, persevering and obstinate. They are filled to the gills with moral principles, respect for the law and all laws, traditions, order, and so on. Provocative clothes and deliberately shocking attitudes make them uncomfortable, but they are not at all prudish. They are simply not much inclined to nonconformist attitudes, and even when they boldly profess one, it is often in the name of some principle or other.

Nevertheless, Oxen do not lack originality. They are, moreover, independent and rather individualistic; but psychologically, they are unable to make comparisons and weigh differences. They are outspoken and not made for subtleties (a waste of time!): everything that matters to them is either white or black, the rest being of secondary importance and without interest.

The Ox is not very sociable. Faithful in his friendships and as dependable in his sympathies as in his antipathies, he rarely goes back on a promise. His best friends are often childhood companions, for he feels more at ease with those who have shared the same paths and smelled the same smells. When childhood friends disappear, snatched away by life and events, he often remains alone, and it will take him some time to recreate a circle of friends — preferably neighbours or colleagues. He is conservative on all levels and rarely welcomes change, although he is capable of dealing with it. If he has doubts about himself, they are private and never expressed. Moreover, if he does have such doubts, he will promptly tell himself that this is really not the time to behave like a weakling. In general he prefers to act, to build, to fashion, to carry out — rather than to reflect on the sex of angels.

Those born under the sign of the Ox are stable, well balanced, solid; you can have confidence in them. In the strict sense the Ox is the most trustworthy of the Chinese zodiac. He is neither talkative nor demonstrative, and seldom amusing. Humour baffles him slightly; he tends to react too late, or not at all, and leaves growling if he thinks that the conversation has become too frivolous. He also does not much appreciate general discussion, the exchange of ideas or debates. To be truthful, he sometimes appears stubborn and sectarian, refusing to allow dissension or acceptance of another's point of view, and therefore seems blind to his own errors. But he is marvellously sincere and knows nothing of lying, hypocrisy or venality. Also, although he can be blinded by fury, he will honestly recognize when he was wrong to have lost his temper.

Oxen are often judged severely, for they make little effort to put their best foot forward, and rarely try to please. Their motto could be, 'If you want me, take me as I am.' For those who value security, there is no lack of charm in those unassuming and determined Ox women, nor those churlish, rather bear-like Ox men. They are worth the effort.

THE OX AS A CHILD

Imagine for a moment that your childhood was spent in a shabby hovel in the centre of a slum, in a country where the weather is cold and windy. You fought hard for yourself and have amassed a fortune. You have a charming wife and are the happy and proud owner of a rubber plantation and several oil wells. You begin to wonder to whom you could leave the fruits of your patient endeavours. Quite naturally, you think of having a child.

But how can you be sure that this squalling little thing, installed in a sumptuous crib, will not grow up to squander the empire you have constructed, stone by stone, by the sweat of your brow? Even if you are very wise and philosophical, such a pill would be very hard to swallow. But if your child is born under the sign of the Ox, this danger will be averted. Rock him to sleep with tales of millionaires, offer him rattles in the form of oil derricks, and with a light heart make him your sole heir. Even if he intensely dislikes the product on which your success is founded, he will never squander his patrimony. For a child born under the sign of the Ox is serious from a very early age, respects the idea of effort and possesses an exceptionally strong sense of responsibility.

Talented or not, he will end up with more than he started with, for he is an assiduous, even plodding, worker. His secret is perhaps simply that he enjoys working, and that he likes to prove to himself that he is capable of being first in the class, winning out over handsome little X who is the teacher's pet and over Y who is so brilliant.

The Ox child is usually a pragmatist: he always has possible job openings in mind as well as the concrete possibilities offered by his knowledge of a subject. Poetry or abstract subjects are rarely his strong point, but he can be talented in maths, grammar and administration. He is a born realist. During play periods, he is often a bit solitary, standing aloof or with a small group of friends with whom he plays chess or naval battles. Your role as a parent is to make him more sociable and to help him to relax. You might almost say to him, 'Well, even if you do not pass your examination, what does it matter!' He will succeed in any case, but your relaxed attitude will help him to pass with flying colours; especially if he is confronted with oral exams, for this perfectionist suffers terribly from stagefright when forced to speak about what he knows.

LOVE LIFE

Being realists rather than romantics, sentiment is rarely the dominant function of those born in the year of the Ox. For them there are the essential things, such as eating, sleeping, working, keeping promises, protecting possessions and the family; then there are other important things which, with a little effort, they can do without, such as love, sex (careful — Oxen are highly sexed but capable of disassociating desire and feeling); finally come the totally superfluous things, such as declarations of love and those small attentions which are the tokens of love.

Like all of us, the Ox needs to feel loved. But he (these remarks apply to the female as well as the male) is extremely independent and prefers to organize his life in his own way, trying, however, not to make life impossible for those he loves. One has to accept that he is rarely hateful on purpose, but rather by default, because he is preoccupied by something else. If you are in love with an Ox, remember that he is full of those classic qualities that are attributed to a good husband or wife: faithfulness, seriousness and an awareness of family responsibilities. He is often the handyman; she the good cook, mother and perfect housekeeper. But if you hope for flowers on your birthday, you will be disappointed: he will not think of such things and, in any case, finds flowers a useless extravagance — you had better remind his secretary! He will offer them on the day you become engaged, but never again. Later, he will have more important irons in the fire.

In short, for an Ox of sound stock, love is often relegated to second place. To him it is not a necessity, but rather a necessary evil. This has nothing to do with the quality of his feelings, which are generally deep and devoted, but he is definitely not a romantic. Sex is an important aspect of his life; the male Ox in particular can relish 'hygienic' liaisons, since physical love is for him as intense an organic need as hunger or thirst; he rarely questions himself on this subject. Mrs Ox also has a strong taste for the opposite sex, but usually prefers the conjugal bed to the excitements offered by transitory pillows.

The Ox is exclusive but not suspicious; he is too preoccupied with his work to play detective. If he marries someone, that means he has confidence in her. Anyway, he will make less of his wife's minor infidelities than of her extravagances or her mishandling of their children's education.

Note carefully, however, that if an Ox is disappointed emotionally he will remain so for life. Once he has lost his confidence in you, it will be almost impossible for you to re-establish it. He will become suspicious, wary, unhappy and disagreeable, and will be incapable of starting again 'from scratch'. Even if he tries to make amends — out of love or goodwill — his memory of 'the error' will remain and poison his attempt — as well as the life of his inconstant spouse.

FAMILY LIFE

Given a little experience, the Ox is a marvellous companion; for one will have learned that his actions speak louder than his words. He is better in the role of the elderly husband than in that of the fiancé or young bridegroom. But above all, Oxen are exceptional parents. To each his speciality. Being a parent is really their virtue. As honest with their children as they are with themselves, they never ask anything of a child which they would be incapable of themselves. They invariably set a good example and watch over their children's development with keen attention. Perhaps because they are steady and equable, and are strongly imbued with the importance of their role as parents, they give their children a constant feeling of security, having a marvellous gift for tempering authority with kindness.

An Ox is not one to stifle his child, nor to try to make him do what he cannot succeed in doing himself. The sign of the Ox always places an emphasis on the free development of the individuality of his children.

All children born under an 'adaptable' sign find it good to have an Ox parent — in particular the Rabbit, Pig and even the Goat — and will make commendable efforts to comply with the demands of their father or mother, who is so stable. The Monkey and the Snake will pretend to obey, but will do as they please. It is with the Rat — enemy of guardianship — the Dragon and the Tiger that the Ox will have difficulties, for these children will never accept rigorous parental guidance. The same is true of the Horse, who will bolt at the first opportunity. Ox parents will have difficulty accepting it if one of their children decides to leave home prematurely. Also, they will have problems with adolescents thirsty for freedom, more so than with children of school age. Mrs Ox, with the best will in the world, will pull a long face if her fifteen-year-old daughter asks if she can go on the Pill. This is your weak point, Ox parents: you find it difficult to accept that your children must grow up.

PROFESSIONAL LIFE

Those born under the sign of the Ox appear calm, obstinate and patient, but they are also ambitious and, no matter what they say, love power. Be careful not to be taken in by an Ox who nobly states, 'Just so long as I am left to work in peace, I don't care a rap whether or not I am in charge.' This is only slightly true. Solitary animals do like to work in peace and hate to be interfered with. Yet although they do not openly seek to be in a position of authority, they find the denial of it intolerable — a subtle difference.

Thus a true Ox will always tend to choose positions which carry heavy responsibilities rather than for reasons of status, for he feels that the work accomplished is in itself a measure of esteem. Although he prefers to be in charge, he will opt, if need be, for some indispensable role within the hierarchy.

Oxen often allow themselves to be overwhelmed by their sense of obligation; they have the impression that no one will be able to do their work as well as they can, and, quite often, they are right. With unreliable assistants or people to whom they cannot delegate for one reason or another, they will, quite naturally, assert: 'I will take over — and then you will see how it should be done.' And they do it. Good enough, but they will be in danger of losing their sense of proportion. From time to time Oxen need to get away, to take long, invigorating walks in the great outdoors. When they become obsessed by work, their colleagues should gently persuade them to take a few days off.

Oxen never abandon a problem. They always find a solution, sometimes an original one. Respectful of their superiors, they are demanding of their subordinates, but not to the point of injustice: they can be relied upon for their fairness. If they happen to be unfair and too rigorous it will be accidental, being due to an inability to put themselves in another's place, which amounts, in effect, to a sort of carelessness.

Oxen tend to be found in administrative and political professions. They are born to direct and administer, which they do conscientiously and competently. But they need concrete and realistic activities; an awareness of psychological subtleties and abstract thinking are not their strong points.

MATERIAL LIFE

The Ox is one of the signs best equipped to cope with practical life, for all the tendencies of his character drive him to act with intelligence and prudence when his security is at stake. Without being a slave to his personal comfort, he knows the value of money, unlike, for example, those born under the sign of the Rat who are hopelessly extravagant. The Ox is thrifty and reasonable, only taking out his wallet after deliberating and having satisfied himself that the expense is justified. With his children or spouse he can be extravagant; otherwise, he can be parsimonious and even a bit stingy.

Unlike certain signs who can experience pleasure from squandering their money, the Ox is happy when he knows that his savings are well invested and his bank account nicely replete. He administers his properties meticulously, pays his taxes on time — neither too early nor too late — and files his bills with care. Mrs Ox budgets carefully and no item is overlooked; next year's holidays and presents for Christmas, as well as medical supplies, are all included, along with food and other household expenses.

All Oxen aspire to leave their mark in the world. This ambition can lead them to construct financial empires, all the more so because they always wish to provide security for their children's futures. For this, time is always available. The perfect Ox, whatever his origins, will always die leaving his finances in good order. Never speculating, this will have been accomplished by borrowing the minimum and repaying it at the stipulated date. The Ox is the banker's dream; he would not have a care in the world if all his clients were like him.

ENVIRONMENT

The Ox is not excessively sensitive to his surroundings. So long as he has enough space in which to move freely, everything is fine. If a pillow's colour clashes with the divan, or if an object is moved without him being told, he will not care. He likes to be at home, in the middle of odds and ends of old things, photographs and mementoes of friends he hasn't seen for ages. His home is comfortable but functional, without any special refinements: he dislikes tables with elaborate tablecloths, fragile knick-knacks or period furniture, preferring a rustic style and highly polished floors.

Although conservative by nature, the Ox is not a stay-at-home. His real domain is nature; minimally, he needs a garden: ideally, to live in the country. Then, every morning, having checked his accounts, he will enthusiastically embark on a long walk, all alone of course. Cold and wind will not deter him; fog will not disturb the voluptuous joy he feels when his feet sink into the soft earth. A man of nature, he is attached to his roots. Rather uncommunicative in daily life, you might be surprised to come upon him during his walk, talking to the flowers and the trees. Naturally, he will have an orchard and a kitchen garden; and Mrs Ox will preserve appetizing fruits in jars which will decorate the top of an old and solid dresser.

A farm is his ideal setting, but if he lives in the city a small house surrounded by a little herb garden will suffice. If he has no choice but to live in a flat, offer him a few green plants — he will care for them lovingly.

A guide to personal relations with an Ox
Methods of seduction:

He: First of all he will observe you and hang around you reticently. Then he will suddenly ask you if you want to or not.

She: Will be calm and peaceful, waiting with an air of 'sooner or later he will see that I am the woman he needs.'

If he loves you: As far as possible, he will avoid saying so, but in the end he will have to: on the day he is overwhelmed with desire for you, it will be the only way for him to possess you. The female Ox will say it only on your wedding day, or when it is the only way she can get you back.

He expects of you: Fidelity, loyalty and respect for his liberty.

To keep you: He will do nothing, for he will not realize that you wish to leave. If pushed, he will come up with some gifts.

If he is unfaithful: He will not feel that he has done anything wrong. After all, he is free, is he not? But in general, he will not be unfaithful.

If you are unfaithful: He will probably not speak about it, but he will be horribly vexed. Take care: it might upset everything; unless you have children he could leave forever.

In case of a break between you: He will try to settle everything because he does not like separations. If the situation is really impossible, he will tell you to go to the devil and clear off, scrupulously taking all his possessions with him.

If you wish to give him a gift: Rummage through the garbage for a sickly green plant. Bring it to him and say, 'You are absolutely the only one who can make it bloom again.'

If you want to seduce him: Accompany him on a long walk (be ready to get up at five o'clock in the morning, at the latest). Say nothing and do not disturb him. When you stop for a rest, simply go to him, undress him and wait for him to ask you to marry him.

If you want to get rid of him: Place your head on his shoulder and amorously say to him, 'When we are married, you will belong to me completely.'

THE OX
AND THE OTHER CHINESE SIGNS

Ox/Rat

The Rat and the Ox get along very well together. Both are individualists and therefore well positioned to respect and allow the independence of each other. In this situation the Rat needs to be taken seriously, and the Ox always takes everything very seriously! A little disposed to gossip, the Ox will nevertheless respect his partner's secrets. Things will go less well when the Rat, for whom the charm of confidences is irresistible — especially when they are somewhat improper — reveals to his closest friends the more intimate appetites of the Ox. The latter will be enraged if this type of information leaks out.

The Rat's passionate nature will perhaps not always be entirely satisfied, for the Ox does not think only 'of that'. Before going to bed, he likes to do his accounts and check that the gas is turned off. But the Ox is faithful and reliable; both the male and the female Ox take their responsibilities seriously. The Rat can count on him, while the Ox, in his everyday life, will enjoy and respond to the intelligence and vivacity of his companion.

Ox/Ox

In everyday life everything will go like clockwork; meals will be served on time and, at the end of the month, there will be no money problems.

Together these two risk being a bit bored. With someone similar to himself, an Ox will too often fall into a dull routine which, paradoxically, will lead him into temptation. The Ox who is not shaken up from time to time, and who has no need to measure himself against the outside world can easily succumb to inertia. Do not forget that this animal needs prodding.

The responsibilities of professional life and the reciprocal independence it involves will create a balance for this couple. Even so, they should not open a shop together, for they are incapable of encouraging extravagance in others and are therefore not very good salesmen.

Ox/Tiger

For the Tiger, everything is possible prey — the Ox included. The eyes of a true Tiger always light up at the sight of possible game, and the Ox is no exception, who, despite his independence, sometimes allows himself to be devoured without even noticing the danger. While the Tiger's eyes may be bigger than his stomach, and he sometimes risks a memorable attack of indigestion, this is no help for the Ox.

Although the Ox does not deter the Tiger from wandering, he will contemplate him with a severe eye and accuse him of being rash, unreasonable and thoughtless. Any type of business relationship is not advised — it will only end in blows. However, on the emotional level, with a male Tiger, Mrs Ox will adapt rather well, provided he is careful to lay in enough fresh meat. The other way round, everything will go well so long as the lady Tiger is very much in love. Afterwards, tied to this Ox, this monument of conscientiousness, she may be bored to death and begin to have flights of fancy.

Ox/Rabbit

This combination is ideal! The Rabbit needs security, calmness and harmony, and the calm and stable Ox offers such a sanctuary. Sometimes the Rabbit is unfaithful — more to prove to himself his seductive powers than through a taste for infidelity — but above all, he values his home life. The Ox, who is not in the habit of going through his spouse's pockets, will prefer to remain as unsuspicious as he is faithful. Both of them fear financial setbacks, disagreeable and unforeseen events and personal confrontations. They always strive to secure their home from any possible hazard.

The Ox, being more independent and better armed to confront difficulties than the Rabbit, is better suited as the active element in this partnership. If his lack of diplomacy causes problems, the more supple and opportunistic Rabbit will give him useful advice.

There is only one obstacle: the Ox likes clear and plain answers, while the Rabbit is hesitant, uncertain, a little unsure and needs to work around a problem to find the ideal solution. By then the Ox will have made his own decision.

This union, while emotionally rich, is ill adapted for business unless there is a third party — a Tiger, for example — to appreciate, and therefore diminish, the risks involved.

Ox/Dragon

The Ox is a person grounded in day-to-day life who, from a very early age, is aware of the danger of going too fast. The Dragon, on the other hand, forewarns of exceptional events involving political, emotional or professional change. In the life of an Ox, the Dragon will pass like a flaming comet; after he has left, nothing will ever be the same again. This will be excellent for the Ox. He will come out of the experience tired but renewed, wiser and more lucid. For a time the Dragon will appreciate the stable and positive side of the Ox, finding repose and an inclination for reflection.

In short, this may be a useful relationship for both, but it will be unlikely to last unless the Dragon is required to travel a great deal. Otherwise, he will become quickly bored — and as quickly elusive. On the other hand, the Dragon may have the good sense to use the Ox to take care of the accounting side of his affairs.

Ox/Snake

A little goodwill on both sides will suffice, for the Snake gets along well with almost everyone. The Ox will think that it is he who dominates — which will please him greatly — and the Snake spouse, who believes that the less effort the better, will certainly not discourage him. The Snake will encircle the Ox as much by understanding as by complimenting him on his seriousness and his sense of responsibility. The Snake, who loves comfort, does not lack will. But if he finds someone ready to work for two, he will only do what is strictly necessary to keep up appearances. And so the Ox will be consumed but remain content, and the Snake will also be content, feeling secure. Assured of the fidelity of his companion, the Snake will indulge in a few discreet 'extras' for amusement, but no one will know about them.

On a business level, they complement each other: one will work, the other reflect. Together, they will be able to amass a handsome fortune.

Ox/Horse

This is not an easy pair to judge. The Ox and the Horse are both egotists and will make little effort to understand each other. And the Horse is forever on the rampage, whereas the Ox is sedentary. The Horse cuts his quick capers, the Ox ruminates. We might wonder if they will ever meet, or just pass each other by. They will have great difficulty adapting to each other's rhythm.

If they do meet and inadvertently fall in love, perhaps their relationship will endure, thanks to the Ox's goodwill. But the Horse will be unhappy: egocentric though he is, he is nonetheless passionate and sentimental, needing not only love but proof of it as well. At the first outbreak of such 'romanticism', the Ox, without meaning to, will throw cold water on him, for such declarations of love are altogether foreign to him.

In other respects, the Horse is sociable while the Ox enjoys nothing better than tranquillity and moments of solitude. For this union to work, it will be necessary for the other dominant signs, Chinese or Western, to be truly in harmony, and these elements should be consulted.

Ox/Goat
If in love one always chose one's total opposite, the Ox/Goat couple would be ideal. Opposed as they are in the Chinese zodiac, and as different as it is possible to be, it would be delightful if they could come lastingly together.

For the Ox, the imaginative and fanciful air that surrounds the Goat like an aura could open a new dimension. For the Goat, whose speciality does not consist in making decisions, let alone wise ones, the Ox's reserves of practicality could be an effective support. All this is written in the conditional because Chinese tradition tersely advises the Ox to avoid the Goat, and vice versa.

It is tempting and easy to say that they will make idiots of each other; better to hope that they meet and fall in love (admittedly very unlikely), for if they do their alliance can prove beneficial to their reciprocal development, and, above all, to their equilibrium.

Ox/Monkey
The Ox will understandably be left nonplussed and dizzy by the Monkey's vivacity. But it will not take much for him to

overcome his natural distrust and come to admire the famous pirouettes of his partner; the Monkey fulfils his need for originality.

For his part, the lucid Monkey can appreciate to a fine degree the Ox's stability and natural equilibrium, for these provide the security necessary for one whose centre of gravity constantly oscillates.

Also important is the fact that these two signs are perhaps the least 'sentimental' of the Chinese zodiac; they do not give love priority in their lives. Each will welcome a partner for whom jealous scenes, displays of emotion and 'stupid' declarations of love are wholly foreign. This will be a sound alliance, both in marriage and in business. On the latter level they will, moreover, be formidable allies, but allies whom it will be unwise to rely on when you are in difficulty, for compassion is not their strong point.

Ox/Rooster

No problems here! The Ox will allow the Rooster to shine in peace, and will be aware of the useful and important role that a sociable spouse can play in his life, since he is so often accused of being too grave and taciturn. Both need freedom, and therefore easily understand each other's need for it. The Rooster likes to sing in peace, and will willingly leave the Ox to organize their daily life. Also, despite his flamboyant nature, the Rooster has a conformist and reasonable side. It is in these latter aspects that he will find most harmony with his Ox spouse.

Obviously, sometimes there will be friction. For example when Mr Rooster unexpectedly brings home a whole carload of friends for dinner; or when the Ox — male or female — sharply criticizes the Rooster in front of friends.

At work the Ox and the Rooster will get along in a highly profitable way. But it must be the Ox who manages the enterprise, while the Rooster takes care of public relations.

Ox/Dog

If a male Dog chooses a lady Ox as his companion, we can

almost be certain that their troubles are over. At the side of this stable, secure and reasonable person, the Dog will forgo his roving rights to devote himself to familial joys, and will no longer be filled with anguish as soon as the slightest difficulty seems to upset his projects. A company director who is a Dog might advisably have an Ox as his second in command to reassure him by always saying, 'No, our cash flow is very good and we will not go bankrupt tomorrow.'

If the female is a Dog, the situation will be more ticklish. Instead of coming to terms with their troubles, lady Dogs sometimes choose to escape them in a blind search for pleasure or by other futile means, which will wear out Mr Ox's reserves of tolerance. Whatever happens, however, they will respect each other. The Ox will admire the Dog's profundity of thought, and the Dog will treasure the Ox's stability. A potentially happy, solid and durable union — except that the Dog will often suffer from the emotional reticence of the Ox, interpreting it as coldness.

Ox/Pig

The Pig thinks himself astute, but often reveals himself to be credulous. However, the Ox will be sceptical enough for two, and both will respect each other's scrupulous honesty.

The Ox likes to have peace and the Pig is a fervent devotee of Peace, which provides a common ground. There are, however, some differences in attitude. Often a gambler, the Pig will tend to resent the parsimonious side of the Ox. Neither will be pleased by the same things, the Ox being satisfied with the strictly necessary and the Pig never sneezing at the superfluous. At home, for example, the Ox will be irritated to see his Pig spouse spend their savings to improve and redecorate when he finds the place comfortable enough as it is.

The Pig will reproach his serious companion with not knowing how to make the most of life, with working too hard when he could relax, with wasting the best years of his life. Happily, this will never go too far because the Pig, although the kind to rush in head first, will not go so far as to endanger a harmony he wishes, above all, to preserve. And the Ox will, perhaps, agree to be dragged off to a restaurant on their wedding anniversary.

SOME OX CELEBRITIES

Aristotle, Bach, William Blake, Richard Burton, Albert Camus, Chaplin, Clemenceau, Cocteau, Dante, Walt Disney, Dubuffet, Dvorak, Erasmus, Geronimo, Giacometti, Heidegger, Hitler, Kipling, Lafayette, Vivien Leigh, Ferdinand de Lesseps, Machiavelli, André Malraux, Napoleon, Pandit Nehru, Nixon, Madame de Pompadour, Renoir, Cecil Rhodes, Richard the Lionheart, Rubens, Van Gogh, Peter Sellers, Vercingetorix, Wellington, Yeats, Zapata.

YOUR COMPANION IN LIFE

生命伴侶

After the Chinese sign of your year of birth, here is the sign of your hour of birth

What is a Companion in Life, as understood in Chinese astrology? It is a sort of 'ascendant' sign corresponding to your hour of birth. This Companion is another animal belonging to the Chinese cycle of the twelve emblematic beasts, who falls into step with you and accompanies you, ever ready to help you brave the traps and ambushes along your route. A permanent and benevolent shadow, he can render the impossible possible.

He is your counterpart, but with his own character and tendencies and with a different psychology. Both guardian angel and devil's advocate, he will be a witness to your life and an actor in it.

Have you ever felt, deep inside yourself, the subtle presence of another 'myself' inhabiting you and with whom you live, at times in harmony, at others in conflict? Another self who sometimes criticizes you and at others encourages you? That is your Companion in Life.

There are times when he will appear to be an imposter or an intruder. Certainly, he often questions your habits and your moral or spiritual complacency. Accompanied by this companion, a shadow within, the route is less monotonous and the voyager multiplies his chances of arriving at his chosen destination. This, however, in itself matters little, for it is the journey and the manner in which it is conducted that are important. Indolence is the greatest danger: your Companion is capable of arousing you from a lassitude of spirit and, to that end, if necessary, robbing you of your certainties, trampling on your secret gardens and, finally, tearing away the great veil of illusion.

It sometimes happens that your Companion is of the same sign as your year of birth, a twin brother in a way — for example, an Ox/Ox. In this case, you must recognize that he will compel you to realize yourself fully and to live the double aspect — the Yin and the Yang — that your bear

within yourself. In any case, you also bear within yourself the twelve animals. So, set out on the long route, ready for the great adventure: the beautiful voyage during which you will encounter the harmoniously entangled, the solemn and the grotesque, the ephemeral reality, the dream and the imagined.

Table of hours corresponding to the twelve emblematic animals

If you were **born** between	11 pm and 1 am	your **companion** is	Rat
	1 am and 3 am		Ox
	3 am and 5 am		Tiger
	5 am and 7 am		Rabbit
	7 am and 9 am		Dragon
	9 am and 11 am		Snake
	11 am and 1 pm		Horse
	1 pm and 3 pm		Goat
	3 pm and 5 pm		Monkey
	5 pm and 7 pm		Rooster
	7 pm and 9 pm		Dog
	9 pm and 11 pm		Pig

These figures correspond to the *solar hour* of your birth. If necessary, you should check the summer times (Daylight Savings Time) and make the appropriate adjustment (sometimes two hours before or after statutory time).

THE OX AND ITS COMPANION IN LIFE

 **Ox/Rat**

Here the Companion is a striking example of a pseudo guardian angel. The aggressiveness of the Rat is tempered by the tranquil force of the Ox. The Rat explores in depth, the Ox on the surface. Both being creators, it is the Ox who sometimes, by butting with his horns, will force the Rat to leave his underground passages, jostling him from his fortifications. A lover of liberty, the Ox will rarely be sidetracked. The Rat symbolizes perpetual movement, the Ox slow deliberation; the Ox dreams of conquering virgin territory, the Rat of impenetrable universes. The Ox/Rat will be realistic, prudent and will know how to reinforce his success.

 **Ox/Ox**

Often a recluse and habitually drawn to isolation and retreat, the Ox is barely able to support his own company. A lover of liberty, always on the search for new lands and virgin soil, the Ox/Ox will be fiercely individualistic and original. He will often disconcert his companions, to whom he will be as sparing of tact as of understanding. Such an unwillingness to compromise borders on sheer egotism. The Ox/Ox belongs to the race of conquerors: nothing can constrain nor attach him.

Ox/Tiger

Born under this alliance, seduction will be your major art. You are hardly likely to lose your way or fall asleep on the march. Conqueror of virgin lands and lord of the jungle, it will be extremely difficult to follow your track, for you are ferociously independent. Imagine a hunter joined to a dreamer, combining intelligence with muscular suppleness. But, Royal Tiger or not, you are also the symbol of temperance. Along with the tenacity and equilibrium of the age-old Ox, you bear within you a potential for sovereign and indomitable power. Alas, modesty and tenderness are not your strong points.

Ox/Rabbit

A home-loving conqueror! The route will be difficult: the Ox/Rabbit will oscillate between anger and silence, and will hesitate between leaving entirely and retiring into contemplation. If at times the Rabbit element is a sort of ball and-chain on the Ox, this will have its uses. Knowing in certain situations how to inspire prudence, calm anger and unknot nerves, the Rabbit can soften the stubbornness in which the Ox becomes entangled and stifled. Meanwhile, Ox will teach his Companion that real space and liberty cannot be measured by surface area alone, such as the size of the Rabbit's burrow. Which will win out — prudence or stubbornness? Take care, Ox/Rabbit, you are in danger of going round the world without leaving your room.

Ox/Dragon

A poisoned gift! A Dragon is always synonymous with luck, but, alas, there is a negative element, above all for a solitary and independent Ox. The Dragon is extremely intelligent but he is inclined to impose his own patterns of life on others. Always on the move, he will do his best to drag the Ox into spaces and dimensions which do not conform to his desires. He will be roused to a fury, which the Ox will oppose with stubborn silence: he is a provoker and able to set the Ox's teeth on edge, and he will have a tendency to goad him; the Dragon dreams of liberty, but it is not the same as his. The Ox/Dragon must therefore take upon himself these two powerful poles, these two disparate forces which inhabit him. Their pressures may be seriously perturbing. Particularly dynamic activity — military, sports or intellectual — may enable the Ox/Dragon to harmonize these contradictory energies.

Ox/Snake

The Ox will often be disorientated by the aggressiveness of his Snake Companion, who can nurture a dormant capacity for violence in him. The peaceful Ox, his eyes fixed on the blue line of the horizon, will not understand the behaviour of the reptile — his attacks, his secret hiding places, his sinuous approach. He will too often be tempted to crush him with a hoof, and in consequence will suffer many internal conflicts. The slow Ox, however, will be stimulated by this mysterious reptile who lures him to a fen and then shows him how he waits, hidden beneath a stone. Although his Snake Companion disconcerts him, the Ox will certainly learn that there are paths that he must sometimes avoid.

 **Ox/Horse**

Shifting from ardour to slow deliberation and back, these two Companions will not share the same concept of their path. The Ox, sure of himself and restrained, likes to take his time; his progress is slow and he is therefore unwilling to put up with the ardent spirit of the Horse, who goads him on, dreaming of honour and sunlit lands while the Ox ruminates on mapped-out paths. The conscientious Ox, desirous of solitude, grinds his teeth in annoyance when faced with the unmethodical and instinctive side of the Horse and his love of crowds and spectacles. Will the Horse's 'fire' heat the body and soul of this Ox, who is sometimes too 'buried' in his earth? If the Ox/Horse can agree on division of labours, he will undeniably hold winning cards. At work, to the seriousness, thoroughness and perseverance of the Ox will be added the passion and creativity of the Horse. On an emotional level, the ardour and vivacity of the Horse will soften the Ox's hard shell of doubt.

 **Ox/Goat**

A little note of capriciousness on the part of our Ox. The light-hearted and carefree Goat will be an excellent Companion. With him, the Ox will remove his blinkers and his deep furrows will be adorned with wild flowers and bouquets of brambles. Retaining a degree of gravity, the Ox/Goat will be capable of unexpected capers. The route will therefore be fascinating, provided that the Ox/Goat knows how to maintain a healthy balance between the real and the fantastic.

Ox/Monkey

The Ox will not resist the Monkey's charm, nor his persuasive and sympathetic magic for very long. Some good advice: if you want peace, give him the illusion that he is stronger but remain attentive and sympathetic. This courageous animal is remarkably agile; physically and mentally he is a first-rate acrobat and gifted with a rare power of persuasion. Take care, for the Monkey is sometimes a sorcerer, capable of transforming all the power of the Ox into mere confetti and mirages.

Ox/Rooster

The Rooster will add a little wine to his water, or, more exactly, he will add a pinch of generosity to his egotism. The Rooster has a sense for sharing and for friendship; admittedly he can behave like a braggart, but then his very ardour and vivacity are so charming that one forgives him everything. From his bravado the Ox will gain a great deal. The morning song of the Rooster will relieve the Ox of a certain torpor and dullness. The ideal would be composed of the Rooster's sharpness on the surface and the Ox's ability in depth.

 **Ox/Dog**

Here is an amalgam that is a little special, for the pessimism of the Dog, added to the slowness and austerity of the Ox, may result in an exceptional and somewhat forbidding gravity. The Dog is the ancient guardian of the Underworld, the Ox of the Labyrinth: this combination of Cerberus and Minotaur will be a bit disquieting. Yet the Dog can bring to the Ox a perspective and power of introspection which he often lacks. The Ox, for his part, will alleviate the doubts, the existential qualms and the tortured questions of the Dog. The Ox/Dog will thus obtain both hope and lucidity; he will know himself a little better, which is the beginning of true wisdom.

 **Ox/Pig**

Both the Ox and the Pig are sometimes slightly egotistical recluses. One is the symbol of fertility, the other of abundance. Their voyage will have every chance of material comfort, but there will be complications. With the Ox in charge, you will face the everyday world with a severe and uncompromising appearance; this will conceal your real life of secret corners and cosy beaches — so enjoyable, luxurious and unconstrained, and made even more pleasurable by discreet weekends, private clubs and closed circles.

If the Pig is in charge, then under the facade of a man who enjoys life to the fullest will lie an indestructible solidity and an unsuspected tenacity which will often make you all the more formidable, especially in business. Some will think they can soften you up by various means; you will appear all smiles, but inside you will remain glacial.

THE OX
AND THE FIVE
ELEMENTS

五行

YOUR ELEMENT

In Chinese astrology, each year is joined to an Element. There are five Elements: *Water, Fire, Wood, Metal, Earth.*

Each of the twelve emblematic animals is linked successively to each of the five Elements. For example, in the year 1900 the Rat was Metal, in 1912 he was Water, in 1924 he was Wood, in 1936, Fire and in 1948 he was Earth. Therefore, for the twelve years from 1900 he was linked to Metal, for the next twelve years to Water, and, for every succeeding period of twelve years, to each of the other Elements, in succession.

In order to determine the Element corresponding to the year of your birth, use the table below:

Years whose digits end in: 2 and 3 — Water
6 and 7 — Fire
4 and 5 — Wood
0 and 1 — Metal
8 and 9 — Earth

The same union of *Animal-Element* repeats every sixty years, for example, Rat-Metal appeared in 1720, 1780, 1840, 1900, 1960 and so on.

The five Elements are the primary forces affecting the universe. It is their particular association with each of the signs which provides the basis for every horoscope. Movement and fluctuation, Yin and Yang, these symbolic forces are in a perpetual state of action and interaction.

Wood gives birth to Fire, which gives birth to Earth, which gives birth to Metal, which gives birth to Water, which in turn gives birth to Wood.

OX/WATER
(you were born in 1913 or 1973)

The cold born of the northern sky descended to earth and gave birth to Water. The Chinese consider Water more a synonym for coldness and ice than the source of heat and fertility.

Characteristics of the Ox/Water
Water of winter nights, rigour and severity; calm and deep water to be feared and respected; still water sheltering demons asleep in its depths; fetid and muddy water of the marsh, the refuge of crawling creatures. Water can be a token of the total arrest of motion; or, for an Ox searching for peace, beauty and harmony, it can be limpid and bracing. Of the Yin tendency and coming from the North, the Ox can become a wall, a closed, placid mask — reserved, distant and mysterious.

Health of the Ox/Water
The Water organ is the kidney; its flavour is salted. As with Ox/Metal, the Ox/Water will experience circulatory problems — in this case of liquids and not of breath, but with similar risk of blockages in general. Everything will depend on how the Ox carries out his projects. Be careful to avoid emotional obstructions and psychological bottlenecks.

Physical characteristics of the Ox/Water
He is by nature round and rather stout, with thick lips and plump hands, but with a dark and marvellously soft skin and thick, glossy hair. This physical type suits the female better than the male. In any case, well-endowed or not, add passion and a touch of audacity.

The Ox/Water and others
Go forward; do not be alarmed, timid and fearful. You know how to listen and are a calm and steady person. You also have a talent for governing the masses while avoiding

excesses, for you are also a humanist. You have a horror of scenes, are a prudent and good salesman, a fine craftsman and an active partisan of peace. Your concern is for your home and children. A fond and doting parent, you take excellent care of your children.

Advice for an Ox/Water
Family life seems highly indicated for you. Build a house in the middle of a green prairie with a flowing river, and have many children. If you decide to move into the active world, then create a business, join a political party or a union, or found a new religion. Do not hesitate to take your place centre stage, for you have it in you to inspire applause.

An Ox/Water year
The culminating point for the Ox/Water year will be winter, a period of gestation. The Yin reinforces the Yin, and the Ox of the North remains in the North, united with Water. You hardly move at all, so make use of this period of immersion to assess your true position, so that you can eventually set forth in a spirit of confidence and boldness. This waiting should not be a period of resignation; do not let things 'go mouldy' but instead recharge your batteries.

Tendency of the year: More favourable for the female Oxen than for the males, and good for creators and artists. Changes are imminent, but reflect more than twice before taking the plunge.

Historical example of an Ox/Water year
1793

At the dawn of the New Year all Europe waited on France. Many people, not least the poet Wordsworth, had greeted the French Revolution with rapture. Two great questions remained: the fate of the French king and the ambitions of the young nation forged by the Revolution.

The first was quickly answered. 'Citizen Capet', as Louis XVI was dubbed, was brought to trial, the death sentence demanded by Robespierre was accepted by a majority of one and Louis suffered death by guillotine on 21 January. The death of an anointed king is said to have outraged the civilized world; in fact what it did was threaten assumptions on which the ruling classes of Europe depended.

The great Whig families of England to a large extent owed their power, wealth and influence to the death by the axe of an English anointed king a century and a half before. Now they found among them French émigrés whose châteaux they had visited and whose instincts and social attitudes they instinctively shared. This induced a natural solidarity of commiseration and reserved friendship. By itself, this had little if any political significance — not because the Whig families had no political weight but precisely because, unlike their French compatriots, they had long carried it. They were not going to raise a war against the new republic on account of the French king's death.

The harder and more thrusting members of English society were indifferent to the plight of the émigrés and unaffected by the fate of their king. They considered the Ancien Régime both tyrannical and futile. However, directly the French opened up the Scheldt it was a different story. The English were thoroughly alarmed by this threat to their trade: overnight, their mood changed from one of indifferent curiosity to one of alarmed belligerence. When the Republic declared war on England Pitt could be assured of their support in what he was convinced would be a short war, for with the defection of the French general Desormiez, the road to Paris seemed wide open. For the first and last time Pitt raised no additional taxes to meet the expenses of the war. He would soon become Paymaster of Europe.

OX/WOOD
(you were born in 1925 or 1985)

To the East, the wind blew in the sky and from its warm caress of the Earth Wood was born.

Characteristics of the Ox/Wood

Wood is of the morning, of springtime, of a temperate nature, loving harmony, beauty and elegance. The Ox/Wood will tend to be more passionate than the Ox on its own; he will be quick to anger — which can represent a danger — and he will have a compulsion to lose his way, a summons to self-destructiveness. He is also in danger of being oversensitive, but his dignified attitude will conceal this. However, the scales will be balanced in his favour due to his strong will and great sense of equilibrium; he will survive. His need for harmony will always win out.

Health of the Ox/Wood

The organ of Wood is the liver; its flavour is acid. Be on your guard against outbreaks of anger, nervousness and narrow-mindedness. In the end these can cause your downfall.

The Ox/Wood and others

He will often be relaxed and calm. He will be creative and imaginative, and will by far prefer his liberty to a brilliant career. He will search for a quality of life rather than for success. A bit of a poet, an artist when he likes, with a feeling for the earth and work well done, the Ox/Wood is con-scientious and has a closer affinity with nature than with people.

Advice for the Ox/Wood

You possess irresistible charm, the soul of a poet and are the very symbol of a free man. Seek to innovate and transform. You are full of ideas — and your feet are on the ground.

Physical characteristics of the Ox/Wood

For an Ox, you are tall, fine boned, slim and hold yourself well. You have the sort of eyes that fascinate, an olive complexion, thick and lustrous hair, soft, smooth skin and red lips. If fortune has neglected to favour you with these knockout looks, what difference does it make — you are a poet! Believe in yourself and others will believe in you. You are, after all, a charming innovator.

An Ox/Wood year

The culminating point for an Ox/Wood year will be spring, a period of growth and prosperity. The Ox will set out from his winter habitat in the North and travel East. His Yin aspect will reach out towards the dynamism of the Yang. Springtime for an Ox is synonymous with birth, life and work. Therefore, no hesitations! Give of yourself fully during this season, so favourable for creation, but remember to be flexible and open, ready to listen and absorb every impression. In this year of renewal you can apply novel techniques and new methods. Open your eyes and prick up your ears because fortune favours you.

Tendency of the year: Be flexible and diplomatic and profit from your good luck, but do not sink into egotism; share happiness and joy throughout the year. Deny your true spirit or thwart your good impulses and you may be faced with your world in ruins.

Historical example of an Ox/Wood year 1805

The campaign leading to the Battle of Austerlitz was one of notable brilliance, even by Napoleonic standards. The unopposed occupation of Berlin which followed completed the military and moral collapse of Prussia.

Europe appeared to have no choice but to submit to a new master, an appearance wholly confirmed two years later by the Peace of Tilsit.

Yet, however secure Napoleon's mastery of the Continent, 1805 was the year in which he was forced to abandon his resolve to invade England: he irrevocably lost the mastery of the sea to the English. The Battle of Trafalgar was the counterpart to Austerlitz. A complete victory, it was not in itself decisive for its outcome; but its strategic effect was nevertheless more profound than that of Austerlitz. As was to be said of Admiral Jellicoe after the naval battle of Jutland in 1916, Nelson could have 'lost the war in an afternoon'. By his victory, however, he secured the sea routes to India, thereby both in that subcontinent and elsewhere abruptly circumscribing Napoleon's global ambitions. The latter, which had extended beyond India to Australia and westwards to the promise of the West Coast of North America, were to be vented in 1812 on a land mass as consuming and uncompromising as the oceans he had lost.

It is said that his particular genius for the land battle rendered Napoleon indifferent to naval affairs. Certainly, he saw in the naval defeat at Trafalgar a matter for peripheral annoyance; but that was a first reaction only. He well understood its import and thereafter sought to emasculate the effect of sea power by the imposition of the continental system, a policy which very nearly forced the English to submit. But until 1805 the conqueror of Egypt hoped to use his naval forces in far-reaching enterprises which depended on that element of surprise for which he was a master on land. Subsequently, he was able to do so on a small scale, but never again could he hope to dislodge the main English fleets from their stations, yet alone destroy them.

OX/FIRE
(you were born in 1937)

Heat was born in the southern sky, descended to Earth and fertilized it. From their union Fire was born.

Characteristics of the Ox/Fire

The Fire element is of the midday, of the South, of summer. Fire is Yang; it is the element which animates; it quickens and transforms. For the Ox, Fire will be a flame to emblazon his feeling for harmony and beauty; for this dreamer it will be a creative. or perhaps even mystical, spark. But it can also blind or devour him. Fire is light or joy — also, at times, the symbol of destruction.

Health of the Ox/Fire

The organ of Fire is the heart; its flavour is bitter. The Ox should be prudent because he is slow and Fire is rapid. He should take care not to squander his energy; he should relax and respect his bodily rhythms. The Ox is a sensualist and should remember that excesses around the age of forty often bring on a heart attack. Enjoy yourself, Ox/Fire, but not to excess.

The Ox/Fire and others

Drawn to politics, but always remaining fiercely individual-istic, the force of his Fire Companion will help to quicken the slowness of the Ox, kindling an ardour for combat and a feeling for the spirit of the game. However, the Ox should take care not to be deceived by the 'game': sometimes one mistakenly thinks that one is pulling the strings while, in the shadows, it is others who are in control of the marionettes. The Ox's fear of failure, joined by the destructive aspect of Fire, can be an extremely dangerous threat to his sacrosanct liberty.

Physical characteristics of the Ox/Fire

The Fire type has a ruddy complexion, wide jaw, aquiline nose and ears with free lobes. While you are not the portrait of a playboy, your high spirits, elegance and wit will work for you. Moreover, your tenacity will get the better of any resis-tance.

Advice for an Ox/Fire

You are not an ordinary animal and, moreover, you are fully conscious of this. You are a conqueror, so do not waste these powerful assets.

An Ox/Fire year

The culminating point for an Ox/Fire year will be summer, a

period of creation and material and spiritual progress; an active year which you will move through at high speed. Take care not to run out of breath, slow down if necessary and do not overdo things.

Tendency of the year: An excellent, rich and productive year, fertile in every sense and in all directions. Nevertheless, try to relax: hypertension can lead to depression. Fire heats and animates, but it also consumes: a single spark can ignite an entire town.

Historical example of an Ox/Fire year 1337

In November Edward III of England sent his formal defiance to Philip VI of France and assumed the title of King of France. The claim had a semblance of legality. Edward was a nephew, Philip a cousin, of the late French king; but Edward was a nephew only through his sister Isabella and this was put forward as a crucial impediment. The point had been argued in Paris the previous year. All agreed, including the English, that no woman could inherit the Crown of France: how therefore could a woman transmit a right she could not possess? The French magnates had no wish for an English king and quickly appreciated the logic of the argument. The 'Salic' law was thus given definition, and it was established that the French Crown could only descend through the male heirs of the French kings.

Edward made a big gesture which had a limited practical aim: he hoped that by yielding his claim to the Crown he could secure the independence of the Duchy of Guienne from French suzerainty. His initial attempts to negotiate these terms came to nothing. Guienne was in far too sensitive an area for the French to renounce all claims to it, and the Pope, when asked to mediate by Edward, supported the French position. In May 1337 Edward declared Guienne to be confiscated to the English Crown, in effect instituting the Hundred Years War. He then threatened ruin to the Flemish cloth trade by prohibiting all exports of

English wool to Flanders. The prospect raised a revolt in Ghent, the flight of the Count of Flanders and the raising of a patrician, Jakob van Artevelte, to the position of a quasi-dictator. This enabled Edward to further his plans. By lifting the embargo and promising subsidies he secured the support of a powerful confederation in the north-west of France, including the support of the Emperor Lewis IV of Bavaria. From that traditional base he prepared to invade France.

It seemed a reckless enterprise. The wealth and population of France far exceeded those of England. The French chivalry was renowned, proud and confident. Yet in this very chivalry lay the French military limitations. The heavily armoured knights were able to fight only in circumstances suitable for their powerful but ill-disciplined charges and the foreign mercenaries, whom they openly despised but in fact depend upon, were crossbowmen with a rate of fire of two bolts per minute. By contrast, Edward commanded an army disciplined from the Scottish wars whose most deadly arm was composed of its longbowmen, archers who could release arrows at the rate of ten per minute. In the early stages of the long conflict, intermittent over more than a century, it was this weapon which was to shatter and demoralize the French chivalry and in the end prove decisive.

OX/EARTH
(you were born in 1949)

Earth was born from the slowly falling elements of the sky at its humid zenith.

Characteristics of the Ox/Earth
This is an afternoon Earth, the humid and hot Earth of summer. For the Ox, this heavy, abundant and fertile earth of rich green grasslands, symbol of retreat and contemplation, is a paradise. Alas, it can also encroach upon him, stick to his hooves and deaden his tread; the grasslands may become a swamp. Although the Ox is close to the Earth, he

should not be its prisoner. He must release it, not be buried beneath it, body and soul.

Health of the Ox/Earth
The Earth's organ is the spleen; its flavour is sweet. The Ox will tend to put on weight; he should avoid rich food and sugar, if he can.

The Ox/Earth and others
As a farmer, winegrower, restaurant owner or director of a supermarket, anything having to do with food will interest you. Work does not frighten you; your life lies before you and you are bound to make good. Or perhaps the Earth will only appeal to you as a refuge, a retreat which entices you to forget the world of men and prefer a life of meditation. Be careful: this might be another form of egotism.

Physical characteristics of the Ox/Earth
Your features are a trifle too heavy (watch your weight). Solidly built yet pleasingly plump, you have a slightly yellowish complexion, thick eyebrows and a rounded back, but a flat stomach. You are slow, prudent and rather set in your ways. Take up a sport and do not ruminate too much, or your morale will suffer with your figure.

Advice for an Ox/Earth
Take a trip, change your ideas, learn how to do without a bit of comfort, lead a healthy outdoor life. Paint, play a musical instrument, do some carpentry and vary your habits. Remember that you are an Ox — become a bull and not a dumb ox.

An Ox/Earth year
The culminating point is summer. The Ox/Earth will be in his element. Because it is a year of abundance and fertility, he will have no material problems. The Ox will feel even freer than usual and will want to discover other lands. He should, however, be prepared for a gregarious life, be outgoing and

keep his egotism under control, rather than wrapping himself up in comfortable solitude.

Tendency of the year: Propitious for creators and productive for businessmen and craftsmen; but do not forget that there are other animals on this earth. The more brilliant and original the talent, the more likely it is to be recognized.

Historical example of an Ox/Earth year 1949

For several years after the end of the Second World War, Great Britain remained withdrawn, its attention focused on problems of social welfare and rigidly opposed to the suggestion of European participation raised by Monnet and Schumann. The austerities imposed by the war had continued into peacetime requiring even the unprecedented rationing of bread. This evidence of a new Puritanism was widely considered to have been prompted by Sir Stafford Cripps, the Chancellor of the Exchequer, whose evident belief in austerity for its own sake was not endorsed by the British people — indeed it was seen by many as an indication of incompetence and was castigated as a desire for controls for their own sake.

Meanwhile, the English were in grave financial difficulty and sought from the Americans both understanding and assistance. The British delegation was greeted by a coldness and incomprehension which only the intervention of the distinguished American diplomat, George Kennan, was able to bend in the interests of friendship. Some trappings of empire were still retained by the British, a grave irritant in Washington, where it was rightly seen as a disinclination to find a new role in Europe. Kennan's view was that there should indeed be a special relationship, one between the United States, Great Britain, Canada and possibly other dominions; for he foresaw that Australian interests would turn increasingly towards the United States. This suggestion was never seriously considered in

Washington or in London; if it had been frankly debated many future misunderstandings might have been avoided. Certainly such a debate would have given a different context to the British contribution to the Korean war the following year. The conjectures remain interesting: the facts mundane.

Of far greater significance was the proclamation of the birth of the Chinese Peoples' Republic on 1 October by Mao Tse-tung.

OX/METAL
(you were born in 1901 or 1961)

In the sky, coming from the West, drought grazed the skin of the Earth and gave birth to Metal. Winds came from the faraway steppes, seeking the vital sap.

Characteristics of the Ox/Metal

Metal is of the night, of the autumn and of cold. It symbolizes clarity, purity and precision. You tend to be rigid, perhaps even austere. You are an excellent administrator and an organizer who will be an incisive and implacable leader. You need the concrete, the real, and to the devil with sensitivity and nice feelings; the important thing is to achieve the goal. A touch moralistic, you are attracted to the mystical and the ascetic. Will you therefore choose isolation and give up society? Does your body, so strongly allied to the Earth, seem so heavy? In short, be careful: there is danger of your being too austere and a killjoy.

Health of the Ox/Metal

Metal's organ is the lung; its flavour is pungent. The Ox/Metal will need oxygen, in all senses of the term, for he is threatened by blockages of all kinds. He must breathe deeply and liberate himself. He needs to loosen up both physically and mentally. The Ox/Metal is coldheaded and coldhearted. Relax, or one day you may forget to breathe.

Physical characteristics of the Ox/Metal

With his fair complexion and lively expression, the Ox/Metal catches the eye. His hands are usually small and his square-jawed face composed harmoniously — in short, a handsome 'animal'. He should try to bring some humour and warmth to his life. Happiness can be a bit like a ship-board romance: it is not necessary to look very far for what exists close to hand.

The Ox/Metal and others

You are full of energy, constant and true to your word; you are also slightly cutting and dry, the very picture of upright-ness and rectitude. You would make an excellent lawyer, judge or tax collector. You like to arbitrate, regulate and command. You are completely above board: there are no 'off-the-record' settlements, bribes or 'under-the-counter' payoffs — you cannot be bought! However, a note of fantasy might lighten your spirit; being so rigorous, you risk becoming sad and morose.

Advice for an Ox/Metal

Do not take yourself so seriously: go to the country and look after the flowers in the garden rather than constructing a pedestal for yourself. Be natural and relax.

An Ox/Metal year

The culminating point in the year of an Ox/Metal will be autumn. He will leave the wintery North to travel West. His Yin tendency will be strengthened by the Yin of autumn, a combination associated with lethargy and a perceptible lessening of dynamic force.

Tendency of the year: Hardening and dryness, both physi-cally and morally. Be careful not to adopt 'regulations' at odds with your nature: at best these will bring you temporary victory, but more likely prolonged depression. One thinks one has won, but one has lost more than from defeat. Too late and one will ask, who was the true victor?

Historical example of an Ox/Metal year
1661

The Stuart line was restored to the English throne and in

December 1660 the body of Oliver Cromwell was exhumed, along with those of his associates Ireton, Bradshaw and Pride, and drawn on a hurdle to Tyburn. All were then hanged in their coffins. It is said that Cromwell's daughter Mary brought her father's headless remains to Newburgh Priory in North Yorkshire. Certainly, there is a sarcophagus in the attic there reputed to contain them.

The Convention Parliament had, by its moderation, effected one of the most remarkable changes in the history of England. This new spirit of revenge was a token of the rising tide of devotion to the restored monarch which was to mark the year 1661. Charles's coronation on St George's Day witnessed a popular enthusiasm unknown since the days of Elizabeth I. The London mob, it is true, had always responded to extravagance and pageantry, but the response was more subtle than a mere reaction against the austerities of the Protectorate. The young Louis XIV had emerged from his tutelage after the death of Cardinal Mazarin. The English felt that they needed a comparable king: it was a matter of pride. Moreover the Dutch were their enemies, rivals not only in commerce but recently victorious at sea, and the Republican emanations from Flanders served to promote enthusiasm for a royal dynasty in England.

Matters were very different in Massachusetts where the New Englanders looked on themselves as a free state and were against owning the English king or having any dependence on England. It was not until August that Charles was proclaimed in Boston, and then without enthusiasm.

In June the negotiations for Charles's marriage to Catherine of Braganza were finally concluded. The marriage treaty, which included the ceding of the island of Bombay and the Port of Tangier, was duly signed; England took over the remnants of the great Portuguese Empire and thereafter its policy was turned towards the wider horizons of maritime empire.

Analogical Table
of the Different Elements

Elements	Wood	Fire	Earth	Metal	Water
Years ending in	4 and 5	6 and 7	8 and 9	0 and 1	2 and 3
Colours	Green	Red	Yellow	White	Blue
Seasons	Spring	Summer	End of summer	Autumn	Winter
Climates	Wind	Heat	Humid	Dry	Cold
Flavours	Acid	Bitter	Sweet	Pungent	Salty
Principal organ	Liver	Heart	Spleen	Lungs	Kidneys
Secondary organ	Gallbladder	Small intestine	Stomach	Large intestine	Bladder
Food	Wheat, poultry	Rice, lamb	Corn, beef	Oats, horse	Peas, pork

Table of Harmony
Between the Elements

		Wood Female	Fire Female	Earth Female	Metal Female	Water Female
○○○ Excellent prosperity	**Male Wood**	● ●	○	○ ○ ○	○	○ ○
○○ Good harmony, understanding	**Male Fire**	○	○	○ ○	●	● ●
○ Effort needed	**Male Earth**	● ●	○ ○	○ ○	○ ○ ○	●
● Rivalries and problems of reciprocal domination	**Male Metal**	○	● ●	●	● ●	○ ○ ○
● ● Misunderstanding and incomprehension	**Male Water**	○ ○	● ●	●	○ ○ ○	○

THE
FOUR SEASONS
OF
THE OX

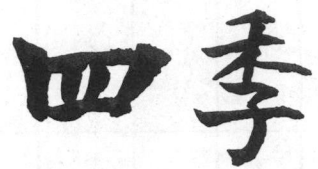

If you were born in spring
Ox/Aries
Many years ago I knew an Ox/Aries whose virile charm and completely indifferent attitude towards women fascinated many of them. His real interest was in land and how he could profit from it quickly. He had an amiable character, although he was a bit brusque because he felt that discussions were a waste of time. If there was a competition, he would set out to win, ramming his competitors' words down their throats. He was always covered with cuts and bruises from sports. And what has he become? A banker who continually calculates his loans and investments before returning home on an enormous and noisy motorcycle.

Most Ox/Aries fit this description. Materialistic, very active, loving speed and quick decisions, insensitive to subtleties, romance or sentiment, they rely on what they can see, touch and measure. Subjective, egotistical, and obvious, incapable of meanness and ready to do anything to protect their family, they are also quick to anger and hot-headed. If you are interested in getting in touch with spirits, avoid the Ox/Aries; but if you want to share a healthy and active life with a solid and sincere person, go ahead! He will never suffer from insomnia, whatever complications he may have to face.

Ox/Taurus
He slightly resembles Ox/Aries, but is more calm, peaceful and stubborn. He will be found amid the rich grasslands, quietly and voluptuously smelling the perfume of flowers, while contemplating the abundant harvests to come and calves ready for fattening. He has a talent for growing things, for nurturing the fruits of the earth and for conservation. Happiest in the countryside, he can profitably adapt himself to commerce, provided he can take time for decisions — he is a slow and deliberate thinker and needs to ruminate over a problem. If he is pressured to hurry he will lose his head, become anxious and nervous and explode with anger. And that, indeed, is formidable. when angry the Ox/Taurus is as

relentless as a bulldozer or an ignited rocket that is impossible to defuse.

Sentimental, but not at all a romantic, he is both faithful and impatient, requiring the sensuality of a sexual attachment without the frills or little attentions; he feels that his being there should suffice.

In old age, one can imagine him belabouring his children with his wise and cunning advice and packing them off to work in the fields day and night. The Ox/Taurus is so intoxicated with nature that he could fertilize a desert. For that matter, he could also strike oil, he is so brimming with practical and profitable ideas.

Ox/Gemini

A curious mixture from which anything can be expected. Here we have the 'heaviest' sign of Chinese astrology crossed with the 'lightest' sign of the Western zodiac. There is plenty to confuse the observer. The Ox/Gemini will be less dogmatic and easier to live with than other Oxen. His mind, his wit and his repartee will be livelier and more humorous. In this respect he will, pleasingly, be able to adapt, but, in another sense, he will be too adaptable and in consequence will seem less 'trustworthy'. One will no longer know for certain that this is the sage Ox one can rely on; the malicious joker sported by a Gemini will always seem to lurk within him.

That being said, he will be a charming Companion, will talk agreeably and knowledgeably and have the gift for making his partner feel secure without smothering him or her. The gift of both the male and female Ox/Gemini is their ability to be more intimate and close than their Ox relatives. But the alliance is not intrinsically stable: the impatience of Gemini allied with the angry temperament of the Ox can be conducive to explosive effects. Do not thwart the eruptive Ox, who will often react when you least expect it. He will probably not go for your throat because his type of violence is not physical; more likely, he will speak out in a torrent of invective. During this maelstrom, every reproach he has stifled since cutting his first milk-tooth will be indiscriminately, but recognizably, loosed upon you.

If you were born in summer
Ox/Cancer

This is the most domestic of the Oxen. He will never leave his grasslands — even if there is a cyclone he will remain with his four hooves buried in the ground that he was born on. Characterized by a rocklike inertia and a capacity for perseverance discouraging to his adversaries, he will cease to pursue his goal only when he has reached it, even though he gives the impression of being completely passive and immobile.

This home-loving Ox fulfils his need to command within the family circle. An authoritarian father who is solid as a rock, an attentive mother, although a little too enveloping, this Ox is the rare pearl, the fairy, who transforms the most neglected of houses into a little paradise.

When in love, the Ox/Cancer is so singleminded and so faithful that once he chooses someone, it is for life — and even after! He finds it difficult to conceive that not everyone is like himself. Undemonstrative in public, he prefers the intimacies of the home to entertaining and social small talk. With his family and friends he is understanding and always available; endless confidences at night under warm blankets are his special treat. If one is in search of adventure, variety or new stimuli, an Ox/Cancer partner is clearly to be avoided. But if one dreams of security, if one suffers from anxieties that need soothing, this partnership will be ideal.

Ox/Leo

It is difficult to imagine the Ox/Leo in a role other than that of 'Great Leader'. His qualities and his defects are all predictable. Ambitious, energetic, authoritarian, tenacious and realistic, he is armed with an analytical intellect. He is never confused by the details of a problem and will sooner or later surmount it. He has a gift for involving other people in his projects, bringing them motivation and direction. And he knows exactly what he wants. He is both lucid and implacable in his own pursuits as well as for others, but his leonine pride is softened by the disinterestedness of the Ox. An excellent strategist, a fighter who is aware of the weak points of his adversaries, he cannot conceive of an insurmountable obstacle. If he really wants something, he will use every means in his power to obtain it, and if these do not suffice, he will somehow find others that will.

Marvellous, you may think. Alas, there is a defect in the Ox/Leo's splendid armour: he cannot stand failure. If he misses his target, he will indict the entire world rather than admit to his own mistake. Whether these blunders are in business or in love, he will have a hard time recovering, taking new conditions into account and starting all over again. Plunging in headlong, his ambition will have taken him altogether too far.

Ox/Virgo

This combination seems as intellectually favourable as it is emotionally delicate. The Ox/Virgo is stable, thrifty and rather conservative, both morally and materially. He is demanding, but does not ask of others more than he asks of himself, knowing to perfection how to gauge the limits of everyone and everything. Reasonable, prudent, hard working, remarkably well organized and scrupulous, he is also sceptical and afraid of being cheated — that his honesty and good faith are being taken advantage of. As an inspector of taxes, controller of works, minister of security or what you will, there is no doubt, as long as he really is in control, that he will succeed in his task. Moreover, he will be above suspicion.

But unless he can resign himself to abandoning his rigidly preconceived idea of the-perfect-relationship-based-on-fidelity-and-duty, our Ox/Virgo is in danger of suffering from many disappointments. All the more so since, lacking confidence in himself, he will be timid and become entangled by his scruples as in a spider's web. If you can shake up his emotions as if in a cocktail shaker and thus resolve his confusion into a forward-moving drunkenness, you may gain his confidence — but you will have to persist with the treatment or he will revert.

If you were born in autumn
Ox/Libra

The Ox's nature is profoundly honest and is coupled with an acute sense of propriety. Libra is sociable, yet will hesitate even before saying 'hello' for fear of being misunderstood. The Ox/Libra will tend to be impartial — or at least will think himself to be so — but will be extremely demanding of others. He will question the authenticity of their methods, their sense of duty, their respect for laws, traditions, and so on. In short, he will be less obliging than he looks: his pleasing smile will often hide an inner judgement from which there is no appeal.

Emotionally he will find it difficult to reconcile his natural distrust with his uncontrollable need for another. He can harbour unjustified suspicions of someone for years whom he nevertheless remains with, and so poison his life. Happily, when he finally acquires true confidence, his affection will hold against any test. Moreover, even though surly and tender in turn, the Ox/Libra has enormous charm. It would take a sadist to wish to be unfaithful to him or to deceive him in any way. Serious yet easy to live with, attached to domestic stability, he is a lover of order, beauty, quiet luxury and even pleasure. The Ox, who is statuesque, is also aesthetic and refined: he watches carefully where he places his great hooves as he progresses for fear of crushing the flowers. To live with him is the simplest thing in the world, on condition that you never deceive him, nor fail him, physically or morally. Elementary. . . .

Ox/Scorpio

The inertia and lethargy of the Ox, combined with Scorpio's tendency to run in circles, to be anxious and guilt-ridden, can produce an uncommunicative, secretive and anxious person who risks bearing all the problems of earth and hell together, but is capable of surprising and liberating explosions. For years on end, the Ox/Scorpio will remain tranquil; it will seem that he is sleeping or meditating, unless one meets his attentive and piercing gaze. Actually, he does not squander his strength. He needs powerful motives to exert it, but if you touch him on a vulnerable point, you do so at your own peril. This is not unlike detonating a charge: the explosion can create an enormous amount of damage.

The Ox/Scorpio combines the passionate, the vindictive and the excessive. His vitality, which is extraordinary, is well directed. He always has a stack of arguments at his disposal, some of the sledgehammer variety, others totally unpredictable. For these reasons, his friendship is to be preferred to his animosity. Also because he possesses life-enhancing qualities: splendidly faithful, he is always ready to give of himself, to take risks and pledge himself for those whom he loves. He is intelligent, reflective, and by far the most perceptive of the Oxen. And, in love, he is not one of those tepid people. Life with him will take place in an atmosphere closer to that created by Dostoyevsky than that of a rose-coloured novel. What intensity!

Ox/Sagittarius

The most sociable of the Oxen, he is also one of the most energetic, but less impulsive than the Ox/Aries and less egocentric than the Ox/Leo . This is probably a good alliance. The indiscriminate sociability of Sagittarius is restrained by the distrust of the Ox; the ponderous attitudes of the Ox benefit from the spark of dynamic fire characteristic of the ninth sign of the zodiac: their complementary qualities and defects will balance each other.

The person born under this configuration is active and realistic, without being self-seeking. Although generous with those he loves, his nature is to conserve his resources in anticipation of difficult days to come. One must not forget that no Ox escapes nightmares of unlucky, lean times. As with the Rat, security is necessary for him but, unlike the Rat, he is not greedy. He is saved from the rigidities of opinion and behaviour by his flair for sensing an opportunity, and so often appears to others to be independent and liberal. This, however, is more apparent than real: he is much more of a conformist than he seems, and his behaviour is based on a scale of values so elaborate that each 'semitone' has been weighed precisely. If this finely graded moral organization is disturbed, he can become biased and sectarian; even if three minutes earlier one would have given him the prize for tolerance. He was born to fulfil an essential role: to maintain a respect for values and to secure a correct balance in things, whether in nature or society. He is a benevolent moralist and an excellent 'father-confessor'. If you heed his advice, you can be assured of the approval of others and that there will be no risk of social blunders. It all depends on whether you wish to be managed or not.

If you were born in winter
Ox/Capricorn

Ferociously individualistic and solitary, this Ox is hardly one to enliven a party. If he makes a joke, it will be awkward or tend towards black humour. The trouble is, he possesses just about all the qualities that one knows only too well in certain people. Reeling off a list of compliments, one acquaintance finished with the comment, 'But, my God, how boring he can be!' Ambitious and authoritarian, he covets power, and to gain it displays a degree of tenacity and purposefulness which can make our contemporary politicians look like amateurs. His sense of duty is often stifling; his opinions, being stubborn and sectarian, are somewhat rigid; but he always finishes what he has begun. He sticks to his word and ignores the meaning of the word 'lie'.

The Ox/Capricorn is fundamentally timid. Although buried under a solid sheet of icy winter soil, his sensitivity remains intensely alive and can often confound him. He might, for example, often appear to be preoccupied with a problem of ready cash, but this is a front: in truth, he does not want to reveal that his heart is in a sling. With him, you must make the first move, but his repayment will be more than worth the effort: his feelings are as lasting as the pyramids — and as self-evident.

Ox/Aquarius
The Ox, like Aquarians, views passionate outbursts with a certain distrust. With the Ox, a precise criterion of choices leaves little place for chance; the Aquarian fears the loss of his sacrosanct detachment if he yields to love: seducing an Ox/Aquarius will prove a lengthy business. You will need all the tricks of seduction, beginning with a show of interest and sheer niceness, alternating to indifference and the use of other and magical potions. Eventually you will go to bed very late, but together.

Happily, the Ox/Aquarius cannot resist friendship. While this may be his best quality, it may also be his weak point. This discreet but profoundly human person is always ready to listen, to help and, eventually, to take care of the lost sheep who come to him for advice. The Ox/Aquarius is less narrow-minded than other Oxen. He sincerely tries to find excuses for others, but only in the context of an ideal he is not prepared to question; he does not like to have it trampled on. An essentially individualistic idealist, charitable and independent, he adores being asked for help, but his charity will never extend beyond the limits of his moral principles.

Ox/Pisces
A curious mixture of an aquatic creature and one forever bound to Mother Earth. The results are variable. In the worst of cases, the Ox/Pisces is ill-defined, slightly muddy, confused and deceptive. Buried to the waist in his grassland, he will look at you with dull, glazed eyes; then, apparently for no reason at all, he will attack. If he knows where he is going, he can be brilliant — but he does not always know. The real problem that confronts the Ox/Pisces is to discover himself and to reconcile the needs of his rational and positive nature with the excesses of his imagination. If he can, his capacities will be remarkable. His rigour, aligned

with his inclination towards fantasy, will give him an efficiency allied to steady creativity. Very adaptable for an Ox, he knows how to make the most of the opportunities within his grasp, restraining his individualism in order to work more effectively as a team with others.

Rather timid and somewhat boorish at times, he is highly susceptible and sensitive. Often more moved by affection than by material ambition, he is capable of passionate, exclusive attachments. He is, perhaps, the most sentimental and the most charitable of the Oxen, but also the most fragile: his hooves are planted in clay, and he knows it. But he can also be an artist, in all senses of the term and in all areas of his life.

THE
I CHING

易经

THE I CHING AND THE OX

In the I Ching game, you ask a question and you obtain an answer. It is therefore a divining game. But the question you ask is posed through your Ox identity; the wheels, the complex mechanism of your mind and spirit, begin to turn. You ask an Ox question and the I Ching answers with an Ox 'solution', on which you then meditate as an Ox before arriving at an Ox conclusion.

The player is presented with a hexagram which contains the 'hypothesis-response' to his question, or, more exactly, a synthesis of forces affecting the concern or event inquired about.

For you, Master Ox, here are the sixty-four hexagrams of the I Ching and sixty-four Ox hypotheses.

How to proceed
1. The question
Ask a question regarding any problem at all, past, present or future, personally concerning you. (If the question concerns a friend, consult the I Ching game in the book corresponding to his Chinese sign.)

2. Method of play
It must be done with concentration:
Take **three ordinary and similar coins** — for example, three 50p coins.
Heads will equal the number 3.
Tails will equal the number 2.
Throw the coins.
If the result is two coins showing Heads and one Tails, write 3 + 3 + 2. You thus obtain a total of 8 which you represent by a continuous line: ———

Draw the same continuous line if you have three coins showing Heads (3 + 3 + 3 = 9).

If you throw two coins showing Tails and one Heads (2 + 2 + 3 = 7), or all three showing Tails (2 + 2 + 2 = 6), draw two separate lines: ▬ ▬

To sum up, 8 and 9 correspond to: ▬▬▬ (Yin)

6 and 7 correspond to: ▬ ▬ (Yang)

Repeat this operation *six times*, noting at the time of each throw the figure obtained on a piece of paper, proceeding from the first to the sixth figure, from bottom to top.

The final result, including a trigram from the bottom, or lower trigram (example: ▀▀ ▀▀), and a trigram of the top, or upper trigram (example: ▀▀▀), will be a hexagram of the I Ching. In our example this would look like:

Now merely look for the hexagram number in the table on page 164, and then consult the list of hexagrams with their descriptions to find the given answer. *In our example,* the hexagram obtained is number 63, entitled **After completion.**

THE HEXAGRAMS OF THE OX

CH'IEN

1  *The creative:* Energy, strength and will. Time is your ally. This is excellent for the slow and patient Ox. The motto 'there is a time for everything' suits you perfectly.

K'UN

2 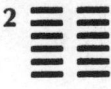 *The receptive:* How can you fail to be close to this earth which is your emblem? Do not forget that if you excavate and cultivate it, it will support you.

CHUN

3 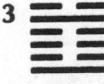 *The initial difficulty:* A bad worker often has bad tools. Search within yourself for the fault; questioning yourself does not mean defeat.

MÊNG

4 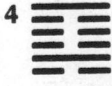 *Youthful folly:* 'It is not I who seek the young fool, but the young fool who seeks me.' There is a time for folly and a time for reason; folly can be good and reason bad.

HSÜ

5 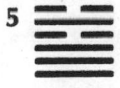 *Waiting:* The meditative Ox will be able to find what he wants. Waiting is the beginning of action.

SUNG

6  *Conflict:* Understand your game, do not charge in with lowered head; agreement is worth more than the risk of defeat. He who fears failure starts out a loser.

Table of Hexagrams

Trigrams	Upper lines ☰	☷	☳
Lower lines			
☰	1	11	34
☷	12	2	16
☳	25	24	51
☵	6	7	40
☶	33	15	62
☴	44	46	32
☲	13	36	55
☱	10	19	54

Use this table to find the number of your hexagrams. The meeting point between the lower and upper trigrams indicates the number of the hexagram that you are seeking.

5	26	9	14	43
8	23	20	35	45
3	27	42	21	17
29	4	59	64	47
39	52	53	56	31
48	18	57	50	28
63	22	37	30	49
60	41	61	38	58

SHIH

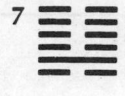

7 *The army:* Submission and discipline are difficult for the independent and solitary Ox. Do not refuse the hand offered you; one day you may need to cling to it. One can feel lonely in a crowd.

PI

8 *Holding together (union):* Should not be a one-way street; before knowing how to give, one must know how to receive.

SHIAO CH'U

9 *The taming power of the small:* There are miniscule objects just as there are majestic splendours. Who is small and who large? Who is important and who unimportant? The flea is small to an elephant, and an elephant is small to a mountain. One can love without measuring.

LÜ

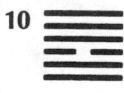

10 *Treading:* 'Tread on the tail of the Tiger, he does not bite man.' Do not charge with lowered head when the door is open. When the tightrope walker balances on his wire, he does not reflect on the void beneath him.

T'AI

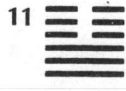

11 *Peace:* Or to know how to find harmony in opposites. During the day the sun, at night the moon; in spring the bud, in autumn the dying leaf. These are the alternations of which harmony and unity are composed. One must gather together rather than separate.

P'I

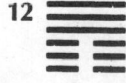

12 *Standstill:* Not a form of resignation or constraint, but a principle, sometimes good to be observed.

T'UNG JÊN

13  *Fellowship with men:* The important thing is to participate. In order to build a wall, one must first position a stone; but one stone does not make a wall.

TA YU

14  *Possession in great measure:* It is one thing to possess; to manage well requires another talent.

CH'IEN

15 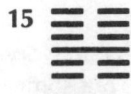 *Modesty:* Seek the right way, moderation and balance. Become master of the great and beautiful as well as of the small. Look with fresh eyes, not merely with different eyes.

YÜ

16  *Enthusiasm:* Simple actions are sometimes better than big ideas. One must learn how to renew, to reconstruct. It is never too late to begin again.

SUI

17 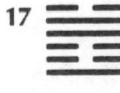 *Following:* Know how to use your charm and innate diplomacy (you have little need for this advice) to get what you want. But remember that your aim is not necessarily shared by your 'neighbour'. Work cautiously with a small brush rather than slamming on the paint with a palette knife.

KU

18 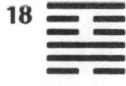 *Work on what has been spoiled:* One must know how to start all over again; a new house is not built on decayed foundations.

LIN

19  *Approach:* It is not yet the route to follow, and the route to follow is not the objective. You must always see further.

173

KUAN

20 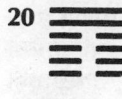 *Contemplation:* Can be a means like any other. Do not set yourself up as an example unless you wish to be confounded. You can observe the world without climbing to the top of a tower.

SHIH HO

21  *Biting through (or clearly defined penalties):* A barking dog does not bite. When the problem seems insoluble, irrevocable decisions are necessary.

PI

22 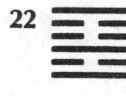 *Grace:* Is a state of mind. Do not erect an ivory tower out of it. Beauty touches you, but sometimes you allow yourself to be seduced by appearances.

PO

23 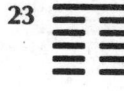 *Splitting apart:* The present is not favourable to you; know how to envisage the future. A building sometimes collapses from the interior. If you concentrate on failure, you will despair; this will slow down your progress and you will never get anywhere.

FU

24 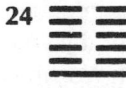 *Return — the turning point:* Leave your labyrinth and work on the surface; the sun will shine on your sweet grasslands.

WU WANG

25  *Innocence:* Trust your intuition; listen to it and let it guide you. Do not become stubborn; your instinct is a guide, not a judge.

TA CH'U

26  *The taming power of the great:* Symbol of power and strength. You must recognize your limits and their possibilities; before adventuring into new fields, question yourself and measure your strength.

I

27  *The corners of the mouth:* Symbolizes the nourishment of body and spirit. Do not sublimate one to the detriment of the other. You must join, not separate.

TA KUO

28  *Preponderance of the great:* Beware of excessively heavy loads which will only diminish you. By no means underestimate yourself; but do not overestimate yourself.

K'AN

29  *The fathomless water:* The danger derives from an ignorance of the terrain. To look over the precipice is a bit like measuring the abyss.

LI

30  *The clinging, fire:* Fire can give you warmth and light, but it can also burn and consume. Stay several steps away. Let go.

HSIEN

31 *Influence:* Fortune favours you, but you must know how to grasp it. It will not seek you out. To presume is already to be mistaken.

HÊNG

32 *Duration:* Waiting does not signify immobility. Changes are not always visible to the naked eye. Duration is an imperceptible movement — but permanent.

TUN

33  *Retreat:* Do not surrender your arms but put them in order, clean them and grease them. Banish the thought of failure from your mind.

TA CHUANG

34 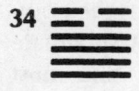 *The power of the great:* Even if you feel like flying, do not lose contact with the earth. The higher the flight, the more violent the fall.

CHIN

35  *Progress:* Accept that you work towards a common objective. If someone is disposed to offer you a place of honour, do not aspire to the throne.

MING I

36 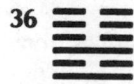 *Darkening of the light:* Night reigns in your labyrinths and on the earth. Simply by accepting this you will have already vanquished it a little.

CHIA JÊN

37  *The family:* For an Ox in love with liberty, it will often be considered a golden prison; there are ties which are necessary to you, others which shackle you. Easing the knot does not mean cutting it.

K'UEI

38  *Opposition:* One does not oppose what one has already in part accepted. Stones on the path are necessary, as are stars in the sky. Do not be stubbornly unwilling.

CHIEN

39  *Obstruction:* Do not shoot down the phantoms of your illusions, nor dig excessively deep trenches; you may be engulfed.

HSIEH

40 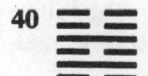 *Deliverance:* After darkness, light. Forget the past, come away from the shadows — better times are coming.

SUN

41 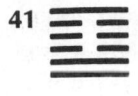 *Decrease:* Times are hard. Be sceptical of bright prospects that are offered. Learn to rediscover the rhythm of the seasons and appreciate again the perfume of flowers.

I

42 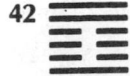 *Increase:* Be opportunistic but know how to leave in time; slowly but surely.

KUAI

43  *Breakthrough:* It is sometimes necessary to speak loudly what others only murmur. The bud must burst before the flower blossoms.

KOU

44  *Coming to meet:* The Ox is not the sort of animal to connive in schemes, so do not be deceived by appearances. Be careful if you do not want to find yourself 'put out to pasture'.

TS'UI

45  *Gathering together:* Learn how to work with others and share a common ideal. However, beware of subversive elements attempting to undermine you or infiltrate; these destructive agents are slow but effective.

SHÊNG

46 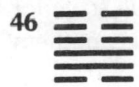 *Pushing upwards:* Be a methodical and tenacious Ox; neglect nothing and take care of details — they will not slow your progress.

K'UN

47  *Oppression:* You are losing energy; know how to adapt yourself to your potential. 'More haste, less speed' should be your watchword.

CHING

48 *The well:* Do not upset the natural order; follow its movement, become a part of it and accept changes and mutations.

KO

49 *Revolution:* Join in; this can be a new, vital and regenerating impulse for you. A change of territory may prove productive.

TING

50 *The cauldron:* Be content with what you have and do your best with it. Do not envy what others have.

CHÊN

51 *The arousing (shock, thunder):* You must follow your slow and tenacious course despite all difficulties. A menacing storm hovers overhead. Do not cringe; there is light at the end of the tunnel.

KÊN

52 *Keeping still:* There are moments for withdrawal, for meditation; this is necessarily a time for retreat. To find tranquillity, to appreciate silence, is a form of art.

CHIEN

53 *Development (gradual progress):* This is a time of trials. They will increase; a difficult stage for you to surmount. Do not be rigid; accept them by adhering to them.

KUEI MEI

54 *The bride:* Be careful. The Ox, loving space and liberty, should weigh well his promises. By nature independent, he should renounce a legal tie which may be too constraining.

FÊNG

55  *Abundance:* Rich soil, bright grasslands, fertility and plenitude. The Ox, as he knows so well, should fully enjoy this richness which must fade. Nature is inexorable. Remember the lean days.

LÜ

56  *The wanderer:* Sometimes it is good and necessary to go away and rediscover virgin lands and wide-open spaces. But clean off your desk before you go; before taking up the future, you must clear up the present.

SUN

57  *The gentle:* Better to be flexible than to strike one's fist on the table adamantly. To attain perfection one must not fear repetition.

TUI

58 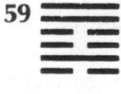 *The serene, the joyous:* Perseverance and courage, as you already know. Remember to try to communicate: once again be flexible.

HUAN

59 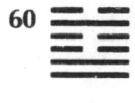 *Dissolution:* Do not try to do two things at once. Concentrate your effort and be less self-centred; peace and contemplation are to be found in all things.

CHIEH

60  *Limitation:* The expanse of the grasslands should not be measured by your eyes alone. Restrain your excesses and extend your boundaries.

CHUNG FU

61 *Inner truth:* The Ox will be more solitary than ever. Finding difficulty in communication, he will be forced to seek refuge within himself. His partner will not be wedded to the same fields.

HSIAO KUO

62 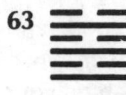 *Preponderance of the small:* You hold few winning cards; do not launch great enterprises. Sometimes one finds consolation in lesser work.

CHI CHI

63 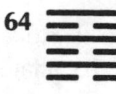 *After completion:* You have reached your zenith and you have earned it. Now, after the climb, you must be capable of undertaking the descent.

WEI CHI

64 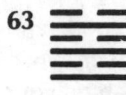 *Before completion:* Show yourself to be thrifty and far sighted, but do not doubt your success — your path is clear. So go forward, take the first step, but do not put the cart before — the Ox.

YEAR OF THE TIGER

 1902·1914·1926
1938·1950·1962
1974·1986·1998

THE DOMAINS OF THE TIGER

十二生肖

THE TIGER AND ITS SYMBOLISM

The Tiger is an animal of the Yang tendency; he comes from the East.

In China the Tiger is indisputably the king of animals. He is the equivalent in the West of the superb and generous lion of Africa, but in Chinese astrology he also possesses a divine armour, symbol of the Yin and of the Yang: his marvellous striped robe. This robe is a veritable protectress, conferring on the Tiger 'this unity in the double aspect Yin and Yang', which gives him a greater role than that of a simple lord of the jungle. 'His stripes are an ostentatious mixture of Yin and Yang. He is the chief of all the animals, the terror of demons and creatures of the hereafter whom he pitilessly devours. He is responsible for the protection of children against the evil spirits. Young boys are often dedicated to the Tiger and wear a hat in the form of a tiger's head to repulse the jealous spirits which plan to carry them off.'

Revered or feared, incarnation of faith or symbol of tolerance, the mount of sages, the Tiger's protection is particularly invoked. This is why man has at times covered the Tiger's claws with silver and with jewels and has strung Tiger teeth round his neck to protect his virility. Without hesitation he will risk his life to secure the tiger's striped coat or proudly display that most marvellous of trophies: mouth agape and terrifying, eyes injected with blood — the head of the man-eater.

Some are white tigers, the symbols of royal valour; others are endowed with immortality when they are mounted by the immortal gods; still others are the companions of sorcerers. There are also Paper Tigers — those housed in zoos or whose fur serves as a bedside rug. However, none of these lack greatness. All — real or symbolic — are exceptional.

Not everyone can ride a Tiger. You can, of course, train on the back of some vulgar alley-cat: if you hear him roar, it means that the weight of your body, added to that of your wisdom, excludes you from following the immortals through the mountains.

Mounted or hunted, the Tiger may both fascinate and terrify. We can learn more from Chinese astrology: The tenth hexagram of the I Ching, named 'Treading', reads: 'Tread upon the tail of the Tiger, it does not bite Man.' One interpretation of this is that 'The situation is really difficult. That which is stronger and that which is weakest are close together. The weak follows behind the strong and worries it. The strong, however, acquiesces and does not hurt the weak because the contact is in good humour and harmless.' This commentary clearly indicates that we should not approach the Tiger as a rival, but nevertheless respect his strength.

Finally, here is a Zen philosophic tale to relish: Every evening, a wise man tossed handfuls of seed round his house. An observant disciple asked him one day:

'Master, why do you throw those seeds round your house?'

'To keep the tigers away,' replied the sage.

The respectful disciple dared to reply:

'But master, there are no tigers in the area!'

'Exactly so, my method is effective!'

A few notes on the Tiger

Principal qualities: Loyalty, courage, enthusiasm, generosity.

Principal defects: Imprudence, toughness, selfishness, excessive impulsiveness.

Work: Brilliant, but only if he is his own master.

Best role: Saviour of the nation, or, second best, monarch or president.

Worst role: Beggar.

Money: Rather spendthrift; ready to take risks, but he is lucky.

Luck: To be born at night. His hunting will be more fruitful, his prey drowsy.

Cannot live without: The unforeseen.

Adores: Wandering about at random without knowing what to expect. To tempt fate, to take his chances.

Hates: Hypocrisy, scandal-mongering, criticism.

Leisure activities: Visiting a country — on foot or on horseback, but certainly not by car — where tourists are scarce. Tibet in 1900 would have suited him perfectly. Now, he quite likes safaris.

Favourite places: The jungle; the impenetrable brush; high finance.

Colours: Orange and dark gold.

Plant: Bamboo.

Flower: Heliotrope.

Professions: This is simple: all those of which he is chief, whether head clerk or head of state, scout leader or leader of a political party. He loves to talk about *his* assistant, *his* secretary, *his* gardener. This makes him feel secure. In fact, being noble and magnanimous, he excels in his role as chief.

The four ages in the life of the Tiger, according to Chinese tradition

The Tiger's *infancy*, although undisturbed in its innocence, will be notable for its physical wounds and bruises. His *youth* will be animated: there will be conflicts, changes, upsets and dangerous passions. If he does not look for adventure, he will nevertheless attract it.

His *maturity* may or may not be serene. This will depend on whether he can profit from past experiences, moderate his appetites and settle down. If not, he will be plagued by instability, above all on the emotional level.

The same diagnosis holds for his *old age*. It is only much later that he will attain tranquillity, by force, perhaps, for he does not much like it and his nature is not equipped for it.

THE PSYCHOLOGY OF THE TIGER

In China the Tiger is the emblem of luck, power and royalty. In this sense it would be easy to depict him as a formidable predator, devouring everything and everyone on his way, like some Chinese Attila. However, we must forgo such zoological prejudices; they are as inappropriate for the Tiger as for the Rat.

In the Chinese zodiac the sign of the Tiger is the richest in both possibility and nuance. To be born under his influence augurs the worst and the best. Epitomizing spirit and animation, the Tiger can either be a savage beast thirsty for blood, or a recognized sage sought by others.

This ambivalence in his nature — one aspect descending towards the submission to instincts, and the other rising towards their domination — depends on a factor closely knit to the history and the symbolism of the Tiger: moderation. It is towards this virtue, combining restraint, tolerance, self-control and objectivity, that the Tiger must constantly extend himself if he is to pluck fortune and secure recognition of his strength throughout the jungle.

Those born in a Tiger year are predisposed to danger. The evidence for this lies, first, in the imprudence often manifested by royal felines, and, secondly, in their pronounced taste for taking risks — both moral and physical — which is well attested. Finally, there is the information provided from observation over thousands of years which, according to Chinese astrologers, proves that the life of those born under the sign of the Tiger is never really calm and that their deaths are sometimes violent. To be born in a Tiger year signifies luck and protection. The Tiger has the *baraka*, which means that he cannot die only because his enemies wish it; in his case this voodoo does not work.

So there are two sorts of Tigers: the Tiger born at night will often appear calm and wise, for the night is his chosen domain and there he is king and melts into the shadows. Born in daytime, the Tiger will be more active and imprudent for, under the light of the sun, he is compelled to meet all dangers.

Tigers are instinctively loyal and honourable. They bristle when faced with falseness; they nobly disdain treachery and, by their actions, seek not only to be proud of themselves but by their courage and generosity to attract the esteem of others. They abominate a narrow and stiff lifestyle or routine. One should never forget that their domain is the jungle — in all senses of the word.

They have an open mind towards the world and are

tolerant and generous, but only so long as their sense of honour is not offended. While daily responsibilities may bore them, they assume them because they do not want to fail. Magnanimously, they will willingly pardon, recoiling from any feeling so petty as spite. Rather than exact revenge, they will simply cut off the acquaintanceship.

Hard on themselves and demanding of their friends, they are rarely easy to live with. It can become tiring to be always saying how admirable they are, to have nothing to reproach them for — except, of course, for being too domineering. But they are unaware of all this, for their good intentions completely isolate them from the outside world.

Essentially, Tigers are generous and, provided they have learned to master their passions, are capable of wise and pertinent advice.

'Provided' is the key to the ·big question: have they dominated their passions? Many have found otherwise, both with Tigers and Tigresses who, despite their splendid qualities, still dumbfoundedly flounder in the most sentimental complications or find it almost impossible to control their swaggering aggressiveness. In both cases they may be terrors to friends and lovers alike. The males will be tall, good-natured men; peaceful in appearance but possessing a strong grip, wills of iron and an admirable confidence. They will be sure of their good luck and of their powers of resistance and success. The females will be exceptionally active, passionate and generous, although slightly authoritarian.

It is often easier to be a Tiger than a Tigress because the male of this sign, despite the current feminism, finds that the world more easily accepts his need to face the realities of existence, to acquire power and to have it recognized. But the females — who are intelligent, virtuous and frank — are sometimes guilt-ridden by their failure to find a true equilibrium in arranging for the education of their children and in household tasks. They would be happier working outside the home and more agreeable than when occupied with mere housekeeping, which, naturally, they do to perfection even though it often bores them. This dissatisfaction — their worth not being recognized — leads them to make emotional demands which can be irritating in private life.

A Tiger or Tigress needs space in which to express him or herself freely and totally. Put in a cage, all their qualities are reduced; behind bars, even abstract ones, they become aggressive, quarrelsome and overwrought. When stubborn, they hold the whole world to blame for their not being able to live as they would have wished. Incapable of conforming to an imposed discipline, of submitting to advice or reflecting before acting, their courage borders on the insensible and can culminate in the rashest of acts, for they are fascinated by any dangerous or gratuitous gesture.

There are Tigers who bloom when taken seriously, who respond, even unconsciously, with a vague pleasure when overhearing flattering murmurs as they pass. This suggestion of warmth and sensitivity is quickly usurped when their way of life no longer suits them. Then they will endlessly quibble about nothing, their egotism takes charge and they refuse to acknowledge their slightest errors. Closely self-seeking, securing their comfort at the expense of others, they will cling at any price to whatever serves their reputation, clutching the prominent image they find necessary to reflect and impose on others.

Now, a metaphor: a splendid tiger imprisoned in a zoo next to the monkeys, growls menacingly to frighten them. This comedy of power, its meanness and lack of possibilities, reduces and saddens him; he is so remote from the true jungle which we should help all Tigers to recover. So what if his bank account is in the red or the dinner has burnt? The world will be so much more interesting that way.

THE TIGER AS A CHILD

This child is likely to give you trouble. He is an absolute stranger to discipline. Quivering with vitality and impatient to pitch himself against the world surrounding him, he is intent above all to live a life forged from his own experience.

You can rely on him never to be sly or cowardly and, since he likes school, he will never play truant. In fact, the family circle is often a trifle too narrow for his taste, whereas school life pleases him because he can measure his strength against his peers, even if not of his calibre. For him this is excellent preparation for adult life.

A tight rein will probably not do much for his education; it will be wiser to follow the example of wild animals who keep their children close to them only until they have been taught how to survive alone in the world. In fact, the young Tiger often leaves his parents' home very early to marry or to work. Or so he says, for that is only an excuse. He actually leaves because he needs to pit himself against the outside world as quickly as possible.

The important thing is to ensure that your budding Tiger does not wake up one day in his future jungle unprepared. Allow him to test himself; do not be overprotective. If he plunges his finger into a wall plug, if he fights with his friends or amuses himself by leaping from the first floor using an umbrella as a parachute, neither faint nor scream. A Tiger or two have gone on to be professional parachute jumpers in this way. It is essential to him that he experience a degree of danger.

But, you will reply, he may get an electric shock or break a leg. Maybe. But this will be of minor importance compared to his central problem — that he is incapable of believing in the existence of a danger unless he has experienced it. It is, however, essential that you make him aware of the risks he takes to prevent him from growing up a rash, hot-headed devil.

Once he has registered this first and indispensable lesson, you can begin the second phase of his education: self-control. It is never too early to teach a Tiger the value of moderation, and, once he has experienced danger, he will be naturally receptive to the idea.

Impress upon him the importance of clear and practical limits in all his activities; his natural bent is to overlook them.

You must make a wise concoction, dosing him with a mixture of permissions and restraints in such a way that he opens up to the external world without being carried away by his hunting instincts. Do not be afraid of exercising authority; he will in any case respect you and, even if he baulks at the time, the outcome will prove to him that you were right.

Finally, the day will come when you must let him go. If, instead of gambolling about, he moves slowly, sure of his strength but prudent and with eyes watchful, you will know that the day has come: he has absorbed your teachings and your little Tiger holds the secrets of success between his claws.

LOVE LIFE

Impetuous and passionate, all Tigers — male and female — are likely to test their powers of seduction at an early age. This active adolescence is necessary because only experience can influence them and moderate and modify their behaviour. There are, however, exceptions: enthusiastic and lured by the prospect of escaping from the authority of the family, they may marry very young.

Tigers are great sentimentalists. They love the exaltation engendered by a new love, and resist day-to-day routine. If their partner is by character the type that can make each day into a new adventure, the relationship is likely to endure. Otherwise, a true Tiger grows tired and bored. Without being exactly unfaithful, a lack of passion will quickly incite him to try his charm elsewhere. One could say that seduction is his way of defining himself, a sport, an act of defiance.

These Tigers and Tigresses think that they are irreplaceable, and one way of holding them is to show them otherwise. They need to be taught — physically and morally — that although interested in them, one can be quite happy independent of them. This goes to the heart of the matter, for the Tiger does not like easy prey. Even when he declares in a burst of sincerity that he has had enough of an unstable life, he forgets that he could not endure to be confined in a day-to-day existence with someone who expects him to turn up at regular hours.

The Tiger is always intensely attentive on the sentimental level. He never lies and he detests any sort of make-believe. But he can burn what he has adored. It is perfectly feasible for him to forget feelings he experienced only two weeks ago. This passionate creature is perfectly capable of crying on Thursday about a disappointed love and going off with someone else on Sunday with his enthusiasm intact. Some Tigers take a very long time to learn not to become involved in complicated experiences from which they only suffer.

The Tiger has a remarkable characteristic envied by many, although his life is no easier for it: his sense of sacrifice. There is no one more noble, loyal, sincere or generous than a deserted Tiger. He specializes in quasi-heroic renunciations: 'Go,' he will declare. 'You will be far better off without me. But remember that I will never forget you.' This said, we must nevertheless admit that Tigers are graceful losers. They make excellent friends — as well as the frankest possible enemies.

FAMILY LIFE

The Tiger is an adventurer and a conqueror; he has a shining image of himself as seen by others. His instincts require him to fight; his deepest satisfaction is to win. Naturally then, with his own family he will consider it normal to be boss. Mr Tiger will both welcome and expect a calm and well-organised wife capable of managing his house in his absence. As for Mrs Tiger, she will either prefer the lure of personal success and independent activity leaving others to execute her order, or play the role of exemplary spouse, perfect mother and efficient housekeeper. She can sustain this role for tradition has it that she is virtuous, but only if her husband is extremely active, travels a great deal and takes her with him.

Tigers and Tigresses are rather flighty parents. When they try to teach their children the qualities of prudence, reflection and reason, when they impress on them that nothing is so important as security, they themselves do not believe a word of it. While delivering these maxims, they will very likely be reflecting on their latest conquest! A Tigress playing the maternal role and recommending the blessings of virtue to her 18-year-old daughter is quite likely to hear her child reply sharply: 'Mother, at my age you were already married and pregnant!'

A disciplined Tiger can be a good influence on his children, extending their horizons beyond those of the family and taking them on exciting excursions. The average Tiger, however, who has not yet learned the great lesson of moderation, will be incapable of hiding his changes in mood, his impulsiveness or anger. His children are likely to feel very insecure with him. In particular, his influence on the life and character of children born under the sign of the Dog, Rabbit, Rat and Goat, can be dramatic; for these signs need, in different ways, a parent's tenderness and attention. Children born under the signs of the Dragon, Horse or Monkey will fare better, for they will admire their parents' enterprise and affectionately seek their advice. With the Pig there may not always be understanding, but there will be mutual esteem. Ox and Snake children will not be on the same wave-length. With the Ox child the Tiger will suffer, for the child's stubbornness will defeat him. The Snake child will make an effort, but in vain; his Tiger parents will retain the impression that they have hatched an ugly duckling.

PROFESSIONAL LIFE

The essence of the Tiger's professional life is simplicity itself: he was born to be in charge, to direct and lead, as the lungs exist to breathe. Whatever his occupation, he needs above all to be the only one responsible for what he does.

Often acting on impulse, his intuition will usually help him avert catastrophe. Highly independent, he is unreceptive to orders from others, which he finds naturally repugnant. Although he loves his parents dearly, he will not acknowledge any debt to them. He has to forge his own character and success must come from his own efforts.

Fertile and enthusiastic, our Tiger will launch new ideas and create new businesses. Even if he begins in a subordinate position, he will soon get to the top. Risks never frighten the Tiger: he has trust in his gifts and in his lucky star. Never doing anything by halves and always involving himself completely his enthusiasm, passion and dynamism are particularly compelling. He will have no trouble finding supporters to back him and invest in his enterprises. But he will never willingly give up control nor be accountable to others. Of course, if he is hopelessly in love or sentimentally grateful, things may be different.

In professional matters — in business or commerce or any sort of trading venture — provided he is really interested, even the most timid of Tigers (there are a few about!) shows considerable nerve and an ability to hang on, impose himself and not let go. With him, everything moves and nothing remains still. One is never bored.

The same applies to the female: the Tigress needs to be independent. Otherwise, unless she has some hobby which satisfies her, she will become bored, aggressive and unstable.

MATERIAL LIFE

The Tiger detests immobility in himself or anything he controls. His natural imprudence predisposes him to risk; the idea of stability is alien to him. As far as money is concerned, he will look for high interest rates and capital growth of his savings. This is not due to greed: he expects money to work and move as he does.

The Tiger is rarely to be pitied. Given his abilities and his luck he can usually extricate himself from misadventures. His ingenuity will rapidly solve the problems which leave others floundering. Usually, Tigers die comfortably well off and their children will not be left on the street.

Whatever his age, the Tiger can always start a new career from scratch. Flexible, he will not hesitate to change professions, return to school or speculate with his money.

But he always has a reserve nearby in case he is thirsty. Despite his unconcerned look, he is shrewd.

The Tiger is never stingy, and in fact he likes to 'lord it' a bit. Generous with his family, and not averse to a certain degree of luxury, he is by no means a puritan. While controlling the household budget is not his strong point, especially if it is limited, he always makes ends meet. Actually, the Tiger is more adept and far quicker to learn in these matters than he can ever be in the emotional field. His success follows this pattern: there are many Tigers whose emotional life is unstable while they are professionally an immense success.

ENVIRONMENT

As we have seen from our study of the Tiger's sign and its symbolic meaning, the Tiger's domain is definitely in the jungle. It may be a real estate jungle, a stock market jungle, a sport's arena jungle or what you will. Fighting against predators satisfies his deepest instincts — that shiver of delight that nothing can equal when winning it all!

Obviously the Tiger also likes the real jungle, with its exotic trees, climbing plants and animals roaming about freely. He dreams of travel, planning impatiently for holidays and plotting safaris, mountain climbs or riding a kayak down rushing rivers. For such adventures he will forgo the simplest of comforts.

In his daily life the Tiger likes to be surrounded by things that are both simple and luxurious. Long low divans adorned with hand-painted silk cushions, fur coverlets, pretty objects, Persian carpets and, if he is sportive, a few mementoes, such as some trophies above a cupboard filled with cups, diplomas and medals. As far as he is concerned, these serve only to impress his guests, no more.

For Tigers, bedrooms are lairs and dangerous territory. How will you feel as you leave — seduced, troubled, overcome? In this intimate cave — straight out of the 'Arabian Nights' — Tigers allow free rein to their fantasies and their imagination. Anything is possible: love potions, miniature jungles, a round bed or walls clad with Oriental hangings. However, take note: photographs are forbidden.

A guide to personal relations with a Tiger
Methods of seduction:

He: Immobile, curled up, he stares at you with the eyes of a hypnotist and with a carnivorous smile. You feel like a prey offered to satisfy his royal appetite.

She: The same. She considers you her prey, and watches you with her eyes half closed and head slightly turned, so that it is not too obvious.

If he loves you: Be ready to follow him wherever he may go — he will give you the most extraordinary experiences of your life. But you must not tire because he will give you no respite.

He expects: That you will follow him, never impede him and always with good grace.

To keep you: He will constantly stimulate you. Anyone else would be sure to bore you horribly.

If he is unfaithful: It is only another trophy and done to demonstrate that he is not dependent on you.

If you are unfaithful: He will take refuge in his dignity and you will never know whether or not he is upset.

In case of a break between you: Noble and magnanimous, he will agree that you should take everything, down to the last teaspoon.

If you want to give him a gift: Ideally this would be an aeroplane ticket to a completely unknown town lost in the middle of a tropical jungle with a beach and palm trees nearby. If this is too expensive for you, buy him some animal skin to put in front of the fire. Avoid cat and rabbit — too common — but tiger, bear or zebra he will covet.

If you want to seduce him: Invite him on a safari, fox-hunting, or, even better, a tiger hunt on the back of an elephant with your old friend the Maharajah. He will not know how to resist such a mixture of the luxurious and the exotic.

If you want to get rid of him: Try to collar and leash him.

THE TIGER
AND THE OTHER CHINESE SIGNS

Tiger/Rat

The Rat is always fascinated by those signs which prove themselves capable of taking risks, and this is one of the more effective ways to earn his admiration. Needless to say, in this respect the Tiger holds all the aces.

The relationship between these two will not be peaceful, but it will certainly be passionate! They will both find great satisfaction in each other, but the Tiger has the soul of a hunter and from time to time, as a good feline must, he will leave his lair to search out available prey.

The apprehensive Rat will have a hard time accepting that such conquests are only a game, a way for the Tiger to prove to himself that he is irresistible. But if he realizes that they are rarely more than escapades, he and the Tiger can establish lasting ties.

One small snag: the Tiger is a realist but at the same time carefree, and the Rat's greed, his fear of tomorrow, are completely foreign to him. He will not give a hoot about such things, although later he may be pleased to find some meat in the freezer which otherwise he would have left to rot. Finally, although they may argue this point, they will prove to be complementary to each other.

Tiger/Ox

For the Tiger everything is possible prey — the Ox included. The eyes of a true Tiger always light up at the sight of possible game, and the Ox, who, despite his independence sometimes allows himself to be devoured without even noticing the danger, is no exception. While the Tiger's eyes may be bigger than his stomach, and he sometimes risks a memorable attack of indigestion, this is of no help to the Ox.

Although the Ox does not deter the Tiger from wandering, he will contemplate him with a severe eye and accuse him of being rash, unreasonable and thoughtless. Any business relationship between the two is not advised — it will only end in blows. However, on the emotional level, with a male Tiger, Mrs Ox will adapt rather well, provided her spouse is careful to lay in enough fresh meat. The other way round, everything will go well so long as Mrs Tiger is very much in love. Afterwards, tied to this Ox, this monument of conscientiousness, she may be bored to death and begin to have imaginative flights of fancy.

Tiger/Tiger

Chinese astrological tradition expressly advises against this alliance, stating that 'two Tigers cannot live together.' First, because their luck — multiplied by two — unlike two negatives making a positive, will be transformed into bad luck. Secondly, the Tiger likes to be the sole master on board; there cannot be two captains with this couple.

These two individuals, tending to extremes of all kinds, do not need to be spurred into action. What each needs — and both are very aware of this — is their opposite, their complement: someone calm, thoughtful but with a will; someone who leaves them free from time to time to breathe alone and yet remains ready to listen to them. No Tiger is capable of waiting idly for his spouse to turn up. Each must follow their own bent and pursue independent activities; only exceptional zodiacal influences can explain their ability to get on with each other.

Tiger/Rabbit

Both in their different ways seek to secure their prey. Each is attached to a certain form of comfort and they share the need for an impression of freedom. Rabbits and Tigers alike will settle by the fireside and then depart, if the mood takes them, to spend the night under the stars. Any attempt to constrain these two is inadvisable.

The Rabbit, however, is more dependent on a life of security, is much more prudent and is likely to shudder with horror at the Tiger's dare-devilry.

If the Rabbit is the less active of the two, their liaison will go very well. The Rabbit will take care of daily comforts and will discreetly restrain his companion's outbursts of audacity. If the contrary, life will be difficult. The undomesticated Tiger with nothing much to do will be furious whenever he sees his Rabbit spouse check the gas meters or the locks on the doors. He could easily lope out of his own house and return to burgle it.

When they disagree, the Rabbit will have a lighter touch than the Tiger; more agile, he will always have the last word, leaving the Tiger spinning round in circles.

Tiger/Dragon

They have many points in common, notably, courage,

energy and an enterprising spirit. The Tiger is a good counsellor, for he never advises anyone to act as rashly as he might do. The Dragon, who is often quite certain that he has got things rights, loves to give advice and will tend to help the Tiger to reflect before he acts, considering his prospects along with his capabilities. Sometimes, too, he will push him, with the best intentions in the world, to pursue adventures from which he will never return.

Their shared tendency to excess will lend a passionate aspect to their lives, but at the expense of stability. This imbalance may be mitigated if the Dragon learns to understand that the Tiger is much more reasonable in his words than in his actions. Things will never go very smoothly; there will be many conflicts and discussions, but their lives will never be boring. Thanks to their frankness, misunderstandings will never last for long. They will succeed like two old friends: each will be pleased with the success of the other, and their deep understanding will ·preclude any rivalry. Even if in business, they may be notorious, but they will work well together — although they will need to hire a good manager.

Tiger/Snake

This liaison is hardly advisable. The vitality of the Tiger is likely to be too much for the contemplative Serpent, who will neither wish nor be able to follow the busy, bustling rhythm that his companion is in the habit of imposing on his entourage.

Indeed, although peaceful, reflective and sometimes lazy, the Snake does not need to be aroused from his natural rhythm. He is capable of managing quite effectively in his own way and hates to be given advice. Sometimes dogmatic — which no Tiger can tolerate — he is also possessive and tortuous, preferring the curved line to the straight, if by this means he achieves his objective. In short, the Snake thinks of the end, while the Tiger also relishes the means, hoping this will be admirable and delightful. They do not really understand each other and will often avoid each other. The Tiger will distrust the Snake's meanderings and the Snake will be intelligent enough to avoid the Tiger, realizing that such an animal cannot be possessed.

On the other hand, it could be a marvellous business alliance: They complete each other beautifully, with one taking the risks and the other calculating behind the scenes. But they should not live together for the Snake would betray the Tiger, who would then certainly destroy him.

Tiger/Horse

These two will go far together! A Tiger and a Horse meet on a level of enthusiasm that is superb. Everything will be for the best, provided the Tiger never grasps the extent of his partner's egotism, which always has priority in the Horse's opinions and desires, unless he is passionately involved. One can only hope that this passion endures and that the Tiger or Tigress are too active to have time to reflect on the why's and wherefore's of the Horse's attitudes. The feeling of deception would be devastating and any dialogue difficult, for the Horse would not understand. Because he is so profoundly convinced of his good faith, he cannot conceive that he could be accused of thinking only of himself; in fact, he does think of others — but only as they relate to him. The Tiger is more open and generous.

This kind of conflict will resemble a Shakespearean tragedy, for neither will understand the meaning of the word 'moderation'. The Horse becomes violent, the Tiger heroic. From a tragedy to a farce, there is only one small step.

Tiger/Goat

The charming Goat, attached to a post, bleats sadly while the feared Tiger silently approaches, licking his fangs in anticipation of the good breakfast he is going to have.

Suspense: will the Tiger devour the Goat? The hypothesis is tempting; but love has its mysteries. The amorous Goat looks to a dynamic person for protection. The amorous Tiger does not tend to devour his partner; on the contrary, he leaves him free — even a little too free for certain tastes.

After reflection this tie, which at first seems strange, can prove to be most positive if sincere feelings are involved. The Goat needs to wander at ease with his nose to the stars if he is to blossom, and the Tiger will not prevent him. The Tiger's courage, loyalty and audacity will provoke the Goat's admiration. It is to be hoped, however, that they have money put aside, for the Goat is a spendthrift, and the Tiger counts more on his luck than his thrift. But they will be happy, for, each respecting the other's liberty, they will acknowledge their partial independence with a touching gratitude.

Tiger/Monkey

Despite his adventurous side, the Tiger is much less supple and adaptable than the Monkey. While he respects his partner's liberty, he likes clear-cut situations: 'What do you mean? Are you with me or with him? You must choose who you want.' But the Monkey, even when really in love, has too great a desire to please to measure the effects of his charm, to remain steadily in place or retain a preconceived or fixed role. He will always escape from the Tiger, who will be outraged at being walked over like a rug.

Then, too, the Monkey mocks, criticizes and is adept at putting his finger on the weak points of those close to him. He will secretly admire the Tiger, but he will not be able to stop himself from tweaking his moustache. Tradition has it that the vexed Tiger will then wait for the Monkey to fall asleep in order to devour him.

The relationship can work though, with much love on the part of the Monkey, and much moderation and tolerance on the part of the Tiger.

Tiger/Rooster

Here, good understanding will not be easy. Although sensitive and loyal, the Tiger is not noted for his reflective abilities. He is neither subtle nor discerning; he judges others by their behaviour, their acts, and even by their reputations. It is their appearance which counts, not their spiritual meanderings. But the Rooster cannot be judged solely by his appearance: it is too elaborate and too brilliant, and one could easily believe that nothing lies behind it.

In the beginning, everything will go well. The Tiger will be flattered by the personality of his fine-feathered Rooster, while the latter will sincerely admire the Tiger's courage. Very quickly, however, the little boasts of the Rooster will irritate his companion, who will not hesitate to criticize. No Rooster can tolerate being constantly reproved, and he will feel himself misunderstood and treated unjustly. He will rapidly set out to seek a more indulgent companion, but, before leaving, he will tell the Tiger a few home truths; he values his reputation for frankness.

These two can be associates, friends or even lovers, but not for long. Essentially, they are not at all on the same wave-length.

Tiger/Dog

Both the Tiger and the Dog are impenitent idealists. The Tiger may often forget to protect his flank and the Dog be reluctant to charge ahead, but let a lost child appear or a famine occur, and they will both be there, ready to abandon everything and fight for the impossible. There will be no mountain too high, no ravine too deep to stem the faith of the one and the enthusiasm of the other. There is nothing like the generous dynamism of the Tiger to snatch a timid smile of hope from the anxious Dog. There is nothing like the prudent instinct of the Dog to arrest a Tiger at the edge of a precipice.

They can be a happy couple, but not very good in the home. As business associates they can be inventive and original. The only hitch is that the Dog needs to be loved and convincingly reassured, and one should not count too much on a Tiger for pretty, sentimental phrases. It is essential that they share a material or spiritual goal if the relationship is to endure; and a goal, work or an enterprise in common which prevents them from having the time to be preoccupied with each other will achieve this, as they walk side by side.

Tiger/Pig

They will be loyal to each other. Their love and friendship will be intense so long as their nights remain passionate; a sense of honour will motivate most of their days.

Often cannier than the Pig, the Tiger will help him to defend himself, to uncover the defects in the armour of his adversaries. Because each loves solitude, each will understand the other's need for liberty and, while being tolerant of each other, will be unlikely to be deceitful: confidence will be the basis of their relationship.

As always, there is a risk. Even a very polite Tiger is and remains predatory. From time to time, without malice but due to curiosity, he will try to push the Pig to the end of his tether or profit from his good faith. On this subject, Chinese tradition cautions, for the Pig, whose defenses are formidable, will win out over the Tiger.

SOME TIGER CELEBRITIES

Beethoven, Emily Bronte, Queen Christina of Sweden, De Gaulle, Isadora Duncan, Eisenhower, Elizabeth II, Goya, Ho Chi Minh, Kandinsky, Jerry Lewis, Lindberg, Louis XIV, Karl Marx, Marilyn Monroe, Lola Montes, Paganini, Pergolese, Robespierre, Steinbeck, Mary Stuart, Sun Yat-sen, H. G. Wells, Oscar Wilde, Molotov, Bolivar, Alec Guinness.

YOUR COMPANION IN LIFE

生命伴侣

After the Chinese sign of your year of birth, here is the sign of your hour of birth

What is a Companion in Life, as understood in Chinese astrology? It is a sort of 'ascendant' sign corresponding to your hour of birth. This Companion is another animal belonging to the Chinese cycle of the twelve emblematic beasts, who falls into step with you and accompanies you, ever ready to help you brave the traps and ambushes along your route. A permanent and benevolent shadow, he can render the impossible possible.

He is your counterpart, but with his own character and tendencies and with a different psychology. Both guardian angel and devil's advocate, he will be a witness to your life and an actor in it.

Have you ever felt, deep inside yourself, the subtle presence of another 'myself' inhabiting you and with whom you live, at times in harmony, at others in conflict? Another self who sometimes criticizes you and at others encourages you? That is your Companion in Life.

There are times when he will appear to be an imposter or an intruder. Certainly, he often questions your habits and your moral or spiritual complacency. Accompanied by this companion, a shadow within, the route is less monotonous and the voyager multiplies his chances of arriving at his chosen destination. This, however, in itself matters little, for it is the journey and the manner in which it is conducted that are important. Indolence is the greatest danger: your Companion is capable of arousing you from a lassitude of spirit and, to that end, if necessary, robbing you of your certainties, trampling on your secret gardens and, finally, tearing away the great veil of illusion.

It sometimes happens that your Companion is of the same sign as your year of birth, a twin brother in a way — for example, a Tiger/Tiger. In this case, you must recognize that he will compel you to realize yourself fully and to live the double aspect — the Yin and the Yang — that your bear within yourself. In any case, you also bear within yourself

the twelve animals. So, set out on the long route, ready for the great adventure: the beautiful voyage during which you will encounter the harmoniously entangled, the solemn and the grotesque, the ephemeral reality, the dream and the imagined.

Table of hours corresponding to the twelve emblematic animals

If you were **born** between	11 pm and 1 am	your **companion** is	Rat
	1 am and 3 am		Ox
	3 am and 5 am		Tiger
	5 am and 7 am		Rabbit
	7 am and 9 am		Dragon
	9 am and 11 am		Snake
	11 am and 1 pm		Horse
	1 pm and 3 pm		Goat
	3 pm and 5 pm		Monkey
	5 pm and 7 pm		Rooster
	7 pm and 9 pm		Dog
	9 pm and 11 pm		Pig

These figures correspond to the *solar hour* of your birth. If necessary, you should check the summer times (Daylight Savings Time) and make the appropriate adjustment (sometimes two hours before or after statutory time).

THE TIGER AND ITS COMPANION IN LIFE

 **Tiger/Rat**

When a rodent is coupled with a carnivorous animal, the voyage will not be very peaceful; count on the Tiger, he will see to it that you do not fall asleep on your laurels! The hunt is his domain, the jungle his universe; the way will be strewn with traps and nothing will escape his watchful eyes. As a sentinel, he is unsurpassed. However, do not forget that the Tiger is a noble lord who will expect to be first. While roaming the Rat's territories he will take them over, and the Rat, due to his individualistic nature, will revolt with violence, which may result in his being emotionally torn. But the Rat should not despair because the Tiger is also a symbol of moderation. He is an excellent guide, in every sense of the word, and the Rat — at times a usurper himself — will gain tolerance and loyalty.

 **Tiger/Ox**

Born under this alliance, seduction will be your major talent. You are hardly likely to lose your way or fall asleep on the march. Conqueror of virgin lands and lord of the jungle, it will be extremely difficult to follow your track, for you are ferociously independent. Imagine a hunter joined to a dreamer, combining intelligence with muscular suppleness. But, royal Tiger or not, you are also the symbol of temperance. Along with the tenacity and the equilibrium of the age-old Ox, you bear within you a potential for sovereign and indomitable power. Alas, modesty and tenderness are not your strong points.

Tiger/Tiger

This animal is a traveller who will keep within his own particular territory, his beloved jungles. A lordly hunter who trusts in his lucky star, he will tend to take over territories for his sole use, relying on fortunes and his prestige to buttress and establish his claims. He risks becoming difficult to deal with beneath his handsome and special fur, that symbol of Yin and of Yang whose principle of alternation he should respect. He will pay dearly if he forgets to do so. His twin signs, blazoned with the same royal stamp under the same striped coat, can only affirm his particular quality of moderation; so he should pull in his claws and hide his fangs.

Tiger/Rabbit

Be careful of this animal; its appearance is deceptive. All gentleness on the outside — softly furry and velvety — he is mistakenly trusted. What makes the Tiger makes the Rabbit, and what makes the Rabbit makes the Tiger — all the better to eat you up. The Rabbit in the skin of a Tiger will find himself perfectly at ease; as for the Tiger, what could be easier than to give the illusion of being a harmless, large, striped tomcat. Essentially, game for the Tiger/Rabbit will involve sowing illusions and creating confusion among other animals: imagine Rudyard Kipling's Tiger meeting up with Bugs Bunny.

Tiger/Dragon

Not one to fall asleep on his way, this terrestrial and celestial mount will be secretive and enigmatic, spreading fear along his route. His isolated condition will compel him to follow his peculiar destiny. The Tiger will awaken the Dragon sleeping deep in a magic grotto; the Dragon will often provoke the Tiger to combat. The Tiger/Dragon is an animal that uses his claws, scales and formidable teeth, sometimes spitting fire. Yet he has a tendency to so overdo things that he can appear a clown. He should be careful of this, by which he may forfeit the fear and respect his majestic appearance inspires. Although it may amuse others to see him clowning, he is not the type — and should not do it.

Tiger/Snake

He is the professional charmer, crafty and sly if the need arises, capable of biting and releasing venom in order to attain his ends. However, moderation will win out over the ill-loved Snake's aggressiveness. Coiled within the Tiger, he can also be a welcome symbol of knowledge and of the underground world. Habituated to the honour due his rank, the Tiger is sometimes forgetful of those who crawl yet accomplish the same ends. The Snake who lies within may pretend humility; this is easy for him, since he is a prince of detours and winding paths. However, he should be careful not to fall into the traps he sets for others.

 **Tiger/Horse**

Spirited but temperate, alert to traps and clearing all obstacles, the Tiger/Horse will accomplish a voyage in which enthusiasm will be joined with patience, and stalking with slyness and galloping. Prudence and balance, calmness and patience will be difficult for the ardent Horse who sleeps within the Tiger: the Horse prefers the sunlit route and applause to the luxuriant semi-obscurity of the jungle. But the Tiger will quickly bring him back to reality; life is more than turning round in circles in a riding-school ring.

 **Tiger/Goat**

A dreamy and artistic Tiger; a wild beast among a mass of clouds, leaping astride the stars. That may make the Tiger/Goat smile, and he has need to. If he loses his Tiger side, which is sometimes too solemn, he will discover that the route can be beautiful — if he travels with his nose raised to the heavens. So, the Tiger should not devour the Goat within him; rather, he should let him caper about his head and his heart; his imagination will bring romance, which will reduce all difficulties to the level of a game.

 **Tiger/Monkey**

Games of hide-and-seek, tricks and hoaxes will blend with feline strategems and bravery. That sorcerer the Monkey has more than one trick up his sleeve. Depend on him to transform you into a skilful tightrope walker or a dazzling juggler. As playful as the Goat, the game with him is one of getting you to accomplish what *he* has decided you should accomplish. The Tiger/Monkey is thus a formidable animal which, combining the proud bearing and temperate skills of the Tiger with the ever-present wizardry of the little Monkey, can be counted on to turn anything upside down and provoke many a sleepless night. For the Monkey, leaping unobserved from branch to branch in the jungle with his eyes shut, one cannot apply the usual formula, 'put a Tiger in your tank.' Rather, 'wrap a Tiger within the skin of a mischievous Monkey, and then you will *really* see something . . . '.

 **Tiger/Rooster**

He detests banality. His creed is based on the need to be first and to dominate. He is unequalled where the question of pride is concerned; be careful, a voyage is always beset with traps and surprises. The Tiger/Rooster will have a tendency to believe himself to be the winner every time. Alas, the higher he climbs, the greater the fall and, striving always to be first, he will be in danger of running out of breath.

Tiger/Dog

He is a double guardian: the one protects from demons and the other protects souls in the next world. He is a virtuous pessimist disguised in the skin of a man-eating Tiger. The Tiger/Dog will be a thoughtful animal, at his ease in the 'invisible' world and prudent in his own territory. Sure of himself, but calm and circumspect, his Dog side brings an awareness of time and distance, an idea of the ephemeral as well as a sense of detachment. The Tiger/Dog knows better than anyone that after this voyage there will be another. He should be careful, however, for his feet are not on the ground and his halo is askew.

Tiger/Pig

He will be the symbol of a successful voyage But then, everything depends on what one calls 'success'. The solitary Pig will lead the Tiger along sombre paths, revealing mysteries and the spiritual world, but he will expect something in return. The Tiger may be a royal lord of the jungle, but the Pig is master of the palace and the symbol of opulence. But what opulence? This unscrupulous hunter will be neither tepid nor moderate; rather, he will be angelic or diabolical. But be careful: those who act like angels sometimes also act like fools.

THE TIGER
AND THE FIVE
ELEMENTS

五行

YOUR ELEMENT

In Chinese astrology, each year is joined to an Element. There are five Elements: *Water, Fire, Wood, Metal, Earth.*

Each of the twelve emblematic animals is linked successively to each of the five Elements. For example, in the year 1900 the Rat was Metal, in 1912 he was Water, in 1924 he was Wood, in 1936, Fire and in 1948 he was Earth. Therefore, for the twelve years from 1900 he was linked to Metal, for the next twelve years to Water, and, for every succeeding period of twelve years, to each of the other Elements, in succession.

In order to determine the Element corresponding to the year of your birth, use the table below:

Years whose digits end in: 2 and 3 — Water
6 and 7 — Fire
4 and 5 — Wood
0 and 1 — Metal
8 and 9 — Earth

The same union of *Animal-Element* repeats every sixty years, for example, Rat-Metal appeared in 1720, 1780, 1840, 1900, 1960 and so on.

The five Elements are the primary forces affecting the universe. It is their particular association with each of the signs which provides the basis for every horoscope. Movement and fluctuation, Yin and Yang, these symbolic forces are in a perpetual state of action and interaction.

Wood gives birth to Fire, which gives birth to Earth, which gives birth to Metal, which gives birth to Water, which in turn gives birth to Wood.

TIGER/WATER
(you were born in 1902 or 1962)

The cold born of the northern sky descended to Earth and gave birth to Water. The Chinese consider Water more a synonym for coldness and ice than as the source of heat and fertility.

Characteristics of the Tiger/Water
Water of winter nights, rigour and severity; calm and deep Water to be feared and respected; still Water sheltering underwater demons asleep in its depths; fetid and muddy Water of marshes, the refuge of crawling creatures.

Tiger/Water, who can make any domain his own territory or his particular universe, will quickly become acclimatised to the humid Element: mud, marshes, reeds or the heat of the rain-forest will stick to his Yin skin. As to the coldness, rigorousness and severity of ice — the symbol of the arrest of all motion — the Tiger will know how to dominate and invigorate it by bringing the dynamic Yang element to Water: in effect, a story of scoring a point and bringing grist to his mill! What is more, the Tiger is almost the only feline who adores swimming.

Health of the Tiger/Water
The Water organ is the kidney; its flavour is salted. The Tiger/Water will probably enjoy mudbaths, but he should not indulge in them for too long for if he does, gently but surely he will get bogged down. He has to keep on the move, take trips and avoid being transfixed by any one place or idea. Water should be his tonic; it is the best way for him to recharge his batteries.

The Tiger/Water and others
The Tiger/Water will be sedate, calm and reserved; he knows how to listen. Not unexpectedly for a Tiger, he will thus govern with ease. By controlling passions and curbing effusiveness he will be a peaceful, prudent leader, an

energetic liberal. Not in the least bit mystical, he will concentrate on political and social issues and humanitarian causes, directing campaigns with firmness and suppleness. Mr Tiger/Water will be a good father, if slightly over-protective and overbearing; and Mrs Tiger, although dominating, will be courageous and generous.

Advice for the Tiger/Water
Beware of taking yourself too seriously: your ideas, noble as they are, should be put into practice, otherwise you and your fur coat will end badly. If you hold back your energy too much you will wander permanently over mined territory and may be blown up. A Tiger/Water must assume his own responsibilities.

A Tiger/Water year
The culminating point for the Tiger/Water year will be winter, a period of gestation. It should be a period for invigorating yourself, not for floundering. Try to give your ideas and projects careful consideration during this period; make use of the time to reflect on them. But do so with a positive attitude; do not be morose or your thinking will deteriorate, bringing about a slow but certain degradation. Too much hesitation can be fatal for you.

Historical example of a Tiger/Water year 1962

On 22 October President Kennedy announced the presence of USSR missile bases on the offshore island of Cuba. Evidently further shipments of material were on their way to complete the installations.

For six days the possibility of a third world war conducted with nuclear weapons appeared to threaten the world. At the time, the crisis appeared to be a terrifying, because brittle, test between two personalities: that of the ardent young American President of known gullibility matched against the volatile nature of President Khrushchev. To an extent this was true. Kennedy had authorized a foolish expedition against the Castro regime in Cuba, the futile 'Bay of Pigs' invasion, and its failure had humiliated him personally, discredited his chosen advisers and encouraged a generous view from any opponent of the ineptitude of both. In Russia, Khrushchev's personal position remained insecure. In the opinion of some members of the Praesidium, the most conservative ruling body in the world, his temperament could not be relied on. Khrushchev needed a victory and a victory which would both match and justify his volatility. Events in Cuba offered, it seemed, the requisite opportunity.

In English terms, and in retrospect, one might say that the episode was not unlike Drake's raid on Cadiz in Elizabethan times known as the 'Singeing of the King of Spain's beard'. There was the same element of playing with the lion's tail, but it was a play that needed to be taken seriously, a play for prestige, for attention and serious recognition. There was also the possibility that an American president already discountenanced by Cuban matters would give up the game: but such a failure of nerve would not have been to the advantage of the Russians, who wished for an ally offshore the United States but not for a nuclear armed weapon base which would inevitably invite destruction. Khrushchev was playing a dangerous game and he seems to have ignored the unwelcome habit of the Americans to over-react. However, he won his game and in doing so he offered a valuable lesson. He both gained prestige for himself in Russia and recovered Kennedy's prestige in the United States. Mutual respect was restored and the future of civilization assured on a marginally sounder basis.

TIGER/WOOD
(you were born in 1914 or 1974)

To the East the wind blew in the sky and from its warm

caress of the Earth Wood was born.

Characteristics of the Tiger/Wood

Wood is of the morning, springtime, a temperate nature, loving harmony and beauty and elegance. Wood brings a little gentleness to our Tiger, softening his aggressive nature and opening his pride to nuances. In the spring, the seed buried deep in the soil during the long winter blossoms, and nature is reborn. Wood symbolizes the breaking of dawn and this will incite the Tiger to leave his hiding place. Wood stretches its branches towards the heavens in the direction of harmony, but also plunges its roots deep into the earth. This double movement is a balancing factor for the Tiger. But Wood is equally the symbol of passion, violence and even destruction and self-destruction. The Tiger/Wood is thus an ambivalent person. Beneath his peaceful exterior his spirit is stirred by excessive and explosive impulses. For this reason others will find his behaviour strange and often disconcerting.

Health of the Tiger/Wood

The organ of Wood is the liver; its flavour is acid. Outbursts of anger and passion are at times necessary. But restrain yourself; if you go too far you will end up an anxious Tiger, turning round in circles in a cage of your obsessions and hallucinations.

The Tiger/Wood and others

The Tiger/Wood will appear relaxed and at ease, giving the impression of taking things lightly. Alas, this is an illusion and a mask, behind which he skilfully hides a highly anxious nature. If he allows himself to be overcome by this anxiety he will head straight for failure. The Tiger/Wood, however, will know how to improvise and give free rein to his fertile imagination; in this way creativity will win out over reasoning.

Advice for the Tiger/Wood

You are passionate, engaging, at ease (at least on the surface) and a lover of liberty. The stage attracts you, the limelight awaits you, the crowd's eyes are fixed upon you. Allow your inspiration free rein.

A Tiger/Wood year

The culminating point for a Tiger/Wood year will be springtime, a period of growth and prosperity. The Tiger will become extremely dynamic due to the Yang force which he bears within him; thus he will be more enterprising and more creative. Profit from this period to start some new enterprise or develop your artistic talents — Wood is by nature poetic. However, always retain your flexibility; in this way you will find it easy to adapt and gain a new lease on life. This is the period to do so because your opportunism will be remarkably well paid.

Historical example of a Tiger/Wood year 1914

On hearing of the assassination of the Archduke Ferdinand at Sarajevo, Emperor Franz Josef is reported to have said that he did not see why the death of one man should lead to war, even if that one man was the heir to his throne. His opinion was not shared by his Foreign Minister and Chief of Staff who had long fostered a desire to humiliate Serbia. But they had no understanding that a mere punitive expedition might lead to general war. Robert Vansittart, then an assistant clerk in the British Foreign Office, was more prescient: he noted 'The unwisdom of a blindly anti-Serbian policy is not at all appreciated in Austria and that is the real point in a rather threatening situation.'

After a month of indecision, Austria delivered an ultimatum to Serbia in terms generally thought to be an intolerable interference in Serbian sovereignty. On 25 July Serbia offered to submit to the ruling of the International Court at The Hague or to the decision of the Great Powers. It was the only rational move the Serbian government could make but, by its very terms, it precluded a punitive expedition by Austria alone. The Serbian reply confounded Kaiser Wilhelm of Germany, for 'it seems that every reason for war has disappeared.' However, he soon stirred the pot by suggesting that Belgrade should be occupied 'as a pledge'. Peremptory advice to this effect was sent from Berlin to Vienna and the efforts of the British Foreign Secretary to gain acceptance for the Serbian suggestion proved ineffective. Austria declared war on Serbia on 28 July.

The German government had exerted pressure on Austria since it realized that here was an opportunity to increase German power by a war with Russia, then in alliance with France, which the German 'Schieflen Plan' disposed of quickly. This, however, required the violation of Belgian territory, and the neutrality of Belgium had been guaranteed by the British. Apart from questions of honour the British were concerned with the prospect of German domination in Europe and the threat to naval supremacy this implied.

The German invasion of Belgium decided the issue. Britain declared war on Germany on 4 August, the day following Germany's declaration of war on France. Thus it was that Europe stumbled into its Armageddon. Those who greeted war with 'an esctasy of joy' in whatever capital city would be lucky if they lived to regret it, and those who welcomed it as a chance to be rid of a sickness their complacent rulers denied were themselves immersed in a greater one.

TIGER/FIRE
(you were born in 1926)

Heat was born in the southern sky, descended to Earth and fertilized it. From their union Fire was born.

Characteristics of the Tiger/Fire
The Fire element is of the midday, the South, the summer.

Fire is Yang; it animates, quickens and transforms. For the Tiger, Fire will be a flame of energy and dynamism, a creative, stimulating and rapid force. Refrain from pulling on this feline's whiskers, for he will leap at your throat. Ideas will flash and fly as fast as lightning and answers will be right on target. But be careful of asking questions to which he can find no solution, for the Tiger/Fire can be as explosive as nitroglycerin.

Health of the Tiger/Fire
The organ of Fire is the heart; its flavour is bitter. The Tiger/Fire should look after his heart. Living under high pressure, he should slow down a little if he wishes to avoid a heart attack.

The Tiger/Fire and others
Fire is often a symbol of war. As an Element of lucidity and clairvoyance, it is also a symbol of passion and violence. Happily, the moderation of the Tiger and his double Yin-Yang nature will balance and temper this sometimes destructive Element. Although the Tiger/Fire is impetuous and ardent, he is also lucid and active; a loyal, royal and virtuous Tiger — unless, of course, he joins a circus.

Advice for the Tiger/Fire
By playing with Fire you risk burning your boats and transforming your life into a desert. A little moderation is called for.

A Tiger/Fire year
The culminating point for a Tiger/Fire year will be summer, a period of creation and spiritual progress. While it is a hyperactive year, do not allow the Fire which devours to overwhelm you. Leaving the East to go South, the Tiger/Fire will be doubly Yang, approaching the 'great Yang'. An overwhelming year: be careful of fire smouldering under ashes and smoking in the bowels of volcanoes.

Historical example of a Tiger/Fire year
1746

The previous year the romantic Charles Edward Stuart had raised his flag for the Stuart cause in Scotland, home of his forebears and his line. The Highland clans flocked to him, along with many of the minor aristocracy and disaffected craftsmen in Scotland. The Stuart Pretender to the English throne soon secured Scotland; he then advanced into England as far as Derby, seeking acclamation and support. But the English did not want him. The Stuarts threatened a double subservience to the Pope and to France, the very combination they had protested against when Charles II was king and had risen against when James II was on the throne. For the English, a Dutchman or a German, be he a Protestant, was altogether preferable as king to a legitimate Stuart.

The result was inevitable: retreat to Scotland, defeat at Culloden, flight and total dispersal. Equally the aftermath was savage, ruthless in conception and ample in execution. In 1746 the glens of Scotland were laid waste, their inhabitants slaughtered instantly or worse. Possibly the humiliation of English arms at Fontenoy the previous year brought an additional rigour to the proceedings.

The final failure of the Stuart cause created its own legend. Unlike his predecessor in 1715, Charles Edward was made on heroic lines. To the Highlanders he represented a moment of hope for five centuries of civilization which retained, on the edge of the European world, a sense of hospitality as a deep-rooted obligation (totally foreign to the Anglo-Saxons) combined with a relish for intellectual pursuit for its own sake which was as alarming in a London drawing-room as it was taken for granted in a French salon. The Young Pretender and his cause remained a legend, their memory engraved in the cryptic hieroglyphic on some of the most beautiful drinking glasses ever made.

The Stuart defeat had been summary but the English were

frightened. George II reluctantly allowed Pitt (later Earl of Chatham) to join the ministry. The consequences were to mark the future of England even more radically than the voids created in the Scottish glens. The survivors from Scotland became the engineers for the empire instigated by Chatham.

TIGER/EARTH
(you were born in 1938)

Earth was born from the slowly falling Elements of the sky at its humid zenith.

Characteristics of the Tiger/Earth
This is an afternoon Earth, the humid and hot Earth of summer. It is a favourable Element for the Tiger, who will blossom. It will be a place of meditation, a refuge and a hiding-place from which he can safely watch out for prey. But he should be careful not to become too dependent on it or allow himself to be trapped by the sticky warmth which saturates his robe. It is important that his Yang aspect should serve as a catalyst for his actions, inciting him to leave his refuge and wander at will. For the Tiger, the Earth Element can be a little too comfortable, and he risks anaesthetizing his irreplaceable dynamic virtues.

Health of the Tiger/Earth
The Earth's organ is the spleen; its flavour is sweet. Unless he leaves his chosen lair, the Tiger/Earth will be reduced quickly to a heavy tomcat. Encroachment of the body means encroachment of the mind. No Tiger sleeps on cotton-wool, and so he must stretch his limbs, roar his war-cry and do his exercises. Do not overeat — choose raw vegetable as your diet.

The Tiger/Earth and others
This Tiger has his feet firmly on the ground. He behaves

prudently, sometimes even egotistically. His sense of propriety is highly developed, but he only attains his objectives at the price of repeated and often endless efforts. He will be crafty enough to intimidate those who question him and will make an excellent financier or a clever banker. Within the family circle he has a tendency to play the despotic patriarch. Mrs Tiger/Earth often appears charming and fascinating, but can also appear slightly vampish.

Advice for the Tiger/Earth
Although you dream of fortresses or impregnable castles, go out a bit, expand your horizons and do not retreat or contemplate too much or stand stiffly by your safe deposit box. The Tiger/Earth is first and foremost a seducer; so, if you do not want to be offered a basket to sleep in, show your fangs, get on the road and stop locking your door.

A Tiger/Earth year
The culminating point for a Tiger/Earth year is summer. The Tiger will find comfort and security, abundance and good hunting during this season. However, profit from this period by finding time to turn towards others. Do not over-cultivate your feeling of superiority; this could rebound and disrupt your peace.

Historical example of a Tiger/Earth year
1938

By January, it was clear to the Austrian Chancellor Schuschnigg that a Nazi *Putsch* was imminent. In 1936 Austrian independence had been guaranteed by Hitler who, in the Chancellor's judgement, would surely denounce it if he was apprised of its details. He judged wrongly. At a meeting in Berchtesgaden in February Hitler demanded that far from the plot being exposed, it should be concealed; that the plotters should be granted an amnesty and that some of them should be admitted to Schuschnigg's government.

Austria was without allies. The 1936 agreement with Hitler had deprived its government of any hope of Italian protection, reversing the policy of Dolfuss, and the Chancellor had only one recourse: to call a plebiscite on the issue of Austrian independence. On 9 March he did so. The Austrians were to determine the issue on 13 March.

Hitler could not risk an anti-German vote. On 12 March his armies entered Austria and he demanded that Austria accept a pro-German government headed by an Austrian Nazi, Arthur Seyss-Inquart. Hitler's policy was not originally aggressive but he wished to establish closer links with Austria, capable of expressing his pan-German views. On his arrival at Linz he was met by wildly cheering crowds; all the suppressed excitement of pan-Germanism had erupted. This could not fail to excite Hitler in turn, and a report that there were crowds in Vienna demanding anschluss decided him. On 14 March he entered Vienna and proclaimed the total union of Austria with Germany. 'I stand here,' he declared in Vienna the following month, 'because I flatter myself that I can do more than Herr Schuschnigg. I have shown through my life that I can do more than these dwarfs who ruled this country into ruins. . .'

After Austria it was to be the turn of Czechoslovakia and the submission by France and England to its partition at Munich.

TIGER/METAL
(you were born in 1950)

In the sky, coming from the West, drought grazed the skin of the Earth and gave birth to Metal. Winds come from the far-away steppes seeking the vital sap.

Characteristics of the Tiger/Metal

Metal is of the night, autumn and cold. It symbolizes clarity, purity and precision. The Tiger/Metal's tendency is to be cutting, rigid and chaste, and his tough comments oscillate between beauty and destruction.

The Tiger/Metal will know how to carry out projects; he will be energetic and unscrupulous and will not encumber himself with sentimentality. Only the result counts for him. The Tiger embodies courage and protection against evil spirits. Because he has a rather limited sense of humour, he can sometimes seem much too sensible. He can perhaps be persuaded to become interested in some 'mystical quest', but he is not always honest about this and may use it as a pretext for majestically crushing his fellows when they visit his royal territory.

Health of the Tiger/Metal
Metal's organ is the lung; its flavour is pungent. The Tiger/Metal, attracted to asceticism and its ecstasy, should take care to control his breathing — that vital element which has to circulate freely — or he will find himself transformed into an ephemeral Paper Tiger. Live in the great outdoors; it is marvellous for the lungs and the mind.

The Tiger/Metal and others
The Tiger/Metal is the symbol of energy. He will be a formidable warrior, a brilliant lawyer or a wily jurist. However, the Tiger/Metal will never be someone's brilliant assistant. His motto could be that of Caesar: 'Better to be first in a village than second in Rome.' As far as he is concerned, subtlety and diplomacy do not exist. His 'tact' is confined to pounding the table with fangs bared; he habitually cuts short discussions, but is easier to wound than to heal. Although this metallic and wild animal is little inclined to tenderness, he remains a noble being — and we all know that nobility makes one duty bound.

Advice for the Tiger/Metal
Be more flexible, file down your claws and your fangs; try some Yoga.

A Tiger/Metal year

The culminating point in a Tiger/Metal year will be autumn.

You will leave the East for the West; your Yin tendency will be strengthened by the Yin aspect of autumn, which sometimes causes a loss of energy and dynamism. Beware of self-destructive or masochistic tendencies; be less stiff and less introverted. Work at becoming physically and mentally supple — otherwise you will be exposed to the worst violence to your feelings.

Historical example of a Tiger/Metal year
1830

The 'Sailor King' William IV succeeded to the throne of England. In personal habits he was a total contrast to his profligate predecessor; not for him the extravagances of Carlton House, the quixoteries of the Brighton Pavilion or the immense debts accumulated while waiting for the throne. But like all the Hanoverians he had a weakness for uniforms: tight trousers on his midshipmen were obligatory. England's answer to this sturdy and unexceptional king, expressed in the mandatory general election which followed his accession, was to return the first 'Liberal' government for eighteen years. The vote, however, as the new king realized, had little to do with him; it reflected one of those occasions across the Channel which occasionally revived the muted hopes of English Radicals.

There, in France, the barricades were up again — the result of the ill-advised July ordinances of a reactionary government under Polignac. The 'July Revolution' followed, prepared by the historian and journalist Adolphe Thiers. What influence this had upon the voters in England was probably due to renewed evidence of the Republican spirit, but in France the ideology seems to have inspired speech rather than action. The basic question there concerned the reliability of the French army. The very soldiers who should have put down the revolt permitted it, and some of them abetted it. For them, the problems were professional and domestic. Promotion came too slowly among the non-commissioned ranks, unlike the careers open to anyone of talent under Napoleon I, and the administration of army affairs and the conditions imposed on the rank and file seemed inefficient and mean, as they always do to soldiers in peacetime who have experienced the profligacies of war.

These aspects passed unnoticed in England, where no standing army of account was supported. The English vote represented a slight shift in inclination. In that lay its significance, for thereafter, whether the administration was Whig/Liberal or Tory/Conservative, a political consenus was established — the two-party system which was to mature under Gladstone and Disraeli and dominate English politics for over a century.

Analogical Table
of the Different Elements

Elements	Wood	Fire	Earth	Metal	Water
Years ending in	4 and 5	6 and 7	8 and 9	0 and 1	2 and 3
Colours	Green	Red	Yellow	White	Blue
Seasons	Spring	Summer	End of summer	Autumn	Winter
Climates	Wind	Heat	Humid	Dry	Cold
Flavours	Acid	Bitter	Sweet	Pungent	Salty
Principal organ	Liver	Heart	Spleen	Lungs	Kidneys
Secondary organ	Gallbladder	Small intestine	Stomach	Large intestine	Bladder
Food	Wheat, poultry	Rice, lamb	Corn, beef	Oats, horse	Peas, pork

Table of Harmony
Between the Elements

Legend			Wood Female	Fire Female	Earth Female	Metal Female	Water Female
○○○ Excellent prosperity		Male Wood	• •	○	○ ○ ○	○	○ ○
○○ Good harmony, understanding		Male Fire	○	○	○ ○	•	• •
○ Effort needed		Male Earth	• •	○ ○	○ ○	○ ○ ○	•
• Rivalries and problems of reciprocal domination		Male Metal	○	• •	•	• •	○ ○ ○
• • Misunderstanding and incomprehension		Male Water	○ ○	• •	•	○ ○ ○	○

THE
FOUR SEASONS
OF
THE TIGER

If you were born in spring

Tiger/Aries

One can truly say of the person embodied by this mixture that he has a 'Tiger in his tank'. He is eager to move, is entranced by action for its own sake and, being reckless by nature, has never really understood what brakes are for.

Tiger/Aries people are fascinating yet tiring individuals for, loyal as they are, and never devious in acts or in words, they are insensitive to the subtleties of language. Scorning what others might think, they lightly reject any principle that is apparently inconvenient to them. Their memory lapses easily because they live with intensity in the present — certainly no further than the near future — and they do not tolerate being contradicted or resisted. Generally, they are loved for their unequalled frankness and because they are truly good and sincere. These qualities help others tolerate their faults for they are quick to anger, flare up and fly into passions. As well, they are rarely aware of their errors, yet will admit them when alone. Those with more reflective temperaments they find difficult to get on with because they consider them to be indifferent. You will not be bored if they love you, but you will sometimes wish you had more time to breathe. It is useless to argue or to quibble with a Tiger/Aries: they are as they are and will never change. Moreover, they are too absorbed with their own affairs to pause for self-reflection or question their motives.

Tiger/Taurus

Efficiency is the hallmark of this Tiger, for the realism and perseverance of Taurus contributes greatly to the Tiger's independent spirit and strength of will. Visualize a royal feline equipped with well-sharpened horns — something to contemplate, is it not?

This animal will be marvellously at ease in the financial jungle and the labyrinths of the stock-market. Within his lairs, behind his desk, he will quietly plan his moment. When he feels that the hour has arrived, he will calmly blow up the bank. Prudent yet bold, courageous yet reflective, he retains the instinctive capacity to know and appreciate the ways of fortune and to attract immense wealth.

In his love life he will wish to establish a mastery over his feelings corresponding to the control he wields over the rest of his life. But this often eludes him and his emotions will then burst forth in splendid blazes, only to be quickly consumed. Once ignited, he will hope these burning passions could last forever, for that is the nature of this touchy conqueror who dreads the prospect of forever setting forth to search for new conquests. Having gained something, he does not appreciate that his right to acquisition may be questioned. He is too busy to respond to those who need reassuring gestures of his affection, which will often exhaust their patience so that they tire of him. He is a dependable head of a family; being loyal and authoritarian; order must reign in his lair or he will roar. Tiger/Taurus is a faithful animal and one can trust his protective paws. But he is also a vindictive enemy: he never forgets underhanded tricks and, for him, vengeance is not an empty word. Be careful: he can be violent and unscrupulous if seriously inconvenienced or upset.

Tiger/Gemini

The Tiger/Gemini is inclined to be reckless. The imagination and experimental temperament of Gemini are combined with the audacity of the Tiger, so that anything rare or peculiar will exert a strong fascination. The most unexpected enterprises can intrigue him and it is impossible to imagine him in the same place for more than five minutes, either materially or morally. Always defending a new idea or engaging in some battle, he is ceaselessly enthusiastic about new ventures. On the other hand, he is always watchful and guarded. Shoot a toy pistol near him and you will never see him again — practically anything can serve as a pretext for his leaving.

Enthusiastic, inventive, original and fluent, the Tiger/Gemini is thoroughly charming, usually extremely intelligent and an opportunist. If fidelity is not his greatest virtue, it is because he has difficulty resisting a desire to please. This is a fascinating game for him, and does not require any great commitment. If he happens upon a tolerant partner the alliance can be lifelong.

On the negative side, this brilliant personality can exhaust himself in pursuing absurd and superficial activities or discussing irrelevancies until blue in the face. But this Paper Tiger is rare. More frequently, he is one of those unreliable adventurers noted for his panache and a courage which excludes an ability to face the consequences. However, he will survive, because he is lucky. Nevertheless, he does lack stamina and, while creative, he finds it difficult to carry anything to its conclusion.

If you were born in summer
Tiger/Cancer

Tiger/Cancer needs an organized life if he is to be well balanced and at ease. He needs to distinguish between his one world devoted to activity, and his other where he can relax. In the first, he will be ambitious, a fighter, courageous and independent, with all the tendencies of the Tiger plus the passive tenacity of Cancer. In the second, he will sprawl delightedly on a sofa among the cushions and fur coverlets, complacent and affectionate as a sated cat. With him, everything depends on equilibrium, style and atmosphere. A contented Tiger/Cancer will embody the best aspects of each sign: faithfulness, generosity, friendliness and protectiveness. But if this tricky equilibrium is not mastered, things will be very difficult. In this case, Tiger/Cancer will be unconventional, free and easy, shirk responsibility, unstable, egotistical and, above all, enormously touchy and easily offended.

In fact, Tiger/Cancer is rather like one of the lesser cats: he requires complete independence while remaining totally attached to his old cushion and to his dear old habits. So long as he is allowed to organize his life as he wishes and his particular rhythm is not disturbed, he will be a delight to live with.

Tiger/Leo

He is truly the royal Tiger, in every sense of the word. The alliance between the king of the animals and the lord of the jungles will never lack in grandeur. The person born of this mixture is proud; he likes to be taken seriously and, moreover, always looks imposing. Whether he is president of some republic or of just a club, he will always have a certain distinction, an appearance of prestige and brilliance. So long as he is treated with deference, he will be staunchly loyal; otherwise he can become touchy and even mean. In fact, he needs an elevated life, whether in dream or in reality, if he is to illuminate the world with his brightest light. If humbled or constrained he will vacillate, protest and hang back, profoundly dissatisfied but more or less incapable of managing within a framework that is not his own. He is made for the jungle, not for suburban hedges.

He has little talent for daily life for he cannot tolerate any moral or physical limitation. He does not know where or when to stop since no obstacle stops him. Children, responsibilities, duty — these are the only calls to which he will respond because a Tiger/Leo loves to transform himself into a furry carpet at home — and into a formidable beast of prey if that home is threatened.

Tiger/Virgo

Even if it does not seem obvious at first glance, this is a marvellous combination, due to the profound disparity of the two signs. There is enough energy and independence in the Tiger to counterbalance the scruples and hesitations of Virgo; and there is a reasonableness, a sense of organization and modesty in the Virgo which can serve to calm the Tiger's foolhardiness and appetite for risk. Thus, a Tiger/Virgo by his dash and by his intrinsic qualities — has everything necessary to impose himself on life, and, thanks to his work, to conserve his prestige and his authority. He can be an esteemed leader, for he feels little contempt and pays attention to all aspects of the enterprise. He could, for example, become one of those formidable trade union leaders who cause sleepless nights to directors of industry. He possesses the prodigious faculty of belonging to all the rungs of the social and hierarchical ladder. He is just about invulnerable, and his few weak points are well concealed.

All Tiger/Virgos are trustworthy in love, for they have a strong sense of responsibility; but their reasonableness does not always mesh with their taste for conquest. For a wild beast to stalk his prey for weeks and then forget about it in order to check his accounts does seem rather surprising; but with a Tiger/Virgo it can and does happen; those close to him will do well to become accustomed to this contradiction.

If you were born in autumn
Tiger/Libra

This Tiger is sentimental and very vulnerable for he tends to risk his emotions and involve himself completely, which can sometimes be dangerous. Passionate and capable of intense attachments, he attracts because he has charm and distinction, is at ease, well dressed (valuable for both sexes) and always extremely attentive and considerate with his partners. In short, he is never lukewarm in any intimate relationship. If deceived he will break off the affair with nobility, but he will be frightfully, horribly unhappy. The Tiger/Libra, in common with other Tigers, cannot endure failure for this calls everything into question — including himself — and he will ask himself if he should not leave this jungle of tears to enter a monastery. Once in the monastery, however, he will simply fall in love again, for that is his natural state. But in between, what highs and lows!

Professionally, on the other hand, the Tiger/Libra is highly efficient for he is unequalled in drawing in his claws. He gets along well with everyone and treats them fairly. No one gets on his nerves, for he is always extremely competent in his own field and, openly at least, does not seek confrontations. A bit of an artist, a bit of a speculator, he can amass fortunes — but also lose them, for love.

Tiger/Scorpio

He is so well hidden at the bottom of the jungle, melting into the shadows and patches of light, that one can barely make him out. If, by an unfortunate accident or because of a tragic carelessness, you poke a poor little tip of your toe into his lair, you will perhaps hear a roar and, stupidly, ask yourself whether it is friendly or menacing. Run for your life — otherwise you will be destroyed, flattened by the scratch of a poisoned claw. For you are confronting the most dangerous and most Tiger of all the Tigers. Sinuous and quick-witted, he knows in advance all the tricks of his adversaries and possesses some unprecedented ones himself. He has a sense for strategy and only enters into combats which he can be certain to win. He triumphs because of his intelligence and because of his gift for surprising his adversary: best of all traps, he appears rather absent-minded. Thought to be inoffensive, he is in fact playing a game as he plays with everything: using and remembering everything.

There is, however, a positive side to this alliance. Tiger/Scorpio defends his friends with as much energy as he defends himself. He is passionate and fascinating with his family and close friends, and has a slightly black sense of humour. His interests are varied, but he does not like to have his hand forced. Respect his independence, recognize his individuality, and he — or she — will be a marvellous and amusing companion.

Tiger/Sagittarius

The Tiger/Sagittarius is quite unpredictable. At times admirable, at others maddening, he is practically incapable of finding the golden mean between two extremes.

First, his good qualities: there is no point in putting oneself out for the Tiger/Sagittarius; he is totally aware of your motives. He is also noble, just, generous, courageous and fearless. He does not know the meaning of pettiness, is enthusiastic about everything he does and is warm and inviting. In him one finds some aspects of Cyrano de Bergerac with a few of Don Quixote's; he likes to conquer, but on a high level. Even the female Tiger/Sagittarius has something of the buccaneer about her. She is not cut out to be a housewife — something one must learn to accept.

If one asks how it is that this hero can sometimes become so odious in everyday life, the simple answer is that it in no way suits him. He will wilt and then exhaust himself in childish attempts to become the conformist, obsessed by power, titles, rank and status and his own sacrosanct authority. The Tiger/Sagittarius would fit very well in a travel agency, but if he got himself into an administrative position, he would cause indescribable disorder. He dreams of the 'Three Musketeers' and 'Star Wars'. He can fascinate crowds by giving them back their childish illusions, since he himself has never stopped being a child.

If you were born in winter
Tiger/Capricorn

This is the rare white Siberian Tiger. At ease in the glacial breeze of the snowy summits of supreme power, he regards the mob stirring beneath him with a vaguely contemptuous eye. The fearlessness of the Tiger and the austerity of Capricorn produce a vigorous yet inflexible person little inclined to tenderness; at this altitude, sweet words, like fragile flowers, do not last long. The strength of Tiger/Capricorn lies in his imperviousness to his surroundings. Buried in the Arctic or the Saragossa Sea, he remains what he is — invulnerable and intractable. He is ambitious, but not for social advantages or financial power. What really interests him are the challenges he places before himself, the progress to be achieved, the record to be broken. Of course, if there are other advantages to be had, he will not spurn them, for he is a hard worker, persevering for a Tiger and does not rely on luck alone. He has an iron will and all his risks are calculated.

Despite his foresightedness and his rare lucidity — which enable him to avoid the natural pitfalls to which all Tigers, because of their natural indiscretion, are prone — the

Tiger/Capricorn can be subject to a miserable feeling of isolation. This is really due to his abrupt temperament. However, he has many fine qualities and is not at all superficial. He can be counted on and depended upon — admirable qualities, but it is useless to take him to a cocktail party.

Tiger/Aquarius

He is the most idealistic, utopian and the most attractive and likeable of all the Tigers, unless you rely on him too much. He is a cloud that has taken the form of a Tiger: you think you hold him and then you discover he is at the other end of the world, distributing rice to poor, starving children. Do not beg for his pity: he will oblige because it is not in him to refuse such requests, but he will immediately cite half a dozen examples of people unhappier than you — frustrating in the extreme!

The active, daredevil side of the Tiger rouses Aquarius, whose intellectual nature compels the Tiger to question his motives and consider the consequences of his actions. The person born under these two signs can thus accomplish great things, but his unawareness of hidden dangers and his tendency to find people better than they are will often land him in difficult and uncomfortable positions. It is not advisable to build something lasting with a Tiger/Aquarius; neither one nor the other of these two signs seems specially made for marriage and independence suits them more comfortably than house slippers. Even a Tiger/Aquarius who is very much in love and very faithful will never remain at home for long. He will not leave simply to gad about, but to enjoy new experiences, become involved and make discoveries. He would be an excellent lawyer, a slightly demanding spiritual leader, a monk, an astronaut — in a word, he is never banal. Also, he will adore speaking into a microphone!

Tiger/Pisces

He is a curious fellow. Both the aggressiveness and fearlessness of the Tiger will be greatly reduced by the Piscean influence, which nevertheless multiplies his imagination and his taste for sacrifice. One must always remember that a true Tiger is noble and proud and that he does not hesitate to make spectacular renunciations. The Tiger/Pisces is slightly melodramatic, adoring impossible or exalting situations. He is a champion of lost causes and tragic loves. He would need to have at his side someone very affectionate yet practical to bring him down to earth. It is very important that this sensitive person, who is slightly marginal, tender and rebellious, should find an exciting job which will enable him to feel useful, even indispensable; or to develop his creative side, for he has a marked gift for artistic expression and a great deal of originality. Even so, he lacks practical sense and the ability to persevere.

It is perhaps easier to be a female Tiger/Pisces because there are psychological tendencies which our minds customarily attribute to the so-called weaker sex. She will be a delicious sprite, a bit feline and tigerish and saturated with charm. The male Tiger/Pisces is equally charming; a slightly mad poet, he has no equal in persuading the worst of shrews to feel terribly maternal. But he does not know how to profit from people. He is agreeable for others, but this does not contribute much to his own material security.

THE
I CHING

易经

THE I CHING AND THE TIGER

In the I Ching game, you ask a question and obtain an answer. It is therefore a divining game; but, in asking your question, you pose it with your Tiger identity. The complex mechanism of your mind and spirit have begun to turn. You ask a Tiger question, the I Ching answers with a Tiger 'solution', on which you can meditate as a Tiger before arriving at a Tiger conclusion.

The player is before a hexagram which contains the 'hypothesis-response' to his question, or, more exactly, a synthesis of forces affecting the concern or event inquired about.

For you, Master Tiger, here are the sixty-four hexagrams of the I Ching with their sixty-four Tiger hypotheses.

How to proceed
1. The question
Ask a question regarding any problem at all, past, present or future, personally concerning you. (If the question concerns a friend, consult the I Ching game in the book corresponding to his Chinese sign.)

2. Method of play
It must be done with concentration.
Take **three ordinary and similar coins** — for example, three 50p coins.
Heads will equal the number 3.
Tails will equal the number 2.
Throw the coins.
If the result is two coins showing Heads and one Tails, write 3 + 3 + 2. You thus obtain a total of 8 which you represent by a continuous line: ——— .
Draw the same continuous line if you have three coins showing Heads (3 + 3 + 3 = 9).

If you throw two coins showing Tails and one Heads
($2 + 2 + 3 = 7$), or all three showing Tails ($2 + 2 + 2 = 6$), draw
two separate lines: ▬ ▬
To sum up, 8 and 9 correspond to: ▬▬▬ (Yin)
6 and 7 correspond to: ▬ ▬ (Yang)
Repeat this operation *six times*, noting at the time of each
throw the figure obtained on a piece of paper, proceeding
from the first to the sixth figure, from bottom to top.

The final result, including a trigram from the bottom, or

lower trigram (example: ▬▬▬), and a trigram of the top,

or upper trigram (example: ▬ ▬), will be a hexagram of
the I Ching. In our example this would look like:

Now merely look for the hexagram number in the table on
page 246, and then consult the list of hexagrams with their
descriptions to find the given answer. *In our example,* the
hexagram obtained is number 63, entitled **After completion.**

THE HEXAGRAMS OF THE TIGER

CH'IEN

 **1** *The creative:* Energy, strength and will. A trinity which is perfectly suited to the Tiger. Create for the pleasure of creating, but take care to persevere — place your desire to create before that of coming in first.

K'UN

 **2** *The receptive:* A nobleman who respects himself should serve; he should not hold his subjects in contempt, nor the earth which bears him, nor the elements which govern him!

CHUN

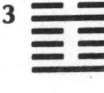 **3** *The initial difficulty:* Seek order from chaos, pour into a new bottle; look for the cause of the trouble. Sometimes the problem can be found within yourself. This will be a painful admission for a Tiger.

MÊNG

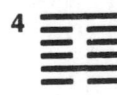 **4** *Youthful folly:* 'It is not I who seeks the young fool, but the young fool who seeks me.' The emperor's place is difficult to take on, therefore take that of the prince instead, to ease the course. A carefree attitude when facing danger must be well timed; do not be obtuse.

HSÜ

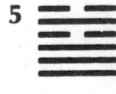 **5** *Waiting:* The Tiger is in the habit of awaiting the arrival of the hunter, but he is often trapped because of his fear of being overtaken by danger. Meditate on this.

Table of Hexagrams

Trigrams	Upper lines ☰	☵	☶
Lower lines			
☰	1	11	34
☷	12	2	16
☳	25	24	51
☵	6	7	40
☶	33	15	62
☴	44	46	32
☲	13	36	55
☱	10	19	54

Use this table to find the number of your hexagrams. The meeting point between the lower and upper trigrams indicates the number of the hexagram that you are seeking.

☷	☶	☳	☵	☱
5	26	9	14	43
8	23	20	35	45
3	27	42	21	17
29	4	59	64	47
39	52	53	56	31
48	18	57	50	28
63	22	37	30	49
60	41	61	38	58

SUNG

6 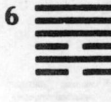 *Conflict:* Even when one represents 'royal virtue' it is necessary to know how to be conciliatory. What is won by force will be wrested away, in your case above all. Persevere with diplomacy rather than attacking head-on.

SHIH

7 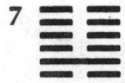 *The army:* Submission and discipline within the group for a common aim. Do not worry, in the army leaders are needed.

PI

8  *Holding together (union):* In order to be elected lord, vassals are needed. Do not forget that you need the devotion of those less important than yourself. Uniting means that you have gained the day.

SHIAO CH'U

9  *The taming power of the small:* Do not set out with the principle that you can never yield and should be obeyed in everything; for one day your followers may outstrip you.

LÜ

10  *Treading:* 'Tread on the tail of the Tiger, he does not bite Man' does not mean that you should tread on your own tail, rather that you should seek equilibrium, the golden mean. Follow the curve rather than negotiate the angle. That is the way in which an emperor behaves.

T'AI

11  *Peace:* From contraries there will develop harmony. Do not impose your personal vision if you wish to be understood, but extend your understanding and so avoid confusion and lack of comprehension.

P'I

12  *Standstill:* It is by moving away from the centre that one sees the centre. Standing back slightly avoids error and corrects distances. To stop does not mean to renounce or stagnate.

T'UNG JÊN

13 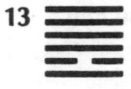 *Fellowship with men:* To associate, to unite, to come together in friendship in the open. The cloth is woven with several threads. Day lights the landscape; the sun illuminates itself. Not to live outside nor inside, but with.

TA YU

14 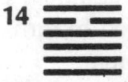 *Possession in great measure:* After coming into possession it is necessary to undertake something if you are to accumulate treasure.

CH'IEN

15 *Modesty:* The lake stretches peaceably, maintaining its level; it does not seek to overflow or to rise. Find equilibrium at your proper level. This is difficult for a Tiger.

YÜ

16 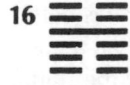 *Enthusiasm:* What remains of the past but impressions? When the party has ended, one must move on. Profit from this occasion and do not stop at mere intentions. Move on; assert yourself today for tomorrow will be too late.

SUI

17 *Following:* Go ahead with your soft, velvety eyes, persevere, but do not forget diplomacy. Unnecessary advice for a Tiger.

KU

18 *Work on what has been spoiled:* To err is human but to persevere in error is diabolical. Indifference and an off-hand manner are more destructive than the original fault.

LIN

19 *Approach:* What is good today will be bad tomorrow; sunshine is good after the rain.

KUAN

20 *Contemplation:* Or the image of the towering mountain visible from afar and to all. It is good to consider things, to meditate; but do not forget that you are awaited at the mountain's foot. If you do not wish to be judged in turn, avoid setting yourself up as an example.

SHIH HO

21 *Biting through (or clearly defined penalties):* The Tiger's bite may prove fatal. Control the power of your jaw, but do not hesitate to illuminate whatever prefers to remain obscure.

PI

22  *Grace:* It is the intention that counts; it is better to receive simple flowers with love than a great bouquet of roses for the principle of the thing. But how to put things in their proper place; roses or daisies, they are only flowers.

PO

23 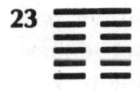 *Splitting apart:* If your wall is cracked, it is not good enough to simply cover it. Strip it down, even though the result is unsightly. Then you will have done the correct thing.

FU

24  *Return — the turning point:* After a long walk in the thick and sombre jungle, here is the light. Returning from an impasse, you can again see clearly.

WU WANG

25  *Innocence:* The Tiger is instinctive. By all means be guided by intuition, but do not be governed by it.

TA CH'U

26  *The taming of the great:* Power and force, the dreamed of duo for the Tiger, so long as he does not fall asleep on his throne and accepts that even the highest position requires competence and responsibility.

I

27  *The corners of the mouth:* Blood-thirsty hunter or royal Tiger, symbol of virtue and courage. Whether feeding oneself on fresh prey or fair words, the importance resides in the character of the nourishment absorbed.

TA KUO

28  *Preponderance of the great:* Do not try to carry all at once a moral or physical burden your shoulders cannot support. If need be, make several trips.

K'AN

29 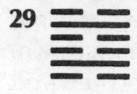 *The fathomless water:* Follow your own path and keep to your own territory; do not venture. A calm attitude will partially disarm your adversary and help you to face danger.

LI

30 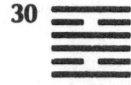 *The clinging, fire:* Do not stiffen before the attack. The wind cannot grasp. Before concentrating your energies in a given direction, ask yourself whether it would not be more sensible to avoid the obstacle.

HSIEN

31  *Influence:* If you condescend to leave your lofty throne you will realize that you are sought after and your presence requested. Even the smallest excursion will be worth the trouble.

HÊNG

32  *Duration:* Time materializes, becomes set; knowing how to stop in order to 'seize the moment' does not involve resting on one's laurels or falling asleep.

TUN

33  *Retreat:* Retiring from the stage and dispossessing oneself signifies control and mastery, an art not to be confused with resignation and defeat, or synonymous with failure and masochism. To retreat is not to abandon.

TA CHUANG

34 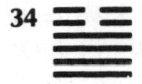 *The power of the great:* Force in movement. Do not allow yourself to be swept up in the spiral of movement and force; losing control, you will be broken. A whirlwind does not signify movement, and intoxication does not signify strength.

CHIN

35 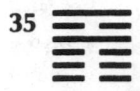 *Progress:* You have the support and assistance of an important person (you are not the only one of importance). Do not spoil your chances by trying to force your way through the doorway first when someone opens it for you and both can easily pass together.

The three Thoughts of the Far East:
Taoism
Confucianism
Buddhism

MING I

36  *Darkening of the light:* The darkness is all around you and within you. Do not struggle like a Tiger in a cage but await the return of the light; and, if you wish to file the bars, do so discreetly.

CHIA JÊN

37 *The family:* To accept a structure is not a sign of imprisonment. Integration into a community does not mean renouncing one's independence.

K'UEI

38  *Opposition:* Has no reason to exist if one does not set oneself up as the holder of the truth, and if one accepts the truth of others. This does not diminish the personality, but rather enriches it.

CHIEN

39 *Obstruction:* Do not confuse ordeals and obstacles with the art of breaking down open doors. Do not disdain a little assistance; even if this makes you smile today, you will regret it tomorrow.

HSIEH

40 *Deliverance:* It is the end of the tunnel, the opening. Start again from the beginning. The horizon and the light lie before you; learn to rediscover them.

SUN

41 *Decrease:* The hunt is difficult, the prey is meagre. Become a vegetarian and avoid luxury for the moment; it can only bring you cruel deceptions. Discover simplicity and sincerity.

I

42 *Increase:* Strike while the iron is hot and seize the prey at the proper moment, it runs fast — and good hunting.

KUAI

43 *Breakthrough:* Lightning heralds thunder, wind the tempest. Do not hesitate to proclaim, publish or denounce, for here you will be first — even if you have to topple others.

KOU

44 *Coming to meet:* Distrust calm appearances; in the heart of the peaceful mountain a volcano is sometimes rumbling. Be prudent in any encounter; it is better to distrust twice than once.

TS'UI

45 *Gathering together:* Know how to regroup and to renew ties; distrust intruders and parasites.

SHÊNG

46 *Pushing upwards:* Neglect nothing and underestimate no one, including the least important. When a flower is growing it seeks the light; as it blooms it reaches ever higher. Do as the flower does, no more and no less.

K'UN

47 *Oppression:* Be careful — you are a Tiger and some have a tendency to take you for a rabbit. There seems to be a loss of tone, energy and confidence in you, which is far graver.

CHING

48 *The well:* Upheavals, transformation and movement do not signify destruction or the negation of structures. Respect them.

KO

49 *Revolution:* You cannot avoid confrontations; mutation and renewal are indispensable.

TING

50 *The cauldron:* Representation of the five Elements — Water, Earth, Wood, Metal and Fire. Spiritual and material nourishment; food for the body and the mind. Excellent for a man-eater.

CHÊN

51 *The arousing (shock, thunder):* Big black clouds are passing in the sky; lightning may strike or hail fall. The noble Tiger should not deviate from his route, but should continue majestically on his difficult way, whatever the opposition.

KÊN

52 *Keeping still:* There must be a small, peaceful corner in the heart of your jungle; hold yourself aloof and create calm and salutary isolation around you before embarking on new actions.

CHIEN

53 *Development (gradual progress):* You will have a difficult time accepting the world of waiting rooms, but if you show too much impatience, you will not inspire confidence. Accept the game and smile nicely; do not bare your teeth.

KUEI MEI

54 *The bride:* Do not leap on your heart's desire as though upon your prey. First of all, it is disagreeable; secondly, springtime is not the whole of life.

. FÊNG

55 *Abundance:* Alas, it is not eternal, and, although a symbol of plenitude, do not forget that with your striped coat you are a symbol of Yin and Yang, embodying the principle of alternation. You should not be surprised if consequences flow from abundance.

LÜ

56 *The wanderer:* Travel and rediscover the great open spaces. Physical and mental health, especially for a Tiger, depends on it. But do not always behave like a conqueror; good masters need and must choose good servants.

SUN

57 *The gentle:* The wave will one day wear away the base of the rock, for its rhythm is gentle but constant perseverance is stronger than force.

THE I CHING

TUI

58  *The serene, the joyous:* Knowing how to share and how to communicate: the river flows nonchalantly into the sea.

HUAN

59 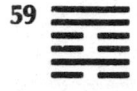 *Dissolution:* You tend to dissipate and lose yourself by concentrating too much on yourself. Call a glass of water a pond if you wish, but do not drown in it.

CHIEH

60  *Limitation:* Do not brandish your rights while minimizing your duties. If you assume the latter, the former will be recognized.

CHUNG FU

61  *Inner truth:* Communication is always difficult. To attempt by words alone is already to be mistaken. Actions count more than words. Be careful of the phrase, 'do as I say, not as I do'.

HSIAO KUO

62  *Preponderance of the small:* Do not hold grand ideas; you will fail. Little steps will cover the same ground as long strides.

CHI CHI

63  *After completion:* A condition of firmness. Meditate on the alternation of the Yin and the Yang. The well-balanced have no reason to fear that they will fall into the void.

WEI CHI

64 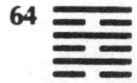 *Before completion:* Already there is accomplishment, but not if you behave like the centipede who, looking at his moving feet and analysing their order of movement, ends up on his back, waving his thousand legs in the air.

YEAR OF THE RABBIT

 1903·1915·1927
1939·1951·1963
1975·1987·1999

THE DOMAINS OF THE RABBIT

十二生肖

THE RABBIT AND ITS SYMBOLISM

The Rabbit is of the Yin tendency; he keeps to the West and belongs to the full moon of mid-autumn.

This animal seems above all to exude a mysterious and elusive essence. It is often our own images which are reflected in our diverse representations of this familiar beast, rather than a true understanding of its nature. Solitary, unusual and enigmatic, the Rabbit is the incarnation of the unsolved mysteries of the world. Subtle and omnipresent, he is the child of dreams and of the night. This smooth, disquieting creature also crystallizes hate and violence, calling forth superstitions. In the Middle Ages, for example, it was a bad omen for a traveller to see a rabbit before setting out on his journey. Yet he also has a history of benevolence and good luck. In pagan times he was worshipped as a sacred animal associated with fertility and the rites of spring. The tradition of a rabbit's paw bringing good luck originates from the eighteenth-century belief that the right paw of a rabbit carried in the left-hand pocket would keep away rheumatism. And, on a more fanciful note, who can forget the wondrous White Rabbit in 'Alice in Wonderland'?

In China the rabbit is common to the Yangtze valley and is the symbol of longevity. For thousands of years he has been associated with the moon, tradition stating that he comes from its vital essence and is therefore strongly influenced by lunar energies. A Buddhist legend relates how a rabbit once offered itself as a willing sacrifice, lying down on a pile of dry grass beneath a full moon; as a reward its soul was delivered to the keeping of the moon.

The Rabbit is said to live one thousand years, turning completely white when it reaches the age of five hundred; a red hare is a symbol of luck and appears when virtuous rulers govern. A very old Taoist tale says that he is the servant of a genie and helps mix the elixir of life.

This little god with a thousand faces should not be tamed or imprisoned in a tiny universe, but should be followed along his path of dreams. His velvet, noiseless tread — is it war, revolution or other such conflict. Their destiny thus depends on external circumstances, the times in which they live and the persons they meet. Their *old age*, however, could be sad or solitary because of their inability or disinclination to make a definite choice.

THE PSYCHOLOGY OF THE RABBIT

Since time immemorial, Rabbits have caused a lot of ink to flow. They have been deified and had statues erected to them; they are at times the emblems of tranquil wisdom, at others the companions of demons. These animals, who cannot really be classified as being 'domestic', always provoke extreme reactions: it is their privilege to be either adored or detested. No one is truly indifferent to them.

In Chinese astrology this sign is one of the most difficult to describe accurately, for it is infinitely shaded and complex. It is as much of a feat to describe the Rabbit in simple and concrete terms as it is to learn acrobatics.

The first and most important ambivalence of the Rabbit is precisely this subtle alternation between dependence and savagery: a taste for comfort and a need for absolute liberty. One can spend a lifetime with a Rabbit in total hapiness, before becoming aware that he escapes all traps and adversaries. His attitude is unforseeable and sometimes ill-adapted to circumstances. When one expects him to be courageous, when there is an ordeal to be faced, he takes cover; when one thinks that he is going to flee, he bravely faces up to any snarling adversary.

This sensitive being, infinitely receptive to currents, climates and sensations, listens only to his intuition, remaining open to and at the disposal of vibrations rather than to analyses or reasoning. It is useless to discuss logic with a Rabbit, even when his profession or his form of intelligence requires that he deal with facts and figures. His real reactions will always lie behind his words, a subjective terrain in which his paws are firmly anchored.

Rabbits are adaptable and can appear to be tame. But if

not the echo of our own fantasies? And that coat of silk, that supple and agile body, are they not the reflection of our own dreams?

A few notes on the Rabbit

Principal qualities: Discreet, prudent, profoundly honest.

Principal defects: Easily offended, egotistic, sometimes pedantic.

Work: Serious and persevering. His motto could be 'It is no good hurrying, you must start punctually'.

Best role: Friend; no one can equal him.

Worst role: Reveller.

Money: Prudent where necessities are concerned; otherwise spendthrift.

Luck: To be born in summer. His destiny will be more serene and he will be less cold.

Cannot live without: A home port.

Adores: Intimate gatherings round a fire while the storm rages outside.

Hates: Being forced to make a decision or to take sides; extreme or conflicting situations, difficult choices.

Leisure activities: Enjoys everything, as long as he is not responsible for its organization or direction and does not have to take risks. Do not take him on an expedition without a first-aid kit.

Favourite places: Nocturnal and silent paths, preferably near his home; paths in the wilderness.

Colour: White.

Plant: Fig tree.

Flower: Queen Anne's Lace.

Professions: Philospher, diplomat, administrator, politician, priest. He can function in all roles except as a front-line fighter.

The four ages in the life of the Rabbit according to Chinese tradition

Rabbits' lives are likely to be peaceful in *childhood, youth, maturity* and *old age*, as long as they do not live in a time of they are not content with their life or with their environment, they will not show it but relegate their dissatisfaction to the recesses of their mysterious beings. If circumstances change, it may one day appear; but if circumstances remain as they are, it may never be expressed.

Like those animals appreciated by the 'fervent lovers and austere scholars' dear to the French poet Baudelaire, those born under this sign behave with discretion and moderation. They are living proofs of suppleness and diplomacy and take an infinite amount of trouble to avoid conflicts and to resolve disputes. Sensitive to harmony, they need a peaceful, temperate climate and a soft ambience in order to blossom. Morally demanding, naturally virtuous, prudent and reflective, they seek comfort, security and tranquillity.

Throughout their lives, Rabbits work to consolidate the structures which make up their psychological and material 'crutches'. Their universe is first and foremost the immediate and the visible. It is only when they have turned everything round in their minds, sniffed in all the corners and provided all the doors with security systems, that they dare go a bit further — but still with prudence and circumspection, carefully placing one paw after the other, watchful, on the alert and vigilant.

This apprehensive attitude derives from the fear nourished by every Rabbit of the disruptions which might unsettle his life. For this sign is neither combative nor aggressive. A Rabbit never derives pleasure from throwing himself head first into difficulties. In fact, he does all he can to avoid them and it is only when he finds himself cornered in an extreme or tense situation that he can be forced into a fight. Rabbits only become dangerous when they are at bay, when baring their teeth is the only resource left to them. Otherwise, they flee from combat and avoid arguments, which they detest.

Their defects include a tendency to hesitate and to be faint-hearted. They do not like to move forward without knowing exactly what lies ahead; they are not made for suspense. Their usual policy is to protect their rear, while examining future possibilities; often, they simply remain in place and miss their opportunities.

Rabbits' deep attachment to security frequently makes them seem indifferent, which they are not, and egotists, which they are. Their moral well-being is essential to them and, although they love to do someone a god turn, they will never do so to the extent of questioning their principles. It may be difficult to believe they are so morally virtuous, but they sincerely believe in the pretexts they put forth.

Rabbits are agreeable to live with, for they are peaceful, sociable and easy-going; they are rarely irritable, remain calm and keep their heads. They are attentive and faithful friends, extremely hospitable, warm, refined and full of delicacy, accepting it as their duty to be understanding and tolerant. Abiding by honourable principles and respectful of traditions, they are rather easily shocked and offended. Just as they are discreet in public, so they love to shine and feel appreciated within their own circle. They express themselves with ease and elegance on many subjects, and their subtlety and facility for assimilation helps them to appear well informed about everything. Not only do they take pride in cultivating their minds, they like others to profit from what they have learned. Rabbits detest being left out of a discussion.

Perfectly at ease in daily life, whose responsibilities they assume easily enough, Rabbits are disturbed by unforeseen situations. Generally, a Rabbit can master any difficulty provided he has also mastered a knowledge of its various aspects and can pull the strings; otherwise he will be nervous, will panic and be inefficient. Most Rabbits are like this. Their success and happiness are dependent on a great variety of circumstances, including external forces at work in the world at large. Peaceful animals, Rabbits are not made for revolutions.

THE RABBIT AS A CHILD

The child born during a year of the Rabbit is usually a delight to bring up. On the whole obedient and disciplined, he rarely questions his parents' advice. He is smiling and approachable, happy to do a good turn, does his homework carefully and spontaneously takes part in school games. But in these and other sports he rarely takes risks, for he is really rather timorous. His parents will have no need to worry about the creases in his trousers or the need to keep bottles of iodine to hand for his wounds; he will prefer the awards of being 'first in the class' to those of the playing fields.

In some cases the young Rabbit is a little lacking in imagination, which may protect him from making stupid errors but will also prevent him from making discoveries on his own. He needs to be stimulated by his parents, which is not a difficult tast for he is adaptable and learns rapidly. His passivity stems from a distaste for personal involvement, and it is only this which restrains his young curiosity. To be truly comfortable and at ease the Rabbit child needs a corner to himself, ideally his own room. If this is not possible, try to arrange a private corner for him, even if it is only protected by a screen, and allow him to arrange this intimate space according to his fancy. He must learn to construct his own personal environment.

If the Rabbit child cries at night, gripped by irrational terrors, reassure him by persuading him that his fears are irrational. But do not pamper him; he needs to become accustomed to the unforeseen and learn to accept risks if he is to confront difficulties later in life. If he is pampered too much, this lunar acrobat and tightrope walker will grow up to be a greedy glutton, plump and wheezing.

Intelligent and diligent, the Rabbit child is likely to do well at school, which will make him slightly vain. One should watch over his choice of subjects for, lacking critical sense in such matters, he is in danger of being too persistent and succeeding in a profession which does not really interest him. He is sensitive to conditioning, heredity, the value of the example and he likes to give pleasure. Remember that he is a Rabbit — and do not try to teach him to fly.

LOVE LIFE

All Rabbits love to be loved; and, because they are far form being fools, it does not take them long to understand that the best way to get love is to give it — before it is given. Consequently they are charming with those from whom they wish to receive affection, as well as with those whom they esteem. They are attentive, affectionate, tender, never forget a birthday and are sensitive to the needs of those around them.

In a climate of shared love, Rabbits blossom and diffuse an aura of happiness. But they need active and constant warmth or all this will fade away. They must feel secure and know that they are loved — that is their oxygen.

Rabbits are faithful and tender by nature and because of their respect for convention. They breathe uneasily during storms of passion and constantly attempt to simplify complex situations in order to feel secure again. If there is too much conflict around them or a situation becomes too tense, they will leave; and if that proves impossible, they will become ill.

Certain Rabbits flit about incessantly and an uninformed observer may think them to be unfaithful, superficial and egotistical. In fact, their inconstant behaviour and fickle seductions express their deep need for a safe home port. As long as their experiences and encounters with others do not seem worthy of their total involvement, they continue to frolic, their ears pricked up. Then one day they meet the provider of the nest they have always dreamt of, and you can be sure that they will then do everything possible not to lose it.

Rabbits detest partings and will hope against all reason that life will untangle the threads of the relationship without wounds or rancour and restore them to their place in the sun.

FAMILY LIFE

Although Rabbits value marriage, intimacy and close

friendships, they sometimes feel ill at ease as parents. It is not that they neglect or scorn their children; in fact, they are indulgent to the point of spoiling them. They will do anything to rear successfully the little marvels they have brought into the world — including a certain toughness, the attitude of a mother rabbit defending its young, even if the emotional relationship is difficult.

While adoring their little ones, Rabbits are easily put out by the great and small upheavals which children inflict on their well-regulated lives. When their children are infants, subject to the hourly feedings and immobilized in a crib, our Rabbits will handle the situation brilliantly. But as soon as the charming baby begins to crawl everywhere, smear the walls and knock over flower vases, things will start to go wrong. Rabbit parents, not being authoritarian by nature, waver between uncontrollable laughter and anger. Many of them, unable to cope, hide behind indifference; the most energetic try to give their offspring a sense of discipline which, with some signs, is indeed a risk.

Everything will go well with Ox, Dog, Snake, Goat, Pig or Rabbit children. Monkey and Rat children will confuse their parents, who will wonder constantly what new catastrophe their child is going to come up with. The independent nature of the Dragon, Tiger and Horse will upset the tranquillity of a father or mother Rabbit considerably.

However this may be, Rabbits, without being slaves to their families — they also attach great importance to their social lives — go to some lengths to preserve harmony. They also know how to find peace and happiness in their daily life: female Rabbits adore housekeeping and receiving guests. But once the word 'divorce' is mentioned, our peace-loving friends are transformed into furious spitting and anxious tigers. For Rabbits, the destruction of harmony is unbearable.

PROFESSIONAL LIFE

Because of his prudence, tact and diplomacy, the Rabbit is

well suited to any profession that involves harmonious relations with others. In short, he can do anything and sustain any role — except, perhaps, that of Robinson Crusoe.

So, you may ask, why do we not see more Rabbits at the top of their professions? There are several reasons. First of all, Rabbits are modest and not given to pretension. Often capable of doing better than others — thanks to their meticulousness, professonal conscience and honesty — they forget to push themselves forwards, leaving the brilliant Dragons or the swashbuckling Roosters to reap the laurels that they themselves merit.

In general, Rabbits are limited in their ambitions: to succeed in their personal, emotional and family lives matters more to them than receiving an award. They refuse a life of compromise which such achievements depend on, dislike complicated plans and hate to get their hands dirty. At most they will ask their subordinates to wash the dirty linen. If they must retaliate, they will command the firing squad from a distance, considering such extreme measures as a 'necessary evil', preferring to set an example through gentleness. Rabbits know instinctively how to avoid conflict.

The more stable professions suit Rabbits best; they like to be recognized and appreciated and feel uneasy in vague situations. They are excellent executors, are organized, precise and like work well done, but are often brought up short if they must innovate, create or start again from the beginning. They adapt very well to changes but do not provoke them. They bloom better in an administrative position — whether it be in the world of finance or research — than in a liberal profession. Rabbits also do not enjoy wars of words, debates or heated arguments. While they prefer to work in a group rather than alone, they tend to leave discussion to others. They try to avoid exposing themselves to criticism, which can upset them considerably and even take away all their self-confidence.

Rabbits are remarkably gifted for the study of history, thanks to their excellent memory, which is quite exceptional; but although this is useful on a professional level, it can become a handicap emotionally, for there are times when it is best to know how to forget.

MATERIAL LIFE

Due to their need for security, Rabbits generally choose the winning side. If unsure they will adopt a neutral position so that their sudden about-faces are not too visible. From idealism they will sometimes uphold the weak side, but at the least sign of real risk they will soon rally to the strong. However, they should not be accused of selfishness or cowardice, because they are the first to suffer from their ambivalence. Sincerely compassionate and generous, they nevertheless lack the strength to do their utmost for a cause — unless, of course, their personal life or the well-being of their family is threatened and therefore dependent on the firmness of their stand.

Rabbits are not really selfish and not at all stingy; they simply plan exactly how much is needed for them to live protected from the unforeseen and, as a result, lack for nothing. It is easier for them to do this if they choose a stable profession within an administrative context, which they usually do.

Once their bank account is well-filled, they will establish deposit accounts for their family, prudence being the mother of security. But this is where their financial know-how completely crumbles: assuming, rightly or not, that they have paid tribute to the prudence which guides them, they easily become spendthrift and unwise, squandering any surplus funds on clothes, decorative objects, rich furnishings, sumptuous parties, travel and so on. It is, perhaps, for this reason that Rabbits frequently remain in a moderate financial position: avarice and hoarding are as foreign to them as the Tiger's love of taking financial risks. Between the two extremes, they eventually find a happy medium.

Intuitive rather than analytical, the Rabbit will sense what is going on around him; his spontaneous judgement is more accurate than his reasoning, which is often obscured by subjective factors.

ENVIRONMENT

Being excessively sensitive to atmosphere, Rabbits attach great importance to their daily lives. They love all that is beautiful and comfortable and, whatever their financial situation, they try to give their homes a touch of refinement, a special perfume. While not necessarily impeccable in their taste, they are orderly, meticulous and zealous house-keepers, known to become ill at the sight of a grease spot on a new rug. Rabbits love to entertain and go to a lot of trouble to treat their guests as royally as possible. They will find out in advance the special tastes of each guest, and will think nothing of preparing a special dish for the one who is slimming. Their guests will be greeted by a blazing fire and vases of freshly cut flowers — part of a Rabbit's natural hospitality.

Even in their offices or in a place they are only visiting, Rabbits know how to create a warm and cosy atmosphere which is special to them. With them, everyone feels at home. Their tastes in furnishing and decoration are rather classical, if not conservative. They adore pretty objects, old lace, candlesticks and romantic paintings. From time to time one finds a horror hanging on their wall, but it is usually a gift from a friend whom they do not want to upset; its sentimental value is worth more to them than its aesthetic or financial value.

Moving house is really heart-rending for them. They can remain for years in a crumbling flat without being able to decide to change. If you have a Rabbit child or friend, open a deposit account for him and oblige him to move.

A guide to relations with a Rabbit

Methods of seduction: For both sexes it begins with a long period of reflection: 'Is it a good match? Is his sincerity total? Can I count on his fidelity?' Finally, at the very moment that you are getting ready to search for more hospitable pastures, he — or she — will literally leap on you saying that he cannot possibly resist you.

If he loves you: It is up to you to take the initiative. You are so intelligent! He will let you speak first and you will be the first to enter his house. If the ceiling falls on you, he will care for you tenderly. But do not complain too loudly because he detests crying and blood.

He expects of you: That you insist that he accompany you to social events, but that you leave his mind free.

To keep you: He will be exceptionally patient and understanding.

If he is unfaithful: Him? never! It is all in your imagination. Anyway, it is his body, not his soul, which is all yours, and he will continue to plead innocent all the way to the scaffold.

If you are unfaithful: He will not make a scene because he hates them. But he will question you remorselessly and will even look in your pockets, feeling guilty all the while.

In case of a break between you: It will not be permanent unless you become truly odious. But do not count on him to take the initiative.

If you wish to give him a gift: You have the choice between a huge patchwork quilt, a soft cushion — or a James-Bond type bodyguard.

If you want to seduce him: Tell him that you represent a company handling bullet-proof doors and wish to show him the latest model. Be well supplied with cushions, have a fire lit and soft music playing.

If you want to get rid of him: Suggest that he join a terrorist group.

THE RABBIT
AND OTHER CHINESE SIGNS

Rabbit/Rat

Delighting in tranquillity and harmony, persons born during the year of the Rabbit hate extreme situations and are ill-equipped to deal with strain or stress.

The Rat, not realizing that his native disquiet creates a common ground with these graceful animals, will immediately label the Rabbit's prudence as pusillanimity. The latter will bristle at the Rat's tart criticism.

There is an undeniable, deep-rooted antipathy between the Rat and the Rabbit; if a Rat loves a Rabbit, he will not understand that the latter is at one and the same time adaptable, unstable and yet clings to security. And the Rat will have nothing to do with tranquillity and harmony; he prefers to live balanced on a tightrope, ever liable to have his fingers burnt. It is, of course, well known that the maxim 'once bitten, twice shy' applies to the Rabbit. Therefore, although the two have to make a strong effort to live together on an emotional level, as brother and sister or as friends, their differences can provide the opportunity for a profitable experience.

Rabbit/Ox

This combination is ideal! The Rabbit needs security, calmness and harmony, and the calm and stable Ox offers such a sanctuary. Sometimes the Rabbit is unfaithful — more to prove to himself his seductive powers than through a taste for infidelity — but above all, he values his home life. The Ox, who is not in the habit of going through his spouse's pockets, will prefer to remain as unsuspicious as he is faithful. Both of them fear financial setbacks, disagreeable and unforeseen events and personal confrontations. They always strive to secure their home from any possible hazard.

The Ox, being more independent and better armed to confront difficulties than the Rabbit, is better suited as the active element in this partnership. If his lack of diplomacy causes problems, the more supple and opportunistic Rabbit will give him useful advice.

There is only one obstacle: the Ox likes clear and plain answers, while the Rabbit is hesitant, uncertain, a little unsure and needs to work around a problem to find the ideal solution. By then the Ox will have made his own decision.

This union, while emotionally rich, is ill adapted for business unless there is a third party — a Tiger, for example — to appreciate, and therefore diminish, the risks involved.

Rabbit/Tiger

Both in their different ways seek to secure their prey. Each is attached to a certain form of comfort and they share the need for an impression of freedom. Rabbits and Tigers alike will settle by the fireside and then depart, if the mood takes them, to spend the night under the stars. Any attempt to constrain these two is inadvisable.

The Rabbit, however, is more dependent on a life of security, is much more prudent and is likely to shudder with horror at the Tiger's dare-devilry.

If the Rabbit is the less active of the two, their liaison will go very well. The Rabbit will take care of daily comforts and will discreetly restrain his companion's outbursts of audacity. If the contrary, life will be difficult. The undomesticated Tiger with nothing much to do will be furious whenever he sees his Rabbit spouse check the gas meters or the locks on the doors. He could easily lope out of his own house and return to burgle it.

When they disagree, the Rabbit will have a lighter touch than the Tiger; more agile, he will always have the last word, leaving the Tiger spinning round in circles.

Rabbit/Rabbit

One cannot see why two Rabbits should not succeed in getting along together. They take such trouble to preserve harmony that the least dispute would be nipped in the bud; the least sly spirit of discord would be whisked away by an angel of light as if by the wave of a magic wand to restore perfect harmony.

What our Rabbits risk is a lack of dynamism; they may go to sleep for too long. But if one is ambitious and the other sedentary, there is no doubt that their life will become a model for family magazines. One can well imagine them receiving awards for conjugal merit.

If the world is ablaze and in turmoil, you can be sure of finding a refuge with them — unless they have transformed their house into an impenetrable nuclear shelter.

Rabbit/Dragon

This relationship will be possible if it is the Dragon who wears the trousers — literally and figuratively. To live for any length of time with his sensational partner — who is not content merely to shine, but needs to collect several awards of distinction that he guards in a small engraved box — a

Rabbit needs to be philosophic and self-sacrificing, qualities he definitely lacks.

Rabbits are patient and peace-loving, but they do not like their paws to be stepped on, whereas Dragons are born paw-crushers. For a while the Rabbit will stoically endure this hurricane which several times a day devastates his chest of drawers, changes objects around and creates draughts (slamming doors are extremely perturbing to the well-bred Rabbit). So, one day, he will confront the Dragon — and it will not be the Dragon who has the last word, for Rabbits only appear to be weak. On the other hand, if the Dragon works away from home and the Rabbit keeps house, each will be free to organize his environment as he wishes, and everything will go well.

Rabbit/Horse
This combination is possible if the Rabbit is very much in love, for love makes him pliable. He is a sentimental and slightly romantic person, and the Horse's enthusiasm, warmth and passion will be irresistible to the Rabbit, who often hesitates to put himself forward; he will be admiring and breathless before the Horse's self-assurance. But when the Horse, in one of his spectacular changes of mood to which he is so often subject, collapses, saying that he is no good and that life is not worth living, the Rabbit will be able to comfort and coddle him.

Rabbit/Snake
They have in common a love of peace, security and aesthetic taste. They will tend to give preference to their home, environment and comfort and will appreciate beautiful objects and places. They would make a good pair of decorators. To have peace the Rabbit will have the wisdom to let the Snake think that he is the boss and master — at least on the emotional level. But the Rabbit's hesitations, and above all his virtuous side, will annoy the Snake whose sense of values is much more elastic.

However, whether it be love or friendship, this tie will be

profitable for both. With patience, the Rabbit will perhaps succeed in persuading the Snake to accept another's opinion; and the Snake, who does not fear danger and adapts to all situations, will teach the Rabbit to be more philosophic.

Rabbit/Goat

A very good alliance. Like the Rabbit, the Goat likes tranquillity, and he adapts to almost any kind of life which allows a minimum of liberty and offers him enough grass to graze on. The Rabbit is affectionate without being too possessive, and his love for the home brings an element of security to those in need of it.

The imagination and fantasy of the Goat will delight the Rabbit and help him escape the daily rut he has a tendency to fall into. The Rabbit's seriousness and his habit of perseverance promise well for the family finances. However, this couple will be vulnerable if an external crisis, a professional setback, an unforeseen loss of money or a domestic accident should occur, for the Rabbit and Goat find it difficult to depend on each other, and their relationship may be difficult to preserve. With each suffering from acute anxiety — the Rabbit for the future, the Goat for the present — they risk making mountains out of molehills and over-dramatizing everything.

Rabbit/Monkey

The intelligent and wily Monkey knows very well how to manage his affairs, but from time to time he enjoys finding understanding and rest with the indulgent and discreet Rabbit. The Rabbit knows all about wiliness, using it himself to get out of many a difficult situation. The Monkey's advice will enable the Rabbit to add several strings to his bow by making him more reasonable.

These two can attain a form of intimacy and complicity which is extremely personal and from which most people will feel excluded. Moreover, they will be so interested in each other that they will barely wish to raise a large family.

In business their understanding can be ticklish because the Rabbit, who is strongly attached to principles, will be scandalized by the occasional nearly illegal convolutions of the Monkey. He will criticize him, even though at bottom he envies him, and the Monkey will make fun of the Rabbit and disregard his virtuous indignation.

Rabbit/Rooster

Whether their relationship is based on friendship, love or professional ties, this duo often risks ending in a fist fight. In fact, no Rabbit has the patience needed to endure the swaggerings and boastings of the Rooster, who often exaggerates — most of the time without reason — just to amuse himself or to see how people react.

The usually patient and peaceful Rabbit will watch his tolerance evaporate quickly. The Rooster makes him literally boil, and our Rabbit cannot stop himself from wanting to snatch at some of the Rooster's feathers in order to diminish his vanity. The Rooster, who actually has no bad intentions, will see the Rabbit's attitude as one of malice — and he will not be entirely wrong.

If the Rabbit is the male, he will seek to confine Mrs Rooster to a role of submissive housekeeper, she, in turn will take advantage of his first absence to fly out the window. If the Rooster is the male, his Rabbit wife will criticize him ceaselessly, which he will not understand.

Rabbit/Dog

With luck, this can result in a happy and stable union. Although commonly regarded as hereditary enemies, these two animals — astrologically and psychologically speaking — have many points in common. Both seek security, both are profoundly honest, even virtuous, and both fiercely protect their property. They will understand, listen to and reassure each other.

But what is the small factor of luck that is needed? It lies in the absence of any great social and political event occurring during the course of their lives together. If such an event should occur, the Dog will heroically swallow his fear and join up as a nurse, missionary or even as cook, since he will do anything to feel useful. The Rabbit, who detests trouble, will ponder for years whether or not to follow him.

Rabbit/Pig

The award for merit and honesty goes to this couple. There is no doubt about it: they will appreciate each other for their true value, holding in esteem those qualities with which they are both bursting. When the Pig wants solitude, the Rabbit will lead his life quietly, perhaps using the time to repaint their flat. Together, these two will carefully avoid revolutions and earthquakes. The intuitive Rabbit will help his Pig spouse to not be taken in by all the tricksters who pass by and, without annoying him, will advise him and make him aware of his errors. There is only one danger: the Pig is sensual, even somewhat lascivious, whereas the Rabbit is slightly prudish, believing that even the most passionate liaisons should be veiled in platonic sentiments and not displayed publicly. The Pig will burst out laughing at this idea and offer the Rabbit a copy of the 'Kama-Sutra'. The Rabbit will not find this terribly amusing.

SOME RABBIT CELEBRITIES

Anne Boleyn, Bolivar, Bonnard, Carlyle, Fidel Castro, Chardin, Agatha Christie, Confucius, Courbet, Marie Curie, Einstein, Max Ernst, Garibaldi, Grieg, Keats, Paul Klee, Luther, Catherine de Medici, Henry Miller, Offenbach, Eva Peron, Edith Piaf, Pirandello, Prokofiev, Racine, Raphael, Rommel, Schiller, Walter Scott, Simenon, Stalin, Stendhal, Toscanini, Trotsky, Queen Victoria, Orson Welles.

YOUR
COMPANION
IN LIFE

生命伴侣

After the Chinese sign of your year of birth, here is the sign of your hour of birth

What is a Companion in Life, as understood in Chinese astrology? It is a sort of 'ascendant' sign corresponding to your hour of birth. This Companion is another animal belonging to the Chinese cycle of the twelve emblematic beasts, who falls into step with you and accompanies you, ever ready to help you brave the traps and ambushes along your route. A permanent and benevolent shadow, he can render the impossible possible.

He is your counterpart, but with his own character and tendencies and with a different psychology. Both guardian angel and devil's advocate, he will be a witness to your life and an actor in it.

Have you ever felt, deep inside yourself, the subtle presence of another 'myself' inhabiting you and with whom you live, at times in harmony, at others in conflict? Another self who sometimes criticizes you and at others encourages you? That is your Companion in Life.

There are times when he will appear to be an imposter or an intruder. Certainly, he often questions your habits and your moral or spiritual complacency. Accompanied by this companion, a shadow within, the route is less monotonous and the voyager multiplies his chances of arriving at his chosen destination. This, however, in itself matters little, for it is the journey and the manner in which it is conducted that are important. Indolence is the greatest danger: your Companion is capable of arousing you from a lassitude of spirit and, to that end, if necessary, robbing you of your certainties, trampling on your secret gardens and, finally, tearing away the great veil of illusion.

It sometimes happens that your Companion is of the same sign as your year of birth, a twin brother in a way — for example, a Rabbit/Rabbit. In this case, you must recognize that he will compel you to realize yourself fully and to live the double aspect — the Yin and the Yang — that your bear

within yourself. In any case, you also bear within yourself the twelve animals. So, set out on the long route, ready for the great adventure: the beautiful voyage during which you will encounter the harmoniously entangled, the solemn and the grotesque, the ephemeral reality, the dream and the imagined.

Table of hours corresponding to the twelve emblematic animals

If you were **born** between		your **companion** is
	11 pm and 1 am	Rat
	1 am and 3 am	Ox
	3 am and 5 am	Tiger
	5 am and 7 am	Rabbit
	7 am and 9 am	Dragon
	9 am and 11 am	Snake
	11 am and 1 pm	Horse
	1 pm and 3 pm	Goat
	3 pm and 5 pm	Monkey
	5 pm and 7 pm	Rooster
	7 pm and 9 pm	Dog
	9 pm and 11 pm	Pig

These figures correspond to the *solar hour* of your birth. If necessary, you should check the summer times (Daylight Savings Time) and make the appropriate adjustment (sometimes two hours before or after statutory time).

THE RABBIT AND ITS COMPANION IN LIFE

 **Rabbit/Rat**

This is a curious mixture, to say the least. Are not these hereditary enemies 'condemned' to travel the same route? But do not be fooled, for this may be the best way to accomplish the voyage. An apprehensive Rat coupled with the eternally stalking Rabbit will not be easily deceived. Suspicious, both adaptable and aggressive, he will be ready to protect himself from predators and to go to any lengths to secure his comfort and vested interests. Also, the influence of the Rabbit will make the Rat less vulnerable to outbursts of passion. Calm and efficient, the Rat/Rabbit illustrates the aphorism 'Better to risk an intelligent friend than indulge a stupid one.'

 **Rabbit/Ox**

A home-loving conqueror! The route will be difficult: the Ox/Rabbit will oscillate between anger and silence, and will hesitate between leaving entirely and retiring into contemplation. If at times the Rabbit element is a sort of ball and-chain on the Ox, this will have its uses. Knowing in certain situations how to inspire prudence, calm anger and unknot nerves, the Rabbit can soften the stubbornness in which the Ox becomes entangled and stifled. Meanwhile, Ox will teach his Companion that real space and liberty cannot be measured by surface area alone, such as the size of the Rabbit's burrow. Which will win out — prudence or stubbornness? Take care, Ox/Rabbit, you are in danger of going round the world without leaving your room.

 **Rabbit/Tiger**

Be careful of this animal; its appearance is deceptive. All gentleness on the outside — softly furry and velvety — he is mistakenly trusted. What makes the Tiger makes the Rabbit, and what makes the Rabbit makes the Tiger — all the better to eat you up. The Rabbit in the skin of a Tiger will find himself perfectly at ease; as for the Tiger, what could be easier than to give the illusion of being a harmless, large, striped tomcat. Essentially, game for the Tiger/Rabbit will involve sowing illusions and creating confusion among other animals: imagine Rudyard Kipling's Tiger meeting up with Bugs Bunny.

 **Rabbit/Rabbit**

He is a mysterious and enigmatic animal, who cultivates a pronounced taste for secrecy; nothing is simple or self-evident for him. Morbidly prudent (he will plan his route meticulously, foreseeing a host of eventual difficulties and how to avoid them), his journey will be transformed into a marathon. Do not hope to get the better of him while he is asleep: he sleeps with one eye open and the other on the look-out. The Rabbit/Rabbit will be a great seducer, refined and perceptive, but beneath his velvet paws, his claws are never completely drawn in. This lover of hiding places and comfortable nooks should overcome his fear of giving himself in a relationship; otherwise he may end up in a lonely corner.

 **Rabbit/Dragon**

This companion will bring him self-confidence, and he will feel his wings growing, be they made of lace or scales. The Rabbit/Dragon will be audacious, equipped with a lively and shrewd intelligence. He will be a seductive prince endowed with a complex brain; a mysterious being gliding among fairy-like worlds and parallel universes. However, he should be wary of a type of aggressiveness revealed in an attitude of 'I know everything; I have seen everything'. He is the guardian of a secret or treasure and has the soul of a fantasist; a lunar vagabond with magical powers, in search of the marvellous.

 **Rabbit/Snake**

A strange creature, whose head is not easily distinguished from its tail. In love with anything strange, but not an adventurer, the Snake/Rabbit will daydream about travelling while curled up in a soft armchair. 'Inhabited' by a price of wanderings, he has a taste for suspense, mystery and the subterranean, discovering hiding places buried under a stone. He will not hesitate to take on the colour of a wall for the pleasure of deceiving, surprising and disconcerting you. Elusive, clever and shifty, he is as dangerous as he is seductive. If you meet up with a Snake/Rabbit, pinch yourself, because he is a professional spell-binder. He will seduce you somehow — with his charm or by blackmail.

 **Rabbit/Horse**

Something of an unprincipled opportunist, he will be slightly mystifying. Irresistibly attracted by all that glitters, he will alternate between being impetuous and prudent. The Horse/Rabbit is a winner; he refuses to run for cover, even when security requires it. For him, a thrilling route is a necessity, and he obtains his goals. This war-horse will not allow others to step on his toes or obstruct him.

 **Rabbit/Goat**

He will be a sweet dreamer, living far from reality in a world of clouds. If he cannot find the comfort which is so dear to him, he will seek it in his dreams. He will love travel, always seeking something more marvellous. He has a supple nature and is intuitive and charming; nothing will seem to ruffle him, for he has the gift of assimilating the most trying situations into his creative universe. Both collar and leash will be rejected by the Goat/Rabbit for he is the type who is always on the loose, ever-ready for adventure.

 **Rabbit/Monkey**

He will be an inventive, lively, rather airy animal. He will have a tendency to be calculating, and will leave nothing to chance. He prefers being a schemer, conjuror and scrounger to labourious and irksome work. The Monkey/Rabbit envisages life as a game which, for the fun of it, he himself strews with traps and mirages, the better to zigzag between them. To attain his ends, he throws scruples to the wind. He will not hesitate to cheat, but who is he deceiving? He does not know himself, unless one day the Sphinx asks him the question.

 **Rabbit/Rooster**

He will always keep his eyes peeled. He must always be entitled to the right to look, to control a situation and to feel he is the master of his destiny. He is not the kind to let himself be guided. He is a curious mixture in which the call of the dawn is coupled with the murmurs of the night. The voyage will be profitable if the prudence of the Rabbit is allied with the tenacity and loyalty of the Rooster. The Rabbit/Rooster is a generous, lively animal with a pure heart. His spur and his claw will be used defensively rather than offensively.

 **Rabbit/Dog**

In this person the Dog element should be recognized as a guide and guardian, a faithful Companion into the invisible world which lies beyond the voyage of life. The egotistical Rabbit will discover that a precious ally lies within him. The Dog/Rabbit is circumspect, sometimes to the point of sickly distrust. While the sun may be shining on him, he will still be thinking only of the darkness to come. This animal is incapable of living in the present and has a tendency to become obsessed with past failures and future difficulties. He will weep for himself, his often imagined ills, and be depressed by the size of his task! In such moods he is incapable of looking at the simple spectacle of life going on around him, let alone enjoying it.

 **Rabbit/Pig**

A solitary animal who is slightly disquieting but perfectly organized. There exists an air of mystery about him; one never knows the real truth. Amassing great wealth, he lives in luxurious comfort but without neglecting the cultivation of his mind. Seductive, he is given to good and bad excesses, a distinction he prefers to ignore. If you corner him, he may either slip away or attack — unless he merely gives you a reply that leaves you breathless. This Rabbit/Pig is often master of a palace of mirages constructed on a base of others' gullibility.

THE RABBIT AND THE FIVE ELEMENTS

五行

YOUR ELEMENT

In Chinese astrology, each year is joined to an Element. There are five Elements: *Water, Fire, Wood, Metal, Earth.*

Each of the twelve emblematic animals is linked successively to each of the five Elements. For example, in the year 1900 the Rat was Earth, in 1912 he was Fire; in 1924 he was Metal, in 1936, Water and in 1948 he was Wood. Therefore, for the twelve years from 1900 he was linked to Earth, for the next twelve years to Fire, and, for every succeeding period of twelve years, to each of the other Elements, in succession.

In order to determine the Element corresponding to the year of your birth, use the table below:

> *Years whose digits end in:* 1 and 6 — Water
>
> 2 and 7 — Fire
>
> 3 and 8 — Wood
>
> 4 and 9 — Metal
>
> 5 and 0 — Earth

The same union of *Animal-Element* repeats every sixty years, for example, Rat-Earth appeared in 1720, 1780, 1840, 1900, 1960 and so on.

The five Elements are the primary forces affecting the universe. It is their particular association with each of the signs which provides the basis for every horoscope. Movement and fluctuation, Yin and Yang, these symbolic forces are in a perpetual state of action and interaction.

Wood gives birth to Fire, which gives birth to Earth, which gives birth to Metal, which gives birth to Water, which in turn gives birth to Wood.

RABBIT/WATER
(you were born in 1951)

The cold born of the northern sky descended to Earth and gave birth to Water. The Chinese consider Water more a synonym for coldness and ice than a symbol of fertility.

Characteristics of the Rabbit/Water
Water of winter nights, cold, rigour and severity; calm and deep Water to be feared and respected, still Water sheltering underwater demons asleep in its depths; foetid and muddy Water of the marshes, a refuge of crawling creatures.

Although not a fanatic about swimming, the Rabbit/Water wil feel at ease in this still water — unless it becomes a swamp, which could quickly absorb him, plunging him into a perilous situation while simultaneously reinforcing his tendency to inaction and a fear of becoming involved. Snug and warm, he can construct a cosy refuge in it and allow himself to be swallowed up; unless it is cold and clear and the Rabbit uses it to remedy his sluggishness.

Health of the Rabbit/Water
The Water organ is the kidney; its flavour is salty. Take care not to lie too long in fresh water: its tonic effect soon wears off and becomes merely soothing. Look after your spine and kidneys; do not remain inactive.

The Rabbit/Water and others
The Rabbit/Water knows how to listen. He is calm and reflective, and refrains from excess and dissipation. However, if he is to govern his life he must overcome a certain timidity and learn the art of indulging those passions he tends to recoil from, while at the same time controlling them. The Rabbit/Water has a horror of difficulties and hates to make a fuss. He will be a good craftsman and a prudent businessman. A pacifist and humanist, he will be more concerned with social problems and the battle against injustice than with spiritual matters.

He will be a good father, but not very stimulating. Mrs Rabbit/Water will be an attentive, tender-hearted mother, but will rarely make decisions.

Advice for a Rabbit/Water
You lack self-confidence. Leave your soft nest from time to time, forego your comfort and discard your slippers. You do not lack the ability to be dashing, but you always remain in the background. Be less passive; unless you want to perish from asphyxiation you must move about more. Do not continually rely on life-jackets; learn the crawl or build a raft.

A Rabbit/Water year
The culminating point of a Rabbit/Water year will be winter, a period of gestation.

A year of reflection rather than of action. However, do not become bogged down nor flounder about too much. If you do not sometimes leave your retreat you will have a false idea of things and of the world around you. Make this a year for projects and leave the flowers in your garden to bloom in their own good time. Practise cultivation in the fresh air, not in a greenhouse.

Historical example of a Rabbit/Water year 1951

In March, General MacArthur counter-attacked in Korea. He recaptured Seoul, the southern capital, and crossed the 38th parallel.

This war was the first to be fought under the idealistic banner of the United Nations and proved to be the last campaign they could support. The former pro-consul of Japan wished to carry the war into the mainland of China and there to assert by use of the nuclear weapon the beneficent powers he had exercised after the destruction of Hiroshima and Nagasaki. He argued that the initial aggression against Korea, although initiated by the Soviets, had been sustained by the Chinese alone who had gambled on the war being limited to the use of conventional weapons. Therefore America could equally gamble that Russia would not resort to their use in order to protect China.

These engaging equations were swiftly dismissed by President Truman. But MacArthur resisted. He resisted all attempts to negotiation, reasserted the need for a nuclear strike and sought thereby to reinstate Chiang-Kai-shek and to assert American dominance in China. Inflamed with the self-esteem he had garnered in Japan, MacArthur failed to appreciate that the vast territories of China were impervious to nuclear destruction and that their occupation under an American aegis would necessarily bring about a potent reaction from the Russians. Truman's policy accorded with the expressed view of the United Nations — to secure the independence of South Korea and otherwise to restore the status quo. Recalled to the Pentagon, MacArthur was greeted by the American people as a hero; but Truman neutralized him. Truman was a statesman. He was prepared to demonstrate that the United States would act to curb aggression; he himself would curb any instincts for wider conquests.

RABBIT/WOOD
(you were born in 1903 or 1963)

To the East, the wind blew in the sky and from its warm caress of the Earth, Wood was born.

Characteristics of the Rabbit/Wood
Wood is of the morning and of springtime. Its temperate nature loves harmony, beauty and elegance. It is an Element which suits the Rabbit perfectly. He will rediscover the mildness of the fertile and creative mid-season, which will restore his equilibrium, release his inventive powers and reinforce his taste for the beautiful. He will be pushed out of

his nest and discover the spectacle of dawn. This Element will develop in the Rabbit a sense of adventure, a passion for travel and a love of nature. But Wood is also a symbol of violence, even of destruction and self-destruction. Although he will not lose his dignity nor his reserve, the Rabbit/Wood will be vulnerable to internal jolts and passionate love storms which will leave him giddy and bewildered. If your instinctive impulses are allowed to dominate you, they will blind you. Overcome your aggressiveness; do not allow yourself to be drowned by your emotions.

Health of the Rabbit/Wood

The organ of Wood is the liver; its flavour is acid. The Rabbit/Wood will often be anxious, anguished and tormented. He will tend to worry and fret. Do not bite your paws, and be careful not to overeat.

The Rabbit/Wood and others

Socially, the Rabbit/Wood is relaxed and calm and well in control of his anguished nature which, if unrestrained, would lead him to fail in all his enterprises and be catastrophic for those around him. His tendency to be self-destructive would be nourished and lead him to ruin. Faced with established rules, the Rabbit/Wood opts for a supple attitude. He prefers to improvise and allow his imagination free rein, which encourages his creative spirit. The Rabbit/Wood has poetic gifts and is attracted to the arts in general — unless he chooses horticulture or landscaping, which can please his sense of beauty and harmony while fulfilling his need for space and liberty.

Advice for a Rabbit/Wood

You possess a good figure and are elegant, poetic and have an artistic soul. You do not appreciate restraints and obligations, so take responsibility for yourself and do not impose rigid restrictions on yourself or you will explode. Leave your anxiety in the cloakroom, polish your act as the aesthetic seducer and allow yourself to enjoy the applause.

A Rabbit/Wood year

The culminating point of a Rabbit/Wood year will be spring, a period of growth and prosperity. He will be alive with a new energy urging him to create, whose principal source of inspiration will be nature. It is a year of harmony and suppleness which he must make use of with art and mastery. In some cases, however, the tendency may be reversed: there are criminal acts and conspiracies in the air.

Historical example of a Rabbit/Wood year 1963

John F. Kennedy's father was remembered in England with anger and resentment. He had not only scoffed at the government but at the country to which he was accredited as ambassador during the years of Hitler's rise to power and the war which followed. He appeared to represent the bleak lack of comprehension of the monied Puritan from the United States, embodying an ignorant contempt for the past and stultifying envy for those who claimed one.

Yet his son, when elected President of the United States, was greeted and acclaimed in England as elsewhere. In the early days of an optimistic decade, he came like a dawn, a new hope for the spirit of integrity and decency in the civilized world. His mistakes were quickly forgiven; his successes as quickly acclaimed. He revived the belief in the power and efficacy of American optimism, its innocence and its urgency, and he appeared to unite an understanding of the nature of the human predicament with a capacity to solve its immediate problems.

Yet Kennedy was probably better regarded anywhere than in his own country. His policies were resented and many of his measures obstructed in Congress. In Texas, he was warned, trouble might be expected when he visited Houston. His policies were not favoured there. To some extent, Houston represented the heartland of the right, bent to the very attitudes which Kennedy had publicly deplored.

Kennedy's assassination both shocked and alarmed the world. The Europeans in particular feared the discovery of some Soviet complicity. This was a foolish misjudgement. Khrushchev and Kennedy understood each other: neither wished the other to be replaced. It was to the credit of both the governments of the United States and of the Soviet Union that this dangerous theme was never allowed to develop. It has been said that Kennedy could never have fulfilled his programmes or his promise. His death marked an end to a potent inspiration to which even de Gaulle seemed willing to respond.

RABBIT/FIRE
(you were born in 1927)

Heat was born in the southern sky, descended to Earth and fertilized it. From their union, Fire was born.

Characteristics of the Rabbit/Fire
The Fire Element is of the midday, the South and summer. Fire is Yang; it is the Element which animates, quickens and transforms.

Fire, in a Rabbit with a Yin tendency, of the full moon in mid-autumn, will make him dynamic. This Element will catalyze your energy, releasing a boldness and rashness which will dominate your instinct for prudence and reserve. It will be an inner flame that strengthens your courage; a creative flame, a keen and rapid force and a giver of light. But it will also be a power which devours and consumes. The Rabbit should learn to control it, lest it become destructive; and maintain it, lest it goes out.

Health of the Rabbit/Fire
The organ of Fire is the heart; its flavour is bitter. Fire of

summer and of the South, it will consume the Yin of the Rabbit. Be careful of changes in temperature. Avoid outbursts of anger and distrust your tendency towards aggressiveness — do not allow yourself to become violent. Keep a close watch on your heart. Eat vegetables rather than meat.

The Rabbit/Fire and others

Fire is often a symbol of war, passion and violence. The Rabbit/Fire prefers aggressiveness and open confrontation to diplomatic compromise; coming to terms is not his strong point. A man of action and combat, he combines energy with daring. However, due to his prudence and reserve, he will not hesitate, if need be, to send others to the frontline so that he can be the first to reap any rewards. The Rabbit/Fire will be artistic, original and anticonformist, and will be happy in this environment provided his life is well-organized.

Advice for a Rabbit/Fire

Although you are strongly attracted to distinguished and bold actions and wild adventures, you should remain faithful to your deepest nature. Reason should always be in control of your excesses, which are not always sincere unless they are symptomatic of an inner crisis and are thus therapeutic.

A Rabbit/Fire year

The culminating point of a Rabbit/Fire year will be summer, a period of creation, material and spiritual uplift and action, but often slightly consuming. The Rabbit will leave the full moon of mid-autumn to warm himself in the summer sun of the South. His Yin tendency will move towards the Great Yang, which will provide him with remarkable dynamism.

Historical example of a Rabbit/Fire year
1867

This was the year of the second Reform Bill in England

enacted by the Conservative government of Derby and Disraeli. Lord Derby later described it as 'a leap in the dark', for it was a measure which Gladstone and the Liberal party might more naturally have put in hand. The cynics regarded it as a measure to 'dish the Whigs' but Disraeli claimed that the policy it enshrined demonstrated that Conservative policy was the policy of true progress. Disraeli's biographer, Robert Blake, writes:* '. . . the picture of what happened has often been distorted. The most popular version . . . is that Disraeli enfranchised the householder at Gladstone's behest, in order to keep office; that the working-class household having received the vote from Disraeli said "thankyou Mr. Gladstone"; and accordingly voted him into power in 1868. His [Gladstone's] amendments were invariably defeated, and he fades into the background during the later stages of the debate. As for the gratitude of the working-class householders [they] . . . did not get on the register in time for the 1868 election . . . but if the Liberal myth dissolves on examination, so, too, does a scarcely less widely held Conservative one . . . . All the evidence of his contemporary papers suggests that Disraeli saw the electorate in traditional terms of rural voters being Conservative, urban voters Liberal; and that he thought of politics as a matter of "management" and "influence" in the old-fashioned sense, not mass persuasion of a new class.' Yet, as Blake concedes, many of the newly enfranchised in the towns did, in fact, tend to vote Conservative. Imperialism and social reform attracted them, a fact intuitively understood by Disraeli. That was not a proper subject for his papers on the Bill, however, which had to be fought on more formal grounds. In those fields Disraeli was a politician of genius and a parliamentarian of unrivalled skill.

*Disraeli, Robert Blake, London, 1966.

RABBIT/EARTH
(you were born in 1915 or 1975)

Earth was born from the slowly falling Elements of the sky at its humid zenith.

Characteristics of the Rabbit/Earth

This is an afternoon Earth, the humid and hot Earth of summer. It is the symbol of the well-cushioned, soft nest, of comfort and abundance; an Earth of slow and profound transformations. It is a blessing for the Rabbit, a warm refuge for repose and solitude, inviting him to meditate and dream. Here he will be far from the aggressions of the outside world, safe from indiscreet looks, trials and tribulations. But care is needed: the Rabbit tends to be a bit of a stay-at-home, and the Earth Element is likely to aggravate this tendency, turning him into a lazy and sated animal.

Health of the Rabbit/Earth

The Earth's organ is the spleen; its flavour is sweet. A sensualist, complete with moustache and cushions, inclined to the good life, the Rabbit/Earth should leave his nest and indulge in sports for the sake of his mental health. If the Rabbit/Earth does not rouse himself he will become a short-winded, fat miser.

The Rabbit/Earth and others

This Rabbit will certainly have his paws on the ground. Materialistic and prudent, he will be a good financier, subtle banker or a shrewd businessman. He will be the kind of whom one says 'he made himself through sheer hard work'. And this is true: he is a hard worker who accumulates the fruits of his efforts and will amass money and speculate with it. He possesses a strong family sense and will often be a despotic parent, brooding over his offspring to the point of smothering them.

Advice for a Rabbit/Earth

Above all, do not become too wrapped up in yourself. Broaden your horizons, take a holiday, mingle with others or participate in group work. Do not confine yourself to a world of mortgages and inventories. You need outdoor activity. Interest yourself in something other than your nest and your clover. Find a hobby. A little passion in your life would help to loosen your overly rigid life style.

A Rabbit/Earth year

The culminating point of a Rabbit/Earth year is summer. It is favourable year in which the Rabbit will no longer have to hunt to feed himself and he will be served on a silver platter. Thus freed from daily obligations, the Rabbit should offer his services to some charitable activity. Be watchful of your attitude towards your personal comforts — you could well become narcissistic.

Historical example of a Rabbit/Earth year 1795

The occupation of Holland by the French, who renamed it the Batavian Republic, directed the attention of the English to the Dutch possessions in the East Indies. In a deep maritime thrust they captured Capetown and Ceylon before investing the former colonies of Holland. Another force was sent to contest the possession of the French West Indian islands, the very troops promised for an attack on the French Riviera designed to coincide with a new campaign by the Austrians. This dispersal of naval forces weakened the blockading fleet off Toulon from which the French fleet escaped intact to secure a great Levenat convoy bound for England. Thus although France was not secure she was no longer in imminent danger; the absolute stringencies imposed by Robespierre and the Terror were no longer acknowledged to be necessary for the public safety. In this young republic given to extremes the reaction was forthright. Robespierre and his chief supporters were arrested, tried and sent to the guillotine on 27 July.

The atmosphere in France changed to one of almost drunken levity. Those younger members of the nobility who had survived took the lead in promoting a reign of pleasure, affecting an extravagance and sophistication of manner as extreme as their dress. Their idol Mme Tallien, on the other hand, affected a minimum of clothing at her celebrated salons. The wealth and interests of the middle classes quickly resumed their sway and the new constitution promulgated in September was expressly designed to produce a weak executive answerable to the propertied class. This development was resented by the royalists of the extreme right and the ultras of the left. Their insurrection proved a turning point in the history of France, for Barras called on the young Napoleon Bonaparte to restore order. It was thus that he came to command the armies with which he would conquer Italy.

RABBIT/METAL
(you were born in 1939)

In the sky, coming from the West, drought grazed the skin of the Earth and gave birth to Metal. Winds come from the far-away steppes seeking the vital sap.

Characteristics of the Rabbit/Metal
Metal is of the night, of autumn and cold. It symbolizes clarity, purity and precision. Its tendency is to be cutting, rigid and chaste, its comments harsh. The Rabbit/Metal will

oscillate between beauty and destruction. He will be expert at putting his plans into effect. At harvest-time, he will be the blade that gleans. Alas, too rigorous a regime will bring sadness and moroseness.

It can be a beneficial time for the Rabbit who is often unselfconscious, detached and prudent, bringing him a sense of responsibility and an indication of the plan he should follow. Unfortunately, rigid plans do not suit his supple spine. Therefore the Rabbit should beware of excess and recognize that strength of purpose does not necessarily mean stiffness. Moreover, the Metal Element is attracted to mystical perspectives which, although not a summons to an authentic vocation, can become an alibi or a dangerous refuge for him. The Rabbit/Metal seeks solitude, but sometimes has difficulty attaining harmony between his body and his soul.

Health of the Rabbit/Metal

Metal's organ is the lung; its flavour is pungent. In seeking an equilibrium, the Rabbit/Metal must keep a watch on his lungs, for their proper function is a source of physical and spiritual harmony. Blockages of all kinds can be dangerous. Do not allow your organs and heart to dry up!

The Rabbit/Metal and others

The Rabbit/Metal is energetic, constant and a man of his word. He can be a warrior or a man of the law. He commands, judges and decides. He has a good feel for organization, but at times may be slightly too blunt in his approach — plain-speaking will come more easily to him than tact and diplomacy. Maintain the moral and physical suppleness of the Rabbit; a stiff neck and a dry, cold heart are not in the nature of your symbolic animal. Rediscover agility, grace and patience. Be energetic, but do not forget that the excessive, in any form, turns against its author. File down your claws and become more supple; indulgence is not necessarily self-indulgence.

Advice for a Rabbit/Metal

Do some relaxing exercises or yoga. Write poems and listen to music; do not encase yourself in an iron corset — it will harm your fur.

A Rabbit/Metal year

The culminating point of a Rabbit/Metal year will be autumn. You will often experience a loss of energy and dynamism, and suffer from depression and a lack of self-confidence. This may perhaps be due to a lack of suppleness or a certain moral stiffness which does not suit your deepest nature. A period of waiting and uncertainty.

Historical example of a Rabbit/Metal year
1519

The Emperor Maximilian I was dead. His eldest grandson, Charles King of Spain and the Two Sicilies, ruler of Burgundy and the Netherlands was the natural claimant by blood. Francis I claimed the historic right as King of France and heir to Charlemagne. Charles put himself forward as a true German and the only person with sufficient resources to resist the Turks, then threatening the entire fabric of Christian Europe. Francis replied that the Empire was not the monopoly of one family, that he alone as the true and historic heir to Charlemagne embodied the chivalry of the civilized world and was the natural guardian of its values against the rapacity of the Spanish King.

However, it was not these formal appeals and dissertations which were to secure the election of the Emperor. The decisive advantage lay with Charles who had immediate access to the resources of the great Fugger banking house in Antwerp. No one could then match them in experience or influence. It was they who secured Charles's election; but not without conditions. The so-called 'Capitulation of Election' bound Charles to observe all princely privileges and to obtain the approval of the

Electors to legislation, treaties, taxes and imperial policy. The hiring of foreign mercenaries was forbidden him.

These were conditions which Francis would have found intolerable but they were acceptable to Charles. At heart he was an ascetic, indeed he was to end his days in monastic seclusion. He wished only to guide imperial policy towards that unity of Christendom laboured for by the medieval papacy.

Analogical Table
of the Different Elements

Elements	Wood	Fire	Earth	Metal	Water
Years ending in	3 and 8	2 and 7	0 and 5	4 and 9	1 and 6
Colours	Green	Red	Yellow	White	Blue
Seasons	Spring	Summer	End of summer	Autumn	Winter
Climates	Wind	Heat	Humid	Dry	Cold
Flavours	Acid	Bitter	Sweet	Pungent	Salty
Principal organ	Liver	Heart	Spleen	Lungs	Kidneys
Secondary organ	Gallbladder	Small intestine	Stomach	Large intestine	Bladder
Food	Wheat, poultry	Rice, lamb	Corn, beef	Oats, horse	Peas, pork

Table of Harmony
Between the Elements

		Wood Female	Fire Female	Earth Female	Metal Female	Water Female
○○○ Excellent prosperity	Male Wood	● ●	○	○ ○ ○	○	○ ○
○○ Good harmony, understanding	Male Fire	○	○	○ ○	●	● ●
○ Effort needed	Male Earth	● ●	○ ○	○ ○	○ ○ ○	●
● Rivalries and problems of reciprocal domination	Male Metal	○	● ●	●	● ●	○ ○ ○
● ● Misunderstanding and incomprehension	Male Water	○ ○	● ●	●	○ ○ ○	○

THE FOUR SEASONS OF THE RABBIT

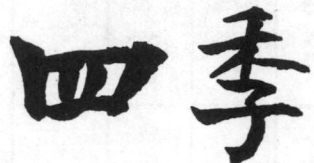

If you were born in spring

Rabbit/Aries

The positive points of this alliance result from the profound differences that exist between a Rabbit and an Aries. The Rabbit is sedentary, prudent and peaceful (do not forget that the sign of the Rabbit is also a Cat, and neither are especially daring). On the other hand, those born under the sign of Aries are impulsive, active and spontaneous. If all that is put into the same pot, boiled and stirred long enough, a harmonious mixture is produced. Thus we find a Rabbit/Aries who is reasonably moderate and active and who, with a shrewd eye, murmurs to us from his comfortable cushion, 'excess in anything is a defect'. Then, quicker than lightning, he snatches a pawful of clover, swallows it whole and licks his lips with an innocent air. In sum, an effective Rabbit who does well in his Rabbit profession.

There is obviously a lively combination of qualities in this mixture which may be usefully exploited in financial and professional areas: daring and prudence combine to avoid the ultraconservative as well as more risky schemes.

However, the Rabbit/Aries also has a slightly superficial quality, a need to shine in any field and to impose his views on matters which he does not really know much about. At the same time, he is sociable and friendly.

Rabbit/Taurus

The Rabbit/Taurus is either a delightful or maddening person, depending on whether or not one can adapt to the kind of life he likes to lead. He is firmly sedentary and attached to his slippers and garden.

For him, security is an end in itself and, to obtain it, he is capable of unusual effort, applying himself with perseverance and a remarkable sense of reality. He will be a prudent, clever, far-sighted businessman. If he does not climb to the top rung in international finance, it will be because at six in the evening something inside his head reminds him with the sound of sweet music that it is time to go home to dinner. He can work overtime in order to buy his son a bicycle, but never in order to hear himself called 'Chief'.

The Rabbit/Taurus is affectionate with his family and friends and likes nothing better than to gather them together at his own fireside. However, harmony is dramatically vulnerable to outside circumstances which might intrude upon him. The unforeseen is his nightmare, and he can be knocked completely off balance by an unexpected event affecting his security or wealth. A true Rabbit/Taurus will have a great deal of trouble not breaking a paw if he falls out of a window.

Rabbit/Gemini

This is the most agile and elusive of Rabbits, as difficult to capture as to hold. Always playing with danger, he never falls for the home-and-hearth life style so fatal for other Rabbits, but travels when he pleases, eats when he is hungry, allows himself to be caressed if he wishes and then disappears. He is very much a Rabbit who walks alone, wherever he feels inclined. There is nothing of the surburban commuter about this Rabbit.

This is not to suggest that the Rabbit/Gemini is not sociable. He likes conversation and to romp in gay company, but never to the extent of having to depend on others. He is as free within himself as he is independent of others. Structures and barriers are unknown to him; he follows only his fantasy and curiosity.

He is certainly unstable, yet remains extraordinarily adroit. He can get out of the most desperate of situations: when he is supposedly in prison for swindling, you will see his photo in the newspaper with the Prime Minister. Seeking surprises, he greatly enjoys causing them.

The Rabbit/Gemini is often unfaithful in love. He prefers variety to the daily routine in love affairs and friendship. Emotional rather than sensitive, it is not easy to move him to pity. Yet in his heart of hearts he fears solitude, and in this state is very vulnerable. It is up to others to know when to try and profit from this.

If you were born in summer
Rabbit/Cancer

These two signs share many tastes, in particular the apparent contradiction between their love of home-life and their taste for independence.

The Rabbit/Cancer draws in its claws, is affectionate and not particularly active. He is ready to make many compromises in order to preserve his security and to defend himself from the outside world. Faced with a problem, he pretends to sleep and develops a formidable case of inertia. But mistrust a sleeping Rabbit; pushed too far, he can become a ball of pins.

The Rabbit/Cancer likes to dream; sometimes he will do no more than daydream instead of setting about his tasks. Given enough encouragement, he will make an effort and complete what he has undertaken to do. He is somewhat erratic in this way. In his own world he likes to be paternalistic and often boasts a bit just to attract attention. Needing to feel in the centre of things, he badly needs to be taken care of. Moreover, everyone excuses his moments of boastfulness and touchiness, for he is amiable and faithful. He prefers the hearth to humid nights outdoors.

Rabbit/Leo

A royal Rabbit: his robe is sumptuous and he cares for it. He also tends to nurse his image and tries to live a life which is basically respectable. He enjoys his ease and tranquillity, but he quivers with pleasurable anticipation at the idea of competition: he immediately sees himself enthroned on a red satin cushion with an Order strung round his neck.

On the whole, he has an even and sociable disposition. He enjoys giving parties in his house, loves luxury and appreciates beauty and lovely objects. He also likes good food. His weak point is that he depends on a settled life. It is not that he lacks courage, but that he is by nature unwilling to face up to unforeseen mishaps or to anything which upsets his plans. He does not like to fail, detests promiscuity, vulgarity or even negotiating a mud-puddle. If totally put out he will at first panic and then, provided he can see his way clearly and is satisfied that the trouble is worth his attention, he will attack. This Rabbit is not bred for navigating in troubled waters; moreover, he hates water.

Rabbit/Virgo

Do not expect this prudent and discreet Rabbit to come up to a stranger and rub against his legs. Distrustful and distant, he advances slowly and methodically, ever on the alert. The Rabbit/Virgo will never willingly expose himself to danger.

He is an attentive and virtuous person, a stickler for honour, justice and duty. He can be annoying because at times he can be tiresomely wordy. He is so afraid of being caught making a mistake — and having to pay dearly for it — that he carefully calculates his approach. 'Once bitten twice shy' fits him like a glove. In fact, one often has the impression that his tenacious memory of past difficulties surfaces whenever he must grapple with a serious problem.

Foreseeing and wise, the Rabbit/Virgo succeeds without creating an uproar and knows how to gain the approval of his fellows, whose liberty he respects. However, in later years he can become dogmatic and grouchy, fuming for hours because his nest has been disorganized or his clover badly prepared.

If you were born in autumn
Rabbit/Libra

Do you remember the Cheshire Cat in 'Alice in Wonderland'? Seated in a tree, he would make himself visible and then disappear; only his smile would remain. There is something of this attitude in the Rabbit/Libra. He dislikes extremes and tense situations. He quietly nibbles his grass, moving slowly, an inch at a time, concerned with preserving the harmony of the moment and its particular ambience. He seeks refinement and certain aesthetic values.

A wordly and sociable Rabbit, he selects those in whom he has noted moral and physical elegance. He behaves with infinite charm, with bows and gracious gestures, preoccupied with a profound desire to please. He is capable of making many concessions to avoid a dispute but he detests being cornered and forced to make a hasty decision. It is then that he will resemble Alice's cat, climbing into his tree and observing you at length, with a debonair and sneering air. You will be the first to give up.

If he is in trouble, he is much more adaptable than the other Rabbits; he always lands on his feet and succeeds tactfully and without haste. Potentially a good diplomat, brilliant lawyer or talented artist, he is not made for manual activities, such as sawing wood.

Rabbit/Scorpio

He is soft, undulating and slightly fiendish. Sociable in appearance, he makes marvellous use of his charm and amiability curling up on your lap. To persuade you of his innocence he would be prepared to play with a doll and rattle.

But as soon as he opens his mouth he becomes scratchy, which comes as a surprise. In fact, the Rabbit/Scorpio is either an accomplished egotist, a refined opportunist, or a chronic neurotic who is anxious and ill-at-ease. He tricks his friends and shamelessly profits from them. The notion of good and evil, dear to our civilization, is simply an inconvenience to him. He would like to be tranquil, which he attains by sitting in the sun. But then night comes and, in spite of himself, he becomes transformed into a magician and a sorcerer. Perhaps the Rabbit/Scorpio remembers, deep in his subconscious, when he was once thrown onto sacrificial pyres, which is why he is uneasy.

His charm is fascinating, his power of conviction astonishing. He likes nothing better than to surprise his associates, alternating softness with sudden aggression. He is extremely prudent, perspicacious and intuitive: do not attempt to deceive him or try to make him believe that the moon is made of green cheese. He will throw himself at you and deliver a beautifully executed right hook.

In love he is sincere, but has trouble putting himself in another's place.

Rabbit/Sagittarius

At first glance this is a truly marvellous Rabbit. He is sociable and well-balanced; his daily routine does not obsess him. He is perhaps the only Rabbit capable of blossoming in his role as domestic as well as wild animal; he has both elements within him and passes from one to the other with marvellous ease. He is easy to live with and always in good humour.

But he is emotional rather than truly sensitive, very ambitious and sometimes egocentric; his generosity is only bestowed on those who are lucky enough to share his point of view. He likes to attract attention — to convince, persuade, seduce and shine. As soon as he sees a podium he wants to make a speech or, if he is timid, dreams of doing so.

An adventurous and audacious Rabbit, he is also a conformist who is strongly attached to his personal principles of honour, independence, and so on. He can be annoying due to his dogmatic side, and seductive due to his spontaneous and warm side. The Rabbit/Sagittarius has many defects, but he will never stab you in the back.

If you were born in winter
Rabbit/Capricorn

If you are feeling lonely one day and go to the pet shop to seek a companion, you will easily recognize a Rabbit/Capricorn; he remains apart from the others and will not come to charm you by rubbing against the bars of the cage. On the contrary, he will be seated at the far end, looking vaguely scornful. If you try to caress him he may even spit, so that you understand that not just anybody is allowed to paw him. But if you take him home and treat him with respect and pay him exclusive attention, you will have won a prize. For the Rabbit/Capricorn is the most faithful and stable of Rabbits. He is neither caressing nor demonstrative, but defends his home better than a watchdog; he can be counted on in all circumstances. He will not adapt in the face of catastrophe, for that is not his strong point, but he will cling heroically.

He is effective and persevering in his material life. Many lost Rabbits will travel over long distances, braving a thousand dangers to find their way home; they must be Capricorns born in a year of the Rabbit.

Rabbit/Aquarius

This combination will diminish considerably the egotistic side of the Rabbit because they are interested in the world surrounding their personal universe. The Rabbit/Aquarius rarely remains a traveller, a vagabond, keeping up friendly relations with almost everyone and enjoying a fair-haired Rabbit in each port. More gifted for friendship than love, he will be spontaneously unselfish. However, he is often a bit absent-minded and distracted.

Extremely creative and completely anticonformist, the Rabbit/Aquarius does not spend much time on reflection but his intellectual activity far exceeds his physical activity. He does not depend on guide lines, and a conventional scale of values will only imprison him. He navigates by guesswork, free as the air and as supple and whimsical as curling breezes. A precious and devoted friend, he knows nothing of jealousy but he is an unstable lover. However, he is marvellously tolerant, even slightly devil-may-care, and does not ask of others more than he does of himself, so one can willingly pardon him.

Rabbit/Pisces

The Rabbit/Pisces often lacks the most elementary practical

sense. Plunged into the most coolly delicious stream, he will dream of having a paraffin heater to increase the temperature. He is never competely content; he always needs a little bit more.

The Rabbit/Pisces is an accomplished dreamer who, if really motivated, can become a formidable opportunist. But this does not happen every day. The rest of the time he is half asleep, imagining terrible dramas, which tires him out. He is neither very persevering nor very active, but he is adorable and affectionate. He also needs a daily ration of affection and tenderness. Give him a tape recording which says 'I love you' every three minutes and do not be stingy with showing him your feelings. Your Rabbit/Pisces will then be in his element.

THE
I CHING

易经

THE I CHING AND THE RABBIT

In the I Ching game, you ask a question and you obtain an answer. It is therefore a divining game. But the question you ask is posed through your Rabbit identity; the wheels, the complex mechanism of your mind and spirit, begin to turn. You ask a Rabbit question and the I Ching answers with a Rabbit 'solution', on which you then meditate as a Rabbit before arriving at a Rabbit conclusion.

The player is presented with a hexagram which contains the 'hypothesis-response' to his question, or, more exactly, a synthesis of forces affecting the concern or event inquired about.

For you, Master Rabbit, here are the sixty-four hexagrams of the I Ching and sixty-four Rabbit hypotheses.

How to proceed
1. The question
Ask a question regarding any problem at all, past, present or future, personally concerning you. (If the question concerns a friend, consult the I Ching game in the book corresponding to his Chinese sign.)

2. Method of play
It must be done with concentration.
Take **three ordinary and similar coins** — for example, three 50p coins.
Heads will equal the number 3.
Tails will equal the number 2.
Throw the coins.
If the result is two coins showing Heads and one Tails, write 3 + 3 + 2. You thus obtain a total of 8 which you represent by a continuous line: ——

Draw the same continuous line if you have three coins showing Heads $(3+3+3=9)$.

If you throw two coins showing Tails and one Heads $(2+2+3=7)$, or all three showing Tails $(2+2+2=6)$, draw two separate lines: —— ——

To sum up, 8 and 9 correspond to: ———— (Yin)

6 and 7 correspond to: —— —— (Yang)

Repeat this operation *six times*, noting at the time of each throw the figure obtained on a piece of paper, proceeding from the first to the sixth figure, from bottom to top.

The final result, including a trigram from the bottom, or lower trigram (example:), and a trigram of the top, or upper trigram (example: ═══), will be a hexagram of the I Ching. In our example this would look like:

Now merely look for the hexagram number in the table on page 320, and then consult the list of hexagrams with their descriptions to find the given answer. *In our example*, the hexagram obtained is number 63, entitled **After completion.**

Table of Hexagrams

Trigrams	Upper lines ☰	☷	☶
Lower lines			
☰	1	11	34
☷	12	2	16
☶	25	24	51
☵	6	7	40
☴	33	15	62
☴	44	46	32
☲	13	36	55
☱	10	19	54

Use this table to find the number of your hexagrams. The meeting point between the lower and upper trigrams indicates the number of the hexagram that you are seeking.

☳	☶	☴	☲	☱
5	26	9	14	43
8	23	20	35	45
3	27	42	21	17
29	4	59	64	47
39	52	53	56	31
48	18	57	50	28
63	22	37	30	49
60	41	61	38	58

THE HEXAGRAMS OF THE RABBIT

CH'IEN

1 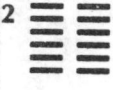 *The creative:* Energy, strength and will, the creative spirit. Master Rabbit will be in his element, he who knows so well how to combine prudence and reserve with a fertile imagination, sometimes reaching beyond the knowable to where dreams and reality are blended.

K'UN

2 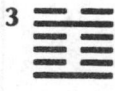 *The receptive:* You are bound to the Earth Mother. It will not be difficult for you to become aware of the elements surrounding you, for they are your tools: even when astride two worlds, do not forget them.

CHUN

3 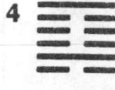 *The initial difficulty:* Unravel, clear away, seek the cause of the trouble. The situation is delicate and there are many obstacles, but a bit of perseverance will enable you to succeed.

MÊNG

4 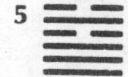 *Youthful folly:* 'It is not I who seeks the young fool, but the young fool who seeks me.' Generously support those who ask your advice, but do not allow yourself to be trapped.

HSÜ

5 *Waiting:* It is unnecessary to draw you a picture; waiting too is an art — and difficult to master.

SUNG

6  *Conflict:* Disguise and diplomacy are better than open warfare. The Rabbit who dislikes becoming involved or being in the forefront will opt for this technique.

SHIH

7  *The army:* Submission and discipline for a collective aim. Know how to join in: although you practise war on your own, with strategies and attacks which have ripened for a long time, know how to bend to the common rule.

PI

8  *Holding together (union):* Strength lies in union. A large bone for the Rabbit to swallow, a defender of 'everyone for himself'.

SHIAO CH'U

9  *The taming power of the small:* This is not the moment to use force, for you do not have enough strength. Goodness and gentleness will give better results.

LÜ

10  *Treading:* 'Tread on the tail of the Tiger, he does not bite man.' Pull in your claws, relax and place your paws between the stripes on the Tiger; it is not difficult, a simple question of balance.

T'AI

11 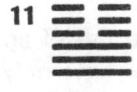 *Peace:* Or the harmony of opposites, which is always delicate to achieve. When dialogue is not possible, confusion reigns; choose peace, but remain vigilant.

P'I

12 *Standstill:* It is better to know how to pull back than to attack when the hour is not right. The art of waiting is a form of action; nothing good can come from hasty acts.

T'UNG JÊN

13 *Fellowship with men:* Even spiritual work is more difficult to accomplish with men than without. But there is work that one cannot accomplish alone. So, forget your egotistical preoccupations and spontaneously help those whose aims are worthy of your esteem.

TA YU

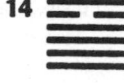

14 *Possession in great measure:* Whether this be material or spiritual, if you neglect it and fail to bring it to fruition good opportunities are likely to be missed.

CH'IEN

15 *Modesty:* Ride out the storm, trim your sails and seek the horizontal; water is its symbol. Exaggeraton in any field will incur disappointments.

YÜ

16 *Enthusiasm:* Although restraint and hesitation are valuable, it is time to take risks; do not play hide-and-seek with reality. You have imagination — use it.

SUI

17 *Following:* After seduction and the use of an 'iron fist in a velvet glove', you now have only to convince with a dose of powerful speech-making.

KU

18  *Work on what has been spoiled:* One does not cure the bad with indifference, nor difficulties with abandon. It is not advisable to make your nest in a minefield unless you know how to defuse the mines.

LIN

19 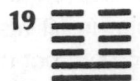 *Approach:* Do not forget that what you call 'today' is already the past. Rather, be preoccupied with the near future. Try to evolve and progress; you will meet with success.

KUAN

20  *Contemplation:* A Rabbit at the summit of a tower will be visible from afar. Your virtue will be put to a difficult test, for in making it public, you expose yourself to the danger of setting yourself up as an example.

SHIH HO

21  *Biting through (or clearly defined penalties):* Lying is not profitable; in giving it shape, think of the consequences. No liaison or association is reliable because the foundations are rotten. The house will fall down. So, burn the bad roots and attack, if only to set an example.

PI

22  *Grace:* Even when planning a sauce for the fish, there will always be bones to swallow.

PO

23  *Splitting apart:* Be on your guard, the edifice threatens to collapse from within. Be careful of what pours down.

FU

24 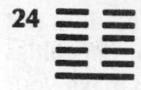 *Return (the turning point):* After spending some time with your head under a cushion, you can come up for air; the danger is past, the wheel turns.

WU WANG

25  *Innocence:* 'Man has received from heaven an essentially good nature to direct him in all his acts.' Your instinct does not mislead you; but it should guide rather than direct you.

TA CH'U

26  *The taming of the great:* Power and strength. This depends on your capacity for renewal. Do not fall asleep on your laurels.

I

27  *The corners of the mouth:* Symbol of nourishment of the body and the spirit: tell me what you eat and read and I will tell you who you are. There is no need to become a vegetarian in order to read the great philosophers. Be authentic.

TA KUO

28 *Preponderance of the great:* It is silly to try and move the mountain when one can go round it.

K'AN

29 *Fathomless water:* The danger comes from outside. Remain calm; pay no attention to fear and master your panic.

LI

30  *Clinging, fire:* Do not concentrate all your energies on a spider when the dogs are barking at the door. The danger is there, so do not weave your own cord but learn to unknot it.

HSIEN

31 *Influence:* You have charm and others are sensitive to it; you have fine qualities and they are noticed. Do not be capricious; drop your mask and take risks. Otherwise you will miss an opportunity — perhaps the opportunity of your lifetime.

HÊNG

32 *Duration:* To avoid stagnating, question yourself; this is painful but effective. Understand that when the wine has been uncorked, it has to be drunk.

TUN

33 *Retreat:* Without constraint or despair, therefore it can even lead to a tactical victory. Do not think of it as a rout.

TA CHUANG

34 *The power of the great:* Might allied with movement becomes a powerful attraction. There is danger of burning one's wings, like the moth and the flame.

CHIN

35 *Progress:* He who possesses radiance does not feel the need to shine. Do not refuse the earthenware bowl and demand a silver bowl; both contain food.

MING I

36 *Darkening of the light:* Do the housework, provide yourself with candles and wait for the storm to pass to relight the flame.

CHIA JÊN

37 *The family:* Has a good deal to be said for it, especially for a Rabbit who loves his tranquillity and comfort. If it seems like a prison, he should not forget that it is he who holds the key.

K'UEI

38 *Opposition:* Does not exist unless one creates it. Respect the harmony of opposites. Do not be opposed to the world.

CHIEN

39 *Obstruction:* Is not equivocal; jump the obstacle, undermine it or go round it. Refuse neither a rope, ladder, nor a helping hand.

HSIEH

40 *Deliverance:* It is today that you must set to work for tomorrow. Do not encumber yourself with painful memories; think of future trials; work to reestablish order.

SUN

41 *Decrease:* Hard to imagine for a fashionable man-about-town, a lover of luxury and ostentation. Flee from pomp, put out the chandeliers and light the candles. They are more poetic and economic.

I

42 *Increase:* Make the most of each minute, involve yourself and be opportunistic; even if you are anxious, keep smiling.

KUAI

43 *Breakthrough:* You cannot make an omelette without breaking eggs; the truth is not always good to hear, but it has to be said.

KOU

44 *Coming to meet:* Do not forget that certain concessions, even if they are humiliating, can reestablish equilibrium — but know how to choose your partner.

TS'UI

45 *Gathering together:* Around a family or a community. However, there is danger of infiltration; distrust unknown elements.

SHÊNG

46 *Pushing upwards:* The Rabbit should prove that he is meticulous and neglects nothing. He will mount the great staircase step by step or, if he feels too tired, will take the lift.

K'UN

47 *Oppression:* Your handsome speeches are no longer effective; they put your audience to sleep; you are losing punch. Do not wait to be backed into a corner before reacting; take a tonic and learn to jump on to the perch.

CHING

48 *The well:* Act on yourself, on nature and things without, however, changing vital structures.

KO

49 *Revolution:* Should not be carried out in the privacy of one's room. Do not fear eventual confrontations, for they will be positive; anticipate them if you do not want them to fall on your head.

TING

50 *The cauldron:* Symbol of the five Elements — Earth, Wood, Fire, Water and Metal. Work to nourish yourself physically and materially. Bread and knowledge do not fall from the sky.

CHÊN

51 *The arousing (shock, thunder):* Will be capable of awakening you and making you aware. Do not, however, change your itinerary; keep calm and accept the trials, for they are a part of your voyage.

KÊN

52 *Keeping still:* Let the tempest pass; find calm within yourself before confronting the tumult outside.

CHIEN

53 *Development (gradual progress):* Accept that you must sometimes bow; it is good for the health and makes one appreciate the vertical position.

KUEI MEI

54 *The bride:* Even if one plays at heartaches, get hold of yourself before succumbing.

FÊNG

55 *Abundance:* Will do no harm, but do not sink into complacence, the mother of egotism. For a time glide in its arms, but be careful of the fall.

LÜ

56 *The wanderer:* Since no one is a prophet in his own country, exercise your talents elsewhere. One must know how to detach oneself, to leave before sinking. Do not grumble — swim!

SUN

57 *The gentle:* The wind blows without violence, but penetrates where it wishes. Do likewise.

TUI

58 *The serene, the joyous:* Learn how to share and communicate. Persevere, but with suppleness.

HUAN

59 *Dissolution:* Be careful of egotism. By turning round and round on yourself, you will end by biting your tail.

CHIEH

60 *Limitation:* Should be understood as a means, not an end. It is not by crawling on your knees that you will be pardoned.

CHUNG FU

61 *Inner truth:* The way is not necessarily the Way. Do not seek to communicate what is incommunicable. Those who enclose God in words may become all-powerful, but only in the realm of words.

HSIAO KUO

62 *Preponderance of the small:* Even the most beautiful sand castles are carried away by the sea. It is folly to build great projects when one possesses only small means.

CHI CHI

63 *After completion:* The prince can become a merchant, but the merchant will never become a prince.

WEI CHI

64 *Before completion:* The seaweed clings to the rock in order to survive, not in the hope of becoming a rock; but joining the rock it welcomes the wave.

YEAR OF THE DRAGON

 1904·1916·1928
1940·1952·1964
1976·1988·2000

THE DOMAINS OF THE DRAGON

十二生肖

THE DRAGON AND ITS SYMBOLISM

It is not exactly a compliment to call someone a 'dragon', and it certainly does not evoke the image of a tolerant or docile person. This creature with scales, guardian of incredible treasures, is a symbol of breathtaking and implacable power. His favourite dwelling place is usually an impenetrable grotto, but the top of a rocky and inaccessible peak will also suit him. The more impregnable his dwelling-place, the more comfortable the Dragon feels: beneath the earth, at the bottom of the sea or in the sky. It is in these secretive, hidden places that adventurers and mythical heroes of the past have sought the Dragon, for whoever crushes him opens the gates to a great mystery and crosses the threshold to another world.

Spitting flames and making the earth tremble beneath his gigantic weight, soaring in the air on jagged and blackened wings, the Dragon tows our most frenzied dreams in his wake; our fears of chaos and annihilation, a procession of obsessions and phantoms which endure from time immemorial. This is why people have always carved the image of the Dragon in stone to decorate their temples and cathedrals: to exorcize and channel his formidable power. In China he is placed on the top of roofs or above doors to banish evil spirits and demons. During the New Year festival in Vietnam, a paper dragon is promenaded through the town and then burned to commemorate the year that has passed and the new one which will be reborn from its ashes.

Men have always contemplated the Dragon with a mixture of fear and respect, as though this creature represented the echo of the most hidden depths, the most unfathomable dimensions of the human soul. Annihilated by the archangel or metamorphosed into a prince charming, the Dragon always incarnates the final step, the ultimate trail before the ideal can be realized, the treasure possessed. He is an esoteric symbol of wisdom and enlightenment.

The Dragon is often portrayed with many heads, which represent the many teeming impulses and passions that lie within the depths of the human psyche. These heads symbolize those desires which haunt the night of the unconscious: if one is severed, another will grow in its place. Thus it is necessary to reach the heart, the root of the human being: in order to conquer the Dragon one must conquer oneself. This is why the blood of the Dragon is supposed to make one invulnerable or immortal.

This Dragon lives in an immense subterranean world filled with palaces, houses, towers and gardens. Sometimes he comes to stay on earth, living in inaccessible mountain caverns.

Generally an enemy of the gods, the Dragon is not against human beings — certain legends even speak of marriages between humans and Dragons.

In India the Dragon is considered to be the ancestor of the inhabitants of Kashmir; he is revered in the form of a half-man, half-dragon who possesses great courage and incomparable beauty. In homage, he is covered with jewels, a crown is placed on his head and his ears are adorned with rings of gold. As a totem of the Dravidians, the most ancient group in India, the Dragon is still venerated in all of the villages of southern India and in certain regions of Kashmir. Moreover, there is a curious connection between this cult and the Seraphs, who occupy an eminent place in the Christian hierarchy of angels. Depicted as surrounding God's throne, the terrifyingly montrous Seraphs remind one of the Dragon. The Seraph is also a fierce guardian of the Absolute, which brings to mind the notion of the Dragon's frontiers, of yet another threshold.

A few notes on the Dragon
Principal qualities: Active, dynamic, scrupulous — and lucky.
Principal defects: Demanding, impatient, intolerant.
Work: Not knowing that a chore is thought impossible, the Dragon will succeed where others have failed.

Best role: Oracle.
Worst role: Diplomat.
Money: Does not mean happiness; but he needs it to safeguard his independence.
Luck: He always has it, but it is better if he is not born during a storm.
Cannot live without: Space, oxygen, fresh air, liberty.
Adores: Being called upon to help when things go wrong.
Hates: To wait calmly and patiently.
Leisure activities: Loves science-fiction, watching for UFOs — in short, anything which takes him far from the good old earth.
Favourite places: The sky, the cosmos, or alone at the helm of a ship.
Colours: Black and yellow.
Plants: Sage and mandrake — sorcerers' plants.
Flower: Lotus.
Professions: Prophet, solicitor, orator, architect, artist, actor, meteorologist, astronomer, astronaut — preferably famous.

The four ages in the life of the Dragon according to Chinese tradition

The *childhood* and *youth* of the Dragon are difficult, for during these periods his need for support and his stubbornness will cause many problems with his family and friends. The gap between his ideal and reality will often make him extremely dissatisfied.

In *maturity* and *old age* he will probably find his equilibrium. However, he should always remember that the Dragon is a legendary, mysterious animal; he must not depend entirely on his brilliant appearance, for the illusion it projects will never last.

THE PSYCHOLOGY OF THE DRAGON

The Dragon is the only animal in the Chinese zodiac to exist solely in legends. He is a mythical, fantastic animal, and those born during his year are exceptional. Contrary to their predecessors, the Rabbits, they can only give their utmost in extreme situations: ordinary, daily life is not their strong point — or else they will transform it in such a way that it becomes exhausting for everyone.

Chinese tradition says that the Dragon is the sign of luck and truth; it is therefore advantageous to be in close contact with a person born under this sign.

Male and female Dragons are extremely overpowering: one must either be their friend or their rival — and it is not a simple matter to be the latter. They see and speak the truth, even though it is not always good to say it, and the advice they give is always worthwhile and wise, even when they announce it publicly rather than whisper it in private.

Alas, our Dragons are not always capable of making good use of their marvellous lucidity: they often point out dangers to their friends into which they will throw themselves headfirst without a thought. They possess intellectual wisdom, but their actions are not always wise.

Dragons are fascinating, gifted and impressively convinced that they hold the keys to success. Everything seems to smile on them, and they are fortunate in love.

Dragons have many qualities: they are full of energy, enthusiasm and vitality; they are frank and scrupulous, try to do their best and succeed, for they do not know the meaning of the word 'failure'. They are also healthy, natural, captivating, and full of charm, sincerity and devotion. Their defects are the reverse of their qualities: they are extremely impatient, cannot bear to wait for anything or anyone, and cannot understand why anyone should resist them. They are irritable and demanding with their friends and relatives. They completely lack the slightest bit of indulgence, and cannot be tactful or diplomatic even if their lives depend on it. Extremely self-assured, they can never understand the doubts or hesitations of others; if *they* feel capable of doing something, they feel that others should be able to do it too — with no further arguments.

Dragons are so convinced that they are infallible that they

behave horribly with those who are not. Intolerant and abrupt, they make decisions too quickly and have difficulty recognizing their mistakes. They barely listen to others, but adore being admired; when they are refused something, they will give an ultimatum and never go back on it.

How is it then that Dragons are so seductive and irresistible? It is simply that they represent life, warmth and light; without them, life would be extremely drab. Their unpredictableness, their good qualities — which are as extraordinary as their defects — give unexpected spice to our lives. They burn themselves out without leaving a trace — but what a beautiful bonfire!

The heroes in children's fairy tales must often fight a flame-spitting dragon bare-handed before attaining their heart's desire. Those born during a year of the Dragon must in a similar fashion confront their own image, which, according to Chinese tradition, is an illusion. It is only by accepting their own fragility, their 'transparence', that they can attain an equilibrium. This is extremely difficult, which is why many Dragons spend a great part of their lives avoiding this disagreeable fact, racing from experience to experience, accumulating successes and forgetting their failures.

Naturally, Dragons are intelligent and, above all, they know how to make use of their knowledge. They often seem more cultivated than they really are. They are fluent and are often found leading demonstrations or are the main speakers at public meetings; Dragons are rarely found in secondary positions.

Because they are made for exceptional situations, Dragons are usually bored and dissatisfied; they wait impatiently for the next storm to arrive.

THE DRAGON AS A CHILD

The young Dragon is independent and inventive. Although not a daredevil like the young Tiger, he needs to be given the freedom to experience things on his own and to assert himself. A routine, a precise timetable or strict discipline should not be imposed on him, for they would only lead to a lamentable lack of communication.

The young Dragon is capable of being an excellent student because he is gifted, brilliant and intelligent; but he does not work very hard, and detests being told to 'work first and play later'. He throws himself into his studies with the same intensity as into his play, wears himself out and then stops when he has had enough. He often appears stupid because he has not bothered to answer a question to which he knows the answer, simply because he is bored or the teacher has irritated him. His relations with his teachers are often difficult, for he is insolent, provocative and very annoying to those in positions of authority.

In fact, the little Dragon does not accept any controls; he does as he wishes and only accepts advice when it is given by someone he has not met before and who therefore seems exotic to him. He is both protective and indifferent towards his parents; he loves them but will refuse caresses or demonstrations of affection. The ideal for him would be to be given food and lodging, and to be left just about free for everything else. This is difficult, even in our permissive times, but if treated with tolerance and generosity — with nothing required in exchange — the little Dragon will become more human and blossom accordingly.

He has his first sexual adventures at a rather early age. It is best to give a girl Dragon some method of birth control during her adolescence without asking too many questions. But there is no need to worry: Dragons never allow themselves to become involved in emotional adventures over which they have no control.

LOVE LIFE

Dragons often behave as though they had 'I am absolutely irresistible' sung to them in the cradle. They are convinced that they possess phenomenal seductive powers — and they do! They have enormous charm and it never occurs to them that someone might be indifferent to it. They have never known an impossible love. If someone pleases them, they make a royal conquest and feel that they are 'honouring' the person by loving them. They believe this with such sincerity and total confidence that the chosen love begins to think so too.

Dragons rarely know what it is to suffer from an unrequited love; they succeed in their amorous endeavours 90 per cent of the time. Then, thanks to an attitude which is a curious mixture of passionate enthusiasm and detachment, they make themselves completely indispensable.

They are passionate, but never blinded by their passion. They know very well what they are doing and what they wish to obtain. Also, they can live very easily without-the object of their desire; Chinese tradition says that the Dragon is happiest when alone.

Neither possessive nor especially jealous, they will remain royally indifferent should their conquests flirt with others, usually in order to attract their attention. They are fully aware that they have only to raise their little finger to regain their 'possession'. They detest emotional outbursts of affection, tears or sentimental blackmail. If inflicted with any of these, they will take flight immediately.

Why is it so hard to resist Dragons? Because they are warm, understanding and dynamic; and their energy is so alive that it acts on others like a euphoric cocktail. With a Dragon, one feels more handsome, more intelligent and more alive. That is the secret of their success in love.

FAMILY LIFE

It is not surprising that Dragons are not family-minded or home-loving. A female Dragon will never accept being relegated to a domestic role. If Dragons marry early, which is often the case, it is simply to prove their independence and autonomy to their parents. They often divorce and remarry; generally, their second marriage is more successful than their first.

Since they are quite reasonable, Dragons will wait until

they are old enough and have enough money before having children. They are good, understanding and encouraging parents who do not stifle their offspring; on the contrary, they seek to encourage independence and the capacity to act alone and get along in life.

Dragon parents are, however, often extremely demanding and their children have trouble keeping up with and satisfying them. An Ox child will never be brilliant enough to please a mother or father Dragon; and a Rabbit child's lack of ambition will irritate his Dragon parents. Young Monkeys, Snakes or Horses will do what they wish with their Dragon parents, for they will know how to flatter, admire and manipulate them. Dragon parents will encourage the artistic gifts of the Goat; will accept the independent spirit of the Rat and will easily gain the obedience of the Rooster and Pig. The Tiger child will not learn moderation, but he will listen to their advice. A Dog child will be catastrophic for Dragons: he will never be duped by their brilliant facade and will criticize them continually.

PROFESSIONAL LIFE

Dragons detest routine; even more, they detest feeling cornered in a web of duties and obligations, required to respect a specific programme or timetable which has been fixed in advance.

They will demolish such structures and recreate programmes to fit their own rhythms. They are surprising and unpredictable: useless at monotonous tasks, they will become super-efficient when it is a question of doing something which others have been unable to because of the difficulties involved. Dragons seem to have been created especially to resolve insoluble problems; on top of which, they are never bored with such tasks.

But our Dragons must often be bored sitting at their desks because their qualities cannot be put to use without revolutions and other social and historical upheavals, which, unfortunately for them, do not happen every day. On the other hand, they can feel some satisfaction and will be appreciated if their work permits them to innovate, create and change; to make things and people come alive. For this reason Dragons should choose to work in new companies where they can become indispensable, rather than in highly organized businesses where they would be mere cogs in a wheel, and therefore miserable.

Because of the multiplicity of their gifts and interests, Dragons often pursue several different professions in the course of their lifetimes. This is because they need to experiment before deciding what it is they wish to do. If your Dragon wife, husband or child should behave in this way, do not become frantic: this instability is simply the astrological baggage of all those born under the sign of the Dragon.

They get along very well with their colleagues — as long as they do not interfere in their personal way of doing things. The slightest intrusion will cause them to spit flames. If you are obsessed with status and fear for your position, one piece of advice: do not hire a Dragon.

MATERIAL LIFE

A Dragon's bank account will be well filled. Because they are gifted and lucky, and because they always find people to believe in them, our winged animals rarely lack the bare necessities, and if they do it is only for a very short time. Generally, they get along very well and adapt to both good years and bad.

However, Dragons often have financial problems, for they are imprudent, get involved too quickly and do not think hard enough about interest and monthly payments. Also, they do not foresee the dishonesty of others, and are sometimes cheated by those less scrupulous than themselves.

It should be added that Dragons are not economical: when they have money, they spend it quickly; earning it in the morning, they will be empty-handed by nightfall.

It is a good idea for them to have the foresighted Ox or the honest Pig as business associates. Otherwise, the cashbox risks remaining empty.

Male and female Dragons spend money for their own pleasure, but they are also generous to their friends and family and like to give presents. In fact, they are the most unselfish people in the world. A lady Dragon would never marry a man for his money; and if Mr Dragon smiles at you, you can be certain that he does not care a fig about your monthly income. Dragons are more interested in the brilliant or inventive side of your profession than in how much you earn. Sometimes they even appear to scorn money; but this does not mean that they are willing to give it all away to charity — Dragons have eminently practical good sense.

ENVIRONMENT

Prince of the clouds, the Dragon is too mythical to need a settled environment. Living between the four walls of a flat, with a suburban garden as his only view, he would soon become depressed, for he cannot stand to be confined. The Dragon is very claustrophobic; he needs space, fresh air and speed, and prefers the whistling of the wind to that of the tea-kettle.

Although not nomadic, Dragons like things around them to move, and they are perfectly capable of adapting to foreign landscape and life style. They are depressed if they must always live in the same place. If they cannot travel they like to have exotic furniture, and will change the style of their living quarters rather often. If they are broke, they will borrow some paint from a friend and transform the walls of their flat into a tropical island. It is rare to find the same colours and decoration in a Dragon's home for more than a year or two.

The ideal home for the Dragon is a fortified castle perched on a rocky peak, overlooking dizzying ravines. Alas, fortified castles are hard to come by, so our Dragons must instead move to an ultra-modern villa, built by a daring architect, with sliding glass windows opening onto a landscape of cliffs and sea. The sound of the waves and the thunder of ocean storms will rock the Dragon to sleep. They would also enjoy living on a boat or flying their own plane.

A guide to relations with a Dragon
Methods of seduction:
He: Is charming and has a free-and-easy manner. No one can ever resist him.
She: Will give you the impression that she is a princess in a fairy tale, courted by every man on earth. She will stimulate your spirit of competition and your taste for conquest.
If he loves you: Start to keep a diary immediately, noting down everything he says and does. He will be delighted, for every Dragon likes to have a personal biographer. Then if he leaves you, you will at least have the material for a best-seller.
He expects of you: That you listen to him with admiration and that you take his advice.
To keep you: He will do nothing in particular. First because he does not consider that you might leave him and, second, he refuses to ask anyone to stay with him.
If he is unfaithful: He does it to show you that you are not indispensable. In any case, he will not let it go too far.
If you are unfaithful: Try not to tell him; you will destroy his ideal. Be discreet.
In case of a break between you: If it is the man's decision, they will remain friends; if it is the woman's, he will disappear — but there will be neither tears nor emotional blackmail.
If you wish to give him a gift: Dragons adore toys. Find out what his hobbies are — your gift will be sure to please him and will show that you truly thought of him.
If you want to seduce him: Buy or borrow a superb sports car — a red convertible — and pass him by, pretending that you do not see him.
If you want to get rid of him: Say to him, 'Amazing, I thought you were taller.'

THE DRAGON
AND THE OTHER CHINESE SIGNS

Dragon/Rat

This is an extremely positive alliance for the Rat; the Dragon's brilliance will compel his admiration, amaze and exhilarate him. The Rat will freely display an attachment both violent and irrational; he, so clever, so clear-headed, will embark without a qualm on the greatest of follies, simply to attract a blazing glance from this Prince of the Sky.

Yet here we may ask, does the Dragon really 'see' the Rat? Well, not always. From time to time he will be taken up with some new enthusiasm and forget him. But the Dragon so loves to be adored, adulated and admired, that the Rat's passion will act like a balm on his scales, as cool rain on his hot, dry breath.

Dragon/Ox

The Ox is a person grounded in day-to-day life who, from a very early age, is aware of the danger of going too fast. The Dragon, on the other hand, forewarns of exceptional events involving political, emotional or professional change. In the life of an Ox, the Dragon will pass like a flaming comet; after he has left, nothing will ever be the same again. This will be excellent for the Ox. He will come out of the experience tired but renewed, wiser and more lucid. For a time the Dragon will appreciate the stable and positive side of the Ox, finding repose and an inclination for reflection.

In short, this may be a useful relationship for both, but it will be unlikely to last unless the Dragon is required to travel a great deal. Otherwise, he will become quickly bored — and as quickly elusive. On the other hand, the Dragon may have the good sense to use the Ox to take care of the accounting side of his affairs.

Dragon/Tiger

They have many points in common, notably, courage, energy and an enterprising spirit. The Tiger is a good counsellor, for he never advises anyone to act as rashly as he might do. The Dragon, who is often quite certain that he has got things rights, loves to give advice and will tend to help the Tiger to reflect before he acts, considering his prospects along with his capabilities. Sometimes, too, he will push him, with the best intentions in the world, to pursue adventures from which he will never return.

Their shared tendency to excess will lend a passionate aspect to their lives, but at the expense of stability. This imbalance may be mitigated if the Dragon learns to understand that the Tiger is much more reasonable in his words than in his actions. Things will never go very smoothly; there will be many conflicts and discussions, but their lives will never be boring. Thanks to their frankness, misunderstandings will never last for long. They will succeed like two old friends: each will be pleased with the success of the other, and their deep understanding will preclude any rivalry. Even if in business, they may be notorious, but they will work well together — although they will need to hire a good manager.

Dragon/Rabbit

This relationship will be possible if it is the Dragon who wears the trousers — literally and figuratively. To live for any length of time with his sensational partner — who is not content merely to shine, but needs to collect several awards of distinction that he guards in a small engraved box — a Rabbit needs to be philosophic and self-sacrificing, qualities he definitely lacks.

Rabbits are patient and peace-loving, but they do not like their paws to be stepped on, whereas Dragons are born paw-crushers. For a while the Rabbit will stoically endure this hurricane which several times a day devastates his chest of drawers, changes objects around and creates draughts (slamming doors are extremely perturbing to the well-bred Rabbit). So, one day, he will confront the Dragon — and it will not be the Dragon who has the last word, for Rabbits only appear to be weak. On the other hand, if the Dragon works away from home and the Rabbit keeps house, each will be free to organize his environment as he wishes, and everything will go well.

Dragon/Dragon

Dragons sparkle and love what glitters; it is not surprising that they attract like magnets. To tell the truth, they are often more in love with themselves as a couple than with their partner as an individual.

Dragons may become irritated very rapidly by their partner's success, not because they are jealous but because they see that he — or she — needs no help or advice. Each will try to go further than the other, to outstrip the other in every way. If they divorce, the courtroom will be filled with malicious abuse — an unforgettable spectacle!

Dragon/Snake

Traditionally this is one of the best friendly alliances for the Dragon — especially when the Snake is the female. Although he must feel he is the stronger, the male Dragon needs to be proud of his wife; and female Snakes are wise, seductive and elegant. Nor will any female Snake be stupid enough to make her power apparent; the 'underground' manoeuvre is much more to her nature.

If the Dragon is female, the relationship will be more delicate: she will hope to be adulated by her Snake husband, a hope which he will satisfy for a while out of kindness, nevertheless coiling round her like a boa constrictor. Unfortunately, female Dragons dislike feeling smothered.

However, despite the Dragon's need to 'shine at any price', and the possessiveness of the Snake, this relationship is to be recommended. These Chinese zodiacal neighbours respect and rarely deceive each other: the Dragon has too much honour to wish to be diminished in someone's estimation, and the Snake is tolerant enough to withhold his criticisms concerning the flames and turbulence of his partner.

Dragon/Horse

Enthusiasm often unites them, especially in the heat of action. One can easily imagine them as loyal rivals in a football game, or companions in some adventure! if committed to a shared purpose, they fit well together. In daily life, however, the problem can be more delicate, particularly if the Dragon is the female, for she needs to be admired and coddled, and the Horse, having conquered her, will be too egotistic to care about her demands. Thus neglected, she will resort to any means — and these, indeed, could be extreme — to demonstrate to her Horse husband that he would have done better to remember her existence.

Things will be easier if the Horse is the female, for the

Dragon is not the kind to invade her privacy too much, even though she does need to roam alone. Preoccupied with herself and what concerns her, she will allow him to shine in peace. He will become a twinkling Dragon before starting to gallop.

Dragon/Goat

This alliance can be either good or bad. Good because the Goat needs to be protected, or at least encouraged and supported. He will listen to the Dragon's advice and, if he succeeds in stifling his desire to yawn, everyone will be content. Indeed, the Dragon can turn out to be a valuable patron for the whimsical Goat.

Unhappily, the Dragon's need for admiration and to feel indispensable will not meet with a ready response from the Goat, for whom any form of adulation is totally foreign. Respect, yes; but it is not his style to compliment. Our poor Dragon risks wilting like a plant without water.

With this couple, one must hope that the Dragon will be the active and dominant element, so that he can find the satisfactions in his work he is unable to obtain at home. But if the Dragon remains at home — and this is almost unthinkable — pity them both: they will make each other's lives impossible, the Dragon will be miserable and the Goat will indulge in resounding follies.

Dragon/Monkey

Avoid this couple if you value the company of those versed in philosophical inquiry. Such pursuits are not their strong point; in fact, both have a tendency to believe that they have delved deeply into a subject when a great deal remains yet to be explored.

They are helped as a couple because each stops at the same point of inquiry, which they will later resume. The Monkey has all the qualities necessary to seduce a Dragon and to keep a hold on him — a rare talent. Knowing how to listen, and then, with a toss of the head, to steal away; to alternate enthusiastic compliments with courteous silences, the Monkey will fascinate the Dragon. The latter, with his unselfish, chimerical and gratuitous side, will know how to captivate the Monkey, who is always seeking a new source of excitement. There will be no rivalry between them; on the contrary, they will complement each other and give each other confidence. Their combination will enable mutual success and other poor mortals, stunned by their charm, will be easily seduced. If a Dog, for example, tries to denounce them as being superficial, they will not hear him.

Dragon/Rooster

They both like to shine, but in totally different ways. The Rooster seeks to please because it reassures him of his personal value; the Dragon dazzles because he is naturally like that.

With these two, everything can go very well indeed. The Rooster will know how to fan the Dragon's flames as their warmth envelops him. He will admire the Dragon, who need make no effort to be seductive, and will be proud of having captured his attention. The adulated Dragon in turn will feel like a proud peacock and will be happy indeed. Danger will come in moments of crisis or misunderstanding, which, alas, can be frequent. The Dragon has little awareness of subtleties and no psychological understanding whatsoever; sometimes he will be tough and intolerant with his Rooster companion, who will then wish to take him down a peg or two.

Dragon/Dog

This liaison is inadvisable, unless they have a common aim or their Western astrological signs offer serious points of understanding. In fact, the Dog is perhaps the only Chinese zodiac sign who cannot be impressed by the Dragon: he is so lucid that he sees the Dragon for what he truly is — brilliant but superficial, devoid of subtleties and emotionally shallow. This is just as well, for a Dog in love with a Dragon would suffer, the Dragon being incapable of giving him the tenderness so necessary, and not caring a rap about his anxieties. The Dragon would also suffer, for, with the best intentions in the world, he could not transform himself into Rodin's 'Thinker' just to please the Dog; he is as he is and he must be accepted, his good qualities along with his bad. This poses a big problem for the Dog who will try to devalue the Dragon in order to establish what he believes to be the truth. Happily, he will not succeed, but it will give the Dragon complexes, as if he did not already have enough!

Dragon/Pig

So much the better for the Dragon, so much the worse for the Pig, who will not be able to distinguish his snout from his tail when caught in the trap of this relationship. Unintentionally, the Dragon will cause the Pig to turn in circles until he becomes dizzy; he will make him believe that the moon is made of green cheese and that big bad wolves eat sweet little pink piglets.

But one should not feel too sorry for the Pig: he will be so busy coddling his Dragon and telling him how wonderful he is that he will not have time to think about himself. And the Dragon will be delighted! And, when the Pig has his usual attack of independence, the Dragon will not say a word; when the Pig returns, his desire for liberty satisfied, the Dragon will smile and give him some words of wisdom. The delighted Pig will listen to him as though he were repeating the Gospel. Luckily, the Dragon usually gives good advice.

DRAGON CELEBRITIES

Joan of Arc, Ataturk, Sarah Bernhardt, Anne Bronte, Pearl Buck, Lewis Carroll, Barbara Cartland, Dali, Danton, Daumier, Louis David, Eiffel, Engels, Anatole France, Franco, Frederick the Great, Freud, Gielgud, Gorky, Cary Grant, Graham Greene, Haile Selassie, Honegger, Edward Heath, Kant, MacArthur, Manet, Mitterand, Napoleon III, Tsar Nicolas II, Nietzsche, Novalis, Oppenheimer, Perrault, Petain, Petrarch, Mary Pickford, Rimsky-Korsakov, Jean-Jacques Rousseau, G. B. Shaw, Stockhausen, Swedenborg, Tito, Vadim, Verlaine, Vuillard, Harold Wilson.

YOUR COMPANION IN LIFE

生命伴侣

After the Chinese sign of your year of birth, here is the sign of your hour of birth

What is a Companion in Life, as understood in Chinese astrology? It is a sort of 'ascendant' sign corresponding to your hour of birth. This Companion is another animal belonging to the Chinese cycle of the twelve emblematic beasts, who falls into step with you and accompanies you, ever ready to help you brave the traps and ambushes along your route. A permanent and benevolent shadow, he can render the impossible possible.

He is your counterpart, but with his own character and tendencies and with a different psychology. Both guardian angel and devil's advocate, he will be a witness to your life and an actor in it.

Have you ever felt, deep inside yourself, the subtle presence of another 'myself' inhabiting you and with whom you live, at times in harmony, at others in conflict? Another self who sometimes criticizes you and at others encourages you? That is your Companion in Life.

There are times when he will appear to be an imposter or an intruder. Certainly, he often questions your habits and your moral or spiritual complacency. Accompanied by this companion, a shadow within, the route is less monotonous and the voyager multiplies his chances of arriving at his chosen destination. This, however, in itself matters little, for it is the journey and the manner in which it is conducted that are important. Indolence is the greatest danger: your Companion is capable of arousing you from a lassitude of spirit and, to that end, if necessary, robbing you of your certainties, trampling on your secret gardens and, finally, tearing away the great veil of illusion.

It sometimes happens that your Companion is of the same sign as your year of birth, a twin brother in a way — for example, a Dragon/Dragon. In this case, you must recognize that he will compel you to realize yourself fully and to live the double aspect — the Yin and the Yang — that your bear within yourself. In any case, you also bear within yourself

the twelve animals. So, set out on the long route, ready for the great adventure: the beautiful voyage during which you will encounter the harmoniously entangled, the solemn and the grotesque, the ephemeral reality, the dream and the imagined.

Table of hours corresponding to the twelve emblematic animals

If you were **born** between		your **companion** is
11 pm and 1 am		Rat
1 am and 3 am		Ox
3 am and 5 am		Tiger
5 am and 7 am		Rabbit
7 am and 9 am		Dragon
9 am and 11 am		Snake
11 am and 1 pm		Horse
1 pm and 3 pm		Goat
3 pm and 5 pm		Monkey
5 pm and 7 pm		Rooster
7 pm and 9 pm		Dog
9 pm and 11 pm		Pig

These figures correspond to the *solar hour* of your birth. If necessary, you should check the summer times (Daylight Savings Time) and make the appropriate adjustment (sometimes two hours before or after statutory time).

THE DRAGON AND HIS COMPANION IN LIFE

 **Dragon/Rat**

This is a lucky combination, for the Dragon is an excellent companion for the Rat. The voyage will be magical. In deepest harmony with himself, the Rat will leave his bottomless depths and will ride his scaled companion across the Milky Way, his muzzle in the stars. But be careful! If you allow yourself to be spellbound by the Dragon within you, you will pay dearly for it. You idolize him; he is fond of you. He reassures you; but in the end makes your decisions for you. The Dragon is prone to terrible rages; you will hide away. You must know how to make the most of your luck. Imagine it as a voyage in the watery depths and through the heavens, which also embraces the terrestrial world and its deeper recesses. Only do not forget that sometimes you must fight the Dragon in order to prevail, and that he is a ferocious sentinel.

Here is a Companion strong enough for the Rat, master of forces from below.

 **Dragon/Rabbit**

This companion will bring him self-confidence, and he will feel his wings growing, be they made of lace or scales. The Rabbit/Dragon will be audacious, equipped with a lively and shrewd intelligence. He will be a seductive prince endowed with a complex brain; a mysterious being gliding among fairy-like worlds and parallel universes. However, he should be wary of a type of aggressiveness revealed in an attitude of 'I know everything; I have seen everything'. He is the guardian of a secret or treasure and has the soul of a fantasist; a lunar vagabond with magical powers, in search of the marvellous.

357

Dragon/Tiger

Not one to fall asleep on his way, this terrestrial and celestial mount will be secretive and enigmatic, spreading fear along his route. His isolated condition will compel him to follow his peculiar destiny. The Tiger will awaken the Dragon sleeping deep in a magic grotto; the Dragon will often provoke the Tiger to combat. The Tiger/Dragon is an animal that uses his claws, scales and formidable teeth, sometimes spitting fire. Yet he has a tendency to so overdo things that he can appear a clown. He should be careful of this, by which he may forfeit the fear and respect his majestic appearance inspires. Although it may amuse others to see him clowning, he is not the type — and should not do it.

Dragon/Ox

A poisoned gift! A Dragon is always synonymous with luck, but, alas, there is a negative element, above all for a solitary and independent Ox. The Dragon is extremely intelligent but he is inclined to impose his own patterns of life on others. Always on the move, he will do his best to drag the Ox into spaces and dimensions which do not conform to his desires. He will be roused to a fury, which the Ox will oppose with stubborn silence: he is a provoker and able to set the Ox's teeth on edge, and he will have a tendency to goad him; the Dragon dreams of liberty, but it is not the same as his. The Ox/Dragon must therefore take upon himself these two powerful poles, these two disparate forces which inhabit him. Their pressures may be seriously perturbing. Particularly dynamic activity — military, sports or intellectual — may enable the Ox/Dragon to harmonize these contradictory energies.

 **Dragon/Dragon**

A route strewn with scales, volcanic earth and tumultuous torrents; the Dragon/Dragon will have a tendency to transform his 'voyage' into a competition in which he must, of course, arrive the victor. It is useless to try to stop him; he will walk right over you and remain deaf to your advice. This animal should learn to relax, otherwise he may 'crack up' en route. Alas, he refuses to listen; he believes in his lucky star, retires into his shell and spits fire. It is advisable that he tone down his showy behaviour — unless he wants a career on the stage.

 **Dragon/Snake**

A lucky and canny animal, the Snake/Dragon is a traveller on whom fortune will smile, and what he cannot obtain by force or charm he will obtain by malice and enchantment. If the Dragon sometimes makes the mistake of being too heavy or conventional, the Snake will lead him to value discretion, patience and the advantages of the indirect approach. A formidable beast, full of charm, he will bring a taste of mystery to his partner, who will shiver either with pleasure or with fear.

Dragon/Horse

Riding may have its charms, but there are inherent dangers in mounting a Dragon which are best avoided, even if he is the companion of a Horse. An impetuous and ardent animal, the Horse/Dragon combines elegance with opportunism, luck with lively intelligence. Few can mount him. The ride will be a sort of mad race in which he may often conquer and attract admiration; but the speed of it all will tend to go to his head and his extraordinary luck make him mad. He needs to learn about that rare flower called modesty; even then, he must be careful not to trample on it while jumping for joy when its bloom is full.

Dragon/Goat

Imagine a terrifying animal — one with multi-coloured scales who spits fire, but wears beautiful boots and is crowned with graceful horns. The Goat/Dragon appears thus, but also very much at ease with himself. The Goat brings reality and substance to the Dragon's wildest dreams, offering him fantasy, imagination and a sense of the marvellous on a platter of clouds. The often too serious Dragon will learn to relax and enjoy himself. The Goat/Dragon, an animal of all territories, will not be merely a complex and well-regulated machine, but will be able to take to the air, becoming a Dragon of subtle azure, soft breezes and capricious clouds.

Dragon/Monkey

Possessing a combination of the supremely gifted synchronized with a talent and taste for walking the tightrope, the Monkey/Dragon — a valiant and fearless guardian — will never unbuckle his armour. Always prepared for war, his days and nights are spent in a state of alertness, much to the continued astonishment of his friends. Alas, he tends to be an extortioner. He has charm, is brilliant and his intelligence is remarkable, but his main defect is his immoderate pride. His company is appreciated, but only in small doses. He will be a phenomenon and his collaboration and assistance will be desired, but you will not be able to breathe freely until you have seen the back of him. So, unwind a little, be natural and glance on your fellow creatures with a less condescending eye.

Dragon/Rooster

He only feels at ease in a high position, both in the geographic and the hierarchical sense of the term. He prefers the top of a tower or a top floor with terrace. The Rooster/Dragon will always be in the first row and nothing will escape his vigilant gaze; he will wish to dominate, control and supervise in all circumstances. He will be kind and possess originality, qualities which the Rooster does not always naturally cultivate. He will also be irresistibly charming.

 **Dragon/Dog**

He is one of those who inspires confidence, and with reason: one can give him one's friendship wholeheartedly and rely on his word. The Dog/Dragon is a loyal, dedicated and faithful animal who appreciates the luck available for him throughout life, not taking it as his due, but as a gift from Providence. The Dog will understand the value of the Dragon sleeping within him; he, in turn, will give to the Dragon a sense of context, humour and an understanding of a subtle world which includes an interior dimension usually incomprehensible to the Dragon. For the Dragon is always on tenterhooks; usually, he cannot pause to reflect, yet alone contemplate or meditate, and has little contact with the invisible and the hereafter.

 **Dragon/Pig**

A solitary wanderer, seeking a treasure that perhaps he did not know how to protect. The Dragon/Pig will tend to gain material and spiritual wealth. Alas, it does not suffice simply to possess matter or mind and spirit — they must be given meaning. Do not sleep before your safe, before the gates of your palace or on the threshold of your mysterious grotto. Ask yourself whether the safe, palace or grotto may be empty; in which case, it is up to you to fill them.

THE DRAGON AND THE FIVE ELEMENTS

五行

YOUR ELEMENT

In Chinese astrology, each year is joined to an Element. There are five Elements: *Water, Fire, Wood, Metal, Earth.*

Each of the twelve emblematic animals is linked successively to each of the five Elements. For example, in the year 1900 the Rat was Metal, in 1912 he was Water, in 1924 he was Wood, in 1936, Fire and in 1948 he was Earth. Therefore, for the twelve years from 1900 he was linked to Metal, for the next twelve years to Water, and, for every succeeding period of twelve years, to each of the other Elements, in succession.

In order to determine the Element corresponding to the year of your birth, use the table below:

> *Years whose digits end in:* 2 and 3 — Water
> 6 and 7 — Fire
> 4 and 5 — Wood
> 0 and 1 — Metal
> 8 and 9 — Earth

The same union of *Animal-Element* repeats every sixty years, for example, Rat-Metal appeared in 1720, 1780, 1840, 1900, 1960 and so on.

The five Elements are the primary forces affecting the universe. It is their particular association with each of the signs which provides the basis for every horoscope. Movement and fluctuation, Yin and Yang, these symbolic forces are in a perpetual state of action and interaction.

Wood gives birth to Fire, which gives birth to Earth, which gives birth to Metal, which gives birth to Water, which in turn gives birth to Wood.

DRAGON/WATER
(you were born in 1952)

The cold born of the northern sky descended to earth and gave birth to Water. The Chinese consider Water more a synonym for coldness and ice than a symbol of fertility.

Characteristics of the Dragon/Water
Water of winter nights, rigour and severity; calm and deep Water to be feared and respected; still, sometimes stagnant Water sheltering underwater demons asleep in its depths; foetid and muddy Water of the marshes, a refuge of crawling creatures.

The Dragon will be in his element, joining the monsters submerged in the depths of still waters, then assuming his role as conqueror when he goes out to challenge the earth and space. His active temperament and the multiplicity of his universes obliges him to live in perpetual movement. However, from time to time Water may stop him short, putting a brake on his flight towards the stars.

Health of the Dragon/Water
The Water organ is the kidney; its flavour is salty. Be sure to drink enough water; swim often; tone up your body. But do not remain in the water for too long — it can be too soothing for a blazing, flaming Dragon.

The Dragon/Water and others
Theoretically, the Dragon/Water should be a calm and reflective person, not given to excesses or upheavals; in fact, his temperament is the opposite of these qualities. However, by learning to control himself he will succeed in synthesizing his Element tendency and the Yin-Yang of his Dragon tendency. He will then possess the art of governing justly and serenely, curbing all excessive passions. At ease in a crowd, he will know how to inspire and lead without violence or anger. The Dragon/Water will be a pacifist and humanist, interested in social problems, the human

condition and justice. Metaphysics will not interest him much; the Water Element will not send him soaring to the stars but instead turn him towards the hearts of men.

Advice for a Dragon/Water
You are dynamic and have confidence in yourself. Do not ruin your chances by wading in a small pool when oceans are what attract you.

A Dragon/Water year
The culminating point in a Dragon/Water year will be winter, a period of gestation. The Yin of Water will balance the Yang of the Dragon.

A year in which action and reflection will alternate. Remain vigilant and distrust sleeping waters. If you go deep-sea diving, do not forget to come to the surface eventually.

Intense effort is needed to avoid having your most grandiose projects and enterprises bogged down.

Historical example of a Dragon/Water year 1712

Queen Anne's reign was entering its final years. Corpulent, sluggish and dulled, she could be implacably obstinate and obtuse in political matters. Luckly this impediment did not affect the real life of the nation and its future, which lay in men she would never know. From these, men of imagination and technical resource, adept at applying their skills, sprung the new middle classes of England. In 1712 mechanical invention was a vital need in two industries in particular — coal and iron.

Hitherto, coal mining had been carried out near the surface, even to the extent of landowners uprooting flowerbeds, lawns and parkland in order to augment their wealth. But the demand for coal was insatiable. Only the mining of the underground seams could satisfy the demand, but this was impracticable since the galleries flooded and there was no known method of pumping the water from the seams. In 1712, Savery and Newcomen, after years of experiment, perfected their steam pump and the underground source became available.

The great problem for the iron industry proved also to be associated with working underground seams of coal. The English iron industry had always depended on charcoal taken from its forests. These had so thinned by the early eighteenth century that the whole future of the industry seemed in doubt. The Darby family of Coalbrookdale turned their minds to the possibility of using coke for smelting. By 1712 their experiments were completed and, by its end, were in active use. Thus, the great iron age of the early industrial revolution was instituted, an indispensable step in the mechanization of resources.

In July the 'Miracle of Denain' recovered the military fortunes of Louis XIV. The omniscience of the coalition armies was exposed and the effect of Marlborough's great victories annulled. The Bourbon dynasty was secured in Spain, the very hegemony that Marlborough had fought so hard against. There was certainly one compensation. From 1712, Handel worked in England.

DRAGON/WOOD
(you were born in 1904 or 1964)

To the East, the wind blew in the sky and from its warm caress of the earth, Wood was born.

Characteristics of the Dragon/Wood
Wood is of the morning and springtime. Its temperate nature loves harmony, beauty and elegance. This mid-season will be fertile and creative for the Dragon; it will bring equilibrium and the power to create; a taste for the beautiful, harmony and nature, inducing him to leave his subterranean grotto or come down from his nest. The Dragon will discover that there are treasures other than those he guards so jealously. Celestial, he will be able to place his feet more firmly on the ground; aquatic, he will

discover the solid earth; and subterranean, he will surface and face the shining dawn. But Wood is also the symbol of excessive passion and anger; the Dragon should be careful of this tendency.

Health of the Dragon/Wood
The organ of Wood is the liver; its flavour is acid. The Dragon/Wood will be perpetually anxious and tormented, often for no good reason, and at times will be tempted to compensate by overeating.

The Dragon/Wood and others
The Dragon/Wood will be relaxed and at ease socially, thus controlling his slightly stiff and inflexible nature. Moreover, the dynamic side of the Dragon will temper the pessimism of Wood and prevent him from sinking into melancholy and self-destruction; it will stimulate him and force him to overcome setbacks.

The Dragon/Wood will often use his imagination and talent to improvise when faced with established structures. He will be a creative inventor and will be attracted to nature and all that symbolizes harmony or beauty.

Advice for the Dragon/Wood
You were born under a lucky star, have good physique, artistic tendencies and a love for harmony. On the one hand you are dynamic and courageous, on the other you like to seduce and please; so, do not ruin your chances by irrational outbursts and careless anger.

A Dragon/Wood year
The culminating point for a Dragon/Wood year will be spring, a period of growth and prosperity.

You will be full of renewed energy and will discover that you have a creative soul; nature will be your source of inspiration. It will bring you beauty, harmony and the suppleness necessary to accomplish your work.

Historical example of a Dragon/Wood year
1244

In June the Khwarismian horsemen, 10,000 strong, swept down into Damascene territory, ravaging the land and burning the villages. Damascus itself was too strong for them to attack, so they rode on into Galilee, past the town of Tiberias, which they captured, and southward through Nablus towards Jerusalem. The Franks suddenly realized the danger. The newly elected Patriarch, Robert, hastened to the city with the Grand Masters of the Temple and the Hospital, and reinforced the garrison in the fortifications that the Templars had just rebuilt, but they did not themselves dare to remain there. On 11 July the Khwarismians broke into the city. There was fighting in the streets, but they forced their way to the Armenian convent of St James and massacred the monks and nuns. The Frankish governor was killed in making a sortie from the citadel, together with the Preceptor of the Hospital. But the garrison held out. No help came from the Franks; so they appealed to their nearest Moslem ally, an-Nasir of Kerak.

An-Nasir had no liking for the Christians and had resented the necessity of their alliance. So, after sending some troops which cowed the Khwarismians into offering the garrison a safe-conduct to the coast if they would surrender the citadel, he then dissociated himself from its fate. On 23 August some 6,000 Christian men, women and children marched out of the city, leaving it to the Khwarismians. As they moved along the road towards Jaffa, some of them looked back and saw Frankish flags waving on the towers. Thinking that somehow rescue had arrived, many insisted on returning towards the city, only to fall into an ambush under the walls. Some 2,000 perished. The remainder, as they journeyed down to the sea, were attacked by Arab bandits. Only 300 reached Jaffa.

Thus Jerusalem passed finally from the Franks. Nearly

seven centuries passed before a Christian army would once again enter its gates.

From Steven Runciman, *A History of the Crusades.* vol. III, Cambridge, 1954.

DRAGON/FIRE
(you were born in 1916 or 1976)

Heat was born in the southern sky, descended to earth and fertilized it. From their union, Fire was born.

Characteristics of the Dragon/Fire
The Fire Element is of the midday, the South, of summer. Fire is Yang; it is the Element which warms, burns, animates, quickens, transforms and destroys.

Fire within the Dragon will strengthen his energy, transforming him into a burning bush and constantly recharging his batteries. If the Fire is within, the Dragon will be in a permanent state of alertness, with a thirst for light and the inexhaustible spring of life; find this spring, but do not drain it empty.

Health of the Dragon/Fire
The organ of Fire is the heart; its flavour is bitter. Fire of summer and of the South, Yang plus Yang: control your anger and aggressiveness and turn away from violence. Reserve your strength; do not burn your energy carelessly. If you need some medicine, do not choose horse remedies.

The Dragon/Wood and others
Fire symbolizes aggression, but also lucidity and clairvoyance. The Dragon/Fire is impassioned and violent and not very diplomatic. A man of action and a daring adventurer — but lucid, artistic and individualistic — he will not be a lukewarm person. Slightly intolerant and tending to live on tenterhooks, he should relax, do some Yoga exercises and learn to meditate quietly.

Advice for a Dragon/Fire

You do not have any choice: you must control yourself and master your impulses or you will become annoying to others and even to yourself.

A Dragon/Fire year

The culminating point in a Dragon/Fire year will be summer, a period of creation. Your Yang tendency will bring you indestructible dynamism.

This will be a year of action and creation, of material success and spiritual elevation. However, do not let your Fire devour your body and soul. At a critical moment, a sudden leap can assure you unexpected triumph.

Historical example of a Dragon/Fire year
1856

After two years of war in the Crimea preliminaries of peace were signed in Vienna. Thus ended hostilities between the English, the French and the Turks on the one side and the Russians on the other. The campaign has been castigated as the most ill-managed in English history. Florence Nightingale brought about a revolution in nursing methods and in the supply of medical provisions, both of which were to have a valuable influence over the practice of medicine generally, but no other lessons were learned in Whitehall from a war which Queen Victoria thought not worth the life of a single grenadier.

In the British army more men were killed from want of firewood than from Russian bullets — yet firewood could easily have been obtained from the nearby forests of Anatolia. Sleeping accommodation consisted of wet blankets and mud. Men died in the field of cholera, of exposure, of malnutrition; of scurvy, gangrene and dysentery. Most of the senior officers were appointed on account of their age rather than their experience in command. Lord Raglan, the Commander in Chief of the

British forces, had never even commanded a company. While the troops were sent to a suicidal and disastrous assault on the Redan fortress near Sebastopol, officers' ladies and visiting gentlemen strolled about a convenient ridge to see the show, entertained by light music from the band of the Rifle Brigade; throughout, Raglan referred to the enemy as the French. This incompetence became a prototype, its lessons unlearned even by the time of the landing in the Dardanelles.

By contrast, the French were well supplied and well directed; and the peace effected in 1856 led to a personal triumph by Napoleon III at the Congress in Paris which he instigated. Praised by all for his moderation, his generosity and his goodwill he acquired both personal prestige and a new confidence in his dynasty.

DRAGON/EARTH
(you were born in 1928)

Earth was born from the slowly falling Elements of the sky at its humid zenith.

Characteristics of the Dragon/Earth
This is an afternoon Earth, the humid and hot Earth of summer. It is the symbol of the well-cushioned, soft nest, comfort and abundance; an Earth of slow and profound transformations.

This Earth will be good for the Dragon, with his caverns and buried treasures. An Earth of reflection, an Earth in which everything germinates, ripens and is strengthened, it will invite him to meditate and concentrate. It is a refuge, a solitary retreat sheltering fairies and monsters, far from the trials, conflicts and aggressions of the external world. Although retreat is sometimes necessary, it should be only a means, a resting-place; there is a time for rest, waiting and reflection, and another for action and discoveries, for climbing to the surface into the fresh open air. The Earth also can be a trap, a prison, a tomb; shake your scales, make the ground tremble, but do not shut yourself up.

Health of the Dragon/Earth

The Earth's organ is the spleen; its flavour is sweet. If the Dragon/Earth does not become active he may become morose and gain weight. If you do not take hold of yourself in time you may suffer from mental paralysis, and a shapeless Dragon will frighten no one — so stand up and exert some energy.

The Dragon/Earth and others

The Dragon/Earth is more realistic than the other Dragons. He is materialistic, prudent and suspicious, and tends to enjoy accumulating wealth and speculating. He will be a hard and conscientious worker, but, due to his fear of taking risks, he may lack imagination. He will be an understanding father, and Mrs Dragon will be exceedingly maternal.

Advice for a Dragon/Earth

You stay at home too much and think too much about your work, becoming maniacal and despotic. If you do not change your habits, people will start to avoid you. Add a bit of feeling to your relationships, become more fervent; learn to dream a little.

A Dragon/Earth year

The culminating point for a Dragon/Earth will be summer, which is favourable for the Dragon. Freed from material constraints, the Dragon can devote himself to creating and research. However, do not close yourself up in your ivory tower; open the doors, widen your horizons, listen to your heart. Isolation could lead to mistakes in judgement and to catastrophe.

Historical example of a Dragon/Earth year
1808

On the 'Dos de Mayo' (2 May) the people of Madrid seized

a brief control of their capital and the hated Joseph, installed as King by his brother Napoleon, fled the city. Although General Murat restored order the following day the uprising seems to have been accepted as a signal throughout Spain for active partisan warfare, conducted not only against the hated invader but also, and if anything more viciously, against any Spaniard suspected of French sympathies. There was no attempt at a general plan. The determination to destroy the invader by any means was instinctive to the Spanish people and the nature of the reprisals which followed indicated the extent of the hatred engendered and something of the extremities and violence fuelled by that hatred among Spanish and French alike. Goya's renowned rendering records the reprisals in Madrid on 3 May, and his *Disasters of War* reflects in all its horror the whole nature of the war in Spain. One of the most gruesome of the series, 'Populardo', depicts peasants torturing a French sympathizer.

Such atrocities were not confined to the guerrilla forces; they were endemic to the nature of the war and perpetrated by the regular forces of France and Spain alike. In July 18,000 men commanded by General Dupont were enmeshed by Spanish regulars. The subsequent treatment of the French prisoners demonstrated, by the nature of their mutilated remains, that the carefully formulated rules of war evolved during the eighteenth century had no application in the Peninsula.

Of the English army, Napier wrote: 'No wild horde of Tartars ever fell with more licence upon rich neighbours than did the English troops upon the Spanish towns taken by storm.' The English showed something near to contempt for their Spanish allies while respecting their French opponents, often to the extent of protecting them against Spanish vengeance. The war in Spain presaged, by its violence, all subsequent wars which called forth partisan resistance. Yet in Spain the English regulars and the Spanish guerrillas were an essential combination.

Neither could have defeated the French without the threat posed by the other.

DRAGON/METAL
(you were born in 1940)

In the sky, coming from the West, drought grazed the skin of the earth and gave birth to Metal. Winds come from the faraway steppes seeking the vital sap.

Characteristics of the Dragon/Metal
Metal is of the night, of autumn and of cold. It symbolizes clarity, purity and precision. The Dragon/Metal will be rigid, chaste and sharp-tongued. He will fluctuate between beauty and destruction. In other respects, he will be expert at putting his plans into effect. At harvest-time he is the blade that gleans. Alas, too rigorous a regime will lead to sadness and moroseness.

The Metal Element will tend to encase the already stiff Dragon in a ready-made suit of armour, isolating him from himself and others. Because the Dragon does not easily give in to feelings, the Metal Element will tend to encourage a dry heart and a lack of suppleness. Try to be circumspect and lucid. You will be attracted to mystical summits, but they could become a dangerous refuge of mirages; once the veil of illusion lifts you could awaken to find yourself falling into an abyss.

Health of the Dragon/Metal
The organ of Metal is the lung; its flavour is pungent. The Dragon/Metal who seeks equilibrium should practise respiratory exercises, which are indispensable for the relaxation necessary to his organism.

The Dragon/Metal and others
The Dragon/Metal will be an energetic and decisive person. He will be a natural-born leader, good at commanding,

judging and deciding. He is uncompromising with himself as well as with others, but is fair, just and honest. He is fanatical about work being done punctually and correctly. In short, he does not have an easy character — and he knows it — which does not make his life any easier. Still, he will follow his route against wind and tide, sure of himself and of his course, as indifferent to blame as he is to compliments, impassive in the midst of tempests that he himself has sometimes brought about.

Advice for a Dragon/Metal
Relax, try to become supple and take the time to play a bit; remember, cemeteries are full of indispensable people.

A Dragon/Metal year
The culminating point in a Dragon/Metal year will be autumn. The Yin tendency of the mid-season will blend with the Yang of the Dragon, making him more temperate and balanced.

Do not confuse suppleness with relaxation or a loss of energy. Use this period to pay more attention to yourself and to others; this will be favourable for you if you do not allow yourself to feel guilty because you are letting go. There are times when it is better to bend than to break, which requires strength and self-control.

Historical example of a Dragon/Metal year 800

By AD 800 Charles, King of the Franks in the Carolingian line, was the sole ruler of the greater part of the ancient Roman Empire of the West. Only at Roncevalles, where Count Roland died, had his armies met a serious reverse. Master of northern Italy and King of Lombardy, he had campaigned against the Saxons, Slavs and Avats to win territory extending from the mouth of the Oder River to the Adriatic Sea.

Wherever Charles the Great conquered, he imposed Christianity, if necessary by torture, massacre or both, thus setting a precedent for many centuries to come. Nevertheless his piety did not interfere with his political acumen; he negotiated with the powerful Caliph of Baghdad, Haroun al Rachid, and exchanged ambassadors with him.

From his capital at Aix-la-Chapelle he exercised a rule over his kingdoms and provinces both resolute and implacable. In the year 800 he summoned the leading Franks to meet him in Rome by Christmastide and forewarned Pope Leo III of his own intended arrival in Rome. The King of the Franks and of Lombardy intended to revive the Roman Empire and to be invested with the accolade of the Imperial Dignity.

On 23 December he was met in St Peter's, Rome, by the Pope and a great assembly composed of Romans and Franks, ecclesiastics and laity. With one accord all supplicated that he should restore the Ancient Empire and accept the title of Emperor. After a suitable show of modest indecision he bowed to their wishes. On Christmas Day King Charles attended Mass at St Peter's. While he knelt to pray the Supreme Pontiff advanced and placed the Crown upon his head. As the Emperor rose from his knees, the enormous congregation acclaimed him: 'To Charles Augustus, Crowned by God, great and pacific Emperor of the Romans, Life and Victory'. To a great hymn of praise, the Pope prostrated himself before the Emperor in the attitude of adoration prescribed by the Byzantine rite.

Analogical Table
of the Different Elements

Elements	Wood	Fire	Earth	Metal	Water
Years ending in	4 and 5	6 and 7	8 and 9	0 and 1	2 and 3
Colours	Green	Red	Yellow	White	Blue
Seasons	Spring	Summer	End of summer	Autumn	Winter
Climates	Wind	Heat	Humid	Dry	Cold
Flavours	Acid	Bitter	Sweet	Pungent	Salty
Principal organ	Liver	Heart	Spleen	Lungs	Kidneys
Secondary organ	Gallbladder	Small intestine	Stomach	Large intestine	Bladder
Food	Wheat, poultry	Rice, lamb	Corn, beef	Oats, horse	Peas, pork

Table of Harmony
Between the Elements

		Wood Female	Fire Female	Earth Female	Metal Female	Water Female
○○○ Excellent prosperity	**Male Wood**	● ●	○	○ ○ ○	○	○ ○
○○ Good harmony, understanding	**Male Fire**	○	○	○ ○	●	● ●
○ Effort needed	**Male Earth**	● ●	○ ○	○ ○	○ ○ ○	●
● Rivalries and problems of reciprocal domination	**Male Metal**	○	● ●	●	● ●	○ ○ ○
● ● Misunderstanding and incomprehension	**Male Water**	○ ○	● ●	●	○ ○ ○	○

THE
FOUR SEASONS
OF
THE DRAGON

If you were born in spring

Dragon/Aries

The Dragon cannot count on Aries to moderate his excess vitality and energy. On the contrary, these two signs multiply their positive and negative traits, for they have many points in common.

The Dragon/Aries is an active, driving person. He radiates charm and is brimming with life and enthusiasm. When he slaps you on the back and gives you one of his frank, warm smiles, you are ready to follow him anywhere. But, just when you are ready to go, he disappears. The Dragon/Aries is very impatient: 'Everything, and immediately, if not sooner' could be his motto. If you love him, you may wear yourself out trying to keep up with him.

He is sincere and loyal, but not at all sensitive or considerate — he does not have time. He often inspires contradictory feelings: he is either adored or hated. He does not realize that he can be curt, abrupt or hurtful. A true Dragon/Aries is apt to confront obstacles with a smile, as he moves from one point to another, his eyes fixed straight ahead, refusing to look either right or left. Only the straight line counts for him as the shortest distance between two points.

Dragon/Taurus

The realistic, patient, pragmatic and constructive side of Taurus can only be positive for the Dragon: before spitting out flames, this Dragon will first make sure that he has enough fuel — he will save energy. The Dragon/Taurus is efficient and energetic. When he has chosen his way, he becomes a tank, capable of clearing the Amazon and transforming it into an English garden. He is indomitable. The Dragon/Taurus is gifted for anything having to do with the material, financial side of life, and he will rarely be in need. He will be capable of constructing a building from a grain of sand, and is not easily brought down.

For a Dragon he is rather sentimental, and if, like the other Dragons, he inspires intense love, there is some chance that he will contribute to it and that it will last. He does not like to be resisted or teased, so do not hestitate if you want him; and, if you wish to seduce a lady Dragon/Taurus, do not wait a week before sending flowers — she needs immediate proof of your devotion.

Dragon/Gemini

This brilliant but often superficial Dragon may pass through your life like a meteor. Gemini fans the flames spit out by the Dragon, which makes for splendid fireworks or a lovely bonfire. Such a fire can light the world, change night into day, winter into summer — for several seconds — then it goes out. That is the problem with the Dragon/Gemini. Inpatient and excitable, he does not always possess the patience and perseverance necessary to keep his promises. Yet he is sincere and does not seek to mislead anyone. It is simply that he goes too far too fast and becomes exhausted before he has reached his goal. He should work with a Rat/Capricorn. There are times when he needs a cold shower so as not to consume himself.

If he learns to regulate his strength early on in life, the Dragon/Gemini will go far for he is intelligent, gifted for everything and possesses the ability to assimilate and judge rapidly. One can have confidence in him — he will always find someone to finish his work for him.

If you were born in summer
Dragon/Cancer

This Dragon is peaceful and stubborn. Born under the water sign of Cancer, the flames he spits out are extinguished and transformed into a comfortable hearthside fire. The Dragon/Cancer gives the impression of being capable of bringing you the security you have always dreamed of. In fact, he is very good with his family and friends and extremely sweet — for a Dragon. However, it would be a gross error to believe that he is patient simply because he does not explode every ten minutes. The Dragon/Cancer is a dormant volcano; he can sleep for ages, trying hard not to become excited, but, at the end of his tether he will become Vesuvius. So do not set his nerves on edge unless you have a weakness for the ruins of Pompeii.

The Dragon/Cancer has a great deal of imagination and easily invents original solutions. Authoritarian but clever, he can succeed in positions that put him in contact with the public, especially politics. But the most important thing for him will be his family, which he will protect like a treasure.

Dragon/Leo

The least one can say is that he is not at all frail or fragile. Whether male or female, the Dragon/Leo is born to govern. He is brilliant, likeable, slightly egotistical and adores being adulated, admired and flattered. He tends to pay attention only to those who compliment him. The Dragon/Leo cares a lot about his appearance: if a man, he will choose an elegant woman who will be a credit to him; if a woman, she will not marry just anyone, and will, moreover, seek to succeed in her own right.

The intelligence of the Dragon/Leo is luminous rather than analytical. He reminds one of the saying, 'All that glitters is not gold'. You will be disappointed if you expect him to reveal deep feelings, but you will never be bored with him. He is amusing, full of vitality and energy, and always has exciting ideas. He detests routine tasks and does not mind ostentation. He likes to surprise as well as to please.

Dragon/Virgo

This Dragon is so precise that when he spits out flames he resembles a laser beam: he finds his target and almost never misses. He is efficient and energetic and uses his potential to its maximum. His discreet appearance is misleading: he is ambitious and will use every trick in order to succeed. However, he will wait for a thick fog to hide in before setting out to crush his enemies. He behaves in this way only when the result is exceedingly important to him; he is a liar or social climber only when absolutely necessary.

春夏秋冬

The Dragon/Virgo is moderately willing to be of service. Generally, he has a clear view of what he wants and gives this priority over his love life. You should avoid him like the plague if you need little touches of tenderness, and also if you are independent by nature. He tends to run the show according to his extremely precise principles, which are not subject to change. He does not know how to smooth things over, to be moved or to play the fool.

If you were born in autumn
Dragon/Libra
The Dragon/Libra shines like a neon light in a dark alley, and not even on purpose. He is an excellent guest at parties, a great host and brilliantly puts forth his point of view without listening to others. You can stop him by telling him that you have heard enough and that it is now your turn to speak; he will be very surprised, but will listen to you. He is the most supple of all the Dragons: his tact and delicacy cause him to seek a middle way rather than to look for extreme solutions. Conciliating and diplomatic, he seems to give in in order to have peace, but, quietly and surely, he pursues his own route with a triumphant and blissful smile.

The Dragon/Libra behaves elegantly in all circumstances. Mediocrity is perhaps the only thing that can enrage him. Naturally, he adores to be loved — by a lot of people. He is extremely attractive and seductive, but his flirtations usually go no further than smiles and words of passion. He is a charmer, not an attacker, and tends to go home peaceably as soon as he has won the battle — in love and in politics.

Dragon/Scorpio
Be careful: if you rub up against him you may be stung. This Dragon resembles those tropical fish that poison you at the slightest touch. Beware of his scales: wear gloves if you wish to caress him; and do not contradict him in front of others (or even when alone with him) for his bite is venomous. The Dragon/Scorpio is a fiercely independent individualist, very

aware of his strength and of the role that he wants to play on earth. To tell him that he reminds you of someone else is a terrible insult, for he likes to think that he resembles no one.

Extremely passionate, he has only a relative idea of fidelity: he will want to be adored, but will explode if you make the mistake of behaving as if you own him. He needs total sexual freedom, which is not always easy to accept.

This belligerent Dragon will find life dull if he cannot discover a worthy adversary; if he can fight 'against' something, he will feel that life is worth living.

Dragon/Sagittarius

This is the most enthusiastic, enterprising and adventurous of all the Dragons. Optimistic and sure of himself, he cannot understand how anyone can resist him, especially since his desires are unselfish and he sincerely wants everyone to be happy. He is slightly tyrannical with his family and friends. He is marvellous when things are going really badly: call him and like Lancelot he will fly to your side, doing everything in his power to get you out of an impossible situation. And he will succeed for he is ingenious and has a gift for seeing things simply and clearly. But in daily life he is painful to live with because he will try everything, whether it will work for you or not — and he has the nerve to be right far too often.

Only love can make him aware of another's desires because the Dragon/Sagittarius is sentimental and loyal. After sowing his wild oats he will become a model of fidelity, although he may feel tempted from time to time. His need to set a good example will always keep him on the straight-and-narrow.

If you were born in winter
Dragon/Capricorn

Capricorn symbolizes long, solitary and laborious plodding to reach a goal. It has a good influence on the Dragon, who learns the patience and perseverance that he so often lacks. The ambitiousness of the Dragon/Capricorn is limitless.

Power interests him: he wants to get it and keep it — and then climb even higher. He tends to be insatiable and so magnetized by his goals that he will not see what is going on around him. You will be taking a great risk if you become attached to him — unless you can become indispensable to the realization of his desires or his ideal.

The Dragon/Capricorn shines like a black diamond — he is incorruptible, pure, unassailable — discouraging! If you succeed in scratching beneath his surface long enough to discover his deepest qualities, you will not be disappointed; but you will need a lot of patience. Have courage: he is one of the best and most faithful friends in the world.

Dragon/Aquarius

He is as independent as the Dragon/Scorpio — if not more so — but he is not as vulnerable. He is so certain of his originality, of his 'irreplaceability', that the criticisms of others have little effect on him. Moreover, he is on a 'higher' plane than most people, if not in height then at least in his mind or ideals. Power interests the Dragon/Aquarius, but merely as a 'human experience'; once he has achieved it, he gives it up easily.

He falls passionately in love, and then when he has discovered all that he wants to know about the other person, he falls out of love, which is why he makes others suffer, although he does not do it on purpose. He is a flying Dragon who cannot be chained down. He is intelligent and handles great problems with ease, but is not at all gifted for routine matters. To tell the truth, he is not always very realistic and needs clever executors to carry out his projects. You may often wonder if he knows what a bill is.

So climb on to the back of this celestial Dragon: you will discover a whole new world — but bring your own sandwiches.

Dragon/Pisces

The sensitivity, imagination and creativity of Pisces are made more dynamic and brightened by the warmth which emanates from the Dragon. This alliance is very positive and gives birth to individuals who are resourceful, full of original ideas and also capable of doing something useful, which is all to the good.

The Dragon/Pisces has a great deal of charm, and he knows how to use it. He deserves an Oscar for his talent in making declarations of love: he is enterprising, bold, romantic and understanding — all at the same time. How is it possible to resist him? He is slightly unfaithful because he needs to prove that he is seductive. Happily, he does not like to hurt anyone; sadly, he is not always aware that he is making someone suffer.

The Dragon/Pisces has such diverse gifts (he is very artistic) that he often spreads himself too thin. Help him get back on the right track and he will be very happy indeed. But realize that he will never do anything banal — it will be all or nothing.

THE
I CHING

易经

THE I CHING AND THE DRAGON

In the I Ching game, you ask a question and you obtain an answer. It is therefore a divining game. But the question you ask is posed through your Dragon identity; the wheels, the complex mechanism of your mind and spirit, begin to turn. You ask a Dragon question and the I Ching answers with a Dragon 'solution', on which you then meditate as a Dragon before arriving at a Dragon conclusion.

The player is presented with a hexagram which contains the 'hypothesis-response' to his question, or, more exactly, a synthesis of forces affecting the concern or event inquired about.

For you, Master Dragon, here are the sixty-four hexagrams of the I Ching and sixty-four Dragon hypotheses.

How to proceed
1. The question
Ask a question regarding any problem at all, past, present or future, personally concerning you. (If the question concerns a friend, consult the I Ching game in the book corresponding to his Chinese sign.)

2. Method of play
It must be done with concentration.
Take **three ordinary and similar coins** — for example, three 50p coins.
Heads will equal the number 3.
Tails will equal the number 2.
Throw the coins.
If the result is two coins showing Heads and one Tails, write 3 + 3 + 2. You thus obtain a total of 8 which you represent by a continuous line: ━━━━

Draw the same continuous line if you have three coins showing Heads $(3+3+3=9)$.

If you throw two coins showing Tails and one Heads $(2+2+3=7)$, or all three showing Tails $(2+2+2=6)$, draw two separate lines: ▬ ▬

To sum up, 8 and 9 correspond to: ▬▬▬▬ (Yin)

6 and 7 correspond to: ▬ ▬ (Yang)

Repeat this operation *six times*, noting at the time of each throw the figure obtained on a piece of paper, proceeding from the first to the sixth figure, from bottom to top.

The final result, including a trigram from the bottom, or lower trigram (example: ▬ ▬), and a trigram of the top, or upper trigram (example: ▬▬), will be a hexagram of the I Ching. In our example this would look like:

Now merely look for the hexagram number in the table on page 392, and then consult the list of hexagrams with their descriptions to find the given answer. *In our example,* the hexagram obtained is number 63, entitled **After completion.**

Table of Hexagrams

Trigrams	Upper lines ☰	☷	☳
Lower lines			
☰	1	11	34
☷	12	2	16
☳	25	24	51
☵	6	7	40
☶	33	15	62
☴	44	46	32
☲	13	36	55
☱	10	19	54

Use this table to find the number of your hexagrams. The meeting point between the lower and upper trigrams indicates the number of the hexagram that you are seeking.

☳	☶	☲	☵	☱
5	26	9	14	43
8	23	20	35	45
3	27	42	21	17
29	4	59	64	47
39	52	53	56	31
48	18	57	50	28
63	22	37	30	49
60	41	61	38	58

龍

THE HEXAGRAMS OF THE DRAGON

CH'IEN

1  *The creative:* Energy, strength and will, as well as creative spirit. The Dragon will not lack energy and strength, but he must also be supple and sensitive. Round off the corners and the tips of your arrows.

K'UN

2  *The receptive:* Mother Earth is a symbol of docility. Water, Fire, Wood and Metal are your tools; even a celestial Dragon must meditate.

CHUN

3  *Initial difficulty:* Seek and you will find the cause of the trouble, the germ in the grain.

MÊNG

4 *Youthful folly:* You cannot do away with danger simply by pretending that it does not exist. Distrust your impulsiveness; do not react quickly or without reflection.

HSÜ

5 *Waiting:* Is painful, but the sun seems warmer after the rain. A little patience will do you good.

SUNG

6 *Conflict:* Is sometimes inevitable, but at the right moment you must depend on your high principles.

SHIH

7 *The army:* The Dragon will feel slightly cramped within the bounds of collective discipline, but he will only seem to be submissive.

PI

8 *Holding together (union):* 'Strength lies in union.' Do not underestimate the assistance that another can bring you.

SHIAO CH'U

9 *The taming power of the small:* The moment has come to forget your spirit of conquest and your haste: by starting at the bottom of the ladder you will arrive at the top.

LÜ

10  *Treading:* 'Tread on the tail of a Tiger, he does not bite man.' You believe in your luck, so stride forward without worrying about obstacles.

T'AI

11 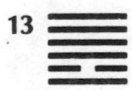 *Peace:* A state of confusion and loss of communication. Do not try to paste the broken pieces together. The vase is broken — find another or plant your flowers in the garden.

P'I

12 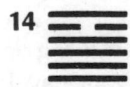 *Standstill:* Control your temper, do not bristle your scales; breathe deeply, practise yoga and meditation — you will attack another day.

T'UNG JÊN

13 *Fellowship with men:* The invulnerable Dragon must learn to leave his rocky peak. There are battles fought on the ground that are as exciting as those fought in the mountains.

TA YU

14 *Possession in great measure:* You were born under a lucky star, but it is not enough simply to know this, you must also believe it and make use of it. A good tool does not necessarily make a good worker.

CH'IEN

15 *Modesty:* It is difficult for the fiery Dragon to maintain stability as he searches for peace. Strength lies in sleeping waters, but he is not attracted to them.

YÜ

16 *Enthusiasm:* The Dragon is enthusiastic, spontaneous and eager to receive; he must learn to give with the same ardour.

SUI

17 *Following:* You are buried in flowers and bouquets. Do not throw them about — you may get a migraine.

KU

18 *Work on what has been spoiled:* Do not waste your energy trying to find the crack in your neighbour's wall when your own is falling down.

LIN

19 *Approach:* Be indulgent towards those whose strength does not equal yours; come closer to them and trust them.

KUAN

20 *Contemplation:* You are in the habit of living on the peaks in order to contemplate your navel; you can do this underground as well, and the result will be the same.

SHIH HO

21 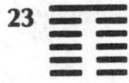 *Biting through (or clearly defined penalties):* This is the moment for the Dragon to charge. Bring out your claws and shoot out your flames as an example; this time you must use your authority.

PI

22 *Grace:* Even if it is said with flowers, it is nevertheless said. Do not make the mistake of accepting candy when you know that it contains poison.

PO

23 *Splitting apart:* It is necessary to improve the situation. Yield to reason: the edifice is cracking everywhere.

FU

24 *Return — the turning point:* Come out of your hole; the storm is over and the crisis past.

WU WANG

25 *Innocence:* Trust your intuition but do not use it as an absolute truth to be flung at your neighbour's head.

TA CH'U

26  *The taming power of the great:* Power and strength. However, do not fall asleep on your laurels. Responsibility and competence are expected of you.

I

27  *The corners of the mouth:* Material and spiritual nourishment. You tend to suffer from attacks of ravenous hunger; overeating will not calm this, nor will it satisfy your body or your mind.

TA KUO

28 *Preponderance of the great:* Do not take too much on your shoulders, morally or physically. An overloaded donkey may be a good donkey, but he is still only a donkey.

K'AN

29  *Fathomless water:* Do not deviate from your route, do not weaken or become discouraged. Remain unruffled.

LI

30 *Clinging, fire:* Do not squander your energy uselessly; anger merely gives the illusion of strength. Create solid ties, but do not trip on the rope.

HSIEN

31 *Influence:* Be opportunistic; profit from the occasion to meet others and join with them. This is not the moment to give yourself airs, even if you are dying to do so.

HÊNG

32  *Duration:* Do not hesitate to criticize yourself, something you are not in the habit of doing; you know so well how to criticize others.

TUN

33  *Retreat:* This is the moment for you to become a hermit, but do not do it in order to be pitied; you are very capable of living alone.

TA CHUANG

34 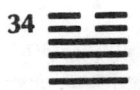 *The power of the great:* Strength, movement, energy. Learn to control them, otherwise you will race straight towards catastrophe. Before charging into the fog, listen to the weather report.

CHIN

35  *Progress:* If you, a celestial Dragon, are offered the Milky Way, do not ask for the moon as well.

MING I

36  *Darkening of the light:* If the darkness is outside you there is no point in showing a white flag or sending out an SOS — rely only on yourself. If the darkness is within, seek out the shadows which are obscuring your being.

CHIA JÊN

37  *The family:* Although it is constraining at times, it also gives a feeling of security: it is up to you to judge.

K'UEI

38  *Opposition:* Although you are hardly the tolerant kind, you must accept the tastes of others. Your freedom is limited by them.

CHIEN

39 *Obstruction:* Do not insist on butting against a concrete wall when a ladder has been offered to you — or else learn to pole-vault.

HSIEH

40 *Deliverance:* Do your spring cleaning and throw out all those old things that are encumbering your life. Live fully in the present.

SUN

41 *Decrease:* Times are hard, even for Dragons. Liking luxury, brilliance and ostentation, rediscover the poetry in soft candlelight, in simplicity and sincerity.

I

42 *Increase:* Mild weather, a period of blossoming. Profit from these fair days, but be careful of getting sunburnt.

KUAI

43 *Breakthrough:* An ideal situation for a Dragon. Advance, be strong, refuse to compromise, elbow your way through, raise your voice if need be.

KOU

44 *Coming to meet:* Be careful of sleeping waters, whose seething depths could well attract you; refuse an alliance with a confused and troubled person, who would hamper your freedom.

TS'UI

 **45** *Gathering together:* Can be favourable if ties have already been established; but beware of sly infiltrators.

SHÊNG

 **46** *Pushing upwards:* You are going to be able to prove your method and your competence; assume responsibilities, take care of small details as you like to do, but do not add to them.

K'UN

 **47** *Oppression:* Alas, you are less convincing and your energy is failing. Analyse the situation, be lucid and realistic — but active!

CHING

 **48** *The well:* Do not turn vital structures upside down; your need to transform, to change, should not destroy. There are those necessities which man must not touch.

KO

 **49** *Revolution:* There is a fight in the offing; you are always ready, but do not play the Boy Scout.

TING

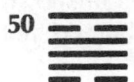 **50** *The cauldron:* Reinforce your position, but do not forget to take others' needs into account.

CHÊN

51 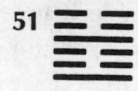 *The arousing (shock, thunder):* There is electricity in the air, trials on the horizon and big clouds floating above your head; you must confront ordeals without modifying anything.

KÊN

52 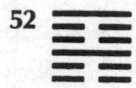 *Keeping still:* Seek solitude in your grotto or on the top of your rocky peak. After the storm, isolation and meditation will be good for you.

CHIEN

53 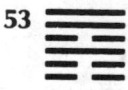 *Development (gradual progress):* You must agree to enter by the side door before attempting a grand entrance. If that hurts your feelings, buy yourself a small red carpet and discreetly unroll it.

KUEI MEI

54 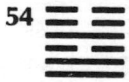 *The bride:* Be on your guard and think before you act.

FÊNG

55  *Abundance:* Moral and physical abundance; make use of it before the wheel turns, which you must accept with the same serenity.

LÜ

56  *The wanderer:* Go far away, discover unknown horizons and new perspectives, but do not always behave like a conqueror.

SUN

57  *The gentle:* It is useless to make the ground tremble and to spew out flames. Be kind and have patience; be stubborn without being surly — you will come out on top.

TUI

58  *The serene, the joyous:* It would be a good idea for you to glance at other human beings; you might then notice that you are not alone.

HUAN

59  *Dissolution:* Rise above your egotism; it stifles you and makes you turn round in circles. Be careful — you are walking on your tail.

CHIEH

60  *Limitation:* Can be profitable for you because you tend to do too much; do not be excessive for yourself, you already are for others.

CHUNG FU

61 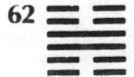 *Inner truth:* If you feel the need to convince others of something, ask yourself if it is really true. Act and leave words for another occasion.

HSIAO KUO

62 *Preponderance of the small:* If you do not have the opportunity to navigate on the high seas, take a canoe and paddle round a pond.

CHI CHI

63 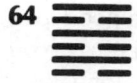 *After completion:* Do not be too impatient to reach the peak; take time to enjoy the climb. Once at the top you will have to plan your descent, which is sometimes more difficult than the ascent.

WEI CHI

64 *Before completion:* Do not sell the skin of the Dragon before you have laid him low! Do not glorify what you have not finished.

YEAR OF THE SNAKE

 1905·1917·1929
1941·1953·1965
1977·1989·2001

THE DOMAINS OF THE SNAKE

十二生肖

THE SNAKE AND ITS SYMBOLISM

The Snake, lord of the tortuous, silent and sinuous, has haunted our dreams and legends since the beginning of time, exciting in turn our anxieties and desires, attracting and repulsing. Whether coiled beneath a stone, winding round our hearts or poised with head high before our astounded eyes, the Snake is always present. Companion of sorcerers and seers, his symbol is the circle — one of the highest because it pertains to the infinite and thus to all esoteric knowledge. In the East, in tantric Yoga and Buddhism, he incarnates the *Kundalini*, those essential and subtle energies that circulate from the base of the spine to the top of the skull, connecting vital mental and suprapsychic spheres. The awakening and liberation of the *Kundalini Snake* constitutes one of the decisive steps towards spiritual discovery, arousing formidable paranormal powers, such as telepathy, clairvoyance and levitation.

The Snake recalls us continuously to his multiple universes, symbols and myths, ceaselessly astonishing and surprising us, even in our sleep. Sacred reptile? Or representative of evil, demon and god of Mother Earth, inhabiting at will waters, marshlands, mud and peat bogs? Crawling from the depths of the earth, emanating from chaos, he rises from the mists of time and from the most obscure depths of our unconscious, which he has always nourished with dreams and illusions.

The Snake's image is inseparable from Chinese culture and civilization, for he is the mythical father of the Chinese emperors. His legend is as follows:

In the beginning was chaos; only animal life existed. Somewhere between the heavens and the earth lay a life composed of forms and matter, replete with marvellous colours, divine sounds and intoxicating perfumes. But no being could perceive these colours, smell these perfumes or hear these sounds.

Fire heated the shell of chaos, licking its enormous egg with thousands of flames, diffusing its creative heat, watching over its hearth, its 'cauldron', its life. All that belonged to lightness formed the sky and all that belonged to heaviness formed the earth.

And then Pan-Ku was born and the organization of the world began. Pan-Ku grew up to become the Great All: he joined the heavens with the earth, his skull touched the summit, the starry vault; his body pierced the heavens and his feet dug deep into Mother-Earth.

The years passed. The sky became higher, the earth heavier and increasingly unfathomable. Pan-Ku created the wind, space and clouds; he caused thunder and lightning to rumble and flash. To heat the earth, he gave the sun; to create cold, he offered the moon. Finally, Pan-Ku gave his own blood, body-fluids, skin and hair. And, with a last kiss, he abandoned his teeth and bones to become stones and metals to solidify the earth.

Through Pan-Ku the sun heated the earth, the moon shone and the planets and stars were born. But until the arrival of Nu-Wa, no human being had appeared. Nu-Wa's beauty was incomparable, his virtues those of the wise. His body was that of a snake and his head of a human being.

Crawling on the earth, Nu-Wa became intoxicated with the thousands of perfumes emanating from it and understood that they were the aroma of life. Using his mouth to dig into the yellow earth, he heaped it up and moulded it for a long time. Thus a human being came into the world from the mouth of Nu-Wa, possessing the head of a man and the body of a monkey. This was the ancestor of the first emperors of China.

A few notes on the Snake
Principal qualities: Reflective, organized, alert and wise.
Principal defects: Jealous and obstinate. Does not listen to a word one says to him.

Work: Wilful, determined. Believes in physical and mental economy, organizing and calculating his actions without any waste of effort and energy.

Best role: Professor of philosophy. He adores Greek and Latin.

Worst role: Assembly-line worker; it would literally make him ill.

Money: Ambiguous. Not very economical, although circumspect. Likes to please himself and lives from day to day, counting on luck, chance and his intelligence.

Luck: To be born on a warm summer day. A Snake born in winter on a stormy night will be in danger all his life.

Cannot live without: Pleasing others.

Adores: Ornamentation and long nightly confidences in bed.

Detests: To be taken in or set up as an example.

Leisure activities: He likes to repaint the walls, change his possessions round and spend tranquil weekends in the country playing classical music and reading.

Favourite places: The desert; dry, wild stretches of land under a limpid sky — and his own home.

Colours: Red and green.

Plants: A rock-garden, ferns.

Flowers: Heather, thistle.

Professions: Professor, philosopher, teacher, psychiatrist, psychologist, diplomat, ambassador, astrologer, clairvoyant, head of personnel — and all professions requiring the skill of divination.

The four ages in the life of the Snake according to Chinese tradition

The *childhood* of the Snake will be happy, but only if calmness reigns within his family, otherwise this age will be critical. His *youth* will be free of problems. On the other hand, in *maturity* he will be at the mercy of all kinds of passions and his emotional life will often be unstable. In *old age* he will finally profit from his wisdom, although the fires of love will die slowly and are likely to cause him problems for a long time.

THE PSYCHOLOGY OF THE SNAKE

There are few animals in the world as rich in symbolic significance as the Snake; an entire book would hardly suffice to enumerate them. From the snake who bites his tail, symbol of eternal renewal, to the snake of the Tibetan 'Book of the Dead' ('I am the Snake Sata who lives in the furtherest reaches of the earth. I die, I am reborn, I am renewed and I become young each day . . .'), to China where he represents wisdom, this crawling creature accumulates dreams and nightmares and serves as an outlet for a plentitude of anxieties. Who does not recoil before a snake? Even when one knows very well it is not poisonous, our initial reaction is one of fear or disgust. If its bite represents a danger — and in some countries a mortal one — our terror knows no limits.

However, if we made the effort to overcome our prejudices, we might admit that, on a strictly aesthetic level, a snake is beautiful. Supple, sinuous and glossy, he fascinates, strangles, poisons or paralyses. He is endowed with an infinity of quasi-magical powers.

The snake of our earliest childhood memories is the one that caused such disorder in God's earthy paradise. No wonder he is feared! We tend to forget that he was only a vehicle adopted by Satan to lead Eve into temptation, an appearance on which our judgement has been based for generations. What a heavy heritage for these poor creatures who certainly never asked for it!

This analogy with sacred history is what brings us closest to the Snake as a sign of the Chinese zodiac. In the zodiac, as in the Bible, he is the *tempter* — the most seductive, fascinating and, in one sense, the most dangerous. Chinese astrological tradition affirms that no other signs, except those of the Tiger, Monkey, and sometimes the Pig, can resist his charm — a natural quality of persons born during the years of the Snake. These creatures are endowed with a kind of inner radiance which has nothing in common with, for example, the sparkling brilliance of the Dragon, but which radiates, charms and wins over the most forbidding and sceptical of individuals.

Those born under the sign of the Snake are distinguished, polished and elegant, refined in their dress and bearing. Handsome or ugly, they all have 'something' which attracts from the start because they are amiable, sociable and polite. In social gatherings they attract attention by their humour and the brilliance of their conversation, and they hold this attention because one senses that underneath this agreeable appearance lies a mystery and depth which is absolutely fascinating. It is this harmonious relationship between a well-prepared, polished exterior and a reflective, lucid personality which makes Snakes irresistible. And they know it, paying attention to both sides, caressing one and cultivating the other.

Endowed with a power of rapid intellectual assimilation, they are constantly learning something new; characteristically, they adore reading and are real library-mice. They use their knowledge to charm their audience and derive great satisfaction from doing so, for they need to exchange ideas and debate opinions. Dialogue is as indispensable to them as the air they breathe. But the dialogue must not be superficial, but rather philosophic and even abstract. Snakes are known to spend entire nights in long intellectual discussions punctuated by reflective silences when one of them pronounces a 'historic phrase' or discovers another way to remodel the world. Conversation with Snakes is always agreeable, for they are profound, intelligent, thoughtful and cultivated, and possess wise answers to many questions. Their judgement, generally free from prejudice, is based on observation. They dislike disputes, violence and vulgarity; loud people who lose control of themselves literally make them squirm, and they will glide rapidly away from them, hissing as they go. They tolerate only music and sotto-voce conversations. I almost forgot: Snakes also love applause — but only when they have earned it and are feeling proud of themselves.

Snakes are intuitive; one can even speak of a 'sixth sense'. They instinctively feel things before they occur and detect the inner thoughts of others when conversing. All this, along with their imagination and mental alertness, makes them well-armed for the battle of life.

Their behaviour is calm and peaceful, for they love harmony and stability. They are also adaptable, well-balanced and endowed with a firm will which they reveal without hesitation when their moral or material comfort is threatened, reacting with the same vindictive vivacity as does their animal sign when someone steps on its tail. The rest of the time they doze. Snakes believe in making the least possible effort: if they can do their work correctly in an hour, they feel there is no point in working longer. The time thus gained will be spent reading a book in a comfortable armchair or stretched out on a soft carpet. When Snakes have nothing to do they can be amazingly lazy. They will yawn, roam around in a state of semi-undress, arrange flowers, water the plants, listen to music and move objects around. Then they will fall asleep, waking very late in the morning.

On the other hand, if they really wish to obtain something they are capable of moving heaven and earth to achieve their ends, even going so far as to discreetly eliminate their competitors. When the motive is strong enough, they are extremely persevering.

Snakes are lucky and, happily for them, often win their battles, for they are bad losers. They take failure as a personal affront and do not tolerate insults.

They are good advisors, understanding and far-sighted, who like to help their friends — as long as money is not involved, for they are quite stingy. But they adore being asked for help.

However, Snakes do have some defects: they do not listen to a word of what is said to them. Nor do they listen to advice, or, if they do, they assimilate it and a year later announce it as their own. They are capable of lying if the 'circumstances' and their wellbeing demand it. Very vulnerable, they detest being put in the wrong, contradicted or criticized, which brings out their aggressive instincts. They then become unkind — even hypocritical and vindicative — and seek revenge, which they will pursue for a long time.

THE SNAKE AS A CHILD

The child born during a year of the Snake is not difficult to raise because his need for peace and tranquillity is such that from his earliest years he will make the effort to adapt to personalities very different from his own. Also, he spontaneously seeks to please and understand his parents and loves to be treated as an adult. He appreciates being told secrets (a proof of confidence in him which reassures him) and does not fear responsibilities.

On the other hand, the Snake child has an enormous need for affection and tenderness; the slightest sign of interest in someone else can make him anxious and demoralize him. Consequently, if you desire a Snake child, remember first of all that he needs to be *preferred*. Extremely exclusive, he would not tolerate sharing his parents' love with a swarm of brothers and sisters: he should be an only child, around whose cradle the good fairies assemble with a chorus of fond and admiring exclamations.

One might well think that if the Snake child were made to share he would become less exclusive and demanding. Perhaps, but more likely this would only arouse a host of anxieties in him for which he would compensate by developing the defects of his sign, becoming introverted, vindictive or even sly. Extremely attached to his parents, the Snake child is sensitive to family harmony. Parental disputes risk scarring him forever, just as the shortest absence is felt to be a painful abandonment. However, if his parents should divorce he will be happier staying with one of them rather than being torn between the two. But the parent in question should be prepared for some problems if he or she should decide to remarry; the step-parent will need a great deal of diplomacy when dealing with the little Snake.

The young Snake works well at school, but erratically: zero in some subjects, brilliant in others. He is often gifted for artistic pursuits and literature. He does not enjoy violent games, preferring creative activities. Irregular in his work rhythm, he needs a lot of rest and relaxation.

LOVE LIFE

The Snake is one of the most seductive signs of the Chinese zodiac. According to tradition, the other animals are advised to flee from the Snake for they cannot resist him.

Why does the Snake have such a dangerous reputation? Because, it is said, he spends an enormous amount of energy seducing his victims, whom he then coils round and stifles. Once his prey has consented and been carefully immobilized, the Snake will seek another adventure, frequenting night haunts in search of his next victim.

Let us try to understand a little better why this is. Snakes are exclusive and jealous people; they love to feel they are the centre of the universe in their partner's eyes. Although they may accept that their spouse is interested in his work (one must, after all, live, and the Snake is realistic), once they believe that their partner has found some greater interest or more stimulating dialogue, they will be dramatically wounded; it will be unpardonable. To the Snake, the best means of avoiding such disquiet and anxiety is to immobilize his or her partner.

Fidelity is another question. Snakes have a very individual conception of it, and the male above all, who believes he is being perfectly faithful if he returns home regularly. The female Snake is more stable, but detests feeling cornered and prefers to retain a minimum of liberty and independence.

Both sexes have a profound need to please and attract, which gives them the impression that they truly exist. It is natural for them to behave charmingly, but this must not be taken advantage of; if they are the victims of a jealous scene they will become even more distant and move even further away.

Snakes are sensual, passionate, and blossom in a relationship based as much on physical compatibility as on dialogue. Even so, good communication with their partner is absolutely indispensable. They love to exchange ideas about books, music or unusual philosophical problems. When Snakes find what they have been seeking, they are easy to live with and are tolerant, understanding and conciliatory. But they will always have a vague idea of possession in the back of their minds — sometimes in spite of themselves.

FAMILY LIFE

If the male Snake does not always have an excellent reputation in Far Eastern countries (he is considered to be a Don Juan and seducer; inconstant, but charming), the female is sought for in marriage, being often beautiful, usually wise and always an excellent housekeeper. Both sexes are faithful to their families and, even when they stretch the marriage contract a bit, their fear of violent ruptures causes them to return regularly to the conjugal home. The fact that they are understanding parents some-times undermines their authority, for 'putting themselves in their children's place', they find they are unable to direct them objectively.

Children born under the sign of the Rat, Dragon or Rooster will get along very well with a father or mother Snake, who in turn will be amused by them. Young Goats and Pigs will be a bit too much under the thumb of their Snake parents, who should encourage them to leave the family nest, however great the effort. A Snake parent will have great difficulty coping with the obstinate character of an Ox child, the independence of a Tiger or a Horse, or the passionate idealism of a Dog; these children will find their parents difficult. With a Monkey child, the relationship will be based more on comradeship than authority, and both will be very happy together. The Rabbit child will feel secure. But if an adult Snake has a child born in his own sign, he will smother it, and the young Snake will suffer acutely in cutting the umbilical cord.

As a rule, Snakes are comfortable in a married state, provided they are given minimal liberty; the legal bond reassures them and allows them the better to possess their partner. But if their choice is not a wise one, they will be exposed to the dangers of adultery and hidden passions. They should therefore reflect carefully before committing themselves, for the slightest error will lead them towards an exceedingly unstable emotional life — the opposite of what they need. They will do better to marry late when they have had some solid experience.

PROFESSIONAL LIFE

Those born under the sign of the Snake have mixed views about success. One has to remember that their principal quality — wisdom — distances them considerably from conflicts, rivalries and other such power struggles. The Snake's ambition can be defined in a single phrase: 'to be able to lead the life I like'. If he is near the point of success he will be remorseless, laying traps for his adversaries and revealing himself to be calculating, canny and even hypocritical. When he has attained his goal he will calm down, often perfectly content to enjoy his acquisitions voluptuously. He will feel no need to go any further, to make enemies or to become a victim of over-work for the sake of additional wealth or power.

Naturally, the Snakes' need for quality prohibits them from attaining the easier satisfactions of life. This is why they continue to struggle on mechanically, never over-tiring themselves. Also, success suits them: they know very well how to use their charm and are masters at insinuating themselves into the good graces of their superiors until they have become indispensable to them. Without getting into trouble, they fulfill marvellously the delicate tasks of mediator, intermediary and public relations. They know how to present an idea and how to outline a programme logically and coolly. When not using their charm, Snakes will keep it in reserve — and put forth another quality: their sense of organization.

If they want to, they can carry out a difficult job without appearing overworked yet without letting others overlook their merit in doing so. They are intelligent, determined and courageous people, and very conscious of their potential. But sometimes, due to their laziness, they will leave it to others to act — and even work — in their place. In the last lap of certain triumph, they will take up the torch; but they will be yawning. The Snake is the most opportunistic of all the Chinese signs: he will know how to seize any valuable opportunity and leave aside those with lesser attractions. He will even go so far as to help you — if you can be of use to him. If this fails, he will try something else. He is never finished with experiences.

MATERIAL LIFE

Snakes love money because it gives them the lifestyle they want: surrounding themselves with pretty objects, holidaying on tropical beaches, buying new clothes regularly and all the books and records they might wish. Without money, they would not be able to do this, and they know it. 'I must have' is their motto. And when a Snake has decided that he needs something, he gets it! They are not at all ashamed to admit this. After all, is it not natural to seek what one desires? Even the idealistic Dog has no answer to that question.

Thus Snakes are self-seeking. They are not the kind to fall in love before investigating their partner's bank account. They accept that they would never have the same tastes as a hippy in ragged blue jeans — unless he or she was the son or daughter of a Greek shipowner. If someone proposes a job, they immediately make inquiries about its financial potential. Snakes have no false modesty.

Being lucky and resolute social climbers, they can be counted on to achieve a certain affluence in their life style; they rarely lack money.

Snakes are not lenders; 'charity begins at home' is another of their mottos. But they are not economical either and spend what they have rapidly for their pleasure and well-being. Unlike Tigers, Snakes do not like to take risks; they are not speculators. As long as they do not have to deprive themselves of anything, their interest in the material side of life will be satisfied; not because they have money put aside, but because they count on luck and destiny to put them in the path of new funds. Nevertheless, Snakes do hanker after a little security, a few investments they can count on. When they are in love or wish to seduce someone, they will find presents enough; and they spoil their family, but only when the mood strikes them.

ENVIRONMENT

The French poet Baudelaire wrote of beds full of gentle aromas, divans deep as tombs and strange flowers adorning rooms. Himself a Snake, the poet's vision is representative of the universe of this sign. Snakes are people of refinement who adore ancient objects, inlaid furniture and delicately coloured Persian carpets — preferably a little worn. Their taste is faultless: they understand the harmony of colour and shape. Their equilibrium requires that they live in an environment they have created in their own image: if you enter a Snake's home you will see immediately whether it was he who chose the decoration because it will *resemble him*. If not, you can be sure that he will soon move — or redecorate the entire place.

Everything in a Snake's home is definitely comfortable and designed for the pleasure of the senses. It is as though our Snake counted on his home to complete his conquests of the outside world, with classical music playing softly, deep cushions, perfumed candles, lovely flowers, a well-filled· library and rare liqueurs and wines.

Naturally, there is the other side of the coin: some cupboards will be in disarray, and he will pass systematically behind you to empty the ashtrays and replace objects that you may have moved by only an inch. He does not do this to vex you; it is a mechanical reaction.

Wherever he goes, the Snake will repaint the walls; he would be a nervous wreck if he had to live with someone else's colour scheme. He detests hotels, anywhere temporary and all furnished places. He often carries with him a pile of ravishing but useless knick-knacks which help him to recreate his personal universe.

It is difficult for him to live with someone because he cannot adapt to tastes other than his own. Environment is perhaps the one area in which he is the least compromising. Male or female, the Snake always needs his own little bachelor flat, office·or room. His well-being depends on it.

A guide to personal relations with a Snake

Methods of seduction: Indescribable. A knowing mixture of detached charm, sensuality, niceness and understanding — all blended differently depending on the Snake, but with the ingredients always the same. And then, to all this physical seduction (they are handsome!), one must add their innate fascination and magic, their astonishing ability to persuade others.

If he loves you: Immediately resist him (he hates it!), for tomorrow it will be too late. He does not need much time to make himself indispensable. If you love him too — good luck! Try to maintain a minimum of independence: he will complain, but will respect you all the more for it; and the respect of a Snake is precious.

He expects of you: That you be unconditionally faithful.

To keep you: He will find your weak point — the chink in your armour — and will use it to soften your heart, to exalt you, listen to you — which he knows so well how to do!

If he is unfaithful: It is for the sheer pleasure of doing so, to be able to murmur under his breath, 'Ah, now I have the better of you!'

If you are unfaithful: He will be deeply shocked. If he loves you a great deal he will try to understand, but it will be difficult for him.

In case of a break between you: If you succeed in getting rid of him, congratulations — you deserve a medal. He will resort to any means to avoid being abandoned, which he hates. He also does not like to initiate the break, unless he wishes to teach you a lesson.

If you wish to give him a gift: It will cost a lot. Offer Mr Snake a work of art or a rare book, or a complete collection of classical records and tapes. Offer Mrs Snake a discreet jewel, but make sure it is real, for Snakes detest fakes and will be contemptuous if you offer one to them.

If you want to seduce him: Make him spend a sleepless night of mad caresses and intimate secrets. But rest up well beforehand.

If you want to get rid of him: Invite him to spend a weekend at your home. Without warning him that another admirer is in the bath, ask him if he wants to freshen up.

THE SNAKE AND THE OTHER CHINESE SIGNS

Snake/Rat

This is a strange mixture. At first glance both appear calm, clever and opportunistic, which makes for a positive common ground, above all in the field of business. But the Rat is active, and the Snake prefers a minimum of effort. The one will shake up the other, who in turn will calm him. Both are possessive, and the Snake has a completely relative notion of fidelity. If unfaithful to his partner, the Snake will only grudgingly accept that his partner is likely to do the same. The Rat will unsheathe his claws, the Snake will try to smother him. Life will become increasingly complicated.

In fact, the Rat and Snake do not need each other, for they are capable, as the occasion requires, of using the same weapons with equal efficiency. But as comrades they respect each other, and, sharing a taste for black humour, have fun together. If they establish an emotional tie, it will depend on mutual tolerance, a quality not notable in either. However, that is the only way they will be able to get along together. Generally speaking, they understand each other, and the Snake's quiet smile always calms the Rat's aggressiveness. But beware: such complicity is deep and secret; only they can sustain it.

Snake/Ox
A little good will on both sides will suffice, for the Snake gets along with almost everyone. The Ox will think that it is he who dominates, which will please him; and his Snake spouse, a willing believer in the less effort the better, will certainly not discourage him. She will surround and net him, as much by understanding as by complimenting him on his seriousness and his sense of responsibility, coiling about him with delight. The Snake, who loves comfort, does not lack will; but if he finds someone ready to work for two, he will only do what is strictly necessary — and then only to keep up appearances. And so the Ox will be consumed but remain content, and the Snake will also be content, feeling secure. Reassured of the fidelity of his companion, the Snake will indulge in a few discreet extras for amusement, but no-one will know about them.

On a business level, they compliment each other; one will work while the other reflects. Together they will be able to amass a considerable fortune.

Snake/Tiger
Hardly advisable. The vitality of the Tiger is likely to be too much for the contemplative Snake, who will neither wish nor be able to follow the busy, bustling rhythm that his companion imposes on his entourage.

Although peaceful, reflective and sometimes lazy, the Snake does not need to be aroused from his natural rhythm. He is capable of managing quite effectively in his own way and hates to be given advice. Sometimes dogmatic, which no Tiger can tolerate, he is possessive and tortuous, preferring the curved line to the straight, if by this he achieves his objective. In short, the Snake thinks of the end, while the Tiger relishes the means, hoping it to be admirable and delightful. They do not really understand each other and will often avoid each other. The Tiger will distrust the Snake's meanderings, and the Snake will be intelligent enough to avoid the Tiger, realizing that such an animal cannot be possessed.

On the other hand, this could be a marvellous business alliance. They complement each other beautifully, with one taking the risks and the other calculating behind the scenes. But they should not live together, for the Snake would betray the Tiger, who would in turn certainly destroy him.

Snake/Rabbit

They have in common a love of peace, security and aesthetic taste. They will tend to give preference to their home, environment and comfort and will appreciate beautiful objects and places. They would make a good pair of decorators. To have peace the Rabbit will have the wisdom to let the Snake think that he is the boss and master — at least on the emotional level. But the Rabbit's hesitations, and above all his virtuous side, will annoy the Snake whose sense of values is much more elastic.

However, whether it be love or friendship, this tie will be profitable for both. With patience, the Rabbit will perhaps succeed in persuading the Snake to accept another's opinion; and the Snake, who does not fear danger and adapts to all situations, will teach the Rabbit to be more philosophic.

Snake/Dragon

Traditionally this is one of the best friendly alliances for the

426

Dragon — especially when the Snake is the female. Although he must feel he is the stronger, the male Dragon needs to be proud of his wife; and female Snakes are wise, seductive and elegant. Nor will any female Snake be stupid enough to make her power apparent; the 'underground' manoeuvre is much more to her nature.

If the Dragon is female, the relationship will be more delicate: she will hope to be adulated by her Snake husband, a hope which he will satisfy for a while out of kindness, nevertheless coiling round her like a boa constrictor. Unfortunately, female Dragons dislike feeling smothered.

However, despite the Dragon's need to 'shine at any price', and the possessiveness of the Snake, this relationship is to be recommended. These Chinese zodiacal neighbours respect and rarely deceive each other: the Dragon has too much honour to wish to be diminished in someone's estimation, and the Snake is tolerant enough to withhold his criticisms concerning the flames and turbulence of his partner.

Snake/Snake
In friendship and in work Snakes appreciate the value of each other. Wearing a sly smile, they will amuse themselves by playing tricks on each other and setting traps for the sole pleasure of seeing the other escape. They will make each other laugh and have a lovely time together. But only in small doses. Chinese astrology is strict on one point: two Snakes cannot live together because they will stifle each other. This is true of all relationships between Snakes, particularly when in love or between parents and children. When these delicious reptiles live too close to one another they fade, as when one snuffs out a candle. And, since they are aware of this and since their discretion is nowhere near great enough to persuade them to take a back-seat, they become furious.

If you are a Snake who loves another Snake, do not live together. Meet from time to time, but if it is more than once a week, you might be in trouble!

Snake/Horse

The Horse will often be seduced by the Snake, and will remain almost faithful to him. He will have the impression — extremely mistaken — of being as free as the air; in fact, his Snake companion, coiled up in a corner of his imaginative brain, will be ceaselessly present and indispensable. On his side, the philosophic Snake will not take offence at being regarded occasionally as a piece of furniture, and will know how to find his own interests. The Horse will amuse him by his shifts in mood and he will have the impression of being at the circus.

But the day will come when the Horse's egotism will cause him to tire of his Snake companion, who will have trouble replacing him. This will not be bad for the Horse: it will allow him to avoid being swallowed up.

Still, this relationship is positive and exalting, especially at the start when the Horse is still blinded by passion and if there is some external obstacle to be overcome. If there is none in sight, they will have no trouble inventing one.

Snake/Goat

There is no problem with their getting along with each other. The Snake infinitely appreciates the fantasy, imagination and creativity of the Goat, and a love of art, beauty and harmony often unites them. And, they will rarely quarrel as it is too tiring.

But which of the two will do the work? On this level, the Goat is irregular and rather badly organized, and the Snake cannot be counted on to keep the accounts. And, when the Goat works and earns money, he wants it for himself — 'me first' — and perhaps a small gift from time to time as well.

If they have inherited some property they will live together peaceably, from time to time doing a little work, not so much to earn money as for the pleasure of it and to prove to others that they can do it. They will pitilessly mock commuters, those victims of the train-desk-sleep syndrome. They will wallow in their respective egotisms, and, even if the Goat occasionally strains on his leash, the relationship will work out in the end; bitterness and divorce are too fatiguing.

Snake/Monkey

Here there will be intellectual compatibility because, on this level, the Snake and Monkey are the most 'endowed' of the Chinese zodiac. They assimilate easily and think fast and effortlessly, adapting themselves to just about everything.

They complete each other: the Monkey is the cleverer on the surface, the Snake in depth. They would make an excellent business team, crammed with ideas and possibilities. They should not hesitate to join forces.

But emotionally, it is another story. The Monkey is traditionally one of the few signs capable of eluding the Snake's grasp. He will not allow himself to be eaten up, and the Snake, disgusted, will not persevere for long but will look for more acquiescent prey. Their reciprocal fidelity would not last for long. They should remain friends — easier and more profitable.

Snake/Rooster

This is the ideal couple of Chinese astrology. Traditionally they represent mind and matter, balancing themselves in harmonious union. They get along marvellously together. From the start they will appreciate each other's elegance: they could even buy matching outfits and look like fashion photographs. They love each other for their flattering appearance as a couple; even more, they understand each other perfectly. The Rooster will be able to sing in peace, and, between cock-a-doodle-do's, will recount his exploits to the Snake, who will comment on them with wit and humour. The Snake will feel secure because of the hard-working side of the farm-yard king, who will finally feel understood, being accepted as he is and not judged only by his brilliant plumage.

The Rooster and the Snake are accomplices. Even if they argue — usually because of an infidelity — their dialogue will always bring them together; they adore philosophizing into the small hours of the morning.

Snake/Dog

In general, Dogs like Snakes very much. They appreciate their wisdom and depth and forget their selfish and ambitious sides. They idealize them willingly, for the Snake's capacity for reflection makes them feel secure. One may well ask why, but that is simply the way it is.

Snakes, on the other hand, sincerely admire the honesty of Dogs, even if they are not disposed to imitate them. As a couple it can work out rather well, as long as the Snake accepts being idealized. But this will not satisfy him for long, because in matters of love he likes difficulty. So, as time goes by, he will glide around all over the place, having completely immobilized his Dog spouse, who will be left in charge of everything. The Dog, however, will remain content, for her Snake will return regularly to coil round her to keep her dependent. With the help of love from one and tenderness from the other, they will go far and be happy. Who are we to complain?

Snake/Pig

Not an obvious alliance. From the start, the Pig runs the risk of being completely taken in by the Snake, whose honesty is relative and highly personal. The unaffected nature of the Pig will often annoy the Snake, who will judge it — sometimes wrongly, but not always — as credulity, even innocence. After all, who would not raise his eyebrows when a Pig lets himself go with some lightly risque remarks?

Despite these difficulties, their powerful sensuality will unite them — even if it is not expressed in the same way.

The Snake, in any case, will eat the Pig in choice morsels. But here comes the surprise: the Pig will react quickly and will know how to extricate himself from the Snake's coils. Like the Monkey and the Tiger, he is capable of resisting the Snake, although not without leaving some skin behind. He should therefore be careful before allowing himself to be buried in the coils of this dangerous reptile; and the Snake should not mistake the Pig for a toy, or he will be in for some unpleasant surprises.

SOME SNAKE CELEBRITIES

Baden-Powell, Bela Bartok, Baudelaire, Borodin, Brahms, Louis Braille, Calvin, Copernicus, Darwin, Dostoyevsky, Flaubert, Faure, Arthur Fleming, Henry Fonda, Gandhi, Garbo, Paul Getty, Andre Gide, Gladstone, Goethe, Gogol, Princess Grace, John Kennedy, Landru, Lincoln, Harold Lloyd, Louis-Philippe, Martin Luther King, Mao Tse-tung, Madame Mao, Matisse, Mendelssohn, Miro, Montaigne, Montesquieu; Nobel, Jacqueline Onassis, Picasso, Edgar Allan Poe, Richelieu, Sartre, Schubert, Tennyson, St Vincent of Paul, Mae West.

YOUR COMPANION IN LIFE

生命伴侣

After the Chinese sign of your year of birth, here is the sign of your hour of birth

What is a Companion in Life, as understood in Chinese astrology? It is a sort of 'ascendant' sign corresponding to your hour of birth. This Companion is another animal belonging to the Chinese cycle of the twelve emblematic beasts, who falls into step with you and accompanies you, ever ready to help you brave the traps and ambushes along your route. A permanent and benevolent shadow, he can render the impossible possible.

He is your counterpart, but with his own character and tendencies and with a different psychology. Both guardian angel and devil's advocate, he will be a witness to your life and an actor in it.

Have you ever felt, deep inside yourself, the subtle presence of another 'myself' inhabiting you and with whom you live, at times in harmony, at others in conflict? Another self who sometimes criticizes you and at others encourages you? That is your Companion in Life.

There are times when he will appear to be an imposter or an intruder. Certainly, he often questions your habits and your moral or spiritual complacency. Accompanied by this companion, a shadow within, the route is less monotonous and the voyager multiplies his chances of arriving at his chosen destination. This, however, in itself matters little, for it is the journey and the manner in which it is conducted that are important. Indolence is the greatest danger: your Companion is capable of arousing you from a lassitude of spirit and, to that end, if necessary, robbing you of your certainties, trampling on your secret gardens and, finally, tearing away the great veil of illusion.

It sometimes happens that your Companion is of the same sign as your year of birth, a twin brother in a way — for example, a Snake/Snake. In this case, you must recognize that he will compel you to realize yourself fully and to live the double aspect — the Yin and the Yang — that your bear within yourself. In any case, you also bear within yourself

433

the twelve animals. So, set out on the long route, ready for the great adventure: the beautiful voyage during which you will encounter the harmoniously entangled, the solemn and the grotesque, the ephemeral reality, the dream and the imagined.

Table of hours corresponding to the twelve emblematic animals

If you were **born** between			your **companion** is	
	11 pm and	1 am		Rat
	1 am and	3 am		Ox
	3 am and	5 am		Tiger
	5 am and	7 am		Rabbit
	7 am and	9 am		Dragon
	9 am and	11 am		Snake
	11 am and	1 pm		Horse
	1 pm and	3 pm		Goat
	3 pm and	5 pm		Monkey
	5 pm and	7 pm		Rooster
	7 pm and	9 pm		Dog
	9 pm and	11 pm		Pig

These figures correspond to the *solar hour* of your birth. If necessary, you should check the summer times (Daylight Savings Time) and make the appropriate adjustment (sometimes two hours before or after statutory time).

THE SNAKE AND ITS COMPANION IN LIFE

 **Snake/Rat**

These two are brothers, but they fight each other mercilessly. Their territory is identical, but they have won it with bites and scratches, venom and trickery. The Rat and Snake are masters of the art of attack; moreover they are intuitive, professional spellbinders, who run the risk of putting each other to sleep by using mutual hypnosis. Alas, in this situation, the Rat cannot reverse roles.

The Snake will not lend himself to this little game. For the Rat the Snake Companion will always remain a mysterious reptile, coiled up under a stone, waiting to drag him at times into perilous labyrinths.

 **Snake/Ox**

The Ox will often be disorientated by the aggressiveness of his Snake Companion, who can nurture a dormant capacity for violence in him. The peaceful Ox, his eyes fixed on the blue line of the horizon, will not understand the behaviour of the reptile — his attacks, his secret hiding places, his sinuous approach. He will too often be tempted to crush him with a hoof, and in consequence will suffer many internal conflicts. The slow Ox, however, will be stimulated by this mysterious reptile who lures him to a fen and then shows him how he waits, hidden beneath a stone. Although his Serpent Companion disconcerts him, the Ox will certainly learn that there are paths that he must sometimes avoid.

435

 **Snake/Tiger**

He is the professional charmer, crafty and sly if the need arises, capable of biting and releasing venom in order to attain his ends. However, moderation will win out over the ill-loved Snake's aggressiveness. Coiled within the Tiger, he can also be a welcome symbol of knowledge and of the underground world. Habituated to the honour due his rank, the Tiger is sometimes forgetful of those who crawl yet accomplish the same ends. The Snake who lies within may pretend humility; this is easy for him, since he is a prince of detours and winding paths. However, he should be careful not to fall into the traps he sets for others.

 **Snake/Rabbit**

A strange creature, whose head is not easily distinguished from its tail. In love with anything strange, but not an adventurer, the Snake/Rabbit will daydream about travelling while curled up in a soft armchair. 'Inhabited' by a price of wanderings, he has a taste for suspense, mystery and the subterranean, discovering hiding places buried under a stone. He will not hesitate to take on the colour of a wall for the pleasure of deceiving, surprising and disconcerting you. Elusive, clever and shifty, he is as dangerous as he is seductive. If you meet up with a Snake/Rabbit, pinch yourself, because he is a professional spell-binder. He will seduce you somehow — with his charm or by blackmail.

 **Snake/Dragon**

A lucky and canny animal, the Snake/Dragon is a traveller on whom fortune will smile, and what he cannot obtain by force or charm he will obtain by malice and enchantment. If the Dragon sometimes makes the mistake of being too heavy or conventional, the Snake will lead him to value discretion, patience and the advantages of the indirect approach. A formidable beast, full of charm, he will bring a taste of mystery to his partner, who will shiver either with pleasure or with fear.

 **Snake/Snake**

Whether a rattlesnake, cobra or adder, he will prefer detours and by-ways to the main roads. But the result will be the same: he will arrive — slowly but surely — at the goal he has fixed for himself. The Snake/Snake will be unable to avoid complicating his life. When it seems too simple, he becomes bored; he always needs a little salt, a tasty sauce, because he is a complicated animal. Always on the defensive and slightly aggressive, he ardently cultivates a sense of property through his home which he makes a veritable refuge, an Ali-Baba cavern, piling up treasures which he jealously protects. If you sight him on your path, make a detour; even if you are not afraid of him, you reaction will give him so much pleasure!

 **Snake/Horse**

He is a wise dandy, combining elegance and ardour with highly developed moral demands which can sometimes conflict with his pride. For the Snake/Horse is a bad loser and does not accept failure. He is a winner and will not hesitate to be opportunistic and sly, restraining neither his tongue nor his heart. Nevertheless, since he is irresistibly charming, the Snake/Horse will be excused for his boastfulness and even his ill-nature. But he should not overdo it!

 **Snake/Goat**

It will be rather dangerous to fall in love with him: it is impossible to expect fidelity from the Goat/Snake. This reptilian Goat is a fickle being charged with fantasy; an artist who will make a 'goat' of you if you try to seduce him. At first he will seem docile, seeking your protection: but he will then pull you joyously along by the tip of your nose. Exclusive and jealous, he is scarcely aware of the contradiction, for his own bad faith is disarming. In life he will enjoy plenty of good luck and have the advantage of good taste and a capacity for finesse; but his instability will cause him considerable damage, some of which he will not recover from, above all during his mature years.

 **Snake/Monkey**

He will be rational and a good organizer, but he will not be able to conceal his strong superiority complex which, unless he takes care, will cause him major problems. An intelligent and quick animal, his tendency to get carried away will be tempered by deep reflection; even so, he will always refuse to listen to the advice of others, because of his pride and self-esteem. He will not entertain any argument about his ideas, still less that his work or his word be questioned. The Monkey/Snake is talkative, courageous and, at times, a liar. However, his ability and his subtlety are major trump cards.

 **Snake/Rooster**

An intuitive and frank animal, he will accomplish his tasks with a generous heart and with much good will and honesty — thus correcting the Snake's tendency to side-track — which will not prevent him from being uneasy, despite his apparent self-assurance. The Snake/Rooster flares up easily, so be careful if it is one of his bad days. He will attack with surprising aggressiveness and be entirely unjust simply to reassure himself. Do not attempt to expose his faults with evidence; he will be narrow-minded and never forgive you for having discovered his weak points. The Snake/Rooster is overly concerned with projecting a good image. He has a need to shine and surround himself with costly and beautiful things; this may appear superficial, but it is vital for his morale.

 **Snake/Dog**

He has a keen moral sense, is intuitive, but has a tendency to be pessimistic. Life with him can become very complicated. He is the kind to torment himself to excess, announcing the onset of a hurricane at the least rising of the wind, or a deluge after a few drops of rain. Ever on the watch and constantly on guard, he risks playing the role of the persecuted, one of those flayed alive, whose company one does not usually seek. This is a drawback, particularly since the Dog/Snake is courageous, warm and understands the meaning of faithfulness. However, he has a great need of love and reassurance.

 **Snake/Pig**

While he is peaceful, secretive and sensitive, he is also a bad loser and his motives are questionable. He does not like to lose and prefers solitude to risking failure. It is useless to try to distract him from his normal routine; he is too obstinate and distrustful. However, this does not stop him from being gullible. It is quite possible to 'take him in'; he will then oscillate between aggressiveness and running away, for at bottom he is tolerant but too proud to admit that his adversary may be right. Although he appears indifferent, the Snake/Pig actually loves money for its own sake and adores amassing treasures and booty. Apparently calm, deep within he is boiling. This solitary reptile is not lukewarm: he is a tough person with a tender heart.

THE SNAKE AND THE FIVE ELEMENTS

五行

YOUR ELEMENT

In Chinese astrology, each year is joined to an Element. There are five Elements: *Water, Fire, Wood, Metal, Earth.*

Each of the twelve emblematic animals is linked successively to each of the five Elements. For example, in the year 1900 the Rat was Metal, in 1912 he was Water, in 1924 he was Wood, in 1936, Fire and in 1948 he was Earth. Therefore, for the twelve years from 1900 he was linked to Metal, for the next twelve years to Water, and, for every succeeding period of twelve years, to each of the other Elements, in succession.

In order to determine the Element corresponding to the year of your birth, use the table below:

Years whose digits end in: 2 and 3 — Water
6 and 7 — Fire
4 and 5 — Wood
0 and 1 — Metal
8 and 9 — Earth

The same union of *Animal-Element* repeats every sixty years, for example, Rat-Metal appeared in 1720, 1780, 1840, 1900, 1960 and so on.

The five Elements are the primary forces affecting the universe. It is their particular association with each of the signs which provides the basis for every horoscope. Movement and fluctuation, Yin and Yang, these symbolic forces are in a perpetual state of action and interaction.

Wood gives birth to Fire, which gives birth to Earth, which gives birth to Metal, which gives birth to Water, which in turn gives birth to Wood.

SNAKE/WATER
(you were born in 1953)

The cold born of the northern sky descended to Earth and gave birth to Water. The Chinese consider Water more a synonym for coldness and ice than a symbol of fertility.

Characteristics of the Snake/Water
Water of winter nights, rigour and severity, calm and deep Water to be feared and respected, still Water sheltering underwater demons asleep in its depths; foetid and muddy Water of the marshes, a refuge of crawling creatures.

The Snake in love with humidity will be attracted to Water: marshes, ponds, stagnant pools, peat and bamboo. Such Water will not be bracing and invigorating for the Snake; it could provoke hesitation or even a halt in his sinuous course, a dangerous effect for this reptile with a Yang tendency, symbol of horizontal energy. The Snake/Water should therefore consider Water a passing Element only — a means or a tool, and not an end in itself.

Health of the Snake/Water
The Water organ is the kidney; its flavour is salty. Seek the bracing waters of the seaside, the torrents and the springs — but not mud baths, although they are excellent for rheumatism — and enjoy them in the sun, which is vital for you.

The Snake/Water and others
The Snake/Water will be calm and wise and his actions will be based on reflection. The Water Element will often be socially beneficial, calming the hyper-active side of the Snake, attracting him to meditation and the possibility of governing, mastery and control. The Snake/Water will then be just and honest; his words will carry weight and men will listen to him, allowing themselves to be guided•by his wisdom and moderation. The Snake/Water will be non-violent, an enemy of anger, aggressiveness and uncontrolled

force. He will be turned entirely towards his fellow men, intent on listening to their problems. An excellent psychologist or a prudent man of the law, he is a cool-headed leader and a warm, good-hearted man.

Advice for the Snake/Water
You have qualities which demand to be used, for the sake of others and for yourself; learn to discover them and put them into practice. Otherwise, they will turn against you, paralyse you and condemn you to be an eternal wanderer.

A Snake/Water year
The culminating point for a Snake/Water year will be winter, a period of gestation. The Yin of Water will balance the Yang of the Snake.

Profit from this year to restore your energies and regain your inner balance. You can be active, and successfully so, but avoid overwork and all excesses, which are so often followed by depression. Maintain your equilibrium and do not waste your energy, otherwise you will ruin everything by wanting to go too far too quickly.

Historical example of a Snake/Water year
1593

Henry of Navarre reverted to the Roman faith. Both the personal decision and its consequences were momentous. In an age when heresay amounted to treason against the state Henry, the legitimate heir to the last of the Valois, was also the avowed leader of the Huguenots, heretics, apostates and schismatics. France was riven by a civil war fired by religious dissension. The Catholic majority would never accept a Protestant as king, preferring to offer the throne to a Guise, even to the son of the Spanish King. The old furies roused by the presence of the infidel in Jerusalem were as nothing compared to the hatred for the schismatic in the sixteenth century. In England papacy was hated because of its threat by an alien authority. Over-governed since the days of Henry II the English temperament required the solitary reliefs afforded by the Protestant faith. The French sensed the need for control, both by their monarchy and the Church.

Henry, by his momentous decision, instinctively recognized this. He had tried but failed to subdue the capital. The resources of the Parisians were too strong for him, not only materially but spiritually; for the indulgent and complacent world of the Roman Church had risen with an iron will to combat the Protestant threat. Thus Henry determined on a policy of appeasement. He should be King of France first, secondly of the Faith, thirdly of that form of the Faith which appealed to his subjects.

On 23 July Henry publicly submitted to the authority of the Archbishop of Bourges and swore to defend the Catholic faith with his blood and his life and to die in it. He renounced the heresies of the schismatics of whom he had long been the leader. A week later he entered Paris, where he was accepted and welcomed as King.

SNAKE/WOOD
(you were born in 1905 or 1965)

To the East the wind blew in the sky and from its warm caress of the Earth, Wood was born.

Characteristics of the Snake/Wood

Wood is of the morning and of springtime. Its temperate nature loves harmony, beauty and elegance. Springtime will be fertile for the Snake, bringing him equilibrium and a sense of creation, encouraging him to develop his taste and desire for harmony and beauty. Nature will become his ally and inspiration, a fountain to which the Snake will go to slake his thirst, to become stronger and to discover nature's multiple powers and secrets. But Wood also contains passion, anger and vulnerability which, if excessive, has a tendency to cause one to lose all sense of proportion and, in turn, become destructive and devastating. The Snake should remain vigilant and lucid and try not to give in to this negative aspect of his Element.

Health of the Snake/Wood
The organ of Wood is the liver; its flavour is acid. The Snake/Wood will be anxious and tormented. He will suffer from a psychosomatic illness and will often need to compensate by over-eating. Cakes and chocolates may then please him, but they will not please his liver.

The Snake/Wood and others
The Wood Element will have a positive influence on the Snake's social life. Aware of his weaknesses, such as his anxiety and self-questioning, he will respond to his predicament with a relaxed attitude, preferring his imagination to run free rather than be constricted by the rigid structures of a society in which he feels asphyxiated. This is a just and reasonable attitude especially suiting the Snake, who prefers the circle to the square and the curve to the angle. With deliberate improvisation, the Snake will extricate himself marvellously from the most difficult situations; he will glide and sneak in and out and let the storm pass; then, when it is all over, he will reappear, tranquil and calm. Inventive and creative, he will be a painter, poet, musician, craftsman, or even a gardener, nurseryman or landscape architect — someone who combines beauty with space.

Advice for a Snake/Wood
You are the symbol of harmony, charm and beauty; you dream of space and liberty. Relax and yield to the imaginative. You have the soul of an artist, so do not close yourself up in an office or allow yourself to be choked by conventional pursuits. Being of Wood, you would end up by drying up.

A Snake/Wood year
The culminating point for a Snake/Wood year will be spring,

a period of growth and prosperity. Beauty and harmony will be your companions during this year. The Snake/Wood will be in his best physical and mental form, supple and intuitive.

Historical example of a Snake/Wood year 1905

In 1904 Admiral Sir John Fisher returned to the English Admiralty as First Sea Lord. The following year Earl Cawdor was appointed his political associate, the First Lord of the Admiralty. Their collaboration, although only lasting nine months, was memorable.

In 1905 Cawdor and Fisher planned for a war they considered likely if not inevitable. Fisher recognized that the great German admiral, Tirpitz, was building a fleet to fight the British navy. Given the intense jealousy of England felt by the Germans engaged in shipping and in foreign trade, and the rapidly increasing influence of these men over German policy, Fisher and Cawdor both understood that the British fleet should be concentrated in home waters and the traditional 'far flung' dispositions abandoned. To camouflage his plan Fisher took half of the Mediterranean fleet from Malta and based it in Gibraltar. There it could operate into the Atlantic. With Cawdor's backing, Fisher laid down the prototypes for England's future battle fleet, the battleship *Dreadnought* and the battle cruiser *Invincible*. Their construction made obsolete not only every British warship but also those of the German fleet. More important, the vast displacements of the new ships far exceeded the dimensions of the Kiel Canal through which any German ships of a comparable size would have to pass. Thus, Britain could build and equip a fleet of between 10 and 14 battleships before a single German ship of their class could be completed.

Politically, this programme was pacific in intention. Cawdor argued that with such a lead against them the Germans would give up the race. Thus war could be averted. However the Campbell-Bannerman government of

1906 was to throw the lead away, a typical 'liberal' measure which incited the Germans to rectify the balance. Furthermore, the Germans greatly improved on the British prototypes, particularly in the field of optics for gunnery and the protection of magazines. When the test came in 1916 the Royal Navy had only one advantage; its ships were accustomed to the sea. Fisher's and Cawdor's creative work had largely been nullified.

SNAKE/FIRE
(you were born in 1917 or 1977)

Heat was born in the southern sky, descended to Earth and fertilized it. From their union, Fire was born.

Characteristics of the Snake/Fire
The Fire Element is of the midday, the South and summer. Fire is Yang; it is the Element which animates; it quickens and transforms.

The Fire that quickens the Snake will perpetually feed and renew his energy. But it could also become dangerous and destructive: A Fire which consumes and devours. The Snake/Fire must learn to control his Element. He must not let it go out or let it flare up, for then all would be consumed in its path.

The health of the Snake/Fire
The organ of Fire is the heart, its flavour is bitter. Fire of summer and southern climes: do not allow yourself to be carried away by anger and control your aggressiveness; all excessive outbursts entail a futile loss of energy. Overwork can lead to a heart attack; slow down and have regular medical checkups.

The Snake/Fire and others
Warrior Fire, but lucid and clairvoyant Fire, too. Passionate and violent Fire, preferring manoeuvres to diplomacy. The

Snake/Fire will be a man of action and of war; an adventurer or an ardent political militant. He will often be a convinced and convincing individualist.

Alas, tolerance will not be his strong point; he will sometimes have to know how to throw water on his Fire, unless he is to end by mounting the pyre that he himself has lit.

Advice for a Snake/Fire
Take things upon yourself, but moderate your flame; you too easily set things ablaze and stir up discord which can turn against you.

A Snake/Fire year
The culminating point for a Snake/Fire year will be summer, a period of creation. Your Yang tendency will stretch toward the 'Great Yang', which will bring an unquenchable dynamism.

Historical example of a Snake/Fire year
1617

Both in England and in France the Monarch was ensnared. James I of England had been compelled to renounce his favourite, Robert Ker, who had accompanied him from Scotland as a page. By the time Ker was attainted and condemned he was the Earl of Somerset and the owner of Walter Raleigh's old manor at Sherborne in Dorset. George Villiers succeeded to the favours of the King. He had risen in much the same way as Ker, from page, cupbearer, gentleman of the bedchamber, to a knighthood, an estate and, in 1617, the Earldom of Buckingham. Buckingham flourished: Ker was to languish in prison until 1622.

The spice of pederasty was not the occasion of the French King's misfortune. He was the victim of his formidable mother, Marie de Medici, Regent of France, who had entrusted the affairs of the kingdom to one Concino Concini, an adventurer who required and was lavished with gifts and the peculations of office.

In 1617 Louis XIII officially came of age. But he was king in form only: the substance was denied him. Louis was not to be subborned. He made arrangements with his captain of the guard, Vitry. On the morning of 24 April Vitry and a group of courtiers stood about the entrance to the Louvre. Warned of Concini's approach he made to intercept him and announced to the astounded Florentine that he was under arrest. Concini, his hand to his sword, called for help but Vitry's accomplices were too quick for him. Five fired, one ball caught Concini between the eyes, one pierced an eye and another his throat; two missed him.

Shortly afterwards, Louis appeared at a window of the Louvre. The crowd gathered below acclaimed him. The young King offered his thanks and exclaimed — 'Now, at this hour, I am King. . .'

SNAKE/EARTH
(you were born in 1929)

Earth was born from the slowly falling Elements of the sky at its humid zenith.

Characteristics of the Snake/Earth
This is an afternoon Earth, the humid and hot Earth of summer. It is the symbol of the well-cushioned soft nest, of comfort and abundance; it is an Earth of slow and profound transformation.

This Earth is blessed for the Snake, inviting rest, meditation and revery; it is an Earth of reflection in which everything germinates, ripens, strengthens and dies. A refuge, lair and solitary retreat, it shelters fairy-lands and monsters. The Snake will feel secure, far from the trials and aggressions of the outside world, and will tend to turn in on himself and coil up under this Earth which invites him to relax, even to be inactive. This Element will be protective and soothing, inciting the Snake to idleness and passivity. Yet he cannot live continually underground: he needs sun, air and humidity. Prolonged hibernation would reduce him to a squeaking rodent.

Health of the Snake/Earth
The Earth's organ is the spleen; its flavour is sweet. The Snake/Earth should not remain inactive; he needs fresh air. He must summon up a certain aggressiveness to stimulate him if he is to maintain his charm.

The Snake/Earth and others
He will be prudent and circumspect, not getting involved lightly, weighing everything carefully and studying the terrain. Distrustful and suspicious by nature, he will be a gifted speculator and a prudent manager, slowly, surely and meticulously amassing wealth — sometimes by debatable means — and adept at concealing it. He has a sense of responsibility and admirably fulfils his role as head of the family, although at times he can be slightly despotic.

Advice for a Snake/Earth
You are often a stay-at-home: go out, communicate with others and keep up with the times; do not close yourself up in your dreams or your past. Put an end to your anxiety and, above all, to old habits — conventional bachelors and spinsters are not attractive. If you cannot overcome your distrust in the business world, at least make an effort to open up on a human level, especially on an emotional one. You will enjoy your success, for you can then breathe security while remaining creative.

A Snake/Earth year
The culminating point of a Snake/Earth year is summer. Summer is favourable for the Snake: free from all material constraints, discover the joys of creation, research and study. But do not close yourself up; leave your hole, come

out from underneath the stone and take a sun — not a sleeping — cure. Be more sure of yourself, reach further towards the world and the people in it.

Historical example of a Snake/Earth year 1809

Defeated in three successive wars and humiliated by the Austerlitz campaign of 1805, the Hapsburgs determined on a war to the finish. They had much to avenge, many humiliations to efface. In the spring of 1809 the signs were propitious. Despite the grave effects on England of Napoleon's 'Continental system' its subsidies were still available. The French armies, embroiled in the Iberian peninsula at deadly cost, appeared over-extended, deployed as they were throughout Europe and along the entirety of its coasts to help enforce the blockade of British goods to Europe. The British also promised diversionary attacks if a new Continental offensive was launched. The Russians, having recovered from Tilsit, were again menacing Poland and in Italy the French had suffered some rough handling from Austrian troops. Moreover, Napoleon's immediate army consisted only of inexperienced conscripts stiffened by troops from the confederation of the Rhine. Any military appreciation would favour an Austrian offensive.

Yet these appraisals proved worthless. A brief four-day campaign disposed of the army of the Austrian Archduke; two weeks later the French army entered Vienna. His first army lost, the Archduke resorted to his second, carefully held in reserve. He contested Napoleon's attempted crossing of the Danube honourably, but forced to battle at Wagram his army was routed and with it the hopes and expectations of the Hapsburgs. The Emperor concluded an armistice bringing an end to a campaign which had lost him one quarter of his estates and decimated his treasury.

Napoleon required more. He demanded and obtained the hand of the Emperor's 18 year old daughter in marriage. By this alliance the Austrian defeat was cemented.

452

SNAKE/METAL
(you were born in 1941)

In the sky, coming from the West, drought grazed the skin of the Earth and gave birth to Metal.

Characteristics of the Snake/Metal
Metal is of the night, of autumn and of cold. It symbolizes clarity, purity and precision. Its tendency is to be cutting, rigid and chaste; its comments harsh. The Snake/Metal will oscillate between beauty and destruction.

Alas, too much stiffness engenders sadness and moroseness. The Snake/Metal to an extent will be protected by his Element, for it is a veritable armour, shielding him from external danger; but not from internal danger, since it also will exclude the sounds and perfumes, feelings and sensations vital to his inner life. Metal will cool the Snake's warm blood, tending to harden him and make him rigid at the cost of his suppleness and intuition. Imagine a Snake that is completely stiff — he would break in two. Moreover, he will be attracted to an inaccessible and pure ideal which will merely bind him in an even more dogmatic rigidity. Pierce a hole in your handsome armour, let in a little oxygen and dream — you need it.

Health of the Snake/Metal
The organ of Metal is the lung; its flavour is pungent. Breathe deeply, seek the open air, sail or climb a mountain; avoid burrowing or deep-sea diving — at least psychologically.

The Snake/Metal and others
The Snake/Metal will be an energetic man — a military officer, top-level government official, judge or priest — all those professions which are regarded as 'serious'. He will always be just, upright, scrupulous and honest; but he will sometimes be fanatical, due to his love of purity. Loving work that is well-done, expecting and demanding perfection

in his own work, he will be pitiless with others, particularly those whom he loves and respects. Clear-sighted and perhaps suffering from his own demands on himself, he is much too proud to recognize his faults and will continue unflaggingly on his way, afraid of letting his resolve be weakened.

Advice for the Snake/Metal

You take yourself too seriously. Be less serious and grave — learn to smile a little. Try to be more humorous, for humour is the best defence against dramas and calamity.

A Snake/Metal year

The culminating point for a Snake/Metal year will be autumn. The Yin tendency of the midseason will unite with the Yang of the Snake, bringing moderation and equilibrium.

Profit from the alternation of Yin and Yang to rediscover your ancestral suppleness; release your armour and relax morally and physically. You have everything to gain, for rigidity is not a necessary element in governing; learn that relaxation and suppleness do not signify weakness.

Historical example of a Snake/Metal year
1521

Francis I of France had not accepted the decision of the Electors whereby Charles V of Spain became the Holy Roman Emperor. He was to contest it until defeated at the battle of Pavia in 1525. The new Emperor had also to contend with a heresy which threatened to fracture the faith of Christendom.

Martin Luther preached that justification was not to be found by work or efforts of the will but through faith alone, the gift of God's grace. His notorious 95 theses aroused strong reactions, and not only in Germany: even Henry VIII of England wrote an anti-Lutheran tract for which he was awarded the title 'Defender of the Faith'.

When the Emperor summoned Luther to the Diet of Worms in 1521 he hoped to force him to recant. Equally Luther, who was nothing if not argumentative, was anxious to expound his views but required and obtained a safe conduct before he appeared. The assembly had no sympathy for his arguments; nor did they approve the manner of his journey. Clad as a monk he had been accompanied by a following fit for a count. At Erfurt and other cities he had preached before massed crowds, exuding physically the pugnacious cast of his mind. Nevertheless he was treated with consideration and allowed time for reflection when asked if he retracted the opinions expressed in his books. Fortified by the night, the solace of the mystic, he appeared the following day, resolute; he retracted nothing. He stood by what he had written.

Thus ended the confrontation at Worms and the unity of the Church. Even Henry VIII, Defender of the Faith, would shortly break with Rome.

Analogical Table
of the Different Elements

Elements	Wood	Fire	Earth	Metal	Water
Years ending in	4 and 5	6 and 7	8 and 9	0 and 1	2 and 3
Colours	Green	Red	Yellow	White	Blue
Seasons	Spring	Summer	End of summer	Autumn	Winter
Climates	Wind	Heat	Humid	Dry	Cold
Flavours	Acid	Bitter	Sweet	Pungent	Salty
Principal organ	Liver	Heart	Spleen	Lungs	Kidneys
Secondary organ	Gallbladder	Small intestine	Stomach	Large intestine	Bladder
Food	Wheat, poultry	Rice, lamb	Corn, beef	Oats, horse	Peas, pork

Table of Harmony
Between the Elements

		Wood Female	Fire Female	Earth Female	Metal Female	Water Female
○○○ Excellent prosperity	Male Wood	● ●	○	○○○	○	○○
○○ Good harmony, understanding	Male Fire	○	○	○○	●	● ●
○ Effort needed	Male Earth	● ●	○○	○○	○○○	●
● Rivalries and problems of reciprocal domination	Male Metal	○	● ●	●	● ●	○○○
● ● Misunderstanding and incomprehension	Male Water	○○	● ●	●	○○○	○

THE
FOUR SEASONS
OF
THE SNAKE

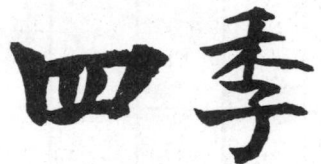

If you were born in spring

Snake/Aries

An extremely contradictory personality: on the one hand we find the less-effort-the-better philosophy of the Snake; on the other, the love of action-for-its-own-sake of Aries. The person marked by this combination is likely to behave unpredictably and suffer rude awakenings. One must not tread on his toes, for he is above all jealous of his independence. He lives at his own rhythm (a euphemism), and is charming if given free-rein materially and emotionally. In this case, he will always return home. But if he is nagged, bothered or bored, he will leave. It is best to accept this in advance.

The Snake/Aries often thinks faster than he acts, but he is very creative. He could become a talented artist, but in practical terms he has a tendency to rely on luck and wait for providence to fill his wallet. Lacking perseverence, he will alter his course whenever he has the impression that he is not getting somewhere. Of all the Snakes he is perhaps the least attracted to difficulties, the most sanely and amiably egotistical — and the most frank.

Snake/Taurus

Charming and a stay-at-home, this Snake loves to warm himself in the sun. His digestion is slow; he is not especially active and does not like to be pushed, being unequalled in his inevitable reply of 'what's the hurry, there's no fire' — he always has time. He is believed to be smug and indifferent. Be careful: the Snake/Taurus is realistic and extremely clear-sighted where his personal comfort is concerned. If it is a question of preserving or improving it, he will stretch, coil to spring and his attack will be as natural and inevitable as the rising tide.

The Snake/Taurus's skin is thick and solid and his personality resistant; but, being also materialistic and acquisitive, he is likely to lose sleep if his shares drop a point or two on the stock exchange (currency devaluation could bring on a depression).

In private he is agreeable and affectionate. Rather faithful for a Snake, he is also horribly jealous and an easier prey for rage than any Othello; the most innocent glance by his companion towards someone else makes him ill. Beware: he may take ten years to react, but when he does he will become wildly furious. Then nothing can stop him, and he will charge like an enraged elephant. If you want to be unfaithful to a Snake/Taurus, be secretive, otherwise buy yourself a coat of armour.

Snake/Gemini
He is rather turbulent for a Snake, but his bite is not fatal. He is not unkind, and if he hurts another's feelings it is always for emotional reasons. In fact, he cannot be held in check: he is inconstant, undisciplined and so sinuous that it is difficult to know where he begins and where he ends. He literally slips between one's fingers.

Emotionally the Snake/Gemini is difficult to live with, but his company is enriching. He is intelligent, intuitive and brilliant, and manipulates his ideas like a magician with his props. He is capable of selling refrigerators to Eskimos or fur coats to the Arabs. Nothing is impossible for him; he loves to convince, to persuade and seduce, which is why he fascinates and twines round Little Red Riding Hoods.

The Snake/Gemini has only to choose. All routes are open to him, particularly those calling for cleverness, diplomacy and eloquence; but working in a coal mine or on the docks is not for him, for he is physically weak.

If you were born in summer
Snake/Cancer
This Snake is sensitive, susceptible and slightly egocentric. He takes himself to be the centre of the world and can quietly doze for hours at a time, coiled about himself. No-one is lazier than a Snake/Cancer: he finds a profound pleasure in doing nothing, nonchalantly stretching himself, savouring his well-being and contemplating the passing

hours. If you suddenly rush at him he will turn mean or close himself up like an oyster — on your fingers. He has a great deal of imagination and remarkable intuition, and he is understanding. The Snake/Cancer is efficient, tenacious and opportunistic, thinks out his projects well in advance and is good in a crisis. That dealt with, he will fall asleep again. He is not made for solitary or constricting jobs, but he does a great deal of work without seeming to take much trouble. This sometimes makes others jealous of him.

Extremely attached to his family, the Snake/Cancer is at his best in intimate surroundings; at his own fireside, surrounded by those he loves, listening serenely to the tempest raging outside, he blossoms. Do not worry about his future: he will never lack for anything. If he has no good reason to be active, he will allow himself to be supported with the greatest of pleasure.

Snake/Leo

This is a handsome alliance, for the conquering energy of Leo dynamically influences the contemplative side of the Snake; and the intelligence of the latter diminishes the defects of the Lion, who, among other things, tends to be authoritarian and to take himself too seriously. The Snake/Leo is a man worth consulting. He reflects before acting, and is not discouraged by obstacles. Strong-willed, he is courageous, well-balanced and adaptable. Be careful: he may seem discreet and modest, but in fact conceals a need for power; he still needs to be number one and to be listened to with wide-eyed admiration. This need for reassurance is his weak point for, at bottom, he only wants to be loved.

Ambitious and hating privation, he generally earns enough money to pay for his pleasures. He is at home living in luxury and is capable of creating it. Luck is often with him, for the days are hot in August and it is good for the Snake to be born in fine, warm weather.

Snake/Virgo

These two signs are outstanding for their organizational ability. The Snake/Virgo does not go just anywhere: he knows very well what direction to take. He is so wise that his capacity for almost always being right can become annoying. Luckily, like all Snakes, he is charming. One can feel secure with him because he is faithful to his way of life and enterprises, to his promises, and always keeps his word.

The Snake/Virgo is often cerebral: he reflects a great deal, is clear-sighted and unequalled in avoiding pitfalls. Of course he makes mistakes, but he manages to keep them hidden; he reveals only what he wishes. Always elegant and beautifully dressed, he never swears or uses bad language in public. But at bottom he is nervous and anxious. Sexual equilibrium is of great importance to him. Deceived in love, he becomes ill-tempered and vindictive, revealing a disposition as poisonous as it initially seemed tolerant.

If you were born in autumn
Snake/Libra

If you have ever met up with a Snake/Libra and have been able to resist his charm, you deserve a medal. This Snake is irresistibly seductive and adores pleasing others. He seduces quietly and sinuously, without seeming to touch his prey, who gaze at him, fascinated.

Acutely sensitive to harmony, refined and aesthetic, the Snake/Libra is not aggressive and sometimes needs to be shaken up a bit to prevent him from indulging in daydreams. He is uncertain, hesitant and rather impulsive. He will respond best if you appeal to his sense of justice and his love of peace — in the noblest sense of these terms. An apostle of nonviolence, he will be capable of tirelessly preserving a certain 'quality of life'. Note well: the Snake/Libra does not make jokes about honour.

Snake/Scorpio

The pairing of these two venomous beasts seems dangerous

enough to make one hesitate before stretching out a hand towards them. Luckily however, the Snake/Scorpio is only moderately aggressive and turns it mostly against himself. He only bites or scratches if faced with unjustified meannesss and is actually rather tolerant, for his exceptional perceptiveness enables him to understand the motives of others. He is a good psychologist and would voluntarily spend his evenings investigating the psyches of his colleagues, philosophizing or being introspective.

Tormented and anxious beneath a peaceful exterior, he often changes his skin to mark the deep existential crises in his life. Yet the Snake/Scorpio is endowed with a fundamental strength of will which always enables him to attain his goals, which, being naturally reticent, he does with discretion. Vindictive as an elephant and possessive as a boa constrictor, he likes to be treated with respect. The best approach is to discuss problems with him openly. But if exposed to an accomplished fact, his pride will be hurt and he will enclose himself within his coils. If you come across him ten years later, do not be surprised if he bites you.

Snake/Sagittarius

A dynamic Snake. Although he has no wish to win the Olympic medal for running, he crawls fast enough to attain his end. The Snake's perceptiveness, intuition and sense of organization prevent the Sagittarian personality from thowing him into mad undertakings and keeping bad company. Highly independent, the Snake/Sagittarius is civilized enough to be relatively tolerant of the behaviour of his friends. But be careful: he is something of a stickler about his moral principles and will not accept the idea that one can play around with them. He is an honest man.

He is also authoritarian and slightly intrusive, always ready to inundate you with advice you have not asked for, then crushing you with abuse and contempt if you have the bad taste not to follow it. The Snake/Sagittarius hates to be contradicted, and if you disagree with him, he will bite.

The Snake/Sagittarius is a realist and cannot resist the tinkling of coins. He has a 'treasure-seeking' side and is irritatingly lucky. When he leaves on a search for some Eldorado, you can follow him in total security: you will not end up sleeping under bridges. But do not assume that he will share his treasure with you. That could be risky, for his generosity is relative. He adores giving presents, but is tight-fisted with his money.

If you were born in winter
Snake/Capricorn

He is a self-controlled animal who, behind a peaceful exterior, controls his emotions and looks at the world with impressive lucidity. His glance has the sharpness of a laser beam. He sometimes takes time to decide what action is necessary but, when he does venture forth, you can be sure that his decision is the right one. A Snake/Capricorn does not have time to make mistakes — an entire lifetime will barely suffice for him to obtain what he desires. Born to conquer summits, persevering and obstinate, he does not seem to have heard of the word discouragement. He is without doubt the most resistant of the Snakes, but he does not enjoy himself — make no mistake about it, he has weightier preoccupations.

If a Snake/Capricorn has decided to seduce you, it is useless to buy an aeroplane ticket for Timbuctoo or to lock yourself up in your house. You will only further inspire him in his desire for conquest. He will never be the first to give up and no difficulty will discourage him; he will use all means in his power to catch you. It is almost impossible to resist a Snake/Capricorn. Moreover, although he is not easy to live with, being demanding and egocentric, he does have compensating qualities: he has a remarkable business sense and does not change his opinion every five minutes; he makes one feel extremely secure; also, he is endowed with a rare form of chilly humour and irony. A truly great Snake.

Snake/Aquarius

A plumed Snake, who lives slightly in the clouds or in a Utopia. He is probably the least materialistic of the Snakes, and earning his daily bread is not his main preoccupation. On the other hand, he is remarkably intuitive, humane and available. He has 'antennae', and reacts with deep emotion to the smallest cry for help.

This Snake has the makings of a scholar or genius inventor; he can also make a fortune in peddling the occult or in areas dealing with investigations of the human spirit. Daily details bore him, and if you bother him about paying end-of-the-month bills, taxes and other such financial matters, he will take off in a flying saucer. He must be allowed to give free-rein to his original and creative spirit; but he needs assistance in channelling himself, for he is slightly erratic.

The Snake/Aquarius often has problems in his love life, for he has difficulty reconciling his need of independence with the emotional demands of others. Although sensual — like all Snakes — he is always thinking of other things, and can be sometimes stupidly jealous, at others vexingly indifferent. Luckily, he is so understanding that one can always find some common ground with him — but you must not try to corner him.

Snake/Pisces

Here is an extremely sinuous mixture and, by turning in circles or swimming between two pools, the Snake/Pisces risks biting his own tail and living within the vicious circle of his imagination. He has difficulty knowing what he really wants, and the multiplicity of his talents does not make his choice easy. Even if it seems a pity, he needs to be put firmly on the track. He will never beat any speed records and will sometimes get lost in the countryside; but he will always end up by doing something interesting. Very receptive and remarkably perceptive, this Snake is supple, adaptable and opportunistic. He organizes himself with deceptive ease, never giving the impression of doing so, and always lands on his feet. If crossed the Snake/Pisces will become sullen and inert, poisoning the atmosphere. Happily, he is not too touchy — or else he rarely listens.

Emotionally he risks sinking into melodrama; he rejoices in crimes of passion. He lives great and ever-complicated passions, asks himself far too many questions and exaggerates everything. In an earlier incarnation, he probably lived through *Gone With the Wind*.

At least he is amusing; one is never bored with him. But an entire lifetime is needed to obtain from him one single, precise answer to any question.

THE I CHING

易经

THE I CHING AND THE SNAKE

In the I Ching game, you ask a question and you obtain an answer. It is therefore a divining game. But the question you ask is posed through your Snake identity; the wheels, the complex mechanism of your mind and spirit, begin to turn. You ask a Snake question and the I Ching answers with a Snake 'solution', on which you then meditate as a Snake before arriving at a Snake conclusion.

The player is presented with a hexagram which contains the 'hypothesis-response' to his question, or, more exactly, a synthesis of forces affecting the concern or event inquired about.

For you, Master Snake, here are the sixty-four hexagrams of the I Ching and sixty-four Snake hypotheses.

How to proceed
1. The question
Ask a question regarding any problem at all, past, present or future, personally concerning you. (If the question concerns a friend, consult the I Ching game in the book corresponding to his Chinese sign.)

2. Method of play
It must be done with concentration.
Take **three ordinary and similar coins** — for example, three 50p coins.
Heads will equal the number 3.
Tails will equal the number 2.
Throw the coins.
If the result is two coins showing Heads and one Tails, write 3+3+2. You thus obtain a total of 8 which you represent by a continuous line: ▬▬▬ .
Draw the same continuous line if you have three coins showing Heads (3+3+3=9).

If you throw two coins showing Tails and one Heads ($2 + 2 + 3 = 7$), or all three showing Tails ($2 + 2 + 2 = 6$), draw two separate lines: ▬ ▬ .

To sum up, 8 and 9 correspond to: ▬▬▬ (Yin)

6 and 7 correspond to: ▬ ▬ (Yang)

Repeat this operation *six times*, noting at the time of each throw the figure obtained on a piece of paper, proceeding from the first to the sixth figure, from bottom to top.

The final result, including a trigram from the bottom, or lower trigram (example: ☵), and a trigram of the top, or upper trigram (example: ☲), will be a hexagram of the I Ching. In our example this would look like:

Now merely look for the hexagram number in the table on page 470, and then consult the list of hexagrams with their descriptions to find the given answer. *In our example,* the hexagram obtained is number 63, entitled **After completion.**

Table of Hexagrams

Trigrams	Upper lines ≡≡≡	☷☷	☶☶
Lower lines			
≡≡≡	1	11	34
☷☷	12	2	16
☶☶	25	24	51
☵☵	6	7	40
☶☶	33	15	62
☴☴	44	46	32
☲☲	13	36	55
☱☱	10	19	54

Use this table to find the number of your hexagrams. The meeting point between the lower and upper trigrams indicates the number of the hexagram that you are seeking.

☵	☶	☴	☳	☱
5	26	9	14	43
8	23	20	35	45
3	27	42	21	17
29	4	59	64	47
39	52	53	56	31
48	18	57	50	28
63	22	37	30	49
60	41	61	38	58

THE HEXAGRAMS OF THE SNAKE

CH'IEN

1 *The creative:* Energy, strength and will, used and controlled according to the time and hour, will favour that creation dear to the prince of sinuous movement.

K'UN

2 *The receptive:* Having allied yourself with time, recoup your strength by returning to Mother Earth. See things in their proper perspective, watch, retreat, and remember that the night brings advice.

CHUN

3 *Initial difficulty:* Do not blame your disappointments on external circumstances. Do not stubbornly continue to sow wheat in a swamp.

MÊNG

4 *Youthful folly:* 'It is not I who seeks the young fool, but the young fool who seeks me.' You are capable of deep thought and reflection; do not allow yourself to be overcome by your speculative powers, and do not take yourself too seriously.

HSÜ

5 *Waiting:* It is your principal ally, your superior quality, your trump card! The more things stir round you, the more it will be in your best interest to remain immobile.

SUNG

6  *Conflict:* If you are sure of being right, this is not the moment to swish your venom round in your mouth. Be careful: knowing how to give way before a towering obstacle is sometimes wise.

SHIH

7  *The army:* Although you are a passionate individualist, you should bend before discipline and feign submission.

PI

8  *Holding together (union):* Take trouble with your friends and colleagues and carefully knot your coils.

SHIAO CH'U

9  *The taming power of the small:* Scorn nothing, underestimate nothing. Do not qualify anything as 'small' before being certain that you are not near-sighted.

LÜ

10  *Treading:* 'Walk on the tail of the Tiger, he does not bite Man.' Even if you turn green with envy under your scales, do not hiss at the sight of stripes. Be a good prince; a little more prudence and generosity.

T'AI

11  *Peace:* All hostility calms down under its kindly reign. Do not stand on your dignity; draw closer to those you love without reserve; be kind and gentle.

P'I

12 *Standstill:* Is useful before attacking. Control your trembling, draw in your fangs and venom; step back, but remain vigilant.

T'UNG JÊN

13 *Fellowship with men:* Fresh air and daylight are good, and not only for relaxing in the sun. Seek to communicate; open yourself up more to the world and to others; avoid mental reservations.

TA YU

14 *Possession in great measure:* The Snake is lucky as long as he takes trouble and is not satisfied with hatching happiness as though it were a rare egg.

CH'IEN

15 *Modesty:* The Snake is the symbol of the horizontal, but in the case of aggression he rears up and becomes vertical. Guard this option even in difficult trials.

YÜ

16 *Enthusiasm:* It is true that you attract, astonish and confuse, but you are going to be forced to give of yourself without expecting anything in return.

SUI

17 *Following:* The fruits of your work or of your seductiveness will be opened to you; do not become too euphoric.

KU

18 *Work on what has been spoiled:* Buy spectacles or contact lenses. Rule out flirtation; you must look directly and closely at the situation.

LIN

19  *The approach:* Should be slow and prudent, for when the sun burns too brightly, a storm is threatening. Multiply your precautions.

KUAN

20  *Contemplation:* A slightly narcissistic period. Be careful not to turn round in circles; do not forget the world about you and its daily demands.

SHIH HO

21 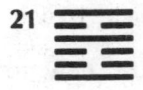 *Biting through (or clearly defined penalties):* Show all your teeth to discourage your enemies and to force destiny. Throw light on lies and you will eliminate the obstacle.

PI

22 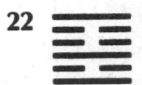 *Grace:* Do not allow yourself to be trapped; that which glitters is not always the light. If you receive a gift, do not throw it into the dustbin while keeping the wrapping.

PO

23 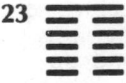 *Splitting apart:* Do not buy a house in which termites have eaten away at the beams. Do not trust appearances too much.

FU

24  *Return — the turning point:* Open your doors and curtains; the sun has risen, the crisis is over and you can go out with complete serenity.

WU WANG

25 *Innocence:* The intuitive Snake can trust completely in his intuition; but he must remain honest and gamble carefully, in case he might be mistaken.

TA CH'U

26  *The taming power of the great:* Power and strength. The Snake changes his skin, renews himself and sloughs off. Do the same if you wish to maintain your force and energy.

I

27 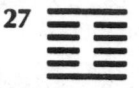 *The corners of the mouth:* Snakes are not all boa constrictors. Do not allow yourself to have eyes bigger than your stomach, nor a head filled with conceit — simply a wisely-filled one.

TA KUO

28 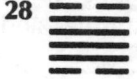 *Preponderance of the great:* Know how to reduce the surplus weight which slows down your sinuous advance.

K'AN

29 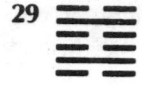 *The fathomless water:* External menace. Do not rear up or coil up; continue tranquilly but discreetly on your way, without attracting attention.

LI

30 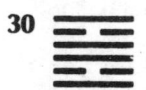 *The clinging, fire:* Remain calm and do not forever be on guard if you hope to be effective when the time comes. Become involved with people and, when you are alone, commune with nature, for she will help you.

HSIEN

31 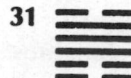 *Influence:* You are fascinated and you fascinate, so do not put off your projects until tomorrow. A piece of advice: do not circle round people and things too much before making up your mind.

HÊNG

32 *Duration:* Examine yourself a bit from the inside; internal mutations are also necessary to good equilibrium.

TUN

33 *The retreat:* Retire quietly, as you have the art of doing, discreetly and without making a sound; this is not flight but wisdom.

TA CHUANG

34 *The power of the great:* Strength added to movement. Do not allow yourself to be carried away by the whirlwind, for you would lose control over what surrounds you, as well as over yourself.

CHIN

35 *Progress:* Do not hesitate to assert yourself, show yourself, to make yourself known, but not for very long. Agree to collaborate; the cake should be shared, so do not be too greedy.

MING I

36 *The darkening of the light:* Do not wait for the electrician, but change the fuses yourself. However, learn too how to move round in the dark; you will easily acquire the habit, and the shadows within you, like the clouds, will disappear.

CHIA JÊN

37 *The family:* Even when you are an unfaithful Snake, at least you have the assurance of your family. When you feel lonely, it makes you feel secure; you would do well to make the effort to be responsible to it and not merely resort to it in periods of dire necessity.

K'UEI

38  *Opposition:* Tastes and colours are not arguable; they are discovered. You must try to understand them. Do not adopt or reject them without reflection.

CHIEN

39 *Obstruction:* If you no longer see anything, buy some spectacles; it is useless to continue to grope your way along, which could even become dangerous. If a hand is held out to you, do not refuse it — perhaps there is one more step you have not seen.

HSIEH

40 *Deliverance:* The storm has passed; set things to rights but also leave your shell.

SUN

41 *Decrease:* In case of difficulty, rediscover simplicity. Put your trust in what is spontaneous and natural; life will become gayer.

I

42 *Increase:* This is the moment to act, the barometer points to the good weather' sign.

KUAI

43  *Breakthrough:* You can attack and, for once, it will be justifiable; your honesty will shine openly. Hold your head high and denounce error; you are in the limelight.

KOU

44  *Coming to meet:* The Snake is no stranger to sleeping waters, but he should be on his guard and more prudent. Although marshes are a part of his universe, he should not choose them as meeting places.

TS'UI

45 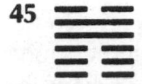 *Gathering together:* Should unite men of all categories and of the most diverse ideas. Seek comradeship but beware of parasites.

SHÊNG

46 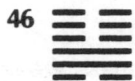 *Pushing upwards:* You are sure of yourself; you can leave. But prepare your itinerary, attend carefully to your voyage, neglect no detail and be careful to note the time of departure.

K'UN

47 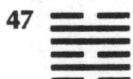 *Oppression:* You are losing speed; your magnetic fluid has stopped flowing; you must reflect on your conduct.

CHING

48 *The well:* It is good to change, transform and slough off; but renewal does not require destruction.

KO

49  *Revolution:* Is sometimes necessary; build barricades and so prepare yourself for an eventual confrontation.

TING

50  *The cauldron:* Symbolizes the five Elements — Earth, Wood, Fire, Water and Metal — the nourishment of the body and spirit. Know how to find a balance between your spiritual and your material needs.

CHÊN

51 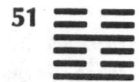 *The arousing (shock, thunder):* Sometimes a nasty jolt can throw light on a subject. Do not make a drama of it, apply a compress and continue on your way — it will perhaps be better illuminated.

KÊN

52  *Keeping still:* Solitude is often a good advisor; for the present be calm and live amid serene surroundings.

CHIEN

53  *Development (gradual progress):* It is more prudent to climb the steps one by one than to bound up them four at a time, risking a fall.

KUEI MEI

54 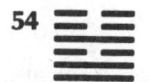 *The bride:* The Snake who hypnotizes should not himself succumb, but should remain prudent and reflective no matter what happens.

FÊNG

55 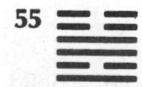 *Abundance:* Prosperity and plentitude. The grass is green and the cherry trees are in flower; do not wait for the grass to turn yellow and the flowers to fade to profit from what life has to offer.

LÜ

56  *The wanderer:* Voyages mould youth, calm passions and soothe grief. Step back for a proper perspective, but also look at what lies behind you.

SUN

57 *The gentle:* The wave ceaselessly caresses the shore and, seeping in, wears away the hardest of rocks.

TUI

58 *The serene, the joyous:* Seek to discover the other bank. If you do not like to swim, build a bridge.

HUAN

59 *Dissolution:* Seek to better perceive and understand those about you. Leave your egotism in the cloakroom.

CHIEH

60 *Limitation:* Although guard-rails are useful and practical, do not impose too narrow limits upon yourself or you will find yourself in a rut.

CHUNG FU

61 *Inner truth:* Do not seek to convey what is incapable of transmission. It is your attitude alone which must convince. Do not raise your voice, determined to be heard, but be profound and sincere.

HSIAO KUO

62  *Preponderance of the small:* If you cannot swim, do not jump into the water, especially without a life-jacket.

481

CHI CHI

63 *After completion:* Know how to admire the blossoming of the rose and detect its fading in the folds of its petals.

WEI CHI

64 *Before completion:* Do not crown yourself with laurels before the prizes are awarded.

YEAR OF THE HORSE

 1906·1918·1930
1942·1954·1966
1978·1990·2002

THE DOMAINS OF THE HORSE

十二生肖

THE HORSE AND ITS SYMBOLISM

'The Horse is the most noble of man's conquests'. However, this depends upon their relationship, for the union between man and horse can either produce a profound, exalting, organic and psychic harmony (the myth of the Centaur), or lead to déath. Allied to the horse and its power, man overcomes distance and appropriates wide-open spaces; disunited from the horse, he will find himself knocked over and stunned.

The thousand-and-one possible combinations of this subtle game are found in a multitude of traditions, rites, myths, tales, legends and poems: horse of the moon or horse of the sun; white horse or black horse; mount of a hero, on parade and splashed with light; or a phantom horse condemned to wander like a lost soul on the borderline of two worlds, between dream and reality.

Man has never truly conquered the horse, even if he has understood his language. The dog, loyal and faithful, is without surprises; the cat is as sure in his way, always independent and mysterious. But the horse is disconcerting, for underneath his apparent submission lies an unfathomable secret. Although he shares with man the most intense and violent adventures — even risking his life— he never gives of himself completely, as though some part of his most intimate self remains inaccessible and sealed from man, who aspires to enslave him.

He is a creature of darkness, emerging from the entrails of the earth or from the depths of the sea. Or, in another sense, he is a black battle-steed, carrying on his rump the goddess of shadows, searching for vagabond souls. But in certain traditions the horse also incarnates the spirit of corn and is the symbol of regeneration. It is he who travels across winter, the country of death and of cold, with the spirit of the sown seed which he transports and protects, replenishing and assuring renewal in the spring.

Certain Celtic rites, notably Irish, are connected with a white horse. During the ceremony of fire at the celebration of St John, after all the peasants had leapt over the embers, a large wooden construction with the head of a horse and covered with a large white sheet hiding the man carrying it would appear. It would be greeted with cries of 'the white horse, the white horse!' The horse would jump over the fire to pursue the spectators, the symbol of the spirit of young wheat and livestock.

A few notes on the Horse

Principal qualities: Loyal, enthusiastic, enterprising.

Principal defects: Unstable, flares up easily, impatient and talkative.

Work: Ambitious and hates to lose.

Best role: Buffalo Bill (who was born under the sign of the Horse).

Worst role: For Mr Horse — accountant; for Mrs Horse — lady of the manor in the Middle Ages, waiting for her knight to return. It is unimaginable that a lady Horse, even of another epoch, could tolerate languorous odes and chastity belts.

Money: Careless and spendthrift, yet generous and unselfish. Luckily, his realism helps him to keep his feet on the ground.

Luck: To be born in winter; it may help to keep his head cool.

Cannot live without: Being supported, encouraged, complimented or even applauded.

Adores: Voyages, change, diversity.

Favourite places: Everywhere, other than where he lives. Often prefers the homes of others. He hates to be hemmed in.

Detests: Silence, lack of communication.

Leisure activities: Fearless and energetic, he likes the sporting life and the competition involved, for he understands the meaning of 'fair play' and will lose with grace.

Colours: Fire.

Plants: Palm and orange trees.

Flowers: Hawthorn, peony and nasturtium.

Professions: Sportsman or monitor of sports, cowboy, technician, union leader, administration, chauffeur, truck driver. Painter, poet, explorer, and all trades or professions involving communication with others, such as lecturer, politician, hairdresser or pub owner.

The four ages in the life of the Horse according to Chinese tradition

The *childhood* and *youth* of the Horse will be critical. He will leave his family when very young and, forced to assert himself so early in life, will meet with difficulties. He will suffer emotionally and financially, often having to sell out in order to start a new project. In *maturity* he will achieve calm and equilibrium, for he will have learned the wisdom of failure and the value of perseverance. His *old age* will be serene.

THE PSYCHOLOGY OF THE HORSE

Unlike the Snake who precedes him in the Chinese zodiac, the Horse has a good reputation. Proud in appearance, for centuries he has been the friend of man, carrying him into the heat of battle or enjoying with him the delights of country retreats.

Since the tractor replaced the horse, riding, jumping and polo have been popular among those who aspire to becoming one with nature. For this, Horses are loved. While there are some who are afraid of them (they stand so tall and are liable to kick), no-one suspects the character of this noble, faithful, loyal and intelligent animal.

But all that is false! In fact, the Horse has a very tiny brain and is as easy to train as he is to frighten. If not controlled, he will panic at any hint of danger and become dangerous. As well, he is physically fragile; even his bones mend badly.

What does the Chinese zodiac sign have in common with this symbolic animal? One important and fundamental thing: he often has a proud and noble bearing, behaves brilliantly and gallops elegantly. For this reason, many, judging him on appearance alone, take him for what he is not, for at bottom the Horse is a weakling, often lacking in composure and too easily carried away and dominated by his feelings.

Those born under this sign are essentially gregarious: they love the social life and crave acceptance. Agreeable companions, glib and eloquent talkers, they know how to please and enjoy pleasing. They are popular, never modest and are adept at attracting attention.

In the face of difficulty they seem sure of themselves and free from all doubts or hesitations. Yet in reality they are uneasy, anxious and vulnerable. The least criticism grates on them, the least sign of contempt undermines their self-confidence. Their dependence on the support of their friends — which cannot be counted on — deprives them of true independence. If disapproved of or rejected, if met with silence or sulkiness, Horses become panic-stricken. For them, dialogue is essential; without it they are lost souls.

A Horse may be regarded as intelligent and be respected in his profession, however his temperament and moods may vary so widely that others will lose confidence in him. He will navigate continuously between two extremes, at times announcing enthusiastically that he will get the better of everyone because he is the best; at others, doubts and self-destructive feelings will convince him that he is good for nothing. Yet at such times he will have the secret hope that someone will come to reassure him, whereupon he will start out again, passionate and frisky. The Horse may be touching, but he is not a very secure person.

Horses are active and impatient; they charge in, obsessed by attaining their objective — yet will sometimes change it along the way. The one thing that really frightens them is the threat of failure. To fail in an undertaking, be it emotional or professional, has such a dramatic effect that it can even lead to threats of suicide. Success means everything to them; they need to live in a state of full intensity. A setback can be a sort of death. Action is a refuge which dissolves obstacles; there is no time for doubt.

The greastest quality of a Horse is *loyalty*: they are frank, direct and know nothing of detours and metaphors. While noble and sincere, they are often too self-absorbed and impatient to reflect on the needs and motivations of others, and so tend to trample on the weak spots of their friends and associates without meaning to.

Horses have many friends, but these are sometimes only superficial, for it is not easy to get to know a Horse behind his deceptive appearance. Although they are eager to communicate, the art of discussion eludes them for they are often intolerant; they are more gifted at self-expression than listening.

Horses are quick-tempered and, when opposed or thwarted, are capable of childish and blind fury — something which does not endear them to their acquaintances. On the other hand, they are experts in smelling out arguments which will be used against them, and this often allows them to have the last word.

Impulsive and rarely foreseeing what they are going to do next, Horses often act on their whims, behaving in an unexpected and unreasonable way; they will not take advice and do only what they please. Luckily, they have a practical, realistic mind which, allied with their enthusiasm and energy, gives them impressive force and remarkable effectiveness.

Horses should fend off people who want to find out what lies behind their brilliant appearance, for they are more gifted than truly intelligent, and sometimes lack depth. They completely lack the power of reflection and the ability for organization. But they have a lively, rapid mind, a gift for repartee and a warm, generous, child-like side which makes them extremely likeable.

Secretly pessimistic, they need affectionate support to blossom, and seek their equilibrium through others. Solitude is painful for them — even intolerable — which results in a curious mixture of dependence and independence, one of the most interesting ambivalences of their complex personality. Their awareness of their need for others, combined with their practical instinct, makes them very strong indeed when it is a question of making use of people — even manipulating them — which they do without bad intentions, for Horses are not wily, vindictive or mean; they are simply egocentric. Louis Pasteur has left us a revealing phrase with which to end this chapter: 'The most beautiful word in our language is "enthusiasm". It comes from the Greek, *en theo*, an internal God.'

THE FIRE HORSE

According to Chinese tradition, every 60 years is the year of the Fire Horse (1906 and 1966 were Fire Horse years; the next will be 2026). This is in a way illogical because the years ending in the number six are dominated by the Water Element. This regular replacement of Water by Fire, insofar as the Horse is concerned, is one of the mysteries of Chinese astrology, and we must forego all rational argument when considering it.

During 1965, the year preceding that of the Fire Horse, the number of abortions in the Far East rose spectacularly: no woman wanted to give birth to a child coming under its influence. Fire Horses are considered ill omens for their family, and their birth supposedly provokes catastrophes among those around them.

It is difficult to verify these beliefs. We know of a man whose birth in 1906 was followed by several deaths in his family; there is a record of a charming girl born in 1966 whose parents separated in an extremely painful fashion several months later. The student of Chinese astrology will ask, is this coincidence, or a reflection of a profound reality? We all must seek the answer for ourselves or for the Horses we know.

On the other hand, to be born during a year of the Fire Horse can also be advantageous. Both the qualities and the defects of the Horse will be multiplied by ten: he will be more ardent and impetuous than other Horses, adventurous, undeniably gifted and, perhaps, ignorant of the notion of good and evil. He will, in any case, be destined for great things. His life will be thrilling, passionate and lively. Luck will be with him. He will be determined to break any ties which might slow down his hallucinating journey.

THE HORSE AS A CHILD

Childhood is a delicate age for the Horse, for the quality of his future and, indeed, his eventual success depends on his ability to adapt to the demands of reality.

The Horse child is independent and impetuous. Naturally confident, he believes that everything he desires will fall from the sky at his mere wish, and that he will never have to make any effort. This carefree side of the Horse causes him to flee from responsibilities, living in joyous disorder and preferring the playground to the school room. But he is so nice, so spontaneous, affectionate and warm, that one does not have the heart to scold him.

It is, however, necessary to use discipline with a young Horse, especially when he reaches school age. He is as clever with his hands as with his mind, learns everything with ease and has a good memory, but he lacks perseverance and discipline, and his performance is uneven. Sometimes he is first in his class, sometimes last, and he is forever being reprimanded and detained after class for his insolence, thoughtlessness, and so on. He has a natural talent for creating chaos behind the backs of his teachers, involving his classmates in the kind of tricks that are severely punished, but which make one laugh in secret.

Even though the little Horse has an amusing time, such slightly anarchical behaviour rarely leads to harmonious study, and so he is threatened by his hereditary enemy —

failure. Confronted with his first setback, the young Horse will be puzzled and lost, unable to understand that reality does not always correspond with his optimistic dreams. Consequently, for fear of encountering such painful situations again, he will often choose a zig-zag course or simply baulk at any obstacles — a reaction well-known to horse trainers.

It is thus important to impress on the Horse child the value and necessity of effort, so that he learns that failure is itself a valuable experience and a useful lesson on the road to success. He must be cured of his tendency to hesitate, and taught to pursue a course free from disorganized impulses. In short, he has to be *educated*, just as stubborn colts are by their trainers. The famous maxim of Winston Churchill (who was a Dog, not a Horse) about going from failure to failure until victory is reached might be repeated frequently to him.

LOVE LIFE

The Horse is passionate and lives according to the rhythms of his heart; and his heart sometimes gets so carried away that his entire physical being is affected deeply: One could say that the Horse is in love with all of himself, morally and physically, and that all of his organs participate in the tempest that he endures when an emotion takes hold of him. He can even be subject to psychosomatic troubles — anguish, breathlessness, palpitations, loss of appetite or ravenous hunger — so great is his emotional involvement and its hold on him.

Sentimental, impatient and avid for love, the Horse seeks to conquer as much as he hopes to be conquered; it is in this context that he is able to live in the present completely and experience intense exaltation. He is subject to immediate attractions: falling in love at first sight, a smile, a look, and there he is, in love. He will then do anything to win his loved one. Male or female, the Horse is subject to desires which will not accept delays nor obstacles. Above all the Horse needs the passion that his strong sexual nature requires, the impression of living for love, without restrictions — even though this may occur every six months.

If seduced, the egocentric Horse is capable of extravagant follies and extreme sacrifices. Yet he is quite capable of coldly trampling on the toes of his colleagues in pursuit of a smile. This apparent realist is actually a romantic whom love renders weak and dependent as a child. For the sake of love he will change his entire life, give up his job and, without hesitation, throw away his memories and ideals. It is, perhaps, this touching passion — the dominating factor in his life — which enables the Horse's friends to overlook those moments when he is egocentric and irritating.

The Horse is not easy to live with: he likes to decide what is best for the other person, without argument, and does not easily understand that they may have wishes or needs different from his own.

Designed to live in the grand manner, routine affections will never satisfy the Horse. Unless his chosen love can match his spirit, he will tire quickly, become bored and gallop off. All the reasoning and wisdom in the world will have no effect upon him when he is in love. Hot or cold, this animal is never tepid.

FAMILY LIFE

Those born under the sign of the Horse cannot abide solitude. They should marry young and establish their own families, removed from the influence and authority of their parents, whom they rebel against as soon as they reach adolescence. Horses usually welcome the age of majority with a marriage vow.

Unhappily, that which encourages such sentiments in the Horse by no means protects him from passion. After several years of marriage have lessened the attraction and calmed the passion which initially invigorated it, the Horse will feel that something new is needed to inflame him again. This is why it is not unusual to see Horses change partners around the age of thirty or forty, or, if they survive as a couple, it will be only through a succession of major crises.

Horses do not bring security to those who need it, but their frankness is disarming and helps them to be forgiven. Unfortunately, they are slightly cowardly, even feeble, when it comes to a parting of the ways, hesitating between the past and present and waiting for their partner to make a decision. They find rational explanations difficult, especially when love is involved, for they abandoned logic when children. One needs to be flexible and patient in order to elicit a straightforward answer, such as 'I still love you', or 'I no longer love you'.

They are erratic in their role as parents — at times consciously present, at others clearly absent — but they are never stifling or boring. They are unequalled in their gift for awakening children to the joys of activity, interesting them in their interests and hobbies and encouraging them to choose their own destinies. Such permissiveness will work well with a Tiger, Rabbit, Dragon, Horse, Goat or Monkey child, but a Dog child will be unhappy and suffer from the egotism of such a parent. The same is true for the Pig child, who will await in vain some protective touch of affection. As for young Rats, Ox's, Snakes and Roosters, they will judge their Horse parent severely and will not be indulgent when it comes to lesser failings. The Horse should expect some scathing criticisms when these children have acquired independence.

PROFESSIONAL LIFE

The Horse is proud and independent; he does not accept failure. These tendencies do not predispose him to a bureaucratic life-style. He will feel more at ease in a completely autonomous occupation which imposes a steady rhythm and allows him to act as though each day were the last. A good maxim for Horses is: 'Work as though you were going to live forever; live as though you were going to die tomorrow.'

The Horse is more a person of ideas than someone who 'executes'. If subject to strict discipline, he will spend his time waiting for better days and will be prone to anxiety and bitterness. Eaten up by doubts, he will be bent on self-destruction. On the other hand, he has a talent for undertaking things or initiating a business deal, leaving others to handle the details.

He likes a change of scene and therefore will be at his best in a profession that requires travelling. Paradoxically, feeling free during the week will open his eyes to the value of peaceful weekends with his family.

The Horse is as receptive to professional brainstorms as he is to love at first sight. He will grasp new ideas and innovations with enthusiasm, open to every risk and pursuing them as exciting adventures in which he must, of course, succeed. But at the least mishap, he goes to pieces and will need the affection and encouragement of those close to him, who alone can give him faith in a new start.

The Horse is adept at persuading and commanding people to join him. Incited by his ambitions, he will dazzle others with his talk, anticipating every argument and, in the end, winning their admiration and consent. A Horse who really wants something — be it a job, budget or subsidy — will always get it. In reality this is all a superb bluff, for someone else will always have to attend to the details.

Those born under the sign of the Horse should remember that, according to Chinese astrology, trouble must precede success. The Horse does not have the luck of Dragons and Snakes, and he will have to exert himself all of his life. Such is his destiny.

MATERIAL LIFE

The Horse is realistic and pragmatic, but not self-seeking. Once he is financially independent he is content and asks for nothing more. This is just as well, for he is not lucky with money and often finds himself with empty pockets: he lacks perseverance, changes his job too often, and is likely to give up regular work for some risky venture which catches his fancy. He is too proud to ask for a raise in salary, and too volatile to qualify for a pension.

The Horse enjoys his pleasures, especially with others; in love, his generosity is unbounded. He hates to forego a holiday or a meal in a three-star restaurant just because he must pay his car insurance at the end of the month.

For financial stability, the Horse needs a regular, assured salary. But are there any truly interesting and challenging jobs available in such a bureaucracy? A teaching position might suit him, but the Horse is not a patient creature, even if he has the gift of convincing others. His independent spirit needs prudence and financial know-how.

For the Horse, material possessions are more of a constraint than a joy. He needs to feel that he can drop everything from one day to the next in order to leave for the North or South Pole. The attraction of distant horizons, the perfume of the unknown and the music of exotic languages commands his imagination. No rustle of banknotes nor tinkling of coins has as much value in his eyes.

At best, the end of the month will not leave him too much in debt. Standing orders for basic bills might help him. Honest but thoughtless, the Horse needs a well-organized and foresighted partner to keep him in order. In any event, he should avoid fanciful spectulations; otherwise, he will find himself bankrupt. His strength lies in other fields.

ENVIRONMENT

The Horse is elegant and well-groomed — especially the mares and fillies — with the males tending to a type of relaxed elegance, even being slightly sloppy and insensitive to their surroundings. In his eyes, objects have an affective rather than aesthetic or material value. He navigates in the midst of highly personal bric-à-brac which he knows intimately and which no one else is allowed to touch.

Mr Horse is often rather disorderly, and dislikes being expected to tidy his cupboards; Mrs Horse likes to decorate her home, but does so in a rather conventional way, without any real originality or imagination. And, just when it is well-organized and clean, she loses interest. Family life and its domestic organization will never take precedence over her professional life.

In fact, for the Horse, home is of secondary importance. His favourite environment is among those who share his interests. He likes crowded places — beaches, sports arenas and fashionable, roomy sitting-rooms. He responds to space and needs elbow-room, adores travel and craves changes of scenery.

A guide to relations with a Horse
Methods of seduction:
He: Impatient and ready to resort to anything to get what he wants. All means will be justifiable, whether playing the clown or kidnapping, including some remarkably well-planned and seductive declarations of love. Do not fall too easily for this champion of passionate declarations!

She: Looks upon you with frankness and lets you see, in a spontaneous and natural fashion, that you please her. You have only to take her up on it.

If he loves you: He is worth listening to; you can even tape what he says and, later, if you are sharing life with a silent and undemonstrative Ox, you can listen to the recording. When a Horse is in love, he says so — with talent and conviction.

He expects of you: That you share his enthusiasm and follow him gaily on his voyages — in body and in spirit.

To keep you: He will intoxicate you with his promises and fabulous projects.

If he is unfaithful: It will be due to weakness; he is incapable of resisting temptation and adores to please and to be agreeable.

If you are unfaithful: If a relationship is coming to an end, be frank because he will accept it and you will remain friends. But if you have a great love affair, conceal it because he would take it as a personal failure, which could destroy him.

In case of a break between you: He will behave in a noble and likeable fashion — unless he feels too diminished; in which case it will be a melodrama full of blood and tears! Be sure to take him seriously: he is sincere but excessive.

If you want to give him a gift: Male and female Horses often like sports, so considering giving camping equipment — or even an aeroplane — it depends on your bank account.

If you want to seduce him: Read up on the subject that interests him most — which could mean spending several sleepless nights and weekends learning enough to be able to discuss it with him. You must follow him everywhere and never leave him. If his passion is flying, good luck!

If you want to get rid of him: At a crucial moment, ask him if he has remembered to turn off the gas.

THE HORSE AND THE OTHER CHINESE SIGNS

Horse/Rat

The Rat and the Horse share a fault: both are egoists and capable of behaving very stupidly when carried away by passion. However, the Rat when passionate remains lucid, and even during his most excessive transports he remains capable of listening to the small voice of wisdom, of recognizing with a flash of lucidity the limits that would really be too dangerous to pass.

Not so the Horse! Acknowledging no limits, the great attraction to him is the love which drives him beyond the frontiers of the possible. He does not think things over; he plunges in like a bumblebee pollinating flowers.

Given their natures, the Rat will always be critical of the excesses and outbursts of the Horse; he will judge him to be superficial. The Horse, on the other hand, will think the Rat is spiteful and ill-natured. Neither of them will be completely wrong.

Understandably, Chinese astrological tradition advises these two signs to avoid an amorous liaison with each other. That is not difficult, for they are not much attracted to each other.

Horse/Ox

This is not an easy pair to judge. The Ox and the Horse are both egotists and will make little effort to understand each other. And the Horse is forever on the rampage, whereas the Ox is sedentary. The Horse cuts his quick capers, the Ox ruminates. We might wonder if they will ever meet, or just pass each other by. They will have great difficulty adapting to each other's rhythm.

If they do meet and inadvertently fall in love, perhaps their relationship will endure, thanks to the Ox's goodwill. But the Horse will be unhappy: egocentric though he is, he is nonetheless passionate and sentimental, needing not only love but proof of it as well. At the first outbreak of such 'romanticism', the Ox, without meaning to, will throw cold water on him, for such declarations of love are altogether foreign to him.

In other respects, the Horse is sociable while the Ox enjoys nothing better than tranquillity and moments of solitude. For this union to work, it will be necessary for the other dominant signs, Chinese or Western, to be truly in harmony, and these elements should be consulted.

Horse/Tiger

These two will go far together! A Tiger and a Horse meet on a level of enthusiasm that is superb. Everything will be for the best, provided the Tiger never grasps the extent of his partner's egotism, which always has priority in the Horse's opinions and desires, unless he is passionately involved. One can only hope that this passion endures and that the Tiger or Tigress are too active to have time to reflect on the why's and wherefore's of the Horse's attitudes. The feeling of deception would be devastating and any dialogue difficult, for the Horse would not understand. Because he is so profoundly convinced of his good faith, he cannot conceive that he could be accused of thinking only of himself; in fact, he does think of others — but only as they relate to him. The Tiger is more open and generous.

This kind of conflict will resemble a Shakespearean tragedy, for neither will understand the meaning of the word 'moderation'. The Horse becomes violent, the Tiger heroic. From a tragedy to a farce, there is only one small step.

Horse/Rabbit

This combination is possible if the Rabbit is very much in love, for love makes him pliable. He is a sentimental and slightly romantic person, and the Horse's enthusiasm, warmth and passion will be irresistible to the Rabbit, who often hesitates to put himself forward; he will be admiring and breathless before the Horse's self-assurance. But when the Horse, in one of his spectacular changes of mood to which he is so often subject, collapses, saying that he is no good and that life is not worth living, the Rabbit will be able to comfort and coddle him.

This tie can be soothing for the Horse and dynamic for the Rabbit, except when the Horse longs to roam wide-open spaces.

Horse/Dragon

Enthusiasm often unites them, especially in the heat of action. One can easily imagine them as loyal rivals in a football game, or companions in some adventure! if committed to a shared purpose, they fit well together. In daily life, however, the problem can be more delicate, particularly if the Dragon is the female, for she needs to be admired and coddled, and the Horse, having conquered her, will be too egotistic to care about her demands. Thus neglected, she will resort to any means — and these, indeed, could be extreme — to demonstrate to her Horse husband that he would have done better to remember her existence.

Things will be easier if the Horse is the female, for the Dragon is not the kind to invade her privacy too much, even though she does need to roam alone. Preoccupied with herself and what concerns her, she will allow him to shine in peace. He will become a twinkling Dragon before starting to gallop.

Horse/Snake

The Horse will often be seduced by the Snake, and will remain almost faithful to him. He will have the impression — extremely mistaken — of being as free as the air; in fact, his Snake companion, coiled up in a corner of his imaginative brain, will be ceaselessly present and indispensable. On his side, the philosophic Snake will not take offence at being regarded occasionally as a piece of furniture, and will know how to find his own interests. The Horse will amuse him by his shifts in mood and he will have the impression of being at the circus.

But the day will come when the Horse's egotism will cause him to tire of his Snake companion, who will have trouble replacing him. This will not be bad for the Horse: it will allow him to avoid being swallowed up.

Still, this relationship is positive and exalting, especially at the start when the Horse is still blinded by passion and if there is some external obstacle to be overcome. If there is none in sight, they will have no trouble inventing one.

Horse/Horse

This is a perfect alliance for those who love a life of passion: together, two Horses can make a lot of noise. The first glance can lead to a mad attraction which obstacles or delays only serve to exalt.

The relationship may continue for a number of years, but, being based in blind love, will endure only so long as it remains blind. As soon as one of the partners recognizes in the other failings he refuses to accept in himself, things will start to go wrong. No Horse has the patience to wait for his partner to change or evolve, and none are endowed with the capacity for clear-sighted and reasonable love. To Horses, 'love' rhymes with 'irrational'; otherwise it is no longer love.

A disappointed Horse will soon leave. If there are shared interests and a child to feed he may continue to take care of everything at home, but he will make his real life elsewhere — intellectually and emotionally. In any case, he will leave for the first passion that is sufficiently strong to lure him away.

Horse/Goat

The lives of Horses are a permanent 'happening'; they need to fall in love — and remain so — and to create a developing and unpredictable relationship. With a Goat for a partner, they are well served. Their mutual dislike of routine, the instability of their behaviour, their irresponsible side, their attitude of 'being ready for anything' does not imply any form of security. A Horse in love with a Goat will often walk a tightrope, but he will never have time to be bored.

The Goat will feel secure, for the Horse's passion will always be self-evident; and the Goat will not suffer from any sense of being neglected or abandoned, both of which he detests.

It will be easier if the man is a Horse, for his Goat spouse will leave it to him to earn their daily bread. Otherwise, let us hope that Mrs Horse is an heiress or has a well-paid job, for Mr Goat rarely likes to work for two.

Horse/Monkey

There is difficult understanding between these two; one is

dominated by emotion, living his passions with intensity and with total, ardent commitment; the other, subject to reason, is always conscious of the traps along the way, of the risks of love, and is forever 'standing back' and doubting the possibility of a lasting attachment.

The sincerity of the Horse might help the Monkey to attain some stability, but the latter will attribute this sincerity to naivety or blindness. On his side, the Horse will not stand for the about-faces of the Monkey, and will accuse him of being calculating or insensitive. They will both be wrong, but that will not alter things.

In any case, this couple is rare because the Horse and the Monkey are not often attracted to each other. Even at first sight, when they do not yet know each other, they share a vague distrust, each suspecting the other of superficiality.

Horse/Rooster

This combination is far from ideal: each needs to have his or her true value recognized and affirmed; appearance is important to them; they are sensitive to the opinion of others — particularly the Horse — and both are very vulnerable. You may think that they thus have many points in common. But in fact they have too many, and both will try to take first place and rank ahead of the other. All the love in the world cannot overcome this reflex.

Also, these similarities do not lead to evolution, but to irritation. The Horse will suffer at seeing his Rooster partner strut about, and will have neither the patience nor the wisdom to allow him to crow in peace. For his part, the Rooster will be dissatisfied because he needs dialogue, and discussion with a Horse is often limited to agreeing that he is right.

Horse/Dog

These two are so dissimilar that it seems hardly possible, at first glance, that they could get along. One is confident, egocentric and enthusiastic; the other sceptical, pessimistic and generous.

However, they could go very well together, but neither is prone to dominate or criticize the other — unless the Horse makes an enormous error.

Each will live his own life, and construct his own system of satisfaction without bothering the other too much. The idealistic Dog will be busy attending to others, leaving the Horse time to attend to himself, and both will be content; Dog is faithful, something the Horse appreciates because it is restful for him.

It could turn tragic if the Horse suddenly became bored and romped around in other pastures. In this case, the sensitive Dog will suffer badly and have a difficult time recovering.

Horse/Pig

Both are honest and share a taste for an easy, agreeable life and the pursuit of pleasure. The egotistical Horse will attempt to take advantage of the Pig's basic decency, but the Pig will know how to protect himself; anyway, his natural indulgence will help him to support his partner. Another positive point: in love the Pig is sensual and imaginative, which will attract the Horse — and keep him.

Unhappily, there will almost always come a time when the outbursts of the Horse will exhaust the patience of the Pig, who will then need to be on his own for a little while in order to relax. The amorous Horse requires complete dedication and the assurance that his partner belongs to him totally. His partner's independence will upset and make him jealous; he will not easily adapt to the mixture of autonomy and candour which is typical of the Pig, and will often tire before coming to terms with it.

SOME HORSE CELEBRITIES

Adler, Josephine Baker, Barnum, King Baudouin of Belgium, Samuel Beckett, Ingmar Bergman, Braque, Buffalo Bill, Charlemagne, Chopin, Shostakovich, Cicero, Davy Crockett, Degas, Delacroix, César Franck, John Huston, Aldous Huxley, James Joyce, Krushev, Lenin, Metternich, Nasser, Newton, Papillon, Pasteur, Puccini, Rembrandt, Jean Renoir, Franklin D. Roosevelt, Theodore Roosevelt, Rossellini, Sadat, Solzhenitsyn, Vivaldi, the Duke of Windsor, Virginia Woolf.

YOUR COMPANION IN LIFE

生命伴侣

After the Chinese sign of your year of birth, here is the sign of your hour of birth

What is a Companion in Life, as understood in Chinese astrology? It is a sort of 'ascendant' sign corresponding to your hour of birth. This Companion is another animal belonging to the Chinese cycle of the twelve emblematic beasts, who falls into step with you and accompanies you, ever ready to help you brave the traps and ambushes along your route. A permanent and benevolent shadow, he can render the impossible possible.

He is your counterpart, but with his own character and tendencies and with a different psychology. Both guardian angel and devil's advocate, he will be a witness to your life and an actor in it.

Have you ever felt, deep inside yourself, the subtle presence of another 'myself' inhabiting you and with whom you live, at times in harmony, at others in conflict? Another self who sometimes criticizes you and at others encourages you? That is your Companion in Life.

There are times when he will appear to be an imposter or an intruder. Certainly, he often questions your habits and your moral or spiritual complacency. Accompanied by this companion, a shadow within, the route is less monotonous and the voyager multiplies his chances of arriving at his chosen destination. This, however, in itself matters little, for it is the journey and the manner in which it is conducted that are important. Indolence is the greatest danger: your Companion is capable of arousing you from a lassitude of spirit and, to that end, if necessary, robbing you of your certainties, trampling on your secret gardens and, finally, tearing away the great veil of illusion.

It sometimes happens that your Companion is of the same sign as your year of birth, a twin brother in a way — for example, a Horse/Horse. In this case, you must recognize that he will compel you to realize yourself fully and to live the double aspect — the Yin and the Yang — that your bear within yourself. In any case, you also bear within yourself

the twelve animals. So, set out on the long route, ready for the great adventure: the beautiful voyage during which you will encounter the harmoniously entangled, the solemn and the grotesque, the ephemeral reality, the dream and the imagined.

Table of hours corresponding to the twelve emblematic animals

If you were **born** between	11 pm and 1 am	your **companion** is	Rat
	1 am and 3 am		Ox
	3 am and 5 am		Tiger
	5 am and 7 am		Rabbit
	7 am and 9 am		Dragon
	9 am and 11 am		Snake
	11 am and 1 pm		Horse
	1 pm and 3 pm		Goat
	3 pm and 5 pm		Monkey
	5 pm and 7 pm		Rooster
	7 pm and 9 pm		Dog
	9 pm and 11 pm		Pig

These figures correspond to the *solar hour* of your birth. If necessary, you should check the summer times (Daylight Savings Time) and make the appropriate adjustment (sometimes two hours before or after statutory time).

THE HORSE AND ITS COMPANION IN LIFE

 **Horse/Rat**

This coupling brings about an interchange between ardour and prudence. The Rat/Horse will go on often tumultuous voyages. What battles lie in wait! It will be difficult to temper the ardour of the Horse galloping under the blazing sun, while the anxious and prudent Rat will be busy securing his underground fortresses.

The ill-loved Rat must take dark and twisting paths to reach the light, while, for the Horse, it is intolerable to gallop in the shade. He needs the luminous Royal Way, and seeks the crowd and worldly success. The poor Rat must, however, straddle this charger and accept him as his guide. Lacking the power to bridle the magician, the Rat can always discover the joys of riding.

 **Horse/Rabbit**

Something of an unprincipled opportunist, he will be slightly mystifying. Irresistibly attracted by all that glitters, he will alternate between being impetuous and prudent. The Horse/Rabbit is a winner; he refuses to run for cover, even when security requires it. For him, a thrilling route is a necessity, and he obtains his goals. This war-horse will not allow others to step on his toes or obstruct him.

 **Horse/Tiger**

Spirited but temperate, alert to traps and clearing all obstacles, the Tiger/Horse will accomplish a voyage in which enthusiasm will be joined with patience, and stalking with slyness and galloping. Prudence and balance, calmness and patience will be difficult for the ardent Horse who sleeps within the Tiger: the Horse prefers the sunlit route and applause to the luxuriant semi-obscurity of the jungle. But the Tiger will quickly bring him back to reality; life is more than turning round in circles in a riding-school ring.

 **Horse/Ox**

Shifting from ardour to slow deliberation and back, these two Companions will not share the same concept of their path. The Ox, sure of himself and restrained, likes to take his time; his progress is slow and he is therefore unwilling to put up with the ardent spirit of the Horse, who goads him on, dreaming of honour and sunlit lands while the Ox ruminates on mapped-out paths. The conscientious Ox, desirous of solitude, grinds his teeth in annoyance when faced with the unmethodical and instinctive side of the Horse and his love of crowds and spectacles. Will the Horse's 'fire' heat the body and soul of this Ox, who is sometimes too 'buried' in his earth? If the Ox/Horse can agree on division of labours, he will undeniably hold winning cards. At work, to the seriousness, thoroughness and perseverance of the Ox will be added the passion and creativity of the Horse. On an emotional level, the ardour and vivacity of the Horse will soften the Ox's hard shell of doubt.

Horse/Dragon

Riding may have its charms, but there are inherent dangers in mounting a Dragon which are best avoided, even if he is the companion of a Horse. An impetuous and ardent animal, the Horse/Dragon combines elegance with opportunism, luck with lively intelligence. Few can mount him. The ride will be a sort of mad race in which he may often conquer and attract admiration; but the speed of it all will tend to go to his head and his extraordinary luck make him mad. He needs to learn about that rare flower called modesty; even then, he must be careful not to trample on it while jumping for joy when its bloom is full.

Horse/Snake

He is a wise dandy, combining elegance and ardour with highly developed moral demands which can sometimes conflict with his pride. For the Snake/Horse is a bad loser and does not accept failure. He is a winner and will not hesitate to be opportunistic and sly, restraining neither his tongue nor his heart. Nevertheless, since he is irresistibly charming, the Snake/Horse will be excused for his boastfulness and even his ill-nature. But he should not overdo it!

 **Horse/Horse**

Thirsty for voyages and adventures, this impatient and impulsive animal will always be a vagabond and his opportunism and risky undertakings will cause him many problems. Others will envy his natural brilliance and elegance: the Horse/Horse will be eloquent, an effective orator and a natural leader; he will attract honours and prestige. Discretion and secrecy are unknown to him. He will need a clear and untramelled path, which he will try to keep all for himself; an avenue in which he can give free rein to his passions and impulses. He will be loyal and honourable, but his unbridled ambition, egotism and boastfulness will irritate his companions. He should curb himself and learn to be more moderate, countering his ardour and impulsiveness with watchfulness and realism.

 **Horse/Goat**

Dream worlds and fantasy will flavour this alliance with a slightly capricious and charming bohemianism, favouring an escape towards enchanted domains of azure and clouds alive with fanciful and diaphanous creatures of the imagination. The Goat/Horse will need an epic existence; his ardour will be conquering, but he will prefer art and heroic poetry to war-like expeditions. His personal universe will open to other dimensions — towards subtle inward spaces that no system of logic can define or measure.

Horse/Monkey

In turn eloquent and courageous, his path will resemble an extended race-course, from which the Monkey/Horse can only emerge victorious. He will be as well-balanced as a race horse, at once mount and rider; a Don Juan or a hermit, — as well as having a touch of Don Quixote — transforming a track into an arena. He will stake his life — from pride, from a delight in taking risks and even from cynicism. Uniting intelligence with a fine appearance, he exploits to the utmost his resources of charm, talent, wiliness and, sometimes, deceit. The Monkey/Horse will often dream of a path haloed by glory and strewn with flowers — that he will stamp upon with superb indifference.

Horse/Rooster

While distinguished, loyal and generous, he is also vain and lacks modesty. His pride drives him, pushing him on against wind and tide, keeping him far in front of the masses, whom he needs to command and carry with him. The Horse/Rooster likes to stand out from the crowd; he is often unique and possesses a sense of honour to the highest degree; his word is his bond. His generosity can be total, his loyalty irreversible. If he gives you his confidence and friendship, nothing — no pressure nor catastrophe — will weaken it.

Horse/Dog

Mount and guide, loyal and faithful, he tenaciously makes his way by day and night, prodded by his intuition. Tempering his impatience and his fire and never doubting his abilities, he is still able to question his ideas and actions and thus improve himself. He succeeds in controlling both his pride and his fear of failure, never hesitating to smile at his defects and his weaknesses, yet he remains ardent and passionate. His Dog side allows him to grasp secrets and dimensions that the Horse can reach only rarely and with difficulty — a world of contemplation and self-questioning in which the Horse's ardour is refined and spiritualized.

Horse/Pig

Endowed with a broad and clear intelligence, the Horse/Pig is well aware of the pride that eats away at him. He has a tendency to overrate the true value of his possessions and conquests, and to overlook their impermanence. He cannot resist collecting 'treasures' which are, in fact, fakes. Actually, he unconsciously seeks a more worthy treasure which lies within him. His ardour and impulsiveness often give way to doubt and mystery, the latter irresistibly attracting him like the promise of a profound accomplishment.

THE HORSE AND THE FIVE ELEMENTS

五行

YOUR ELEMENT

In Chinese astrology, each year is joined to an Element. There are five Elements: *Water, Fire, Wood, Metal, Earth.*

Each of the twelve emblematic animals is linked successively to each of the five Elements. For example, in the year 1900 the Rat was Metal, in 1912 he was Water, in 1924 he was Wood, in 1936, Fire and in 1948 he was Earth. Therefore, for the twelve years from 1900 he was linked to Metal, for the next twelve years to Water, and, for every succeeding period of twelve years, to each of the other Elements, in succession.

In order to determine the Element corresponding to the year of your birth, use the table below:

Years whose digits end in: 2 and 3 — Water
6 and 7 — Fire
4 and 5 — Wood
0 and 1 — Metal
8 and 9 — Earth

The same union of *Animal-Element* repeats every sixty years, for example, Rat-Metal appeared in 1720, 1780, 1840, 1900, 1960 and so on.

The five Elements are the primary forces affecting the universe. It is their particular association with each of the signs which provides the basis for every horoscope. Movement and fluctuation, Yin and Yang, these symbolic forces are in a perpetual state of action and interaction.

Wood gives birth to Fire, which gives birth to Earth, which gives birth to Metal, which gives birth to Water, which in turn gives birth to Wood.

HORSE/WATER (Fire Horse)
(you were born in 1942)

The cold born of the northern sky descended to Earth and gave birth to Water. The Chinese consider Water more a synonym for coldness and ice than a symbol of fertility.

The Horse/Water (Fire Horse)
Of the sixty Animal/Element couples in Chinese astrology, the year of the Horse/Water is the only one whose Element undergoes a curious mutation, by which a person born in the years concerned (1846; 1906, 1966, and so on) is called a *Fire Horse.*

A year ending in the number six is no less influenced by the Water Element: the Horse born in such a year will possess all of the characteristics of the Water Element, as well as the specific traits of the Fire Horse (see page 25).

Characteristics of the Horse/Water
Water of winter nights, rigour and severity; calm and deep Water to be feared and respected; still Water sheltering underwater demons asleep in its depths, foetid and muddy Water of the marches, a refuge of crawling creatures.

The ardent and impulsive Horse will seek to conquer and dominate the Water Element, becoming the aquatic Horse of Indian legends. But he must surface on to this earth, a symbol of space and liberty and more suited to serve his insatiable need for action and movement. Water will not be an impediment to the Horse; his dynamism and Yang tendency will always drive him into the depths of himself and those universes which, for him, are synonyms of conquest. The effect of the ardent energy of the Horse on Water is so frenzied that it can even make it come to a boil, a phenomenon from which derives the expression 'Fire Horse', to designate the Horse/Water.

Health of the Horse/Water
The Water organ is the kidney; its flavour is salty. The Horse

should transform this Water to make it invigorating and fertile, invigorating himself at the same time. He must always strive to be dynamic and active: too much humidity and inaction will only paralyze him, if not physically at least morally, a state of affairs which the Horse will find difficult to endure.

The Horse/Water and others
Bizarre deaths often fall on his family and friends, but this Horse is endowed with rare power. Thus he can dominate his impulses, control his passions and master his excesses better than others. He may even be able to listen to other's advice. However, make no mistake, the Horse's temperament remains active, violent and inhabited by wild dreams. If he succeeds in channelling all this dynamism, he can become a great adventurer, in the noblest sense of the term, or a master in the art of governing, leading crowds and heading nations. The Horse/Water can also be a humanist; he believes in the individual and will often plead his cause against the state, justice and society. It is not that the spiritual universe leaves him indifferent, but that he has a difficult time combining it with his need for action. And it is in this field that he can hope to obtain victory over his latent egotism.

Advice for a Horse/Water
Allow your dynamism to drive you along; believe in yourself and in your lucky star; do not be afraid to take over the reins and lead. You possess the power to stir sleeping waters.

A Horse/Water year (Fire Horse)
The culminating point for a Horse/Water year will be winter, a period of gestation. The Yin of Water is brought to the boiling point by the Yang of the Horse, from which arises the Fire Horse.

Seek equilibrium through a balance between action and reflection. Do not weaken your energies by impulsively throwing yourself into excessive physical or emotional adventures — reflect before becoming involved to avoid deceptions and failures. Do not allow yourself to be attracted to sleeping waters, but seek the invigorating source; you will succeed in doing many great things.

Historical example of a Horse/Water year 1942

By 1942 huge tracts of Europe were sunk in the barbarism of Hitler's Europe. The policy of reprisals continued unremittingly; the inhabitants of the village of Lidice were exterminated following Heydrich's assassination in May, with which not one of them had any connection, and over 1,000 Czechs were slaughtered in Prague as an appetizer. The 'Night and Fog' Decree just issued formulated a spurious legal basis for terror in the West whereby those merely suspected of anti-German opinion were either to be shot out of hand or transported to the 'Night and Fog' of the Reich, never to be seen or heard of again. As Martin Gilbert has written: *'The murder of Russian prisoners of war, of hostages and of critics of Nazism in the West was a consistent operation. There was never a time when it was suggested that Russians should be released, or hostages imprisoned in tolerable conditions, or the victims of "Night and Fog" left unmolested in their place of exile; death was the object of all decrees.'

He continues: 'No such unanimity of purpose existed as far as the German policy towards the Jews was concerned. As well as being the Germans' greatest imagined enemy, they were also their greatest embarrassment. There were so many of them; every conquest added more; by 1942 there were upwards of six million whereas in 1939 there had been under a million.' The 'Final Solution' was only agreed on in the spring of 1942.

Already forced labour camps, adjacent to factories, had been established; the largest, at Auschwitz, where only 450

* *The European Powers, 1900-1945,* London 1965.

of the 12,000 Russian prisoners of war directed to its building survived, was begun in November 1941. The new solution required a change of emphasis; extermination rather than forced labour was to be its predominant purpose.

There was a faint promise of some halt to these horrors by the end of the year, for by then the Germans were on the brink of surrender at Stalingrad, Rommel had been comprehensively defeated at the battle of El Alamein and in November the Americans landed their forces in Morocco and Algeria. But the terrorism in Europe continued and the policy of the 'Final Solution' was pursued until the end of the war.

HORSE/WOOD
(you were born in 1954)

To the East the wind blew in the sky, and from its warm caress of the earth Wood was born.

Characteristics of the Horse/Wood
Wood is of the morning and springtime. Its temperate nature loves harmony and beauty. This season will be fruitful and creative for this elegant Horse. It will bring equilibrium and power and, by moderating his impetuous spirit and strengthening his creative powers, develop his sense of beauty and need for harmony to the maximum. Nature in its entirety will be offered to the Horse, attracting him far from the stable, offering him the promise of new spaces to conquer and lands to discover, which will satisfy his impatient, passionate nature. But, like the Horse, Wood is also passionate, excessive and easily carried away, and the Horse/Wood will thus often be vulnerable, jealous and possessive.

Health of the Horse/Wood
The organ of Wood is the liver; its flavour is acid. The

Horse/Wood will be anxious at times, even anguished, and his fear of failure may become obsessive. This can cause all kinds of difficulties, including depression and even psychosomatic illnesses. Try to remove emotional drama from difficult situations; even the worst setback may hold the seeds of regeneraton.

The Horse/Wood and others
The Wood Element is fundamentally ambivalent, since, alongside an uneasy fervour, it contains relaxed and restful tendencies. These will enable the Horse to overcome his fear of failure. If opposed by established structures, the Horse/Wood will improvise, preferring the creative and imaginative to reason and discipline. Forgetting his doubts and fears, he will tend to attack an obstacle, and this audacity will often be repaid. Such an attitude, while perhaps confusing to others, will surely astonish and seduce. The Horse/Wood will not hesitate to exploit his charm, elegance and good taste. Deliberately opportunistic, he will succeed, yet without shocking or crushing others.

Advice for a Horse/Wood
You are an ardent and elegant Horse, scorn routine and the banalities of life and hate to lose. Play the romantic juvenile; never retreat nor submit to doubt.

A Horse/Wood year
The culminating point for a Horse/Wood year will be spring, a period of growth and prosperity.

This will be a creative year, full of new energy and strength, ideas and projects. Apparently insoluble conflicts and problems can be resolved.

Historical example of a Horse/Wood year
1954

In this year the political and ideological features of the

people of South East Asia were still in the balance; but the odds were already heavily loaded against the old colonial powers. Yet the Americans sought to redress them. American interests required a stability in the area and American policy was inclined to succeed to the influence hitherto exercised by the colonialists whose yoke they had shed and whose policies they were quick to denounce.

Members of popular movements inspired by a passion for independence and fired by Communist ideology had taken up arms in Malaysia, Burma and Laos. President Sukarno of Indonesia called for an end to the Union of the Netherlands. In Indo-China the élite of the French army had been fighting the Vietminh for seven years and were now under siege in their great fortress of Dien Bien Phu.

The eyes of the world were on the French defenders, snaffled in the gut of their fortifications. The Americans had resisted the Chinese in Korea; now the French asked that they should do so in Indo-China where the Chinese, in breach of the Korean Treaty, were supplying the Vietminh. On 13 March two key positions fell to them and the French commander, General Navarre admitted that his position was not inviolable. The French sent General Ely to Washington where he was sympathetically received. Various studies were put in hand for the relief of the French. The English, allies in Korea, were asked by the Americans if they would assist. General Eisenhower pronounced the situation akin to a game of dominoes — the first to fall would bring down the pack. Rightly, he decided against an intervention doomed to be ineffective because too late. The great fortress fell on 7 May.

The French overtures were not without consequence. The South Vietnamese came under American protection, a role which would eventually bring upon them a humiliation unequalled in their history.

HORSE/FIRE
(you were born in 1906 or 1966)

Heat was born in the southern sky, descended to earth and fertilized it. From their union, Fire was born.

Characteristics of the Horse/Fire
The Fire Element is of the midday, the South, of summer. Fire is Yang, the Element which warms, burns, animates, quickens, transforms and overthrows. The Fire inside a Horse will become a formidable source of energy, a constant reservoir he can resort to. His need for perpetual movement, action and voyages; physical, emotional and intellectual adventures will all be supported. The Horse/Fire will always thirst for light, in all its forms; forever unsatisfied, he will always wish for something better, something just beyond his grasp. However, he should beware of the Fire within him which, if he does not remain its master, will quickly consume him. All of the Horse's strength depends on his capacity to transform energy, a task he should never neglect.

Health of the Horse/Fire
The organ of Fire is the heart, its flavour is bitter. Do not allow yourself to be overwhelmed by anger and feelings of violence. Spend your energy in small doses; do not waste it. Your egotism will often be an excellent regulator.

The Horse/Fire and others
Symbol of war, Fire is also clear-sighted and clairvoyant. Passionate and violent, this person's anger will scorn diplomacy and compromise. His character will lead him towards a military career and risky and adventurous paths. Of an artistic nature and aesthetically gifted, he will never quite join the 'establishment' and will ignore the world of fashion and others' opinions.

Advice for a Horse/Fire
You must be responsible for yourself, however difficult this

may be. If you do not, you will quickly become unbearable to others, as well as to yourself.

A Horse/Fire year

The culminating point for a Horse/Fire year will be summer, a period of creation. Your Yang tendency will incline towards the Great Yang, bringing dynamism and vitality.

A favourable year for action and creation. You should be successful in many areas.

Historical example of a Horse/Fire year
1066

Edward the Confessor died in January leaving no heirs. His vow of chastity had remained unbroken to his death, despite his marriage, for Edward had been brought up in a Norman monastery and was always a monk at heart. He was unfitted for kingship, ineffectual, incompetent and colourless. Nor, aged 40 when he assumed the crown, did he take to English habits. He introduced the French way of life to the English court and insisted that French should be its official language. He left behind him a group of dangerous, cunning and unprincipled Normans whom he had injected into the political and ecclesiastical life of England. These were resented by the English, a resentment which seems to have its origins in 1051, the year Duke William visited England and was promised, he later asserted, the nomination as Edward's successor.

Edward's kingship needed a buttress, a power behind the throne, and the House of Godwin were determined to provide it. Of the blood royal of Denmark they were, on the failure of Canute's direct line, natural aspirants to the throne of England and on Edward's death Harold Godwin was his natural successor. He was acclaimed King and the claims of the Duke of Normandy were not even considered. William was essentially a Dane and a bastard Dane at that; he could claim neither royal nor simple

English blood. There was no English precedent on which he could base his claim.

But when Harold had been in William's power he had given an oath to secure William's succession after Edward's death, or so William averred; and to rebut in advance the charge that it was extracted under duress, he skilfully secured a judgement in his favour before the Roman Curia and thus took to the field against Harold under the Papal banner in September. He may also have arranged for Tostig's invasion of Northumbria at the vital moment, an important element in his success for Harold met him at Hastings, after a series of forced marches, with an exhausted and depleted force. No adult of the House of Godwin survived the battle, leaving William the only remaining claimant for the Crown. William's victory as profoundly affected the future of north-west Europe as the Norman incursions in southern Italy and Sicily in 1058 the course of history in the Mediterranean.

HORSE/EARTH
(you were born in 1918 or 1978)

Earth was born from the slowly falling Elements of the sky at its humid zenith.

Characteristics of the Horse/Earth

This is an afternoon Earth, the humid and hot Earth of summer. It is the symbol of the well-cushioned, soft nest, of comfort and abundance; an Earth of slow and profound transformations. It is an Earth blessed for the Horse who tramples, works and conquers it. But the Earth is also a symbol of refuge, repose and revery, inviting the Horse to reflect and meditate. Although in communion with the Earth Element, the Horse should not be its prisoner, for then he will be reduced to a beast of burden and will lose his celestial character, deprived of his starry course among the angels of heaven. The Earth will claim him as it supports his hooves.

Health of the Horse/Earth
The Earth's organ is the spleen, its flavour is sweet. The Horse/Earth should take care to remain active and sportive, otherwise he will be in danger of becoming neurotic and fat — a hired hack in a livery stable.

The Horse/Earth and others
The Horse/Earth is usually a realist, even a materialist, who advances prudently and sceptically. Lucky and calculating, he is inclined to speculate and could amass a fortune. But he will sometimes lack breadth, and will be less ambitious than other Horses. He will be conscientious and scrupulous, but possessive and jealous and often unduly suspicious of his friends. Full of ardour and initiative in his early years, later he will become preoccupied with his need for comfort and security, devoting himself to the needs of his family and investments.

Advice for a Horse/Earth
Do not sink into a rut; this could be unfortunate for your figure and your image in the world. Preserve what you can of your youth and dynamic qualities; the Horse is first and foremost an elegant and seductive conqueror. You will get nowhere by boring people with the state of your heart, let alone of your investments. Slip into your golden hooves and your coat of light; banish the word 'failure' from your vocabulary.

A Horse/Earth year
The Earth is a productive Element representing the centre.

The culminating point for a Horse/Earth year will be summer. The Horse will no longer be constrained to seek his daily bread and, free of all constraints, will recapture his taste for wide-open spaces and rediscover his freedom of movement. But he should guard against his excessive and fervent nature, for its lively and uncontrolled expression could lead him to make catastrophic errors.

Historical example of a Horse/Earth year 1918

General Ludendorff was the architect of Germany's defeat in the west in 1918. It was his insistence that German submarines sink American ships which brought the United States into the war in April 1917.

German hopes now depended upon breaking the stalemate in the West before the massive resources of the Americans could effectively intervene. The Russian Revolution which led to the end of hostilities in the east gave Ludendorff his chance. With the huge armies thus released for the Western Front he would be in a position to launch a massive and final offensive. He planned a general attack on the French and British armies and this may have delayed his preparations, a crucial factor since time was on the side of the Allies. It was not until March 1918 that he launched his offensive and, by then, American forces were already in France although not yet integrated into the Allied armies.

The Germans rapidly drove back the French armies, advancing 30 miles towards Paris through Peronne to Montdidier; but their artillery and transport could not keep with them and the advance lost its impetus. On their right flank they were held up by the British along the line from Arras to Armentières. By May, each side had lost nearly a quarter of a million men. Ludendorff regrouped his forces and, on 27 May, launched a concentrated drive on Paris. Within two days his armies were at Soissons and by 2 June within 40 miles of Paris. Two hazards awaited them. The great wine cellars of Champagne lay beyond Soissons and the Germans indulged in an orgy of looting, particularly at Frismes. This time it was ill-discipline and drunkenness which slowed the German impetus. By then the Americans, well trained and marvellously confident, were disposed behind Château Thierry which the Germans were attempting to negotiate. The Americans counter-attacked and after hard fighting lasting 19 days captured the key feature of Belleau wood. This success put new life and energy into the weary and despondent Allies. The British struck effectively and reached Peronne, and by 15 September the Americans attacking the vital sector of the St Mihiel salient had captured it and advanced half-way to Metz. On 26 September the 'Grand Assault' by the British, American and French forces began. Ludendorff had exhausted his reserves and was unable to contend with the mass of men and material all directed against his forces with a new-found enthusiasm inspired by the Americans. As early as 29 September he asked the German War Council to agree to an immediate Armistice. He had lost the War in the West.

HORSE/METAL
(you were born in 1930)

In the sky, coming from the West, drought grazed the skin of the Earth and gave birth to Metal. Winds come from the far-away steppes seeking the vital sap.

Characteristics of the Horse/Metal
Metal is of the night, of autumn and of cold. It symbolizes clarity, purity and precision. The Horse/Metal will be cutting, rigid and chaste, his comments harsh. He will be effective and expert; at harvest-time he will be the blade that gleans. Yet, this severity, if overdone, will engender sadness and moroseness.

Metal will tend to restrain the Horse, imposing a fixed direction and a slightly too-rigid attitude for such an ardent and passionate animal. The Metal Element will enclose the Horse in a straitjacket of such rigidity and weight that his natural feelings, impulses and longings for the wild will be stifled. Metal is unequivocal, settling questions out of hand. Its severity will shackle the supple Horse, bridling his actions and restricting his scope. Mystical aspirations attract the Horse/Metal, but if dominated by such mirages, he will find himself thrown pitilessly into the abyss. He must not confuse sanctity with extravagance.

Health of the Horse/Metal

The organ of Metal is the lung, its flavour is pungent. The Horse/Metal should draw in oxygen, breathe the pure air, be active and repel physical and moral restrictions which impede his circulation.

The Horse/Metal and others

Just and honest, unhesitant when acting on a decision, he has the mentality of a leader. An ardent idealist, he is slightly sectarian, the prototype of the horse with blinkers who works conscientiously to the very end, is intolerant of any lapses and is as tough on himself as on others. His curt remarks can make enemies of those who feel their cut. Effective and brilliant enough to remain in the forefront, he often does so only at the expense of his nerves.

Advice for a Horse/Metal

Be more relaxed and less of a stickler for principles.

A Horse/Metal year

The culminating point in a Horse/Metal year will be the autumn.

Revive your suppleness; be aware of your body and your instincts. Learn to relax and set aside your armour. In order to maintain perfect self-control, you must align yourself with your natural rhythms and movements — otherwise you will experience a revolt from the obscure forces of your psyche.

Historical example of a Horse/Metal year
1270

Louis IX of France, the St Louis of history, was a fierce lover of peace and a hater of schism. His ardour was reserved for the Holy War against the Infidel, to which end he directed his foreign policy, wasted the resources of his kingdom and expended the best of his own energies. His first Crusade in 1249 ended in disaster with his imprisonment. Twenty years later he was anxious to try again. His health was failing; he was in a hurry.

Louis called on his brother, Charles of Anjou, King of Sicily, to join him. Charles's shadow was the longest in the Mediterranean and it was already touching Constantinople, capital of the Empire of the East, which he was determined to invade. He knew however that he could not deter his brother from his single-minded purpose, so he decided to turn it to his own advantage by suggesting that the Crusade should first sail to Tunis where King Mustanir had been withholding annual tributes due to him. Charles skilfully suggested that Mustanir might be won over to the Christian faith and that a small show of force would overcome the objections of his generals and imams. The prospect of converting a whole country to the faith aroused Louis' enthusiasm. With a formidable army he sailed from Aigues-Mortes for Tunis where he arrived on 17 July 1270. It was agreed that Charles should follow.

When the French army disembarked, the actions of King Mustanir suggested nothing of the eager convert; he retired to his capital and manned the fortifications. Louis set up his camp among the ruins of ancient Carthage. The African summer took its toll; half the French army were soon stricken with dysentery and typhoid. After three weeks on his sick bed King Louis died, at 3 am on 25 August. Charles anchored his fleet in the bay later that morning. He was able to save the French army and in October concluded a satisfactory treaty with Mustanir. Both knew that Edward I of England was on his way to join the Crusaders and understood the advantage of concluding matters before his arrival.

Analogical Table of the Different Elements

Elements	Wood	Fire	Earth	Metal	Water
Years ending in	4 and 5	6 and 7	8 and 9	0 and 1	2 and 3
Colours	Green	Red	Yellow	White	Blue
Seasons	Spring	Summer	End of summer	Autumn	Winter
Climates	Wind	Heat	Humid	Dry	Cold
Flavours	Acid	Bitter	Sweet	Pungent	Salty
Principal organ	Liver	Heart	Spleen	Lungs	Kidneys
Secondary organ	Gallbladder	Small intestine	Stomach	Large intestine	Bladder
Food	Wheat, poultry	Rice, lamb	Corn, beef	Oats, horse	Peas, pork

Table of Harmony
Between the Elements

		Wood Female	Fire Female	Earth Female	Metal Female	Water Female
○○○ Excellent prosperity	Male Wood	● ●	○	○ ○ ○	○	○ ○
○○ Good harmony, understanding	Male Fire	○	○	○ ○	●	● ●
○ Effort needed	Male Earth	● ●	○ ○	○ ○	○ ○ ○	●
● Rivalries and problems of reciprocal domination	Male Metal	○	● ●	●	● ●	○ ○ ○
● ● Misunderstanding and incomprehension	Male Water	○ ○	● ●	●	○ ○ ○	○

THE FOUR SEASONS OF THE HORSE

If you were born in spring

Horse/Aries

The Horse/Aries is fast enough to win races, but he lacks stamina. For him, a good start is essential; he is not made for long distances — his enthusiasm is for beginnings — however, with a good jockey on his back, he can go far.

But here lies his principal difficulty: his ardent, warm, sincere, naive, subjective and passionate nature does not easily accept the influence of others. Yet in order to be really effective in life, he needs to be led to do things (in the sportive sense of the term, otherwise it would be he who would lead) and to cease fearing the loss of his independence. This must be accomplished in such a subtle manner that he does not notice it, which is actually not too difficult, for the Horse/Aries does not have much perspicacity or sense of psychology, and is therefore open to suggestion. In love, he is capable of marvellous devotion, and it does not enter his head that he might be repulsed. He is not understanding, but he is good.

Horse/Taurus

Contrary to his predecessor, this Horse is well-suited for running long distances. Capable of sustaining huge weights, he has the strength of an elephant. He also has the same ability to bear a grudge: if he is relegated to the sidelines, or cannot use his energies to the full and materialize his dreams, he will complain and fume for a good many years.

This alliance considerably develops his imagination. A veritable creative torrent flows through the veins of the Horse/Taurus; if he can learn to rationalize and look outside of himself, he is capable of remarkable things.

The Horse/Taurus is sentimental, affectionate and less egotistical than the other Horses. He likes to make the people around him happy; indeed, this is indispensable to him. Generous but intolerant, he tires quickly if his passion is not returned. Because he lives on an intensely emotional level, his behaviour can vary surprisingly depending on whether or not he is in love. For him, the confusion of passion is a normal state, like breathing. Needless to say, not everyone is up to following him on this path.

The Horse/Taurus is peaceful but his anger, although rarely expressed, is devastating. Engulfed by his own suffering, no appeal to reason will help. The best remedy is to wait until he calms down and make him a nice cup of camomile tea — or immobilize him with a bridle.

Horse/Gemini

The Horse/Gemini is a circus horse, in the noblest sense of the term. He will leap over hoops of fire, dance the tango or play dead on hearing a revolver shot. His principal sport is to play and parade. While he does not take himself very seriously, like all Horses he hates being treated casually.

The Horse/Gemini has the makings of an actor or orator. He is self-assured and easily adaptable. But by making people laugh and turning everything into a farce, he risks creating a false image of himself and becoming a victim of his own drama. If a man dressed as a clown performs an heroic deed, who is remembered, the hero or the clown? The Horse/Gemini is brave but impatient and is constantly agitated. He likes the grandiose and is adept at bluffing, throwing dust in others' eyes with grand gestures and loud laughs. If he cries, everyone assumes he is putting on an act; they misunderstand the true nature of this melancholic, the concealed tragedy of the clown.

The Horse/Gemini rarely knows what he wants, although gifted for everything, and should not choose a profession requiring application and perseverance. He would make an excellent sports reporter, for eloquence is one of his principal qualities; it helps him to seduce. In love, he is slightly irresponsible, being unaware of the feelings of others, not from malice but from thoughtlessness.

If you were born in summer
Horse/Cancer

The Horse/Cancer has a considerable imagination which

requires rich pastures. Security is important to him. At a well-managed stud farm he will be unequalled in performance; running wild in nature he will become fearful and bitter. He is the most tender and affectionate of Horses. His private life matters more to him than anything, and he devotes himself with unfailing energy to the happiness of his family. It is for them rather than for glory that he will win races and master difficult jumps. Certainly, he can sometimes be slightly boastful and he likes to be admired, but when a Horse/Cancer receives a medal, his family is his real audience.

The Horse/Cancer needs comfort, which is why he works hard and obstinately at his tasks, most of the time thinking of other things. He is marked by a certain reticence and is often pulled up short by an obstacle, doubting his ability to clear it; in his corral, he will careen around but not dare to neigh too loudly. However, he has as many possibilities for success as other Horses, even though he is too sensitive to trample remorselessly on others.

Horse/Leo

A champion in any obstacle race, nothing can stop him. Moreover, he loves it because it adds spice to his life. As soon as he is capable of standing on his own legs, he prepares for the Olympics. Small-town competitions do not interest him: what he wants with all his heart is to win — and to win big!

The Horse/Leo detests delays; he has to be on the move. If thwarted he will paw the ground; if prevented from going at his favourite gallop, he kicks out. Even at his most lucid and intelligent, the Horse/Leo has difficulty curbing his ambition, being driven by an insatiable thirst for breaking records. He cannot stand to wait around because his personal ideals leave him no rest. He is proud, authoritarian and has a dramatic fear of failure.

His principal defect is his egotism. He rarely thinks of others and, even when passionately in love, will not understand the modesty, hesitations and scruples of the object of his desire. If you ask him to put himself in your place, you will become a carpet — and he will not even realize it. His great quality is courage. He is stifled by inaction. Believe in him and let him know it — that will give him a good puff of oxygen!

Horse/Virgo

The Horse/Virgo is well balanced, for the support of the Earth-sign protects the Horse and enables him to avoid disorder. Reasonable, honest and diligent, he achieves his aim by hard work. Although he is less brilliant than the other Horses, he has the chance of obtaining a more solid, if less spectacular, success, for fame does not turn his head. He is very resourceful and does not ignore practical problems. This alliance is also favourable for those born under the sign of Virgo, for it gives them what they lack most: self-confidence and enthusiasm. Virgos born in a year of the Horse are sociable, gifted for personal contacts with others and persuasive. This natural facility, joined with their sense of duty, can work miracles on the professional level.

Emotionally, the Horse/Virgo is very attached to his home but, beneath his timid exterior is an authoritarian with principles who likes them to be observed. His rules of life are strict, and, like all Horses, he is extremely surprised when those he loves have the bizarre need to exist on their own.

If you were born in autumn
Horse/Libra

This is an elegant and refined Horse, with a lustrous coat and abundant mane. When he leaves his stall, no pieces of straw will spoil his immaculate appearance. He prefers a buoyant and harmonious trot, neither too fast nor too slow. The influence of Libra gives him a feeling for the nuances and contrasts of life. A Horse/Libra is more tolerant than other Horses; the only thing he cannot abide is bad taste.

The Horse/Libra is eloquent and will defend passionately his ideals of justice and harmony, yet leaves action to others because his role is to convince and gain adherents by speech rather than by action. The Horse/Libra can do many things, for he adapts easily. He is as agreeable socially as in the bedroom, ready to overlook secondary points for the sake of agreement. However, he will never sacrifice himself: if he loves you, he will appear weak but will have well-defined limits as to the extent that he is prepared to be manipulated. Not everyone can saddle him.

Horse/Scorpio

This lucid and mistrustful Horse is difficult to tame, and if he permits you to ride him it will be because he finds it useful to allow you to. Madly independent, hypersensitive, impassioned and revengeful, he has an essential need of liberty. At times he can be unscrupulously ambitious: at the start of a race it is he who kicks out at his competitors, without a shadow of remorse.

On the other hand, the Horse/Scorpio is distinguished from his brothers by his understanding of others. He is not stifled by his principles, and so does not need to crush his entourage; as long as his independence is respected, he can be agreeable to live with. But he is defenceless against passion. With unrestrained sensuality he will throw himself into a conquest with the enthusiasm of a pollinating bee. If one attempts to escape from him, or if one resists him without a valid reason, he will become a wild stallion. If you feel that you have the strength of a rodeo champion, all will be well. If you keep astride him for more than a minute, you will have won.

Horse/Sagittarius

A competition Horse, he has great breathing power and adores running. The problem is that, unlike the Horse/Leo, he does not run to win, but simply for the intoxication of hearing the winds of liberty sing in his ears. It is very important for the Horse/Sagittarius to have some spiritual, material or emotional aim. Otherwise he will run joyously but to no purpose, as unaware of the beauties of the landscape as of his responsibility to the children he has left behind in the stable. So long as the Horse/Sagittarius is governed by a purpose and knows where he is going, there is no need to worry, for he will get there. He will do well because he has a sense of honour and has an air about him which assures success. Naturally immodest, he will talk about his triumphs to everyone for the next twenty years. He is the kind to accomplish an unprecedented feat, and then spend the rest of his life giving conferences on it.

Emotionally the Horse/Sagittarius is generous and tries gallantly to understand those about him. But be careful: he does not laugh at family values. There are those things which are done, and those which are not!

If you were born in winter
Horse/Capricorn

This noble and honest Horse is the most virtuous, persevering and courageous of them all. He needs time to feel his way, but once decided on his course, he is resolute and gives of everything he has. For this reason he will appear to care more about his work, or more exactly the results of his work, than his wife's or children's birthdays. In serious moments he is capable of great affection, but he has a clear hierarchy of obligations: the necessary prevails over the superfluous. He is not demonstrative but needs a stable family life; once he has obtained it, he rarely calls it into question. He is secretly passionate and not so lacking in a sense of humour as some may think.

The Horse/Capricorn can disconcert others by the rigor of his demands. He despises weakness, detests compromise and is his own source of justice. Although he needs to hope in order to undertake, he is capable of persevering in the face of failure, something which is rare among Horses. He is farsighted and is the kind who enjoys posthumous glory.

Horse/Aquarius

This combination is a curious mixture of egotism and generosity. Intuitive but unstable, his imagination — which he has difficulty controlling — drives him to ignore the present in favour of a vague and nebulous future. If you have a Horse/Aquarius child, 'A bird in the hand is worth two in the bush' should be repeated often. Soon enough he will probably understand. Subconsciously the Horse/Aquarius knows where he is going but he is incapable of explaining it, which causes a great deal of misunderstanding. Attempts to restrain him result only in his becoming nervous and irritable. A good solution is to face him squarely with his responsibilities, for he has a sense of duty and a fine moral judgement.

If he is not expected to involve himself personally, the Horse/Aquarius is understanding, devoted and adorable. Otherwise he can be unbelievably egotistical, insensitive and detached. He may be unhappy to see you suffering, but he will take care never to show it. It is a difficult and delicate business to get him to live on the mundane level of daily life.

Horse/Pisces

As everyone knows, horses often sleep standing up. Born under Pisces, they are particularly susceptible to dreams and, consequently, the Horse/Pisces is at the mercy of currents he cannot control, without being consciously aware of them. Very susceptible to influence, sentimental and even slightly naive, he sees himself in the role of the sacrificial hero. He does not really distinguish between dream and reality and is capable of living both intensely, cheerfully confusing the two.

Romantic and liking security, the Horse/Pisces is both available to others and self-seeking. Charming with his friends, he always retains, in the depths of his unconscious, the idea of what is in it for him. He is not really calculating, but he is living proof of a rather remarkable opportunism which comes naturally to him. If you tell him that you find him greedy, he will leap for your throat, citing a jumble of good works in which he has been involved. You will never know if he is the benefactor or the beneficiary. Always deeply sincere at the time, he constantly adapts himself to new truths. But he is seductive and charming. It is up to you to choose.

THE I CHING

易经

THE I CHING AND THE HORSE

In the I Ching game, you ask your question and you obtain an answer. It is therefore a divining game; but in asking your question, you pose it with your Horse identity. The wheels, the complex mechanism of your mind and spirit, have begun to turn. You ask a Horse question and the I Ching answers with a Horse 'solution', on which you then meditate as a Horse before arriving at a Horse conclusion.

The player is before a hexagram which contains the 'hypothesis response' to his question, or, more exactly, a synthesis of forces affecting the concern or event inquired about.

For you, Master Horse, here are the 64 hexagrams of the I Ching and the 64 hypotheses of the Horse.

How to proceed
1. The question
Ask a question regarding any problem at all, past, present or future, personally concerning you. (If the question concerns a friend, consult the I Ching game in the book corresponding to his Chinese sign.)

2. Method of play
It must be done with concentration.
Take **three ordinary and similar coins** — for example, three 50p coins.
Heads will equal the number 3.
Tails will equal the number 2.
Throw the coins.
If the result is two coins showing Heads and one Tails, write 3 + 3 + 2. You thus obtain a total of 8 which you represent by a continuous line: ———— .
Draw the same continuous line if you have three coins showing Heads (3 + 3 + 3 = 9).

If you throw two coins showing Tails and one Heads (2 + 2 + 3 = 7), or all three showing Tails (2 + 2 + 2 = 6), draw two separate lines: ▬ ▬ .

To sum up, 8 and 9 correspond to: ▬▬▬ (Yin)

6 and 7 correspond to: ▬ ▬ (Yang)

Repeat this operation *six times*, noting at the time of each throw the figure obtained on a piece of paper, proceeding from the first to the sixth figure, from bottom to top.

The final result, including a trigram from the bottom, or lower trigram (example:), and a trigram of the top, or upper trigram (example: ▬▬▬), will be a hexagram of the I Ching. In our example this would look like:

Now merely look for the hexagram number in the table on page 548, and then consult the list of hexagrams with their descriptions to find the given answer. *In our example,* the hexagram obtained is number 63, entitled **After completion.**

Table of Hexagrams

Trigrams	Upper lines ☰	☵	☶
Lower lines			
☰	1	11	34
☷	12	2	16
☳	25	24	51
☵	6	7	40
☶	33	15	62
☴	44	46	32
☲	13	36	55
☱	10	19	54

Use this table to find the number of your hexagrams. The meeting point between the lower and upper trigrams indicates the number of the hexagram that you are seeking.

☵	☶	☴	☳	☱
5	26	9	14	43
8	23	20	35	45
3	27	42	21	17
29	4	59	64	47
39	52	53	56	31
48	18	57	50	28
63	22	37	30	49
60	41	61	38	58

THE HEXAGRAMS OF THE HORSE

CH'IEN
1 *The creative:* Energy, strength and will; unhoped-for winning cards for an impetuous and passionate Horse, but he must also learn how to wait and not buck from impatience.

K'UN
2 *The receptive:* Ardour is not enough for creative work. You must think of the earth that you trample, and in which you can also sink.

CHUN
3 *The initial difficulty:* Anger and rage will not free you from the brambles which paralyze you. You must search within yourself; perhaps there you will find the clue.

MÊNG
4 *Youthful folly:* 'It is not I who seeks the young fool, but the young fool who seeks me.' Do not wear blinkers under the pretext of fearing danger, and do not set yourself up as an example, even if you are a circus horse.

HSÜ
5 *Waiting:* It is useless to become over-excited before the start of the race; just leave on time.

SUNG
6 *Conflict:* Even if flinging out and gnashing your teeth, retain some prudence and show yourself to be approachable; this is better than running a victory lap.

SHIH

7 *The army:* There are, perhaps, honours you can win, you who love prizes and heroics, but you must submit to a minimum of discipline.

PI

8 *Holding together (union):* Unite and participate with your squadron; solidarity is all.

SHIAO CH'U

9 *The taming power of the small:* There are no small obstacles; all art consists of the ability to leap.

LÜ

10 *Treading:* 'Tread on the tail of a Tiger, he does not bite Man.' Don your suit of light, be lordly, diplomatic, elegant; you are in the arena, but this time the roles are reversed — you are the jockey and must be careful, for your mount has stripes.

T'AI

11 *Peace:* Do not seek to convince, you are not on the same wavelength. If need be, turn back; when you come across an obstacle it is useless to gallop on until you have no breath left.

P'I

12 *Standstill:* Control your ardour and temper your fervour. If it calms you, dig a trench to pass the time — in any case, you are going to be forced to wait.

T'UNG JÊN

13 *Fellowship with men:* Even if you are a wild and solitary Horse, you should leave your prairies and become sociable: communication is essential for success.

TA YU

14 *Possession in great measure:* You hold precious winning cards, so weigh your chances and do not ruin them by impatience and empty boasts.

CH'IEN

15 *Modesty:* You will find it difficult to secure your equilibrium because you are an impatient and eager Horse. If necessary, adopt the horizontal position. Reflecting before taking action never does any harm, especially for a feverish Horse.

YÜ

16 *Enthusiasm:* At the very least, a Horse will tend to become too easily excited, to be carried away or to bolt. This time you can let yourself go, but bluffing will no longer suffice.

SUI

17 *Following:* You are in the middle of the arena; the cameras are trained upon you. Do not let the applause allow you to behave like a third-rate actor or to succumb to your passion for the spectacular.

KU

18  *Work on what has been spoiled:* Know how to admit your errors; do not persist when the race is lost, but analyze the reasons for your failure.

LIN

19 *The approach:* You are susceptible to flattery and to those who fawn on you. Beware of them; you may end by being trampled on.

KUAN

20 *Contemplation:* The Horse will have intuitive flashes, the powers of a medium and psychic and visionary gifts. It is useless to gallop to the top of the tower where fever and turbulence will only cloud your vision.

SHIH HO

21 *Biting through (or clearly defined penalties):* You should bite steadily, lash out with your hooves, charge at full speed and generally attract attention; in any case, you must show your authority.

PI

22 *Grace:* Do not fall into the trap of trusting appearances, even if they are flattering. There is nothing to stop you from dining by candlelight, but do not forget the oppressive realities of the external world.

PO

23 *Splitting apart:* Do not undertake anything; the structure is rotting from the inside, do not remain underneath.

FU

24 *Return — the turning point:* After galloping among the shadows, you are in full sunlight. The crisis lies behind you and it is useless to turn back. Remember Lot's wife, who was turned into a pillar of salt.

WU WANG

25 *Innocence:* Intuition guides you, which will be good provided you remain impartial. If it only leads you to the stable, you probably need rest.

TA CH'U

26 *The taming of the great:* Power and strength. Others have wagered on you; you must not disappoint them. Refresh your spirit and increase your chances.

I

27 *The corners of the mouth:* Food for the body and spirit. For the spirit, discipline is necessary; for the body, perhaps a diet.

TA KUO

28 *Preponderance of the great:* Do not overload yourself morally or physically; if you wish to win the race, call for help.

K'AN

29 *Fathomless water:* Do not alter your direction; maintain it even if a storm threatens. Rearing back will not prevent it.

LI

30 *Clinging, fire:* If ardour is necessary, there is a time for displaying it and another for curbing it. The rage from losing is as powerful as the rage to win; be particularly circumspect.

HSIEN

31 *Influence:* Know how to profit from opportunities and propitious encounters or associations, but do not get carried away: a walk may not be an epic journey, but do not refuse it. Perhaps it will rain tomorrow.

HÊNG

32 *Duration:* Question yourself: however difficult this may seem, you need to do so; the result will exceed your wildest hopes.

TUN

33 *Retreat:* Knowing how to withdraw is not to flee the field but a sign of wisdom; hold your head high without foaming at the mouth.

TA CHUANG

34 *The power of the great:* Strength, movement, energy. Marvellous winning cards for a race horse, but he must know when to stop — at the winning post.

CHIN

35 *Progress:* If you are finally able to prove your competence, do not hesitate to show your trump cards. Even so, welcome collaboration and remain loyal to your friends.

MING I

36 *Darkening of the light:* It is pointless to neigh when the night is impenetrable. If your fuses have blown, do not look for candles but wait for dawn.

CHIA JÊN

37 *Family:* It is more than a warm and comfortable stable; become a part of it and respect the structure. You have a family and should understand that you need it.

K'UEI

38 *Opposition:* Although you are naturally talented in jumping fences, you cannot afford to dispense with discipline. Too much facility could be fatal.

CHIEN

39 *Obstruction:* It must be said that you possess the art of running to meet a challenge. This is a valuable technique in its own right, but if a hand is held out to you, do not refuse it. Overtaking an obstacle with assistance is more important than breaking your teeth because of pride, and all alone.

HSIEH

40 *Deliverance:* Make a clean sweep, without waiting. Start again at zero with sound hooves.

SUN

41 *Decrease:* Times are difficult for Horses in flight, lovers of display and luxury. Learn how to rediscover simplicity and sincerity.

I

42 *Increase:* You are an opportunist and this is the time to be one. Seize the moment. A period of blossoming and abundant oats.

KUAI

43 *Breakthrough:* 'Advance with strength and without compromise'. Circle before the judges and descend into the arena; neglect nothing, denounce scandal; a favourite role for the Horse.

KOU

44 *Coming to meet:* Bridles, harnesses and constraints do not suit you, so reject them. Distrust sleeping waters — sometimes they contain terrible poisons.

TS'UI

45 *Gathering together:* A meeting has been called. Ensure that you are not overwhelmed by uncontrolled elements; your fear of failure could become panic.

SHÊNG

46 *Pushing upwards:* Leave nothing to chance, demonstrate your competence and take on responsibilities. You will feel at one with the deepest part of your being.

K'UN

47 *Oppression:* It is useless to rear up or foam with rage. You must accept that your energy has diminished and that you are stalling. Recover your breath but keep alert.

CHING

48 *The well:* You feel the need of change, to overturn your life and your habits. This will be positive if you respect the rules which govern the evolution of the body and the blooming of the spirit.

KO

49 *Revolution:* You who love to be in the forefront are going to be well served. Mutations, confrontations and even disturbances are sometimes indispensable.

TING

50  *The cauldron:* Symbol of the five Elements — Earth, Wood, Fire, Water and Metal. Physical and spiritual nourishment. Respect them and you will finish your race as a celestial Horse.

CHÊN

51 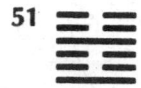 *The arousing (shock, thunder):* Trials and conflicts loom on the horizon; do not deviate from your chosen route. Perhaps light will emanate from discord; keep calm.

KÊN

52  *Keeping still:* Stay quietly in your stable; it is in calm solitude that you will renew your strength; keep to this for the time being.

CHIEN

53  *Development (gradual progress):* Do not try to leap over stages but cross them methodically. You will save your energy and retain your self-respect.

KUEI MEI

54  *The bride:* Is perhaps a good match to consider, without, for the moment, any formal obligation.

FÊNG

55  *Abundance:* Here, for the time being, is a state of plenitude, of green prairies and wide-open spaces. The wise Horse will prepare himself for arid soil and restricted space, thus respecting the alternations of Yin and Yang.

LÜ

56 *The wanderer:* Move off and withdraw temporarily, the better to rejoin space and its liberty.

SUN

57 *The gentle:* As the reed bends before the wind, so should the Horse avoid direct conflict. His true strength lies in going with currents, not in breaking himself apart in frenzied assaults.

TUI

58 *The serene, the joyous:* Discover that the joy of giving is as great as that of receiving.

HUAN

59 *Dissolution:* Working towards a common end for its own sake, unselfishly and without ulterior motives or constraint is a fine lesson to be learned.

CHIEH

60 *Limitation:* You must not impose limits on yourself arbitrarily; you have first to understand why they are needed.

CHUNG FU

61 *Inner truth:* Shouting from the rooftops means nothing; applying rules in daily life, without showing off, is more convincing.

HSIAO KUO

62 *Preponderance of the small:* Your means are limited. This is not the time to launch big projects; to accept limitation is to overcome it.

CHI CHI

63  *After completion:* Even in a state of maturity, equilibrium and control, you must foresee a reversal. After every apogee comes the decline — but not necessarily a fall into hell.

WEI CHI

64 *Before completion:* You have not yet received the medal or the great prize.

YEAR OF THE GOAT

1907 · 1919 · 1931
1943 · 1955 · 1967
1979 · 1991 · 2003

THE DOMAINS OF THE GOAT

十二生肖

THE GOAT AND ITS SYMBOLISM

'Stubborn as a goat' is a well-known but somewhat misleading saying, for the Goat is also intuitive, unselfconscious and eccentric. The Goat in three colours — white, black and red — straddling the clouds, seems only a visitor on earth. Indeed, the sky, infinity and space constitute his domain and his personal universe. The Goat plays; he cavorts and gambols with ease. Before you can catch a glimpse of his horns, he is likely to have disappeared behind a large cloud — which he will slash with a kick of his hooves, laughing merrily at the rain drops as they spill into the chalice of a luminous dawn. But be careful — if you do not take him seriously he will trigger off a storm, tickling the lightning and exciting the thunder. The little Goat is a rainmaker, a friend of lightning and an inhabitant of the starry canopy of heaven.

The Ancient Greeks called him the nurse of Zeus, but our Goat does not give two hoots for such legends. With him all is fantasy and caprice, a pretext for making fun of men and their seriousness. Nevertheless, the Goat is not insensitive to the earth. A maternal and protective animal, he participates in its virtues and its cycles, in the growth of the grain and the fertilization and blossoming of nature. Profoundly intuitive and sensitive, he is strong in the face of difficulty and never yields, no matter what happens. Neither wolves nor ogres can succeed in making him listen to reason, or cause him to overthrow his deepest convictions. Generous and frivolous, he is always elusive and obstinate. In India, where his name is 'Aja' ('the unborn'), the Goat is considered the mother of the world and of all nature.

Of the three colours of the Goat, black reveals a tendency to veil, to mask and to hide, belonging to that which disguises divine reality behind the illusions of the intellect. White, on the other hand, is the symbol of light, the power which dissipates illusion. Finally, red represents action, the creative dance of worlds in perpetual metamorphosis. The

Goat thus appears as changeable and multifaceted — a veritable magician intoxicated by winds and reflected lights.

Let him gambol and spin round with his airy hooves; but listen to his intuitions and learn to appreciate his finesse and good taste, while he browses among the flowers in his celestial garden. Whoever knows how to win him over sits astride the clouds, head in the stars and open to the most intimate and subtle understanding of nature.

There was once a little goat who possessed the gift of seeing into the future. He was a charming tri-coloured goat — white, black and red — who lived peacefully within his flock. One day he discovered that the neighbouring shepherds, jealous of his master's pasture, nurtured sinister designs on him and desired his death. The Goat immediately went to warn his master.

'They want to kill you,' he said.

'What do I care, let them do it,' the shepherd replied. 'But you must bury me in the middle of my flock along with three flutes. When the wind blows, the flutes will whistle and the little goats will weep tears of blood.'

'But what should I say to the people in the village?'

'That I have gone away on a voyage, and that I have married a queen.'

The obedient Goat did not wish to go against his master's wishes, and so, ever since, with all the other members of the flock, he weeps tears of blood each time the wind blows in the branches of the trees.

This tale illustrates well the tenderness and sweetness, the sensitive and whimsical nature of the Goat, as well as his vulnerability, his artistic spirit and his fidelity to memory — which can indeed become an obsession.

A few notes on the Goat
Principal qualities: He is peaceful and adaptable and has a gentle and easy character.
Principal defects: They begin with the negative prefixes,

'ir-' 'in-' and 'un-' — irresponsible, irrational, inconstant, unsatisfied, undisciplined.

Work: What a horrible idea! The Goat loves art, but considers it to be a pleasure, not work.

Best role: Guest. He makes a party 'go'.

Worst role: Administrative director or financier.

Money: Ah, if one could only get along without it!

Luck: To be born on a rainy day — his fate will be more peaceful and happier.

Cannot live without: Beauty.

Adores: Tranquillity.

Hates: To be put face to face before responsibilities which he has no wish to assume; to be made to choose.

Leisure activities: A blend of visiting art galleries, weekends in the country and visits to the doctor for check-ups (he pays a great deal of attention to his health).

Favourite places: Parks and gardens with fountains and marble statues.

Colour: Sky-blue.

Plants: Anise, wormwood.

Flower: Honeysuckle.

Professions: Actor or actress, painter, musician, landscape artist, weaver, potter (all crafts); also, courtesan, gigolo, professional dance partner — and tramp.

The four ages in the life of the Goat according to Chinese tradition

Childhood is a delicate time for the Goat, who depends on the harmony and security of the family. His *youth* will be marked by uncertain and hesitant emotional behaviour — at times inconstant and timid — amounting to instability. On the other hand, he will be lucky during *maturity,* and in *old* age will want for nothing.

THE PSYCHOLOGY OF THE GOAT

Following closely in the steps of the passionate Horse is the ardent Goat. He has as much elegance, but more delicacy.

He cavorts with equal facility, but, whereas the Horse simulates thunder when he gallops, from the Goat only a rhythmic and discreet tapping will be heard. The purpose of the Goat's hooves is not to keep him in contact with the ground (like those of the Buffalo), but to sustain his leaps among the clouds, his favourite domain. Walking with elastic steps, his nose in the air, the perfumes caught by his palpitating nostrils have, in his eyes, far greater importance than the ground upon which he treads. Goats have an airy and often dreamy nature. They are inspired by everything which brings about harmony and adds to the 'quality of life', rather than from any material necessity, which they prefer to ignore. If they are forced to pay attention to the material side of existence, the effort can provoke so much anxiety as to cause psychosomatic illness.

Creative, imaginative and ingenious, Goats would like to devote all their free time to the arts, which to them, are the equivalent of a religion. Writing cheques, paying bills, and so on, are activities they consider shocking, even indecent. Goats believe that the truth is no truer for being said, and that not all realities should be experienced.

From his refusal to see the material side of life, one might easily suppose the Goat to be detached from anything which derives from the possession of wealth, comfort, regular meals, security and the like. This, however, is not the case, and herein lies his main contradiction. Goats are not 'pure spirits'. Although some of them approach mysticism on an abstract level, there are certain pleasures they find extremely difficult to renounce. Legend has it that a Goat attached to a stake will pull ceaselessly on the rope tethering him if the grass is scarce, but will remain peacefully if the field is grassy and green.

It is simply that the Goat, needing stability and support, relies on others to provide it rather than creating it himself. Is he amoral? Unaware? Neither one nor the other. It is his nature, and one must take him as he is without trying to change him; otherwise he will flee, gambolling away, and nothing will hold him back. Both independent — nothing can make him settle down except love, and that we shall see later — and profoundly dependent — his physical and moral well-being is conditioned by others — the Goat has a slightly profiteering side, but he is not hypocritical. If you are insistent, if you start nagging him, he will wash his hands of the whole affair.

Chinese tradition says that if they are to blossom and give the best of themselves, Goats need a patron to take charge of administration, leaving the Goat to develop his creative talents. This can take several forms: a father-protector; a stable, hard-working and understanding spouse; a manager or devoted accountant.

Those born under this sign all possess charm, and are also amiable, attractive and calm. Their fantasy and their imagination give pleasure, which in turn, because of their goodness and their indulgence, retain the sympathy of others. It is against their nature to criticize; rather, they seek and find excuses for the behaviour of others; they are also adept at finding excuses for themselves.

If the victims of some treachery or underhanded dealing, they are forgiving, considering anger and vengeance to be callous and useless. Rather than brood over old sores, they prefer to seek new and greener pastures.

Detesting anything routine, in their attempts to escape from constraints and obligations Goats sometimes behave somewhat eccentrically, enough to provoke curiosity but without shocking, for they do not want to antagonize others. They are repelled by cold and hostile atmospheres, are peace-loving and believe in compromises. If need be, they will stifle their resentment to preserve good will, for this is essential to them. They are never mean; if they are the cause of suffering it is because they have been thoughtless or careless. They are often a bit timid, especially to start with, but become quickly at ease, talkative, amusing and sparkling.

Goats also have their defects, which are accentuated in

their youth but lessen in their adulthood due to the responsibilities thrust upon them, which, moreover, are not agreeable to them. They are by nature carefree, impulsive and lazy. They hesitate to take the initiative or to commit themselves and are easily influenced. Dreamy and pliable, their natures are 'plastic'. They find it difficult to be punctual, having no sense of time, and, when thwarted, will sulk before trying to make up. When really pressured Goats will initially lose their heads and become extremely upset, but in the end they will come to terms with the problem, realizing that action is the only way out. Then they will be stubborn.

Oddly enough, their general lack of organization is relatively unimportant, for they are capable of skilled and precise action. While they may not especially like work, they prefer that it be done well if it is to be done at all.

Some Goats, lacking the will — and above all the desire — to deal with an unpleasant situation, take to feeling sorry for themselves, blaming those around them and determinedly refusing to recognize their own errors. By indulging in self-pity rather than action, they risk being caught within a vicious circle from which there is no escape.

Although Goats have their own mad rhythm of life, to please you they will willingly adapt to yours; on the whole they are agreeable, discreet and easy to live with. They will listen to your confidences but never try to give advice because they do not want to become involved, which can sometimes be pleasant. Goats are determined not to get mixed up in what does not concern them — to such a degree as to call into question the existence of any real friendship; one can never really know if they can be counted on. If reproached for this they will reply with disarming sincerity, 'But I never told you that you could depend on me.' Actually, this is not surprising, for they already have more than enough troubles of their own.

By the simple power of words and the magic of a gesture, Goats alone know how to create an ideal ambiance, to transform the most oppressive atmosphere into an earthly paradise. Unless one begs to be allowed to follow them into this fairy-like universe, into their dream palaces, one must accept them as they are and demand nothing.

THE GOAT AS A CHILD

Children born during a year of the Goat are timid and sometimes uncertain. It is essential that they are kept warm and secure and that their parents are at ease with each other, for they need to lean on someone in order to find their equilibrium. This is by no means conventional, since moral structures are important to them only because they sometimes create obstacles. Consequently, the young Goat will be more at ease and more sure of himself with a divorced parent who is relaxed and likeable, than with perfectly united but narrow-minded parents haunted by rigid principles. In an atmosphere full of fantasy, love and indulgence he will blossom; constrained by strict middle class rules or the insincere and unhealthy comedy of estranged parents, he will wilt.

Even if one seems a bit authoritarian with a Goat child, it is tempting to impose one's will and influence him. But — and here Chinese tradition is emphatic — one must never try to change the Goat child. He is not made to become a Tiger or a Dragon, and to try and force him to become so would cause him deep unhappiness. It is therefore important — despite the temptation, for the Goat child is adaptable, pliable and does not always seem to know what he wants — to allow him to seek for himself and discover his nature on his own, while always remaining available, ready to intervene at the least sign of alarm, but otherwise keeping one's thoughts to oneself.

For some parents this is almost impossible. The Ox, for example, believes that without his advice his little child will be sure to get into terrible trouble. However, the Goat child must be allowed to contend with his own difficulties; otherwise he will never become aware of reality nor of his responsibilities, and will become no more than an amiable dilettante, sponging off his parents. Twenty years on they will be sick and tired of it.

At school the Goat child is unpredictable. All will depend on whether his teachers can awaken his imagination and interest. Whether they do or not, an artistic orientation is likely to be the most favourable for him, for then he will be able to shine without worrying that he is rather different from the others. In this way his aesthetic and creative senses will be aroused and he will not be left to vegetate, 15th in a class of 30.

LOVE LIFE

From their earliest years, the lives of Goats are transmitted through their emotional reactions. It is a mistake to expect logical and objective reasoning from them. They are wholly involved in their sympathies, their refusals, in the *feelings* they experience. Expecting much from others, they are ready to give everything in return. What a dream! But we must now look into this in a little more detail, and examine what it is they expect and what they offer.

What do Goats expect? Above all, a form of moral and material protection: they need to be able to assure themselves that 'No matter what happens, he (or she) will stay with me, will never betray me. Whatever the temptations offered, whatever the risks involved, our tie will be protected from storms and misunderstandings.'

Next, Goats wish to be either relieved of all material concerns, or to be supported when they must face up to responsibilities. In this respect, they are not indifferent to the social standing of their partner. They are often mistakenly dubbed self-seeking climbers or spongers; in fact, they do not seek the help of others and do not run after money, but simply need a certain comfort — which they avow openly. They rarely have the kind of pride which requires them to say 'I have arrived by myself and I owe nothing to anyone.'

What do Goats offer? Simply, themselves — they give

spontaneously of their qualities, faults, impossibilities and their own special talents. Being open and uncalculating, they never try to adapt their behaviour to suit the personality of the other. They are originals: either one loves them and so takes, or one does not love them and so refuses. Each is free. Those who take on a Goat companion will enjoy a unique experience, as long as they do not require that he or she should change. Naturally happy and optimistic, Goats live in the present, do not ask indiscreet questions, respect other people's liberty and are polite and affectionate. Anguish and anxiety are absent from their repertoire (except when their supply of grass runs out, but then, their appetite is not gargantuan); and, if they have difficulty recognizing their faults, they do not invite discussion or disputes.

Goats have a special gift for creating an agreeable ambiance round them which contributes to their social success, including frequent invitations to weekends in the country. But be careful! If your Goat guest is comfortable in your house, you will not get him to leave easily, for Goats are capable of installing their belongings anywhere and, provided the lodging and food are worth the trip, they will suffer no qualms from making the most of it.

For Goats, feeling counts at least as much as the sexual act itself; before approaching the pleasures of the night, they require a romantic sunset. They love the preliminaries, games of love and chance and slow seductions; 'paratroop' behaviour is not their strong point.

Are they faithful? Yes, so long as they are not abused, and so long as their partner dedicates himself to them exclusively or, in return for their fidelity, they can expect something which they value in return. Without being altogether immune to temptation, Goats have a light touch when dealing with it, and can resist it if necessary. A little flirtation here and there, for their own amusement and to verify their seductive powers, will suffice. But they know how to reserve themselves for really great occasions — especially Mrs Goat.

On the other hand, if their life is currently uncertain or

insecure, they are capable of many adventures. Passion? That is not really the point; it is more a matter of curiosity. If the moment is right, if the grass seems young and green and some spirit of the devil is in him, the Goat's natural curiosity will prevail.

FAMILY LIFE

Marriage? Why not, if you really want to. But those born under the sign of the Goat do not enter a church for the pleasure of hearing a discourse on the state of marriage. Society's rules leave them indifferent; when it comes to signatures and contracts, they prefer a somewhat wanton liberty.

A Goat will light-heartedly marry for the best and forget to imagine the worse. If there is some crisis in the marriage, he will refuse to recognize its existence and concentrate on something else. Like Rabbits, Goats recoil from tense situations.

If there is open disagreement, their reactions are positive: they try to mediate, to find some common ground for a reconciliation. If this fails, if their partner will hear none of it, they shut themselves up in their room to listen to music or sublimate their misery by painting a picture. They ask for a divorce as rarely as they marry for conventional reasons. If you are insistent about something, they will agree with you, for they want, above all, to have peace.

Mr Goat has no sense of family responsibility in the conventional sense. He is quite likely to take his children to museums two days before their final examinations, or to buy a diamond for his wife without thinking for a moment of the sorry state of his bank account. Mrs Goat will forget the roast in the oven while she recounts the story of Little Red Riding Hood to her delighted children. She will then serve up a sort of burned picnic, with another charming little tale to take the place of good food. But her children will adore her and never sulk. Some lady Goats can occasionally forget they even have children.

Slightly irresponsible, Goat partners are adorable. They have no authority, but then they do not mind if their children are lacking in respect. Their system of education may be lax, but it does have the advantage of encouraging creative and imaginative talents in their children — none of them will ever be stifled.

Goat, Dragon, Snake or Monkey children will bring out the best in their Goat parents, and the family atmosphere will be idyllic. Young Dogs, Rabbits or Pigs will feel rather insecure, but will avoid quarrels and, except for the Rabbit, will eventually reverse roles and come to the aid of their parents. Things will not go very well with the aggressive Rat ('What on earth have I done to deserve such a child?'); or with the Tiger who detests nonchalance, or with the impenetrable and independent Horse.

The Rooster child, who is very attached to his rights, will not stand for seeing his Goat parent slide here and there, not caring a whit for the opinion of others. The Ox Child, outraged, will close in on himself or will constantly criticize his parents. Goats would be well advised to avoid giving birth to a child belonging to these two signs, for it will be difficult to attain, yet alone conserve, any mutual understanding.

PROFESSIONAL LIFE

Those born under the sign of the Goat are neither especially active nor especially ambitious. Sometimes lazy, often erratic, they find no value in the competitive spirit — a form of rivalry which, in their eyes, will necessarily involve them in conflicts and disputes. A spirit of 'live and let live' will always be more important to them than the pursuit of power. They are advised never to mix work with friendship, and even to refuse to help a friend in trouble, however selfish this may seem. If the work they are doing interests them, Goats are perfectionists and scrupulously careful, leaving nothing to chance. If for some reason they do take on responsibility for the failings of a friend they have helped, they will be placed in an unpleasant and confused situation. However, they are capable of sacrificing a well-earned success or of deliberately botching some details to avoid a dispute or a separation.

In the employment jungle, among predators armed with diplomas and attaché cases, Goats are as out of place as a rhinoceros in a Venetian glass factory. Have you ever heard someone say 'after you' when it was a question of obtaining a higher position? If so, it must have been a Goat.

In professions requiring a certain cheek coupled with self-interest, material ambitions and a taste for confrontation, Goats are defenceless. They lack one essential thing: belief in this kind of enterprise. For this reason they are usually to be found content in secondary roles, making no effort to gain promotion. It is not that they are unhappy, they are simply asleep — or, more exactly, dreaming.

But let a good fairy, a tolerant parent or a bright manager lean over their cradle; let an intuitive producer offer them a role in the arts or in the theatre, and these modest caterpillars become brilliant butterflies. They need only a little beauty round them to sparkle and dazzle. The most timid become talkative, the most lazy become highly active. Their voices, perhaps inaudible in everyday life, will sound warm over the microphone. In this kind of atmosphere, Goat-like qualities bubble over.

This is not to say that Goats can only blossom in the arts; only that they will do other things less well, lacking enthusiasm, finesse and belief. Imagine James Dean (Goat 1931) or Johnny Halliday (Goat 1943) behind a desk in a bank or a window at the Post Office. They would be charming but 'absent'. Without an aesthetic or artistic contact, Goats wilt like plants deprived of water.

MATERIAL LIFE

Natives of this sign need money, but they do not like to have to get it. They find no pleasure in manipulating vast sums and their own money slips between their fingers like a river under a bridge. Goats are neither acquisitive nor hoarders.

If they earn more than enough for their needs, they would be well advised to consult a stockbroker as to investment of the surplus; but they should first check on his reputation, for Goats are gullible and, being slightly naive, all too ready to believe in Eldorado. They are the perfect juicy prey for predators of all kinds.

Another solution for Goats is to find a practical and well-organized spouse who will hold the purse strings and, naturally, take care of their material concerns.

If you should find yourself in the noble role of patron-protector of a Goat, observe the following advice: never give him all his month's allowance on the first of the month, for after a very few days he will have spent it all. It is better to give him a little at a time; in that way, the ingenious Goat will get the most out of it.

Goats are honest but rather careless about their own property which they give away too easily to their friends before learning better. At times a benefactor and at times a parasite — but always polite and agreeable — the Goat will find it impossible to be truly motivated for material reasons. However, he as readily adapts to the role of the carefree millionaire living among palm trees and gambling casinos as to that of an artist living in a bohemian community.

ENVIRONMENT

While Goats are particularly sensitive to the beauty of objects and the harmony of forms and colours, like the Snakes their appreciation is not dependent on a pride of possession. This indifference to possessions stems from their restlessness; they like to be able to go away at will, leaving everything behind them. You can be sure that if they are the happy owners of real estate this is neither from taste nor from avarice, but simply because a well-intentioned friend has proved to them that it is the best possible investment.

In fact, Goats are perfectly capable of living in furnished rooms; but the furniture will be beautiful and the surroundings attractive. Some of them, vagabonds in spirit and repudiating any ties, will spend at least a part of their lives wandering indifferently from city to city, guitars slung across their shoulders, their belongings on their backs. There is often a little of the 'smiling hippy' among Goats.

They readily adapt themselves to others' homes, where they will create their own universe — on a corner of a sofa if need be. They have the magical gift of seeing only what is beautiful, and in a dark and smelly room will install a rare and superb object, indirectly lit, and everything else will melt into obscurity before the work of art.

A guide to personal relations with a Goat

Methods of seduction: About the same for both sexes — pleasantness and delicacy, a touch of fantasy, and then it is your turn (otherwise, the game would become tiring).

If he loves you: He will give a great deal, but will take a great deal in exchange. You will have to have some moral and material reserves, as well as a good deal of patience. If you do not feel capable of supporting so much fantasy, imagination and uncertainty, then look elsewhere.

He expects of you: That you follow him in his search for the beautiful and the true, and that you take charge of the management side of his life.

To keep you: He will frolic to keep you guessing.

If he is unfaithful: It is because he has a need for variety or, possibly, for an instant he has forgotten that you exist.

If you are unfaithful: He is not suspicious but subtle and intuitive. He will sense your indiscretion and do the same, and then he will sulk, complain and speak of you to the entire world as the most ignoble individual that our planet has ever seen.

In case of a break between you: There will be much wrangling, a lot of shouting, departures, returns and beating about the bush, until the moment comes when he will decide that finally he no longer cares. By then it will be too late. But a final rupture is not inevitable, for the Goat is slow to quarrel with those he loves.

If you wish to give him a gift: Offer him a nice little sum for life — in other words, give him an income! More modestly, give him a rare and delicate object. However, be careful if you do because he has infallible taste and the ability to detect imitations.

If you want to seduce him: If you can afford it, be grandiose. Organize a costume ball, 17th century, with clever lighting, fireworks, ballets, and a musical background of silvery notes from a clavichord. If that is too costly, invite him to the country.

If you want to get rid of him: Ask him to help you fill out your income tax forms.

THE GOAT AND THE OTHER CHINESE SIGNS

Goat/Rat

Here is a relationship scarcely encouraged by tradition. It is accepted that the specific traits of these two signs are not in harmony: the Rat is too assiduous, too selfish, too critical and too lucid to tolerate for more than a very short time the casual unconcern and the fantasies of the Goat. And, although imaginative, the Rat is neither supple nor subtle enough, nor enough of an aesthete to follow the Goat in his quest for 'beauty at any price'.

The Goat will be disappointed in this relationship. He will feel misunderstood and will hate the Rat's criticisms. The

581

Rat, irritated by what he feels to be an inconsistency in the Goat, will become even more biting. Since one belongs under the earth and the other lives in the clouds, it is, in any case, difficult for them to meet on any level.

A true Rat likes security, but he admires those who are capable of procuring it for themselves. This is not at all the Goat's 'forte'; he usually needs a patron. Unless the Western signs are especially encouraging, this relationship between such different personalities is hardly advisable.

Goat/Ox

If in love one always chose one's total opposite, the Ox/Goat couple would be ideal. Opposed as they are in the Chinese zodiac, and as different as it is possible to be, it would be delightful if they could come lastingly together.

For the Ox, the imaginative and fanciful air that surrounds the Goat like an aura could open a new dimension. For the Goat, whose speciality does not consist in making decisions, let alone wise ones, the Ox's reserves of practicality could be an effective support. All this is written in the conditional because Chinese tradition tersely advises the Ox to avoid the Goat, and vice versa.

It is tempting and easy to say that they will make idiots of each other; better to hope that they meet and fall in love (admittedly very unlikely), for if they do their alliance can prove beneficial to their reciprocal development, and, above all, to their equilibrium.

Goat/Tiger

The charming Goat, attached to a post, bleats sadly while the feared Tiger silently approaches, licking his fangs in anticipation of the good breakfast he is going to have.

Suspense: will the Tiger devour the Goat? The hypothesis is tempting; but love has its mysteries. The amorous Goat looks to a dynamic person for protection. The amorous Tiger does not tend to devour his partner; on the contrary, he leaves him free — even a little too free for certain tastes.

After reflection this tie, which at first seems strange, can prove to be most positive if sincere feelings are involved. The Goat needs to wander at ease with his nose to the stars if he is to blossom, and the Tiger will not prevent him. The Tiger's courage, loyalty and audacity will provoke the Goat's admiration. It is to be hoped, however, that they have money put aside, for the Goat is a spendthrift, and the Tiger counts more on his luck than his thrift. But they will be happy, for, each respecting the other's liberty, they will acknowledge their partial independence with a touching gratitude.

Goat/Rabbit

A very good alliance. Like the Rabbit, the Goat likes tranquillity, and he adapts to almost any kind of life which allows a minimum of liberty and offers him enough grass to graze on. The Rabbit is affectionate without being too possessive, and his love for the home brings an element of security to those in need of it.

The imagination and fantasy of the Goat will delight the Rabbit and help him escape the daily rut he has a tendency to fall into. The Rabbit's seriousness and his habit of perseverance promise well for the family finances. However, this couple will be vulnerable if an external crisis, a professional setback, an unforeseen loss of money or a domestic accident should occur, for the Rabbit and Goat find it difficult to depend on each other, and their relationship may be difficult to preserve. With each suffering from acute anxiety — the Rabbit for the future, the Goat for the present — they risk making mountains out of molehills and over-dramatizing everything.

Goat/Dragon

This alliance can be either good or bad. Good because the Goat needs to be protected, or at least encouraged and supported. He will listen to the Dragon's advice and, if he succeeds in stifling his desire to yawn, everyone will be content. Indeed, the Dragon can turn out to be a valuable patron for the whimsical Goat.

Unhappily, the Dragon's need for admiration and to feel

indispensable will not meet with a ready response from the Goat, for whom any form of adulation is totally foreign. Respect, yes; but it is not his style to compliment. Our poor Dragon risks wilting like a plant without water.

With this couple, one must hope that the Dragon will be the active and dominant element, so that he can find the satisfactions in his work he is unable to obtain at home. But if the Dragon remains at home — and this is almost unthinkable — pity them both: they will make each other's lives impossible, the Dragon will be miserable and the Goat will indulge in resounding follies.

Goat/Snake

There is no problem with these two getting along with each other. The Snake infinitely appreciates the fantasy; imagination and creativity of the Goat and a love of art, beauty and harmony will often unite them. They will rarely quarrel — it is too fatiguing.

But which of the two will do the work? On this level the Goat is irregular and rather badly organized; the Snake cannot be counted on to keep the accounts, and when the Goat works and earns money, he wants it for himself — 'me first' — and perhaps a small gift from time to time as well.

If they have inherited some property they will live together peaceably, from time to time doing a little work, not so much to earn money as for the pleasure of it and to prove to others that they can do it. They will pitilessly mock commuters, victims of the train-desk-sleep syndrome. Both will wallow in their respective egotism and, even if the Goat occasionally strains on his leash, this relationship will work in the end — bitterness and divorce are too fatiguing.

Goat/Horse

The lives of Horses are a permanent 'happening'; they need to fall in love — and remain so — and to create a developing and unpredictable relationship. With a Goat for a partner, they are well served. Their mutual dislike of routine, the instability of their behaviour, their irresponsible side, their attitude of 'being ready for anything' does not imply any form of security. A Horse in love with a Goat will often walk a tightrope, but he will never have time to be bored.

The Goat will feel secure, for the Horse's passion will always be self-evident; and the Goat will not suffer from any sense of being neglected or abandoned, both of which he detests.

It will be easier if the man is a Horse, for his Goat spouse will leave it to him to earn their daily bread. Otherwise, let us hope that Mrs Horse is an heiress or has a well-paid job, for Mr Goat rarely likes to work for two.

Goat/Goat

At least they will not ask of each other more than they can give, which will spare them many dissatisfactions. They will spend hours, days and weeks improving their home, buying pretty objects, only to move house until they have found the ideal setting. When they have, they will eat a delicious meal to celebrate and afterwards take a nap.

Divine indeed! So where lies the flaw in this match? You will have spotted it — neither work nor money have been mentioned. Goats being spendthrift, who will keep the pot boiling? If both are artists, living at their own unconstrained rhythms, then all will be well if they have invested wisely and enjoy a decent income. Even so, they will need a good accountant; otherwise, they will forget about their taxes until it is too late to escape a penalty. If they have a child, raising it will develop their sense of responsibility. Ideally, they need a patron or a manager to promote them.

Goat/Monkey

This is a relationship full of gaiety and fantasy. These two will never be bored together and will be very amusing for others, ceaselessly inventing new pranks and using their imagination and intelligence with remarkable virtuosity. They will know how to make the most of each other, tossing the ball back and forth.

In fact, everything will go well so long as they remain friends or associates — or even lovers. However, if they decide to live together they will run the risk of things becoming less rosy and idyllic.

In spite of himself, the Monkey will preserve his reasonableness, whereas the Goat will need to be told over and over again that he is loved, so that he may feel truly cared for and secure.

Once the initial enthusiasm has passed, the Goat will be disappointed; the Monkey, even with the best intentions in the world, will not be able to become what he is not — not even to please the Goat.

Goat/Rooster

They do not have much in common except, perhaps, a love of the countryside and a certain flair for socializing. They do not really understand each other. The Goat will feel secure, for the Rooster will work for two, but he will expect in return understanding, permanent companionship and a form of encouragement amounting to moral support which the Goat will be unable to provide.

Although he may pretend to be unconcerned, the Rooster will be deeply upset and will withdraw into himself, a role at which he is a specialist. The Goat, assuming the truth to be revealed by the role, will retreat within his vagabond spirit — and the rift between the two will continue to widen.

If the man is a Goat and the woman a Rooster, she will nag him ceaselessly and will not tolerate his 'bohemian' side. But if she can be his manager, she will be excellent and do great things for him. In this way they will reach a better understanding and the mutual respect they gain will cement their alliance.

Goat/Dog

While Goats are often anxious about the present and the near future, the anxiety of the Dog is more extensive and more profound. Each needs to be reassured of the fidelity of others and the depth of their feelings for them. Both to different degrees are pessimistic: the Goat will be philosophic, the Dog anguished.

It is better not to put them in the same boat or they will travel from Charbydis to Scylla without catching their breath, which will merely augment their anxieties. They will be found filled with tranquillizers, predicting the end of the world and modern industrial society. Another obstacle is that the Dog is a stranger to fantasy. He is serious and responsible, but rarely amusing, and the Goat's outbursts of fantasy will insult his good sense. No, it is hard to imagine them as a couple together — unless they found a mystical and ecological sect in which to be together.

Goat/Pig

A profitable alliance for both signs: each gets something out of it. The Pig, master of the palace, is born under the sign of opulence and is generous. The Goat adores palaces, so long as he can do as he likes. This poses no problem, for the Pig, who is not possessive, will let him run about as he pleases. The Goat also adores opulence, to which he has the gift of bringing a sense of comfort and harmony, which will not displease the Pig, who also loves beauty.

Indeed, a feeling for beauty is their greatest common ground; each associates it with a calmness refined to an ideal of peace. To preserve this, both will be capable of making the necessary concessions. Even when there is coldness between them, they will make up by going on a tour of the art galleries.

The only risk is that the Goat, aware of his partner's indulgence, will go too far and become temperamental and altogether irrational. The amiable Pig will then become a severe and stubborn critic and will slap the Goat's fingers like a schoolmaster — and will have the last word.

SOME GOAT CELEBRITIES

Balzac, Empress Josephine, Simone de Beauvoir, Cyrano de Bergerac, Boucher, Cesare Borgia, Cervantes, Pierre Curie, Claudette Colbert, Daguerre; James Dean, Catherine Deneuve, Thomas Edison, John Ford, Douglas Fairbanks, Johnny Halliday, Franz Kafka, Lizst, Daphne du Maurier, Michelangelo, Alberto Moravia, Mussolini, Laurence Olivier, Pushkin, Proust, Swift, Thackeray, Mark Twain, Rudolph Valentino, John Wayne.

YOUR
COMPANION
IN LIFE

生命伴侣

After the Chinese sign of your year of birth, here is the sign of your hour of birth

What is a Companion in Life, as understood in Chinese astrology? It is a sort of 'ascendant' sign corresponding to your hour of birth. This Companion is another animal belonging to the Chinese cycle of the twelve emblematic beasts, who falls into step with you and accompanies you, ever ready to help you brave the traps and ambushes along your route. A permanent and benevolent shadow, he can render the impossible possible.

He is your counterpart, but with his own character and tendencies and with a different psychology. Both guardian angel and devil's advocate, he will be a witness to your life and an actor in it.

Have you ever felt, deep inside yourself, the subtle presence of another 'myself' inhabiting you and with whom you live, at times in harmony, at others in conflict? Another self who sometimes criticizes you and at others encourages you? That is your Companion in Life.

There are times when he will appear to be an imposter or an intruder. Certainly, he often questions your habits and your moral or spiritual complacency. Accompanied by this companion, a shadow within, the route is less monotonous and the voyager multiplies his chances of arriving at his chosen destination. This, however, in itself matters little, for it is the journey and the manner in which it is conducted that are important. Indolence is the greatest danger: your Companion is capable of arousing you from a lassitude of spirit and, to that end, if necessary, robbing you of your certainties, trampling on your secret gardens and, finally, tearing away the great veil of illusion.

It sometimes happens that your Companion is of the same sign as your year of birth, a twin brother in a way — for example, a Goat/Goat. In this case, you must recognize that he will compel you to realize yourself fully and to live the double aspect — the Yin and the Yang — that your bear within yourself. In any case, you also bear within yourself

the twelve animals. So, set out on the long route, ready for the great adventure: the beautiful voyage during which you will encounter the harmoniously entangled, the solemn and the grotesque, the ephemeral reality, the dream and the imagined.

Table of hours corresponding to the twelve emblematic animals

If you were **born** between		your **companion** is	
11 pm and 1 am			Rat
1 am and 3 am			Ox
3 am and 5 am			Tiger
5 am and 7 am			Rabbit
7 am and 9 am			Dragon
9 am and 11 am			Snake
11 am and 1 pm			Horse
1 pm and 3 pm			Goat
3 pm and 5 pm			Monkey
5 pm and 7 pm			Rooster
7 pm and 9 pm			Dog
9 pm and 11 pm			Pig

These figures correspond to the *solar hour* of your birth. If necessary, you should check the summer times (Daylight Savings Time) and make the appropriate adjustment (sometimes two hours before or after statutory time).

THE GOAT AND ITS COMPANION IN LIFE

Goat/Rat

Here is an excellent companion for the Rat, very different from him, whose nature is gay and free from care. An intuitive and subtle artist, the Goat will be prodigiously therapeutic for our ill-loved and anxious rodent. Moreover, the Goat responds to charm and appreciates sympathetic magic, and will not be bored by these qualities in the Rat.

Both will have a tendency to float about in a world of illusions, but, since they will get something worthwhile out of it, it is no matter if they seem blind and deaf; for these two it can be a useful technique.

Goat/Ox

A little note of capriciousness on the part of our Ox. The light-hearted and carefree Goat will be an excellent Companion. With him, the Ox will remove his blinkers and his deep furrows will be adorned with wild flowers and bouquets of brambles. Retaining a degree of gravity, the Ox/Goat will be capable of unexpected capers. The route will therefore be fascinating, provided that the Ox/Goat knows how to maintain a healthy balance between the real and the fantastic.

Goat/Tiger

A dreamy and artistic Tiger; a wild beast among a mass of clouds, leaping astride the stars. That may make the Tiger/Goat smile, and he has need to. If he loses his Tiger side, which is sometimes too solemn, he will discover that the route can be beautiful — if he travels with his nose raised to the heavens. So, the Tiger should not devour the Goat within him; rather, he should let him caper about his head and his heart; his imagination will bring romance, which will reduce all difficulties to the level of a game.

Goat/Rabbit

He will be a sweet dreamer, living far from reality in a world of clouds. If he cannot find the comfort which is so dear to him, he will seek it in his dreams. He will love travel, always seeking something more marvellous. He has a supple nature and is intuitive and charming; nothing will seem to ruffle him, for he has the gift of assimilating the most trying situations into his creative universe. Both collar and leash will be rejected by the Goat/Rabbit for he is the type who is always on the loose, ever-ready for adventure.

 **Goat/Dragon**

Imagine a terrifying animal — one with multi-coloured scales who spits fire, but wears beautiful boots and is crowned with graceful horns. The Goat/Dragon appears thus, but also very much at ease with himself. The Goat brings reality and substance to the Dragon's wildest dreams, offering him fantasy, imagination and a sense of the marvellous on a platter of clouds. The often too serious Dragon will learn to relax and enjoy himself. The Goat/Dragon, an animal of all territories, will not be merely a complex and well-regulated machine, but will be able to take to the air, becoming a Dragon of subtle azure, soft breezes and capricious clouds.

 **Goat/Snake**

It will be rather dangerous to fall in love with him: it is impossible to expect fidelity from the Goat/Snake. This reptilian Goat is a fickle being charged with fantasy; an artist who will make a 'goat' of you if you try to seduce him. At first he will seem docile, seeking your protection: but he will then pull you joyously along by the tip of your nose. Exclusive and jealous, he is scarcely aware of the contradiction, for his own bad faith is disarming. In life he will enjoy plenty of good luck and have the advantage of good taste and a capacity for finesse; but his instability will cause him considerable damage, some of which he will not recover from, above all during his mature years.

Goat/Horse

Dream worlds and fantasy will flavour this alliance with a slightly capricious and charming bohemianism, favouring an escape towards enchanted domains of azure and clouds alive with fanciful and diaphanous creatures of the imagination. The Goat/Horse will need an epic existence; his ardour will be conquering, but he will prefer art and heroic poetry to war-like expeditions. His personal universe will open to other dimensions — towards subtle inward spaces that no system of logic can define or measure.

Goat/Goat

His sense of reality will be precarious, which does not bother him in the least. The Goat/Goat will love travel and will be ever ready to leap about and cavort. His tendency to be in a state of confusion will attract enemies who dislike his carefree attitude, lack of gravity and disregard for conventions. You can preach to him the errors of his ways as much as you like, but he will escape you with a graceful pirouette, his nose in the air. It is an understatement to say that the Goat/Goat enjoys the good life. Even if his route is strewn with traps, he will never be discouraged, and will take it all with good will, humour and in a free and easy manner.

Goat/Monkey

Intuitive and intelligent, he will be extremely restless. At times pride will curb his fantasies and his ideas will then gain in constancy and consistency, though there is no certainty that he really wants to pursue them to their logical end. The Monkey likes to leap from branch to branch, and the Goat leaps ceaselessly from cloud to cloud. Thus, their alliance will be particularly lively and eventful. As for love, the Monkey/Goat can be a real heartbreaker!

Goat/Rooster

Generous and outgoing, this animal will be honest and pure, but, alas, his character will often prove unreliable and difficult to pin down. The Goat/Rooster will tend to kick out and back away, for he will not accept ties, advice or any form of dependency. His needs for liberty is expressed to a marked degree. He also needs to be reassured and coddled, but dislikes revealing his weaknesses and takes care not to expose himself.

His principal motivation seems to be to set himself apart from other animals, for his pride will always win out. He wants to be original and fanciful at any price. If you are unlucky enough to come up against these qualities, he will become aggressive and capricious, even a bit cruel. However, he does not hold grudges and the next day you will see him trotting along, eyes shining and flowers for you in hand.

Goat/Dog

He will be gifted with remarkable intuition. Unfortunately he tends to complicate his life, forever changing his moods, ideas and decisions, constantly retracing his steps and becoming distrustful and pessimistic. However, he will be both faithful and courageous. Even though his nature causes him to constantly put himself in danger, he will never capitulate; he will always see things through to the end. Basically, he needs recognition and devotion; he cannot endure solitude or a lack of affection.

Goat/Pig

He will not be easy to tame. Of a suspicious nature, the Goat/Pig will seek solitude in thickets and among hidden, rocky paths. In character he is stubborn, obstinate and sometimes even narrow-minded. He is often credulous, but clear-sighted, which is why he prefers to work alone, far from danger and unpleasant encounters. Also, being proud, the Goat/Pig is slow to recognize his errors, but that does not prevent him from being tolerant and always ready to forgive. It is sometimes said that he is a bit of a sorcerer; if you meet up with him, do not forget that at bottom he is tender-hearted and vulnerable.

THE GOAT AND THE FIVE ELEMENTS

五行

YOUR ELEMENT

In Chinese astrology, each year is joined to an Element. There are five Elements: *Water, Fire, Wood, Metal, Earth.*

Each of the twelve emblematic animals is linked successively to each of the five Elements. For example, in the year 1900 the Rat was Metal, in 1912 he was Water, in 1924 he was Wood, in 1936, Fire and in 1948 he was Earth. Therefore, for the twelve years from 1900 he was linked to Metal, for the next twelve years to Water, and, for every succeeding period of twelve years, to each of the other Elements, in succession.

In order to determine the Element corresponding to the year of your birth, use the table below:

> *Years whose digits end in:* 2 and 3 — Water
> 6 and 7 — Fire
> 4 and 5 — Wood
> 0 and 1 — Metal
> 8 and 9 — Earth

The same union of *Animal-Element* repeats every sixty years, for example, Rat-Metal appeared in 1720, 1780, 1840, 1900, 1960 and so on.

The five Elements are the primary forces affecting the universe. It is their particular association with each of the signs which provides the basis for every horoscope. Movement and fluctuation, Yin and Yang, these symbolic forces are in a perpetual state of action and interaction.

Wood gives birth to Fire, which gives birth to Earth, which gives birth to Metal, which gives birth to Water, which in turn gives birth to Wood.

GOAT/WATER
(you were born in 1943)

The cold born of the northern sky descended to Earth and gave birth to Water. The Chinese consider Water more a synonym for coldness and ice than a symbol of fertility.

Characteristics of the Goat/Water
Water of winter nights, rigour and severity; calm and deep Water to be feared and respected; still Water sheltering underwater demons asleep in its depths; fetid and muddy Water of the marshes, a refuge of crawling creatures.

The Goat will be in his real Element, that which splits the clouds apart, fertilizes vegetation and helps in the growth of grain. The Goat is invigorated by contact with this Element, which itself becomes spring-water, rain and running brooks. The Goat/Water cavorts among the clouds and leaps about the fields, jumping streams to follow their winding courses. The Water Element can only be a symbol of fertility and a token of good health for Goats throughout their lives.

Health of the Goat/Water
The Water organ is the kidney; its flavour is salty. Remain active and thus conserve your youth and your strength. Drink water in quantity to hydrate your body.

The Goat/Water and others
The nature of the Goat/Water will be temperate and reflective and capable of listening to others. By keeping a watch on himself he will avoid excess and accept eventual trials calmly and serenely. In this way the Goat will be master of himself and able to gain a leading position, which he will turn into a game and a personal experience. He will also be at ease in a crowd, which will respond to him, since he will appeal to it not with violence but with restraint, perspective and humour.

The Goat/Water will be peace-loving. Resolutely humanitarian, he can devote himself to social problems and to the cause of justice. But his preference will always be for the arts, which will be a means of communication and a language more than for purely aesthetic reasons.

Advice for the Goat/Water
Your nature is lively and active. Have confidence in yourself, even during difficult periods. The Goat/Water is the very symbol of success.

A Goat/Water year
The culminating point for a Goat/Water year will be winter, a period of gestation. The Yin of Water will balance the Yang of the Goat.

You will be at the height of your physical form, and this year will bring you the success you will have earned by your perseverance and dynamism. Turn aside from sleeping waters, they are bad for the Goat; even if they attract you — avoid them.

Historical example of a Goat/Water year
1223

The barbarians of the twentieth century, Hitler and Stalin, were not unlike their predecessor, Genghis Khan. All three of them were slaves to cultures they overthrew but whose fruits they wished to garner without in the least understanding them. Like all provincially minded conquerors, they assumed they deserved the best and indiscriminately ransacked their conquered territories to secure it. The Soviet cry of 'Kulturny' is no more than a blown echo from the Great Khan of 1223 who transported half a million craftsmen from Persia to the depths of his original kingdom, there to exercise their fastidious tastes among a horde of indifferent subjects. Offered delights, the Mongols fed from troughs.

In 1223 the Great Khan confronted the Russians, a people who had long known where they were and expected to remain there. Loosed among them, the Mongol cavalry wrought devastation. Insensible to those whose lands they traversed, they senselessly and pitilessly exterminated them. This 'scorched earth' policy succeeded for a generation or two but the procreative powers of the Mongols could not sustain the task of inhabiting and populating the Russian Steppes. Nor could their horses survive. The vast Russian empyrean exposed the folly inherent in Genghis Khan's declared purpose of forging a world empire. What remained was sorrow, an enduring bitterness and faction among the conquerors. The more solid ambitions of the Great Khan were never to be realized and the physical and political effects of the prodigious energies expended in 1223 were to vanish without trace. To those mirrors whereby the Mongols sought to reflect, in their violent advent, the traces of an acceptable rule the Russians disposed a total indifference.

GOAT/WOOD
(you were born in 1955)

To the East, the wind blew in the sky and from its warm caress of the Earth Wood was born.

Characteristics of the Goat/Wood
Wood is of the morning and springtime. Its temperate nature loves harmony, beauty and elegance. Springtime is a symbol of gentleness, a period in which all of nature awakens and opens itself to the forces of youth, creation and growth. This Element will be fruitful for the Goat, bringing him equilibrium and the power of creation, a taste for beauty and harmony. What could be more ideal for an artistic, discriminating and sensitive Goat, the mother of nature? You will descend from the clouds, your walk nonchalant and your eyes bright. Your curiosity will be satisfied, for you will go tirelessly from discovery to discovery. Your life will be lived in gentleness, full of charm and good humour and imbued with art and harmony. However, be careful: Wood is an ambivalent Element subject to anger, passion and

excess. This influence could impel you to outbursts and intemperate and disconcerting violence.

Health of the Goat/Wood
The organ of Wood is the liver; its flavour is acid. The Goat/Wood will be anxious, worry a lot and suffer from fits of bad temper. Some days will seem as harmonious as paradise itself, others sombre and tortured. In these sad periods the Goat/Wood will tend to compensate by over-eating — pay attention to your weight.

The Goat/Wood and others
The Goat/Wood is aware of his perpetual distress when socializing and will opt for a relaxed style to mask his anxiety. It will seem as though nothing can touch him, but at the least alarm he will tend to take refuge in his ivory tower, returning with one bound to his universe of fantasy and clouds. This will be his basic defensive technique when faced with doubt, failure and depression. When rigid structures are imposed upon him, the Goat/Wood will escape with a pirouette, and will intelligently improvise, his fertile imagination being of precious assistance to him. Inventive and creative, the arts and nature will be his principal interests. There, the full measure of his subtleties and his sensitivity will flower, thus joining the useful with the agreeable.

Advice for a Goat/Wood
You have been born under a good star and are the symbol of luck and success. You are a subtle, sensitive artist, endowed with an excellent physique. The future is yours; do not trample on it in childish rage.

A Goat/Wood year
The culminating point for a Goat/Wood year will be spring, a period of growth and prosperity. The Yang tendency of the Goat will be added to the Yang of springtime.

You are going to have a harmonious year, evolving with

good humour and curiosity by way of the arts and nature. So take care; control your vulnerability and ensure that it does not break this vernal gentleness.

Historical example of a Goat/Wood year 1715

Louis XIV of France, the Sun King, ruler of France for 72 years, died on the morning of 1 September. In the same month, the Earl of Mar rallied the clans in Scotland in a futile attempt to revive the Stuart cause in England, now supported by the dissaffected Tory minister, Bolingbroke, who had secretly fled to France as Queen Anne lay dying. Although each country was to develop culturally in a manner so distinct that one wonders how any single taste could have been acceptable to both, 1715 marked a sea change in the history of each.

The peace of 1713 was to last until 1739. During this period both France and Great Britain intensified their maritime policies, seeking to invigorate their trade and wealth in the West Indies, the North American continent and India. The English merchant classes condemned the peace, feeling that they were the dupes of the French who now remorselessly undermined the commercial advantages England had gained by the war. For there was a significant change of policy in France. The Regent, Phillipe d'Orleans, understood the folly inherent in the Continental wars of the previous reign, an appreciation which Louis himself had shared as he lay dying.

Equally, 1715 marked the end of English commitment to war in Europe. England was to learn that so long as she pursued an expansionist trading policy she could protect her interests in Europe more effectively with money than with troops. Indeed, after 1715, the English genius lay in technological invention and its commercial exploitation. The abortive rebellion in Scotland was significant in that it enhanced the status of the new house of Hanover which was not to be threatened again by the Stuart cause for thirty years. Thus the English wars of the eighteenth century were essentially trade wars against rival French interests, and the English successes encouraged the French in their great cultural adventures at home.

GOAT/FIRE
(you were born in 1907 or 1967)

Heat was born in the southern sky, descended to Earth and fertilized it. From their union, Fire was born.

Characteristics of the Goat/Fire
The Fire element is of the midday, of the South, of summer. Fire is Yang; it is the Element which animates, quickens and transforms. The Fire inside a Goat will bring an increase in energy. It will be a force of inspiration, a catalyst for expressiveness; a source of inventive ardour and original images for this artistic and creative sign. However, the Goat should scrupulously attend to his Fire: should it become smothered and go out, the Goat will be reduced to a state of anxiety followed by repression and self-criticism, leading to a permanent and, finally, sterilizing self-doubt.

Health of the Goat/Fire
The organ of Fire is the heart; its flavour is bitter. Fire of summer, Yang plus Yang, the Goat should guard against aggressiveness, violence and anger. He should not waste his energy or spread himself too thin, for his energies would then turn into smoke.

The Goat/Fire and others
Symbol of war, passion and violence, Fire is also lucid and clairvoyant. The Goat will need all his natural tact to restrain the latent aggressiveness of this Element. He could become a brilliant lawyer, sharp and anti-conformist, or a particularly dynamic fire-brand. If you are a Goat/Fire, be careful of your

604

incorrigible tendency to dissipate your energy by amusing your entourage and uselessly exhausting your talents. Slow down your rhythm and learn to relax.

Advice for a Goat/Fire

You have a strong personality; while there is no need to repress it, be careful not to make too much of it or you will become burdensome and overwhelming. Fire's heat is necessary, but not so much so that it smothers.

A Goat/Fire year

The culminating point for a Goat/Fire year will be summer, a period of creation.

An active year in which you can give free rein to your imagination, which will express itself in a concrete form and bring you much satisfaction. However, use your talents economically; do not dissipate your energies or they will go up in smoke.

Historical example of a Goat/Fire year
1187

The Christian kingdom of Acre was in peril before the assaults of Saladin. King Guy sought the aid of the Hospitallers and the Templars who summoned all their available knights; the Templars gave further aid. Henry II of England, in expiation of the murder of Thomas à Becket before the altar of Canterbury cathedral, had remitted funds to them. The Templars agreed that the emergency justified their appropriating them to the defence of Acre rather than banking them against the day of Henry's arrival on his own promised crusade. The Templars were scrupulous. Every soldier so equipped carried a banner emblazoned with Henry's arms.

Guy encamped his army at Sephoria in a position immune to serious attack and he refused to compromise his main chances by going to the aid of his wife who was under attack in Tiberias. But the Grand Master of the

Templars beguiled him into thinking that it was shameful not to attack the besiegers of a city only six leagues away. Guy's weakness was to listen and to act on the last words of advice he heard. Persuaded, he encamped his army above the Horns of Hattin. His soldiers were weary after a waterless march. The prayers and songs of the Moslems greeted them from the watered valley below. Shortly before dawn Saladin fired the scrub on the hillside and Guy found his army encircled. Faced by the prospect of annihilation, the Franks fought desperately but eventually were forced to surrender. Saladin, as always gracious and magnanimous in victory, treated Guy honourably: 'A king does not kill a king', he told him. But the crimes, treachery and greed of Reynald de Castellon he could not forgive and he beheaded him with a stroke of his sword.

The great merchant city of Acre was surrendered on 10 July and by 20 October Jerusalem itself was forfeit. Saladin granted generous terms but he took care to contrast his clemency with the actions of the Christian conquerors of the first Crusade.

GOAT/EARTH
(you were born in 1919 or 1979)

Earth was born from the slowly falling Elements of the sky at its humid zenith.

Characteristics

This is an afternoon Earth, the humid and hot Earth of summer. It is the symbol of the well-cushioned, soft nest, of comfort and abundance; an Earth of slow and profound transformations.

Element of all things deeply rooted and of germination, Earth is a marvellous refuge for the Goat, giving shelter to his reveries and meditations. However, he must remain close to the surface of nature — its winding roads, steep-banked streams and small grottoes — which will be favourable to his repose and his unpredictable mental habits. A deep cavern would be an alien and slightly uncomfortable universe for the extroverted and celestial Goat. For him, the Earth must be a passage, a springboard — the pirouette preceding action. He should make use of the Earth, but be careful not to shut himself up in it or he will lose his vitality and his unselfconscious zest, the essential traits which make up his charm and which are necessary for his equilibrium.

The health of the Goat/Earth
The Earth's organ is the spleen; its flavour is sweet. The Goat/Earth should make sure to remain active, otherwise he will become morose and gain weight, which would considerably impede his excursions into the world of dreams and fantasy. Meditation would then rapidly become lax and self-destructive. Live outdoors: you have nothing in common with the underground crawling creatures; above all, you are light and airy and belong to the heavens.

The Goat/Earth and others
The Goat/Earth will be more realistic than the other Goats, which will cause him to be both more prudent and more mistrustful. Unlike the others, he will prefer to make money, accumulate it and speculate with it. He will possess some talent for work and a professional conscience, but will rarely have any breadth of vision, for his carefree and whimsical character will always get the upper hand. However, in an artistic profession — above all the stage — he will bring seriousness to everything he undertakes, and still amass some savings for rainy days. His dreams, tinged with a certain gravity and slightly romantic melancholy, can push him towards philosophy, religion or the occult sciences. While this will soothe his anxieties and provide a secure channel for his secret fears, his need for friendship and universal love will become inflamed by his passion for ritual and daily devotion.

Advice for a Goat/Earth
The studious and far-sighted character of your earthly nature

will never put an end to your tricks and impulsive pranks. So do not keep your head lowered, staring down at the toes of your boots: raise your eyes and contemplate the stars.

A Goat/Earth year

The culminating point for a Goat/Earth year is summer, when the Earth is hot and humid. You can turn towards what attracts you — the arts in general — for this year you will be free of material constraints and so, simply free. Know how to make the most of this year; avoid idleness and inertia, which would not be good for you. You need the broad daylight, the fresh open air and space.

Historical example of a Goat/Earth year
49BC

Two men dominated Rome, Caesar and Pompey. Pompey represented the aristocratic element in Roman society; Caesar was the idol of the people and of the legions who had fought with him. All the elements of civil war were present.

Caesar wished to avoid a confrontation but the constitution was worked against him by a small faction in the Senate, spurred by Cato and helped by the power and prestige conferred by Pompey's armies, illicitly on Italian soil under the guise of recruitment. The pro-consul refused to yield. The precise legal points at issue in Caesar's claim to stand for the consulate in absence and also retain his province until the end of the year remain unclear, but the flavour of the political crisis can be identified. Caesar was not the first to have thwarted or suspended the constitution in the past and he now asserted both legal and moral rights to preferential treatment. His enemies thrust upon him the choice between civil war and political extinction; for Caesar, the latter involved the loss of his personal honour.

Pompey's promoters, well briefed by Cato, secured the vote which declared Caesar a public enemy unless he lay down his command by a given date, but they wholly misjudged the extent to which popular feeling was on Caesar's side. They expected that the respectable and solid classes in Italy would rally to their side. They did not. Nor did any armed legion rise to Pompey's call. Even Picenum, his own barony, went over to Caesar. With only one legion to hand, Caesar swept down the east coast of Italy, gathering troops, momentum and confidence as he went. Within two months he was master of Italy.

The crowning victory at Pharsalus was secured by luck, the devotion of his veteran legionaries and the divided counsels of his adversaries.

Based on Ronald Syme, *The Roman Revolution*, Oxford, 1963.

GOAT/METAL
(you were born in 1931)

In the sky, coming from the West, drought grazed the skin of the Earth and gave birth to Metal. Winds come from the far away steppes seeking the vital sap.

Characteristics of the Goat/Metal

Metal is of the night, of autumn and of cold. It symbolizes clarity, purity and precision. Its tendency is to be cutting, rigid and chaste, its comments harsh. The Goat/Metal will oscillate between beauty and destruction. In other respects, he will be expert at putting his plans into effect. At harvest time, he is the blade that gleans. Alas, too rigorous a regime will engender sadness and moroseness.

For an intuitive and artistic Goat, Metal's contribution will be to restrain him in his race to the stars, wrapping him in an armour tightly closed against vibrations, perfumes and music — the very things on which the equilibrium of this animal often depends. If he is not careful, the Goat/Metal risks having his heart and soul dry up if, by using a code of ethics, a religion or a philosophy as a pretext, he imposes upon himself a way of life which does not correspond to his nature. He should therefore remain vigilant and not enclose himself in dogmas or in a constraining philosophy which is sometimes illusory.

However, the Goat's finesse cannot be completely destroyed by this Element. If he can learn to exploit its virtues, to forge a strong sense of reality, a sharpness of judgement and reason without smothering his creative talents, he will become formidable.

Health of the Goat/Metal

Metal's organ is the lung; its flavour is pungent. In order to maintain his equilibrium, the Goat/Metal should get a great deal of air and not remain closed up indoors, morally or physically. Rediscover the delights of mountains!

The Goat/Metal and others

The Goat/Metal is more energetic and resolute than the other Goats, with a tendency to judge and penalize. He will also be more equitable, rigorous and a perfectionist. His curious mixture of fantasy and exactitude, of tolerance and stubbornness may seem disconcerting: he will be light and easy in some situations, uncompromising in others. This ambiguity sometimes poses problems for him and makes him suffer. Always deeply obstinate, he has difficulty in recognizing his faults. Do not try to contradict him too much, even if it is for his own good. Even if a thunderbolt were to fall on his head, he would still find a way to buck. Luckily, the Goat/Metal is staunchly resistant at all levels.

Advice for a Goat/Metal

The joints of your armour should always be flexible and perfectly lubricated. It is vital for you to remain supple and vivacious. In this way you will have everything to gain from Metal: as heavy as lead in the head and with fingers of gold.

A Goat/Metal year

The culminating point in a Goat/Metal year will be autumn. The Yin tendency of the mid-season will balance the Yang of the Goat, bringing tolerance and moderation.

Profit from this year to find again your suppleness and freedom. Leave your armour and your shield in the closet. A certain rigour will be all to the good if you can then accomplish a delicate piece of work. Use it, but keep a light touch and an open mind; this will be a gust of fresh air which it will be up to you to prolong.

Historical example of a Goat/Metal year
1871

The English historian, R.C.K. Ensor writes of the French predicament in 1871: 'Later still persisted the 131 days siege of Paris itself, the very heart of the world's luxury, with its long agony of torn hopes and tarnished heroisms, vain sorties and remorseless hunger; an object lesson for London at its doors. And last of all, after the surrender to the Germans, the appalling episodes of the Paris Commune of 1871 revealed for the first time in modern history — what Thucydides had known, and what in 1917-19 we saw on a much vaster scale — that when shock and defeat have battered an organised society beyond a certain point not only its external but its internal walls collapse, and the worst atrocities of war may be eclipsed by those of revolution.' He continues, 'time was yet to show ... how much the liberal spirit, which for so long had been radicated through Europe from England and France, was to be checked and dampened through the catastrophic defeat of what was then the larger of those two nations.'*

These measured yet elegiac sentences were published just as Hitler assumed absolute power in Germany. Undoubtedly they were written when Hitler was no more than a doubtful portent yet one finds in them a prescient voice, a determined if ineffective call for civilization by one immersed in its values and peculiarities. Yet Ensor was wrong. The horrors of the Commune saved France, if only for three decades. After 1871 the French offered to the world an artistic liveliness and genius unmatched since the days of the Italian Rennaissance. It was as if a third dimension had blossomed, freed at last from the constraints of the great Capetians and the squalid languors of empire.

* England, 1870-1914, Oxford, 1936.

Analogical Table
of the Different Elements

Elements	Wood	Fire	Earth	Metal	Water
Years ending in	4 and 5	6 and 7	8 and 9	0 and 1	2 and 3
Colours	Green	Red	Yellow	White	Blue
Seasons	Spring	Summer	End of summer	Autumn	Winter
Climates	Wind	Heat	Humid	Dry	Cold
Flavours	Acid	Bitter	Sweet	Pungent	Salty
Principal organ	Liver	Heart	Spleen	Lungs	Kidneys
Secondary organ	Gallbladder	Small intestine	Stomach	Large intestine	Bladder
Food	Wheat, poultry	Rice, lamb	Corn, beef	Oats, horse	Peas, pork

Table of Harmony
Between the Elements

		Wood Female	Fire Female	Earth Female	Metal Female	Water Female
○○○ Excellent prosperity	Male Wood	● ●	○	○ ○ ○	○	○ ○
○○ Good harmony, understanding	Male Fire	○	○	○ ○	●	● ●
○ Effort needed	Male Earth	● ●	○ ○	○ ○	○ ○ ○	●
● Rivalries and problems of reciprocal domination	Male Metal	○	● ●	●	● ●	○ ○ ○
●● Misunderstanding and incomprehension	Male Water	○ ○	● ●	●	○ ○ ○	○

THE FOUR SEASONS OF THE GOAT

四季

If you were born in spring
Goat/Aries

Those born under the sign of Aries are independent and impulsive beings who like to 'shock' those around them, if only to amuse themselves. Goats are dependent but eccentric. The person marked by these two signs thus risks being provocative, aggressive and unstable, according to his various enthusiasms. He needs some guidance, but this should not be oppressive. A spacious park surrounded by walls hidden by trees where he can frisk about will suit him perfectly, for total security with an impression of liberty is his ideal. Otherwise, a Goat/Aries left too much on his own is all too likely to commit many little blunders: making light of the business of others, stamping joyously on their susceptibilities and, by his lack of perseverance and of any sense of responsibility, forfeiting their good will.

The Goat/Aries is sociable and optimistic (some think he is devoid of any conscience) and needs to evolve within a relaxed circle of people who do not ask boring questions and with whom he can allow free rein to his fantasy, which he needs. In such conditions, he is charming. His gifts are artistic but they need active expression, for example on radio or television where he can become an excellent interviewer. His talent is to comment on those who take risks, to praise them; it suits him better than running them himself.

Goat/Taurus

This alliance of the most stable of the earth signs and of the 'cloud' is positive, for it contributes a great deal to bringing the wandering hooves of the Goat back to earth. On the other hand, Taurus is ruminating and slow, and these qualities will not help the Goat to be strong and decisive. The Goat/Taurus is calm and intuitive. Artistically, he needs to touch in order to appreciate. He works at leisure, without regard for time limits, which he considers absurd. If you irritate him by saying that you need him to finish a piece of furniture before the 15th, he will leave you standing there with a doorless wardrobe on your hands.

This rather dreamy individual detests sudden changes or any atmosphere of violence and conflict. He would be happiest living a bucolic life with everything to hand. Otherwise he may tire of the game and pick on the most accessible attraction. The Goat/Taurus is affectionate, slightly timid, but amusing in a small group.

He is adaptable, but needs some plan of action to be prepared for him in advance.

Goat/Gemini

The influence of Gemini amplifies certain defects in the Goat — such as instability, irresponsibility and capriciousness — but it does develop his mental capacities. The Goat/Gemini is a veritable masterpiece of fantasy and humour. There is no doubt about his gifts as an entertainer and story-teller. When he feels secure and confident, he can become as talkative as a magpie, never pausing between anecdotes yet giving them a continuity. Verbally, nothing is impossible for him, although his reasoning is sometimes far-fetched.

The Goat/Gemini has a remarkable gift for imitation. At ease in all roles, adoring changing costumes, he can be excellent as a clown. A bureaucrat, no. If he cannot become a pop singer he might make a good businessman — if he has some material or emotional connection with an accountant who will take on his administrative and financial problems, for these are not his strong point. He is no pleader of causes because he listens too much to others and, simply because he is 'available' and not very sure of himself, is influenced by the last person to speak.

If you were born in summer
Goat/Cancer

In this couple, Cancer sees many of his deepest traits magnified, including a predilection for ambivalences. A Cancer born during a year of the Goat is especially torn between a need for security and an attraction to fantasy. It is only with great difficulty that he succeeds in reconciling the two, for he is tormented if he lacks either. Often dissatisfied or romantically melancholic, he surprises others by his behaviour, which oscillates between an instability which can shock and a tenacity which can astonish. The choice is dictated more by his mood of the moment than by circumstances.

Cancer is dependent on his affections; the Goat is simply dependent. Unless there is a loving and patient person capable of making him feel secure and capable of jostling him around from time to time, this alliance will not do well. But once the Goat/Cancer is engaged on a path which pleases him, things will go well. The tragedy of the Goat/Cancer lies in his difficulty in getting off the ground and getting started. Five minutes after departure, he is capable of sitting down on the ground and dreaming of his arrival. He must be spurred on incessantly. This is not easy to understand, for he really believes that he is ever so tired — and this can be very touching.

Goat/Leo

Be careful, this Goat is endowed with special powers: he has golden horns. With the dynamism of Leo to support him, he can become brilliant, satisfied by a success obtained thanks to a subtle mixture of naive audacity, opportunism and an ability to show only his best side. Everything he does looks easy; but it is often the result of strenuous work. The person marked by these two signs intends to succeed. He is much less dependent than the other Goats, but retains their capacity to exploit what is offered to him and make full use of generous patrons. Here, interest and emotion are so dissociated as to obtain the maximum efficacy.

The Goat born under the sign of Leo is really the most qualified to get along alone, with just a few stepping-stones to help. But his sometimes unhealthy susceptibility (due, at bottom, to a lack of self-confidence) often leads him to react with wounded pride and consequently to brag. For he is more vulnerable than he seems. He really needs the support of a family; without it, and by running after success, he will become worn out and lonely.

Goat/Virgo

The influence of the sign of Virgo considerably alleviates the unstable and slightly eccentric side of the Goat. On the other hand, it accentuates his tendencies of uncertainty and hesitation. The Goat/Virgo is often an anxious person. Nervous when he should make a rapid decision, his confidence in his capacities is rather limited. From being capricious, he becomes timid and, instead of frisking around, tends to advance with measured steps, fearing he might slip on a banana peel or fall into a trap laid for those who are impulsive.

The Goat/Virgo is skilful and can do anything with his hands, so long as it is work which pleases him and offers some measure of aesthetic value. For a Goat he is extremely conscientious and careful; in fact, considerable talent will emerge from this mixture.

It is in the world of the emotions that the Goat/Virgo will experience the greatest difficulties. Being naive and romantic, he easily becomes unjustifiably distrustful if the smallest grain of sand intrudes into the personal relationships he has established. Difficult to seduce, he would do well to avoid, so far as he can, all ruptures and clashes.

If you were born in autumn
Goat/Libra

Above all the problem of the Goat/Libra is to find his equilibrium. His extreme sensitivity to his surroundings and his need for 'harmony at any price' sometimes makes his social life uneasy, even though he is otherwise agreeable and civilized, possessing that little grain of fantasy necessary to elicit the comment: 'What a charming, polite person — and not at all boring either.'

The Goat/Libra rarely finds his right domain at the first attempt, for his choice depends on an infinite number of details which he must dwell on and, in so doing, loses a lot of sleep. On the other hand, once in his domain he will stay there and concentrate on making it increasingly agreeable and welcoming. He lacks any gift for competitiveness and is somewhat indecisive. Sustained pressure is beyond him, although his ability to adapt and his diplomacy bring him occasional success. Very much the aesthete, the Goat/Libra is also hyper-affectionate and is very dependent on those he loves. He is incapable of living alone.

Goat/Scorpio

Persons born during a year of the Goat are peace-loving and unaggressive. The influence of Scorpio will not inject them with venom. But in this alliance they become devilishly susceptible and defensive. As capricious as the other Goats but less dependent, they sport a light and playful style. This cannot be relied on since, generally, they know very well what they do not want, as opposed to what they do want. If you try to influence or protect them you may well receive a solid butt from their horns. Goat/Scorpios are gifted and their intuition is remarkable. They adore long conversations, personal confidences and are very passionate in their intimate moments. They can also be extremely vindictive. Always anxious, even tormented, they need a stable life if they are not to lose themselves in a jungle of complications.

Goat/Sagittarius

This idealistic Goat is attracted to far-away horizons and is a natural vagabond. If some new landscape is not offered every day he will compensate by filling his home with exotic or slightly baroque objects — but also with some comfortable divans.

The Goat/Sagittarius is less creative than the other Goats, but he is more decisive and, above all, more adventurous. He even risks under-estimating the dangers he runs. Independent in his behaviour, easy and free in his manner and possessing an innate elegance, he remains totally devoid of sophistication. However, he is dependent on a few moral precepts which serve as a basis for his actions.

When young he is a potential rebel, somewhat irresponsible and impulsive; his work will often lack preparation. When older, he will tend to calm down and conform. Not always, however, for certain Goat/Sagittariuses continue their curious wanderings until they draw their last breath. Foot-loose and optimistic, this Goat should never be constrained. If he is herded into a pasture, even though it is green and rich, he will leap over the barriers. Do not shut him up — please!

If you were born in winter
Goat/Capricorn

More serious and reflective than most, this Goat will love art like other Goats, but his creations will be marked with a label of authenticity. The Goat/Capricorn will never dwell on a subject that he does not know. His growth periods will be long and his births often fastidious. On the other hand, relatively sure of his talent (and 'relatively' should be stressed for he will never be totally sure of it), the Goat/Capricorn's inventiveness will prove inexhaustible.

He is discreet, has a sense of humour and relaxes easily in any intimate circle; but in public he can appear proud and even hostile. Simply, he is timid. To become and remain his friend you must accept that he detests a worldly life; remember never to ask him to do a piece of work rapidly or to improvise; and be resigned to his apparent lack of feelings, since he rarely reveals them. On the other hand, you can be sure that he would not accept you in his circle if he did not like you. It is a good idea from time to time to ask him several searching and possibly indiscreet questions; they will shake him up a little, and for the better. Having tried to avoid any direct answer, he will come out with the truth; basically, he is honest. He is also rather impressionable. A Goat to be gentle with.

Goat/Aquarius

There is nothing here to restrain the Goat's tendencies to eccentricity and off-handedness; his altruism or his detachment, even his disdain of material responsibilities. Also, the Goat/Aquarius's need for comfort is limited: he can live as easily with sandwiches, guitar in hand, sleeping on public benches as in a palace eating caviar. His behaviour will not change one iota: he will sit in his grand house casting longing eyes beyond the open windows where freedom beckons. It is important to understand that the Goat/Aquarius is not self-seeking; you cannot bribe him with the promise of two square meals a day. He may accept the situation for a while, but only for the new experience it offers. Then he will leave, without remorse or regrets.

The Goat/Aquarius can attain the best or achieve the worst: at times he will reach the summits, at others he will flounder in total unreality. If you wish to live with him, follow him. Take with you some simple provisions and an umbrella to protect him when it rains, otherwise he will catch a pulmonary infection. Be his guardian, patron, father, mother and best friend: he will never leave you, even though you cannot be sure that he will always be aware of your presence. Do not forget that the 'cloud' which symbolizes the Goat, blended with the air of Aquarius, does not produce a solid mixture.

Goat/Pisces

Sentimental and devoted, the Goat/Pisces feels the need to be useful to those around him; also, and more than the other Goats, the need to be protected. He has a pleasant character, is slightly dreamy and imaginative. His resources for escaping from annoying realities are infinite. An artist to the tip of his hooves, he creates as he breathes, scarcely thinking of the market value of his works. Backed by someone who is resourceful and practical, he will produce wonders.

The Goat/Pisces is not abrasive and he dislikes hurting people. His parents should be careful of the influence they have on his choice of profession. In fact he is capable of vegetating for years in an office without daring to protest or seeing the point of doing so, since he will be uncertain of being able to do anything else, even though he is deeply dissatisfied.

His subconscious is a vast, cosmic chaos and genius boils within the same pot as maladjustment and madness. His conscious mind is hardly more orderly. How to make a coherent choice between so many possibilities? How to know what one wants or does not want, what one loves and what one detests, when all one's feelings are in perpetual movement? Help him with your affection, but do not seek to rein him in too much. Beware: it is often in losing himself that he finds himself. Nothing is simple.

THE
I CHING

易经

THE I CHING AND THE GOAT

In the I Ching game, you ask a question and you obtain an answer. It is therefore a divining game. But the question you ask is posed through your Goat identity; the wheels, the complex mechanism of your mind and spirit, begin to turn. You ask a Goat question and the I Ching answers with a Goat 'solution', on which you then meditate as a Goat before arriving at a Goat conclusion.

The player is presented with a hexagram which contains the 'hypothesis-response' to his question, or, more exactly, a synthesis of forces affecting the concern or event inquired about.

For you, Master Goat, here are the sixty-four hexagrams of the I Ching and sixty-four Goat hypotheses.

How to proceed
1. The question
Ask a question regarding any problem at all, past, present or future, personally concerning you. (If the question concerns a friend, consult the I Ching game in the book corresponding to his Chinese sign.)

2. Method of play
It must be done with concentration.
Take **three ordinary and similar coins** — for example, three 50p coins.
Heads will equal the number 3.
Tails will equal the number 2.
Throw the coins.
If the result is two coins showing Heads and one Tails, write 3 + 3 + 2. You thus obtain a total of 8 which you represent by a continuous line: ▬▬▬ .
Draw the same continuous line if you have three coins showing Heads (3 + 3 + 3 = 9).

If you throw two coins showing Tails and one Heads (2 + 2 + 3 = 7), or all three showing Tails (2 + 2 + 2 = 6), draw two separate lines: ▬ ▬

To sum up, 8 and 9 correspond to: ▬▬▬ (Yin)

6 and 7 correspond to: ▬ ▬ (Yang)

Repeat this operation *six times,* noting at the time of each throw the figure obtained on a piece of paper, proceeding from the first to the sixth figure, from bottom to top.

The final result, including a trigram from the bottom, or

lower trigram (example: ☵), and a trigram of the top,

or upper trigram (example: ☵), will be a hexagram of the I Ching. In our example this would look like:

Now merely look for the hexagram number in the table on page 626, and then consult the list of hexagrams with their descriptions to find the given answer. *In our example,* the hexagram obtained is number 63, entitled **After completion.**

Table of Hexagrams

Trigrams	Upper lines ☰	☷	☶
Lower lines			
☰	1	11	34
☷	12	2	16
☶	25	24	51
☵	6	7	40
☶	33	15	62
☴	44	46	32
☲	13	36	55
☱	10	19	54

Use this table to find the number of your hexagrams. The meeting point between the lower and upper trigrams indicates the number of the hexagram that you are seeking.

☷	☶	☵	☲	☳
5	26	9	14	43
8	23	20	35	45
3	27	42	21	17
29	4	59	64	47
39	52	53	56	31
48	18	57	50	28
63	22	37	30	49
60	41	61	38	58

THE HEXAGRAMS OF THE GOAT

CH'IEN

1 *The creative:* Energy, strength and will. The creative and artistic Goat should gauge time and form an alliance with it to carry out his work.

K'UN

2 *The receptive:* Symbol of Mother Earth, the intuitive Goat cannot fail to derive strength and inspiration from it.

CHUN

3 *The initial difficulty:* Do not be stubborn and insist on unravelling the skein of confusion; return to the source rather than dally with superficial causes.

MÊNG

4 *Youthful folly:* 'It is not I who seeks the young fool, but the young fool who seeks me.' Although a star bears your name, it is not because of it that you shine. The carefree Goat, denying the existence of danger, should prove more reasonable.

HSÜ

5 *Waiting:* Be careful of lashing out and butting with your horns: patience has to be self-taught and is its own reward.

SUNG

6 *Conflict:* Be a good sport and accept this arrangement; that is the wiser course and the more advantageous.

SHIH

7 *The army:* Although you are not of a submissive nature, you must make an effort to enlist among the ranks, at least momentarily.

PI

8 *Holding together (union):* A steep and solitary plateau is preferable as a place for your goat-pen if you wish to assure your defense.

SHIAO CH'U

9 *The taming power of the small:* It is sometimes the small cloud which spurts forth a great deal of rain.

LÜ

10 *Treading:* 'Tread on the tail of a Tiger, he does not bite man.' After having met up with the wolf, bravely face the Tiger. One piece of advice: it will be more prudent if you are tactful.

T'AI

11 *Peace:* To keep it, evade the issue; escape from it without offering explanations.

P'I

12 *Standstill:* Is often necessary for it favours reflection before any action is taken, and it avoids your butting with lowered head into a void.

T'UNG JÊN

13 *Fellowship with men:* The independent Goat should come down from his rocky promontories and meet with men. Cease to isolate yourself on top of the mountain, moaning about your solitude.

TA YU

14 *Possession in great measure:* Success is imminent, so do not waste it by being lax or capricious.

CH'IEN

15 *Modesty:* Seek equilibrium and the Golden Mean — but not necessarily on the edge of a precipice.

YÜ

16 *Enthusiasm:* Your good intentions will not suffice; go out to meet circumstances without bucking, or take a personal share in the work.

SUI

17 *Following:* After the enthusiasm, the gates to the garden and the orchard will be open to you; so enjoy a feast — but do not chew on the rose bushes.

KU

18 *Work on what has been spoiled:* There is danger of a landslide; change your course; do not allow mere bravado to make you careless.

LIN

19 *The approach:* It will be slow and progressive, but enriched with a multitude of different perspectives.

KUAN

20 *Contemplation:* Climb to the top of the tower: it is perfect there if you need a better view. But if you wish to execute a balancing exercise, aim lower — or have a net placed under you.

SHIH HO

21 *Biting through (or clearly defined penalties):* Bring out your horns and sharpen your hooves: the punishment is sometimes a painful test for he who inflicts it, but just and necessary when face to face with lying and its results.

PI

22 *Grace:* Even if the bottle attracts you, do not forget its contents — they alone matter.

PO

23 *Splitting apart:* The foundations are rotting; do not hesitate to raze the structure; you can take care of the decorating later — or elsewhere.

FU

24 *Return — the turning point:* Leave your hiding place, your hole; the storm has passed and the black clouds have dispersed.

WU WANG

25 *Innocence:* Is synonymous with intuition; the Goat can use it as a guide, but only if he remains honest and lucid. Do not remain obstinate in face of error.

TA CH'U

26 *The taming power of the great:* Power and strength; but in order to retain them you must know how to renew yourself. If you pull on the cord, it will end by breaking; better to learn how to untie it or to ease out the stake.

I

27 *The corners of the mouth:* Do not have eyes bigger than your stomach, and do not saturate your head with useless knowledge. To digest well, you must learn how to select and refine.

TA KUO

28 *Preponderance of the great:* Do not wait until you have collapsed from the weight of your burden; abandon part of it along the way; dead heroes serve no purpose.

K'AN

29 *The fathomless water:* If you walk along the side of a precipice, do not look over the edge.

LI

30 *The clinging, fire:* If you go in for mountain climbing, do not weep for your fear of heights — secure a rope.

HSIEN

31 *Influence:* Mutual attraction, the need to draw close together; you will cavort and trot about on your own another day.

HÊNG

32 *Duration:* Be lucid about yourself and shake yourself up a bit. To endure takes strength of character.

TUN

33 *Retreat:* Walking on tiptoe can be synonymous with wisdom and intelligence — unless there is someone who lies in wait for you at the bend in the road.

TA CHUANG

34 *The power of the great:* Do not allow yourself to become intoxicated by your talent for leaping across crevices; a fall could be fatal; slow down.

CHIN

35 *Progress:* Do not hesitate to get up on the stage or the podium and reveal your gifts to the public, but be careful to acknowledge a collaborator, even if he does remain in the background.

MING I

36 *Darkening of the light:* After storms and tempests comes the night; wait its passing, inside as well as out: patience and cleverness.

CHIA JÊN

37 *The family:* Despite your fickle nature, you still look to it for security and comfort. So for once, make an effort.

K'UEI

38 *Opposition:* Not everyone is a celestial Goat; be tolerant. Harmony is born of diversity; your intuition and your finesse will take care of the rest.

CHIEN

39 *Obstruction:* There are several ways to clear it; envisage all the possibilities and you will multiply your chances.

HSIEH

40 *Deliverance:* It is time for the Goat to leave his pen; winter is over, spring is here.

SUN

41 *Decrease:* The Goat likes beautiful things and luxury, but now, alas, he must be content with more modest surroundings while awaiting the return of good times.

I

42 *Increase:* Seize the occasion, for you are under a good star. Your blossoming will depend on your sense of opportunity.

KUAI

43 *Breakthrough:* The Goat will walk with his head high, his fur white and pure, denouncing errors or faults; be careful, you are being watched and listened to; for once, be serious.

KOU

44 *Coming to meet:* Do not be beguiled by a resting-place for you will find yourself deprived of your freedom. Beware particularly of sleeping waters — they are a dangerous mirror.

TS'UI

45 *Gathering together:* Distrust parasites and strengthen those structures which bring a meaning to your life — family, culture and political or philosophical ideals.

SHÊNG

46 *Pushing upwards:* Seductive for the Goat so attracted by rocky peaks, but be sure to take equipment and provisions: prepare carefully for the expedition and take good care of the details.

K'UN

47 *Oppression:* Do not panic if you are not in high spirits; accept it and look for the cause. Be careful of your credibility.

CHING

48 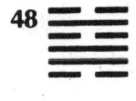 *The well:* You like to call your life and your ideas into question; this is a good thing, but do not forget that after moving out you must move in. Do not leave the furniture by your front door.

KO

49  *Revolution:* Is a necessary evil. If you wish to avoid it, consider it as an alternation of white and black, of Yin and Yang.

TING

50 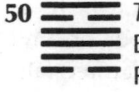 *The cauldron:* Representation of the five Elements — Earth, Wood, Fire, Water, Metal. Physical and spiritual nourishment. Vegetable broth or witch's broth, whichever it may be, be sure to keep it hot.

CHÊN

51 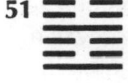 *The arousing (shock, thunder):* There are strokes of love and strokes of bad luck. Sometimes their purpose is to forewarn of a situation which threatens to explode. The Goat will accomplish several leaps and will, perhaps, receive some black-and-blue marks, and then resume his route calmly.

KÊN

52 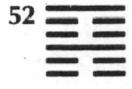 *Keeping still:* You will find the serenity necessary to your equilibrium in solitude. Accept the present moment without asking for more.

CHIEN

53  *Development (gradual progress):* Useless to mount the stairs four at a time in order to arrive first; you will have to wait on the landing.

KUEI MEI

54 *The bride:* Fortune and happiness. Tempting, but remain on your guard.

FÊNG

55 *Abundance:* Period of prosperity and of plenitude; take advantage of it so that you have the moral calibre to deal with later shortages.

LÜ

56 *The wanderer:* Decamp, clear off, bolt, get away as far as you can; in short, tear the tethering cord apart. But be sure you have a place to fall back on, without rancour or any spirit of conquest, otherwise it could be free-fall to disaster.

SUN

57 *The gentle:* Like a cloud and a light breeze, unflaggingly it passes and repasses, prevailing over any force or influence.

TUI

58 *The serene, joyous:* The Goat should share his fantasies and dreams.

HUAN

59 *Dissolution:* Be less airy and detached and more attentive to others. Off-handedness is a form of egotism.

CHIEH

60 *Limitation:* Is not imposed by constructing mental or physical barriers; it is therapeutic — do not apply them if it does not agree with you.

CHUNG FU

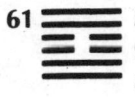

61 *Inner truth:* Do not spread it like butter on a slice of bread; the evidence of your attitude alone can demonstrate clearly it is there. Acts, not words!

HSIO KUO

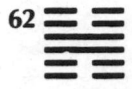

62 *Preponderance of the small:* It is useless to amuse yourself by leaping over large crevices and spraining your ankle; act according to your means — for the moment, they are limited.

CHI CHI

63 *After completion:* If you feel in a state of euphoria, of bursting out all over, make the most of it; after the apogee comes the decline.

WEI CHI

64 *Before completion:* Do not announce the death of the wolf before you have killed him. Remember, he can answer you back!

YEAR OF THE MONKEY

 1908·1920·1932
1944·1956·1968
1980·1992·2004

THE DOMAINS OF THE MONKEY

十二生肖

THE MONKEY AND ITS SYMBOLISM

'The Monkey is considered by some as both Yin and Yang. It is the symbol of intelligence and a sometimes slightly dishonest ingenuity. Does not the Monkey-God owe his immortality to the peach that he stole in the garden of the Sovereign Mother of the West? His life-span is several thousand years. From his youth until eight hundred years, he is not always benevolent, but he improves with age, and, when he is transformed into a baboon, he becomes charming and helpful.'

'Sharp as a monkey' is a common expression, but the term 'crafty' fits the monkey better. Crafty, agile, clownish, the monkey is a disconcerting animal which continues to surprise us, to baffle us. Leaping from branch to branch, he symbolizes the consciousness of the palpable world. 'The mastery of the Monkey' is that of the heart; it is thus that he is described in certain methods of Buddhist meditation, expressing a control of perpetually roving emotions. In the beautiful Chinese book of the *Si-yeou-KI*, the Monkey is designated as 'Son of Sky and of Earth'. In India he is found as the extremely adroit, spontaneous, agile and whimsical monkey called Hanumänn. This personage represents the perfect servant of God, the perfect adorer. 'He disposes of immense strength. But he does not use this power for egotistical ends, for the satisfaction of his own desires, for his own glory, but puts it entirely at the service of his master, his God, and attributes to himself no merit.'

In Asia the Monkey is also synonymous with wind — the West wind. Like the wind, he suddenly rises up, gambols, flies away and disappears with one bound. Is he white or is he black? Is he Yin or is he Yang? He is both, this magician, this acrobat. He is intelligent and ambiguous and master of the instinctive and creative forces that he liberates. He roves his universe and the irrational, jumping about on the spokes of the Wheel of Time. He is the tightrope walker, vigilant and superciliously bantering; for ever on the lookout for the fall of his fellow creatures. At times indifferent to notions of good and evil, but perfectly lucid, he is a wily confederate, ready to disappear at a moment's notice, carrying off the stolen fruit.

But let us return to the Monkey of the *Si-yeou-KI*.

In China, within the border of the eastern regions, the Monkey was a rock which, since the beginning of the world, received the rays of the moon and of the sun. One day the rock swelled and burst, giving birth to a stone egg. A hurricane broke, the egg split, and from it emerged a stone monkey. He possessed all five senses: sight, hearing, smell, taste and touch. After much training, he succeeded in travelling to the North, South, East and West, nourishing himself on the fruits of the trees and the water of the rivers. Later, he lived in the mountains, sleeping at night on the lower slopes and climbing to the summits during the daytime. In this way he became friendly with other monkeys, the gibbons.

One very hot day, the Monkey, accompanied by the gibbons, went into a little wood of pine trees, in the middle of which bubbled a deep and cool stream. At the sight of such pure, sparkling water, they decided to plunge in to find its source and measure its depth. The Monkey's companions agreed to proclaim King whoever could descend to the bottom of the stream. The stone monkey dived in first. Having arrived at the bottom, he opened his eyes. He discovered not water but a large palace on which was engraved, 'Mount of flowers and of fruits, land of happiness, celestial cavern'.

The Monkey hurried back to the surface to tell the gibbons what he had discovered. The gibbons were happy and danced with joy. Then the stone monkey said to them 'We are going to live in the palace. We will be sheltered from the sun and the rain.' All the monkeys then plunged into the water and took possession of the Palace of Happiness. The stone monkey installed himself on a seat and had himself proclaimed King, as had been agreed. He was named Perfect Monkey-King.

However, despite his glory as a sovereign, laden with riches and power, the Perfect Monkey-King was melancholy: he feared old age and death.

One day, he decided to leave the Palace to search for immortality. Riding on the wind, he looked in the furthest reaches of caverns and in the azure of the sky. In the course of his quest, the Monkey's body and spirit little by little changed completely, and he ended by becoming a man.

This tale nicely illustrates a typical Oriental idea: intelligence, courage, prestige, fortune and power — all are worthless unless the fundamental mysteries of life and death are studied and understood thoroughly.

A few notes on the Monkey

Principal qualities: Intelligence, clear-sightedness, keenness of mind.

Principal defects: A slight superiority complex and often indulges in a low opinion of others.

Work: Able, ambitious, gifted in everything, the Monkey's powers are far-ranging. All doors are open to him.

Best role: A gentleman-thief such as Raffles.

Worst role: He has none because he can be the best around, so long as he wants to be.

Money: Rich from time to time — due to luck or cleverness — but too spendthrift to remain so for long.

Luck: He is the animal most adapted to life on earth; and if he is born in summer, his luck will be all the greater.

Cannot live without: Movement, discussion, the exchanging of ideas.

Adores: Taking care of others, for he has a feeling for chivalry.

Detests: Feeling excluded, ignored or another's indifference and, above all, for his self-confidence to be shaken.

Leisure activities: He is sociable and likes to circulate. He loves social meetings, cocktails, smart parties, and, above all, to be adulated.

Favourite places: Everywhere, provided life is intense and he is not bored; he enjoys being on holiday, and even his office, if he likes his work.

Colour: Violet.

Plants: Sandalwood and cedarwood.

Flower: Elderberry.

Professions: Politician, diplomat, ambassador, writer, spokesman, storyteller, orator, salesman, actor — and thief.

The four ages in the life of the Monkey, according to Chinese tradition

The infancy of the Monkey will be happy and without problems: he is intelligent, hard-working and adapts easily. His *youth*, however, will be unstable, full of changes and emotional difficulties. In *maturity*, the Monkey will achieve some tranquillity and success — but watch out for *old age* when he will often be solitary and cut off from family and loved ones.

THE PSYCHOLOGY OF THE MONKEY

For the layman, Chinese astrology poses a problem similar to that found in Western astrology: that of dividing humanity into twelve different psychological types. We are imbued with a sense of our individuality, our tastes, our times and of our culture — and we cling to these sacrosanct distinctions. It is sometimes difficult to admit that our neighbour upstairs, that insupportable creature, has the nerve to share a sign of the zodiac with us, be it Oriental or Occidental. How much more comforting it would be to relegate what we pompously call the 'dregs of humanity' to a thirteenth undetermined sign, a depository of our rancours and our prejudices.

Given that there is no such 'sign' in astrology, some of the people we encounter have inherited unfortunate, and not always justified, reputations. In Western astrology, the signs of Virgo and Scorpio have attracted many unflattering epithets; the same occurs in Oriental astrology, and the Monkey is one such zodiacal 'scapegoat'.

Tradition accords him with an expansive and magnanimous nature, the greatest intelligence and the keenest lucidity. Equally, it also dispenses a litany of faults with which to categorize him: he is a liar, garrulous, hypocritical and unstable.

Being interested in Chinese astrology, I have never been able to resist the temptation to seek out among my circle of friends and acquaintances the influence of certain signs and psychological or other constants which they are supposed to express. These little studies have resulted in a high percentage of statistical accuracy. There was, however, one exception: of the twelve signs of the Chinese zodiac, only the Monkey remained obscure and apparently remote from his human counterparts. In an attempt to establish what they had in common, I closely observed and listened to my friends born under his sign, and studied long lists of celebrities born in his year. This proved difficult and often inconclusive, and I have the distinct impression that those born under the sign of the Monkey must feel ill-at-ease in reading about some of the character traits ascribed to them.

Evidently, there is a lack of agreement between the moving, complex reality of the 'nature' of the sign and the slightly arbitrary simplicity of the texts describing it. One then asks why this is. For one reason, classic Chinese astrological literature seems to judge those born under the sign of the Monkey on their *appearance* (the same is true, though less so, for those born under the sign of the Rooster). This is misleading. Monkeys are indeed jokesters, actors and manipulators of ideas; but they do not always behave so either on purpose or with bad intentions. They are accused of wishing to dominate others, to decide everything for them, and of having a frightening superiority complex. This is true. But one forgets that, due to their superior intellectual capacities, they naturally tend to dominate others, and that they frequently make wise decisions which many would do well to imitate.

In fact, Monkeys are indeed special. The best adapted to the world we live in, they are the most likely to get the best out of it. No wonder they provoke jealousy and misunderstanding.

Among the Monkeys I know personally, I have noticed some common characteristics: they share an entirely unique blend of vivacity, fantasy and detachment. In a matter of minutes, one acquaintance of mine will change from a joyous, playful, devil-may-care person to a haughty and responsible intellectual; all done with a slight, secretive and ironic smile.

Another close friend will burst out with a stream of ideas so disorganized and irrational that he would dazzle any psychoanalyst — and then return to his office to manage his little world with an iron hand.

Monkeys also share a natural facility for expressing themselves in a·clear, precise and convincing manner. Their behaviour is professional, efficient and responsible. They are remarkably adaptable and show a young, fresh and enthusiastic side that is ready to embark on any crusade to seek the Holy Grail, the unknown or the unprecedented. Monkeys hate regularity and abhor routine and repetitive tasks. When they are solicited, even hustled, the adrenalin flows and they find the incentive to use their ingenuity and their capacity to make swift decisions. Outsiders do not easily understand this facility. It is so disconcerting; is there *nothing* they cannot do?

Monkeys are independent, swift people with particularly lively minds and a gift for repartee, but they sometimes lack perseverance and concentration. Liking variety and change, they will find concentrating on a single problem desperately boring. They easily spread their interests far and wide among a wide variety of things, and show an infinite curiosity about anything and everything. Their thirst for knowledge is unquenchable. They actually do know a great deal, but their impulsive, lighthearted manner disguises this and consequently they are considered to be more superficial than they really are.

Their gregarious nature, the ease with which they sidestep the problems of others, does not cause people to feel indulgent towards them.

It is here that we find the real secret, the true drama of those born under the sign of the Monkey: by flitting about, criticizing, propounding and dominating, they bring about reproaches and are misunderstood. One might think that they do not care, for they always lightly evade the issue even, if necessary, cruelly mocking themselves. They have, in fact, a great sense of humour and rarely take themselves seriously. In truth they may suffer profoundly from this feeling of exclusion, becoming pessimistic, bitter and sceptical, but without revealing a hint of these feelings to others.

Monkeys wish to be admired, loved with indulgence and affection and understood. But they hardly even confide in others, opening out to them and revealing their true nature. They seem to need to evade understanding. It is difficult to know whom or what they are defending.

So, never hesitate to hold out your hand when you see a Monkey somersaulting on the flying trapeze of his fantasy; perhaps, waiting only for that, he will in turn lay his head on your shoulder.

The Monkey has a generous nature; he wants to be chivalrous. He takes great care of others, is tactful, adroit and sensitive. But he is also too rational and, finding it difficult to put himself in the place of others, regrets this bar to his comprehension, for at bottom he is always reasonable.

With friends, he cannot keep quiet. He loves to talk about himself and them. In dialogue he blossoms: the exchange enhances! He is forceful rather than violent; his crown sits on a world of language and of literature, not of war.

He may seem unfeeling, but that is a misconception. Quite simply, he cannot prevent himself from filtering his emotions and feelings through an intelligence as agile as his gestures. He is both a child and an old man. Deep within him the two carry on an interminable dialogue, the old man throwing cold water on the child, the child rejecting the pessimism of the old man. The Monkey, always ironically self-absorbed, is highly personal, different and original — even when he tries to agree with everyone. Even in moments of great sociability, he will find it difficult to avoid throwing out an accurate and rather cutting remark about the personal characteristics of the person facing him. He has, in fact, observation as sharp as a laser beam.

THE MONKEY AS A CHILD

Here is one of the easiest of children to educate — at least Chinese tradition believes so. If you are worried about potential problems, bear a Monkey child.

The young Monkey is 'easy' to raise because learning is not difficult for him. Intelligent, gifted, brilliant, sociable, he adapts marvellously to school life; in particular, he often has a gift for languages.

If he returns home from school to a horrible slum where an alcoholic father beats him regularly, and a schizophrenic mother and a tubercular little sister await him, he will still have an excellent chance of surviving without traumas. Where, for example, a young Dog would be marked for life and would attempt to hide the shameful defects of his family, the Monkey will write a play or a novel about his unhappy childhood. Dickens was a Monkey.

If unhappy with his family, our young Monkey will quickly find others — intellectuals or athletes — and join their communities and clubs; he does not lack imagination.

To keep a hold on him, you must above all interest him. He needs dialogue and surprises; he likes to share your problems and your occupations. I have a Monkey girlfriend who speaks tenderly about the years of her childhood when she assisted her busy midwife mother. Perhaps a mother who had worked quietly in a dull office would have filled her with less admiration.

With this kind of child, the parents' role consists above all in gently curbing an accelerated mental development. They must encourage their little Monkey to wait for others, to put himself in their place, to be less ironic — or at least to learn the difference between an amusing joke and a hurtful criticism. That is about all. Oh, no, I almost forgot — they must also reread their Classics if they are to keep up with a child who learns and assimilates with remarkable facility.

LOVE LIFE

Among the Monkeys whom I know, all have acquired an honourable, even exceptional, success in their professions. All have a rather lively social life and are surrounded by friends. But — all are also alone, or are on the point of becoming so, or have just become so. The Monkey is too rational for his love life to be an easy one. Excepting, naturally, the first moments of passion and enthusiasm, the intoxication of doing everything together, they rarely remain in a state of loving bliss for more than a few months. Sometimes, because of their intelligence and clarity of mind, without meaning to, Monkeys will quickly sense in their loved one the slightest slackening of tension or interest. This will undermine their self-confidence and provoke them into running away to protect the most intimate recesses of their psyches. Usually, it is the Monkeys who give up; they are too aware of the minute detail that is amiss. It is well known that love, if it is to last, must be touched by blindness, and that the most difficult moment is when one discovers the faults of the other. For those born under the sign of the Monkey, this is as hard to weather as Scylla and Charybidis combined. The strength of their attachment is not strong enough for them to resist the stark landscape that their pitiless eyes and their sharp lucidity reveal. I know one female Monkey who is profoundly taken with a gentleman whom she cannot refrain from criticizing. I know another who cannot find her soul-mate, because she quickly discovers 'the point on which we could never get along'. In fact, if Monkeys ever have a really marvellous memory of a liaison, it is usually because it was impossible anyway, or quickly curtailed by absence. In such circumstances they can remain very much in love.

These animals always behave with great charm and kindness, for they love to please and vaguely fear that they will not be liked. They are easily carried away, seducing you with a flick of the wrist and throwing themselves with intensity into each new love. But be careful: it is temptation and conquest they adore. Otherwise, they will follow instantly the first member of the opposite sex who passes by.

FAMILY LIFE

Those born under the sign of the Monkey often marry young, when their passions are fully aflame and their reason is inhibited. Later, they come to a different point of view because their reasonableness causes them to look without illusion upon the romantic world of fairy-tale love which has led other signs to divorce or estrangement. Marvellously adapted to reality, Monkeys know how to be content with it; it is rare to see them drop the substance for the shadow. If they are told that 'the grass is always greener...', they will not budge without first getting a sample and an analysis of the terrain. These Monkeys are not crazy....

By nature Monkeys are not faithful, but they can become so, naturally. The family is neither their end nor be all, nor their universal panacea; but once there, they decide, why run elsewhere? And do not, unless certain that something better is to be found.

And then, Monkeys adore children. They themselves are the most eternally young of all the Chinese zodiac, and neither the lines on their faces nor worldly experience will deprive them of that eternal 'youthfulness of spirit' which is their principal charm. It is not naivety nor romanticism, but simply an unfailing resilience which makes them always ready to begin again. For their children, who find themselves at once carried away, stimulated and understood, this enthusiasm is wonderfully enlivening. The Monkey parent always has an indulgent and complicitous eye, for he is aware, despite his children's most colossal blunders and their most catastrophic stupidities, of his own capacity to do worse. Do not expect rigorous lectures nor moralizing from him: he would not last five minutes without laughing. But he has no equal when it comes to sharing in the games, reading and the work of his children — all done with total sincerity.

For varying reasons, children of the Ox or the Dog will adapt badly to a Monkey parent: they either need disciplining or moral protection; precautions that are totally foreign to the Monkey. Such children will be unhappy and dissatisfied. On the other hand, Goat, Rabbit, Tiger, Snake, Pig, Dragon and Horse children — and Monkey children too — will learn a lot from the tricks of their Monkey parent. The little Rat, as well as the young Rooster, will do everything they can to follow, but their Monkey parent will not always reciprocate the intense, blind love they bring and dream of receiving in return.

PROFESSIONAL LIFE

Those born under the sign of the Monkey are independent, crafty and ambitious. Although they clearly prefer to succeed on their own without owing anything to anyone, they are capable of assessing how to profit from the goodwill of those around them, or from the assistance that a relative or a friend in the 'right place' can give them. Diversity is a spur, and they hate tasks that are too routine, preferring situations requiring ingenuity and resourcefulness. When the unexpected fails to occur, they prove capable of inventing it, either by sowing disorder and discord among their professional colleagues (at worst), or by inventing original and distracting hobbies. In the latter case they do their daily job with diligence and vivacity — while thinking of everything they are going to be able to do once the day's work is done.

Monkeys have a speciality in which they are champions: they always occupy their time to the full; not a minute is wasted. Where Snakes or Rabbits spend hours asking themselves vaguely what there is to do, Monkeys will finish off their eight-hour working day by going to the gym or the swimming pool, getting out their accounts or reading a story to their children — in between which they will have started the washing machine, fed the pets and turned on the iron. They are unequalled in their ability to do thirty-six things at once, while being perfectly relaxed and efficient.

This virtuosity brings excellent results in their professional life. Intelligent and gifted with an almost perfect memory and a remarkable facility for adaptation, Monkeys are capable of anything — in the best sense fo the word. No avenue is closed to them — it is enough that they wish to arrive. They will, however, be more at ease in professions requiring contacts, movement and communication; in any case where solutions must be worked out and utilized. They are excellent intermediaries. Supple and opportunistic, they are also decision-makers and will not hesitate to shake up everyone if their business seems to be succumbing to routine. They love to be in the forefront, responsible only to themselves, free; in short, to move around as they please.

MATERIAL LIFE

Monkeys are not noted for their altruism. It is rare to run into them at a charity event — unless they have a personal fortune or need to display a flattering, philanthropic image of themselves. They are preoccupied with profitability, comfort, love and the independence that money can buy. They are quite capable of asking for a loan when they are broke. They are generous only to their families, especially their children, for whom they stop at nothing and would plunder Eldorado to give them Christmas presents. But the rest of the time they prefer to spend money on their own pleasure.

Mr Monkey likes to play lord of the manor. As for Mrs Monkey, it is inadvisable — unless you wish to face immediate ruin — to open an unlimited credit account for her at a large department store. She is capable of spending a month's salary on eccentric trifles that she will wear once and then give to her maid; the next day she will go to her boss and charm him into giving her an advance on her salary. Monkeys are improvident in this way.

However, their ingenuity usually suffices to get them out of the most difficult corners: it is always at the moment when you believe them to be on the point of going to prison for debt that you see their photograph in a newspaper, shaking the hand of Mr Rockefeller and concluding a particularly fruitful and juicy deal. You simply never can tell about Monkeys.

Their spendthrift and carefree side often coexists with great financial ability. This is, to say the least, surprising: they are as ready to administer and multiply their money as they are to throw it out of the window. However that may be, in their material life there is a guiding thread: they cannot bear to deprive themselves, and they never fail to buy pretty and original things. In any case, they are too skilful to go bankrupt. If one day you recognize sprawled in the back seat of a gold Rolls-Royce the person you have seen many mornings begging in front of the bus stop, you can be sure that he is a Monkey.

ENVIRONMENT

Although not slaves of their environment, nor passionately attached to places and objects belonging to their childhood, Monkeys are refined and have good tastes. They enjoy decorating, repainting and moving house; and, when they do not travel with their own furniture and objects, it amuses them to change their surroundings with original and varied accessories: a pagoda or possibly some 16th century French object. Their favourite environment embodies variety: they would adore a flat with walls made of movie screens on which to project different landscapes each day, changing the colours as they wished. Male or female, they are generally remarkable handymen, often with a touch of genius. They are also willing helpers: whenever I have to use a hammer or a drill, I call on my Monkey friends for help — an immediate solution is guaranteed. The toolbox holds no secrets for them; they know how to do everything, from fitting bookshelves to putting up a partition, hanging tapestries or framing a picture.

However, when it comes to tidying up, it is better to put them in an armchair with a glass, lest you find the sausages in your makeup kit and your socks in the fridge. Their wardrobes are always filled to bursting with clothes and forgotten papers, all piled with joyous abandon. Once every ten years they will clear everything out in order to choose what to keep, and will burst out laughing or become sentimental over their incredible mountain of possessions — mementoes of their rich, full life.

A guide to personal relations with a Monkey
Methods of seduction:

He: Before your dazzled eyes, he holds out bright prospects of a fascinating future, rich in the unexpected and the exciting. He makes you drunk on his words and gestures and persuades you that your life with him will be different (which is absolutely true!).

She: Carries on an intelligent conversation and gives you the impression that you are the most brilliant individual ever born. She does this vivaciously and radiantly, and, in truth, with just a little provocation.

If he loves you: He will do everything he can to seduce you, even if it involves kidnapping you, renting a plane or setting fire to your house so that he may be your shining knight. There are two possible solutions: flee or give in, depending on whether or not you have a taste for risk.

He expects of you: That you are always available and that you need him.

To keep you: He is the best armed of the Chinese zodiac and, if he truly wishes, he will transform your life into such a giddy whirl that, without realizing it, you will wake up one day to your golden wedding anniversary.

If he is unfaithful: It is only for pleasure, because he wants to. Do not try to be moralistic — unless you want to hear that if you were more amusing he would not want to.

If you are unfaithful: Beware; this is a dangerous game. Though neither exclusive nor jealous, the Monkey hates to be made a fool of. He is capable of Machiavellian vengeance and it is you, in the end, who will often appear ridiculous. Equally, it is useless to try to hide anything; he is so observant, so astute, that he will scent the danger before you are even aware of it.

In case of a break between you: Try to remain friends; it is worth it. You will succeed in this if you avoid emotional blackmail and jealous scenes.

If you wish to give him a gift: Give him something to be transformed — from a piece of cloth to make a dress with to an old hut overrun with weeds. With a single wave of his magic wand he will create a fashionable gown or a lovely country cottage. Never hesitate to appeal to his resourcefulness and his imagination.

If you want to seduce him: Take him to the airport and buy a ticket for the first flight out. (You will buy the necessary clothes when you get there.)

If you want him to leave: Tell him, preferably in public, 'Oh no, not that one again, you have told it so many times!'

THE MONKEY AND THE OTHER CHINESE SIGNS

Monkey/Rat

It is difficult in the case of a Monkey/Rat relationship to advise that they should avoid each other like the Plague. If you did, they would escape many difficult problems and complications; but it is precisely complications that they love, along with the risk that the relationship is likely to be somewhat tortuous.

Alike on many levels, the Rat and the Monkey are capable of being accomplices and can enjoy themselves together. But one will always be trying to get the better of the other, to dominate without seeming to do so. Each will say in turn, 'I am stronger; I got him that time.' But they will both be mistaken.

If they are friends or associates, their alliance will be unstable but dynamic. If they are in love, their situation becomes more critical, for the rational Monkey is incapable of following the Rat into the depths of his passion or of paying him the attention he requires. When it suits him, the Monkey will be variously charming, attentive and considerate, intoxicating his Rat with flowery phrases; then he will turn cold, indifferent and inconsiderate. This can shatter the Rat, who must take care, for his equilibrium is in danger, and the Monkey will dominate him too often for comfort.

Monkey/Ox

The Ox will understandably be left nonplussed and dizzy by the Monkey's vivacity. But it will not be long before he overcomes his natural distrust and comes to admire those famous pirouettes of his partner; for the Monkey fulfils his own need for originality.

For his part, the lucid Monkey appreciates to a fine degree the Ox's stability and native equilibrium, for these provide the security necessary for one whose centre of gravity constantly oscillates.

Also important is the fact that these two signs are perhaps the least 'sentimental' of the Chinese Zodiac. They do not give love priority in their lives. Each will welcome a partner for whom jealous scenes, emotional displays and 'stupid' declarations of love are foreign. This will be a sound alliance, both in marriage and in business. In the case of the latter, they will, moreover, be formidable allies, but it will be unwise to rely on them when you are the one in difficulty, because compassion is not their strong point.

Monkey/Tiger

Despite his adventurous side, the Tiger is much less supple and adaptable than the Monkey. While respecting his partner's freedom, he likes clear-cut situations: 'What do you mean? Are you with me or with him? You must choose whom you want!' But the Monkey, even when really in love, has too great a desire to please, to measure the effects of his charm and to remain steadily in place to maintain the Tiger's preconceived and fixed role of him. He will always escape from the Tiger, who will be outraged at being walked over like a rug.

Then too, the Monkey mocks, criticizes and is adept at putting his finger on the weak points of those close to him. He will secretly admire the Tiger, but he will not be able to stop himself from tweaking his moustache. Tradition has it that the vexed Tiger will then wait for the Monkey to fall asleep in order to devour him.

However, with much love on the part of the Monkey, and much moderation and tolerance on the part of the Tiger, the relationship can work.

Monkey/Rabbit

The intelligent and wily Monkey knows very well how to manage his affairs, but from time to time he enjoys finding understanding and rest with the indulgent and discreet Rabbit. The Rabbit knows all about wiliness, using it himself to get out of many a difficult situation. The Monkey's advice will enable the Rabbit to add several strings to his bow by making him more reasonable.

These two can attain a form of intimacy and complicity which is extremely personal and from which most people will feel excluded. Moreover, they will be so interested in each other that they will barely wish to raise a large family.

In business their understanding can be ticklish because the Rabbit, who is strongly attached to principles, will be scandalized by the occasional nearly illegal convolutions of the Monkey. He will criticize him, even though at bottom he envies him, and the Monkey will make fun of the Rabbit and disregard his virtuous indignation.

Monkey/Dragon

Avoid this couple if you value the company of those versed in philosophical inquiry. Such pursuits are not their strong point; in fact, both have a tendency to believe that they have delved deeply into a subject when a great deal remains yet to be explored.

They are helped as a couple because each stops at the same point of inquiry, which they will later resume. The Monkey has all the qualities necessary to seduce a Dragon and to keep a hold on him — a rare talent. Knowing how to listen, and then, with a toss of the head, to steal away; to alternate enthusiastic compliments with courteous silences, the Monkey will fascinate the Dragon. The latter, with his unselfish, chimerical and gratuitous side, will know how to captivate the Monkey, who is always seeking a new source of excitement. There will be no rivalry between them; on the contrary, they will complement each other and give each other confidence. Their combination will enable mutual success and other poor mortals, stunned by their charm, will be easily seduced. If a Dog, for example, tries to denounce them as being superficial, they will not hear him.

Monkey/Snake

With this couple there will be excellent intellectual understanding because, on this level, they are the most 'endowed' of the Chinese zodiac. Both assimilate easily, think quickly and effortlessly and adapt themselves to just about everything.

They complete each other: the Monkey is cleverer on the surface, the snake in depth. They make an excellent professional team — unbeatable and crammed with ideas and possibilities — and should not hesitate to become associates.

Emotionally, it is another story. The Monkey is traditionally one of the rare signs capable of eluding the Snake's grasp. He will not allow himself to be eaten and the Snake, disgusted, will not persevere for very long and will look for more acquiescent prey. Their reciprocal fidelity will not last for long.

They should remain friends — something easier to attain, and more profitable.

Monkey/Horse

There is difficult understanding between these two; one is dominated by emotion, living his passions with intensity and with total, ardent commitment; the other, subject to reason, is always conscious of the traps along the way, of the risks of love, and is forever 'standing back' and doubting the possibility of a lasting attachment.

The sincerity of the Horse might help the Monkey to attain some stability, but the latter will attribute this sincerity to naivety or blindness. On his side, the Horse will not stand for the about-faces of the Monkey, and will accuse him of being calculating or insensitive. They will both be wrong, but that will not alter things.

In any case, this couple is rare because the Horse and the Monkey are not often attracted to each other. Even at first sight, when they do not yet know each other, they share a vague distrust, each suspecting the other of superficiality.

Monkey/Goat

This is a relationship full of gaiety and fantasy. These two will never be bored together and will be very amusing for others, ceaselessly inventing new pranks and using their imagination and intelligence with remarkable virtuosity. They will know how to make the most of each other, tossing the ball back and forth.

In fact, everything will go well so long as they remain friends or associates — or even lovers. However, if they decide to live together they will run the risk of things becoming less rosy and idyllic.

In spite of himself, the Monkey will preserve his reasonableness, whereas the Goat will need to be told over and over again that he is loved, so that he may feel truly cared for and secure.

Once the initial enthusiasm has passed, the Goat will be disappointed; the Monkey, even with the best intentions in the world, will not be able to become what he is not — not even to please the Goat.

Monkey/Monkey

Relationships between persons who resemble each other are often advised against or criticized; though interesting and easy, only rarely are they constructive and capable of development. Here, however, is the exception to the rule, for those born under the sign of the Monkey are too clear-sighted and too intelligent to set themselves up as rivals. On the contrary, this relationship enables them to become even more intelligent and efficient — and above all, close accomplices. Understanding each other without effort, each encouraging and stimulating the other, our two Monkeys will go far and will have a marvellous time together.

Naturally, it would be best if they shared some intellectual or material goal. Mad passion will not interest them forever, and they will need something else to bind them as time passes. Since neither of them will make particularly passionate demands on the other, the relationship should work.

Monkey/Rooster

This alliance can work, but only superficially. While the astute, clever Monkey and the honest, frank Rooster complete each other, the former will always have a tendency to mock, criticize and treat the Rooster as a superficial, naive person. The Rooster, on the other hand, will for a while admire the acrobatic games of his partner, but will end by saying: 'Ah, I didn't realize that he was so superficial!'

By judging each other solely on external appearances, they will methodically detect the mote in their companion's eye and not the dust in their own.

Their problem is that they cannot accept that they are on an equal footing, and so they live at war with each other as perpetual rivals. However, a little indulgence and acceptance of the other 'as he is', without wishing to change him, would enable this couple to live in comparative peace.

They can agree on one level: their mutual taste for parties and social life. They will squabble ceaselessly, but what a handsome couple they make!

Monkey/Dog

These two both have a tendency to criticize and are slightly cynical; they have few illusions about their neighbours and voluntarily cultivate the bitter flowers of irony. But there is a snag: the Dog is profoundly idealistic; he is the kind to shout 'All is lost save honour!' and similar, which will seem completely unrealistic to a Monkey, who is more of an opportunist and not at all altruistic.

Between a Dog child and a Monkey parent, between childhood friends or between a brother and sister who have grown up together, a relationship would be possible. But as a couple? The Dog will be profoundly disappointed but will not dare to say so. Little by little he will build up an enormous amount of resentment, being jealous of the Monkey's carefree attitude and, indeed, of his lack of scruples. He will harbour this resentment, feeling that the Monkey is quite disgraceful, but that his tricks work for him, and unjustly so.

As for the Monkey, he will quickly become bored, and make off. Deep down, he is too uneasy to accommodate another's misgivings.

Monkey/Pig

The Pig is perhaps the only sign capable of disarming the manipulative instincts of the Monkey, who will remain mesmerized and admiring in the face of such loyal, indeed royal, honesty. What is this bizarre animal who gives himself without expecting anything in exchange; and who, in his very guts, believes in a good and charitable humanity? Is he a madman, or is he a wise man modestly imbued with the Truth?

The Monkey will find himself caught up in this relationship before having had the time to ask such questions. Though good at seeing through the underhandness of his adversaries, the Monkey is flabbergasted by genuine frankness and generosity. He will do no harm to the Pig, and, seeing himself reflected in such a positive fashion in his partner's eyes, he will believe himself to be a better person — and will become so.

The Pig will rub his hands and laugh in his beard. He knew perfectly well that he would have the last word: his apparent naivety hides a cleverness and abilities far superior to that of the Monkey, simply because he is not in the least bit self-seeking.

SOME MONKEY CELEBRITIES

Byron, Julius Caesar, Chamberlain, Captain Cook, Couperin, Descartes, Diaghilev, Dickens, Dos Passos, The Dumas, Fellini, El Greco, Lyndon Johnson, Buster Keaton, Jack London, Milton, Modigliani, Paderewski, Bertrand Russell, de Sade, Scaramouche, Schopenhauer, Elizabeth Taylor, Spinoza, Chekov, Truman, Leonardo da Vinci.

YOUR COMPANION IN LIFE

生命伴侶

After the Chinese sign of your year of birth, here is the sign of your hour of birth

What is a Companion in Life, as understood in Chinese astrology? It is a sort of 'ascendant' sign corresponding to your hour of birth. This Companion is another animal belonging to the Chinese cycle of the twelve emblematic beasts, who falls into step with you and accompanies you, ever ready to help you brave the traps and ambushes along your route. A permanent and benevolent shadow, he can render the impossible possible.

He is your counterpart, but with his own character and tendencies and with a different psychology. Both guardian angel and devil's advocate, he will be a witness to your life and an actor in it.

Have you ever felt, deep inside yourself, the subtle presence of another 'myself' inhabiting you and with whom you live, at times in harmony, at others in conflict? Another self who sometimes criticizes you and at others encourages you? That is your Companion in Life.

There are times when he will appear to be an imposter or an intruder. Certainly, he often questions your habits and your moral or spiritual complacency. Accompanied by this companion, a shadow within, the route is less monotonous and the voyager multiplies his chances of arriving at his chosen destination. This, however, in itself matters little, for it is the journey and the manner in which it is conducted that are important. Indolence is the greatest danger: your Companion is capable of arousing you from a lassitude of spirit and, to that end, if necessary, robbing you of your certainties, trampling on your secret gardens and, finally, tearing away the great veil of illusion.

It sometimes happens that your Companion is of the same sign as your year of birth, a twin brother in a way — for example, a Monkey/Monkey. In this case, you must recognize that he will compel you to realize yourself fully and to live the double aspect — the Yin and the Yang — that your bear within yourself. In any case, you also bear within yourself the twelve animals. So, set out on the long route, ready for the great adventure: the beautiful voyage during which you will encounter the harmoniously entangled, the solemn and the grotesque, the ephemeral reality, the dream and the imagined.

Table of hours corresponding to the twelve emblematic animals

If you were **born** between			your **companion** is	
	11 pm and	1 am		Rat
	1 am and	3 am		Ox
	3 am and	5 am		Tiger
	5 am and	7 am		Rabbit
	7 am and	9 am		Dragon
	9 am and	11 am		Snake
	11 am and	1 pm		Horse
	1 pm and	3 pm		Goat
	3 pm and	5 pm		Monkey
	5 pm and	7 pm		Rooster
	7 pm and	9 pm		Dog
	9 pm and	11 pm		Pig

These figures correspond to the *solar hour* of your birth. If necessary, you should check the summer times (Daylight Savings Time) and make the appropriate adjustment (sometimes two hours before or after statutory time).

THE MONKEY AND ITS COMPANION IN LIFE

 **Monkey/Rat**

Before leaving on a trip, these two should prepare a first-aid kit: their journey is more likely to resemble a hazardous adventure than an agreeable outing. These two Companions believe in the principle of 'an eye for an eye and a tooth for a tooth', and will repay each other accordingly. The Monkey will have but one idea — to devour the unhappy little rodent. The Rat will use all his tricks, including the most perverse, to cause his Companion to fall into physical, moral and even spiritual traps. These two strange companions will have no tenderness for each other and will give each other no respite. Their journey will be staged in a prize-fighting ring, where all blows are allowed and no rules are observed. May the stronger win!

 **Monkey/Ox**

You will not resist the Ox's charm nor his persuasive and sympathetic magic for very long. Some sound advice: if you want peace, create the illusion that he is the stronger, but be attentive and sympathetic as well. This courageous animal is remarkably agile; physically and mentally he is a first-rate acrobat, gifted with a rare power of persuasion. Take care: the Monkey is sometimes a sorcerer capable of transforming the power of the Ox into mere confetti and mirages.

 **Monkey/Tiger**

Games of hide-and-seek, conjuring tricks and hoaxes will blend with feline strategems and intrepidity. That sorcerer the Monkey has more than one trick up his sleeve — depend on him to transform you into a fearless tightrope walker or a dazzling juggler. As playful as the Goat, for him the game is a matter of getting you to accomplish what *he* has decided you should accomplish. The Monkey/Tiger is a formidable animal that, by combining the proud bearing and temperate skills of the Tiger with the ever-present wizardry of the little Monkey, can turn anything upside down and provoke many a sleepless night. For the Monkey, leaping unobserved from branch to branch in the jungle with his eyes shut, one cannot apply the usual formula, 'put a Tiger in your tank'. It will have to be, 'wrap a Tiger in the skin of a mischievous Monkey and then you will really see something!'

 **Monkey/Rabbit**

He will be an inventive, lively, rather airy animal. He will have a tendency to be calculating, and will leave nothing to chance. He prefers being a schemer, conjuror and scrounger to labourious and irksome work. The Monkey/Rabbit envisages life as a game which, for the fun of it, he himself strews with traps and mirages, the better to zigzag between them. To attain his ends, he throws scruples to the wind. He will not hesitate to cheat, but who is he deceiving? He does not know himself, unless one day the Sphinx asks him the question.

 **Monkey/Dragon**

Possessing a combination of the supremely gifted synchronized with a talent and taste for walking the tightrope, the Monkey/Dragon — a valiant and fearless guardian — will never unbuckle his armour. Always prepared for war, his days and nights are spent in a state of alertness, much to the continued astonishment of his friends. Alas, he tends to be an extortioner. He has charm, is brilliant and his intelligence is remarkable, but his main defect is his immoderate pride. His company is appreciated, but only in small doses. He will be a phenomenon and his collaboration and assistance will be desired, but you will not be able to breathe freely until you have seen the back of him. So, unwind a little, be natural and glance on your fellow creatures with a less condescending eye.

 **Monkey/Snake**

He will be rational and a good organizer, but he will not be able to conceal his strong superiority complex which, unless he takes care, will cause him major problems. An intelligent and quick animal, his tendency to get carried away will be tempered by deep reflection; even so, he will always refuse to listen to the advice of others, because of his pride and self-esteem. He will not entertain any argument about his ideas, still less that his work or his word be questioned. The Monkey/Snake is talkative, courageous and, at times, a liar. However, his ability and his subtlety are major trump cards.

 **Monkey/Horse**

In turn eloquent and courageous, his path will resemble an extended race-course, from which the Monkey/Horse can only emerge victorious. He will be as well-balanced as a race horse, at once mount and rider; a Don Juan or a hermit, — as well as having a touch of Don Quixote — transforming a track into an arena. He will stake his life — from pride, from a delight in taking risks and even from cynicism. Uniting intelligence with a fine appearance, he exploits to the utmost his resources of charm, talent, wiliness and, sometimes, deceit. The Monkey/Horse will often dream of a path haloed by glory and strewn with flowers — that he will stamp upon with superb indifference.

 **Monkey/Goat**

Intuitive and intelligent, he will be extremely restless. At times pride will curb his fantasies and his ideas will then gain in constancy and consistency, though there is no certainty that he really wants to prusue them to their logical end. The Monkey likes to leap from branch to branch, and the Goat leaps ceaselessly from cloud to cloud. Thus, their alliance will be particularly lively and eventful. As for love, the Monkey/Goat can be a real heartbreaker!

 **Monkey/Monkey**

He will be by nature chivalrous, slightly boastful and often proud. He will have some difficulties in staying on a straight course; in fact, he will be tempted to take detours and shortcuts for the sheer pleasure of discovery and a taste for novelty. He cannot stay in one place and epitomizes the born traveller. If he comes across an obstacle, he will be tempted to get round it by using guile rather than by overcoming it directly. The Monkey/Monkey will be diabolically intelligent and lucid. However, though luck and happiness are apt to favour him, he will often be incapable of enjoying these gifts; he is too preoccupied with himself and blinded by a narcissism which will rob him of his best opportunities.

 **Monkey/Rooster**

Very proud and full of himself, he will not be, to say the least, modest and self-effacing. He will see to it that he never goes unnoticed and will care a great deal about the effect he produces on others. Lacking neither intelligence nor good taste, he will still be irresistibly attracted by all that glitters. A word of advice: do not call too much attention to his weaknesses because the Monkey/Rooster will never forgive you!

 **Monkey/Dog**

A supremely intuitive animal, it will be difficult to put him off his trail; he will always find his way despite obstacles and difficulties. However, he has a tendency to complicate his life because, to him, everything is a voyage. He hates simplicity, straight lines and mapped-out routes. The Monkey/Dog will often be a character with marked phases of exaltation and depression. Today full of spirit and sure of himself — even a little too much so — tomorrow he will see everything as completely black, questioning his projects, ideas and decisions. Avoid following him if you like to travel in peace.

 **Monkey/Pig**

He will adept at living in solitude, an extremely clear-sighted person to whom it is inadvisable to talk humbug. In fact, he has a built-in lie-detector that sometimes resembles clairvoyance. He has a horror of speaking without purpose. The Monkey/Pig will not be easy to live with: he has his own conceptions of life and will not tolerate having others' imposed on him. He likes to bury his treasures — material or psychological — which are not always of a very clear origin. The Monkey/Pig has, at times, a rather peculiar idea of honesty.

THE MONKEY AND THE FIVE ELEMENTS

五行

YOUR ELEMENT

In Chinese astrology, each year is joined to an Element. There are five Elements: *Water, Fire, Wood, Metal, Earth.*

Each of the twelve emblematic animals is linked successively to each of the five Elements. For example, in the year 1900 the Rat was Metal, in 1912 he was Water, in 1924 he was Wood, in 1936, Fire and in 1948 he was Earth. Therefore, for the twelve years from 1900 he was linked to Metal, for the next twelve years to Water, and, for every succeeding period of twelve years, to each of the other Elements, in succession.

In order to determine the Element corresponding to the year of your birth, use the table below:

> *Years whose digits end in:* 2 and 3 — Water
> 6 and 7 — Fire
> 4 and 5 — Wood
> 0 and 1 — Metal
> 8 and 9 — Earth

The same union of *Animal-Element* repeats every sixty years, for example, Rat-Metal appeared in 1720, 1780, 1840, 1900, 1960 and so on.

The five Elements are the primary forces affecting the universe. It is their particular association with each of the signs which provides the basis for every horoscope. Movement and fluctuation, Yin and Yang, these symbolic forces are in a perpetual state of action and interaction.

Wood gives birth to Fire, which gives birth to Earth, which gives birth to Metal, which gives birth to Water, which in turn gives birth to Wood.

MONKEY/WATER
(you were born in 1932)

The cold born of the northern sky descended to earth and gave birth to Water. The Chinese consider Water more a synonym for coldness and ice than the source of heat and fertility.

Characteristics of the Monkey/Water
Water of winter nights, rigour and severity; calm and deep water to be feared and respected; still water sheltering demons asleep in its depths; fetid and muddy water of the marsh, the refuge of crawling creatures.

The Water Element will tend to confirm the Monkey's irrational impulses, thus cutting him off from the realities of the world and its constraints. The Monkey/Water perceives the world in a global and uncertain manner, through foggy and slightly confused vision. But the Monkey is both Yin and Yang, and it is in his power to enliven Water, to render it bracing and dynamic. Thus by his own power of will he can act upon this Element, inclining it towards the positive and the creative. So, Monkey/Water, find your source, then flee the marsh.

Health of the Monkey/Water
The Water organ is the kidney. Its flavour is salted. The Monkey is active and should remain so. If quiet waters attract him, he should be careful not to sail on them too often: they could be dangerous for his nervous and mental equilibrium.

The Monkey/Water and others
The Monkey/Water will be tolerant and thoughtful, capable of subduing his pride and of listening to others. He is inclined to moderation rather than excess, and will make his mark in a responsible position which he will assume calmly and serenely. However, this can be simply a game, another form of experience for the Monkey. He needs to test his potential and then the reactions of his friends. Yet he will

almost never lose his sense of humour and detachment and will rarely take himself seriously. But boredom can sour his good humour and flights of fancy. The Monkey needs to communicate with men, to compel them to vibrate; he must lead them, if sometimes from a distance. The Monkey/Water will be more of a humanist than a mystic. His deepest anxiety is the boredom of routine and its stagnation.

Advice for a Monkey/Water
You need action, movement, change, novelty and discoveries. Respect your need to question everything because it is one of the keys to your success.

A Monkey/Water year
The culminating point for any Monkey/Water year will be winter, a period of gestation.

It is a year of ripening. Try not to preempt the harbingers of success, which bring in their wake the harvest and the fruits of your work. On the other hand, do not build on still waters: a groundwell may lurk beneath. In short, beware of the unforeseen: it can devastate you.

Historical example of a Monkey/Water year
1812

By 1812 the French Empire had reached its greatest extent; its 152 departments contained fifty million of the one hundred and seventy five million of inhabitants of Europe. Yet this was the year which relieved England, Paymaster of Europe, in its attenuated struggle against Napoleon.

The accord with Russia, symbolized by the floating raft at Tilsit, had been abrogated. In 1810 the Tsar Alexander I found it necessary to discontinue his participation in the 'Continental System' by which Napoleon sought and very nearly managed to reduce Great Britain to starvation and surrender. The Russians, urgently needing industrial goods that the French were unable to provide, concluded an agreement covering preferential tariffs with the British.

Napoleon was determined to assert the System of Tilsit and did so, at first by provocative action in Poland and Turkey, finally by military action against Russia itself. Securing levees from Prussia and Austria by demand rather than by negotiation, he assembled an army numerically larger than any previously recorded. But it lacked any natural cohesion. Its unwilling drafts, conscripted throughout Europe, were awed but not moved by Napoleon's aspirations. The Polish contingents possibly relished the prospect of revenge against a hereditary enemy; certainly, the armies of Austria flinched from the association. Imbued with the professional standards common in the eighteenth century, they had no sympathy for the system of total war conducted by Napoleon. They considered it barbaric and themselves to be dishonoured by participating in it.

However, Napoleon's object was not total war — he wanted a quick victory and a rapid peace. He misunderstood the Russians as he had misunderstood the Spanish. Dumbfounded and obstinate, he stayed on too long. He had counted on the niceties of diplomacy but by forgoing the formality of actually declaring war he forfeited every consideration.

MONKEY/WOOD
(you were born in 1944)

To the East the wind blew in the sky, and from its warm caress of the earth Wood was born.

Characteristics of the Monkey/Wood

Wood is of the morning, springtime, temperate nature, loving harmony, beauty and elegance. This season will be fruitful and creative for the Monkey, bringing him equilibrium and creative power.

The Monkey/Wood will appreciate the art of living, be sensitive to nuances and tradition, and quite often will be an artist. Understanding and tolerant, he will be a humanist. When angry or impassioned, the Monkey/Wood will find quietness in nature and solitude to appease his anger and obsessions. The Wood Element will moderate the Monkey's abundant activity and offer him stability. His only fault: susceptibility.

Health of the Monkey/Wood
The organ of Wood is the liver; its flavour is acid. The Monkey/Wood sometimes needs to overcome his black moods and stop fussing about details. When he is really true to himself, the Monkey/Wood cannot only exercise a remarkable control over his deepest impulses, but also over his metabolism, for he knows how to listen to his body's needs. This will enable him to develop his will when very young.

The Monkey/Wood and others
The Monkey/Wood will often have an apparently relaxed attitude, but this will only be a facade, a technique for hiding his weaknesses and secret qualms. He will usually succeed, and few will guess at the conflicts and tensions at work behind his jovial and debonair mask. Against the rigidity of certain institutions, the Monkey/Wood will set his imagination and sense for improvization, and here he will work miracles. You will be convinced that he is perfectly sure of himself, relaxed, playing with words and circumstances. You will never suspect that he is in fact using a defensive technique so carefully constructed that it becomes in truth an art of living exemplified by an attention to detail and an insistence on perfection.

Advice for a Monkey/Wood
You know perfectly well how to cope with real difficulties, so do not question your abilities simply because the occasional wave rises around you.

A Monkey/Wood year
The culminating point in a Monkey/Wood year will be

spring, the time of growth and prosperity.

A harmonious year in which you will be able to give free rein to your imagination and to your gift for life. However, control your weaknesses: do not allow your garden to be invaded, lest it become overrun with weeds.

Historical example of a Monkey/Wood year 1944

This was the climactic year of the Second World War and should have seen the end of it in the west. According to plan, and by coincidence on the same day, 6 June, the Russian summer offensive coincided with the Allied invasion of Europe. By 25 July the Russian armies had destroyed 25 divisions of the German armies and were advancing to the Vistula. On 19 August General de Gaulle entered Paris to a triumphant reception disturbed but, in its enthusiasm, not diminished by intermittent sniping from the rooftops. For this he owed much to the chivalry and good sense of the German commander who refused to act on orders from Berlin to desecrate the city; also, to his courage, for it was a brave man who refused to carry out orders after the failure of the Stauffenburg plot to kill Hitler on 19 July.

More serious sniping followed between the Allied generals and their governments. Field Marshal Mont-gomery, in the tradition of Marlborough, appreciated that the essential problem lay in supply, particularly in the supply of petrol for the armoured groups. He pressed for a single deep thrust into the Ruhr, Germany's industrial heart. He would necessarily have been in command of the operation and in command of American armies for the purpose. The idea was politically unacceptable to the Americans and the suggestion resented by their generals whose troops out-numbered the British. The supreme commander, General Eisenhower, had no choice. He could neither accept the British plan nor release his own forces for a single thrust to the south of the Ruhr. More-over, Montgomery's ability to strike fast was suspect and Patton, the best tank general on either side after Rommel's death, would not have served under him. A general advance was therefore ordered. Predictably, the supplies available were insufficient to support it.

Retribution followed. Ignoring the lessons of history the Ardennes was left lightly defended by the Allied command. In effect, their armies had gone into winter quarters. On 12 December the German panzers broke through and threatened to re-enact the great manoeuvre of 1940.

As so often happens, the threat of disaster bought cohesion to the Allies. Montgomery assumed command of all forces in the area and deployed them with precision. The Americans held out courageously and bought time at Bastogne; and Patton himself executed a rapid redeploy-ment of which any other general would have been incapable of contemplating. Even so the Allies were lucky. The panzers missed the great petrol dump which alone could have taken them to the Channel. The attack petered out. The alarm was over.

Alarm it was, but the outcome of the battle would not have affected the outcome of the war. More significant for the future was President Roosevelt's withdrawal from the Morgenthau plan which would have reduced Germany to an agrarian economy after victory had been won.

MONKEY/FIRE
(you were born in 1956)

Heat was born in the southern sky, descended to earth and fertilized it. From their union, Fire was born.

Characteristics of the Monkey/Fire
The Fire Element is of midday, of the South, of summer. Fire is Yang; it is the Element that heats, burns, transforms, confuses.

Fire will multiply the Monkey's energies, accentuating his

need for perpetual movement; but Fire will also tend to consume much of his power. This is why the Monkey should avoid wasting his reserves of energy and squandering his resources, lest he destroy himself. He must learn to restrain himself and to control his overactive nature. This Fire could also be an inner fire, a devouring flame, keeping him on the alert but allowing him little time for sleep and recuperation. Luckily, the Monkey possesses the Yin tendency, a calming and balancing factor.

Health of the Monkey/Fire

The organ of Fire is the heart, its flavour is bitter. Avoid becoming entrapped by aggressiveness and anger to the point of all control; for then you will lose cohesion, dissipate your energies and be condemned to wander endlessly like a mad comet.

The Monkey/Fire and others

Fire is often synonymous with war. It is lucid and clairvoyant, but also violent, irascible and impassioned. You will certainly not be very diplomatic, and your aggressiveness will often win out. You are a man of action and leadership; you also cultivate a kind of tolerance and a vehement anti-conformism. Your fervour and your inner demands may press you towards the monkish solitude of a philosopher. The Monkey/Fire will seesaw between the satisfaction of his strong material needs and his mystical aspirations, tending at times to fanaticism, isolating him from his fellowmen and cutting him off from reality.

Advice for the Monkey/Fire

Businessman or mystic, allow your energies free rein but moderate your judgements and your actions with understanding and indulgence. Learn the meaning of the word 'tolerance'.

A Monkey/Fire year

The culminating point for a Monkey/Fire year will be

summer, a period of creation. Your Yang tendency will be reinforced by the Yang of your Element, giving an abundance of energy.

A year full of action, surprises and forging ahead — the kind of year you like. However, do not lose your cohesion or you will spoil your chances, which are based on your strong will and good physical condition.

Historical example of a Monkey/Fire year
1956

It does nobody any good to be Crown Prince for too long. This was undoubtedly true of Sir Anthony Eden: when he finally assumed his inheritance and became Prime Minister he had lost the nerve essential for the exercise of power.

When President Nasser of Egypt nationalized the Suez Canal on 26 July Eden regarded it as an affront, which it was intended to be, and as a direct and dangerous attack on the vital interests of Great Britain, which it was not.

For a period rarely before equalled the French and British governments conspired and connived together. The two former great powers were reliving, in unnatural harmony, their preoccupations of a century before. Protracted and diffuse negotiations ensued, based rather on legalistic rights and their moral and commercial appeal to other nations than on the priorities of national interest to which the two powers pretended, and the loss of which they greatly feared. A laborious military build-up accompanied these public discussions, Cyprus being the appointed launching place.

Nasser's policy presented an immediate and practical threat to the State of Israel, whose government accordingly joined secretly in the Anglo-French talks. Together they resolved on war. Initially the Israelis were to attack, affording the two Western powers a moral justification for 'putting out the forest fire', a phrase greeted with the derision it deserved when uttered by Eden on British television. The American reaction was prompt: a financial threat which Harold Macmillan, then Chancellor of the Exchequer, could not ignore. The power of the dollar was too great.

The hypocrisy of the Americans could be sustained; that of France and England could not. The Soviet Union, then engaged in ruthless suppression of a patriotic rising in Hungary, threatened more physical action. Eden gave in, followed quickly by the French. A truce was declared and the Allied Forces were withdrawn; the Israeli forces remained in the positions they had conquered.

MONKEY/EARTH
(you were born in 1908 or 1968)

Earth was born from the slowly falling Element of the sky at its humid zenith.

Characteristics of the Monkey/Earth
This is an afternoon Earth, the humid and hot Earth of summer. Earth is the symbol of a downy nest, of comfort and abundance; of slow and profound transformations.

Like the eleven other emblematic animals, the Monkey is only passing through on Earth, but the Monkey/Earth will arrange things so that his stay will be as comfortable as possible; to this end no sacrifice will be too great. He will often be egotistical and proud, slightly forgetful of the Earth which carries him and which is a cauldron, the symbol of docility. In the best of cases, the Monkey/Earth will take refuge in his Element with the object of recharging his energies. But most of the time the Earth will be a lair — a cavern in which to bury his treasures rather than a temple for meditation.

The Monkey/Earth will be first and foremost a materialist, placing his imagination at the service of his need for power.

Health of the Monkey/Earth
The Earth's organ is the spleen, its flavour is sweet. The Monkey/Earth will remain active and keep a close eye on his

weight. In fact, strongly inclined towards greediness and overeating, he will have a tendency to gain weight, above all in old age.

The Monkey/Earth and others

The Monkey/Earth is more pragmatic and realistic than the other Monkeys. All of his enterprises are motivated by an overriding need for expansion and a desire for an increasing number of possessions. But he also likes activities that bear fruit and will be attracted to speculation, banking and real estate — in short, tangible values. His main preoccupation will be the accumulation of goods, the harvesting and gathering of crops. The Monkey/Earth will often be distrustful and suspicious of those near to him, which will sometimes make him difficult to live with. He is easily worried about his future, and will be constantly tormented by his need to be financially secure. He cannot, however, be reproached for his lack of courage: his fortune is always built by the sweat of his brow and at the price of laborious and conscientious work. With the Monkey/Earth, greed has its roots in fear, and is all the more intense because this fear of insecurity is buried deeply in his unconscious.

Advice for the Monkey/Earth

Dreams have no value on the stock market and weigh little in the balance; but they are the honey that is the balm for our wounds. So, keep a secret garden in which to cultivate your dreams; they will soothe your anxiety more than all the gold in Fort Knox.

A Monkey/Earth year

The culminating point for a Monkey/Earth will be summer, the season of hot and humid soil. Your savings account and barns will be full, so turn your eyes towards the summits or the starry canopy of heaven. Profit from this period to widen your perspective and discover new horizons.

Historical example of a Monkey/Earth year 1968

In 1968 the British and French governments were beset by a common problem, student unrest. Not for the first time, the students of Europe found their inspiration in the United States. The hybrids from the campuses flowered in England and in France; in both countries students attacked the authority of their teachers and of the university they were paid to attend. They campaigned against the politics of the politicians responsible for paying both the universities and their teachers to exercise authority over them and to teach them the rudiments of learning, trimmed by some old-fashioned refinements. The students, good anarchists at heart, considered the refinements out of date and thoroughly resented the rudiments.

The English government wisely refused to intervene directly. However, lest it should be accused of being wholly insensitive to the clamours of the young, it determined that they should be enfranchised at the age of 18, the silent argument being that those impelled by the offer of a grant to study should have the right to vote for those able to offer the grant. This enfranchisement was duly proclaimed by Act of Parliament.

In France it was a different story. De Gaulle, for whom barricades erected by students (or by anyone else) were little more than an historical coda to Parisian behaviour, was aloof to the pragmatic considerations which determined the actions of the Anglo-Saxons. Nor was he inclined to accept the advice of his Minister of Culture, André Malraux, that a violent insurrection of students, in which the trade unions and the parties of the Left had joined, amounted to a veritable 'crisis of civilization', a calling into question of the traditional values of France. A noble and austere man, he vacillated, possibly for the first time in his life. He disappeared, but he did so to think. On 30 May he returned to Paris and then announced a referendum inviting the nation's support. He was given it. Later he was to say: 'I recovered myself and I recovered France.'

MONKEY/METAL
(you were born in 1920 or 1980)

In the sky, coming from the West, drought grazed the skin of the earth and gave birth to Metal. Winds come from the faraway steppes, seeking the vital sap.

Characteristics of the Monkey/Metal
Metal is of the night, of the autumn and of cold. It symbolizes clarity, purity and firmness. Metal is decisive; it cuts through; its temperament is rigid and chaste; its remarks stinging. It oscillates between beauty and destruction. In other respects, it is expert at putting plans into effect. At harvest time it is the blade that gleans. Alas, too much rigour engenders sadness and moroseness.

The Monkey/Metal will often be unsatisfied. He will be apt to look for the impossible, the inaccessible, and will often be attracted to mysticism and have a tendency to shut himself off. Removing himself from the world and from life, he will suffer from his inability to deal with the day-to-day struggle. Paradoxically, the Monkey/Metal loves glittering success; he feels the desire to lead, supervise and control, and in these he is formidable. He is uncompromising, inflexible, sometimes even fanatical. The Metal Element will often be dangerous for the Monkey by enclosing him in a rigid armour and restraining him; sometimes imposing upon him a way of life, rules of conduct and ethics so that the Monkey will lose his freedom of movement, if not his liberty. This is a kind of straitjacket in which he may suffer and be destroyed.

Health of the Monkey/Metal
Metal's organ is the lungs, their flavour is pungent. Since summits of all kinds attract you, take to mountain climbing. But above all, control your breathing; it is the key to your equilibrium.

The Monkey/Metal and others

The Monkey/Metal will aim for high positions and great responsibilities, but he will need diversity and innovation in his work. He will not tolerate the routine of the daily grind. He will be an inventor, but the Monkey's imagination will often be subordinate to rigour and severity. Mixing the exigent with the meticulous, he will have a tendency to make abrupt decisions. Rather stiffnecked and obstinate for a Monkey, he will not accept compromises easily.

The Monkey/Metal may be a remarkable man of law, whether a judge or practising lawyer — but he will be neither obliging nor flexible. He will apply the law, statute or article strictly. He often behaves in an enigmatic and closed manner: besides his repugnance for explaining and justifying himself, he is prompted by a constant desire to stand apart and to be different, from which comes a taste for solitude and some difficulty in communicating with his fellows.

Advice for the Monkey/Metal

You suffer from your isolation and your narrow-mindedness, so make an effort to come down to earth; soften your judgements and burst open the iron collar of your prejudices. Rules that are too austere generate anguish and disorder.

A Monkey/Metal year

The culminating point for a Monkey/Metal year will be autumn. The Yin tendency of the midseason will balance the Yang of the Monkey, encouraging tolerance and moderation.

This year will be the symbol of openness and flexibility, so lay down your arms, soften your movements and round off the corners; freedom of gesture and of heart will bring you a breath of fresh air.

Do not prevent yourself from breathing freely because you wish to demonstrate your self-control; you will only reveal your narrow-mindedness when great liberation is within your reach.

Historical example of a Monkey/Metal year 1260

The idea of universality in human affairs still held good in the late thirteenth century. The Papacy was still infused with the concept of a Christian dominion; the Angevins sought to dominate the Mediterranean world and aspired to the conquest of the Byzantine Empire; the Mongol Empire attained its apogee with the reign of Koubilai, who assumed the throne in 1260, thirty-three years after the death of Ghenghis Khan. Tibet had been absorbed and the armies of Batou had penetrated Finland. Hougalou, the brother of Koubilai, captured and sacked Baghdad and asserted his dominion.

Yet Koubilai brought order and prosperity, even an apparent stability, to his immense empire. He was a great administrator and capable of valuable innovations. He understood about cities, a priceless asset for his subjects in the West; and not only did he organize their development, he also arranged for their citizens the human necessities of urban life. He introduced paper money, a remarkable experiment for his day, built hospitals, and funded care for the sick and the poor. He opened schools and established a national alphabet. On a scale almost equal to the Romans he constructed roads and canals throughout his empire. He also paid his armies on a regular basis, thus securing their obedience while restraining their greed. Since his administration was orderly it was accepted as just, and his levies were carefully related to the income of his subjects rather than to their capital wealth.

Marco Polo, reporting on these aspects of Koubilai's empire to the Venetians, is said to have been met by a total incredulity: the sophisticated Venetians could not understand how 'barbarian hordes' could so rapidly absorb the elements of an ancient civilization. Yet the Normans had already done so a century before in their Kingdom of Sicily.

Analogical Table
of the Different Elements

Elements	Wood	Fire	Earth	Metal	Water
Years ending in	4 and 5	6 and 7	8 and 9	0 and 1	2 and 3
Colours	Green	Red	Yellow	White	Blue
Seasons	Spring	Summer	End of summer	Autumn	Winter
Climates	Wind	Heat	Humid	Dry	Cold
Flavours	Acid	Bitter	Sweet	Pungent	Salty
Principal organ	Liver	Heart	Spleen	Lungs	Kidneys
Secondary organ	Gallbladder	Small intestine	Stomach	Large intestine	Bladder
Food	Wheat, poultry	Rice, lamb	Corn, beef	Oats, horse	Peas, pork

Table of Harmony
Between the Elements

		Wood Female	Fire Female	Earth Female	Metal Female	Water Female
○○○ Excellent prosperity	Male Wood	● ●	○	○○○	○	○○
○○ Good harmony, understanding	Male Fire	○	○	○○	●	● ●
○ Effort needed	Male Earth	● ●	○○	○○	○○○	●
● Rivalries and problems of reciprocal domination	Male Metal	○	● ●	●	● ●	○○○
● ● Misunderstanding and incomprehension	Male Water	○○	● ●	●	○○○	○

THE
FOUR SEASONS
OF
THE MONKEY

四季

If you were born in spring

Monkey/Aries

It is good for a Monkey to be born under the sign of Aries, just as it is good for an Aries to be born in a Monkey year. However, those born under the sign of Aries are sometimes too frank and too instinctive. They have a tendency to rush into things whatever the visibility, without taking heed of the weather forecast. The Monkey is crafty and intelligent; he never loses sight of his best interests. His opportunism will lend increased efficiency to the active Aries and the latter will endow the Monkey with a basic honesty, for which his friends can only be thankful.

The Monkey/Aries is capable of making total use of the many resources of these two emblematic animals. A born fighter — at times skilful and diplomatic, at others taking dangerous risks in order to impress his public — he is extremely resourceful in business, capable of keeping several irons in the fire at the same time and carrying on several conversations simultaneously. He has a good memory and will not make the same mistake more than once. He is brilliant, direct and seductive. He is courageous and has a flair for recognizing and assessing danger; he is a strategist as well as a fighter.

Monkey/Taurus

This Monkey is a far cry from a marmoset; he is, rather, a member of the gorilla or orangoutang species. For a Monkey he is slow and reflective. He is also sentimental and capable of covering up his escapades with the help of some pious lies; when he lies, it is with the best intentions in the world. The Monkey and Taurus both have a good business sense, and their alliance will strengthen it considerably. It also strengthens his memory, while diminishing a tendency towards fantasy and the dispersion of energies.

The Monkey/Taurus is sociable and enjoys life. He is a born possessor: as soon as he sees something which pleases him, he wants to have it. If he does not get what he wants through his work, he will exploit his cleverness, ready to bend the rules a little. In any case, he will lack for nothing. He is as gifted at earning money as he is at spending it; he will not let his gold lie in a bank vault. He could be a broker or a brilliant speculator. Endowed with a practical and constructive intelligence, he has the capacity to deepen his knowledge and put it to good use. On the emotional level, he will do well to marry an heiress.

Monkey/Gemini

We have seen how delicate a task it is to find analogies between the Western and the Chinese zodiacs. With perhaps one other exception, the Monkey and Gemini are so alike that one could be mistaken for the other. This alliance therefore represents the 'pure Monkey' or the 'pure Gemini'. All of his qualities and defects are magnified: he is remarkably intelligent (if you meet an illiterate Monkey/Gemini, take him immediately to have an IQ test — you may be rendering society a great service), high-spirited, eclectic, quick-witted, resourceful and eloquent. He is also nervous, unstable, flighty, lacks perseverance and concentration and is often flying off in several directions at once.

If you fall in love with a male or female Monkey/Gemini, try to tolerate their escapades: their passions never last. And you will be repaid in a few years . because the Monkey/Gemini becomes the most charming, liveliest and youthful of old people.

If you were born in summer
Monkey/Cancer

The Monkey's activity is, as a general rule, essentially mental; that of Cancer, emotional. The former experiences only surface emotions; the second feels deeply. The individual who has within himself these contradictory tendencies — if he is not a genius, and that is a rare breed — may feel himself to be like an animal derived from two different species.

It is important to the Monkey/Cancer that he control his life rather than submit to it. In the latter case, he will become a wanderer, unstable and suffering from his instability, always frustrated emotionally and a bit of an obsessive liar. In the former case, on the other hand, the Monkey/Cancer, if he adapts himself to the possibility of making use of the qualities of the two signs, will not allow himself to be overcome by hypersensitivity and will retain the perspective necessary to have a healthy view of life. He will then succeed in his professional life without making too many enemies (thanks to the soothing influence of Cancer), and be capable of a successful love-life, and even fidelity, something difficult for all Monkeys.

Monkey/Leo

Except for his appearance, he is a savage baboon. To understand this, look at the monkeys in a zoo. You will see that they are formidable, having long, sharp teeth over which they draw back the lips of a wild animal. They do not hesitate to attack and appear to take themselves with the utmost seriousness. The Monkey/Leo is the same. It is inadvisable to pull his mane, and before starting a discussion with him it is best to prepare one's arguments carefully and to refresh one's knowledge of the Classics. Address him formally and assume a respectful air when approaching him; and, naturally, avoid contradicting him, as he will not take this lightly. The Monkey/Leo seems physically large, even if he is actually quite short and slim. You can be sure that he has the means to get what he wants; he is cultivated, brilliant and exceedingly well-informed. His vital energy equals his vivacity of mind: he is both head and feet.

Monkey/Virgo

Here, nervousness is the dominating factor. Deep inside himself the Monkey/Virgo is in turmoil, but he forces himself to present an outwardly stable appearance and to keep solid control of himself. This constant battle to maintain his equilibrium is as fatiguing as the twelve tasks of Hercules. He is not particularly malleable; in fact, he is as taut as a violin string. In him, perfectionism and fantasy, the strictest honesty and the wildest tricks confront each other constantly. He may have unsuspected reactions, sometimes prudish and moralizing, at others imaginative and provoking.

The positive side of this alliance is his kindness. The Monkey is sociable and has an engaging manner; he helps Virgo to overcome his timidity and to forget the small bag of complexes that he has dragged along with him since childhood. Virgo's feeling of inferiority and the Monkey's sense of superiority create an equilibrium in which Virgo's qualities of devotion can be seen to their greatest practical advantage. To sum up, the Monkey/Virgo, although often ill-at-ease, is perhaps the least dangerous to love, all the more because he has an excellent understanding of reality and is a capable and lucid worker.

If you were born in autumn
Monkey/Libra

A lengthy and thorough search among all of the combinations of the Eastern and Western astrologies will not reveal an alliance as sociable as the Monkey/Libra. He is an open, amiable, engaging and eloquent individual who is never more at ease than in the role of intermediary or of public relations consultant. In his hands the worst conflicts are always resolved. This he does, almost before you can look twice at him, with a few engaging words and a good deal of conciliation. One can well imagine him discoursing on world peace or walking about waving a banner inscribed, 'Come to me, I will arrange everything.' And it is true that he has a gift for arranging things. Behind a lighthearted and somewhat offhand exterior, he is humane, alert and available.

Of course he has his faults, but they are not big ones. This Monkey is very easy to live with. One piece of advice however: if you do not like background noise, buy ear plugs, for he never stops talking — about everything and nothing.

Monkey/Scorpio

As with the Monkey/Virgo, nervousness dominates, but here it is deeper. The Monkey/Scorpio is in a state of permanent anxiety and poses questions about everything and everybody. He surprises with his cynical attitude, his sombre side, which will suddenly explode into a thousand particles of fantasy. He is an intelligent being of foolproof lucidity who, when caught up in an activity or an emotion, always gives the impression that he is playing in a tragicomedy in which he is both actor and spectator.

The Monkey/Scorpio is gifted with an unlimited curiosity and a remarkable capacity for assimilation. Everything that is hidden, mysterious or complicated interests him. He would make a fine detective, an implacable and wily strategist, knowing in advance the tactics which could be turned to account: there should always be a Monkey/Scorpio in government to foresee and analyse the methods of the opposition. A piece of advice if you love him: buy a bulletproof vest; you will need it to survive his stings. It is not that he is disagreeable, but he cannot keep from criticizing and taking things apart just 'to see'.

Monkey/Sagittarius

This is an excellent alliance for a politician, a diplomat, or, better still, an ambassador. More modestly, careers such as those in a large-scale commercial undertaking are favourable. The Monkey/Sagittarius has good sense, lucidity tempered by a good nature, a perspicacity moderated by indulgence. Who can ask for more? Besides, he asks fewer questions than other Monkeys, being more intent on realizing his ambitions. Extremely sociable, but none too selective, he never feels so at home as when in the middle of a talkative and excited group. Interest the Monkey/Sagittarius in tourism, and in no time he will have trailing behind him a group of top businessmen out on a spree.

Very easy to live with for those who resemble him, he is frantically independent and has a strong predilection for action. On the other hand, if you are a sensitive, sentimental little thing, avoid him like the Plague: you will break your gold teeth on him. In fact, it is absolutely impossible to attach this Monkey to his perch. He needs wide-open windows in order to be happy.

If you were born in winter
Monkey/Capricorn
Those born under the sign of the Monkey are not simple people. If Capricorn is added, such a special cocktail is made that, even in noting down all the ingredients, it would be difficult to make it again. If it is Capricorn who dominates, his rigid influence risks freezing the Monkey into a sort of stereotyped fantasy. If the Monkey is the stronger there results a social — albeit tremendously selective — individual, excessively observant, uneasy, distrustful and nervous: in equal measure he is intelligent and, without repudiating his real nature, adaptable.

His behaviour can alternate between icy immobility and feverish activity. His attitude towards money is ambiguous: times he is sordidly avaricious, at others he throws money out of the window. In fact, he is hopeless about finding himself, knowing who he is or creating his own unity. He is, in general, more balanced in maturity than in adolescence: like wine, he grows better with age. He lacks neither courage nor ability, but his unconcerned, even unfeeling, appearance discourages some people.

Monkey/Aquarius
The Monkey/Aquarius is endowed with a remarkable ingenuity and an inventiveness without equal. He has something about him of the sorcerer's apprentice and of the hypnotizer; or the scholar or scientist who is unappreciated because he is ahead of his time. As a child, it is the Monkey/Aquarius who terrorizes his neighbourhood with barbarous

devices and regularly detonates 'bombs' in the cellar of the house. But do not dismiss him completely: under his roguish little face smeared with soot may lie the brain of an Einstein. With him, however, the end result is unpredictable: with his agile fingers he will create either a rocket or a wire to cut butter. Give him the benefit of the doubt.

Charming, pleasant, somewhat absentminded but always ready to listen to confidences, the Monkey/Aquarius is an agreeable companion, but not of much help if you are in need of security. Basically, he needs too much reassurance himself to be able to reasssure others. He is an investigator, but to be effective he needs, as do all investigators, materials, recognition and three meals a day. He is an intellectual, not a businessman. Like the road to hell, his is paved with good intentions.

Monkey/Pisces

Elusive, floating here and there, slipping cunningly through the mesh of a net, here is the delicious Monkey/Pisces. He is utterly charming, persuasive and adaptable to an incredible degree; parachuted into high society, he will seem to be as at ease there as in a Ukrainian farm or a colony of penguins. He knows instinctively how to adopt the language suited to the occasion and the attitude required; he is a chameleon. Do not forget that the Monkey is an animal with a remarkable gift for imitation. The supple Pisces amplifies this tendency which comes close to mimicry. The Monkey/Pisces often loses his way. He is a specialist in unanswerable questions and metaphysical interrogations. It would not take much for him to forget to eat.

The Monkey/Pisces is a willing helper, but he is careful to guard his own little world. He hates to be confined, so, if you want to keep him, buy him a pretty cage — with the door left open — or, even better, an aquarium opening into the sea. He will reappear regularly, flapping his fins, and perhaps he will bring you the treasure from a sunken galleon — or an old shoe. He is so very unpredictable!

THE
I CHING

易经

THE I CHING AND THE MONKEY

In the I Ching game, you ask a question and you obtain an answer. It is therefore a divining game. But the question you ask is posed through your Monkey identity; the wheels, the complex mechanism of your mind and spirit, begin to turn. You ask a Monkey question and the I Ching answers with a Monkey 'solution', on which you then meditate as a Monkey before arriving at a Monkey conclusion.

The player is presented with a hexagram which contains the 'hypothesis-response' to his question, or, more exactly, a synthesis of forces affecting the concern or event inquired about.

For you, Master Monkey, here are the sixty-four hexagrams of the I Ching and sixty-four Monkey hypotheses.

How to proceed
1. The question
Ask a question regarding any problem at all, past, present or future, personally concerning you. (If the question concerns a friend, consult the I Ching game in the book corresponding to his Chinese sign.)

2. Method of play
It must be done with concentration.
Take **three ordinary and similar coins** — for example, three 50p coins.
Heads will equal the number 3.
Tails will equal the number 2.
Throw the coins.
If the result is two coins showing Heads and one Tails, write 3 + 3 + 2. You thus obtain a total of 8 which you represent by a continuous line: ━━━ .
Draw the same continuous line if you have three coins showing Heads (3 + 3 + 3 = 9).

If you throw two coins showing Tails and one Heads (2 + 2 + 3 = 7), or all three showing Tails (2 + 2 + 2 = 6), draw two separate lines: ▬ ▬

To sum up, 8 and 9 correspond to: ▬▬▬ (Yin)

6 and 7 correspond to: ▬ ▬ (Yang)

Repeat this operation *six times*, noting at the time of each throw the figure obtained on a piece of paper, proceeding from the first to the sixth figure, from bottom to top.

The final result, including a trigram from the bottom, or lower trigram (example:), and a trigram of the top, or upper trigram (example: ▬ ▬), will be a hexagram of the I Ching. In our example this would look like:

Now merely look for the hexagram number in the table on page 704, and then consult the list of hexagrams with their descriptions to find the given answer. *In our example,* the hexagram obtained is number 63, entitled **After completion.**

THE HEXAGRAMS OF THE MONKEY

CH'IEN

1 *The creative:* Energy, strength and will. Monkey of the irrational, often immune to reality, you will need much patience and tenacity to carry out your projects.

K'UN

2 *The receptive:* Do not neglect or scorn your tools; let them guide your hand; follow your intuition.

CHUN

3 *The initial difficulty:* Practise introspection. Listen to what lies deep within you; you will thus lift the veil of confusion.

MÊNG

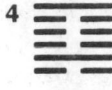

4 *Youthful folly:* 'It is not I who seek the young fool but the young fool who seeks me.' You who hold masters in contempt, do not set yourself up as a master. In order to eliminate danger, it is not enough simply to deny it.

HSÜ

5 *Waiting:* Difficult for a Monkey who cannot stand still; you must, however, be resigned and know how to make the best of it.

SUNG

6 *Conflict:* Try to reach an amicable arrangement. This way of going about things agrees much more with your nature than do quarrels and confrontations.

Table of Hexagrams

Trigrams	Upper lines ☰	☷	☳
Lower lines			
☰	1	11	34
☷	12	2	16
☳	25	24	51
☵	6	7	40
☶	33	15	62
☴	44	46	32
☲	13	36	55
☱	10	19	54

Use this table to find the number of your hexagrams. The meeting point between the lower and upper trigrams indicates the number of the hexagram that you are seeking.

5	26	9	14	43
8	23	20	35	45
3	27	42	21	17
29	4	59	64	47
39	52	53	56	31
48	18	57	50	28
63	22	37	30	49
60	41	61	38	58

SHIH

7 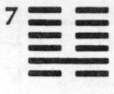 *The army:* A little discipline never harmed anyone. In any case, the Monkey is skilled in the art of getting round the rules and using them to his own advantage.

PI

8  *Holding together (union):* You will only win through unity. Your true power lies in your capacity for bringing people together.

SHIAO CH'U

9  *The taming power of the small:* Little streams make big rivers. Neglect no detail. The stream's murmur is sometimes enough to launch an avalanche.

LÜ

10  *Treading:* 'Tread on the tail of thé Tiger, he does not bite man.' The king Monkey will not allow himself to be intimidated; however, pirouettes and tricks are indispensable to him.

T'AI

11  *Peace:* Accept the harmony of contraries. The Yin and Yang Monkey should understand the principle of alternation, but neither seek to explain it nor confine it within a cast-iron rational structure.

P'I

12  *Standstill:* Even if it is painful for you; it will be a wise counsellor. Before jumping onto a branch, make sure that it is not rotten.

T'UNG JÊN

13  *Fellowship with men:* The Monkey understands this very well, but not necessarily in broad daylight, as advised by the I Ching. Beware of schemes, deceptive intrigues and obscure sidestreets.

TAYU

14  *Possession in great measure:* Possession is only a means and not an end. The Monkey prefers to eat the fruit rather than to help it grow.

CH'IEN

15  *Modesty:* Symbol of moderation, equilibrium, stability. Difficult for the Monkey who is perpetually agitated. His agility should serve the equitable.

YÜ

16 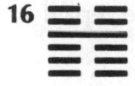 *Enthusiasm:* You have the gift of gab, but the day always comes when the magician must explain his tricks — even if he loses some of his prestige and mystery.

SUI

17  *Following:* Thanks to your seductive charm, you have entered the queen's orchard. But do not misuse this charm: it will not extricate you from perilous or ambiguous situations forever.

KU

18  *Work on what has been spoiled:* If you sometimes vent a devious wit, at least do not indulge your pleasantries so far as to provoke a breach; you could be the first victim.

LIN

19  *Approach:* According to the principle of alternation, today's good fortune is likely to turn against you tomorrow.

KUAN

20 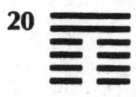 *Contemplation:* The Monkey likes to climb to the tops of trees or to the summit of a mountain less to appreciate the landscape than to be conspicuous and visible from afar. Take care: you are a marvellous target.

SHIH HO

21 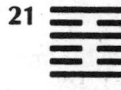 *Biting through (or clearly defined penalties):* Become a little like a gorilla: sharpen your cutting teeth in preparation. The lie is familiar to you, but its consequences may be fatal.

PI

22 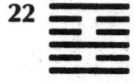 *Grace:* You possess many gift-wrapped presents; do not hesitate to offer them. Your gifts — abstract or material — will be repaid a hundred times over.

PO

23 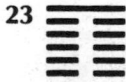 *Splitting apart:* Despite a taste for risk, do not install yourself in a castle whose walls threaten to collapse.

FU

24 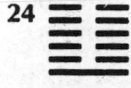 *Return — the turning point:* The prodigal Monkey. After the shadows comes light. Know how to turn back before going too far.

WU WANG

25  *Innocence:* It is not exactly your outstanding virtue, however, you will need it. Avoid devious schemes and complicated calculations.

TA CH'U

 26 *The taming power of the great:* Power and success, on condition that you know how to renew your character. The Monkey will be in his element: everything should smile on him.

I

 27 *The corners of the mouth:* Mentally, the Monkey is forever hungry. But, like the boa, his digestive capacity is prodigious — happily for him, since his appetite is limitless.

TA KUO

 28 *Preponderance of the great:* To leap correctly from branch to branch, you must feel free in your movements. So, do not take on too much, even to amaze the audience.

K'AN

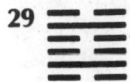 29 *The fathomless water:* It laps all around you. Be vigilant, and remember that the straightest route is always the shortest.

LI

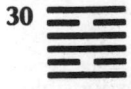 30 *The clinging, fire:* Prestige, fortune and power are illusory golden prisons: it is better to avoid such enclosures than to be reduced to looking feverishly for the key.

HSIEN

 31 *Influence:* You exercise a certain fascination, and in conversation easily cast a spell on those with you. Take advantage of this to win new adherents, renew commitments and strengthen alliances. Everything depends on your powers of persuasion.

HÊNG

32 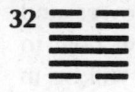 *Duration:* You who are lucid should first of all be lucid about yourself; in this way you will avoid becoming too set in your ways and obtain better results. Even your charm will be more effective.

TUN

33  *Retreat:* Should be done quietly, without constraint or any feeling of impotence or guilt. It is a veritable art, sometimes a master stroke which represents an enormous victory.

TA CHUANG

34 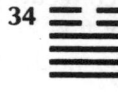 *The power of the great:* Although you are extremely flexible and agile — the symbol of perpetual movement — it is in your interest to place a safety net beneath you before you jump; without it, the void may swallow you up.

CHIN

35 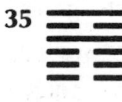 *Progress:* You are going to be able to make use of your gifts in broad daylight, but do not refuse to share the glory with your collaborators for fear they may eclipse you.

MING I

36 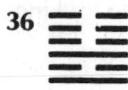 *Darkening of the light:* Being solely responsible, you must seek the cause within yourself. Light the candles or wait for dawn, but do not count on outside help; no one is going to bring you a light bulb.

CHIA JÊN

37 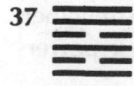 *The family:* The Monkey has a rather patriarchal view of the family: he has to assume all of the duties, and also all of the obligations.

K'UEI

38  *Opposition:* You often speak of tolerance and harmony; bring these words from your heart and remember that reconciliations are always possible.

CHIEN

39 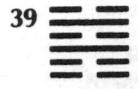 *Obstruction:* Or the courage to face an ordeal. You can obtain some pleasure from this by proving that nothing can stop you; but do not overestimate your strength; do not tempt the devil.

HSIEH

40  *Deliverance:* After the thorns, here, at last, are the flowers! Take advantage of this to relax and wholeheartedly enjoy the harmony.

SUN

41 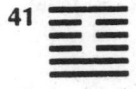 *Decrease:* The Monkey does not relish hard times. He will, however, know how to cheer himself up with superfluous and charming little nothings. Graceful and artistic poverty suits him better than boring and routine comfort. He will always enjoy a candlelit dinner, even though the plates are bare.

I

42 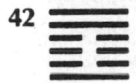 *Increase:* You are going to be forced to be opportunistic. How else can you blossom? You will not be told twice.

KUAI

43  *Breakthrough:* The curtain is about to rise; make your entrance. The Monkey will take malicious pleasure in exposing error or causing scandal; he never hesitates to pour oil on the fire.

KOU

44 *Coming to meet:* Do not associate with the flawed; distrust still waters — they reflect a false image and often flatter an image of which you are the first to be taken in.

TS'UI

45 *Gathering together:* Get rid of the hangers-on and concentrate your available energies. New and fruitful ideas will be born from them.

SHÊNG

46  *Pushing upwards:* Even if you climb to the top of the mountain faster than anyone else, take time to pause and catch your breath in the resting places provided. Before leaving, do not forget to check your equipment carefully.

K'UN

47 *Oppression:* You are losing liveliness and tone. Instead of prancing up and down, take the opportunity to recuperate. But take care: do not pretend to have recovered your confidence if you remain depressed.

CHING

48 *The well:* There are times in which to turn everything upside down and to question everything, and others to put everything in its place and restore order. Do not rely on others to take responsibility; you alone know your real needs.

KO

49 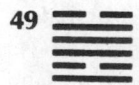 *Revolution:* It has its place in the indispensable cycle of alternation, and sometimes its logic proves inescapable; but do not make a dogma of it, for it will turn against you.

TING

 **50** *The cauldron:* Symbol of all five Elements — Earth, Wood, Fire, Water and Metal. Nourishment for the body and the mind. One must understand and respect the mysteries of this delicate alchemy.

CHÊN

 **51** *The arousing (shock, thunder):* The Monkey will know how to profit from ordeals; he has often emerged the victor, if at the price of executing some particularly acrobatic and painful pirouettes.

KÊN

 **52** *Keeping still:* Even though you need constant excitement and people around you, you will have to seek equilibrium in solitude and meditation. Accept reality; live for the present. Your inward commitment to things is the token of your success.

CHIEN

 **53** *Development (gradual progress):* As with the hare and the tortoise, it is enough to leave on time -- and useless to tread on the head of your competitor.

KUEI MEI

 **54** *The bride:* 'Fortune and happiness', the Monkey will declare. 'On condition', Prudence will reply.

FÊNG

 **55** *Abundance:* To gorge oneself on all the fruit from the orchard, while preparing for an imminent journey across the desert.

LÜ

56 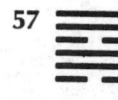 *The wanderer:* Very favourable to the Monkey, provided he abandons all ideas of conquest and gives serious thought to his destination. Take to the road; be free of ties and dependencies.

SUN

57  *The gentle:* Symbol of wind and clouds. The Monkey should feel at ease. He will insinuate himself, nip in and out everywhere; the least chink will suffice. He will end by surreptitiously triumphing over even the worst influences.

TUI

58  *The serene, the joyous:* It is the time for sharing and the joy it brings.

HUAN

59 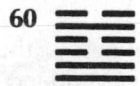 *Dissolution:* Conquer egotism. This promises to be a rough battle requiring an exceptionally ardent spirit.

CHIEH

60 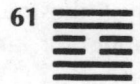 *Limitation:* This should be like a dressing on a wound. It is a technique, no more, but is better than gangrene, or amputation.

CHUNG FU

61 *Inner truth:* Your attitude alone should bear witness to it, so put away your suave words and cajoling airs.

HSIAO KUO

62 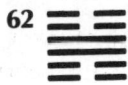 *Preponderance of the small:* Even though you dream of using extreme measures, you must content yourself with the options available to you at the moment. If shipwrecked — even if you have thrown a bottle into the sea — you should think seriously about how you are going to survive. Help does not fall from the sky.

CHI CHI

63  *After completion:* Maturity, plenitude, perfect equilibrium, but there is always a precipice nearby. If you leap, do not forget that you must yield to the laws of gravity.

WEI CHI

64 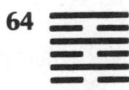 *Before completion:* Do not crown yourself nor proclaim yourself emperor, even if you sometimes take yourself for Napoleon.

YEAR OF THE ROOSTER

 1909 · 1921 · 1933
1945 · 1957 · 1969
1981 · 1993 · 2005

THE DOMAINS OF THE ROOSTER

十二生肖

THE ROOSTER
AND ITS SYMBOLISM

When one thinks of the Rooster, one symbol that comes to mind is the Gallic cock. However, this particular Rooster is a completely recent notion and possesses no mythological foundation, being only the warriorlike expression of an animal that represents the pride, daring and vigilance of the French soldier. Nevertheless, the Rooster found on the tops of monuments commemorating the dead has a tendency to evoke a creature of death and devastation and the memory and suffering of millions of men fallen in battle for their country.

The Rooster is above all a solar symbol, announcing the sun's rising with his morning song. In India he personifies solar energy; in Japan he incarnates the first manifestation of light; and in China he is designated by the character K, symbolizing the five virtues. He is a Rooster of good omen, favourable in his aspect and bearing, with his cockscomb giving him an air of authority. The way he carries his spurs symbolizes military virtue, the courage displayed during battles and his goodness, for the Rooster shares his food. Finally, he portrays confidence because of the assurance with which he greets the sunrise. All of which runs contrary to the aggressive and swaggering bird of popular imagery.

The Rooster is also the emblem of the hero and of the guardian and protector of life: is he not often at the top of buildings? Surmounting a weather vane, or roof, the Rooster is on the watch, looking down on men and scanning the horizon. In announcing the break of day he disperses ghosts and phantoms, the powers of illusion and darkness. He is the incarnation of the forces of youth, hope and clarity.

The following is from a 19th-century history of animals for young people and reflects the admiration with which the Rooster has been regarded for many centuries and in all civilizations:

'Rooster of proud bearing and sober walk, of a bold and

courageous character, Rooster distinguished by the fine lines of your body, by your plump blazing red crest, by the richness and the variety of your feathers, as well as by the agreeable contour of your tail feathers, your song is the clock of our countrysides, night and day. You are kind, obliging and attentive to your hens; you warn them of danger, call them to share with you your good fortune, generous to the point of foolishness. Alas, you are extremely jealous, and will suffer no rival. If your song is imitated, you become uneasy and alarmed, assemble your hens, protecting them assiduously. If you should fight another, you will do so courageously and until death rather than survive a shameful defeat . . . Sentinel, protector and guardian, you can be as dangerous and as wily as the worst rogue when it comes to protecting your own.'

With his mixture of conformity and eccentricity, aggressive impulses and meditative leanings, the Rooster is a rather strange and paradoxical animal. This captive king is a bizarre and contradictory creature, a ruler and a slave whose bravery and despotism are confined by the narrow limits of the farmyard. In this sense the Rooster is an analogy for the frailties of prestige and power, confined within the inevitable enclosure of time and death.

A few notes on the Rooster

Principal qualities: Honest, frank, obliging, courageous.

Principal defects: Vain, thoughtless, preoccupied with his appearance.

Work: Gives of himself completely. Tradition has it that he would find an earthworm in the desert.

Best role: Military hero or comic figure.

Worst role: Spy (he is too conspicuous).

Money: Very extravagant; he cannot resist temptation. His bank account often will be in the red.

Luck: He does not have much. All his life he will be forced to scratch the earth to find food. But if he is born in spring, he will be less of a braggart.

Cannot live without: Seducing. Admiring looks from others are a drug to him, even though he might not admit it.

Adores: From time to time to spend quiet holidays in an isolated and comfortable place.

Hates: Any attempt to probe his private being or expose his motives. In short, any attempt to lift his feathers to look underneath.

Leisure activities: Evenings spent socializing or reading.

Favourite places: He likes to have a corner of his own, decorated by him, where others can only enter by invitation. A kind of 'secret garden'.

Colour: Yellow.

Plants: Gentian; orange and palm trees.

Flowers: Sunflower, hawthorn.

Professions: Any commercial profession from salesman to sales director or sales representative; military officer; restaurant owner, hairdresser, public relations, farmer, aesthete, manicurist, teacher — and village cock!

The four ages in the life of the Rooster according to Chinese tradition

During his *childhood*, *youth* and *maturity*, the Rooster will often have problems and his life will be strewn with ups and downs. He will know the greatest joys and suffer the greatest sorrows; sometimes he will be rich, sometimes poor; sometimes he will be surrounded by friends, sometimes alone. But as soon as he attains emotional stability and becomes settled in a profession, his life will become calm. In any case, he will enjoy a happy *old age*.

THE PSYCHOLOGY OF THE ROOSTER

The personality of those born under the sign of the Rooster consists of three levels: *appearance*, *reality* and *emotion*. The first is so blinding that it often prevents us from the reaching the second, let alone the third.

According to tradition, Roosters are much above the common run of men. When one observes them — or rather when one has them before one's eyes, for they are hard to miss — one is struck first by their elegant gestures and rich colours. They are generally well-dressed, sometimes a bit ostentatiously. They like people to turn to look at them and they rarely pass unnoticed; their presence is unavoidable. Even a young Rooster wearing the strangest rags or patched blue jeans always leaves behind a half-admiring and half-irritated audience. Is it their aura? Their charm? This is hard to know.

These animals, whose role it is to announce the dawn, do not wish to be seen carelessly dressed. Some, more arrogant, even seem to think that the rising sun is simply obeying their cry. Scrupulous about their appearance, they become ruffled before others' lack of taste, and are never completely satisfied with their own warbling or plumage, even though they may seem to be sure of themselves.

Agreeable in society, easy and relaxed, wherever they may mingle, Roosters will be met with a cordial smile, be it in Buckingham Palace or a sitting room in a semi-detached in the suburbs. In either case, the hostess will find them charming and invite them back, which is why Roosters have a rather active social life.

Roosters are highly cultivated, and, beneath their light manner, are capable of serious conversation. Having read a great deal, they are knowledgeable and up-to-date on everything and possess an excellent memory. Yet, curiously, they rarely display their knowledge — as though they prefer to be judged by their famous feathers. Their crowning is an aspect of the second level, which we shall now look into.

Roosters only reveal themselves to their family and intimate friends, for they abhor being used as fodder for social conversations or as guinea pigs for amateur psychologists. Sooner or later one begins to question whether their superficiality is real or a game. The answer is that they conceal their inner selves with near desperation, obstinately camouflaging their lack of self-confidence and the fact that, at bottom, they are only fragile birds. What remains of a Rooster when one takes away his feathers and his cock-a-doodle-do? It is up to you to find out — he will not want to know.

Roosters are charming but sometimes difficult to live with, for they are very egocentric and completely preoccupied with their own needs, desires and longings. They serve themselves first — in all senses of the word — with total innocence and touching good faith. At table, if you are shocked to see them take the best morsels, they will reply angelically 'But it is only to see if it is good'.

Completely indifferent to the state of mind of others, they follow their own little route. In daily life they hate others to interfere in their affairs — and avoid interfering in those of others. If you pull at their feathers to tell them about a clogged sink or your baby having the measles, they will send you packing very brusquely indeed.

However, then comes the miracle which often makes these Roosters so adorable and appreciated — and with good reason. At the very moment when you hold in your arms your smallest child who is suffering from the flu, and your house has been flooded by a burst pipe, the Rooster will appear, stethoscope in one hand and plumbing tools in the other. With a charming smile he will arrange everything in a matter of minutes: your child will be sleeping peacefully, having been given the proper medicine, and your pipe will be mended. Roosters are extremely pleasant and obliging, especially in times of dire necessity. They love to be asked for help but do not like being asked direct questions about themselves.

Their greatest qualities are their honesty and frankness. Actually, they sometimes go too far! They say what they think with the delicacy of a bulldozer. They do not mean to hurt anyone's feelings, they simply think that it is helpful for you to know that your pudding is inedible or that your new hair style is a disaster. Mrs Rooster is even more guilty of this than the male, although she is almost always forgiven because everyone knows that she is not naturally malicious. So, although friendly, generous and charitable, Roosters cannot be counted on to be careful of the feelings of others. It is best to understand this from the start.

While loyal, sincere and capable of giving sensible advice, Roosters do not like to confide in others and prefer to solve their problems on their own. Their relationships thus lack give-and-take and confidence. Decidedly independent, they refuse to owe anything to anyone.

Roosters often seem original, even slightly eccentric, but at heart they are rather conforming. Although their rhythm of life is often unstable, their morality is as solid as a rock. They also give the impression of being adventurous, but in fact prize security, their home and their family. Yet in times of danger they are the most courageous and heroic persons in the Chinese zodiac.

As for the third level, we shall speak of their sensitivity, which is well hidden, even from themselves. Roosters fear their vulnerability, and, lest they be discovered, are distrustful and hide what they are feeling, preferring to appear insensitive. Most of the time they succeed, and are unhappy because of it. Sharing life with a Rooster is exciting, but not simple. They are gay, amusing, always ready for adventure and to discuss things. Understanding and available, and never appearing to be bored in your company, they often fall silent for a moment and then joke and change the subject. Be careful: although not on purpose, you have touched upon their secret garden. Perhaps one day they will open the door to you, but it is they who will choose the moment. If you try to force an entrance, you will only find a void, for if a Rooster does not wish to reveal something, he will make it invisible.

THE ROOSTER AS A CHILD

The young Rooster is alert, open and full of vivacity. Everything interests him, and, like his animal sign, he has a tendency to peck about from right to left, trying everything and spreading himself widely. Naturally gifted for many things, intelligent and curious, he likes to learn but has difficulty choosing. He often becomes passionate about a subject, takes a great deal of trouble to become knowledgeable about all aspects of it, and then becomes totally disinterested and passes on to something else with the same enthusiasm and intensity.

This 'touching on everything' side of the young Rooster deserves to be encouraged, for the knowledge he acquires might be useful later on. But the parents of a Rooster child must guide him in his choice of profession, which is not always simple for his capacities are extremely varied and, should he feel imprisoned in a field he finds dry and unrewarding, he will rebel and become discouraged. Invite your Rooster child to share your interests, open new horizons for him and travel with him — discovering new things enchants him. Encourage his hobbies, but do not become too excited if he reveals himself to be exceptionally gifted in something bizarre, since his enthusiasm may well be. short-lived.

Try to prepare him for a reasonable and stable profession and encourage him to persevere; he appreciates comfort and security and from a young age will respond to your practical arguments. Persuade him to earn a diploma or degree; with this in hand he can afford to sow his wild oats. The important thing is that he plan for his future and that his impractical tendencies are held in check.

Rooster children are charming, easy to live with and, whether boys or girls, often daredevils. They need to be independent: avoid asking too many questions and respect their secrets.

Although capable of adapting to a slightly rigid educational system, the Rooster cannot bear injustice: the sight of it can turn him into an absolute rebel. On the other hand he is always particularly nice with his brothers and sisters, and, as an elder brother or sister, he is ideal. He dislikes solitude and will blossom more readily in the centre of a large family, where he will delightedly play the role of the little chieftain, and will assist in educating the others, for he is a very well-organized child.

LOVE LIFE

Neither Mr nor Mrs Rooster lack charm and both are precocious. In adolescence, the young female Rooster trails a crowd of admirers behind her, whom she leads by the nose. There is no need to worry about her future, for she is reasonable and will almost always choose someone who is at the very least acceptable, or even brilliant, but in any case well able to support a family. She will adapt to married life with wisdom and humour. Mrs Rooster is sociable, communicative and very active. If she is a housewife, there is no doubt that she will be perfect; otherwise she will not care a fig about housework and will devote herself to her career. She is frank and honest, agreeable and gay, never conceals anything and will be faithful to her duty and true to her promises. She can be carried away by passion, but will never lose her footing or her head, for beneath a sometimes carefree and frivolous appearance, she has a keen sense of her responsibilities.

Mr Rooster is often a swaggering braggart. When young he collects conquests, rapidly discarding those who give in too quickly, for difficulty attracts and inspires him. He likes to have an entire hen house, with a well-organized hierarchy, at his disposal. Like a sultan and his harem, he will have 'favourite' and 'regular' girlfriends — and others kept in reserve. His fidelity is completely relative. Certainly he is faithful, but to several women at a time.

Roosters are not always easy to live with for they jealously protect their independence and refuse to allow interference. Tradition has it that they make better friends than lovers because their off-hand manner and sometimes outrageous frankness causes those who love them to suffer.

They are, however, jealous, and this is true of both the males and females. They hate to be supplanted by a rival, but take care not to show it for they dislike displaying their deeper emotions. They are often mistakenly thought to be indifferent.

One piece of advice if you are in love with a Rooster: do not overwhelm him or her with devouring passion nor insist on conversation. They adore long philosophic discussions, provided they are not personally nor directly involved. They are extremely sensual and greedy on all levels.

FAMILY LIFE

Although relaxed and whimsical in appearance, Roosters are aware of their familial responsibilities, and when they have made a commitment on this level, they keep it. At bottom they are conformists, endowed with an impeccable moral sense, and respect conventions from the moment they choose family life. They can live the joyously irregular life of a dashing bachelor and then change to a married life that is perfectly peaceful and well-organized.

They are usually against divorce and try to avoid it — but if there is a total breakdown of understanding, they will accept it, for they are too frank to live hypocritically.

Roosters are firm yet warm parents, and their children will never want for anything. However, the children, especially if they are sensitive, could suffer from the independence of their Rooster parents, who egotistically, will rarely sacrifice their personal pleasures for the needs of their offspring. This is unconscious on the Roosters' part; they have clear consciences and hardly ever suffer from guilt. Their aim is to give their family the essentials — but no more. On the other hand, if a family member is in trouble or if the family security is threatened, they become generous, courageous and will not lose their heads, whatever difficulties they must contend with.

Rat, Rabbit or Dog children — who have a need to be pampered — will feel misunderstood and resent their

Rooster parent. Ox, Goat and Pig children will submit to discipline without too much difficulty. But there will be trouble with Tigers, Dragons and Horses, all of whom will systematically refuse to bend to the will of the Rooster, who will consequently often lose some of his feathers. Monkey and Snake children will reap many rewards from their Rooster parent, for communication will be open and continuous. The rest will have to rely on being philosophic.

PROFESSIONAL LIFE

Roosters can succeed in all professions that demand self-assurance, nerve and brilliance. Intelligent and skilful, they know how to convince and persuade others. Their taste for comfort and security encourages their desire for a good salary and their appreciation of efficiency and practicality, but they dislike routine, and prefer independence to subordinate positions.

This is why Roosters do so well in the acting profession, where they can behave like strutting peacocks; and in positions which involve travelling and in which their qualities will be recognized.

Roosters generally prefer to impose their own self-discipline rather than submit to outside demands, but they are conscientious. They are reasonably ambitious, yet prefer to become department heads and maintain their sanity, rather than managing directors and risk a heart attack. Thanks to a harmonious mixture of perseverence, frankness and energy, they rise easily in the social scale. They are both appreciated and feared for their stony sincerity and their systematic refusal to take catastrophies seriously — at least in appearance; their smile is their best weapon, but there are occasions when it is uncalled for.

Many Roosters have an unstable working life, changing jobs according to their dreams and not worrying too much about the future. Only the dependence of their family will have a truly stabilizing effect on them, and only their moral responsibilities to their family will keep them from being short-sighted and unreasonable. Unlike Rabbits, they face extreme situations more easily than small obstacles. Impressionable beneath their cool and sure exterior, they sometimes get lost in details, forgetting the essentials. It is useless to intervene: they prefer to handle their problems on their own.

In their work they are highly organized, even meticulous, and become furious when someone moves their papers; but they are enthusiastic and face difficulties with a smiling courage that is unequalled in the Chinese zodiac. They are quite dashing!

MATERIAL LIFE

If you are married to a Rooster, one piece of advice: earn your own money and keep your own accounts because Roosters are incapable of organizing a budget and are real spendthrifts. They simply love to spend money, first on themselves (believing that charity begins at home) and then on their families. The only exceptions are those Roosters who suffered from poverty in their early lives.

Paradoxically, Roosters can be extremely stingy if out with friends whom they consider able to pay. If you invite Mrs Rooster to dinner because you find her attractive, do not expect her to offer to share the bill; but with girlfriends, she will be spontaneous and generous. Roosters' bank accounts are often in the red, or about to become so. This, however, does not bother them very much. Financial power does not interest them in the least: they only want to satisfy their needs and not have to deprive themselves. The hoarders among the Rats or Ox's would do well to imitate this healthy philosophy. Whether a Rooster must be careful of what he spends, or whether he spends without thinking of tomorrow, he has the same relaxed attitude. Roosters possess the wisdom to take life as it comes.

ENVIRONMENT

It is not uncommon for a Rooster to claim that he can sleep anywhere, adapt himself to any climate and dress in any old way. However, in his daily life he is likely to take at least two showers a day, and spend a great part of his free time buying new gadgets for his home in order to make it more comfortable.

He is a good example of the ambivalence of those born under this sign: capable of having the wildest fantasies on holiday, he will be maniacal and finicky at home. A Rooster's home is harmonious and comfortable, with simple but expensive objects, soft sofas and well-organized cupboards.

It must not be forgotten, however, that Roosters are adaptable, which helps them to feel fine anywhere. They are sensitive to anything pretty or agreeable, are smiling and at ease, and are able to create a special universe around themselves. They rarely feel out of their element, except when faced with ostentation or filth. If you lack imagination or the taste for interior decorating, ask a Rooster friend over — he will change your objects around, move the furniture and help you choose or change your colour scheme.

A guide to relations with a Rooster
Methods of seduction:

He: Courts you in three stages. He puts everything into the first stage — amazing, stunning, impressing and exciting you. In the second stage he will try to make himself indispensable to you. And finally, the third stage — must be censored.

She: Is flirtatious and has a free and easy manner. You may think that you are the one and only, but beware! In any case, you will have to show your credentials — and they had better be impressive — before she makes up her mind.

If he loves you: There will be great romantic moments in the style of 'I never thought such complete understanding to be possible'. Take care, however, that you share interests and responsibilities. Be exceptional, or you will find yourself imprisoned in a hen-house and lost in the crowd, for the Rooster is not faithful by nature and quickly resumes his old habits.

He expects of you: That you be his accomplice and that you speak or remain silent depending on his mood. This requires some training.

To keep you: He will make as few concessions as possible — just enough to keep you from throwing a plate at him.

If he is unfaithful: He will be very lordly indeed, and she will play the great lady: 'But, have you forgotten? I told you that you were perfectly free to do as you wished.'

In case of a break between you: He, or she, will remain a faithful friend and will not hold a grudge.

If you wish to give him a gift: It is the feeling that counts, so you can buy clothes or anything for the house and not make an embarrassing mistake. Not something too expensive, because then he will feel obliged to do the same and may dislike this. Think of the gift as merely a gesture — something bought on a trip, for example, which you can tell him cost practically nothing; he will be comfortable and happy that you thought of him.

If you want to seduce him: Tell him not only how handsome he is, but how intelligent and profound!

If you want to get rid of him: Suggest sweetly that it might be a good idea to see a psychoanalyst!

THE ROOSTER AND THE OTHER CHINESE SIGNS

Rooster/Rat

One always fears that the Rat sees only the defects of the Rooster and becomes hypnotized by them. Then and there he will refuse to engage with this individual, so horribly sure of himself, and will pronouce him vain and superficial.

If the Rat takes the trouble to delve beneath appearances, he will discover qualities in the Rooster which please him. Once they get together, they will merrily criticize their circle of friends and acquaintances.

On the other hand, if they should turn their aggressions and their critical capacities against each other, a real boxing match will develop. Then, too, neither of them has any idea of economy. They would become broke and ruin each other in no time, at first with gifts and then with lawsuits.

A combination of a male Rat and female Rooster works better, because the female Rooster is level-headed and knows how to handle day-to-day life, even though it irritates her. If it is the Rat who is female, they will do well to open a shop for cut-rate goods, hire an amiable sales-girl and contrive not to eat up all their capital.

Rooster/Ox

No problems here! The Ox will allow the Rooster to shine in peace, and will be aware of the useful and important role that a sociable spouse can play in his life, since he is so often accused of being too grave and taciturn. Both need freedom, and therefore easily understand each other's need for it. The Rooster likes to sing in peace, and will willingly leave the Ox to organize their daily life. Also, despite his flamboyant nature, the Rooster has a conformist and reasonable side. It is in these latter aspects that he will find most harmony with his Ox spouse.

Obviously, sometimes there will be friction. For example when Mr Rooster unexpectedly brings home a whole carload of friends for dinner; or when the Ox — male or female — sharply criticizes the Rooster in front of friends.

At work the Ox and the Rooster will get along in a highly profitable way. But it must be the Ox who manages the enterprise, while the Rooster takes care of public relations.

Rooster/Tiger

Here, good understanding will not be easy. Although sensitive and loyal, the Tiger is not noted for his reflective abilities. He is neither subtle nor discerning; he judges others by their behaviour, their acts, and even by their reputations. It is their appearance which counts, not their spiritual meanderings. But the Rooster cannot be judged solely by his appearance: it is too elaborate and too brilliant, and one could easily believe that nothing lies behind it.

In the beginning, everything will go well. The Tiger will be flattered by the personality of his fine-feathered Rooster, while the latter will sincerely admire the Tiger's courage. Very quickly, however, the little boasts of the Rooster will irritate his companion, who will not hesitate to criticize. No Rooster can tolerate being constantly reproved, and he will feel himself misunderstood and treated unjustly. He will rapidly set out to seek a more indulgent companion, but, before leaving, he will tell the Tiger a few home truths; he values his reputation for frankness.

These two can be associates, friends or even lovers, but not for long. Essentially, they are not at all on the same wave-length.

Rooster/Rabbit

Whether their relationship is based on friendship, love or professional ties, this duo often risks ending in a fist fight. In fact, no Rabbit has the patience needed to endure the swaggerings and boastings of the Rooster, who often exaggerates — most of the time without reason — just to amuse himself or to see how people react.

The usually patient and peaceful Rabbit will watch his tolerance evaporate quickly. The Rooster makes him literally boil, and our Rabbit cannot stop himself from wanting to snatch at some of the Rooster's feathers in order to diminish his vanity. The Rooster, who actually has no bad intentions, will see the Rabbit's attitude as one of malice — and he will not be entirely wrong.

If the Rabbit is the male, he will seek to confine Mrs Rooster to a role of submissive housekeeper, she, in turn will take advantage of his first absence to fly out the window. If the Rooster is the male, his Rabbit wife will criticize him ceaselessly, which he will not understand.

Rooster/Dragon

They both like to shine, but in totally different ways. The Rooster seeks to please because it reassures him of his personal value; the Dragon dazzles because he is naturally like that.

With these two, everything can go very well indeed. The Rooster will know how to fan the Dragon's flames as their warmth envelops him. He will admire the Dragon, who need make no effort to be seductive, and will be proud of having captured his attention. The adulated Dragon in turn will feel like a proud peacock and will be happy indeed. Danger will come in moments of crisis or misunderstanding, which, alas, can be frequent. The Dragon has little awareness of subtleties and no psychological understanding whatsoever; sometimes he will be tough and intolerant with his Rooster companion, who will then wish to take him down a peg or two.

Rooster/Snake
This is the ideal couple of Chinese astrology. Traditionally they represent mind and matter, balancing themselves in harmonious union. They get along marvellously together. From the start they will appreciate each other's elegance: they could even buy matching outfits and look like fashion photographs. They love each other for their flattering appearance as a couple; even more, they understand each other perfectly. The Rooster will be able to sing in peace, and, between cock-a-doodle-do's, will recount his exploits to the Snake, who will comment on them with wit and humour. The Snake will feel secure because of the hard-working side of the farm-yard king, who will finally feel understood, being accepted as he is and not judged only by his brilliant plumage.

The Rooster and the Snake are accomplices. Even if they argue — usually because of an infidelity — their dialogue will always bring them together; they adore philosophizing into the small hours of the morning.

Rooster/Horse
This combination is far from ideal: each needs to have his or

her true value recognized and affirmed; appearance is important to them; they are sensitive to the opinion of others — particularly the Horse — and both are very vulnerable. You may think that they thus have many points in common. But in fact they have too many, and both will try to take first place and rank ahead of the other. All the love in the world cannot overcome this reflex.

Also, these similarities do not lead to evolution, but to irritation. The Horse will suffer at seeing his Rooster partner strut about, and will have neither the patience nor the wisdom to allow him to crow in peace. For his part, the Rooster will be dissatisfied because he needs dialogue, and discussion with a Horse is often limited to agreeing that he is right.

Rooster/Goat

They do not have much in common except, perhaps, a love of the countryside and a certain flair for socializing. They do not really understand each other. The Goat will feel secure, for the Rooster will work for two, but he will expect in return understanding, permanent companionship and a form of encouragement amounting to moral support which the Goat will be unable to provide.

Although he may pretend to be unconcerned, the Rooster will be deeply upset and will withdraw into himself, a role at which he is a specialist. The Goat, assuming the truth to be revealed by the role, will retreat within his vagabond spirit — and the rift between the two will continue to widen.

If the man is a Goat and the woman a Rooster, she will nag him ceaselessly and will not tolerate his 'bohemian' side. But if she can be his manager, she will be excellent and do great things for him. In this way they will reach a better understanding and the mutual respect they gain will cement their alliance.

Rooster/Monkey

This alliance can work, but only superficially. While the

astute, clever Monkey and the honest, frank Rooster complete each other, the former will always have a tendency to mock, criticize and treat the Rooster as a superficial, naive person. The Rooster, on the other hand, will for a while admire the acrobatic games of his partner, but will end by saying: 'Ah, I didn't realize that he was so superficial!'

By judging each other solely on external appearances, they will methodically detect the mote in their companion's eye and not the dust in their own.

Their problem is that they cannot accept that they are on an equal footing, and so they live at war with each other as perpetual rivals. However, a little indulgence and acceptance of the other 'as he is', without wishing to change him, would enable this couple to live in comparative peace.

They can agree on one level: their mutual taste for parties and social life. They will squabble ceaselessly, but what a handsome couple they make!

Rooster/Rooster

This relationship is rather lively. They are either extremely fond of each other, but squabble a lot — or they do not like each other at all, and do not mind saying so. Those who have difficulty accepting their own faults are usually incapable of accepting them in others; without realizing it these Roosters get on their high horses and a cock fight will quickly ensue.

This mini-war is of no great importance between a man and a woman, but it can become quite dumbfounding between the same sex. A valuable alliance can only really exist between parents and children whose apparant contempt hides a secret esteem, which, curiously, usually occurs between two Roosters.

Rooster/Dog

These two signs share a common attribute: a critical mentality. The Rooster manifests this in a rather systematic way — sometimes criticizing simply to talk, sometimes to be interesting and at others just to make people laugh — but he never considers the wounds he is inflicting in the process. The Dog will be critical deliberately and consciously, particularly when his nerves are on edge, as they are by the typical defects of the Rooster — his boasting, bragging side; his constant use of 'me' and 'I'; his ease and freedom from care. Given his anxieties, this seems personally injurious to the Dog. So their relationship easily degenerates into a war of words. Each will suffer, for both are sensitive.

However, if they can control themselves and hold their tongues — if one rejects a taste for the tough, hurtful remark and the other his moral rigidity — they could really help each other; for their qualities are complementary. But will they make the necessary effort?

Rooster/Pig

Everything is possible with the tolerant Pig, who has a thick skin and is not excessively disturbed by the pricks of the Rooster. He is even one of those rare persons who can recognize the Rooster's goodness and kindness which lie hidden beneath his brilliant feathers. The Pig disarms the Rooster's aggressiveness, understands him and tranquillizes him.

However, the Rooster will never try to take advantage of the Pig. They get along very well together, although their relationship will be one of comradeship rather than passionate love or intellectual stimulation. They will take life easily, but will be ready to fly to help each other at the least sign of danger. What could be better? A little spice perhaps, for the unforeseen, the delicious surprise, will often be lacking with these two.

SOME ROOSTER CELEBRITIES

Alexander I and Catherine II of Russia, Colette, Fenimore Cooper, Copernicus, William Faulkner, Fulton, Goebbels, Kierkegaard, La Fontaine, Marie Laurencin, Andre Maurois, Marie de Medici, Princess Caroline of Monaco, Yves Montand, Patton, Madame Recamier, Richelieu, Johann Strauss, Strindberg, Telemann, Verdi, Queen Victoria, Wagner.

YOUR
COMPANION
IN LIFE

生命伴侣

After the Chinese sign of your year of birth, here is the sign of your hour of birth

What is a Companion in Life, as understood in Chinese astrology? It is a sort of 'ascendant' sign corresponding to your hour of birth. This Companion is another animal belonging to the Chinese cycle of the twelve emblematic beasts, who falls into step with you and accompanies you, ever ready to help you brave the traps and ambushes along your route. A permanent and benevolent shadow, he can render the impossible possible.

He is your counterpart, but with his own character and tendencies and with a different psychology. Both guardian angel and devil's advocate, he will be a witness to your life and an actor in it.

Have you ever felt, deep inside yourself, the subtle presence of another 'myself' inhabiting you and with whom you live, at times in harmony, at others in conflict? Another self who sometimes criticizes you and at others encourages you? That is your Companion in Life.

There are times when he will appear to be an imposter or an intruder. Certainly, he often questions your habits and your moral or spiritual complacency. Accompanied by this companion, a shadow within, the route is less monotonous and the voyager multiplies his chances of arriving at his chosen destination. This, however, in itself matters little, for it is the journey and the manner in which it is conducted that are important. Indolence is the greatest danger: your Companion is capable of arousing you from a lassitude of spirit and, to that end, if necessary, robbing you of your certainties, trampling on your secret gardens and, finally, tearing away the great veil of illusion.

It sometimes happens that your Companion is of the same sign as your year of birth, a twin brother in a way — for example, a Rooster/Rooster. In this case, you must recognize that he will compel you to realize yourself fully and to live the double aspect — the Yin and the Yang — that your bear within yourself. In any case, you also bear within yourself

the twelve animals. So, set out on the long route, ready for the great adventure: the beautiful voyage during which you will encounter the harmoniously entangled, the solemn and the grotesque, the ephemeral reality, the dream and the imagined.

Table of hours corresponding to the twelve emblematic animals

If you were **born** between		your **companion** is	
11 pm and	1 am		Rat
1 am and	3 am		Ox
3 am and	5 am		Tiger
5 am and	7 am		Rabbit
7 am and	9 am		Dragon
9 am and	11 am		Snake
11 am and	1 pm		Horse
1 pm and	3 pm		Goat
3 pm and	5 pm		Monkey
5 pm and	7 pm		Rooster
7 pm and	9 pm		Dog
9 pm and	11 pm		Pig

These figures correspond to the *solar hour* of your birth. If necessary, you should check the summer times (Daylight Savings Time) and make the appropriate adjustment (sometimes two hours before or after statutory time).

742

THE ROOSTER AND ITS COMPANION IN LIFE

 **Rooster/Rat**

The Rooster, announcing the rising of the sun, and the Rat, busy with his nocturnal activities, are two companions who will hardly have time for sleep. For these two dissimilar characters, a true understanding may seem impossible, yet it is precisely in this that they may prove to be complementary to each other. The Rooster will perch; the Rat will burrow. Each has a lively nature. The one is a sun symbol, the other a symbol of night. They will mutually strengthen each other. Rat will offer his world of the underground on a gold platter to the Rooster at the very moment when the Rooster, ruffling his feathers, is rising on his spurs awaiting the moment of dawn's song. This is a daily offering on which the Rat would do well to meditate. For Master Rat, so often taking but rarely giving, this generous Rooster will be a source of strength, if he knows how to take what is offered.

 **Rooster/Ox**

The Rooster will add a little wine to his water, or, more exactly, he will add a pinch of generosity to his egotism. The Rooster has a sense for sharing and for friendship; admittedly he can behave like a braggart, but then his very ardour and vivacity are so charming that one forgives him everything. From his bravado the Ox will gain a great deal. The morning song of the Rooster will relieve the Ox of a certain torpor and dullness. The ideal would be composed of the Rooster's sharpness on the surface and the Ox's ability in depth.

743

Rooster/Tiger

He detests banality. His creed is based on the need to be first and to dominate. He is unequalled where the question of pride is concerned; be careful, a voyage is always beset with traps and surprises. The Tiger/Rooster will have a tendency to believe himself to be the winner every time. Alas, the higher he climbs, the greater the fall and, striving always to be first, he will be in danger of running out of breath.

Rooster/Rabbit

He will always keep his eyes peeled. He must always be entitled to the right to look, to control a situation and to feel he is the master of his destiny. He is not the kind to let himself be guided. He is a curious mixture in which the call of the dawn is coupled with the murmurs of the night. The voyage will be profitable if the prudence of the Rabbit is allied with the tenacity and loyalty of the Rooster. The Rabbit/Rooster is a generous, lively animal with a pure heart. His spur and his claw will be used defensively rather than offensively.

 **Rooster/Dragon**

He only feels at ease in a high position, both in the geographic and the hierarchical sense of the term. He prefers the top of a tower or a top floor with terrace. The Rooster/Dragon will always be in the first row and nothing will escape his vigilant gaze; he will wish to dominate, control and supervise in all circumstances. He will be kind and possess originality, qualities which the Rooster does not always naturally cultivate. He will also be irresistibly charming.

 **Rooster/Snake**

An intuitive and frank animal, he will accomplish his tasks with a generous heart and with much good will and honesty — thus correcting the Snake's tendency to side-track — which will not prevent him from being uneasy, despite his apparent self-assurance. The Snake/Rooster flares up easily, so be careful if it is one of his bad days. He will attack with surprising aggressiveness and be entirely unjust simply to reassure himself. Do not attempt to expose his faults with evidence; he will be narrow-minded and never forgive you for having discovered his weak points. The Snake/Rooster is overly concerned with projecting a good image. He has a need to shine and surround himself with costly and beautiful things; this may appear superficial, but it is vital for his morale.

Rooster/Horse

While distinguished, loyal and generous, he is also vain and lacks modesty. His pride drives him, pushing him on against wind and tide, keeping him far in front of the masses, whom he needs to command and carry with him. The Horse/Rooster likes to stand out from the crowd; he is often unique and possesses a sense of honour to the highest degree; his word is his bond. His generosity can be total, his loyalty irreversible. If he gives you his confidence and friendship, nothing — no pressure nor catastrophe — will weaken it.

Rooster/Goat

Generous and outgoing, this animal will be honest and pure, but, alas, his character will often prove unreliable and difficult to pin down. The Goat/Rooster will tend to kick out and back away, for he will not accept ties, advice or any form of dependency. His needs for liberty is expressed to a marked degree. He also needs to be reassured and coddled, but dislikes revealing his weaknesses and takes care not to expose himself. His principal motivation seems to be to set himself apart from other animals, for his pride will always win out. He wants to be original and fanciful at any price. If you are unlucky enough to come up against these qualities, he will become aggressive and capricious, even a bit cruel. However, he does not hold grudges and the next day you will see him trotting along, eyes shining and flowers for you in hand.

Rooster/Monkey

Very proud and full of himself, he will not be, to say the least, modest and self-effacing. He will see to it that he never goes unnoticed and will care a great deal about the effect he produces on others. Lacking neither intelligence nor good taste, he will still be irresistibly attracted by all that glitters. A word of advice: do not call too much attention to his weaknesses because the Monkey/Rooster will never forgive you!

Rooster/Rooster

This animal will not pass unnoticed. Others will turn to look at the Rooster/Rooster, who is always dressed in the latest fashion, is rather proud, and tries to stand out among his companions — not because he scorns them, but simply because of his love for originality. He dreams constantly of always being in the forefront, in a high position, at the top of a tree or tower. He is a symbol of vigilance, both protector and look-out. But he will often be aggressive, susceptible, intolerant and rebellious if contradicted. Alert to the external world, he may close up within himself due to his fear of discovering his own weaknesses, as well as those of others.

Rooster/Dog

Imbued with honour and fidelity, the Dog/Rooster will be a sentinel and guardian, yet capable of questioning his handsome self-assurance and looking into himself and tempering his aggressiveness. He will make his way by night as well as day, straddling the two worlds of shade and sun. He will be belligerent, pessimistic and active, but the ordeals he endures will not discourage him. He will persevere, but without any wish for conquest or revenge. The Dog/Rooster will seek to improve himself but remain susceptible to those around him. He will be a man of his word and of his heart.

Rooster/Pig

He is a strange and solitary traveller, due more to personal conviction than to a love of originality. The Rooster/Pig seeks to stand out in a crowd by his attitude towards life rather than by appearance. In order to achieve this, he will seek a hiding place in which to bury his treasures, far from the eyes of the world. He will work hard to acquire wealth and knowledge, but will take care to disguise them so as to be the only one to enjoy them — an expression of his pride and egotism.

THE ROOSTER AND THE FIVE ELEMENTS

五行

YOUR ELEMENT

In Chinese astrology, each year is joined to an Element. There are five Elements: *Water, Fire, Wood, Metal, Earth.*

Each of the twelve emblematic animals is linked successively to each of the five Elements. For example, in the year 1900 the Rat was Metal, in 1912 he was Water, in 1924 he was Wood, in 1936, Fire and in 1948 he was Earth. Therefore, for the twelve years from 1900 he was linked to Metal, for the next twelve years to Water, and, for every succeeding period of twelve years, to each of the other Elements, in succession.

In order to determine the Element corresponding to the year of your birth, use the table below:

Years whose digits end in: 2 and 3 — Water
6 and 7 — Fire
4 and 5 — Wood
0 and 1 — Metal
8 and 9 — Earth

The same union of *Animal-Element* repeats every sixty years, for example, Rat-Metal appeared in 1720, 1780, 1840, 1900, 1960 and so on.

The five Elements are the primary forces affecting the universe. It is their particular association with each of the signs which provides the basis for every horoscope. Movement and fluctuation, Yin and Yang, these symbolic forces are in a perpetual state of action and interaction.

Wood gives birth to Fire, which gives birth to Earth, which gives birth to Metal, which gives birth to Water, which in turn gives birth to Wood.

ROOSTER/WATER
(you were born in 1933)

The cold born of the northern sky descended to earth and gave birth to Water. The Chinese consider Water more a synonym for coldness and ice than a symbol of fertility.

Characteristics of the Rooster/Water

Water of winter nights, rigour and severity, calm and deep Water to be feared and respected, still Water sheltering underwater demons asleep in its depths, foetid and muddy Water of the marshes, a refuge of crawling creatures. The Rooster/Water, of the Yang tendency, will not risk being immobilized by his Element; rather, he will seek to make use of its dynamic aspect. For him, Water will be fresh and sparkling, a symbol of movement and youth. After all, Water is needed to make the grain grow, which in turn feeds the Rooster.

Health of the Rooster/Water

The Water organ is the kidney; its flavour is salty. The Rooster should remain dynamic and active. Water must cicrulate through him; he must take care to avoid blockages and be careful of what he eats.

The Rooster/Water and others

The Rooster/Water should take himself in hand and moderate his aggressiveness and avoid excesses; he should learn to manage his life calmly and serenely. It will be possible for the Rooster to govern the masses (which he dreams of doing), if he places his pride and honour in the service of men and justice and seeks to improve social conditions and human relations. The Rooster/Water will be a humanist rather than a mystic. He will prefer the concrete, excel in manual work and remain honest throughout his career. The Rooster/Water is not a man of compromises and does not mind becoming personally involved and taking responsibility for his actions. Thus he is first and foremost a man who acts from the heart.

Advice for a Rooster/Water
Like your Element, Water, you are pure and possess the energy necessary to direct, command and control. Do not ruin these gifts because of your pride.

A Rooster/Water year
The culminating point for a Rooster/Water year will be winter, a period of gestation. The Yin of Water will balance the Yang of the Rooster.

Turn towards what is dynamic and do not allow yourself to be attracted by sleeping waters, which are too still for your needs. Take the time to reflect upon yourself and your life. Relax by gardening, for example.

Historical example of a Rooster/Water year 1453

In Constantinople the roses were in bloom as the month of May drew to a close but the moon, once the symbol of the thousand year old city, was on the wane. After seven weeks of siege by the Turkish armies, led by the young Sultan Mehmet, the hopes of the Christians within the walls were fading. Yet there was a feeling of frustration in the Turkish camp. Badly damaged though they were by the great siege engines set against them, the city walls had not yet been penetrated by a single Turkish soldier. It was known that the old Vizier Halil continued to disapprove of the venture; relief might be on the way; a Venetian fleet was reported at Chios; the Hungarians might cross the Danube.

Mehmet attempted a last overture for peace which neither he nor the Emperor believed in. He then met with his commanders and notables. Zaganos Pasha and the younger generals called for an immediate assault, and

Mehmet acceded to their views. His heralds toured the army and, as the customs of Islam allowed, promised a three-day sack of the city. Monday was declared a day of rest and atonement and the troops were ordered to be ready for the assault the following day. Mehmet again spoke to his ministers and commanders. He reminded them of the booty which would soon be theirs, that the city was not impregnable, that its defenders were few and exhausted, and that for centuries its capture had been the sacred duty of the faithful. He personally would never give up the fight until the city was taken.

On Monday, while quietness pervaded the Moslem camp, a great procession was formed in Constantinople and the icons and sacred objects carried through the streets. The Emperor likewise spoke to his people and to his Greek and Italian commanders, of their duty to die for their faith, their families, their country and their sovereign. The populace moved to a service of intercession held in the great church of the Holy Wisdom, heedless that its sacred liturgy had been defiled by the Latins. For this moment before destruction there was unity in the Church of Constantinople.

The afternoon of the following day Mehmet entered the city, heir and possessor of the ancient Roman Empire.

ROOSTER/WOOD
(you were born in 1945)

To the East, the wind blew in the sky and from its warm caress of the the earth Wood was born.

Characteristics of the Rooster/Wood
Wood is of the morning and of springtime. Its temperate nature loves harmony and beauty. This Element is flattering for the preening Rooster, so careful of his appearance. This season will be fruitful and creative if the Rooster blends with and becomes impregnated by the beauty surrounding him,

opening himself to an internal world whose door he tends to leave closed. However, Wood is also passionate, susceptible and excessive, and the Rooster already possesses these defects. He should use his clear-sightedness to avoid letting himself get carried away. But the Rooster/Wood knows his limits, which will doubtlessly permit him to maintain his equilibrium, giving him self-assurance and an ability to share with and love others.

Health of the Rooster/Wood
The organ of Wood is the liver; its flavour is acid. An awareness of your weaknesses should not cause you to become anxious or depressed and indulge in over-eating.

The Rooster/Wood and others
The Rooster/Wood will often behave calmly and seem sure of himself. But this is misleading, for at certain moments he is full of self-doubts. His self-assured attitude, which is purely defensive, will be pleasing for those around him, who will enjoy his relaxed and smiling air. He will have a talent for improvising in difficult situations. He has a fine imagination, which he will put to use, particularly if he turns towards the arts, such as poetry or painting. He will take refuge in nature in order to fulfil his need for liberty, space and harmony.

Some advice for a Rooster/Wood
Your unaffected nature increases your charm; maintain your simplicity and live at your own rhythm. Refuse to put on an iron collar or a coat of armour — you are not made for them.

A Rooster/Wood year
The culminating point for a Rooster/Wood year is spring, a period of growth and prosperity.

Profit from this year to recharge your batteries. Be creative, discover Mother Nature and do not give in to anger; be supple, tolerant and seek harmony.

Historical example of a Rooster/Wood year
1945

At the Potsdam conference in July the decision was taken to drop the first two atomic bombs on Japanese cities. Hiroshima was annihilated on 5 August; 'sweet Nagasaki, the flower of Kuyushu' four days later. The barbarism extended by Hitler and the SS to Europe was now extended by the Americans and their international team of scientists to Japan.

In August 1945 Japan was, for all practical purposes defeated and ready to sue for terms — but 'terms' there could not be because the doctrine of unconditional surrender enforced on Germany had also to be enforced on Japan. In that context, Churchill's reaction when hearing of the successful testing of the bomb at Los Alamos is understandable: he recorded that 'the nightmare vision of conventional air bombing and invasion by huge armies had vanished.' More important to the Americans, Japan could be defeated without the help of the Russians. It was altogether clear that the Americans, whatever they would agree to in Europe, had no wish for a Russian presence in Japan. To these considerations the scientists added their own: 'The bomb simply had to be a success — so much money had been expended on it . . . the relief to everyone concerned when the bomb was finished and dropped was enormous.'* That was the view of one engaged on the project. Truman's chief of staff Admiral Leary emphasized that the military were anxious to demonstrate the bomb's effectiveness — two billion dollars had been spent on it.

Dropped, demonstrated or kept in store, there is no doubt that the technology of the bomb could not have been kept a secret. Stalin knew of its development and his agents were deployed to gather the information needed. The balance of terror would have dominated postwar strategy whether or not the bomb had been used. Yet its actual release was a gesture of moral impotence from which the victors have never recovered.

* B. Liddell Hart in *New Cambridge Modern History*, vol.XII, 1968.

ROOSTER/FIRE
(you were born in 1957)

Heat was born in the southern sky, descended to earth and fertilized it. From their union, Fire was born.

Characteristics of the Rooster/Fire

The Fire Element is of the midday, of the South, of summer. Fire is Yang; it is the Element that warms, burns, animates, quickens, transforms and overthrows. Fire in a Rooster of the Yang tendency will strengthen his rashness, audacity and argumentativeness. This could be dangerous, because the Fire might devour, becoming a violent and flashing power. The Rooster/Fire should learn to control this force which can flare up within him and could turn against him. If he allows it to gain the upper hand it could be transformed into aggressiveness and be destructive to others as well as to himself.

Health of the Rooster/Fire

The organ of Fire is the heart, its flavour is bitter. Fire of summer and of the South, Yang plus Yang; be careful of over-work and excesses of all kinds. If you burn your wings, you may well lose your feathers.

The Rooster/Fire and others

He will often be violent and passionate. His life will not be easy: although he needs to be surrounded by flattery and applause, he is also aware of his weaknesses and thus the admiration of others ends by making him scornful and sceptical. The Fire Element will strengthen the belligerence of the Rooster/Fire: he can be a man of action, a soldier or a formidable leader; but the Rooster/Fire can also be an outsider who likes to stand apart as a means of seducing and conquering. He will often be an exceptional person, an adventurer of wide-open spaces or of the intellect. Gifted with a strange and powerful personality, he will evolve within a special universe, far from other men and their run-of-the-mill reactions.

Advice for a Rooster/Fire

Warrior, statesman, emperor or revolutionary, you run after phantoms that you can never grasp. This is the basis for your greatest successes as well as for your worst failures. Be especially vigilant and discerning.

A Rooster/Fire year

The culminating point for a Rooster/Fire year will be summer, a period of creation.

This will be an active and enriching year, both materially and spiritually, and you will be full of energy. However, do not do too much nor spread yourself too thin or you will tire and lose confidence.

Historical example of a Rooster/Fire year
1477

This was a period, both in England and France, of rapidly shifting alliances. Actions at least nominally traitorous were prompted by a political climate so uncertain that the principle of loyalty had little, if any, relevance. By 1474 Edward IV had secured his position in England. By good luck and good generalship he had weathered the Lancastrian revolutions — their king was dead, his supporters scattered and the power of the Neville family destroyed for ever.

The embers of the old war between England and France remained, potent if dulled. Edward's policy was to revive the war once he had secured his position at home. The rivalry between Louis XI of France and Charles the Bold of Burgundy offered him his opportunity. He and Charles made a firm agreement to invade the territories of the French king in 1475. The money was raised, a large army collected together and Edward crossed to Calais. But, as

Louis recognized, Edward's resources were already stretched. If Edward could be detached by a bribe he would be free to deal with his main enemy who would then be isolated. In consideration of a large payment and a pension Edward withdrew his army.

Thus it was that Charles of Burgundy, already committed to an act of insurrection, found that this principal ally had deserted him. In his chagrin he set about antagonizing the very people who might still have rallied to him. In 1477 he arrived before Nantes with a depleted force, as weary as his treasury was impoverished. Duc René of Lorraine lay in wait for him, supported by German and Swiss contingents. Charles was slain and his army melted away. Louis had won his victory; money had detached Edward and money had secured the services of the German and Swiss mercenaries.

ROOSTER/EARTH
(you were born in 1969)

Earth was born from the slowly falling Elements of the sky at its humid zenith.

Characteristics of the Rooster/Earth
This is an afternoon Earth, the humid and hot Earth of summer. It is the symbol of the well-cushioned, soft nest, of comfort and abundance; an Earth of slow and profound transformations.

The Rooster/Earth will not be much of an adventurer: he will be afraid of becoming too involved and of taking risks. He often will be rather egotistical. Mainly preoccupied with his own success, security and appearance, he will not hesitate to profit from others' work, and will not be overly imaginative. However, the Rooster's vivacity will encourage the flourishing of his body, mind and heart. He will have a tendency to bury his treasures and wealth away from indiscreet glances: his Element will be less a symbol of meditation and reflection than a safe deposit box or Ali Baba's cave.

Health of the Rooster/Earth
The Earth's organ is the spleen, its flavour is sweet. The Rooster/Earth should not remain immobile or he may suffer from sluggishness and become fat in his old age.

The Rooster/Earth and others
He will be realistic, pragmatic, and often shrewd rather than intelligent. Due to his egotism, he will not be burdened with too many principles. Moreover, he will be prudent and distrustful; he will reflect at length, carefully weighing the pro's and con's before becoming involved in any enterprise. He will rapidly climb to the top in professions such as banking, property or insurance, not hesitating to elbow others out of the way. If a Rooster/Earth goes into politics he will be successful, especially in the economic sector. He seems to be loyal and sincere; he needs an activity which flatters his pride while assuring him fame and comfort. As a parent, the Rooster/Earth will be rather authoritarian, sometimes smothering his children with care.

Advice for a Rooster/Earth
Fulfil your heart's desire and become a man in the public eye. By expressing your need to be seen and admired, perhaps you will succeed in unlocking certain internal tensions and exorcizing your terrible fear of poverty. Otherwise, become a rich farmer.

A Rooster/Earth year
The culminating point for a Rooster/Earth year will be summer.

It will be a favourable time for the Rooster, who will no longer need to worry about how he is to eat. Freed from this constraint, the Rooster/Earth should overcome his egotism, open his heart and enlarge his horizons beyond his 'territory'.

Historical example of a Rooster/Earth year
1789

On 5 May, after many delays, the Estates General of France assembled at Versailles. The event was taken note ot but not particularly remarked on in the capitals of Europe. Little more than two months later the Bastille was stormed and the most stratified society in western Europe extinguished. Mirabeau's pledge to 'yield only to the bayonet' had been fulfilled. In August the National Assembly formally abolished the feudal orders of France and relieved the peasantry of its ancient obligations to the seigneurial system. Thenceforth, all classes in France were free from restrictions in terms of office holding and trade. The events of 14 July were thus ratified. The public administration ceased to function, the army declared itself dissolved and the National Guard, created by Lafayette to temper the wilder enthusiasms of the Revolution, comprehensively embodied those who were the most prone to them.

The French Revolution was the first in the modern world to demonstrate the power of radicalism — not to reform by degrees but to overthrow by violence.

The English radicals responded with enthusiasm; a vigorous correspondence developed with members of the new regime. The French even followed English example and established political clubs. But English enthusiasm responded to the spirit rather than the substance of the revolution. By temperament the English radicals were attached to the constitution embodied in the 'Glorious Revolution' of 1688; they were proud to be its heirs and were not alone in thinking that the French would be content to accept it as a model. The Americans had a better understanding of events and good cause for pride when the French declaration of the Rights of Man was published on 2 August. It closely followed the Virginia Bill of Rights of 1776.

ROOSTER/METAL
(you were born in 1921 or 1981)

In the sky, coming from the West, drought grazed the skin of the earth and gave birth to Metal. Winds come from the faraway steppes seeking the vital sap.

Characteristics of the Rooster/Metal
Metal is of the night, of autumn and of cold. It symbolizes clarity, purity and precision. The Rooster/Metal will fluctuate between beauty and destruction, with an appetite for material success and a need for spiritual fulfilment. He will suffer because he is a realist and painfully clear-sighted. The Metal Element tends to encase him in an iron collar, to cut him off from his roots and to push him into a desperate quest for the sap of vitality, for contact with the earth, which resembles an obsession for a lost paradise. The Rooster/Metal may therefore find himself bound within a psychological prison made up of constraints and rigidity. These qualities, however, are not in the Rooster's nature, being as he is attracted to society, sophistication and luxury. He will therefore feel torn, lost and ill-at-ease. In order to recuperate and bandage his wounds he will be forced to endure periods of solitude or retreat to create the harmony to which his body and soul aspire.

Health of the Rooster/Metal
The organ of Metal is the lung, its flavour is pungent. The Rooster/Metal should pay attention to his heart and his breathing because he seeks an equilibrium which is difficult to attain.

The Rooster/Metal and others
The Rooster/Metal is energetic, a man of his word and an honest and sincere friend. But he is not very sensitive to the simple beauty of things; he must always have structures, a fixed framework, regulations and reasons. Not much of a diplomat, he will make decisions, without taking special

cases or attenuating circumstances into account. He will like to command, programme and organize everything. He will leave little space in his life for chance; in fact, he insists that everything depend upon *his* decisions. He often lacks an awareness of subtleties and depends mostly on his critical faculties. In short, he will not be agreeable to live with because he is as demanding of those close to him as he is of himself.

A Rooster/Metal year
The culminating point for a Rooster/Metal year will be autumn.

Do not neglect your physical form; do the necessary exercises, for this will improve your general equilibrium. Take care not to be too excessive or you will stiffen and suffer from an erroneous vision of the world. Take time to listen to your body and your heart. In this way you will become more sensitive to the needs of others.

Historical example of a Rooster/Metal year
1981

The English Labour party, fractured within and open to every form of dissension under a leader so obtuse that he regarded it his duty to stay where he was, awaited the results of the French presidential election. The Americans had moved decisively to the right when they voted for Reagan and the English no less so when deciding for Margaret Thatcher. If President Giscard d'Estaing was returned to office the Labour left in England could claim to be the true voice crying in the wilderness of Western reaction. However, if Mitterand succeeded, his old-fashioned policies would surely founder as had those of previous Labour governments in England, cast in the same model; and all the more so since Mitterand would have time to implement them, the guaranteed continuity of power given by de Gaulle's constitution. Thus the prospect of a Socialist victory in France did not really appeal to the English Socialists. The moderates preferred that their own failed policies should not be given, as it were, a re-run in France; the extremists sought the martyr's garb which a strong Socialist government in France would render otiose.

The French Communists formed an extension to these equations. The stronger they proved to be in a government formed by Mitterand the more they could be blamed for the failure of its policies, a result therefore satisfactory to the moderates in the Labour party; whereas the weaker their representation, the more persecuted they would appear, a result which would suit the English Left. Such were the political equations being composed in England in 1981.

The significance of Mitterand's victory for Anglo-French relations lay in the possibility of a new approach, freed from the long shadows of the Gaullist past. It certainly led to an increase in candour during the early exchanges between the President and the English Prime Minister.

Analogical Table
of the Different Elements

Elements	Wood	Fire	Earth	Metal	Water
Years ending in	4 and 5	6 and 7	8 and 9	0 and 1	2 and 3
Colours	Green	Red	Yellow	White	Blue
Seasons	Spring	Summer	End of summer	Autumn	Winter
Climates	Wind	Heat	Humid	Dry	Cold
Flavours	Acid	Bitter	Sweet	Pungent	Salty
Principal organ	Liver	Heart	Spleen	Lungs	Kidneys
Secondary organ	Gallbladder	Small intestine	Stomach	Large intestine	Bladder
Food	Wheat, poultry	Rice, lamb	Corn, beef	Oats, horse	Peas, pork

Table of Harmony
Between the Elements

Legend		Wood Female	Fire Female	Earth Female	Metal Female	Water Female
○○○ Excellent prosperity	Male Wood	● ●	○	○○○	○	○○
○○ Good harmony, understanding	Male Fire	○	○	○○	●	● ●
○ Effort needed	Male Earth	● ●	○○	○○	○○○	●
● Rivalries and problems of reciprocal domination	Male Metal	○	● ●	●	● ●	○○○
● ● Misunderstanding and incomprehension	Male Water	○○	● ●	●	○○○	○

THE
FOUR SEASONS
OF
THE ROOSTER

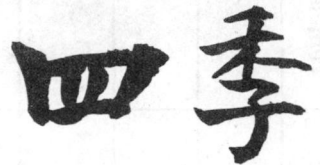

If you were born in spring
Rooster/Aries
This alliance considerably magnifies the qualities and defects of the Rooster, for he has many points in common with Aries.

The Rooster/Aries is above all courageous: he will face up to the most desperate situations, behaving heroically and with an awareness of the useless but nevertheless superb gesture. In this he resembles the hero of a cloak-and-dagger film. He is sincere and never lies; when in love he will never express feelings that he does not have. But he is often disappointed in love, for, being idealistic and naive, he is easy to fool; moreover, he cannot understand why anyone would lie or disguise their feelings. And here we begin to perceive his defects.

The Rooster/Aries is so exasperatingly frank that he can become a danger to himself and to others. He is also totally unaware of the sensitivity and vulnerability of others. It is difficult not to become enraged when he starts to tell you a few home truths; but he should be forgiven because he does not hurt you on purpose.

Rooster/Taurus
This is a stable and warm Rooster, an epicurean who likes the good things in life. He derives great satisfaction from helping people and will never refuse assistance. If you are in a horrible situation he will stand by your side, cheer you up and hold your hand. But if things are going well for you, he will not accept any capricious behaviour. The Rooster/Taurus is courageous and energetic; he also does not like to waste precious time and is therefore permeated with the idea of utility. Like all Roosters he has the unfortunate habit of hitting his friends over their heads with rather indigestible truths, which are usually based on long observation and almost always true. Yet he does not wish to hurt anyone's feelings, and if he realizes that he has, while he will not excuse himself, he will do something especially nice in order to be forgiven.

The Rooster/Taurus loves his liberty but needs to feel admired and appreciated. He is secretly hypersensitive. Extremely sensual and sociable, he loves to receive friends and is a fine host. He would also like to have a harem, to which he would be marvellously faithful.

Rooster/Gemini

This Rooster is a bit of a weather-vane, not because he is constantly changing his opinions, but because he is always moving. He is hyperactive and so full of contradictory plans that he seems agitated, and therefore can become tiring. Living with him is like sharing a house with a pneumatic drill.

The Rooster/Gemini is always prepared to do something, whether it be brilliant or stupid. However, do not misunderstand him: he is agitated, but also fairly constant in his affections. As long as he is allowed to spin around as he pleases he remains attached to his hens and is not interested in those belonging to his neighbours. He is enthusiastic, but also a dreamer; dreaming about everything fascinating that he might do — and he usually ends up doing it, for at bottom he has good common sense. Despite his detached air he is rather clever in business — he has a good 'nose' for it.

Extremely obliging, he is easy to live with because he leaves others in peace. He asks only one thing — that you do the same for him. His kindness is based on a solid foundation of egotism: 'Charity begins at home'.

If you were born in summer
Rooster/Cancer

In order to achieve material and emotional success, the Rooster/Cancer must first overcome his contradictions, which is not easy. He is, in fact, particularly sensitive, vulnerable and vindictive. Disappointments often have an indelible effect on him, and for this reason he needs to be praised and reassured. However, this is difficult because he is so emotional and subjective that he cannot adapt easily to new circumstances or surroundings. A homebody, and basically a conformist, he is the kind who never leaves the barnyard, while dreaming of being a bird of paradise, flying over exotic lands.

The Rooster/Cancer has tenacity and inner strength, but needs time to think about what he is going to do, which can make him seem passive or absent-minded. Take care! If you attack his family he will become a fighting cock. He is never so happy as when surrounded by members of his family. As long as he is treated with respect and kindness he is affectionate, tender and stable. Tell him that you love him and smooth his feathers; this adorable person lacks self-confidence and may wear himself out showing off if he feels unappreciated.

Rooster/Leo

All Roosters are slightly vain and appreciate luxury. Leos are also proud — and love luxury. In other words, if he is born in a slum, the Rooster/Leo will not rest until he has escaped from it. His dream is to live in a penthouse atop a pure gold building, where he can crow out loud to show off his success. This may seem like a defect, but it is often a form of wisdom — knowing how to be satisfied with what one has accomplished.

The Rooster/Leo is honest and even possesses a certain nobility. He is always aware of the effect he is going to produce, and he wants that effect to be good. Of course he is an egotist, like all Roosters, but in his case it is less obvious because he wishes to appear generous and magnanimous. He succeeds in this, and it is only those who are extremely close to him who understand that giving pleasure to others reassures him and gives him a good opinion of himself.

At work, the Rooster/Leo is authoritarian and energetic. He has only concrete dreams; his building is solid and you can live safely within it.

Rooster/Virgo

A Virgo born in a year of the Rooster will gain self-confidence and the dash of audacity that he usually lacks in order to succeed. But his confidence is only a facade, for the Rooster/Virgo is an anxious individual. He works and works, never stopping for an instant, imposing strict discipline on himself and his subordinates. This is because he does not know what tomorrow may bring.

He might be thought modest, but this is not really true for Virgo is a summer sign and it is those Roosters born in the spring who are less flamboyant. In fact, the Rooster/Virgo needs to shine, but only among a select few. He crows quietly, but he does crow; try to silence him and you will see — he will attack you immediately. The Rooster/Virgo is madly attached to his principles and ideas and will not accept being contradicted. Be a good friend and leave him his crutches, which are so well waxed.

If you were born in autumn
Rooster/Libra

At first glance this alliance seems extremely positive. Those born under the sign of Libra are diplomatic and have a sharp awareness of subtleties. It is rare to find a Libra taking an extreme position, which will be favourable for the Rooster who so often overstates his case. This does not mean, however, that a Rooster/Libra is a tactful and delicate spokesman, but at least he will try to avoid exaggerating and will not shock too many people.

The Rooster/Libra is extremely talkative; he loves to discuss and argue, but he does not say just anything. He could be a good lawyer or orator. He is sometimes slightly ostentatious and is very concerned with his appearance and his home; he is rather spendthrift where his comfort is concerned. Rather prudent for a Rooster, he will nevertheless behave somewhat stupidly when in love because of his tendency to judge others by their appearance and to idealize them.

The Rooster/Libra is very much a conformist and he always remains well within the law. In fact, he would be happy as a lark if he were given a medal or decoration.

Rooster/Scorpio

A piece of advice: before starting a discussion with a Rooster/Scorpio, watch where you are walking; and while you are at it, avoid competing with him. He is formidable: first, because he is energetic and courageous; second, because he knows how to wield authority and make others behave as he wishes. Above all he is a smooth talker and his gift of the gab is incredible! His critical faculties are easily provoked, and his latent aggressiveness is expressed in his speech. He can appear to be extremely disagreeable. This is not always the case, but he does take a lot of pleasure in cutting people to the quick, even when they are relatives or friends. The only remedy is to burst out laughing and reply sharply with a smile. He will not mind, for he has a sense of humour — black, naturally.

The Rooster/Scorpio likes to dominate and to this end tries to surprise people and catch them up short when they least expect it. Consequently he is often misunderstood because at bottom he is insecure, above all when in love. If he is master of the barnyard, his hens will be plump and contented; but if he is running wild, he will wreak havoc in all the neighbouring hen-houses. This is an important thing to know about him.

Rooster/Sagittarius

He is the most boastful of the Roosters. He never stops talking about his projects, which, of course, are grandiose. He may plan to convert the entire world, to fight for humanity's survival, but even this is too modest for him; words such as 'cosmos', 'universe', and so on are more like it. At a party he will tell you in a whisper — loudly enough so that others will overhear — about his last meeting with some extra-terrestrials. He is not a liar, simply enthusiastic — and slightly excitable.

However, the Rooster/Sagittarius rarely carries out his mad plans, for he likes his comfort. He is an adventurer only in a dream world of his own making; he is unequalled when it comes to telling stories to children.

This warm-hearted, relaxed, independent person has a lot of charm, but he needs liberty, especially during his adolescence. As he matures he can become slightly dogmatic and want to make everyone else profit from the fruits of his experience. But he is always ready to take care of orphans in distress. His courage, loyalty and fidelity to his friends make it easy to excuse his blunders.

If you were born in winter
Rooster/Capricorn
The Rooster's tendency to boast too much in this case is transformed into a sort of iciness. The Rooster/Capricorn is just and full of integrity, but he cares little for subtleties. His outrageous frankness if not appreciated by most people, especially since it tends to be irreproachable. He is not really hard and actually has a good heart and is a faithful and dependable friend. But his innate honesty makes it impossible for him to tell white lies or to twist the truth.

He is also the most hard-working and clear-sighted of all the Roosters. Obsessed with the desire to finish what he has started, he cannot stop working. He is a perfectioniist who is as interested in the means as the end result.

The Rooster/Capricorn is well-liked socially, for he is courteous and behaves with ease and discretion; also, his conversation is interesting because he always knows what he is talking about. Some Rooster/Capricorns have a tendency to philosophize and to play with abstract ideas; their intellectual life may then be richer than their emotional life which is sown with periods of solitude.

Rooster/Aquarius
The alliance of these two signs considerably increases the tendency in both to be idealistic. The Rooster/Aquarius is an

absolute idealist who thinks sincerely and generously of the well-being of humanity in general, and of his friends and relations in particular. Although he does not launch into mad adventures like the Rooster/Sagittarius, he is willing to give a great deal of himself in order to arrange things for others. His mind is full of ingenious ideas destined to lessen the hardships of life, both on a practical and human level. He is a born advisor, filled with amiable intentions, good-will and devotion — all of it crowned with a good dose of naiveté. He has an answer for everything and adores being asked for his opinion or advice, but he sometimes lacks logic and objectivity.

Socially, the Rooster/Aquarius is amiable and eloquent; he gives the impression of knowing a great many things; he is as good at listening as he is at talking, which is always agreeable for others.

On the other hand, this master of conversation is not very reliable on an emotional level. Because he likes to give pleasure, he has a tendency to promise more than he can give, and will then disappear like smoke as soon as his back is up against the wall.

Rooster/Pisces

This is an elusive Rooster who is difficult to catch. His feathers are smooth, damp scales and impossible to grasp. However, he has great qualities: he is humane, sensitive and devoted. He will listen to you compassionately for hours as you recount your miseries, and will then give you his opinion, sprinkling it with reflections in the style of 'of course, I am not sure', 'perhaps I am mistaken', and the like. And that precisely is his problem: he is unsure of himself. He is often torn between two choices, one romantic, the other materialistic. He never really knows whether he is a bird of prey or a victim, whether he is going to sacrifice himself or cheerfully eat everyone up.

He is a dreamer and a scatter-brain, sometimes here, sometimes there. Those around him sometimes have an intense desire to tie him to his perch. But even then he would escape — in his thoughts.

The Rooster/Pisces is very talkative. He lets go a river of words which flow and seduce, for he likes to please and is a master at it. Never caught off guard, clearheaded and resourceful beneath his dreamy exterior, he will always survive — but not without scars.

THE
I CHING

易经

THE I CHING AND THE ROOSTER

In the I Ching game, you ask a question and you obtain an answer. It is therefore a divining game. But the question you ask is posed through your Rooster identity; the wheels, the complex mechanism of your mind and spirit, begin to turn. You ask a Rooster question and the I Ching answers with a Rooster 'solution', on which you then meditate as a Rooster before arriving at a Rooster conclusion.

The player is presented with a hexagram which contains the 'hypothesis-response' to his question, or, more exactly, a synthesis of forces affecting the concern or event inquired about.

For you, Master Rooster, here are the sixty-four hexagrams of the I Ching and sixty-four Rooster hypotheses.

How to proceed
1. The question
Ask a question regarding any problem at all, past, present or future, personally concerning you. (If the question concerns a friend, consult the I Ching game in the book corresponding to his Chinese sign.)

2. Method of play
It must be done with concentration.
Take **three ordinary and similar coins** — for example, three 50p coins.
Heads will equal the number 3.
Tails will equal the number 2.
Throw the coins.
If the result is two coins showing Heads and one Tails, write 3 + 3 + 2. You thus obtain a total of 8 which you represent by a continuous line: ▬▬▬ .
Draw the same continuous line if you have three coins showing Heads (3 + 3 + 3 = 9).

If you throw two coins showing Tails and one Heads ($2+2+3=7$), or all three showing Tails ($2+2+2=6$), draw two separate lines: ▬ ▬ .

To sum up, 8 and 9 correspond to: ▬▬▬ (Yin)

6 and 7 correspond to: ▬ ▬ (Yang)

Repeat this operation *six times*, noting at the time of each throw the figure obtained on a piece of paper, proceeding from the first to the sixth figure, from bottom to top.

The final result, including a trigram from the bottom, or lower trigram (example:), and a trigram of the top, or upper trigram (example: ▬▬ ▬▬), will be a hexagram of the I Ching. In our example this would look like:

Now merely look for the hexagram number in the table on page 778, and then consult the list of hexagrams with their descriptions to find the given answer. *In our example,* the hexagram obtained is number 63, entitled **After completion.**

Table of Hexagrams

Trigrams	Upper lines ☰	☲	☷
Lower lines			
☰	1	11	34
☷	12	2	16
☳	25	24	51
☵	6	7	40
☶	33	15	62
☴	44	46	32
☲	13	36	55
☱	10	19	54

Use this table to find the number of your hexagrams. The meeting point between the lower and upper trigrams indicates the number of the hexagram that you are seeking.

☵	☶	☴	☲	☱
5	26	9	14	43
8	23	20	35	45
3	27	42	21	17
29	4	59	64	47
39	52	53	56	31
48	18	57	50	28
63	22	37	30	49
60	41	61	38	58

THE HEXAGRAMS OF THE ROOSTER

CH'IEN

1 *The creative:* Energy, strength and will. You are the symbol of K, signifying the five virtues — so do not impatiently claw the air with your spurs.

K'UN

2 *The receptive:* You who sing to welcome the sunrise cannot be unaware that the heat of the sun regenerates the Mother Earth which bears us.

CHUN

3 *Initial difficulty:* Master Rooster will know how to disentangle himself from the straw — on condition that he looks closely at himself and recognizes his errors.

MÊNG

4 *Youthful folly:* 'It is not I who seeks the young fool, but the young fool who seeks me.' Although you are master of the hen-house, do not rise on tiptoe and puff out your feathers — bravado will not dissolve the danger.

HSÜ

5 *Waiting:* What you expect will come by day, but it would be ridiculous to sing too soon. You would be laughed at, and your pride would not stand for that.

SUNG

6 *Conflict:* Although combat is your domain, do not make a principle of it; there are wiser and gentler methods.

SHIH

7 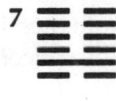 *The army:* You are the emblem, the flag. Submission and discipline should not be a problem for you — and leaders are always needed.

PI

8  *Holding together (union):* This is a word you know well. The moment is ripe to assemble all your available forces and to seek out your friends.

SHIAO CH'U

9  *The taming power of the small:* Widen your horizons; do not say that the earth is too small while you remain on your perch.

LÜ

10  *Treading:* 'Tread on the tail of the Tiger, he does not bite man.' If you wish to obtain someone's support, do not stiffen your crest nor puff out your feathers; pull in your spurs and do not utter ear-piercing cries.

T'AI

11  *Peace:* Dig your trenches, build your barricades; do not hesitate to surround yourself with protective barriers.

P'I

12 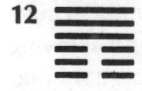 *Standstill:* If it is difficult to stand on a promontory, climb down and wait comfortably until the storm has passed. Otherwise, nothing can break your fall.

T'UNG JÊN

13 *Fellowship with men:* 'Community with men in broad daylight brings success.' Any sincere alliance will be profitable to you.

TA YU

14 *Possession in great measure:* If you inherit a 'full granary' do not be in a hurry to empty it to celebrate a windfall; instead, make it bear fruit.

CH'IEN

15 *Modesty:* Seek to completely relax any physical, emotional or mental tensions. This is difficult to achieve when perched on high. Find a happy medium, but do not use this to show off your feathers.

YÜ

16 *Enthusiasm:* The Rooster is exhilarated, and he knows how to make others share in his excitement. But more is expected: some initiative, ideas and responsibility.

SUI

17 *Following:* Your powers of seduction and your fine presence will get the better of others' reticence. When you really want to, you know how to play with words without hurting anyone's feelings.

KU

18 *Work on what has been spoiled:* Do not accuse your friends of having been asleep and allowing the fox into the hen-house while you continue to take sleeping pills.

LIN

19  *The approach:* The sun may shine in the midst of clouds, but it will not prevent rain from falling. This is the moment to sharpen your discrimination.

KUAN

20 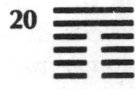 *Contemplation:* Perch on the top of the tower; you will enjoy a wider view. But do not show yourself on the day of the hunt.

SHIH HO

21 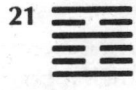 *Biting through (or clearly defined penalties):* Stand up; fight with your spurs and your beak; set an example. Your sense of honour cannot endure lying, and your righteousness is horrified by false promises.

PI

22 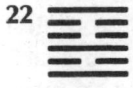 *Grace:* You are sensitive to appearances and all that glitters. Scratch through the varnish, scour the facade, strip and analyse. Truth is so much more beautiful when naked.

PO

23  *Splitting apart:* Do not undertake anything; the terrain is unhealthy and the edifice fragile; even the grain is mouldy and the water foetid.

FU

24 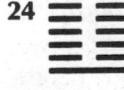 *Return — the turning point:* The shower has stopped. Profit from the return of the sun: the elements are once again lucky for you. Learn how to pardon and recognize your errors.

WU WANG

25  *Innocence:* Even if one is intuitive one does not necessarily possess the truth. Do not try to impose your opinions on your neighbours.

TA CH'U

26  *The taming power of the great:* Power and strength. You are honest and a man of your word; you are going to be able to prove it, but you must avoid rigidity and introversion. What is good for you is not necessarily good for those around you.

I

27  *The corners of the mouth:* Food for the body and the mind. You are neither a camel, a boa constrictor, nor a walking encylcopaedia. The moral is: absorb what you need; an insatiable appetite will give you apoplexy.

TA KUO

28  *Preponderance of the great:* You are the symbol of the warrior, but this is no reason to attack your own terrain by boasting. Do not do more than what is asked of you.

K'AN

29  *The fathomless water:* Be vigilant and on guard; there is aggression in the air. But do not change your itinerary: you know your route, but you ignore the dangers outside of it.

LI

30  *The clinging, fire:* Do not exhaust yourself by beating your wings and emitting ferocious war cries; perhaps the attack was a sham. Renew your ties with allies and others, but do not encumber yourself.

HSIEN

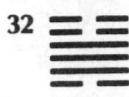 **31** *Influence:* The time is favourable — do not put off an association or meeting. Profit immediately from the least hopeful occasion: your charm may not operate with the same vigour tomorrow.

HÊNG

 **32** *Duration:* You are admired and followed. This will have the happiest of consequences for you, on condition that you know how to ask relevant questions — a sometimes painful but effective operation.

TUN

 **33** *The retreat:* It is useless to call the masses together to announce your decisions, or to drape yourself in your resolutions — you could lose your footing.

TA CHUANG

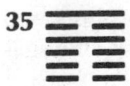 **34** *The power of the great:* Strength, movement, energy. If the tempest is favourable for you to take wing, verify the direction of the wind before taking off. Know how to make use of the currents: they can lift you to the summits, or toss you into the abyss.

CHIN

35 *Progress:* If you are offered a brilliant position as second in command, do not turn your back on it because you are aiming for a higher post. You are skilful at climbing the rungs of the ladder.

MING I

36  *The darkening of the light:* Count only on yourself; fraternity is, alas, often only a pretty word. If you are submerged in a night of solitude, tell yourself that the sun never fails to rise.

CHIA JÊN

37  *The family:* It is extremely important to you; in all circumstances and under all conditions you should think of creating a home for yourself.

K'UEI

38 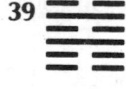 *Opposition:* If you wish to have your liberty respected, think first of liberty for others. You will then see that there will be no more opposition, and you will feel free.

CHIEN

39 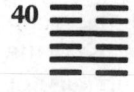 *Obstruction:* If the fence is too high, perhaps you can pass beneath it. The most important thing is to be clear of it. On the other hand, if you are offered a leg-up, stop digging. Do not waste your energy when help is offered.

HSIEH

40  *Deliverance:* The storm has passed. Put things in order and consolidate your ties. Give your attention to the present: each problem should be treated in due time.

SUN

41 *Decrease:* Will be hard for a Rooster who loves luxury. Put aside your ostentatious tastes and discover the beauty of wild flowers. A little self-denial may lead to plenitude.

I

42 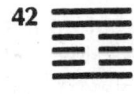 *Increase:* Luck is with you: profit from it immediately. You are in a state of happiness. Your need for ostentatious display will be gratified to the full.

KUAI

43  *Breakthrough:* Use your authority and do not accept any sort of compromise. Be upright and control the situation; you possess everything that is needed to succeed.

KOU

44 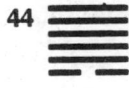 *Coming to meet:* Do not seek to swim in troubled waters or you will lose your feathers. Turn away from still waters, but do not forget that in times of drought you will need them.

TS'UI

45 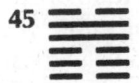 *Gathering together:* Usually it is you who rings; answer the call, even if it comes from outside.

SHÊNG

46  *Pushing upwards:* You may finally be offered a job that is worthy of you. Take care of the details, study the terrain; your success depends on your meticulousness.

K'UN

47 *Oppression:* There is nothing to worry about: a lessening of vitality does not signify a loss of your good image. Lack of self-confidence is much more dangerous than passing fatigue, and is your real enemy.

CHING

48 *The well:* Call things into question, but do not raze to the ground. Make decisions, alter and renovate — but do not uproot the foundations.

KO

49 *Revolution:* Minds are heated, the battle is imminent, but perhaps you can envisage other methods. Such seething excitement could be fatal for you.

TING

50 *The cauldron:* Symbol of the five Elements — Earth, Wood, Fire, Water and Metal. Physical and spiritual nourishment. The Rooster should both find and share the food.

CHÊN

51 *The arousing (shock, thunder):* Follow the weather forecasts carefully; large, menacing clouds which threaten to obscure the horizon are approaching. Do not change direction; you might add the dangers of the unknown to those of the storm.

KÊN

52 *Keeping still:* It is useless to struggle or to fight in a void. Stop moving about excitedly, let the hurricane pass and take refuge in solitude, which, for the moment, will be your best friend.

CHIEN

53 *Development (gradual progress):* Do not attempt to climb the rungs of the ladder four at a time, but take them as they come. Distrust your pride and your vulnerability.

KUEI MEI

54 *The bride:* Despite the favourable aspect, remain prudent and vigilant. Wait for what follows; do not be too quickly seduced by charming and sparkling appearances.

FÊNG

55 *Abundance:* Profit from it to heap up reserves. Winter will be arduous.

LÜ

56 *The wanderer:* By fixing your eyes on the horizon you know how to evaluate distances. Take the proper perspective needed for your equilibrium and for the planning of your enterprises.

SUN

57 *The gentle:* By repeating a gesture, one attains perfect ease; a quality which cannot be opposed since it does not seek opposition, but suppleness, adhesion and integration.

TUI

58 *The serene, the joyous:* Your gifts will be repaid a hundredfold. Giving will bring intense joy and unhoped for advantages.

HUAN

59 *Dissolution:* You must try, at any price, to overcome your egotism. Cease to revolt continually against the rules of the group and of the community.

CHIEH

60 *Limitation:* It is practised without violence, but is inescapable. It is a law that cannot be broken.

CHUNG FU

61  *Inner truth:* You will not be heard any better on top of a hen-house or a church, or in a public square. Evidence is not proclaimed, but witnessed in daily actions.

HSIAO KUO

62 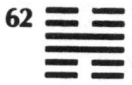 *Preponderance of the small:* Do not waste your energy. Do not row a boat in the fog during a tempest.

CHI CHI

63  *After completion:* You are majestic and resplendent at the top of the spire, but now you must think of climbing down.

WEI CHI

64 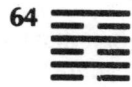 *Before completion:* Do not sell the skin of the fox before the hunter arrives; do not descend from your tree prematurely.

YEAR OF THE DOG

1910 · 1922 · 1934
1946 · 1958 · 1970
1982 · 1994 · 2006

THE DOMAINS OF THE DOG

十二生肖

THE DOG AND ITS SYMBOLISM

In tales and legends, we often find the Dog condemned to wander between two universes, in the disquieting greyness of intermediary worlds, on the threshold of twilit wastelands marking the portals to obscure regions of the soul.

The nature of the Dog has always been considered pessimistic and anxious, but the origin of his torments is rarely investigated. Yet the Dog is the faithful companion of man: an affectionate pet, a familiar in our midst, a part of our lifestyle sometimes even a status symbol. Unlke the rabbit, who imposes his own mystery and independence upon us, deigning to be affectionate when it pleases him, the Dog submits to a man's will with love. Perhaps the Dog hides his true identity beneath this apparent servitude, life being for him simply a passage or antechamber into another world.

Poor Dog, we might reflect consolingly. But does he not exist in order to reassure, protect and love us? We ask no more than that. And it is precisely this 'more' that the Dog desperately attempts to communicate and express to us; yet somehow we remain deaf to his appeal, apparently incapable of translating his language. So the Dog returns to lie docilely at our feet, licking the hand which caresses him. He awaits nightfall, when he will prowl, a guide and companion of the underground invisible worlds traditionally associated with earth and water — and also with the moon, which he either insults or pleads with.

If the Dog accepts his servitude, it is perhaps because of the heavy weight of his heredity: the world of death, hells, crossroads of the beyond, kingdoms of darkness and ice. Under the features of Anubis, found in the Egyptian 'Book of the Dead', he guides souls during their funereal voyage; or he howls at the full moon, haunting cemeteries with the terrifying Hecate, lunar goddess of the dead, magician and sorceress 'presiding over the apparitions of phantoms and spells.'

In the third and last constellation of the ancient Mexican zodiac, called the constellation of the Dog, we find it is he who introduces ideas of death, the end, the subterranean world, a symbol of initiation into death and rebirth.

One recalls the famed Cerberus of Greek mythology: 'Lying down in a cave by the river Styx, entwined with serpents, he guarded the gates of Hell and of Pluto's palace. He caressed the shades of night as they entered, and with his three howling heads, jaws agape, menaced those who aspired to leave.'

Let us now leave this Dog of darkness and enter the world of La Fontaine and his fable of the wolf and the dog.

A skinny, ragged, mangy wolf, consisting literally of skin and bone, met up with a sleek, beautiful and powerful dog. This miserable wolf would willingly have traded in his rags for the dog's handsome livery, but this would have involved flattering the household and pleasing the master. When he saw the harness around the dog's neck, he asked what it was, and the dog replied that it was merely a collar to keep him attached. The wolf, surprised, cried: 'Then you cannot run about freely!' 'But where should I run to, what difference does it make?' the dog replied. At that point, the wolf ran away — and he is running freely still.

Poor Dog! Not content with having stolen his soul, man has also stolen his liberty. Despite this, the Dog pleads man's cause, interceding for him with the gods. Guardian of the gates and bridges, eternal guide and prowler, he remains a faithful companion.

A few notes on the Dog

Principal qualities: Loyal, faithful, unselfish.
Principal defects: Anxious, pessimistic, doubting everything; his life is a vale of tears.
Work: Very active and honest. He is appreciated by his superiors as well as by his subordinates, for he is a good manager and often gives priority to their collective interests rather than his own.

Best role: Prophet of disaster.

Worst role: Actor in a theatrical company.

Money: His family needs it, so he earns it. But at bottom he thinks of it as mere paper; he would have been happier in an age of barter.

Luck: To be born in the daytime. The Dog born at night will spend his life on the alert, an immovable sentry.

Cannot live without: Tenderness.

Adores: Anything occult, mysterious, bizarre, paranormal, parapsychological, para-everything! Also, he likes lightning rods because he is afraid of thunder and lightning.

Hates: To be shown by means of A plus B the existence of a reality that he is not disposed to accept.

Leisure activities: Films, particularly horror movies and those dealing with the fantastic; also peaceful evenings by the fireside, far from the 'madding crowd'.

Favourite places: He has a weakness for wild and romantic landscapes, remote regions alive with legends. He would feel at home in Scotland, Ireland, Cornwall or Brittany.

Colours: Black, navy blue; the colours of the night.

Plants: Poppies and water-lilies.

Flowers: Orange-blossoms, red poppy (which fades when cut).

Professions: Head of a company or labour union; in any case, he cares about the 'quality' of the enterprise and the living standards of the employees. Then: priest, missionary, teacher of retarded children, nurse, magistrate, judge, lawyer, doctor, scientist, researcher, preacher or critic.

The four ages in the life of the Dog, according to Chinese tradition

The life of the Dog is often unstable except during *childhood*, but only then if his parents are protective enough. His *youth* is often tormented by difficult love affairs, which rarely leave him with good memories.

His *maturity* will be haunted by nightmares, and his *old age* saddened by regrets at failing to have profited from life when he was young enough to do so. But there is a remedy: to learn during his childhood how to see joy in life as he lives it.

THE PSYCHOLOGY OF THE DOG

'In vain I could cheat and keep my eyes tight shut: there will always be a lost dog somewhere who will keep me from being happy . . .

The best qualities that can be found in a man — as in an animal friend of man — are united under the sign of the Dog, who, willy-nilly, brings upon his oh-so-stubborn head the admiration and respect of Chinese astrology, from its origins until the present day. 'For myself,' says the Dog, 'I would have preferred quite simply to be lucky, like those who make so much noise; you know, the Dragons, or the Goats who always find a protector.'

And this brings us to our first verified finding: Dogs are never content!

It is true that Dogs are not systematically favoured by that faithless gambler we refer to as 'luck'. It is also true, according to tradition, that 'each dog has his hour of glory'.

As with the other eleven signs of the Chinese zodiac, a 'constant' exists within those born under the sign of the Dog. This constant serves as a 'rallying point' for all the varied, possible and imaginable varieties of behaviour that beings born during the same year are susceptible to. There may indeed be many different species of dog, but a dog is always a dog, just as a rabbit is always a rabbit.

For the Dog, this constant is expressed as *anxiety*, and it must not be forgotten when considering the subtleties and complex psychology of this next-to-the-last of the Chinese zodiac animals. Everything is based on and derives from it, and the most contradictory attitudes can result, just as a calm river or a violent torrent can spring from the same source.

THE DOG

Who would not willingly thank Buddha for his many Dog friends, all of them exceptional personalities? Yet, although unlike in appearance, they are all horribly and forever anxious. One Dog will give every sign of extreme activity breathing heavily when pacing round his office like a bear in a cage, telephone in hand, busily resolving weighty problems. This Dog behaves in the classic fashion described by psychoanalysts as 'the flight forward'.

Another type will seem quiet, for he seeks, with a sort of persevering pessimism, the ideal place to shelter from his insomnia. People think him peaceful and carefree — not at all!

A third will profess a carefree attitude in public about his professional prospects. But he cannot stop working for even three minutes, is considered a tyrant by his family and also suffers from terrible insomnia.

The point in common between these three Dogs is their perpetual anxiety, the eternal temptation to say 'What is the point of it all? I am only on a visit to this earth and anything I build is doomed to fall to dust.'

This heroic attitude, at once detached and sceptical, this strange certitude about the fleeting character of reality, finds poetic expression in the Sumerian myth of Gilgamesh, symbolically linked with the Western zodiac (applicable to Aquarius and Pisces, the last of the 12 signs). In this last passage, the hero Gilgamesh has forever lost his most faithful friend. He roves and wanders the earth, seeking to evoke his spirit:

'Tell me, my friend, tell me, my friend, tell me the law
of the subterranean world that you know.'
'No, I will not tell you, my friend, I will not tell you; if I
tell you the law of the subterranean world that I know,
I will see you sit down and weep!'
'What you have had that is most dear to you, that you
have caressed and which pleased your heart, like an
old piece of clothing, is now eaten by worms.
What you have had so dear to you, that you caressed

and which pleased your heart, today is covered with
dust.
All is plunged into dust
All of it plunged into dust.'

For those born under the sign of the Dog, it seems as if an
ill-humoured fairy imbued them at birth with a philosophy of
fatalism. They arrive on earth burdened with unrealized
hopes and old guilts from earlier incarnations, which they
courageously act out again. But they do so without an eye to
any immediate result, for they are awaiting the inevitable
moment when they will breathe their last and enter a future
life — that place where they will finally come to know
peace: Nirvana — a serenity they cannot know in this life.

In order to understand this curious psychological
development, one's spirit has to be open — as with the
Orientals — to the notions of Karma and beliefs in
reincarnation. Otherwise it is not possible to have any real
understanding of those born under the sign of the Dog. An
appreciation based only on character traits do not amount to
much if the philosophic and spiritual dimensions are
disregarded, and any knowledge gained will be superficial.

Dogs often seem as if their thoughts are far away, almost as
if they are 'doing penance':
'She is in suffering but only in *passing through*
A soul which suffers without anger
And how limpid are her morals.'

(Paul Verlaine)

More than all the other animals, Dogs have a tendency to
ask themselves, 'What on earth am I doing here?' Yet they
remain obstinate, firm against all opposition and courageous
and persevering. They are always aware of their duties and
responsibilities, even to the point of obsession.

Although they are capable of blossoming and of being
warm and amusing in private, they detest and put into the
same basket (which they would cheerfully consign to the
bottom of the sea) noisy family reunions, smart cocktail

parties, society gatherings, and so on. If a Dog sees a friend happily dressing up for a party, he may well remark, acidly: 'Do you really want to go and act the clown with that lot of idiots?'

Even those Dogs adapted to society, the most communicative and gregarious, after the first drinks and a few hors d'oeuvres, will be unable to refrain from cynically criticizing the assembled guests. Except for those who receive their barbs, their comments are generally regarded as witty.

A sense for ridicule prevails among all born under the sign of the Dog. They are aware enough of their own weaknesses to mock themselves frequently; but their humour is as black as the darkest tunnel, as black as night itself. Often sharp, tart and snappish with someone they despise, they cannot abide anyone greedy for power, superficial or inconstant. Yet they are unequalled in understanding the troubles of others, in putting themselves in another's place or lending a helping hand to those who are drowning. They will never expect thanks; they do it because it is their role on earth. Doubtless, this reflects one of the bizarre teachings of the fairy we mentioned previously.

General and disinterested, noble, loyal and admirably faithful, the Dog is not made for this brutal world in which aggression, competition and disloyalty reign. It is no wonder that Dogs can rarely adapt to circumstances and feel at ease or that they are in their proper place.

One of the reasons for their uneasiness is their basic mistrust of strangers, for Dogs often behave as if they are in the Middle Ages guarding some castle: 'Who goes there? Where are your letters of introduction? How can we be sure that you are not an enemy, that you are not going to set us on fire, kidnap the women and violate the young girls?' Strangers do not find it easy to supply a ready answer.

Dogs are entirely trustworthy. Although highly emotional, hypersensitive and by nature timid, they do not show it. They are strict with themselves and their honesty is unimpeachable. But they suffer from their pessimism. Although never discouraged themselves, they are often discouraging for those around them who do not enjoy perpetually waiting for a catastrophe to occur. The somewhat static aspect of their nature recoils from anything unforeseen which might threaten their established frontiers, leading them to be frequently misunderstood. This explains their timidity, grim outlook and lack of self-confidence. However, the Dog will say, 'What does it matter; my kingdom is not of this world.'

The anxious Dog does not like the unexpected. He has spent so much time setting up the limits of his territory, arming his frontiers and restocking his battlements with buckets of boiling oil, that he has difficulty coming to terms with an external event alien to his organization. So, take care: his structures are fragile; never take away his crutches without immediately holding out a friendly hand — beaten Dogs never forget.

A special paragraph is necessary for Mrs Dog because Chinese tradition describes her as rather different from the male — although she possesses the same qualities of honesty and kindness, as well as suffering from the same anxiety and vulnerability.

Mrs Dog is ambitious and aspires more to material security than 'her man'. Gifted and creative, she is slightly lacking in perseverance and tends to leave things half-finished, justifying herself with some pretext, such as, 'Ah, if I had not had children, I would have continued my studies, taken that job . . .' While fame interests her, she dislikes compromises or concessions, and backs away if she no longer feels at ease with herself.

She is attractive, impatient and adores conversation, being more sociable than Mr Dog. However, she is happiest when surrounded by friends, children and pets — be it in a palace, a suburban house or a flat. Her fault lies in a tendency towards narrow-mindedness; an inability to appreciate things which are not part of her immediate universe.

THE DOG AS A CHILD

A sensitive and affectionate child, he is easy to live with if he has attentive and understanding parents. They can do a lot to help their Dog child find happiness on this earth, rather than spending his life dreaming of the past or the future without appreciating the present. He can be subject to fits of morbid imagination and be terrorized by the dark, even thinking up fears and anxieties the better to savour later the joy of feeling secure in his nice, warm bed.

If he likes stories about Dracula rather than Tom Thumb, let him read as he likes, but please, never tell him that Dracula — accompanied by his friend Frankenstein — is going to come at night to eat him up! If you do, he will suffer from insomnia for the rest of his days. In fact, the young Dog remains marked for a long time by all that happens to him and, during his early years, finds it difficult to distinguish between dreams and reality. What at first seems only an exciting game can become a terrifying experience for him if his father or his mother — infallible divinities — suggest that it is grounded in reality.

It will also help the Dog child if you give him the opportunity to be close to nature. Its eternally rotating cycles will reassure him and also encourage his spiritual side, for he often has a mystical turn of mind.

Rather exclusive, he tends to resent the arrival of younger brothers or sisters, fearing that he will lose his parents' love. He needs to *be preferred* over others and surrounded by love. But never fear, he will be unequalled in his defence of his little brother, and will help his little sister with her homework. He is profoundly obliging and devoted.

While he is introverted and has difficulty in adapting to school life, he will get along well with children who share his sign and experience the same problems. On the other hand, if he feels rejected in any way, that he has been abandoned or excluded (and he all too easily does), he is capable of intense resentment, becoming vindictive towards his parents, closing up within himself and living a solitary existence. This will not help him later in life. So, love him a lot and do not stifle him (he loves liberty, reflection and calm). Listen to him and help him without trying to form him in your own image. In this way he will learn to love life without feeling that it is an obligation to live it.

LOVE LIFE

Dogs are faithful by nature and prefer long, secure affairs to passing adventures. If you meet a Dog who is busy chasing girls and fooling around, do not be misled: he is searching for a soul sister. As soon as he feels he has found her, he will stop running around and heave a sigh of relief. For most of the time, these animals are, in their private lives, affectionate, tender, sensual and even passionate. Once involved, they respect their commitment and, without being impervious to temptation, they know how to resist it, for protecting their home is the most important thing to them.

Despite all these qualities, Dogs are not always happy in love. They are jealous, anxious and constantly need to be reassured about the feelings of their loved one.

Their pessimistic side, their strong tendency to imagine possible catastrophes, becomes tiring and discouraging in the long run, even to those partners with the best of intentions. In fact, although their moral solidity and their emotional fidelity indicate stability, their strange sense of humour — extremely dependent on atmosphere and the attitudes of others — does not encourage those around them to feel secure. They are highly emotional and intuitive and, while they 'feel' the feelings of others, they see everything in varying shades of black. It takes a Dog quite a while to feel relaxed, truly to have confidence in someone. It can even take a life-time. Some of them never gain confidence and continue to watch for any possible sign of indifference or infidelity in the loved one, poisoning his or her life with perpetual suspicions. They are often poets of solitude; or disappointed, remote and inaccessible loves.

For a Dog, marriage is advisable as a legal institution and a rampart against temptation, betrayal and predators — but he should marry an optimist.

Dogs are, on the other hand, faithful friends always ready to help when things go wrong. During the bad moments in your life, count the friends who stick with you; you will find a high percentage of Dogs among them.

FAMILY LIFE

Dogs are often fussy parents, anxious to do well by their children and slightly smothering them, above all when the child is of the opposite sex. If you want to seduce the charming daughter of a Dog, you had better watch your step. Do not try to sneak in secretly or you will set off an alarm and find yourself thrown out bodily by Mr Dog, guardian of threatened virtue.

Extremely conscious of their duty, Dog parents will attend all parent-teacher meetings and will devour every book available on education and childhood diseases. Moreover, they are positively touching when panicked by the sight of the smallest bruise or the slightest scratch. They love their children so much because, for them, they are a justification of their time on earth. In the eyes of others, they give their children far too important a role, willingly sacrificing themselves to their well-being. They will even feel guilty if they are unable to have children.

Dog parents will get along well with a young Tiger, to whom they will teach prudence, and with a young Horse, whose egotism they will tame. With Rabbit, Rat and Dog children, there will be affectionate understanding and a climate of tenderness which will help both to swallow much distasteful medicine.

The contemplative young Snake and the too-whimsical Goat will irritate the active Dog; but it is the Pig who can teach this Dog parents how to enjoy life!

If possible, the Dog should avoid bearing an Ox child (lack of understanding), a Dragon child (too touchy), a Rooster child (traumatized by the anxiety surounding him, he will lose all his feathers) or a Monkey child (they are too dissimilar, and the Monkey is so independent!).

PROFESSIONAL LIFE

Dogs have everything necessary to succeed in their professional lives except, at times, motivation. They must be able to believe in what they are doing and feel committed to a mission on behalf of humanity if they are to give the best of themselves. If they do not have faith (which moves mountains), they remain seated melancholily before their kennel, forever brooding over bitter thoughts, dreaming of everything they could have done and did not do.

They possess original gifts, but lack sufficient independence and aggressiveness to make the best use of them; also, when they are adolescent, they hesitate to act contrary to their parents' wishes for their future, which can result in their pursuing studies for which they are unsuited, or adopting a profession which cannot satisfy their deepest needs.

On the other hand, those Dogs free to act as they please and spontaneously to enter the profession of their choice prove themselves excellent workers. They work strenuously, never leaving a job half-done, and when they are at the head of a business they are just to their subordinates. The know how to make themselves appreciated by their employees, for they have the rather rare gift of behaving simply and naturally, of being accessible to everyone without losing one iota of their authority. Only their anxiety, which is always present, runs the risk of 'spoiling the tone', unless they succeed in controlling it.

Dogs do not attach any particular importance to attaining the highest rungs of the hierarchical ladder. If they do climb, it is because they have the impression that it will be best for everyone, since at least then they will not be at the mercy of greedy people. They are modest, kindly and magnanimous. But take care: if they encounter dishonesty or hypocrisy, they will be transformed into wild Dogs; do not forget that they are the champions of justice.

Intelligent and provided with the ability to grasp quickly a situation, the small grain of sand in the gearbox rarely eludes them. This ability can even amount to a defect, for they have an exaggerated tendency to be over-critical. They can allow themselves to become obsessed by the missing detail, to make mountains out of molehills in their determination to come to grips with minor details of no particular significance.

They are particularly suited for professions in the sciences, research and social work. It is unwise for them to become devoted solely to earning money, for material gain alone will not satisfy them for long.

MATERIAL LIFE

The Dog has no talent for juggling with speculations or building financial empires — he would succeed only if he was very clever in choosing his associates or advisers. His nature is too generous and unselfish; it is not egotistical enough. Success in business requires a certain cynicism towards others, a certain toughness absent in the Dog, who is tender and whose cynicism is not material but philosophic. He will recoil before the necessity of ruining a rival, will forgive the person who has offended him and will be true to his word — something that crafty predators will know how to take advantage of.

When times are good, the Dog will be spendthrift, even profligate: nothing will be too good for his family. Also, he will spend vast sums on decorating and improving his home. But, during lean times, he will have a tendency to dramatize the situation, imagining himself ruined and about to be imprisoned for debt. Hopefully, in his difficult moments he will be able to turn to a realistic spouse who will persuade him to see things as they are, and keep his head on his shoulders.

Rather than taking on financial responsibilities, Dogs should choose one of the helping professions — they are so gifted at defending the rights of widows and orphans — or official or administrative problems.

ENVIRONMENT

Dogs are often sedentary and deeply attached to the places where they were born. They love to keep a home-port, and jealously conserve the old family home, full of dust and haunted by memories and souvenirs from their childhood; on this level they are conservatives. Some of them, to sustain the memories of their imagination, will even derive pleasure from leaving their family homes as they always were — happily washing in a basin whose enamel was worn away years before, and leaving their familiar ghosts in peace.

There was once a Dog who, infatuated with the fantastic and the bizarre (like many of his sign), was a fanatic when it came to early horror films. His happiest holidays were spent in the old, freezing, creaking and cracking family home tht had sheltered his first anguishes and nourished his first phantasms and illusions.

However, in general Dogs give infinite care to the decoration of their homes. They have great taste, are demanding — even meddlesome — and analyse with care the view, the height of the ceilings or the style of a building (they prefer the 17th century), totally forgetting that the shops are ten kilometres away!

Dogs who are fairly reasonable concerning their dress — hesitating and fearing to make a mistake in colour or style they can make a salesperson bring them 25 pairs of shoes, then leave without having bought anything — forget the meaning of money when it is a question of interior decoration, heading straight for the most sumptuous materials, and choosing only Aubusson tapestries (17th century as usual) and Sevres vases.

A guide to personal relations with a Dog
Methods of seduction:

He: When he is no longer twenty, appeal to his instinct for protection, which lies within all of us. This will be in the style of, 'I no longer believed in anything, my life was worthless, and then I met you and the impossible became true; it is astonishing — love does exist!' All this is said with great sincerity, which is all the more touching since the Dog says it with his ears hanging down and his eyes misty with adoration. When he is twenty, or thirty, his determination is untiring and he pays court as discreetly and romantically as one could wish.

She: Mrs Dog plays the inaccessible, or even the ravaged heroine. One could often believe that both are inspired by a cloak-and-dagger novel or old fairy tales.

If he loves you: His mood will be ardent, punctuated with moments of emptiness. Comfort him!

He expects: That you be at once father, mother, nurse, psychiatrist, mistress and old chum. He needs to be constantly reassured and coddled, as does Mrs Dog. A good way of keeping her is to give her many children; she adores them.

To keep you: He will give the impression that his feelings for you will never change — 'for better and for worse'.

If he is unfaithful: What could you have done to make this happen? Seek within your own conscience . . . .

If you are unfaithful: It will be a catastrophe. He will pretend to laugh, but his hidden tears will eat away inside him like acid.

In case of a break between you: If it is he who has decided to leave you, he will do it with incredible awkwardness, floundering in his loyal and sometimes vexing explanations. If it is you who leave, it would be nice if you could find him or her a replacement — he or she will be so unhappy alone!

If you wish to give him a gift: Offer him a mascot, a souvenir or a stuffed animal to which he can give a special name or a protective amulet.

If you want to seduce him: Tell him that you believe you have loved each other in a previous life; or, invite him to a seance.

If you want to get rid of him: Tell him that his life is a failure — just as he has said so many times — and that he has only himself to blame.

THE DOG
AND THE OTHER CHINESE SIGNS

Dog/Rat

Why not? The Rat, who is always haunted by the morsels of grain which he will need when he is old, can easily understand the deep anxieties of the Dog. The Dog, who carefully protects his territorial limits, will not be offended by his companion's mania for secrecy. They will accept their differences without conflict and will delight in their similarities. They will pursue their way, discreet accomplices, travelling only at night and never speaking to strangers.

This alliance will develop their reciprocal taste for mystery and, curiously enough, make them feel secure, for they give each other confidence: the Dog because he is faithful — which the Rat needs — and the Rat because he knows how to defend himself in case of difficulties. In short, this is an advisable relationship, in both the emotional and business domains.

Dog/Ox

If a male Dog chooses a lady Ox as his companion, we could almost be certain that their troubles were over. At the side of this stable, secure and reasonable person, the Dog will forgo his roving nights to devote himself to the joys of family life, and will no longer be filled with anguish as soon as the slightest difficulty seems to upset his projects. A Dog company director might advisably have an Ox as his second in command, who could reassure him by saying, 'But no, our cash flow is very good and there is no chance of bankruptcy.'

If the female is a Dog, the situation will be more ticklish. Instead of coming to terms with their troubles, the ladies sometimes choose to escape in a blind search for pleasure or other futile means, which will wear out Mr Ox's reserves of tolerance. Whatever happens, however, they will respect each other. The Ox will admire the Dog's profundity and the Dog will treasure the Ox's stability. A happy, solid and durable union — except that the Dog will often suffer from the emotional reticence of the Ox, mistaking it for coldness.

Dog/Tiger

Both the Tiger and the Dog are impenitent idealists. While the Tiger may often forget to protect his flank, and the Dog be reluctant to charge ahead, let an orphan or a lost child appear, or a famine occur, and they will both be there, ready to abandon everything and fight for the impossible. There will be no mountains too high nor ravines too deep to stem the faith of the one and the enthusiasm of the other. There is nothing like the dynamism of the Tiger to snatch a timid smile of hope from the anxious Dog. There is nothing like the prudent instincts of the Dog to arrest a Tiger at the edge of a precipice.

This can be a happy couple, but not very good in the home. As business associates, they can be inventive and original. There is only one hitch: the Dog needs to be loved and convincingly reassured, and one should not count too much on the Tiger for pretty, sentimental phrases. It is essential that they share a material or spiritual goal if their relationship is to endure. And a goal, work or an enterprise in common that prevents them from having the time to be preoccupied with each other will achieve this, as they walk side by side.

Dog/Rabbit

With luck, this can result in a happy and stable union. Although commonly regarded as hereditary enemies, these two animals — astrologically and psychologically speaking — have many points in common. Both seek security, both are profoundly honest, even virtuous, and both fiercely protect their property. They will understand, listen to and reassure each other.

But what is the small factor of luck that is needed? It lies in the absence of any great social and political event occurring during the course of their lives together. If such an event should occur, the Dog will heroically swallow his fear and join up as a nurse, missionary or even as cook, since he will do anything to feel useful. The Rabbit, who detests trouble, will ponder for years whether or not to follow him.

Dog/Dragon

This liaison is inadvisable, unless they have a common aim or their Western astrological signs offer serious points of understanding. In fact, the Dog is perhaps the only Chinese zodiac sign who cannot be impressed by the Dragon: he is so lucid that he sees the Dragon for what he truly is — brilliant but superficial, devoid of subtleties and emotionally shallow. This is just as well, for a Dog in love with a Dragon would suffer, the Dragon being incapable of giving him the tenderness so necessary, and not caring a rap about his anxieties. The Dragon would also suffer, for, with the best intentions in the world, he could not transform himself into Rodin's 'Thinker' just to please the Dog; he is as he is and he must be accepted, his good qualities along with his bad. This poses a big problem for the Dog who will try to devalue the Dragon in order to establish what he believes to be the truth. Happily, he will not succeed, but it will give the. Dragon complexes, as if he did not already have enough!

Dog/Snake

Dogs in general like Snakes very much: they appreciate their wisdom and depth and forget their selfish and ambitious side. They willingly idealize them, for the Snake's capacity for reflection makes them feel secure. One may well ask why, but that is the way it is.

Snakes, on the other hand, sincerely admire the honesty of Dogs, even though they are not disposed to imitate them. As a couple, this union can work out rather well, as long as the Snake accepts being idealized by the Dog; but this condition cannot satisfy him for very long, since, in matters of love, he likes difficulty. As time goes by, he will slide around all over the place, having completely immobilized his Dog spouse, who will be left in charge of everything. The Dog will remain contented, for his Snake will return regularly to coil round him, to keep him dependent. With the help of love from the one and tenderness from the other, they will go far, and be happy with their situation; so who are we to complain?

Dog/Horse

These two are so dissimilar that it seems hardly possible, at first glance that they could get along. One is confident, egocentric and enthusiastic; the other skeptical, pessimistic and generous. However, they go very well together, for neither is prone to dominate or criticize the other — unless the Horse makes an enormous error.

Each will live his own life and construct his own personal system of satisfactions without bothering the other too much. The idealistic Dog will be busy attending to others, leaving the Horse time to attend to himself, and both will be content, all the more so because the Dog is faithful, something the Horse appreciates because it is restful for him.

It could turn tragic if the Horse suddenly became bored and romped around in other pastures. In this case the sensitive Dog would suffer badly and have a difficult time recovering.

Dog/Goat

While Goats are often anxious about the present and the near future, the anxiety of the Dog is more extensive and more profound. Each needs to be reassured of the fidelity of others and the depth of their feelings for them. Both, to different degrees, are pessimistic: the Goat will be philosophic, the Dog, anguished.

It is better not to put them in the same boat or they will travel from Charybdis to Scylla without catching their breath, which will merely augment their anxieties. They will be found filled with tranquillizers, predicting the end of the world and modern industrial society. Another obstacle is that the Dog is a stranger to fantasy. He is serious and responsible, but rarely amusing, and the Goat's outbursts of fantasy will insult his good sense. No, it is hard to imagine them as a couple — unless they found a mystical and ecological sect together.

Dog/Monkey

They both have a tendency to criticize and are slightly cynical, have few illusions about their neighbours and voluntarily cultivate the bitter flowers of irony. But there is a snag: the Dog is profoundly idealistic, the kind to shout 'All is lost save honour!' and similar, which will seem completely unrealistic to a Monkey, who is more of an opportunist and not at all altruistic.

Between a Dog child and a Monkey parent, between childhood friends or between a brother and sister who have grown up together, a relationship would be possible. But as a couple? The Dog will be profoundly disappointed but will not dare say so. Little by little, he will build up an enormous amount of resentment, being jealous of the Monkey's carefree attitude and his lack of scruples. He will harbour this resentment, feeling that the Monkey is quite disgraceful, but that his tricks work for him, and unjustly so. As for the Monkey, he will quickly become bored and leave. Deep down, he is too uneasy to cope with another's misgivings.

Dog/Rooster

These two signs share a common attribute: a critical mentality. The Rooster manifests this in a rather systematic way — sometimes criticizing simply to talk, sometimes to be interesting and at others just to make people laugh — but he never considers the wounds he is inflicting in the process. The Dog will be critical deliberately and consciously, particularly when his nerves are on edge, as they are by the typical defects of the Rooster — his boasting, bragging side; his constant use of 'me' and 'I'; his ease and freedom from care. Given his anxieties, this seems personally injurious to the Dog. So their relationship easily degenerates into a war of words. Each will suffer, for both are sensitive.

However, if they can control themselves and hold their tongues — if one rejects a taste for the tough, hurtful remark and the other his moral rigidity — they could really help each other; for their qualities are complementary. But will they make the necessary effort?

Dog/Dog

Why not? Those who resemble each other, assemble together. And these two will be united by their love of children, family, security and the need for protective frontiers — perhaps also by a love of love. But if this couple seem easy together, do not trust appearances: it is merely a facade. In fact, they are infinitely dependent on each other;

and an absence or an abrupt remark can knock their emotional crutches out from under them. In the end, however, they are saved by the similarity of their needs. Naturally, it will help if their financial situation is solid, their children in good health and the world at peace. Otherwise, each will lose sleep by listening to discover whether the other is able to sleep.

Happily, Mrs Dog, less anxious than her husband, is capable of unselfish heroism and will help him to start out again hale and hearty after he has come up against some insurmountable obstacle. She will battle alongside him. This couple is interesting to contemplate and their life together quite fascinating.

Dog/Pig

They will have an excellent understanding, from which the Dog in particular will profit. The high-living Pig will bring him the zest, carefree attitude and optimism which he lacks. Both are honest, generous and understanding. They respect these qualities in each other, comforting and persuading each other that, after all, the important thing is to live and to love; leave the wolves to devour themselves and the devil with the rest!

The Dog, reassured, will be happy and serene. Even in friendship and in business he should listen to the Pig, who will give him only useful advice.

The Pig, who is sometimes awkward and naive, will benefit from the Dog's mistrust, whereas the Dog, if need be, will defend him to the end. From time to time the more philosophic Pig will become annoyed with the Dog's customary anxiety and will want to tell him to relax and keep cool. The Dog will have less fear of thieves if his spouse is a Pig, for he will have acquired a sense of proportion. Not a bad gift.

SOME DOG CELEBRITIES

Jean Anouilh, Brigitte Bardot, Bizet, Brecht, Blücher, Chou En-lai, René Clair, Debussy, Dumas, Eisenstein, Empress Eugenie, Foujita, Benjamin Franklin, Yuri Gagarin, Gambetta, Garcia Lorca, Gershwin, Hemingway, Victor Hugo, Madame de Lafayette, Leibnitz, Lenin, Sophia Loren, Louis XVI, Magritte, Marconi, Maupassant, Millet, Molière, Elvis Presley, Marcel Proust, Rasputin, Saint Louis, Schönberg, Madame de Staël, Robert Louis Stevenson, Talleyrand, Titian, Voltaire, Von Zeppelin.

YOUR
COMPANION
IN LIFE

生命伴侣

After the Chinese sign of your year of birth, here is the sign of your hour of birth

What is a Companion in Life, as understood in Chinese astrology? It is a sort of 'ascendant' sign corresponding to your hour of birth. This Companion is another animal belonging to the Chinese cycle of the twelve emblematic beasts, who falls into step with you and accompanies you, ever ready to help you brave the traps and ambushes along your route. A permanent and benevolent shadow, he can render the impossible possible.

He is your counterpart, but with his own character and tendencies and with a different psychology. Both guardian angel and devil's advocate, he will be a witness to your life and an actor in it.

Have you ever felt, deep inside yourself, the subtle presence of another 'myself' inhabiting you and with whom you live, at times in harmony, at others in conflict? Another self who sometimes criticizes you and at others encourages you? That is your Companion in Life.

There are times when he will appear to be an imposter or an intruder. Certainly, he often questions your habits and your moral or spiritual complacency. Accompanied by this companion, a shadow within, the route is less monotonous and the voyager multiplies his chances of arriving at his chosen destination. This, however, in itself matters little, for it is the journey and the manner in which it is conducted that are important. Indolence is the greatest danger: your Companion is capable of arousing you from a lassitude of spirit and, to that end, if necessary, robbing you of your certainties, trampling on your secret gardens and, finally, tearing away the great veil of illusion.

It sometimes happens that your Companion is of the same sign as your year of birth, a twin brother in a way — for example, a Dog/Dog. In this case, you must recognize that he will compel you to realize yourself fully and to live the double aspect — the Yin and the Yang — that your bear within yourself. In any case, you also bear within yourself

the twelve animals. So, set out on the long route, ready for the great adventure: the beautiful voyage during which you will encounter the harmoniously entangled, the solemn and the grotesque, the ephemeral reality, the dream and the imagined.

Table of hours corresponding to the twelve emblematic animals

If you were **born** between		your **companion** is	
11 pm and	1 am		Rat
1 am and	3 am		Ox
3 am and	5 am		Tiger
5 am and	7 am		Rabbit
7 am and	9 am		Dragon
9 am and	11 am		Snake
11 am and	1 pm		Horse
1 pm and	3 pm		Goat
3 pm and	5 pm		Monkey
5 pm and	7 pm		Rooster
7 pm and	9 pm		Dog
9 pm and	11 pm		Pig

These figures correspond to the *solar hour* of your birth. If necessary, you should check the summer times (Daylight Savings Time) and make the appropriate adjustment (sometimes two hours before or after statutory time).

819

THE DOG AND ITS COMPANION IN LIFE

Dog/Rat

He can be the ideal Companion for the Rat. The Dog is the guide for souls during their 'voyages' and is the guardian of the beyond. Like the rodent, he moves between subterranean and invisible worlds, He is, moreover, a faithful and mysterious Companion, slightly pessimistic for, symbolically, he is often associated with the idea of death. Since the Rat shares this association, the Dog's presence is not always welcome.

Perhaps one day the Rat will try to kill the Dog within him and, in battling against this guardian of the gates, he will break through his constraints. The Companion is sometimes a victim who must be sacrificed during the voyage.

Dog/Ox

Here is a mixture that is a little special, for the pessimism of the Dog added to the slowness and austerity of the Ox may result in an exceptional, if somewhat forbidding, gravity. The Dog is the ancient guardian of the underworld and the Ox of the labyrinth. This combination of the Cerebus and Minotaur will be a bit disquieting. Yet the Dog can bring a perspective and power of introspection to the Ox which he often lacks. The Ox, for his part, will alleviate the doubts, existential qualms and the tortured questions of the Dog. The Dog/Ox will thus obtain hope and lucidity. He will know himself a little better, which is the beginning of true wisdom.

 **Dog/Tiger**

He is a double guardian: the one protecting from demons, and the other protecting souls in the next world. He is a virtuous pessimist disguised in the skin of a man-eating Tiger. The Dog/Tiger will be a thoughtful animal, at ease in what is called the 'invisible' world, and prudent on his own territory. Sure of himself along the route, and calm and circumspect, his Dog side brings an awareness of time and distance, an idea of the ephemeral, as well as a sense of detachment. This Dog/Tiger knows better than anyone that, after this voyage, there will be another to be traversed. He should be careful, however, for his feet are not on the ground and his halo is askew.

 **Dog/Rabbit**

In this person the Dog element should be recognized as a guide and guardian, a faithful Companion into the invisible world which lies beyond the voyage of life. The egotistical Rabbit will discover that a precious ally lies within him. The Dog/Rabbit is circumspect, sometimes to the point of sickly distrust. While the sun may be shining on him, he will still be thinking only of the darkness to come. This animal is incapable of living in the present and has a tendency to become obsessed with past failures and future difficulties. He will weep for himself, his often imagined ills, and be depressed by the size of his task! In such moods he is incapable of looking at the simple spectacle of life going on around him, let alone enjoying it.

 **Dog/Dragon**

He is one of those who inspires confidence, and with reason: one can give him one's friendship wholeheartedly and rely on his word. The Dog/Dragon is a loyal, dedicated and faithful animal who appreciates the luck available for him throughout life, not taking it as his due, but as a gift from Providence. The Dog will understand the value of the Dragon sleeping within him; he, in turn, will give to the Dragon a sense of context, humour and an understanding of a subtle world which includes an interior dimension usually incomprehensible to the Dragon. For the Dragon is always on tenterhooks; usually, he cannot pause to reflect, let alone contemplate or meditate, and has little contact with the invisible and the hereafter.

 **Dog/Snake**

He has a keen moral sense, is intuitive, but has a tendency to be pessimistic. Life with him can become very complicated. He is the kind to torment himself to excess, announcing the onset of a hurricane at the least rising of the wind, or a deluge after a few drops of rain. Ever on the watch and constantly on guard, he risks playing the role of the persecuted, one of those flayed alive, whose company one does not usually seek. This is a drawback, particularly since the Dog/Snake is courageous, warm and understands the meaning of faithfulness. However, he has a great need of love and reassurance.

 **Dog/Horse**

Mount and guide, loyal and faithful, he tenaciously makes his way by day and night, prodded by his intuition. Tempering his impatience and his fire and never doubting his abilities, he is still able to question his ideas and actions and thus improve himself. He succeeds in controlling both his pride and his fear of failure, never hesitating to smile at his defects and his weaknesses, yet he remains ardent and passionate. His Dog side allows him to grasp secrets and dimensions that the Horse can reach only rarely and with difficulty — a world of contemplation and self-questioning in which the Horse's ardour is refined and spiritualized.

 **Dog/Goat**

He will be gifted with remarkable intuition. Unfortunately he tends to complicate his life, forever changing his moods, ideas and decisions, constantly retracing his steps and becoming distrustful and pessimistic. However, he will be both faithful and courageous. Even though his nature causes him constantly to put himself in danger, he will never capitulate; he will always see things through to the end. Basically, he needs recognition and devotion; he cannot endure solitude or a lack of affection.

 **Dog/Monkey**

A supremely intuitive animal, it will be difficult to mislead him; he will always find his way, despite obstacles and difficulties. However, he too has a tendency to complicate his life by making everything a voyage. He hates simplicity, straight lines and mapped-out routes. The Dog/Monkey will often have marked phases of exaltation and depression. Today full of spirit and sure of himself — even a little too much so — tomorrow he will see everything as being completely black, questioning his projects, research and decisions. Avoid following him if you like to travel in peace.

 **Dog/Rooster**

Imbued with honour and fidelity, the Dog/Rooster will be a sentinel and guardian, yet capable of questioning his handsome self-assurance and looking into himself and tempering his aggressiveness. He will make his way by night as well as day, straddling the two worlds of shade and sun. He will be belligerent, pessimistic and active, but the ordeals he endures will not discourage him. He will persevere, but without any wish for conquest or revenge. The Dog/Rooster will seek to improve himself but remain susceptible to those around him. He will be a man of his word and of his heart.

 **Dog/Dog**

He will make his way with fear in his heart, forever on guard and rearing up at the slightest sound. He will be a pessimist and riddled with anxiety: the only remedy will be communication with people which will oblige him to get out of himself, go beyond himself and finally, to believe in himself. The Dog/Dog cannot abide solitude; he will go well out of his way if, by so doing, he will find companions to surround himself with and cause him to feel loved. For the Dog/Dog, an offer of affection is the equivalent of a stimulant; it acts as a tonic. Love is his motor. Without it, the Dog/ Dog crawls along unsure of himself, going so far as to question why he is alive at all.

 **Dog/Pig**

The Dog/Pig will be capable of adapting to solitude: he will not hesitate to take wooded paths far from the main roads. By doing so, he will gain self-confidence and his natural self-doubt will be less apparent and weigh less on his companions. He is conscious of his individuality and will tend to turn towards the spiritual world, which attracts and fascinates him. Seeking to pass beyond the threshold of which he is guardian, he will also seek to pass that imperceptible frontier which separates the two universes. While generally favoured in social and material success, the Dog/Pig will remain an enigmatic and mysterious animal to his companions.

THE DOG AND THE FIVE ELEMENTS

五行

YOUR ELEMENT

In Chinese astrology, each year is joined to an Element. There are five Elements: *Water, Fire, Wood, Metal, Earth.*

Each of the twelve emblematic animals is linked successively to each of the five Elements. For example, in the year 1900 the Rat was Metal, in 1912 he was Water, in 1924 he was Wood, in 1936, Fire and in 1948 he was Earth. Therefore, for the twelve years from 1900 he was linked to Metal, for the next twelve years to Water, and, for every succeeding period of twelve years, to each of the other Elements, in succession.

In order to determine the Element corresponding to the year of your birth, use the table below:

> *Years whose digits end in:* 2 and 3 — Water
> 6 and 7 — Fire
> 4 and 5 — Wood
> 0 and 1 — Metal
> 8 and 9 — Earth

The same union of *Animal-Element* repeats every sixty years, for example, Rat-Metal appeared in 1720, 1780, 1840, 1900, 1960 and so on.

The five Elements are the primary forces affecting the universe. It is their particular association with each of the signs which provides the basis for every horoscope. Movement and fluctuation, Yin and Yang, these symbolic forces are in a perpetual state of action and interaction.

Wood gives birth to Fire, which gives birth to Earth, which gives birth to Metal, which gives birth to Water, which in turn gives birth to Wood.

DOG/WATER
(you were born in 1922 or 1982)

The cold born of the northern sky descended to Earth and gave birth to Water. The Chinese consider Water more a synonym for coldness and ice than a symbol of fertility.

Characteristics of the Dog/Water

Water of winter nights, rigour and severity; calm and deep water to be feared and respected; still water sheltering underwater demons asleep in its depth; fetid and muddy water of the marshes, the refuge of crawling creatures.

The Dog/Water, who is of the Yin tendency, will feel so at ease in his Yin Element Water, which so permeates and infiltrates, that he will be tempted to indulge too much. It may slow him in his course, even if it does not stop him completely. He will seek in it a refuge from his anxieties, doubts and pessimism. Belonging to the earth-water-moon trilogy, the Dog forever seeks a lost paradise, wandering on the edge of obscure worlds.

Health of the Dog/Water

The Water organ is the kidney, its flavour is salty. The pessimistic and anxiety-ridden Dog should be aggresive and dynamic, seeking energy in the Water Element, which is also a tonic and ensures that the salty taste will not come from his own tears.

The Dog/Water and others

The Dog/Water will be active and enterprising, and always scrupulous and virtuous. One of his principal qualities will be perseverance. He will not back away from an obstacle, will be ready to listen to others and will be accessible to advice. Alas, he will lack self-confidence and with his first mistake will fall into a state of self-doubt. Sometimes those around him will be tempted to take advantage of his retreats into himself and his emotional imbalance and set out to exploit them. While the Dog/Water will be perfectly aware of this, he will refuse to accept it, preferring to blame himself rather than question his relationships or his friends. Moreover, he will tend to dramatize certain situations, finding pleasure in their misty outlines and blurred and illusory meanings. Advise him to see with a clearer eye, even if this requires great effort.

Advice for the Dog/Water

You are pure, faithful and hold to your convictions. Do not acquire a taste for troubled and muddy waters, as this is no place for a Dog. Do not criticize your nature; rather, seek to know yourself.

A Dog/Water year

The culminating point for a Dog/Water year will be winter, a period of gestation. You are not only meditative, you are also belligerent. Balance is necessary; divide your time between reflection and action. Do not allow yourself to be attracted to sleeping waters, mist and fog; go to a spring where the water is limpid and running. Believe in yourself: chase away your doubts and you will recover your energy and vigour — do not resign this right.

Historical example of a Dog/Water year
1682

Louis XIV moved his court and his government to his great creation at Versailles. Here the 'Sun King' reigned in a splendour unparalleled since the Roman Empire and as intricate and demanding in its ceremonials as the movement of a clock. The Louvre had been plundered of its treasures and the great cabinet makers, jewellers and rare metal workers unremittingly employed for its embellishment. The new palace resembled a vast museum of all that France had invented or could create for the enhancement of living. Its fountains and terraces surpassed the great gardens of the d'Este family and were open to all to visit, so long as they were decently dressed. As a seal of its splendour, Mme la Dauphine was there delivered of a son, Louis, Duke of Burgundy, on 6 August amid a torrent of illuminations, fireworks, cannonfire and carillons of bells.

By contrast, the English scene was one of comparative poverty and evident dissension. Charles II has been criticized for his pro-French policies but it was French money which supplied him with the funds Parliament refused to vote, whatever his policies might be. Increasingly the English monarch would escape to his small residence in Newmarket and from there take to the sea in one of his yachts, free from the fret and greed of the London mob. In 1682 his brother, the Duke of York, was able to return to England, a Catholic excluded from office by the Test Acts, his future children excluded from the throne to which he was the heir by Acts of Exclusion. For both of them, things would have been ordered better in France.

DOG/WOOD
(you were born in 1934)

To the East, the wind blew in the sky and from its warm caress of the earth wood was born.

Characteristics of the Dog/Wood

Wood is of the morning, of springtime. Its temperate nature loves harmony, beauty and elegance. Springtime is a symbol of gentleness, a period in which all nature awakens and opens itself to the forces of youth, creation and growth.

The Dog/Wood, who is intuitive, even a seer, will be sensitive to this blossoming and to the tenderness which impregnates it. In it he will find a poetic vision which will ease his passage on earth and encourage him in the expression of subtle emotions aligned to the world of the arts and other creative activities. This can lead the Dog/Wood to find his proper equilibrium, but he must not exceed its limits, for Wood is a passionate Element and capable of sudden outbursts of violent anger. Generally, the doubts and anxieties which the Dog is heir to could be sublimated in this aesthetic contact with nature and the world.

Health of the Dog/Wood

The organ of Wood is the liver; its flavour is acid. If you are anguished or let yourself be carried away by terrible outbursts of anger, do not turn to over-eating as compensation.

The Dog/Wood and others

The Dog/Wood hides his lack of self-confidence beneath a calm and relaxed exterior. This is a defensive reaction, for he feels ill-at-ease when not in his own world. With his ever-ready imagination, he is always adept at improvisation, able to convince, confuse and attract. In fact, the Dog/Wood is a seducer; his charm lies in his unaffected behaviour, his love of the arts and his feelings for the countryside. There, sheltered from tumult and chaos and far from the noise and excitement which make him want to run away, he will love to spend his time. This Dog is a lover of natural harmony and poetry; without them liberty has no meaning for him.

Advice for the Dog/Wood

By overcoming your anxiety, you can come to feel perfectly at ease. Essentially, you are a well-balanced person with great charm who knows how to attract others; so, above all, change nothing!

A Dog/Wood year

The culminating point for a Dog/Wood year will be springtime, a period of growth and prosperity.

You who seek harmony and beauty will be gratified to the full, above all if you are an artist who is sensitive to nature. Be careful, however, of losing your temper or of being intolerant.

Historical example of a Dog/Wood year
1214

In vigour and sagacity Philip Augustus was probably the greatest, certainly the most successful, of the Capetian Kings of France. Philip not only recovered great tracts of territory from the English; he recovered them into his direct possession. The Angevin lands formerly held through Eleanor of Aquitaine, wife of Henry II of England, and those of the Norman barons held through Henry's youngest son, John, were all taken into the patrimony of the French Crown. In 1214 Philip Augustus assured the future of his kingdom and his dynasty.

Philip had his share of luck for in John, King of England, he who was to submit to the Magna Carta the following year, he faced an incompetent.

In 1213 Philip had, with the Pope's blessing, been ready to launch a crusade against England, then under interdict. The threat united the English despite the character of their monarch. However, John was not prepared to surrender his French possessions and, instead of luring Philip into the trap posed by invasion, set about an adventure in France. He made peace with the Pope, set up alliances in Germany, secured the support of the new Count of Flanders and attached the Emperor Otto IV to his cause.

The plan was for Otto to invade northern France while John struck north from Aquitaine. John hardly put up a fight; his campaign was an ignominious failure. Meanwhile, Philip routed the Emperor's forces at Bouvines and put his achievements of the previous decade beyond the reach of any foreseeable counter-attack, either from England or the Empire.

DOG/FIRE
(you were born in 1946)

Heat was born in the southern sky, descended to Earth and fertilized it. From their union, Fire was born.

832

Characteristics of the Dog/Fire

The Fire Element is of the midday, the South, of summer. Fire is Yang; it is the Element which animates; it quickens and transforms.

The Fire inhabiting a Dog will bring him the strength necessary to vanquish his doubt and his pessimism; it will give him energy and vitality. But this Fire could also be an interior Fire, and the Dog — respectful of rites, sensitive to symbols and as the guardian of the afterworld — will seek the key to this mysterious portal and to this lost language known only to initiates. In this way he would no longer be condemned to stand before the threshold of the afterworld which haunts him and desperately attracts him. So compelled, he will truly assume his role of secret guide, his phosphorescent eyes chasing away the shadows and piercing through the darkness.

Health of the Dog/Fire

The organ of Fire is the heart, its flavour is bitter. You are animated by a formidable energy which could turn against you and become destructive. Control your impulses and distrust hyperactivity, which can lead to depression.

The Dog/Fire and others

The Dog/Fire will not be easy to live with. Always on tenterhooks, he will be perpetually agitated and eternally unsatisfied. Impelled by violent passions and sudden anger, he will often appear to be impossible. Belligerent and untiring, but also honest and pure, nothing can make him change his mind or lessen his resolve. As a leader he will be implacable and as hard on his collaborators as on himself; he will not permit any form of opposition.

Sometimes he is attracted to mysticism and will decide that he should cut himself off from the world and all contact with his fellow men. Concerned exclusively with spiritual realities, he will live completely isolated, confined within a rigorous and ardent asceticism.

Advice for the Dog/Fire
You are an exceptional person. Make full use of your potential — in the end you will be accepted for what you are.

A Dog/Fire year
The culminating point for a Dog/Fire year will be the summer, a period of creation.

An active, aggressive year, full of energy, which will bring you material success or attainment of that spritual universe which so attracts you. But be careful: do not disperse your energy nor consume yourself with vain display.

Historical example of a Dog/Fire year 1886

Gladstone, Prime Minister of England, brought in the Home Rule Bill for Ireland and thus split the Liberal party. There followed a twenty-year period of almost uninterrupted Conservative rule characterized by the 'enlightened' imperial policies espoused by Joseph Chamberlain. Judged solely from the point of view of The Irish Question Gladstone's was the only practical solution, and if his party had had the full support of the country it had once enjoyed, its political representatives would not now have been subject to the divisive influences which rent it apart.

However, a significant element of the Liberal support in the country had, for social and economic reasons, shifted to the Conservatives. Despite the Second Reform Act of 1867 English political society remained restricted in the main to the upper and middle classes and in the counties the landowners were its nexus. Impoverished by the 'great depression' many of the lesser members of the rural aristocracy sought to revive their fortunes and retain their land by marrying their children to those of successful industrialists. The latter were generally Conservatives, and a subtle but significant change occurred in influential London society which determined the flavour and sometimes the course of events at Westminster.

In 1886 protectionist countries such as the United States, Germany and Japan brought about a partial decline in English industry. The Labour movement was forced to look to its political future. This would lie in the formation of an Independent Labour Party which was to sap the springs of traditional Liberal support.

DOG/EARTH
(you were born in 1958)

Earth was born from the slowly falling Elements of the sky at its humid zenith.

Characteristics of the Dog/Earth

This is an afternoon Earth, the humid and hot Earth of summer. It is the symbol of the well-cushioned, soft nest; of comfort and abundance. It is an Earth of slow and profound transformations.

Usually the Dog/Earth is something of an egotist; absorbed by his anxieties and fearful of committing himself, he shrinks from taking risks. On the other hand, he is preoccupied with material success. Avid for notoriety, tormented by a powerful need for public recognition, he devotes himself heart and soul to his schemes and social ambitions. He sometimes seems to be generous and devoted; but this is usually a simple piece of opportunism, for he does not hesitate to use the work of others for his own profit, as though it were naturally his due. These particular aspects of the Earth Element are not very easy for a Dog to integrate into his personality, since they conflict with his essential nature. Nevertheless, there remains for the Dog/ Earth the opportunity to adjust himself to these conditions by a process of self-examination. If he succeeds, he can then use the Earth Element as a symbol of refuge and meditation.

Health of the Dog/Earth

The Earth's organ is the spleen, its flavour is sweet. The Dog/Earth should discipline himself with physical exercise and not give in to self-indulgence. Otherwise, he will become obese in old age.

The Dog/Earth and others

The Dog/Earth will be realistic and pragmatic. He will also be canny, imaginative and creative, especially in business or commerce. Moreover, being both shrewd and sceptical, he will not engage himself lightly. Capable of being an excellent banker, company chairman, property developer or politician, he will choose a profession which will offer him the scope to build a reputation or a fortune, which he will manage meticulously and jealously, not even trusting those close to him. The Dog/Earth will not hesitate to exploit his partners or members of his own family to attain his ends. Despotic and authoritarian, he may often seem like a vampire to his family or associates. Yet the Dog is faithful and loyal and will thus be capable of sincere friendship, while remaining indifferent to the contradictions of his nature. He will take back with one hand what he has given away with the other; at times he will seem to be a victim of amnesia.

Advice for a Dog/Earth

Reach down a little into your own Element; let the honest and faithful Dog part of you speak — that Dog who seeks paradise and is a guide and companion to men.

A Dog/Earth year

The culminating point for a Dog/Earth year is summer, the symbol of fertility and abundance. At this time the Dog will be relieved of his daily task of seeking food, the lot of every animal. Reserve this season for your mind and your heart: examine yourself and open yourself up to others; try and stretch your limits; enlarge your horizons and your vision of the world.

Historical example of a Dog/Earth year
1958

The United Arab Republic was established, a step, but only a step, towards the cause of Pan-Arab unity pursued by President Nasser of Egypt.

Harold Macmillan, who had succeeded Eden as Prime Minister, set about the task of restoring England's morale, gravely bruised by the Suez fiasco in 1956. By securing an independent nuclear armoury he encouraged the impression that England was still a power to be reckoned with, and by his policies at home and his speeches he cleverly persuaded the English of their material prosperity, a conviction amply reflected when his party was returned to power the following year. In 1958 Macmillan etched in firm outline his image of the 'unflappable'.

The French situation posed more complex problems than the English. The war in Algeria was beyond the power of the fourth Republic to solve for, ultimately, its constitution allowed of too great a disparity for its ministry to pursue any policy to a firm conclusion. Only one man could solve the crisis — de Gaulle. On 1 June he laid claim to the leadership of France before the National Assembly. He evoked the menaces of civil war, outlined the principles which should govern the new constitution he sought, and demanded unrestricted powers for six months. He was accorded them. Thus the fifth Republic was born and the future of France and of Europe reorientated.

DOG/METAL
(you were born in 1910 or 1970)

In the sky, coming from the West, drought grazed the skin of the Earth and gave birth to Metal.

Characteristics of the Dog/Metal
Metal is of the night, the autumn and cold.

The Dog/Metal will oscillate between beauty and death, and at times, unhappily, between material success and spiritual preoccupations, seeking glittering success but also an internal, secret light. Alas, like a moth, he will tend to destroy himself in that light. The Dog/Metal is discerning and lucid, but he cannot seem to avoid torturing himself by curbing his natural impulses, throttling his impetuous instincts and cutting himself off from his deepest roots. He thus erects his own prison, and, by forging his own chains, puts on an iron collar of rules and regulations, and a straightjacket of dogmas.

However, he will remain a Dog, gifted with intuition and subtle vision. But his armour condemns him to solitude and doubt, compelling him to grope blindly towards the light.

Health of the Dog/Metal

Metal's organ is the lung, its flavour is pungent. The Dog/Metal possesses the remedy to his ills, on condition that he really wishes to pay attention to his body and that he stops stifling himself.

The Dog/Metal and others

The Dog/Metal will not be encumbered by scruples: to attain success he will frequently transgress the Dog's principles of loyalty and honesty. For him there are no useless feelings, no gratuitous acts, no wasted time or useless diplomacy. If he attains a top position requiring heavy responsibilities, the Dog/Metal will show a highly developed sense of leadership. Everything will be organized and carefully programmed; nothing will be left to chance and everything will be subservient to his will. However, his doubts will persist and, to protect himself, he will insist on settling things, refusing to round out the angles, to see subtleties or to temper his judgements. Thus he will be difficult to live with and, if he does not take care, will end his life alone, facing himself and his contradictions.

Advice for the Dog/Metal

There is a chink in every armour; you alone can pinpoint it, provided you really want to. That is what is meant by free will.

A Dog/Metal year

The culminating point in a Dog/Metal year will be autumn.

Try to enlarge your horizons, open your heart and pay attention to your body's needs. Your general equilibrium depends on this. Learn to be attentive to others and meditate on 'a healthy mind in a healthy body'

Historical example of a Dog/Metal year 1610

Referred to as the 'wisest fool in Christendom' and, equally derisively, as 'the British Solomon', James VI of Scotland ruled in England as James I. Conciliation was the keynote to his reign, in foreign policy, in religion and between Crown and Parliament; but James lacked the political finesse necessary for success.

This mattered less in matters of foreign policy than in home affairs. He quickly concluded a peace with Spain and was later asked to mediate between Spain and France. In religion he attempted to follow Elizabeth's middle way but was suspected, rightly, of Papist sympathies and past Papist practices. In finance, he inherited a depleted treasury and what is now called an inflationary problem and sought to remedy this by the system known as 'impositions', a tax that he had a prerogative right to levy but unwisely did so at the time he was seeking a reconciliation with Parliament by his scheme for the Great Contract. In 1610 he gave way on the heaviest of the impositions but failed to secure parliamentary co-operation. In this predicament the fanciful side of James's nature came to his aid. He thought up a new hereditary order of knighthood, the Knight Baronet. The following year he floated the issue; it was eagerly taken up by the new families who had founded landed estates under the Tudors whose sons would now inherit the benefit of the patent.

Analogical Table
of the Different Elements

Elements	Wood	Fire	Earth	Metal	Water
Years ending in	4 and 5	6 and 7	8 and 9	0 and 1	2 and 3
Colours	Green	Red	Yellow	White	Blue
Seasons	Spring	Summer	End of summer	Autumn	Winter
Climates	Wind	Heat	Humid	Dry	Cold
Flavours	Acid	Bitter	Sweet	Pungent	Salty
Principal organ	Liver	Heart	Spleen	Lungs	Kidneys
Secondary organ	Gallbladder	Small intestine	Stomach	Large intestine	Bladder
Food	Wheat, poultry	Rice, lamb	Corn, beef	Oats, horse	Peas, pork

Table of Harmony
Between the Elements

		Wood Female	Fire Female	Earth Female	Metal Female	Water Female
OOO Excellent prosperity	Male Wood	• •	O	O O O	O	O O
OO Good harmony, understanding	Male Fire	O	O	O O	•	• •
O Effort needed	Male Earth	• •	O O	O O	O O O	•
• Rivalries and problems of reciprocal domination	Male Metal	O	• •	•	• •	O O O
• • Misunderstanding and incomprehension	Male Water	O O	• •	•	O O O	O

THE FOUR SEASONS OF THE DOG

四季

If you were born in spring
Dog/Aries
There is quite a lot to be said for the Dog born under the sign of Aries, whose influence will lighten the seriousness of his make-up, increase his energy and help him to be more open towards others. The Dog/Aries is less meddlesome than his fellows. He reflects, likes to analyse situations, but is also capable of acting quickly. In short, he is something of a complete being.

Extremely idealistic and little concerned with his personal comfort, the Dog/Aries will make more of an effort to improve the daily life of his family than to ensure there is money for new clothes. His appearance does not interest him and he is quite likely to wear the same shirt over and over again — clean enough, but with frayed cuffs and collar; he will give away the new ones to the poor. He is too generous to have a sense of ownership. Do not offer him gifts if you like them to be well cared for; it is not that he is negligent, but that he sincerely believes that someone else needs a thing more than he does.

The Dog/Aries is an exceptional fighter when motivated by the knowledge of an injustice which he is convinced he must set to rights. But he has no sense of strategy and will need a companion who can formulate his battle plans.

Dog/Taurus
This alliance is also positive. The Dog will profit from the good sense, constructive bent and healthy sensuality of Taurus. He will lose some of his scepticism and will learn to profit from life. Intelligent, with a capacity for rapid assimilation, he will gain and learn from experience. The Dog/Taurus can make a successful businessman, and will be appreciated not only for his realism but also for his sense of justice and simplicity. He is not a snob, and likes to be at ease, both morally and physically.

However, he risks running into some emotional difficulties because, passionate, faithful and loving, he is constantly in fear of losing the person he loves. Seeking to reassure himself of the strength of the other's feelings, he sometimes becomes extremely irritating. On the material level, he is very attached to his possessions and loathes giving anything up. Chauvinistic, attached to his home, his family and his origins, he obstinately guards his security: a true Watch-Dog. If you love a Dog/Taurus and he returns your love, you will be tranquil for life. But take good care of him and be tactful; he is a bundle of sensitivity, a bit clumsy and awkward and needs tenderness.

Dog/Gemini

The nervousness and latent instability of Gemini is not good for the Dog. He will not be able to keep still and will not know if he should remain at home to protect his house or take a walk to see what is happening outside. His curiosity helps him to surmount his anxiety. He is sociable, likes company, but can surprise others by his sudden changes of mood: one minute chattering away, the next withdrawing into quiet introspection and then, suddenly, reversing the process.

In fact, the Dog/Gemini is alway seeking a stability within himself, which he has difficulty finding. By sniffing everywhere and ferreting about he may find a treasure, but he is just as likely to be scratched by a marauding cat; for he is not distrustful nor selective enough in his relationships. His enthusiasms — as well as his discouragements — are intense and cause him to live either at great heights or among the depths during a good part of his life; his fighter's path closely resembles the motions of a seesaw.

The Dog/Gemini could blossom and become more relaxed, even brilliant, if sustained by a stable, peaceful person who would help him organize his life and define his aims, limits and frontiers. He is not made to live alone.

If you were born in summer
Dog/Cancer

If you meet a Dog/Cancer, do not trust appearances. He often seems completely indifferent, blasé and total encased in protective armour. Abandoned by everyone, criticized and misunderstood, he will respond with a slight and scornful smile, which will make you think that he feels nothing. But you will be wrong: the Dog/Cancer is, perhaps, among all the possible alliances between Chinese and Western signs, the most sensitive, emotionally fragile and vulnerable. Although he is a master at projecting a semblance of tranquillity, under his steely self-protectiveness he is covered with wounds — and he heals badly.

The Dog/Cancer resembles an inexhaustible reservoir, replete with that 'milk of human kindness' of which Shakespeare wrote. Always putting himself in the place of others, he understands them, feels sorry for them and would like to defend them. To say that this eliminates him from careers in which an aggressive spirit is indispensable is to state the obvious; but there is one exception: if he becomes involved in aiding the oppressed. He will do very well in some kind of social work, willingly going to peel vegetables for a poverty-stricken family, watched by the incredulous eyes of their starving children. The soup will be salted by tears.

Dog/Leo
A sleigh-Dog. If he is properly motivated (always essential for a Dog), he will, without apparent fatigue and without complaining, travel round the world dragging a heavy burden of responsibilities that he shoulders with remarkable elegance. He profoundly believes that he is someone of value, that he has a power, a magnetism, that most others do not possess, and he wishes to use this to an unselfish end. The Dog/Leo is a great gentleman.

Obviously, he has his weak points: since his mission is to help, he finds it incomprehensible if his protection is refused. Also, if he finds himself standing in a queue, he will devour the other dogs until his supremacy is recognized. He does this not because he is cruel, but because he is not sure that he can have confidence in others; it is better for everyone if he is the leader. No one combines to this degree such a certitude of his own value with such a lack of egotism. Be careful: if he begins to doubt himself, the consequences will be terrible and he will become bitter and vengeful. Help him to believe in his own worth and usefulness.

Dog/Virgo

Eyes anxious, always watchful, he remains in his kennel, hoping that no one will come to attack his perfectly structured universe; for then he would be obliged to fight, something he detests. This peace-loving but nervous and anxious Dog will resort to any means to forestall dangers which he cannot be certain he is equipped to face. He underestimates himself, has complexes, is complicated and perpetually on edge.

Gentle and faithful, he takes his role as guardian of the hearth and of moral virtues very seriously and believes that without them society would be no more than a terrifying jungle. He has the soul of a sentinel. All will be well for him if he can be certain that the army is behind its fortifications, ready to fall upon the invader — for that is not part of his job as sentinel.

His need for security requires evidence of order. He is scrupulously careful and precise, pigeon-holing every one of his emotions to ensure that none of them overwhelms him. Modest and timid, he does not know how to declare himself, gazing at you with limpid eyes in which all the tenderness in the world lies hidden. One gesture, and he will be devoted to you forever; one unfeeling word and he will run for cover to his kennel, ears dragging. Sensitive and thin-skinned, security is his deepest need. Give him an efficient alarm system — then he will finally be able to sleep in peace.

If you were born in autumn
Dog/Libra

The Dog/Libra is a sociable individual, but hesitant because he is a perfectionist. In seeking the ideal balance he becomes, in spite of himself, so demanding and selective that he often ends up without a flower to his name. In which case he will demolish his previous construction and begin all over again. After several centuries he will have succeeded in recreating the Garden of Eden — but without the Snake, of course.

He is filled with gifts ranging from an understanding of organization and a feeling for aesthetics to a developed sense of tact supported by a sensitivity to nuance. He is marked by a certain delicacy, never forgetting a birthday and delighting in the giving of flowers. He is wary of conflict, dislikes making a fuss and rarely imposes his knowledge or ideas on others. An apostle of non-violence, he is a conciliatory lover of justice who resolves problems with discretion and diplomacy. He often risks being surrounded by a mass of parasites whom he is incapable of throwing out due to his soft-heartedness.

If he really wishes to achieve something concrete in life, he should ally himself with someone energetic and enterprising; otherwise, he may slide into becoming a dilettante. Because personal conflict is rather contrary to his nature, he needs to develop the will to engage in it when necessary. He depends a little too much on the company of others.

Dog/Scorpio

The Dog/Scorpio is not at all sociable: plunged into a superficial atmosphere (superficial in his eyes at least), he will cheerfully criticize the company, furniture, neighbourbood and paintings, leaving behind a petrified audience. A specialist in sharp phrases perfumed with acid, he figures that he can be more useful to others by serving up a well-thought out analysis of their behaviour, rather than by covering them with syrupy flattery.

His problem centres on the profound differences which separate him from the rest of humanity. Incapable of lightening his life by little compromises, the Dog/Scorpio is often a solitary person and can easily develop an exclusion complex. He feels rejected and repulsed by others, even when this is not at all the case. Anxious, suffering from qualms and torments, he is gifted with a lucidity which does not allow comforting illusions. He can become cynical and disillusioned. While he has fine qualities — courage, inner strength, resistance and self-sacrifice — he cannot apply them to his daily life. As far as possible, avoid attacking him. He is extremely distrustful, and, in combat, willingly adopts the expedient philosophy of 'shoot first and talk afterwards'.

Dog/Sagittarius

This is an independent Dog who needs space, liberty and will never be content with being taken out twice a day. His vitality is so great that he tends to race about and bark at anyone in sight. It is important that he is taught from a very young age at least some discipline and respect for decorum. If he learns these, he may be capable of accomplishing great things.

The Dog/Sagittarius is a warm-blooded idealist who would certainly have felt more at ease as a knight in the Middle Ages, wearing his beloved's colours, than today, obliged to stand in a queue at the Post Office or the Social Security office. He is not against these services, but he wants them to move fast.

He is also a moralist and a defender of human rights, provided they have sufficient justification. He tends to qualify daily cares as petty, and forever active, he would willingly drag everyone along his quest for the Holy Grail. In love, the Dog/Sagittarius is faithful, not because he is a moralist but because of his sense of honour. Any deception is odious to him, and he suffers greatly when another's disloyalty is exposed.

If you were born in winter
Dog/Capricorn

He is not unlike one of those marvellous shepherd dogs that takes care of large flocks of sheep, apparently peaceful but always on the alert, ever ready to recover lost sheep and recalcitrant lambs. The Dog/Capricorn has a very high conception of his duties and responsibilities. He sleeps with one eye open. Reserved, cold and distant, when he smiles one has the impression that he is grimacing, because it is not his habit to smile. Because he is not demonstrative, talkative nor eloquent, he is considered detached, glacial and insensitive. However, when you are in deep trouble, he will help you — and not with comforting words (they are not his style), but with actions; which is indeed agreeable!

The Dog/Capricorn is an emotionally suppressed person who hides behind a handsome edifice of irony. But when he is invaded by some strong feeling, he loses his way, blushes and becomes as mute as a carp.

Although he makes one feel secure, he is not easy to live with, being incapable of the slightest compromise. Of inflexible honesty, he calmly conforms to his numerous moral principles and does his duty.

Dog/Aquarius

Ingenuous and idealistic, he rarely takes on commitments equal to the high level of his ambition for, despite his good will, the necessary stimulus is often lacking. Consequently, a vague feeling of bitterness and dissatisfaction results, which he disguises behind caustic behaviour. The Dog/Aquarius's humour tends to be cynical and clear-sighted and he plays with this marvellously, even while asking himself what he is doing. If attacked, he turns a deaf ear, and if those he loves are attacked, he bites. Be careful: do not assume that his peaceful expression means that he is a mummy's boy. Despite his absent air and apparent vagueness, the Dog/Aquarius is more than capable of fighting back. The playwright Jean Anouilh's phrase could refer to him: 'If soldiers began to think, there would be nothing left to do but to place chairs on the battlefield.'

He possesses to an intense degree the sort of courage that causes some to risk their lives for a cause in which they do not even completely believe. Faithful and generous to his friends, he is devoted and indulgent to his family without finding it necessary to be authoritarian. He is also discreet in the extreme: if you can extract a confidence from him it will be a miracle, but do not be surprised if he disappears for several weeks in order to recuperate.

Dog/Pisces

In imaginative and charitable Dog, he needs a stable emotional life in order to be happy and well balanced. Unless he can openly express his feelings, he is capable of interminable suffering and of subsiding into pessimism and melancholy.

The Dog/Pisces has a passion for being of use to others. He is happiest when he is told 'I could not do without you'. This gives him the impression that he truly exists and that his existence is justified. He willingly leaves material responsibilities to others, although he is neither ambitious nor selfish. He is not unlike one of those smiling hippies who can melt you with nostalgic ballads celebrating a world of peace, love and harmony. But, after several years, you will regret that he only sings.

The Dog/Pisces is suited to a professional life which does not demand discipline nor precise structures. He is happy living at his own rhythm, having just enough to eat and a roof over his head. Above all, be careful not to jostle or hustle him, or he will become enraged.

THE I CHING

易经

THE I CHING AND THE DOG

In the I Ching game you ask a question and obtain an answer. It is therefore a divining game; but, in asking your question, you pose it with your Dog identity. The wheel, the complex mechanism of your mind and spirit have begun to turn. You ask a Dog question and the I Ching answers with a Dog 'solution', on which you can meditate as a Dog before arriving at a Dog conclusion. The player is given a hexagram which contains the 'hypothesis-response' to his question, or, more exactly, the synthesis of forces affecting the concern or even inquired about.

For you, Master Dog, here are the sixty-four hexagrams of the I Ching and their sixty-four Dog hypotheses.

How to proceed
1. The question
Ask a question regarding any problem at all, past, present or future, personally concerning you. (If the question concerns a friend, consult the I Ching game in the book corresponding to his Chinese sign.)

2. Method of play
It must be done with concentration.
Take **three ordinary and similar coins** — for example, three 50p coins.
Heads will equal the number 3.
Tails will equal the number 2.
Throw the coins.
If the result is two coins showing Heads and one Tails, write 3 + 3 + 2. You thus obtain a total of 8 which you represent by a continuous line: ━━━

852

Draw the same continuous line if you have three coins showing Heads $(3+3+3=9)$.

If you throw two coins showing Tails and one Heads $(2+2+3=7)$, or all three showing Tails $(2+2+2=6)$, draw two separate lines: ▬ ▬

To sum up, 8 and 9 correspond to: ▬▬▬ (Yin)

6 and 7 correspond to: ▬ ▬ (Yang)

Repeat this operation *six times,* noting at the time of each throw the figure obtained on a piece of paper, proceeding from the first to the sixth figure, from bottom to top

The final result, including a trigram from the bottom, or lower trigram (example: ≡ ≡), and a trigram of the top, or upper trigram (example: ≡ ≡), will be a hexagram of the I Ching. In our example this would look like:

Now merely look for the hexagram number in the table on page 854, and then consult the list of hexagrams with their descriptions to find the given answer. *In our example,* the hexagram obtained is number 63, entitled **After completion.**

Table of Hexagrams

Trigrams	Upper lines ☰	☵	☶
Lower lines			
☰	1	11	34
☷	12	2	16
☳	25	24	51
☵	6	7	40
☶	33	15	62
☴	44	46	32
☲	13	36	55
☱	10	19	54

Use this table to find the number of your hexagrams. The meeting point between the lower and upper trigrams indicates the number of the hexagram that you are seeking.

☵	☶	☲	☳	☱
5	26	9	14	43
8	23	20	35	45
3	27	42	21	17
29	4	59	64	47
39	52	53	56	31
48	18	57	50	28
63	22	37	30	49
60	41	61	38	58

THE HEXAGRAMS OF THE DOG

CH'IEN

1  *The creative:* Energy, strength and will, together with the creative spirit. The anxious Dog should accept that time is on his side rather than an instrument of his anxieties; he must cease to worry about the future — to do so is obsessive and sterile.

K'UN

2  *The receptive:* You are sensitive and intuitive; you cannot disregard this earth which supports you so receptively — it is your partner.

CHUN

3  *Initial difficulty:* You cannot continue to walk in a fog, despite your good eyesight, and all the more so since you have the power of influencing time. So make the utmost of this precious faculty.

MÊNG

4  *Youthful folly:* 'It is not I who seek the young fool, but the young fool who seeks me.' One does not need to teach a puppy to be playful. To deny that the obstacle exists does not avoid danger — to acknowledge a peril is already to limit its effects.

HSÜ

5  *Waiting:* This should not be the source of anxiety, but of self-control. Forget everything which is not *before you here and now.*

856

SUNG

6 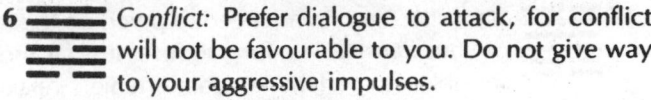 *Conflict:* Prefer dialogue to attack, for conflict will not be favourable to you. Do not give way to your aggressive impulses.

SHIH

7 *The army:* Seek unity the better to fight the battle; the obedience asked of you is only a question of good will. It will be in your best interest from every point of view.

PI

8 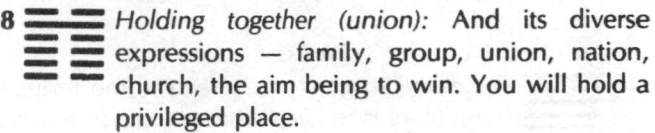 *Holding together (union):* And its diverse expressions — family, group, union, nation, church, the aim being to win. You will hold a privileged place.

SHIAO CH'U

9 *The taming power of the small:* Do not measure your distance according to the length of your leash; such reasoning could lead to tragic errors.

LÜ

10 *Treading:* 'Tread on the tail of the Tiger, he does not bite man.' Even for a police dog, the operation is delicate and requires skill and tact. Custom and protocol must be scrupulously respected.

T'AI

11 *Peace:* It is as short-lived as a truce between dogs and cats. Do not be insistent, but mark out your territory and remain tranquilly at home. Do not provoke your neighbours — the least spark could blow everything up.

P'I

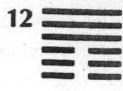 12 *Standstill:* You do not need to perch on the top of your kennel, in a formal pose. It is far more sensible to adopt a comfortable, relaxed position and let the storm pass.

T'UNG JÊN

 13 *Fellowship with men:* Live your life openly and move in the full light of the sun and of nature. Be confident, for your success is assured. Above all, do not listen to the inner demons who are urging you to retreat within yourself.

TA YU

 14 *Possession in great measure:* The most difficult thing of all is to keep what you have; above all when consumed with chronic and almost pathological anxiety.

CH'IEN

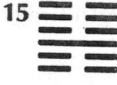 15 *Modesty:* Seek equilibrium and be constant to its principles and to its guiding thread in life. This is possible for a Dog, so long as he does not repeatedly doubt his destiny and its possibilities.

YÜ

 16 *Enthusiasm:* You must overcome your pessimism and become sharper and more pungent. Become a young wolf and slip your collar: by yourself, completely independently, you can undertake great things.

SUI

 17 *Following:* Or, the result of your capacity to enchant; your particular charm. Your rather strange and melancholic magnetism is now fully effective.

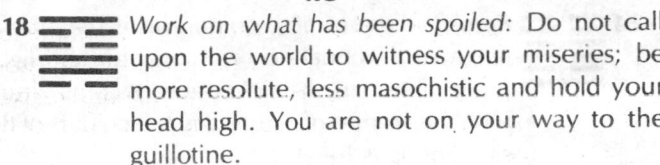

KU

18 *Work on what has been spoiled:* Do not call upon the world to witness your miseries; be more resolute, less masochistic and hold your head high. You are not on your way to the guillotine.

LIN

19 *Approach:* Consider what you wish to achieve and carefully assess your chances before undertaking anything. Premature decisions could be fatal.

KUAN

20 *Contemplation:* Climb to the summit of the tower to meditate, but remember that you must come down. Unless you do, your solitude could make its own prison.

SHIH HO

21 *Biting through (or clearly defined penalties):* Attack, bare your teeth and bite. Make an example: are you not the guardian, the manacing Cerebus? To resort to lying will prove ineffective.

PI

22 *Grace:* Even if you are offered a tasty bone, make sure that it is not in fact some explosive device. Exploit your flair and the intrigues of your enemies will rebound against them.

PO

23 *Splitting apart:* Do not enter marshy terrain; if you are in the mountains, beware of an avalanche or landslide at first not visible to the naked eye. Be doubly prudent, but do not panic or be faint-hearted.

THE DOG

FU

24 *Return — the turning point:* This is the time to leave your kennel, to rediscover air and light. Frolic about in the fields and become drunk with the aromas of nature and the colours of the sky. Spring is here!

WU WANG

25 *Innocence:* You are intuitive and instinctive and have a flair for things, but you can make mistakes. Beware of following a false trail; if you persist, it could lead you to the dog-pound.

TA CH'U

26 *The taming power of the great:* Power and strength. For once, do not doubt yourself, but do think of questioning yourself. If you are to avoid being dragged down, you must move.

I

27 *The corners of the mouth:* Feeding of the mind and of the body. Even if you possess the hunger of a wolf and a thirst for knowledge, remember that it is not enough to swallow — one must know how to digest. The more material and spiritual nourishment you absorb, the more delicate its assimilation.

TA KUO

28 *Preponderance of the great:* You are faithful and loyal, but, even in the name of friendship, do not take on burdens and responsibilities beyond your capacities. Be careful of your tendency to sacrifice and to play the saviour.

K'AN

29 *Fathomless water:* You, a guardian, should remain on your guard and on the alert. This is no time to abandon your post; the enemy would seize the opportunity to break in and destroy you.

LI

30 *The clinging, fire:* Do not strain on your chain, rather, slip your collar. True independence resides in a profound understanding of the intimate ties which unite you with the rest of the universe.

HSIEN

31 *Influence:* Do not squander your trump cards and all your chances by putting off until tomorrow what should be done today. Start to work immediately and refuse to allow any difficulty to discourage you.

HÊNG

32 *Duration:* It is pointless to ask yourself indefinitely about the value of the result; it is acquired, that is the essential. Frivolous questioning will get you nowhere, but lucid and rigorous self-examination will. Do not hesitate to question your inner being, but never brood on the past; you will only bore yourself.

TUN

33 *Retreat:* Although you can barely endure solitude, it will be good for you; but do not announce your decision. Retire discreetly, without drum or trumpet. Silence is your surest ally today.

TA CHUANG

34 *The power of the great:* Force, movement, energy. Do not allow yourself to become intoxicated by your journey. You could end up in a ravine with your paws bloodied. Your initial direction is constructive, as long as you keep a cool head.

CHIN

35 *Progress:* If you are offered the number two position, do not feel too badly; this does not mean that you will be left in the shade. Get used to the light progressively, otherwise you risk being dazzled, blinded and even destroyed. It is in obscurity that one best perceives the clarity outside.

MING I

36 *Darkening of the light:* Do not be discouraged — you alone know the emergency exit; therefore, you are indispensable. Your support will be requested on all sides; you will be begged to intervene and to show the way.

CHIA JÊN

37 *The family:* Your equilibrium will depend on it. But do not be content with a passive role; your family needs your protection. More than ever, be their guide and counsellor.

K'UEI

38 *Opposition:* Dogs and cats are both needed to make a world. As for you, you are only requested not to meow — to each his own language.

CHIEN

39 *Obstruction:* You are capable of leaping the wall in one bound, but beware of what awaits you on the other side: you could meet disagreeable surprises.

HSIEH

40 *Deliverance:* You are out of the swamp. Take up your old life; no longer remain alone; friends will come to you spontaneously and success will smile on you, provided you chase away the bad memories.

SUN

41 *Decrease:* When there is no more meat, there are, perhaps, some bones. You must accept the situation and learn to see good intentions concealed, sometimes, by forbidding faces and ambiguous gestures.

I

42 *Increase:* For once, do not hesitate to be an opportunist; believe in the chance offered to you and learn how to exploit it. You may not get another so soon.

KUAI

43 *Breakthrough:* Adopt a firm and authoritarian attitude and, if need be, show your fangs. Do not be intimidated or impressed. You have the strength to resolve the most critical situations and to obliterate your enemies.

KOU

44 *Coming to meet:* You are not a man of compromise or one who inhabits troubled waters; so destroy your bridges and distrust the cat who purrs as he sleeps — he has claws.

TS'UI

45 *Gathering together:* In order to participate, you must feel concern and possess real affinities with the group. However, there is no need to mix with the crowd. Also, distrust the enemy within, the infiltrators: you are easy prey for them.

SHÊNG

46 *Pushing upwards:* You are going to be promoted rapidly and experience a brilliant rise in your position and status. Do not slip backwards; be meticulous, precise and firm. Do not change your itinerary on the way.

K'UN

47 *Oppression:* You are not in your best form; accept this passing depression without bowing your head or being obsequious. Do not be oppressed by signs of impatience or negative and hostile attitudes.

CHING

48 *The well:* Do not deny the past on the pretext of progress; you must rebuild while conserving the foundations. But do not overestimate your strength; a defeat would have dramatic consequences for you.

KO

49 *Revolution:* Turn over a new leaf and start again, hale and hearty. Otherwise, abstain from any action or engagement. The situation is ambiguous; the issue can turn out to be for the best or for the worst.

TING

50 *The cauldron:* Representation of the five Elements — Earth, Wood, Fire, Water and Metal. Spiritual and material nourishment. Do not scorn one for the benefit of the other — respect balance. What you attribute to the mental is often of physical origin, and vice versa.

CHÊN

51 *The arousing (shock, thunder):* Pessimist or not, anxious or not, you must accept the facts — the weather is not set fair. However, do not alter your timetable or your itinerary — you would only add to your problems.

KÊN

52 *Keeping still:* Do not fight against windmills; calm down, momentarily isolate yourself and think of better days. Try to cast out your demons: they can only be destructive.

CHIEN

53 *Development (gradual progress):* Even in climbing to the roof of your kennel, you will not catch the stars. Work out something which is possible for you to achieve and try to attain it, step by step.

KUEI MEI

54 *The bride:* Do not rush about like a dog after a bone. Tenderness, tact and gentleness should be the order of the day.

FÊNG

55 *Abundance:* This is the moment to harvest and gather, to make provision for difficult days. However, for the moment, fortune smiles upon you.

LÜ

56 *The wanderer:* You must know how to leave the boat, the table or the kennel — liberty and space await you at the end of the voyage.

SUN

57 *The gentle:* Seek to influence; convince with a light touch, as the wind insinuates itself under the door.

TUI

58 *The serene, the joyous:* The Dog, faithful companion, knows only too well the price of sharing. Do not always accept what you cannot return.

HUAN

59 *Dissolution:* You must combat egotism, fear and doubt. Overcome incertitude and do not allow yourself to be discouraged. Do not hesitate to seek alliances or to ask for assistance.

CHIEH

60 *Limitation:* It can be imposed by chains and barbed wire, or freely accepted as a discipline. Better to opt for the second method.

CHUNG FU

61 *Inner truth:* Do not seek to convey it by flowery phrases; all you will be doing is throwing dust in someone's eyes. Rather, testify to it by your conduct and your behaviour; be a living example.

HSIAO KUO

62 *Preponderance of the small:* Do not go on your own in the middle of the wood, even if you are a sporting dog suddenly taken by an urge to track down game.

CHI CHI

63 *After completion:* So hard to imagine for a pessimistic and anxious Dog. However, remember that even in a state of equilibrium and mastery there remains after every ascent the inevitable descent — to foresee it is to avoid the fall.

WEI CHI

64 *Before completion:* Your permanent doubt can be transmuted into wisdom and courage, provided that it does not resolve itself into a form of anxiety, but rather of patience.

YEAR OF THE PIG

1911 · 1923 · 1935
1947 · 1959 · 1971
1983 · 1995 · 2007

THE DOMAINS
OF
THE PIG

十二生肖

THE PIG AND ITS SYMBOLISM

A Wild Boar in China, a Pig in Vietnam; an animal from the next world, master of the palace, solitary guide — or symbol of pleasure, representing ignorance and overweening passions — who are you really? A noble boar? A toy bank in the shape of a pig? A porker who evokes debauchery and brute force? Dazzling and dim in turn, depending on how we imagine you, you appear and disappear, leaving us perplexed and defenceless in the face of your mysterious presence, which disturbs and fascinates us. Intangible and wild, you are a powerful and solitary animal who feeds on acorns; a terrible beast who devastates harvests; a slippery creature who wallows in sombre pig sties. But in the end it is out puzzlement which gives rise to our repulsion. What hesitation and secret anguish we feel when we regard you! Your darkest legends come from the ancient and primitive forests rooted in our collective memory.

The Pig is a solitary animal whose secretiveness evokes the Druids hidden in the far reaches of a Celtic forest. In many myths the Pig represents spiritual authority; hunting him down and killing him is a metaphor in which the temporal (the hunter and the hunt) tracks down the spiritual (the noble Pig).

In Christian tradition the Pig usually projects a baleful image: he incarnates the devil, as well as an obscene glutton incapable of controlling his passions, and a destroyer of fields, orchards and vineyards.

In the Chinese zodiac, the Pig symbolizes courage, prosperity and nobility; and in Japan he sometimes represents the god of war. However, it is among the Celts that he plays a very important role. The Celts were great breeders of pigs, and the swineherd was regarded with the utmost respect. In Celtic mythology the Pig is a supernatural animal. The story goes that when the Celts were vanquished and exiled by the Gauls they were fed seven supernatural pigs which were killed each evening and were reborn each morning. In another tale from the Middle Ages, the hero is seduced by a luminous white Pig who has taken the form of a beautiful young girl; he is no longer the black, terrifying being of the night, hunted at the risk of one's life.

However, our fear and lack of understanding make it difficult for us to accept the existence of the Pig's virtues. In any case, he will always be a solitary master, the companion of the Druids; and the path to him — bordered with trees and hedges, leading, perhaps, to his secret garden in the shade of the sacred oak — will be difficult.

A few notes on the Pig

Principal qualities: Honest, rigorous, tolerant.

Principal defects: Profoundly egotistic despite his generosity, his own well-being always comes first.

Work: Persevering and steady, but lacks competitive spirit.

Best role: A gentleman-farmer.

Worst role: Political spokesman for an opposition party.

Money: He likes it but spends it as soon as he earns it; however, he manages to always be prosperous.

Luck: He has more than enough, but it will be best if he is not born near New Year's Day, for then he runs the risk of being eaten.

Adores: Beauty, liberty, fresh air and greenery.

Hates: Hypocrisy, social-climbing, unkindness, lying, injustice.

Cannot live without: Physical love.

Leisure activities: He likes to walk along a beach or in the woods with a book of poetry in his hand, listening to the sounds of nature and observing the animals.

Favourite place: A country house with a view of a mountain or on the sea, shared with someone he loves.

Colours: Blue and pale green.

Plants: Acacia, lavender, hazel.

Flowers: Genista, broom.

Professions: Doctor, mediator, judge, confessor, poet, painter, forester, benefactor — and millionaire.

The four ages in the life of the Pig according to Chinese tradition

The *childhood* of the Pig will be calm, peaceful and protected. His *youth* will be burdened with many emotional problems and his *maturity* with family problems. He should make an effort to attain emotional stability. He will enjoy a prosperous *old age*.

THE PSYCHOLOGY OF THE PIG

Our Western imagery is extremely meagre concerning the Pig, the last of the twelve signs of the Chinese zodiac. Our good old Pig is regarded at best as a gastronomical delight; we know more recipes for cooking him than about his psychological characteristics and his symbolism as portrayed in Chinese astrology.

However, there are quite a few analogies between Oriental tradition and our Western 'digestive' image of the Pig. Both are in the habit of putting a Pig on the menu for the New Year feast. Also, in both traditions the Pig is considered to be incapable of resisting mud, and because of this he has a reputation for lewdness. Happily, these sweet and debonair animals ask only to be allowed to live in peace; and their courageous and serene nature enables them to overlook the opinion of others.

Pigs are the most honest and scrupulous of all the animals in the Chinese zodiac. They come into the world with a trunk full of slightly old-fashioned sentiments, such as goodness, altruism, indulgence and tolerance, seasoned with optimism and an admirable belief in the perfectability of mankind. Needless to say, the vultures immediately pounce on this tender prey and make mince-meat of him. Because of this, we believe Pigs to be naive, credulous, over-confident, easy marks and vaguely stupid.

But distinctions are necessary. Pigs are rather credulous, but only in the sense that they prefer to see the good side of people and things. They try to put themselves in the place of others, and to understand the worst depravities. They believe that there always exists, somewhere, a pure little flame of goodness that must be protected and maintained.

Endowed with one of the rarest of virtues — *compassion* — Pigs avoid making snap judgements. Abhorring disputes and conflicts, they unhesitatingly choose to compromise, which gives them the reputation of being weak. But they do not care in the least. They believe in a better world, insist that they are right and refuse to listen to the howling of pessimistic wolves. Naturally, such extreme tolerance at times causes them to go astray: they are the kind to shelter a criminal and then, during the trial, testify how sweet he was with their children.

Like those born under the sign of the Dog, Pigs are in love with justice, and rape is the only crime that they feel merits the worst possible punishment. They cannot tolerate any form of fanaticism, and can even become dangerous, for they are not lacking in courage. Also, they lack the Dog's critical sense; and, contrary to the Dog, they wish to create their happiness here on earth rather than in the next world.

Pigs are stable and calm, perfectly at ease and adapt easily to their environment and to neighbours. They delight in sensual pleasures, especially eating. They love the pleasures of life with every fibre of their being and asking them to give them up before they have had a taste would be terribly cruel. Materialistic sensualists and slightly coarse, they are avid for pleasure, but naturally and frankly so, and with perfect simplicity. They are the kind to slap you on the back and exclaim 'Do not worry! Just so long as you are healthy.'

Pigs are sociable and like to be with people, but they rarely shine in society. They prefer to remain silent because they are afraid of putting their foot in it, and they do not express themselves easily. On the other hand, in private they can be extremely talkative, even long-winded, speaking happily about everything and nothing. Pigs are, moreover, intelligent and eager to learn, even though they do not always show it. Their knowledge is broader than it appears, but they prefer to tackle diverse subjects superficially rather than devote themselves to long-term, intense study.

Stubborn and obstinate, Pigs are slow and take a long time to get started, but nothing can stop them once they have made a decision. They also hesitate to take the initiative and tend to rely on others' assistance, which, curiously, is almost never refused. For this reason, their friends often believe that they are incapable of existing on their own. But they are quite mistaken! If the assistance requested is withdrawn, our Pigs get down to brass tacks, peaceably, serenely — and efficiently.

Pigs are sometimes the victims of their own kindness. If taken advantage of, the strongest among them will not lose faith and they will remain apostles of non-violence against wind and tide. Others, less principled, compensate with suspicion and distrust, which keeps them from being taken a second time. But this weakness hides great strength: they can resist negative influences. It is said that the Pig, along with the crafty Monkey, is the only sign capable of resisting the Snake's charm — and of dominating him.

These gentle and sensitive people make marvellous friends; they are always ready to help or to make excuses for you, even if you have behaved very badly indeed. They are extremely comforting.

The psychoanalyst Carl Jung was a Pig. His research into the human psyche, although perhaps less striking and provocative than that of Freud (a Dragon), is stamped with profound tenderness and a great love of humanity.

Pigs love to do good; they take great trouble to be useful to their fellow-men. They become disheartened when faced with slander, nastiness or hypocrisy; if their fingers get burned they will learn from experience, but will remain sensitive to the suffering of others. However, be careful: they are still wild animals, and when they become angry — which is rare — they can be violent and destructive. It is not advisable to waken a sleeping Pig.

THE PIG AS A CHILD

The Pig child is not especially difficult to raise. He is slightly slow, stubborn, hyper-sensitive and secretive. He will not be demanding nor critical; he often leaves the limelight to his more extroverted and demonstrative brothers and sisters. He is a well-behaved and reasonable child who listens to advice and follows it with the best faith in the world. However, such confidence in others can have a questionable side, for one can easily make a young Pig believe that the moon is made of green cheese. He will believe in fairy tales and Santa Claus when small, and then will pretend to believe to please his grandmother, who enjoys telling stories. What difference does it make, the Pig will say with an angelic smile, the world is so much nicer when inhabited by fairies.

These children like tranquillity and comfort: the boy will often prefer reading to sports; and, from her earliest years, a girl will be feminine to the tips of her fingers.

At school the little Pig will have his ups and downs because his carelessness will work against his natural gifts. He will be the one who hides spiders in his desk or blows up the school during a chemistry experiment. He is gifted and has a lively mind, but he is often lazy, dreamy and absent-minded. He needs consistent rhythm in his work and regular periods devoted to sports, nature and fresh-air activities. From time to time he also needs to be alone, for he likes to meditate and reflect in peace.

Although it is never necessary to be severe with him, it is extremely important that he is directed towards a profession adapted to his capacities, and in which there is a minimum of competitiveness, for the young Pig scorns rivalry and the fight for power. If he comes to grips with life holding winning cards in his hands he will easily be able to find his place in the sun; otherwise he may remain slightly uncertain, afraid to embark on a doubtful course. He is not a competitive animal, which must be taken into account — without, however, allowing him to shirk his responsibilities. In any case, his taste for material well-being will always be an incentive.

LOVE LIFE

Pigs love life, they know how to make flowers grow in the desert. Above all, and this is even more rare, they know how to *imagine* flowers. They are the poets of reality and of joy.

Given such a nature, they are of course fascinated by love. From their earliest years Pigs are motivated and conditioned by the pleasure of loving, and in this they are remarkably precocious. Extremely sensual, passionate and imaginative, they are forever transforming the desires that haunt their dreams into actual experiences. And, because they care so little about what others might say, this can lead them to all kinds of experiments which they engage in without shame, malice or depravity. They are the kind of people who will say with a smile that vice does not exist, only vicious people, and that everything is beautiful when one is in love. This healthy philosophy brings them a great deal of success.

Mrs Pig meets life with the same sensual appetite. Ardent and bursting with life, she differs from other females in her enthusiasm, which is mixed with greediness — 'everything and immediately!'

Pigs are faithful by nature, but demanding and highly discriminating: they sometimes take quite a long time to unearth, among the mass of their admirers, the soul sister who will gratify their desires to the full. Once they have found her they will happily construct a life which includes the best (a great deal), the worst (the least possible) and, above all, the deliciously superfluous.

Jealous and possessive by nature, Pigs expect their partners to be as honest and total in their feelings as they are; which is why they should be careful when choosing a mate, and thus avoid those who may turn out to be fickle and unfaithful.

When they are satisfied and happy with a relationship, they are extremely reliable, peaceful and optimistic; they remain emotionally dependent on the object of their love, even when they seem to behave with great independence.

FAMILY LIFE

When the Pig has found a pleasant home, he rarely moves about, devoting his efforts to leading an agreeable life in harmonious surroundings. If possible these will be rather luxurious, for it must be admitted that he has a weakness for well-heeled comfort, even if he seems satisfied with only a sleeping bag.

The very idea of divorce is shocking to him, for he is a conformist, loyal to and respectful of commitments; in later life some Pigs become traditionalists and moralizers. Their heart will be broken by separation or breaking up with a loved one. Ideally, they would like to be able to reconcile their need for exclusivity with their desire to keep all those they have once loved.

The Pig is a naturally possessive and often over-protective parent, who is concerned with the well-being of his offspring. He is a stickler for education and respect for principles. He tries to allow his children to blossom freely, while at the same time giving them some sense of morality. Although severe, he is also quite tender.

The only negative side of a Pig parent is that he may keep his children tied to him emotionally, so that they have trouble cutting the cord later on. In short, they are too possessive, but with the best intentions in the world. Curiously, it is Mr Pig who is most guilty of being over-protective; Mrs Pig is more reasonable, although she is more authoritarian.

Those children born under the adventurous and independent signs of the Ox, Tiger, Dragon or Horse will give their Pig parent trouble, who will be in a state of permanent anxiety, and will buy out the entire stock of bandages from all the local chemists. The indifference and off-hand manner of Rabbit and Goat children will amaze their Pig parent, but they will feel secure and happy because they can count on his support. The young Rat, the little Rooster and the playful facetious Monkey will get along very well with such a

879

parent, who will offer them understanding and affection. The Dog child will be able to calm his anxieties before they become too deeply imbedded, and, finally, the Snake child will be able to do as he wishes.

PROFESSIONAL LIFE

It is rare that unbridled ambition will ever keep a Pig awake at night, but they do like success because of the independence and material comfort it brings. Thus, with tranquil perseverance and hidden passion, they try to attain what really interests them — prosperity.

Before making their place in the sun, Pigs must often face several setbacks. There are various reasons for this: the first is that they do not always choose their profession in a reasonable way. For example they might completely overlook the job market or the possibilities for promotion in a profession. Thus, they often find themselves stuck in blocked or over-staffed situations.

Secondly, if a Pig is caught in the middle of a crowd, he runs the risk of getting lost in it, for competitiveness is not his strong point. He is too loyal to compromise, too proud to lick his superior's boots, too lazy to work twice as hard as the others. He needs time — and a few mistakes — to learn to be distrustful and thus prevent his little friends from copying his work during study period. Also, when he is encouraged to fight back, he tends to shrug his shoulders, implying that it would be beneath his dignity to crush his adversary's toes. It is only when he has been swindled or knocked about a number of times that the Pig sees red and will attack. In which case, his enemy should be careful that he does not also lose the use of his arms and legs.

Yet such setbacks do not undermine the Pig's confidence, for he is philosophic. But it is very important for him to feel satisfied professionally, or he will regret his missed opportunities for the rest of his life. So if you love a Pig here is a piece of advice: prod him, encourage him, shake him up a little, and do not be upset if he growls. His future stability depends on it. One thing is certain though: he will never sacrifice his private life to professional success.

MATERIAL LIFE

If you ask a Pig whether he loves money, or whether he can do without it, he will shrug his shoulders and reply with the utmost sincerity that of course he needs money in order to live, but he does not especially care for it, and he is sure he could do without it by living very simply. You will leave with the impression that Pigs are totally uninterested in material things, capable of living on love and scorning those who spend their time studying their bank accounts.

Be careful — this is absolutely false! Pigs are not liars, but in this they are mistaken. in fact, their attitude towards money is rather ambivalent. They adore comfort, luxury and beauty and hate to do without them. But they sometimes forget how to count and are capable of spending a month's pay on totally useless things. They will economize for a year by living frugally, then on impulse will spend a week in the most expensive, palatial hotel in the south of France — when they should have taken their family to the country for a month. Mrs Pig will fill a milk bottle with change in order to repaint her kitchen, then one day will take the money to buy a pair of Dior boots that she will rarely wear. Pigs also love to give presents and to spoil their family and friends; they can be called spendthrifts but not egotists.

Happily, Pigs are lucky with money: when they do not earn it themselves, they always find someone to give it to them, and they invariably end their days rather wealthy. At least this is what Chinese tradition says.

ENVIRONMENT

Enamoured of their domestic comfort, but in love with nature and long walks in the forest, the Pig's ideal is a house in the country, in the mountains or at the seaside — so long as it is surrounded by a spacious garden and sufficiently removed from neighbouring houses so that the Pig can live in peace.

The great majority of Pigs live in the country; if they have to live in town it will be in a small garden flat. They will not be prepared to move into a larger flat without a garden, and the moment the sun shines they will leave town to visit friends in the country, with a great sigh of relief.

Pigs need space and oxygen; they wilt within a closed space and cannot stand to be confined. Modern flats depress them, basements or garrets cause them anguish and elevators give them fits of dizziness. Remember: they are wild animals, kings of the forest.

According to Chinese tradition, they are also Masters of the Palace. They therefore pay particular attention to their home, pottering and tinkering about, putting down new carpets and repainting walls the moment any smudge appears. They are often Rubinsteins with an electric drill and Paganinis with a screwdriver. They spend money easily, filling their homes with costly and ravishing things that they adore to look at.

Mrs Pig is more reasonable than her male counterpart, and not as prone to redecorate at the drop of a hat. But she is an excellent hostess and will not hesitate to spend a lot of money to entertain her friends in a grand but warm and comfortable style. In fact, Pigs should run restaurants and hotels — in the country, of course.

A guide to relations with a Pig

Methods of seduction: Both male and female Pigs are exceedingly frank: 'You please me, and I suppose that I please you, otherwise you would not be here. So, shall we go to your place or to mine?'

If he loves you: He will follow you wherever you go like Ruth and her mother-in-law Naomi in the Bible: 'Whither thou goest, I shall go; whither thou liveth, I shall live; thy people shall be my people and thy god shall be my God. . . .'

Expects of you: That you share in his moments of passion and respect his need for solitude. In short, live in his den, but do not track him down; the Pig does not like hunters.

To keep you: You will enjoy first place in his life. This is rare, comforting and flattering.

If he is unfaithful: It is perhaps your fault. Are you aware that the Pig needs a great deal of passion in his life? The only solution: a sleeping tablet for him and an aphrodisiac for you.

If you are unfaithful: You must have an enormous physical appetite and be very healthy!

In case of a break between you: He will start by demanding explanations or by giving them, of which there will be a veritable torrent. Naturally, you will not understand anything, and neither will he. Then there will be tears and despair. He is always sincere. Do not leave sleeping pills lying around.

If you wish to give him a gift: He will love anything; his joy will be caused by the fact that you thought of him. Do remember his birthday and holidays. He is very sensitive, and his admiring looks will be a handsome repayment — even if you only give him a key-ring.

If you want to seduce him: Invite him to share an erotic-gastronomic weekend with you in a luxurious country inn.

If you want to get rid of him: Suggest a game of poker — and cheat.

THE PIG AND THE OTHER CHINESE SIGNS

Pig/Rat

The Rat and the Pig have in common the fact that they are unrepentant sensualists who like to profit from life, and sometimes go so far as to burn the candle at both ends. There is no doubt that they derive great pleasure from being together, goad each other on and will have fantastic experiences on all levels.

However, the Rat runs the risk of being irritated by the Pig's naivete, especially if he is not in love or if the relationship is of the professional or family order.

But if passion is involved, our Rat, gratified by the kindness, the attentiveness and serenity of his partner, will never fail to take up his defence, encourage him and push him to be more dynamic. He will also teach him some profitable little tricks, such as how to avoid paying parking fines without getting caught. The Pig will be a bit shocked, but will then come round.

Pig/Ox
The Pig thinks himself astute, but often reveals himself to be credulous. However, the Ox will be sceptical enough for two, and both will respect each other's scrupulous honesty.

The Ox likes to have peace and the Pig is a fervent devotee of Peace, which provides a common ground. There are, however, some differences in attitude. Often a gambler, the Pig will tend to resent the parsimonious side of the Ox. Neither will be pleased by the same things, the Ox being satisfied with the strictly necessary and the Pig never sneezing at the superfluous. At home, for example, the Ox will be irritated to see his Pig spouse spend their savings to improve and redecorate when he finds the place comfortable enough as it is.

The Pig will reproach his serious companion with not knowing how to make the most of life, with working too hard when he could relax, with wasting the best years of his life. Happily, this will never go too far because the Pig, although the kind to rush in head first, will not go so far as to endanger a harmony he wishes, above all, to preserve. And the Ox will, perhaps, agree to be dragged off to a restaurant on their wedding anniversary.

Pig/Tiger
They will be loyal to each other. Their love and friendship will be intense so long as their nights remain passionate; a sense of honour will motivate most of their days.

Often cannier than the Pig, the Tiger will help him to defend himself, to uncover the defects in the armour of his adversaries. Because each loves solitude, each will understand the other's need for liberty and, while being tolerant of each other, will be unlikely to be deceitful: confidence will be the basis of their relationship.

As always, there is a risk. Even a very polite Tiger is and remains predatory. From time to time, without malice but due to curiosity, he will try to push the Pig to the end of his tether or profit from his good faith. On this subject, Chinese tradition cautions, for the Pig, whose defenses are formidable, will win out over the Tiger.

Pig/Rabbit

The award for merit and honesty goes to this couple. There is no doubt about it: they will appreciate each other for their true value, holding in esteem those qualities with which they are both bursting. When the Pig wants solitude, the Rabbit will lead his life quietly, perhaps using the time to repaint their flat. Together, these two will carefully avoid revolutions and earthquakes. The intuitive Rabbit will help his Pig spouse to not be taken in by all the tricksters who pass by and, without annoying him, will advise him and make him aware of his errors. There is only one danger: the Pig is sensual, even somewhat lascivious, whereas the Rabbit is slightly prudish, believing that even the most passionate liaisons should be veiled in platonic sentiments and not displayed publicly. The Pig will burst out laughing at this idea and offer the Rabbit a copy of the 'Kama-Sutra'. The Rabbit will not find this terribly amusing.

Pig/Dragon

So much the better for the Dragon, so much the worse for the Pig, who will not be able to distinguish his snout from his tail when caught in the trap of this relationship. Unintentionally, the Dragon will cause the Pig to turn in circles until he becomes dizzy; he will make him believe that the moon is made of green cheese and that big bad wolves eat sweet little pink piglets.

But one should not feel too sorry for the Pig: he will be so busy coddling his Dragon and telling him how wonderful he is that he will not have time to think about himself. And the Dragon will be delighted! And, when the Pig has his usual attack of independence, the Dragon will not say a word; when the Pig returns, his desire for liberty satisfied, the Dragon will smile and give him some words of wisdom. The delighted Pig will listen to him as though he were repeating the Gospel. Luckily, the Dragon usually gives good advice.

Pig/Snake

Not an obvious alliance. From the start, the Pig runs the risk of being completely taken in by the Snake, whose honesty is relative and highly personal. The unaffected nature of the Pig will often annoy the Snake, who will judge it — sometimes wrongly, but not always — as credulity, even innocence. After all, who would not raise his eyebrows when a Pig lets himself go with some lightly risqué remarks?

Despite these difficulties, their powerful sensuality will unite them — even if it is not expressed in the same way. The Snake, in any case, will eat the Pig in choice morsels. But here comes the surprise: the Pig will react quickly and will know how to extricate himself from the Snake's coils. Like the Monkey and the Tiger, he is capable of resisting the Snake, although not without leaving some skin behind. He should therefore be careful before allowing himself to be buried in the coils of this dangerous reptile; and the Snake should not mistake the Pig for a toy, or he will be in for some unpleasant surprises.

Pig/Horse

Both are honest and share a taste for an easy, agreeable life and the pursuit of pleasure. The egotistical Horse will attempt to take advantage of the Pig's basic decency, but the Pig will know how to protect himself; anyway, his natural indulgence will help him to support his partner. Another positive point: in love the Pig is sensual and imaginative, which will attract the Horse — and keep him.

Unhappily, there will almost always come a time when

the outbursts of the Horse will exhaust the patience of the Pig, who will then need to be on his own for a little while in order to relax. The amorous Horse requires complete dedication and the assurance that his partner belongs to him totally. His partner's independence will upset and make him jealous; he will not easily adapt to the mixture of autonomy and candour which is typical of the Pig, and will often tire before coming to terms with it.

Pig/Goat

A profitable alliance for both signs: each gets something out of it. The Pig, master of the palace, is born under the sign of opulence and is generous. The Goat adores palaces, so long as he can do as he likes. This poses no problem, for the Pig, who is not possessive, will let him run about as he pleases. The Goat also adores opulence, to which he has the gift of bringing a sense of comfort and harmony, which will not displease the Pig, who also loves beauty.

Indeed, a feeling for beauty is their greatest common ground; each associates it with a calmness refined to an ideal of peace. To preserve this, both will be capable of making the necessary concessions. Even when there is coldness between them, they will make up by going on a tour of the art galleries.

The only risk is that the Goat, aware of his partner's indulgence, will go too far and become temperamental and altogether irrational. The amiable Pig will then become a severe and stubborn critic and will slap the Goat's fingers like a schoolmaster — and will have the last word.

Pig/Monkey

The Pig is perhaps the only sign capable of disarming the manipulative instincts of the Monkey, who will remain mesmerized and admiring in the face of such loyal, indeed royal, honesty. What is this bizarre animal who gives himself without expecting anything in exchange; and who, in his very guts, believes in a good and charitable humanity? Is he a madman, or is he a wise man modestly imbued with the Truth?

The Monkey will find himself caught up in this relationship before having had the time to ask such questions. Though good at seeing through the underhandness of his adversaries, the Monkey is flabbergasted by genuine frankness and generosity. He will do no harm to the Pig, and, seeing himself reflected in such a positive fashion in his partner's eyes, he will believe himself to be a better person — and will become so.

The Pig will rub his hands and laugh in his beard. He knew perfectly well that he would have the last word: his apparent naivety hides a cleverness and abilities far superior to that of the Monkey, simply because he is not in the least bit self-seeking.

Pig/Rooster

Everything is possible with the tolerant Pig, who has a thick skin and is not excessively disturbed by the pricks of the Rooster. He is even one of those rare persons who can recognize the Rooster's goodness and kindness which lie hidden beneath his brilliant feathers. The Pig disarms the Rooster's aggressiveness, understands him and tranquillizes him.

However, the Rooster will never try to take advantage of the Pig. They get along very well together, although their relationship will be one of comradeship rather than passionate love or intellectual stimulation. They will take life easily, but will be ready to fly to help each other at the least sign of danger. What could be better? A little spice perhaps, for the unforeseen, the delicious surprise, will often be lacking with these two.

Pig/Dog

They will have an excellent understanding, from which the Dog in particular will profit. The high-living Pig will bring him the zest, carefree attitude and optimism which he lacks. Both are honest, generous and understanding. They respect these qualities in each other, comforting and persuading each other that, after all, the important thing is to live and to love; leave the wolves to devour themselves and the devil with the rest!

The Dog, reassured, will be happy and serene. Even in friendship and in business he should listen to the Pig, who will give him only useful advice.

The Pig, who is sometimes awkward and naive, will benefit from the Dog's mistrust, whereas the Dog, if need be, will defend him to the end. From time to time the more philosophic Pig will become annoyed with the Dog's customary anxiety and will want to tell him to relax and keep cool. The Dog will have less fear of thieves if his spouse is a Pig, for he will have acquired a sense of proportion. Not a bad gift.

Pig/Pig

This is an excellent alliance. They have the same qualities, the same defects and the same indulgence towards the weaknesses of others. They are excellent accomplices and will not be able to get along without each other.

They should share a business, or at least work together, otherwise even the briefest separations will lead to terrible jealous scenes and all the dishes will get broken.

They will argue constantly about how to bring up their children, even after they have grown up.

If they do not work together, it will be best if either they both work or neither of them works, because the one who remains at home will feel frustrated and resent the other; and the one who works will resent the fact that he has been left to work alone. This is an all or nothing relationship.

PIG CELEBRITIES

Albert I of Belgium, D'Annunzio, D'Artagnan, Beria, Berlioz, Bismarck, Cézanne, Cromwell, Chagall, Duke Ellington, Emerson, Henry Ford, Garibaldi, Géricault, Hemingway, Henry VIII, Hitchcock, Ignatius Loyola, Jung, Mann, Mistinguett, Montgomery, Murat, Pascal, Pompidou, Prince Rainier, Ravel, Rilke, Rothschild, Saint Just, Albert Schweitzer, Francoise Sagan, Thérèse of Avila, Van Dyck, Velazquez.

YOUR COMPANION IN LIFE

生命伴侣

After the Chinese sign of your year of birth, here is the sign of your hour of birth

What is a Companion in Life, as understood in Chinese astrology? It is a sort of 'ascendant' sign corresponding to your hour of birth. This Companion is another animal belonging to the Chinese cycle of the twelve emblematic beasts, who falls into step with you and accompanies you, ever ready to help you brave the traps and ambushes along your route. A permanent and benevolent shadow, he can render the impossible possible.

He is your counterpart, but with his own character and tendencies and with a different psychology. Both guardian angel and devil's advocate, he will be a witness to your life and an actor in it.

Have you ever felt, deep inside yourself, the subtle presence of another 'myself' inhabiting you and with whom you live, at times in harmony, at others in conflict? Another self who sometimes criticizes you and at others encourages you? That is your Companion in Life.

There are times when he will appear to be an imposter or an intruder. Certainly, he often questions your habits and your moral or spiritual complacency. Accompanied by this companion, a shadow within, the route is less monotonous and the voyager multiplies his chances of arriving at his chosen destination. This, however, in itself matters little, for it is the journey and the manner in which it is conducted that are important. Indolence is the greatest danger: your Companion is capable of arousing you from a lassitude of spirit and, to that end, if necessary, robbing you of your certainties, trampling on your secret gardens and, finally, tearing away the great veil of illusion.

It sometimes happens that your Companion is of the same sign as your year of birth, a twin brother in a way — for example, a Pig/Pig. In this case, you must recognize that he will compel you to realize yourself fully and to live the double aspect — the Yin and the Yang — that your bear within yourself. In any case, you also bear within yourself

the twelve animals. So, set out on the long route, ready for the great adventure: the beautiful voyage during which you will encounter the harmoniously entangled, the solemn and the grotesque, the ephemeral reality, the dream and the imagined.

Table of hours corresponding to the twelve emblematic animals

If you were **born** between		your **companion** is
11 pm and 1 am		Rat
1 am and 3 am		Ox
3 am and 5 am		Tiger
5 am and 7 am		Rabbit
7 am and 9 am		Dragon
9 am and 11 am		Snake
11 am and 1 pm		Horse
1 pm and 3 pm		Goat
3 pm and 5 pm		Monkey
5 pm and 7 pm		Rooster
7 pm and 9 pm		Dog
9 pm and 11 pm		Pig

These figures correspond to the *solar hour* of your birth. If necessary, you should check the summer times (Daylight Savings Time) and make the appropriate adjustment (sometimes two hours before or after statutory time).

THE PIG AND HIS COMPANION IN LIFE

 **Pig/Rat**

On the one hand, the Pig is eager to cultivate the 'art of solitude'. He will avoid the main routes, preferring bushy paths with their odour of humus and a quiet night lying under the stars. On the other hand, a Rat/Pig is a complete materialist. Hoarder and profiteer, he will know how to capitalize not only on money, but on the fruits of his experiences.

The Rat/Pig will know only white or black; for him there are no shades of grey, no half-measures. His route will be scattered with obstructions which he will ruthlessly overcome. Do not count on him to have scruples; he will not know the meaning of the word.

Be careful! The Pig is credulous and this. added to the curiousity of the Rat, will spring a few traps. So, Rat/Pig, before you set forth, lay in your provisions of cheese and acorns.

 **Pig/Rabbit**

A solitary animal who is slightly disquieting but perfectly organized. There exists an air of mystery about him; one never knows the real truth. Amassing great wealth, he lives in luxurious comfort but without neglecting the cultivation of his mind. Seductive, he is given to good and bad excesses, a distinction he prefers to ignore. If you corner him, he may either slip away or attack — unless he merely gives you a reply that leaves you breathless. This Rabbit/Pig is often master of a palace of mirages constructed on a base of others' gullibility.

 **Pig/Tiger**

He will be the symbol of a successful voyage. But then, everything depends on what one calls 'success'. The solitary Pig will lead the Tiger along sombre paths, revealing mysteries and the spiritual world, but he will expect something in return. The Tiger may be a royal lord of the jungle, but the Pig is master of the palace and the symbol of opulence. But what opulence? This unscrupulous hunter will be neither tepid nor moderate; rather, he will be angelic or diabolical. But be careful: those who act like angels sometimes also act like fools.

 **Pig/Ox**

Both the Ox and the Pig are sometimes slightly egotistical recluses. One is the symbol of fertility, the other of abundance. Their voyage will have every chance of material comfort, but there will be complications. With the Ox in charge, you will face the everyday world with a severe and uncompromising appearance; this will conceal your real life of secret corners and cosy beaches — so enjoyable, luxurious and unconstrained, and made even more pleasurable by discreet weekends, private clubs and closed circles.

If the Pig is in charge, then under the facade of a man who enjoys life to the fullest will lie an indestructible solidity and an unsuspected tenacity which will often make you all the more formidable, especially in business. Some will think they can soften you up by various means; you will appear all smiles, but inside you will remain glacial.

 **Pig/Dragon**

A solitary wanderer, seeking a treasure that perhaps he did not know how to protect. The Dragon/Pig will tend to gain material and spiritual wealth. Alas, it does not suffice simply to possess matter or mind and spirit — they must be given meaning. Do not sleep before your safe, before the gates of your palace or on the threshold of your mysterious grotto. Ask yourself whether the safe, palace or grotto may be empty; in which case, it is up to you to fill them.

 **Pig/Snake**

While he is peaceful, secretive and sensitive, he is also a bad loser and his motives are questionable. He does not like to lose and prefers solitude to risking failure. It is useless to try to distract him from his normal routine; he is too obstinate and distrustful. However, this does not stop him from being gullible. It is quite possible to 'take him in'; he will then oscillate between aggressiveness and running away, for at bottom he is tolerant but too proud to admit that his adversary may be right. Although he appears indifferent, the Snake/Pig actually loves money for its own sake and adores amassing treasures and booty. Apparently calm, deep within he is boiling. This solitary reptile is not lukewarm: he is a tough person with a tender heart.

 **Pig/Horse**

Endowed with a broad and clear intelligence, the Horse/Pig is well aware of the pride that eats away at him. He has a tendency to overrate the true value of his possessions and conquests, and to overlook their impermanence. He cannot resist collecting 'treasures' which are, in fact, fakes. Actually, he unconsciously seeks a more worthy treasure which lies within him. His ardour and impulsiveness often give way to doubt and mystery, the latter irresistibly attracting him like the promise of a profound accomplishment.

 **Pig/Goat**

He will not be easy to tame. Of a suspicious nature, the Goat/Pig will seek solitude in thickets and among hidden, rocky paths. In character he is stubborn, obstinate and sometimes even narrow-minded. He is often credulous, but clear-sighted, which is why he prefers to work alone, far from danger and unpleasant encounters. Also, being proud, the Goat/Pig is slow to recognize his errors, but that does not prevent him from being tolerant and always ready to forgive. It is sometimes said that he is a bit of a sorcerer; if you meet up with him, do not forget that at bottom he is tender-hearted and vulnerable.

 **Pig/Monkey**

He will adept at living in solitude, an extremely clear-sighted person to whom it is inadvisable to talk humbug. In fact, he has a built-in lie-detector that sometimes resembles clairvoyance. He has a horror of speaking without purpose. The Monkey/Pig will not be easy to live with: he has his own conceptions of life and will not tolerate having others' imposed on him. He likes to bury his treasures — material or psychological — which are not always of a very clear origin. The Monkey/Pig has, at times, a rather peculiar idea of honesty.

 **Pig/Rooster**

He is a strange and solitary traveller, due more to personal conviction than to a love of originality. The Rooster/Pig seeks to stand out in a crowd by his attitude towards life rather than by appearance. In order to achieve this, he will seek a hiding place in which to bury his treasures, far from the eyes of the world. He will work hard to acquire wealth and knowledge, but will take care to disguise them so as to be the only one to enjoy them — an expression of his pride and egotism.

Pig/Dog

The Dog/Pig will be capable of adapting to solitude: he will not hesitate to take wooded paths far from the main roads. By doing so, he will gain self-confidence and his natural self-doubt will be less apparent and weigh less on his companions. He is conscious of his individuality and will tend to turn towards the spiritual world, which attracts and fascinates him. Seeking to pass beyond the threshold of which he is guardian, he will also seek to pass that imperceptible frontier which separates the two universes. While generally favoured in social and material success, the Dog/Pig will remain an enigmatic and mysterious animal to his companions.

Pig/Pig

This is a solitary and unsociable animal who likes to get away from the main by-ways and planned routes; he is an 'original' who dislikes the company of passing animals. He loves to travel on new and unknown paths, seeking out the mysteries of life, taking shelter in the thickets and shrubs while waiting for night to fall before continuing on his way. He is also an attacker; one should not bar his way unless prepared to face a formidable foe. He does not allow himself to be imprisoned by conventions and regulations and will tend to live on the fringes of society. He is instinctive and intuitive, obeying only his own law, staking out his territory and savagely defending it from intruders.

THE PIG AND THE FIVE ELEMENTS

五行

900

YOUR ELEMENT

In Chinese astrology, each year is joined to an Element. There are five Elements: *Water, Fire, Wood, Metal, Earth.*

Each of the twelve emblematic animals is linked successively to each of the five Elements. For example, in the year 1900 the Rat was Metal, in 1912 he was Water, in 1924 he was Wood, in 1936, Fire and in 1948 he was Earth. Therefore, for the twelve years from 1900 he was linked to Metal, for the next twelve years to Water, and, for every succeeding period of twelve years, to each of the other Elements, in succession.

In order to determine the Element corresponding to the year of your birth, use the table below:

> *Years whose digits end in:* 2 and 3 — Water
> 6 and 7 — Fire
> 4 and 5 — Wood
> 0 and 1 — Metal
> 8 and 9 — Earth

The same union of *Animal-Element* repeats every sixty years, for example, Rat-Metal appeared in 1720, 1780, 1840, 1900, 1960 and so on.

The five Elements are the primary forces affecting the universe. It is their particular association with each of the signs which provides the basis for every horoscope. Movement and fluctuation, Yin and Yang, these symbolic forces are in a perpetual state of action and interaction.

Wood gives birth to Fire, which gives birth to Earth, which gives birth to Metal, which gives birth to Water, which in turn gives birth to Wood.

PIG/WATER
(you were born in 1923 or 1983)

The cold born of the northern sky descended to earth and gave birth to Water. The Chinese consider Water more as a synonym for coldness and ice than as a symbol of fertility.

Characteristics of the Pig/Water
Water of winter night, or rigour and severity, calm and deep Water to be feared and respected, stagnant Water sheltering underwater demons asleep in its depths, foetid and muddy Water of the marshes, refuge of crawling creatures.

The Pig/Water is of the Yin tendency and runs the risk of splashing and floundering about in his Element, taking pleasure in it and being fascinated by it. Attracted to oozing mud and slimy bogs, he should take care not to be sucked in; not to choose a dream over reality; not to cut himself off from the world and retreat into his illusory or mythical universe. Only the Pig's aggressiveness, obstinacy and pride can perhaps drive him to take action and to make his strongest impulses into something concrete.

Health of the Pig/Water
The Water organ is the kidney; its flavour is salty. To remain inactive is bad for your physical and mental health. Seek running water, spring water, which will give you energy and stimulate your aggressiveness.

The Pig/Water and others
The Pig/Water can be energetic and alert, if only to prove that he is capable of taking action; in fact, social conflict does not interest him in the least. What really matters to the Pig is his freedom and tranquillity, and he will be prepared to make many sacrifices to protect them. Once he has proven that he is capable of taking action, he will hasten to return to his retreat, far from the madding crowd. He will not tolerate having his territory encroached upon or his

independence interfered with. He will be solitary and uncommunicative — unless he decides to become wealthy, in which case he will play the game and act the part of financier to perfection. However, he will always have but one idea in his head: to earn enough money to leave it all behind and live within a closed and comfortable universe, surrounded by rare and sumptuous objects. Then he really will be the 'Master of the Palace', and faithful to the image found in Chinese legends.

Advice for a Pig/Water

Follow your dream, but take care: awakenings are sometimes rude and painful.

A Pig/Water year

The culminating point for a Pig/Water year will be winter, a period of gestation.

Use this year to take stock of things; reflect at length before taking action. Be distrustful of proposals and dangerous situations, prefer running spring water to a marsh. Remember, however: reflection does not mean immobilization.

Historical example of a Pig/Water year 1863

For two years the United States had been ravaged by Civil War. In January, Abraham Lincoln feared that the North was on the brink of defeat. Under General Robert Lee, the finest strategist on either side, the Confederates of the South had gained remarkable successes at Bull Run, Fredericksburg and in May, with some difficulty, at Chancellorsville in Virginia. The way to the North lay open. Avoiding Washington, Lee crossed Maryland and advanced on Harrisburg, aiming to cut communications between the Atlantic and the Great Lakes. On 3 July he came up against a numerically superior army under

General Meade, disposed in heavily fortified positions among the hills near the village of Gettysburg. A heavy artillery bombardment failed in its intended effect and the cream of the Southern armies of Virginia, launched to attack supposedly pulverized defences, were checked and forced to retreat by a murderous fire from defensive positions still wholly intact. Barely a quarter survived to return to their lines. Lee was forced to retreat behind the Potomac.

In the South, 1250 miles away, General Grant forced the capitulation of the Confederate armies at Vicksburg. The armies of the Confederacy were effectively isolated from each other.

Gettysburg was the decisive battle of the war. Despite Lee's victories in the field the South was unable to break the supremacy of the North in men and materials; above all the greatly accelerated production of articles of war enabled it to recoup material losses. Thus Lee, although he could win battles, has not been able to force a decisive conclusion and was faced after each victory with an increasingly powerful enemy. After Gettysburg, however, Lee could not prevent General Sherman's 'scorched earth' marches through Georgia and Carolina. He delayed the final outcome for two years but in April 1865 surrendered unconditionally to General Grant at the Appótomax courthouse.

PIG/WOOD
(you were born in 1935)

To the East, the wind blew in the sky and from its warm caress of the earth Wood was born.

Characteristics of the Pig/Wood
Wood is of the morning, of springtime. Its temperate nature loves harmony, beauty and elegance. Springtime is a symbol of gentleness, a period in which all of nature awakens and

opens itself to the forces of youth, creation and growth.

The Pig is an animal who loves the woods and the earth that he treads upon and digs into; he is a friend of nature, which is his universe, his palace, his lair. Wood will play the role of the Muse for the Pig, impelling him to express himself through the arts, sharpening his sensitivity and intuition. The Pig/Wood's extremes of passion, anger, excess and vulnerability will act as a sort of filter, from which harmony and equilibrium will flow. He will be keenly aware of the aesthetic value of things and thus will savour the beauties of the world with intensity.

Health of the Pig/Wood

The organ of Wood is the liver; its flavour is acid. The Pig/Wood may have crises of anger and vulnerability which will be dangerous and harmful to his equilibrium; he should not make himself ill by pouncing on rich food and filling himself with delicacies.

The Pig/Wood and others

The Pig/Wood cares little for formality or climbing the social ladder. Faced with a structured, bureaucratic society which is the epitome of everything he detests, he prefers to be relaxed, supple and sometimes even careless. He will often feel ill-at-ease and cramped if confined within a highly organized and rational universe. An artist by nature, thanks to his imagination he will manage very well, knowing how to improvise at the right moment, how to baffle and seduce when necessary. Thus he is blessed with an excellent defensive technique.

The Pig/Wood will prefer the country to the city, the arts to the world of business, freedom to a Swiss bank account. Although he is extremely attracted to luxury and rare and valuable objects, the Pig/Wood will not sacrifice his independence for such things. He is capable of building a veritable little palace for himself with his own hands, and owing to his good taste and refinement, it will be exquisite.

Advice for a Pig/Wood

You seem to be very much at ease and are certainly a well-balanced and charming person, so do not pay attention to those who are jealous or frustrated — simply close the door and your heart to them.

A Pig/Wood year

The culminating point for a Pig/Wood year will be spring, a period of growth and prosperity.

A harmonious and balanced year, favourable for artists and creators. Remain in contact with nature, which will sharpen your sensitivity. Be more diplomatic and tolerant; accept the fact that others may not always thinks as you do.

Historical example of a Pig/Wood year
1815

On the island of Elba Napoleon, the erstwhile scourge of Europe, seemed resigned to his fate. Surrounded by a handful of faithful followers he lived a comfortable, indeed elegant life in the petty principality accorded him by the Treaty of Fontainebleau. The English government did not trust him and openly canvassed for a remoter place of exile. However, the European powers were intent on the proceedings at the Congress of Vienna. They wished Napoleon out of their way and out of their minds; and that is how they regarded him.

Evading British security measures, Napoleon took ship and landed on French soil on 1 March accompanied by a few hundred men. He told them that he would reconquer France without a shot being fired. So it proved to be. Outlawed by the Bourbons in Paris he was everywhere received with acclamation and delight; his physical presence and the aura of his past sufficed. Marching by way of Grenoble and Lyons he reached Auxerre where Marshal Ney went over to his cause. Two days later the royal family furtively left the Tuileries and made for

Belgium; a few hours after that Napoleon had installed himself at the Louvre.

It was the French army which forced Napoleon to abdicate in 1814; yet ten months later it rallied to him and, as he had predicted, without a shot being fired. There was no real paradox. Peace had brought with it boredom and disaffection and Napoleon appeared to offer a return to the great days. The veterans of his campaigns were without a role; spontaneously, they seized on the hope of one. Alerted to the dissensions in Vienna Napoleon probably counted on a similar dissension among the armies the statesmen disposed of. In this he was mistaken. The single accord at the Congress was that Napoleon should be kept in isolation. Yet Napoleon correctly judged the mood of the French nation and, despite his defeat at Waterloo and lonely exile at St Helena this mood prevailed into memory and through memory into substance. Two subsequent Empires bore his name and de Gaulle revived and sustained his idea of the greatness of France.

In Vienna, the English wished to ensure that France remained a great if accountable power. They were amenable to the argument of Talleyrand that the nation had been led astray as also to the Congress System espoused by Metternich. They knew that once a balance of power in Europe had been safely established they could resume their maritime preoccupations.

PIG/FIRE
(you were born in 1947)

Heat was born in the southern sky, descended to earth and fertilized it. From their union, Fire was born.

Characteristics of the Pig/Fire
The Fire Element is of midday, the South, of summer. Fire is Yang; it is the Element which warms, burns, animates, quickens, transforms and destroys.

Fire is the symbol of energy and vitality; it will bring passion and audacity to the Pig. The Pig/Fire will be a fighter, a warrior, a sort of Attila. He will always get around an obstacle by relentlessly overthrowing it; it is advisable never to stand in his way. Fire can also be internal, endowing the Pig with ardour and enthusiasm in the realm of ideas; intellectually he will be endlessly curious and nothing will be able to interfere with his quest. This strange and solitary person will often be an enemy of narrow-mindedness, a lover of mystery and the imaginative.

Health of the Pig/Fire
The organ of Fire is the heart; its flavour is bitter. You are a reservoir of energy; learn to make good use of it. But remember: even a perfectly regulated machine can some-times break down.

The Pig/Fire and others
The Pig/Fire will not be the charming prince whom romantic young girls dream of; he will be a solitary and sometimes unstable person, looking for the exit, having just entered a room. He will be tempted by adventure and will tend to rush into dangerous enterprises, due to his taste for risk and novelty. He will be a reckless gambler, never ensuring a means of escape. Passionate and quick to anger, he will usually act impulsively; his colleagues will be able to profit from his weakness or to exploit his gullibility. A big-hearted man, the Pig/Fire will give of himself blindly. But even when his back is to the wall or he is forced to look the facts in the face, he will continue to deny his mistakes. His defects can be quite destructive, but, strangely enough, he will always be forgiven. Is it his mystery which fascinates us, or his magical presence? It is simply that the vulnerable and elusive Pig/Fire is so special that he is extremely attractive.

Advice for a Pig/Fire
You are an exceptional animal, a professional charmer, and

you know it — so please, there is no need to burn your boats in order to surprise and seduce.

A Pig/Fire Year

The culminating point in a Pig/Fire year will be summer, a period of creation.

This will be a year of action; you will be able to use your energies to be aggressive and courageous. Luck will smile on you during the entire year. However, learn how to control yourself: do not give in to outbursts of anger and avoid dispersing your gifts too widely. A year full of creativity lies before you.

Historical example of a Pig/Fire year 1587

On 6 February Mary Queen of Scots was executed at Fotheringay Castle after months of vacillation by Elizabeth I of England; even after the execution, she denied that she had ordered it. For Elizabeth, both from instinct and experience, was opposed to such a deed. The horrors and insecurities of her childhood, when her own life seemed to be in the balance, had impressed on her the transient nature of the Estate of Princes and the personal conduct of her own rule was to assert its permanence and vigour. In this she resembled her father, Henry VIII, but she shrank from his easy habit of shedding blood and, in the case of Mary, the example it might set. It was not only that Mary was her cousin; she was an anointed Queen and her execution would breach the hierarchical order of the Tudor world and undermine the sacred character of the Crown.

Her advisers were concerned with the safety of a kingdom only recently recovered to the Protestant religion. They had pressed for Mary's execution for years past on the grounds that she was the natural, indeed almost indispensable centre for any Catholic plot abetted or inspired by Philip II of Spain. Indeed, Elizabeth had seriously contemplated her death after the Ridolfi plot of 1572, the Massacre of St Bartholomew and the triumph of the League in France. Eventually it was Walsingham, 'Prince of Spies', who encompassed Mary's final ruin by facilitating her involvement in the Babington Plot of 1586, for which she was brought to trial and sentenced to death. By February the following year the Council, with certain news of the preparations for the Great Armada, was determined that the sentence should be carried out.

Mary dressed for the ceremony of her death in the same flamboyant style she had favoured during the years of her freedom. Her dress incorporated the varied colours of flames alight, which some saw as a presage to the fires of hell. The story ended on a bizarre and sordid note. Her executioner bent to lift her severed head aloft but raised only her wig. The grey hairs of the head itself tumbled to the bloodstained platform.

PIG/EARTH
(you were born in 1959)

Earth was born from the slowly falling elements of the sky at its humid zenith.

Characteristics of the Pig/Earth
This is an afternoon Earth, the humid and hot Earth of summer. It is the symbol of the well-cushioned, soft nest, of comfort and abundance; an Earth of slow and profound transformations.

The Pig/Earth will tend to be an egotist, snug in his solitary lair; he will rarely like to go out and will not be at all daring. In spite of this he will care a great deal about his popularity, because social success is very important to him. He will do anything to give the impression of being generous and humanitarian, but in fact his thoughts and acts are motivated only by his need for success. He will use the work done by those around him without any scruples or sign of remorse.

However, his Element may inspire a form of equilibrium; perhaps in solitude and meditation the Pig/Earth will find the awareness and conscience necessary for improving his character and will then open himself to the world and to humanity.

Health of the Pig/Earth
The Earth's organ is the spleen; its flavour is sweet. The Pig/Earth should exercise and engage in sports; he should not isolate himself or cut himself off from the world; he should take care not to compensate for his problems by overeating.

The Pig/Earth and others
The Pig/Earth is shrewd and imaginative, but perfectly realistic and materialistic. He will be attracted to the world of business, banking, prudent speculation and commerce in general. Politics will fascinate him because he will see a means to shine and to assure his worldly success. The Pig/Earth is calculating and not at all given to risk-taking; instead he will create detailed plans and projects, evaluating risks and weighing the pro's and con's. He will be distrustful, suspicious and haunted by a fear of being cheated. His life will often be devoted to accumulating wealth, which he will try to hide from the eyes of those whom he believes to be curious and envious. As a husband and father he will be a trifle despotic, sometimes causing difficulty for his children because of his tendency to make decisions for them concerning their marriages or careers. Mrs Pig/Earth will appear to be submissive, but in fact will control everything from behind the scenes, actually leading her little world by the nose.

Advice for a Pig/Earth
Do not spend you life dreaming in front of your safe-deposit box; break out, change your habits, be imaginative and think less of profit.

A Pig/Earth Year

The culminating point in a Pig/Earth year will be summer, which is favourable for the Pig.

Summer, symbol of warmth and abundance, will deliver the Pig from daily cares. Since he will no longer be forced to struggle for the essentials, he will be able to devote himself to studying, research or simply to his friends and family, whom he tends to ignore. Expand your horizons, cast your gaze far and wide, extend your field of vision.

Historical example of a Pig/Earth year
1719

The year 1719 marked the apogee in the career of a Scotsman, John Law, born in Edinburgh in 1671, the son of a silversmith. The 'Système Law' became the wonder of European financiers. In his youth, Law was renowned for his exceptional intelligence and his proficiency in mathematics. Profligate in talent, he tended also to profligacy in behaviour. He came to London burdened by debts he could not meet, quarrelled, fought a duel, was arrested, tried and condemned to death; but, with the connivance of the authorities, he was able to escape to Europe.

There he applied his mind to the subject he knew so well, indebtedness — but on the grand scale. He conceived a scheme designed to restore the credit of the French Kingdom. Through the influence of the Duc d'Orleans his paper was brought to the notice of Louis XIV who dismissed it; its author was a Protestant, sufficient condemnation. However, M. le Duc later became Regent of France and Law's paper was re-examined and found favour. His expedient, then unheard of, was to form a bank entitled to issue paper exchangeable on sight for gold. By 1719 the bank had become the Banque Royale and Law had also founded a Company of the Mississippi and a Company of Senegal.

If Law's enterprise illustrates the propensity of the Scots to work anywhere but in their own country the accession of the House of Hanover to the English throne introduced another form of disaffection, one between father and son. In 1719 the Prince of Wales and his wife, Caroline of Ansbach, attracted the lively younger generation to their separate court at Leicester House, for George I had banished his son from the Court of St James. There, Robert Walpole formed an alliance with the Princess Caroline which was to prove invaluable to him throughout his long years as Prime Minister during the next reign.

PIG/METAL
(you were born in 1911 or 1971)

In the sky, coming from the West, drought grazed the skin of the earth and gave birth to Metal. Winds come from the far-away steppes seeking the vital sap.

Characteristics of the Pig/Metal

Metal is of the night, of autumn and of cold. It symbolizes clarity, purity and precision.

The Pig/Metal will feel prepared to overcome any obstacle, to bring down any mountain; he will be extremely proud, which will tend to blind him. This Pig will not seek out shadowy corners and wooded paths, but rather will walk in full daylight, enjoying success and glory.

The Pig/Metal will be energetic and ambitious, but he will remain clear-sighted, which sometimes will be painful: he will question himself, dig into his inner being and feel magnetized by the mystery of his soul and his subconscious. But the heavy armour of Metal will weigh him down, slowing his course and making his quest difficult. Wishing to defend himself, he will succeed only in closing himself in his own prison, imposing limits and regulations which will only bring doubt and solitude.

Health of the Pig/Metal

The organ of Metal is the lung; its flavour is pungent. The Pig/Metal should take care of his body, in which he at times feels a prisoner, or else he will be in danger of blockages of all kinds. Learn to breathe calmly and to relax.

The Pig/Metal and others

The Pig/Metal will not be a scrupulous person; he will often be very ambitious, ready to sacrifice his private life to attain his end — in other words, success at any price. He will be devoid of real feeling, and will not always keep his word. He will be exceedingly tactless and will demand that he be followed without question. If the Pig/Metal feels he is misunderstood, he will cut off all communication, turn on his heels and, without any explanation, take refuge in his ivory tower, far from those who are incapable of recognizing his obvious superiority.

Advice for a Pig/Metal

You are difficult to live with; choose solitude — which in fact attracts you — and profit from it to 'descend' into yourself and seek equilibrium.

A Pig/Metal Year

The culminating point for a Pig/Metal year will be autumn.

Be less bigoted; listen to the needs of your body and open up your heart — life will seem simpler and easier. In finding your equilibrium you will discover the pleasure of moving about without armour or a shield. Lay down your arms, pack your bags, go on a trip, discover new horizons.

Historical example of a Pig/Metal year 1851

On 1 May 1851 the Great Exhibition in Paxton's Crystal Palace in Hyde Park was opened by Queen Victoria. The following morning *The Times* proclaimed: 'There was yesterday witnessed a sight the like of which has never happened before, and which, in the nature of things can never be repeated ... In a building that could easily have

914

accommodated twice as many, twenty-five thousand persons, *so it is computed*, were arranged in order round the throne of our *Sovereign*. Around them, amidst them, and over their heads was displayed all that is useful or beautiful in nature or in art. Above them rose a glittering arch far more lofty and spacious than the vaults of even our noblest cathedrals. On either side the vista seemed almost boundless ... there was so much that seemed accidental and yet had a meaning that no one could be content with simply what he saw ... all contributed to an effect so grand and yet so natural, that it hardly seemed to be put together by design, or to be the work of human artificers.'

Throughout the generation after Waterloo the idea of 'progress' gradually took hold of the English imagination. In this the Prince Consort, the instigator of the Great Exhibition, certainly believed; but not in a mundane way. A week before the opening he spoke at the Mansion House: 'We are living at a period of most wonderful transition, which tends rapidly to accomplish that great end to which indeed all history points — the realization of the unity of mankind.' *The Times* described the morning of the opening as 'the first since the creation of the world that all peoples have assembled from all parts of the world and done a common act.' The distinctive flavours of these announcements, however incorrect their historical statements, indicate the difference between the idealism of the German prince and the triumphant congratulations awarded by the English to themselves for achieving, in a setting of material progress, an evangelical example good in the sight of God.

Analogical Table
of the Different Elements

Elements	Wood	Fire	Earth	Metal	Water
Years ending in	4 and 5	6 and 7	8 and 9	0 and 1	2 and 3
Colours	Green	Red	Yellow	White	Blue
Seasons	Spring	Summer	End of summer	Autumn	Winter
Climates	Wind	Heat	Humid	Dry	Cold
Flavours	Acid	Bitter	Sweet	Pungent	Salty
Principal organ	Liver	Heart	Spleen	Lungs	Kidneys
Secondary organ	Gallbladder	Small intestine	Stomach	Large intestine	Bladder
Food	Wheat, poultry	Rice, lamb	Corn, beef	Oats, horse	Peas, pork

Table of Harmony
Between the Elements

		Wood Female	Fire Female	Earth Female	Metal Female	Water Female
○○○ Excellent prosperity	Male Wood	● ●	○	○ ○ ○	○	○ ○
○○ Good harmony, understanding	Male Fire	○	○	○ ○	●	● ●
○ Effort needed	Male Earth	● ●	○ ○	○ ○	○ ○ ○	●
● Rivalries and problems of reciprocal domination	Male Metal	○	● ●	●	● ●	○ ○ ○
● ● Misunderstanding and incomprehension	Male Water	○ ○	● ●	●	○ ○ ○	○

THE
FOUR SEASONS
OF
THE PIG

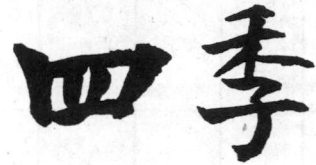

If you were born in spring
Pig/Aries

These two signs share a hatred of hypocrisy and an incapacity for lying. He has the ability to wield authority, is scrupulous and an excellent adviser. The Pig/Aries is touchingly sincere, loyal, spontaneous, impulsive and takes everything said to him as being the Gospel truth. As a result he is always deeply involved and has a terrible time getting the proper perspective on things. He leaps from enthusiasm to enthusiasm and, with an almost total lack of reason, has blind faith in the most naive beliefs.

The problem with the Pig/Aries is that he is naive without being aware of it — for an Aries will often believe himself to be shrewder than he is and will not admit that he has been 'had'. The Pig, on the other hand, is aware, but his Aries side eliminates this objectivity. Thus a Pig/Aries risks making many errors, thinking that it is he who is pulling the string, when in truth he is the marionette. Finally, when he is completely covered with scars, he will perhaps understand that his good faith is unequalled in this evil world. At this point he will be able to develop and make use of his more profound qualities.

Take care: a disappointed or discouraged Pig/Aries will charge head first at the source. It is best to avoid placing yourself in his path.

Pig/Taurus

This is the ideal host or hostess. Gracious, hospitable, warm and not at all snobbish, he is unequalled in organizing relaxed and enjoyable parties. At bottom, he most likely nourishes a hidden fascination with Roman orgies and sees himself lying in a milk bath with several voluptuous odalisques in attendance.

The Pig/Taurus is a sensual epicurean who adores the pleasures of the flesh. Yet he is neither greedy, possessive, nor stingy; he simply aims to live well. His faults? He does not adapt easily to change and refuses to compromise; he is stubborn as a mule and hangs on desperately to his idealistic convictions. It is surprising to see someone who so enjoys the sensual pleasures of life brandishing the flag of justice. Thus there is some contradiction between the Pig/Taurus's sensory world and his abstract desires, but he finds this perfectly normal. If you love or are friends with a Pig/Taurus, it is never too late to convince him that he needs to slim from time to time.

Pig/Gemini

The vivacity, the knack of doing or saying the right thing and the shrewdness of Gemini are excellent for the Pig, whose natural kindness in turn lessens the caustic side of Gemini. It is a fine alliance. The Pig/Gemini is supple, adaptable, sociable and ready to see the good side of things without being taken in. His intellectual curiosity and intelligence are highly developed: he is interested in many things and he loves to learn and to improve himself. It is difficult for him to concentrate however, and he must make a great effort to get to the bottom of things and to understand what makes people tick.

Sometimes the Pig/Gemini may play a game, behave contrary to his ideal and reveal himself to be less honest than he should be; but he will stop such nonsense rather quickly and then feel extremely guilty about it. He is not very farsighted and will often build his house with matchsticks, like the little pigs in the fairy tale. He tends to believe that everything will work out thanks to chance. Happily, he is so charming that he will always find refuge with someone.

If you were born in summer
Pig/Cancer

The Pig/Cancer is born to be a parent. He will be, of course, slightly possessive and stifling, and will fill his children's heads with a mass of orthodox and 'correct' ideas. Since he is emotional, sensitive and vulnerable, he will spend his life perpetually defending himself. He shields those he loves from sin and suffering, but he also shields himself from everything, which sometimes causes him to lose precious time. His sceptical and slightly cantankerous attitude is really a mask he uses to protect himself from attack, so that he may be tranquil and happy.

The Pig/Cancer has trouble resisting temptation, but he knows it. He also knows that once he has fallen in love he will go to the bitter end, giving himself completely, for better or for worse. For this reason he tries at all costs to avoid making a mistake.

Both gentle and authoritarian, conciliatory and stubborn, he is remarkably faithful and will tolerate a lot from the person he loves. Be careful though: pushed to the end of his tether, he attacks like the dangerous animal he can be.

Pig/Leo

A Pig/Leo would make a wonderful king: he is pure, chivalrous and generous; he is not the kind to eat lobster if his subjects are hungry or to ride in a Rolls-Royce during an oil crisis. He has such a lofty and exalted idea of his sacred duties that he will always be ready to set a good example, to share in work and problems and to risk his own skin. He is perhaps as naive as the Pig/Aries, but in his case the choice is deliberate. The world is good and beautiful because he says so.

The Pig/Leo does have one failing: he can have an immoderate love of extravagance and luxury. His drug is adulation, and, despite his objectivity, he has trouble resisting flattery, praise, commendation, excessive homage and deference. But he will never use his power at the expense of another.

If you are in need of security, comfort and fidelity, if your soul has been wounded by searing disappointments, marry a Pig/Leo and you will be happy.

Pig/Virgo

Here is a mixture which goes from one extreme to another,

without, alas, passing through the in-between stages.

The Pig/Virgo is generally a model of honesty, rectitude and fidelity. He has just about all the qualities a mother-in-law could hope for. He is a perfectionist who leaves nothing to chance, is forever on the look out for errors in taste, and is always scrupulously careful. He is a purist who sometimes sees evil everywhere, for his notion of good is extremely demanding. But the smallest temptation can make him topple over into the opposite extreme and roll about with pleasure in vice and degradation, easily tossing aside the pious principles which had served as his crutches.

Therefore, when you meet a Pig/Virgo, do not trust in appearances; think of the reverse side of the coin. Of course, you will never be bored with him. If *you* are a Pig/Virgo, try to be aware of the fact that you are both Dr Jekyll and Mr Hyde and try to resolve it. Nothing can resist you.

If you were born in autumn
Pig/Libra

The Pig/Libra is extremely hesitant and prone to beat about the bush. He is a model of restraint and tolerance, but he will do anything to have peace, to avoid disputes or conflicts, to preserve harmony. An energetic and determined person might easily become irritated living with this individual, who spends most of his time weighing the pro's and con's, seeking an ideal solution yet at the same time respecting the established order. This Pig/Libra should win the Nobel Prize. The only way to force him to react is to confront him with an example of gross injustice, but even then he will put himself in the offender's place. He is capable of finding excuses for the worst possible criminal, absolving a wife-killer or Jack the Ripper. Use him as a father confessor if you do not like recriminations or reprisals.

Pig/Scorpio

These two complement each other perfectly. It is good for a Scorpio to be born in a year of the Pig: it relaxes him, makes him more indulgent towards others and, above all, inspires him to seek peace and harmony. A Pig born between 23 October and 22 November will be less credulous, more selective, more critical.

Thus, this alliance is positive, for it brings the Pig what he lacks — discernment, the survival instinct, scepticism and shrewdness. He is a Pig who will be clever and far-sighted.

However, less advantageous tendencies also spring from this alliance. The Pig/Scorpio is extremely sensual and this can lead to some negative excesses; a Pig who happens upon a nice mud puddle will always have a desire to wallow in it, and a Scorpio will never stop short of the very end. The search for heightened pleasure can lead this individual to go too far — with pleasure becoming an end in itself.

The Pig/Scorpio may often feel torn between his desire for tranquillity and his tendency towards destructiveness.

Pig/Sagittarius

This Pig is bubbling with good intentions: he is full of honourable principles, of pious ideas and remembers an impressive number of proverbs and axioms. He would willingly become the spokesman for the wisdom and experience of all humanity. For the Pig/Sagittarius there is no problem that cannot be solved, with a little ingenuity and a lot of good will. He believes that, given the opportunity, he could reconcile the Jews and the Arabs, transform the Mafia into a charitable organization and cannibals into vegetarians. He has the gift for convincing others through his intense good faith and unbridled enthusiasm. His stubborn optimism, however, does cause him some problems, for he absolutely refuses to see any flaws in those he loves. In fact, he considers it an act of treason to question their perfection, and insists on giving them the benefit of the doubt.

If deceived or disappointed the Pig/Sagittarius does not mope around for long, but begins again with someone else. His faith in humanity is admirable and touching. One would like to invent a paradise on earth just for him. He is a happy person who carries his own paradise within himself.

If you were born in winter
Pig/Capricorn
The influence of Capricorn accentuates the authoritarian tendencies of the Pig. The Pig/Capricorn elevates honesty to the level of a religion, and his need to defend his principles is such that he will delicately strangle all who would wish to transgress them. He is extremely hardworking, a bit rigid, very persevering and terribly attached to his ideas. Unless you have a suitcase crammed with irrefutable proof, it is difficult to make him change his mind. Even then, it will take time.

The Pig/Capricorn will probably be extremely cultivated, for his insatiable intellectual curiosity is allied with Capricorn's gift for deep thought.

Faithful to his promises, and exacting, he often takes himself with the utmost seriousness, lacks a sense of humour but not an awareness of the practical, and is very courageous. He can be an inflexible boss, a redoubtable father and is an unequalled disciplinarian. But he is not terribly amusing, and can never tell a joke properly.

Pig/Aquarius
If he succeeds in controlling his internal contradictions, the Pig/Aquarius has every chance of becoming a particularly well-balanced individual. Aquarius is idealistic, while the Pig is extremely interested in hard cash; the mixture of these two tendencies will allow them to avoid excesses in one direction or the other. As well, the spontaneous detachment characteristic of Aquarius will often save the Pig from the slippery slopes of sexual temptation. At the gate to the pig sty, Aquarius will sound a little alarm which says 'Be careful, you are going too far.'

The Pig/Aquarius may be more preoccupied with purity than other Pigs. There will be times when he will feel torn between the angel and the beast, who fight to dominate his mind. Although he will spend a lot of time hesitating between sensual pleasures of the domestic variety and the exciting exoticism of new conquests, he will make up for lost time on the financial level. He is capable of making a fortune without even cheating — people can never understand how he does it.

Pig/Pisces

Peaceable and accommodating, the Pig/Pisces is rarely carried away by anger. If he should find himself in the middle of a dispute, you can be certain that his exceptional thoughtlessness was the cause of it. He will not seek a fight for anything in the world — unless he is playing a game — and, at the least sign of danger, our Pig/Pisces will don his enigmatic Chinese smile and give in.

He is a clever, polite and obliging person, who knows how to make friends and keep them. However, due to thoughtlessness or naiveté, he can commit enormous blunders and be stupifyingly tactless, which he is the first to regret. The materialistic influence of the Pig, and his taste for opulence, are a good omen for a Pisces who will become more opportunistic and clever in business. He will learn how to distinguish between dream and reality, work and relaxation. Agreeable and understanding, the Pig/Pisces is very well adapted to life. He will take an enormous amount of trouble to avoid circumstances which might unveil his weak point: cowardice.

THE I CHING

易经

THE I CHING AND THE PIG

In the I Ching game, you ask a question and you obtain an answer. It is therefore a divining game. But the question you ask is posed through your Pig identity; the wheels, the complex mechanism of your mind and spirit, begin to turn. You ask a Pig question and the I Ching answers with a Pig 'solution', on which you then meditate as a Pig before arriving at a Pig conclusion.

The player is presented with a hexagram which contains the 'hypothesis-response' to his question, or, more exactly, a synthesis of forces affecting the concern or event inquired about.

For you, Master Pig, here are the sixty-four hexagrams of the I Ching and sixty-four Pig hypotheses.

How to proceed
1. The question
Ask a question regarding any problem at all, past, present or future, personally concerning you. (If the question concerns a friend, consult the I Ching game in the book corresponding to his Chinese sign.)

2. Method of play
It must be done with concentration.
Take **three ordinary and similar coins** — for example, three 50p coins.
Heads will equal the number 3.
Tails will equal the number 2.
Throw the coins.
If the result is two coins showing Heads and one Tails, write $3 + 3 + 2$. You thus obtain a total of 8 which you represent by a continuous line: —— .
Draw the same continuous line if you have three coins showing Heads ($3 + 3 + 3 = 9$).

If you throw two coins showing Tails and one Heads $(2+2+3=7)$, or all three showing Tails $(2+2+2=6)$, draw two separate lines: ▬ ▬ .

To sum up, 8 and 9 correspond to: ▬▬▬ (Yin)

6 and 7 correspond to: ▬ ▬ (Yang)

Repeat this operation *six times,* noting at the time of each throw the figure obtained on a piece of paper, proceeding from the first to the sixth figure, from bottom to top.

The final result, including a trigram from the bottom, or lower trigram (example: ▦), and a trigram of the top, or upper trigram (example: ▦), will be a hexagram of the I Ching. In our example this would look like:

Now merely look for the hexagram number in the table on page 930, and then consult the list of hexagrams with their descriptions to find the given answer. *In our example,* the hexagram obtained is number 63, entitled **After completion.**

THE HEXAGRAMS OF THE PIG

CH'IEN

1 *The creative.* You possess energy, strength and will but that is no reason to attack indiscriminately anything that moves on the borders of your territory.

K'UN

2 *The receptive:* You are going to have to learn to walk without crushing flowers and bushes — a good lesson in tact and docility. But you are intuitive enough to sense the right attitude to have.

CHUN

3 *Initial difficulty:* You will not find the bad seed by devastating your garden. Rather, seek within yourself — calmly, coolly and with determination.

MÊNG

4 *Youthful folly:* 'It is not I who seeks the young fool, but the fool who seeks me.' The true master is often a solitary person who does not spend his life on the stage and does not display his power. Confront danger without disdaining or minimizing it.

HSÜ

5 *Waiting:* You know that you are either the hunter or the hunted. Study yourself and the situation in depth. You will perhaps have some surprises.

Table of Hexagrams

Trigrams	Upper lines		
Lower lines			
☰	1	11	34
☷	12	2	16
☳	25	24	51
☵	6	7	40
☶	33	15	62
☴	44	46	32
☲	13	36	55
☱	10	19	54

Use this table to find the number of your hexagrams. The meeting point between the lower and upper trigrams indicates the number of the hexagram that you are seeking.

䷇	䷗	䷓	䷢	䷪
5	26	9	14	43
8	23	20	35	45
3	27	42	21	17
29	4	59	64	47
39	52	53	56	31
48	18	57	50	28
63	22	37	30	49
60	41	61	38	58

SUNG

 6 *Conflict:* You are not the sort to beat about the bush. Nevertheless, try to smooth things over and be slightly diplomatic; the slightest incident could degenerate into open warfare.

SHIH

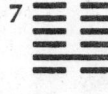 7 *The army:* Even though you are a solitary person, there are times when you must fall into line and bend to discipline. This will be the price of success. Too much individualism will lead to disaster.

PI

 8 *Holding together (union):* Unite together, form a group, tighten your familial, friendly and professional ties. You are going to need your fellow men and their understanding.

SHIAO CH'U

 9 *The taming power of the small:* Do not attack head-first in the fog. Wait until it has disappeared — and look where you step.

LÜ

 10 *Treading:* 'Tread on the tail of a tiger, he does not bite man.' You must keep calm and smiling. Do not seek a fight — it is not to your advantage.

T'AI

 11 *Peace:* Is not possible between the hunter and the Pig. Polish up your defences and ready yourself to cross swords. Remember that 'If you wish peace, prepare for war.'

P'I

12 *Standstill:* Choose solitude, retire to your refuge, look at the world's agitation from afar. The tumult will always pass; only silence will remain.

T'UNG JÊN

13 *Fellowship with men:* Difficult for a Pig who loves isolation and the cool shade of the underbrush; but you will have success if you go out a little, hold out your hand to others and interest yourself in their problems.

TA YU

14 *Possesson in great measure:* Makes sense only if a man knows how to use it. The treasure lies in the manner of possessing not in the possession itself. Dedicate yourself completely to your enterprise but remain detached from its results.

CH'IEN

15 *Modesty:* You must continue with what you have imposed on yourself. Respect the balance between life and principles, between the needs of nature and the necessities of the social order.

YÜ

16 *Enthusiasm:* Go to meet others and anticipate their desires, but not just with nice words. Give of yourself completely; be at one even with your slightest gestures.

SUI

17 *Following:* It will depend on your charm and your good will. Handle problems with openness and suppleness. Adapt to others and to circumstances without disowning your personality.

KU

18 *Work on what has been spoiled:* Do not accuse the wolf of having rabies just because you want to get rid of him. Resolve your problems on your own. Do not project the cause of your difficulties onto a scapegoat, or the irritation in the air may turn against you.

LIN

19 *Approach:* Analyse the situation and the terrain, look further than the end of your nose. This is the moment to make long-term plans and to think of the future.

KUAN

20 *Contemplation:* Climb to the top of the tower, but come down before it is razed or the base of your pedestal comes unscrewed. Do not become hypnotized by your glorious but precarious isolation.

SHIH HO

21 *Biting through (or clearly defined penalties):* Attack to bring down the obstacle and destroy the lie. Nothing can stop you; nothing should stand in your way or make you hesitate.

PI

22 *Grace:* To see clearly, sharpen your wits and make a decision; choose the natural light of the sun; avoid subdued and flattering illumination.

PO

23 *Splitting apart:* Do not set out on a swamp or a cliff which threatens to crumble: your itinerary is filled with invisible dangers. Be prudent; trust nothing and no-one.

FU

24 *Return — the turning point:* Leave your ditch, the danger has passed. Frolic freely in the bushes; put down your burden of cares and fears.

WU WANG

25 *Innocence:* You tend to rely on your intuition, but it is not always infallible; if an error occurs, be a good sport, and admit to it, even proclaim it if necessary, and you will change failure into a triumph.

TA CH'U

26 *The taming power of the great:* Power and strength, but on condition that you do not fall asleep on your laurels. This is the moment to redouble your efforts and to give your full measure.

I

27 *The corners of the mouth:* Material and spiritual nourishment; a healthy mind in a healthy body. Even if you are sometimes prone to excess, try to maintain a proper balance between the physical and the mental.

TA KUO

28 *Preponderance of the great:* Do not hesitate to lighten your burden: 'A good hero is a live hero'. Follow your courtly impulses, but act with caution and spare your strength — you will be more effective that way.

K'AN

29 *Fathomless water:* Despite hail or bullets, do not deviate from your route or you will confront even greater perils.

LI

30 *Clinging, fire:* Do not go against the current, follow the direction of the wind, even during a tempest. By becoming one with a fall, by riding with it, you will avoid breaking your bones.

HSIEN

31 *Influence:* Despite your need for isolation and your deep-rooted individualism, do not turn away if others come to greet you. True friends are sometimes hidden in the middle of a crowd.

HÊNG

32 *Duration:* A bridge spans the river, so do not swim across it. Do not persist in an uncertain and complicated undertaking when an obvious and simple solution is to hand.

TUNG

33 *Retreat:* You know that it is the source of joy and control. Keep to your convictions and remain faithful to your deepest nature. Solitude will be good for you.

TA CHUANG

34 *The power of the great:* Do not allow yourself to become intoxicated by your speed — you risk falling into the hunter's net. Take a step back and look closely at everything; the balance sheet perhaps will prove to be less exalting than expected.

CHIN

35 *Progress:* Your projects have every chance of succeeding on condition that you leave your retreat and collaborate in full daylight. Any new proposal must be examined in a positive frame of mind.

MING I

36 *Darkening of the light:* Outside it is a moonless night. Within you it is also dark. It is useless to send out distress signals; you will only increase your anxiety; wait for the dawn.

CHIA JÊN

37 *The family:* You are solitary and retreat even within your family circle. Make an effort to become integrated, or else you will create tensions that will be difficult to bear.

K'UEI

38 *Opposition:* The diversity of trees, flowers and plants creates the harmony of nature; it is the same for men and their ideas — their differences make for equilibrium. The secret of true happiness lies in respecting this interdependence.

CHIEN

39 *Obstruction:* You are ready to attack, but the obstacle may be only one more illusion. Ask yourself about the real nature of the problem: you will perhaps find that it is non-existent.

HSIEH

40 *Deliverance:* From now on everything is cleared up, you can leave, begin again, rebuild. No more setbacks, no more uncertainty: the route is straight and clear.

SUN

41 *Decrease:* Sincerity and purity of intention are more touching than the greatest gestures or the handsomest words: learn to discover them.

I

42 *Revolution:* Preparing for it is already to undertake it. It is sometimes inevitable and necessary, but if you want to change the world, begin by changing yourself.

KUAI

43 *Breakthrough:* A situation in which the Pig should feel at ease. Walk straight ahead, do not accept compromises and lash out at errors. However, remain tolerant and avoid taking on an extremist position.

KOU

44 *Coming to meet:* Do not let yourself be attracted to swamps or confused situations; you will lose your liberty. If the meaning is confused, do not take steps.

TS'UI

45 *Gathering together:* Do so in order to vanquish or protect yourself, but take care not to be 'swamped'. Crafty enemies may try to insinuate themselves into your confidence.

SHÊNG

46 *Pushing upwards:* If you feel sure of yourself, set out on the path to glory with arms and equipment. Do not turn back nostalgically towards what you have left behind.

K'UN

47 *Oppression:* You are not at the peak of your moral and physical form. Do not give up however, and do not allow anguish to destroy you; stoically accept this lessening of energy and this negative situation.

CHING

48 *The well:* You feel the need to upset everything, but do not shake the foundations or you may damage the edifice that is your life. Make only indispensable changes.

KO

49 *Revolution:* Preparing for it is already undertake it. It is sometimes inevitable and necessary, but if you want to change the world, begin by changing yourself.

TING

50 *The cauldron:* Symbolizes the five Elements — Water, Wood, Fire, Metal and Earth, material and spiritual nourishment. Scorn nothing, neglect nothing; everything serves to feed the body and regenerate the spirit.

CHÊN

51 *The arousing (shock, thunder):* Trials and troubles are on the horizon; however, they may bring 'illumination' and understanding. Know how to accept them without changing anything in your daily life.

KÊN

52 *Keeping still:* You are adept at living in solitude; this is the moment to profit from it and regain calm and peace.

CHIEN

53 *Development (gradual progress):* You must bend, make your spine more supple — an indispensable discipline if you wish to progress. Advance harmoniously with small, gracious and measured steps.

KUEI MEI

54 *The bride:* Perhaps a good match, and most seductive: the sensual Pig will not be indifferent.

FÊNG

55 *Abundance:* Or fat days; take advantage of this state of plenitude and build up your reserves for winter and its privations. Know how to enjoy living for the moment, but do not forget that the day of reckoning approaches.

LÜ

56 *The wanderer:* Burn your bridges and break your ties. Take to the road without regret or hatred.

SUN

57  *The gentle:* Be gentle and persuasive; you must infiltrate rather than smash or shatter. Let masks and illusions fall, but without clamour or scandal, instead do so with tact and refinement.

TUI

58  *The serene, the joyous:* Tighten existing ties and create new ones. In order to do this you must leave your thickets and bushes; mix with your fellow men and interest yourself in their problems.

HUAN

59 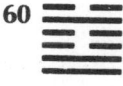 *Dissolution:* In order to overcome egotism, begin by leaving your retreat; go into the world and society, leave your ivory tower.

CHIEH

60 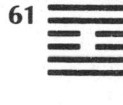 *Limitation:* If you insist on running after several hares at the same time, you will not catch any at all. Impose self-discipline, not with severity but seriously. The important thing is to respect your own rules of the game.

TUI

61  *Inner truth:* If you think you have attained your goal and have carried out what you wished to do, there is no need to announce it from the rooftops. Rather, put it into practice and set an example.

HSIAO KUO

62 *Preponderance of the small:* One does not build cathedrals on quicksand.

CHI CHI

63 *After completion:* Once the work is completed, one must fiddle with it to achieve perfection. Never consider a piece of work or situation as finished.

WEI CHI

64 *Before completion:* Do not anticipate prematurely; remain prudent, do not come to hasty conclusions.